D0941440

THE LIFE OF JESUS

THE
LIFE
OF
JESUS

by Conrad Noel

SIMON AND SCHUSTER

New York · 1937

All rights reserved
Copyright, 1937, by Simon and Schuster, Inc.
Published by Simon and Schuster, Inc.
386 Fourth Avenue, New York

LIBRARY
FEB 11 1969
UNIVERSITY OF THE PACIFIC

195296

Printed in Great Britain

DEDICATED

TO

HAROLD MASON
Vicar of Sneyd, Burslem

CONTENTS

PART III

THE ADVENT OF THE MESSIAH

MAPS

by J. F. HORRABIN

PREFACE

I HAVE throughout this work followed the usage of the Authorized and Revised Versions, and of such writers as the late Bishop Gore in the matter of small letters instead of capitals for 'he' and 'his' in describing the Christ. I have used the term 'the Christ' generally, instead of 'Christ,' in order to remind my readers that the title is not a surname but a synonym for the Messiah.

The fact that I am a priest of the English Catholic Church and a member of the 'Order of the Church Militant' makes it unnecessary for me to lay stress on my acceptance of the Catholic tradition and of its Christology, although it may be necessary to point out that conventionality and orthodoxy are completely different matters, and that many who boast the name of Catholic would be surprised and shocked at what the tradition actually involves.

But here in these pages Christian theology is not obtruded and it has been my endeavour to write a life of Jesus which will interest both orthodox and unorthodox alike. I have tried to see his life and teaching from the angle of those who actually came across him for the first time and were drawn within the orbit of his influence. Theological deductions as to his nature and his relation to the Godhead are of a later period. My hope has been to recover something of the life itself, its spontaneity and freshness, and to interpret it in relation to its actual environment.

My thanks are due to the present Archbishop of York and the Dean of Canterbury for permission to reprint sections originally published in their respective quarterlies, *The Pilgrim* and *The Interpreter*, both now unfortunately defunct.   I am also indebted to the editors of the *Crusader Christendom*, *Optimist*, *Commonwealth*, *Catholic Crusader*, and *Challenge* for a like permission.

My thanks are also due to Fr. Harold Mason, Vicar of Sneyd, to Miss H. O'Toole, B.A., and Mr. John Hart, for their invaluable assistance to me in completing this work since my blindness, and to the authors and publishers of the books to which reference has been made, particularly to Mrs. Chesterton and Evelyn Underhill; the executor of Harriet King; and Mr. Vyvyan Beresford Holland, executor of Oscar Wilde; T. & T. Clark for the extracts from Burkitt's *Gospel History and its Transmission*; Heinemann Ltd. for the extracts from Swinburne's *Songs before Sunrise*; Macmillan & Co. for the extracts from Warde Fowler's *The City State* and Walter Pater's *Marius the Epicurean*; and Watts & Co. for the extracts from Bertrand Russell's *Why I am not a Christian*.

CONRAD NOEL.

THAXTED
December 1936.

INTRODUCTION

THERE are such innumerable lives of Christ published nowadays that it has become the fashion for their authors to apologize to the public on their appearance. If I do not follow the fashion, it is because this *Life of Jesus* breaks entirely new ground. It will be unusual and provocative, not by means of any conscious effort to achieve originality, nor even because it will look at the life of the Christ and interpret his teaching in the light of the economic and political background of his times, but because the conclusions drawn will often be the opposite of those given by authors who have travelled the same road. If it does provoke the public, I hope it will not provoke them to fury but to thought.

The work will dwell on the social content of Christ's teaching, but it will at the same time try to keep the balance between his plan for world liberation and his intimate dealings with the individuals with whom he came in contact. It is indeed my aim to show that these two things are in reality one, namely the understanding of the individual and the understanding of world affairs. Many people are so engrossed in world politics that they forget the individual men and women for whom the world should be put straight, while others are so taken up with the needs of individual people that they ignore the fact that those very needs are largely the result of an evil environment and an evil political outlook. Man, as has often been said, is 'a political animal,' and the individual salvation depends largely upon what the New Testament calls the 'common salvation.'

Something must here be added about the modern challenge as to the character of the Christ, a challenge represented by such books as that of Bertrand Russell. The old Victorian assumption shared by Christians and Agnostics alike to the effect that Jesus was, in any case, the greatest moral genius who ever existed is going by the board.

Many critics now challenge the validity of his moral teaching. They neither allow it to be original nor what is called by Christians 'final.' They attempt to dethrone him from the central position he has for so long held in the world's history. Albert Kalthoff writes of 'the fiction that there was in the historical Jesus an absolute principle of Christianity and (as Christianity was considered the standard religion) of religion generally, so that it gave men an ideal by which they might test the religious and moral value of the whole of life. On such a fiction the whole of liberal theology was bound to be shipwrecked. The autonomous spirit of our time will not suffer a man who lived at a certain time and place to be made the absolute law of its own life.'

Bertrand Russell[1] defines carefully what he means by 'Christian.' To have any claim to the title you must at least believe in God and immortality. If you do not believe that the Christ was very God of very God you must at least 'have some kind of belief about Christ. . . . I think, at the very lowest, you must have the belief that Christ was, if not divine, at least the best and wisest of men . . . therefore, I take it that when I tell you why I am not a Christian I have to tell you two different things; first, why I do not believe in God and immortality; and secondly, why I do not think that Christ was the best and the wisest of men, although I grant him a very high degree of moral goodness.'

With the problem of the existence of God and of personal survival this *Life of Jesus* will not directly deal; but with that other problem, the moral pre-eminence of Jesus, we are here directly concerned.

Most of Bertrand Russell's charges are concerned with the inconsistencies of the Church and not of its Founder, but he suggests that in many matters he takes Christ's maxims more seriously than most professing Christians, although he does not make any boast of always living up to them. But Bertrand Russell questions the Christian assumption that the Christ was the best and wisest of men. When Jesus

[1] *Why I am not a Christian.* Watts & Co.

makes splendid ethical assertions, they have often been made before him; this challenges his originality (a question to which a special chapter has been devoted) which, by the way, Bertrand Russell is inclined to deny. But Christ, it is argued, made positive mistakes, and that on all important questions such as that of his second coming. 'In that respect clearly he was not so wise as some other people have been, and he was certainly not superlatively wise.'

It is, however, not only his wisdom, but his morality that is called in question. He believed in everlasting torment which would seem to be a definitely immoral belief; you do not find that attitude in Socrates. 'You find him quite bland and urbane towards the people who would not listen to him; and it is, to my mind, far more worthy of a sage to take that line than to take the line of indignation.' Lord Russell reminds us of the sort of things Socrates was saying when he was dying, but forgets what the Christ was saying on the cross and what the first martyr St. Stephen, inspired by him, was saying about his enemies. The author fails to appreciate that 'righteous indignation' which figures largely in the teachings of the Christ; not a vindictive malice, but a burning and generous indignation against the oppressor and the hypocrite. 'Ye serpents; ye generation of vipers.' Russell comments: 'That was said to people who did not like his preaching.'

When we come to describe the actual situation which called forth this deep and passionate indignation, the objector will perhaps perceive how inadequate and almost grotesque the comment sounds, as if our Lord had flown into a rage because the congregation had not quite liked one of his sermons. It was not petulance but pity that dragged that denunciation from the Christ. Perhaps he was not a philosopher or a 'sage' and the thing as Bertrand Russell says was certainly not in 'quite the best tone.' Jesus was not always faultlessly 'correct,' and his sayings were often uncouth. He did not move in the best circles.

Bertrand Russell is pained by the words of Jesus about the sin against the Holy Ghost, words which have been the inspiration of such poets as Ibsen, who can hardly be accused of a narrow orthodoxy. He does not like the story of the Gadarene swine and, I think, misunderstands it. Perhaps he has more cause for doubt when he comes to the cursing of the fig - tree; his conclusion is as follows: 'I cannot myself feel that either in the matter of wisdom or in the matter of virtue Christ stands quite as high as some other people known to history. I think I should put Buddha and Socrates above him in those respects.' Alas! Jesus fails to get his degree in the Russell-Kalthoff academy. So would elemental nature with its discords and harmonies, its shattering storms and serene silences.

Bertrand Russell says a few good things about the conventional Christian teaching, and asks if it is really true that we should all be wicked if we did not hold to the Christian religion. 'It seems to me that the people who have held to it have been for the most part extremely wicked.' But have they in fact held to it? It is hardly true to add that fear was the chief ingredient of Christ's teaching. A careful study of the gospels will show courage and not fear as his message to mankind. 'Fear not' is his repeated motif. This and many other points will be brought out in my story of Jesus and, after all, it must be the telling of this story itself which will either convince or fail to satisfy the modern world of his right to proclaim 'Before Abraham was, I am.'

Lenin, to whom as a revolutionary and constructive statesman, my debt is incalculable, classes all religions alike and every form of the Christian religion as poisonous and reactionary. He is illogical, for he admits that the early Christians were revolutionaries against the Roman Empire. Lenin was a very busy man, and it would be as absurd to take him seriously as a student of the New Testament or of Christian history as it would be to take the opinions of some physical scientists seriously when they pose as experts and specialists on every question under the sun. Religion, said Karl Marx, is the opium of the people, but I would remind my readers that Charles Kingsley, Canon of the English Church and most popular of novelists, was saying the same thing, and at the same time. Writing of the generality of the clergy of his day he says: 'We have never told you that the . . . true poor man's book, the true God's voice against tyrants, idlers, and humbugs, was the Bible. Ay, you may sneer, but so it is. It is our fault, our great fault, that you should sneer, sneer at the only news that ought to be your glory and your strength. It is our fault. We have used the Bible as if it were the special constable's handbook—*an opium dose for keeping beasts of burden patient while they were being overloaded*—a mere book to keep the poor in order.' (May 1848.)

There have been moments, not only in early Christian history, but in the medieval period, when the Christian religion, so far from being the opium of the people, has been the dynamic which drove them to revolt against the 'powers that be.' It was so when the armed labourers went forth with their priests and Catholic leaders with the crucifix and the banners of the saints to do battle in the peasants' revolt against their plutocratic enemies, and their battle cries were the slogans of modern communism. It was so when the towns of Europe fought their way to freedom under the fiery inspiration of the Catholic Faith against popes and bishops and abbots, and secular lords. Catholic officialdom was against them, *but they could quote and did quote the great Catholic schoolmen as on their side*. It was with full knowledge of the law of resistance to tyrants laid down in scripture and in the writings of the recognized doctors and divines of the Church that they fought and often won. Not only the smaller rebellions of cities, but even national rebellions were fought under the banners of the Christian religion. The revival of this type of religion in such modern bodies as the Church Socialist League, the Catholic Crusade, and the Order of the Church Militant is no mere eccentricity, but is inspired by Holy Scripture and the most living of the Church's traditions.

C. N.

PART I

THE POLITICAL, ECONOMIC, AND RELIGIOUS BACKGROUND

B

CHAPTER I

THE ROMAN SCENE

THE City States were built on the foundation of the slave. The Greek democracies were, for the most part, aristocratic oligarchies. At Sparta there was some attempt made in a communistic direction, but Sparta had its industrial proletariat and was a city of stock - jobbers, speculators, and usurers. The civil wars of Athens were in reality 'economic struggles in which the small free proprietors rebelled against the continual and rapid concentration of wealth.'[1] Thi concentration of capital in the hands of a few, and th absorption of small properties, took the heart out of t' nation and rendered it indifferent to foreign invasion.

By the first century of the Christian era, Rome, ir origin a small republic some twenty miles square, become an industrialized empire, dominating the West world and thrusting its imperial conquests far into the Ea

Some centuries before Christ, it had been a communit of free peasants occupying an area of nearly four hundrec square miles, with a population almost entirely dispersec over the countryside. Most of the families 'had a small holding and a cottage of their own where father and sons lived and worked together, growing corn for the most part, with here and there a strip of vine or olive. Their few head of cattle were kept at pasture on the neighbouring common land: their clothes and simple instruments of husbandry they made for themselves at home. . . . Occasionally they would visit the capital, with its temples of the gods, its houses of the wealthy, its artisans and traders, where corn, oil, or wine could be bartered in small quantities for salt or rough tools or weapons of iron.'[2]

[1] Nitti's *Catholic Socialism*.
[2] H. G. Wells (quoting Ferrero), *Outline of History*. Although this book has been subjected to adverse criticism on certain points, his summary of recent research on Roman history seems on the whole both lucid and accurate.

For a couple of hundred years or more, patricians and wealthy plebeians contended perpetually for the mastery of the State, but their struggle was more or less a matter of indifference to the mass of slaves, 'free' workers, and other unpropertied persons, 'who were entirely outside and beneath the struggle.'

After 366 B.C. the struggle began to lessen, the aristocratic families were growing poorer and the plebeians richer, and there was now a considerable intermixture of the two classes. The freed slave, sometimes an artisan, often a trader, was rising to positions of power in the growing republic. Even so late as 390 B.C. Rome was still a comparatively insignificant city, but within little more than a hundred years 'she was ruling and unifying all Italy from the Arno to the Straits of Messina.'

Her greedy expansions abroad were at first softened by the comparatively generous policy of incorporating her sturdiest antagonists on terms of equality with herself. But the half-century between 200 and 150 B.C. ushers in a harsher policy. There were no more extensions of the franchise at home, and attempts to incorporate foreign populations ceased. 'Rome was taxing the foreigner to release her home population from taxation.' Without such taxation the position of the Roman population would have been desperate, for the people were flocking into the city from the countryside, uprooted from their ancient holdings by rich landlords who were acquiring the land and working it by means of cheap slave labour.

'The land of Italy is in this period slowly and surely passing into the hands of wealthy Romans, plebeians as much as patricians: and as cattle-breeding pays better than tillage, and winter pasture is needed for the vast herds which occupy the higher lands in summer, the small freeholder of the valleys is gradually got rid of by fair means or foul and his land absorbed into the great man's estate. Nor is he even maintained as a day labourer . . . for all that was needed could be done by slaves at a much smaller expense.' [1]

[1] Warde Fowler, *The City State.*

Although a more humane philosophy about the slave was creeping in, and many thinkers would now repudiate the earlier conception of him as mere property like timber or livestock, yet Warde Fowler, who is on the whole a defender of the Roman system, records that 'the unskilled slaves, captured or kidnapped in Spain, Gaul, Epirus, Thrace or Asia Minor were cheap in the Roman market and would do well enough to run a farm with, especially if that farm were chiefly pastoral with flocks and herds needing no great experience or skill to look after. This cheapness and the physical conditions of rural life in a mountainous country, made cattle running and sheep-tending a profitable industry. Large districts of Italy, especially in the centre and south, became covered in this period with huge estates owned by capitalists and worked by rough and often savage slaves, who were locked up at night in underground prisons and treated simply as "living tools." No ray of hope ever broke in on these miserable beings. No free citizen gave a thought either to their condition or to the economic danger of the system . . . incredible cruelty, recklessness of human life, callousness in dealing with the vanquished and subject peoples, meet us at every turn.' He continues: 'As a result of plunder and extortion in the provinces, most men of the upper classes had some capital in money, and this was almost always invested in public works and State undertakings of all kinds, e.g. the raising of taxes and the fitting out of fleets and armies. These things were all done by contract, and the contracts were taken out by companies in which every man was a shareholder who had anything to invest . . . the forum of Rome became a kind of stock exchange in which the buying and selling of shares was always going on, and where every man was trying to outwit his neighbour.'

We might trace through the centuries the history of property in the Roman republic, its gradual concentration in the hands of the few, encouraged by the granting of liberty to bequeath by will, but the evils caused by this 'were much less serious, much less disastrous than those produced by the banking system and the concentration of capital.'[1]   During several centuries all economic legislation in Rome did but serve the interests of the great proprietors.

Mr. H. G. Wells shows that the eastern expansion of the empire was mainly a hunt for treasure, and Döllinger supports these writers, and remarks that war was not only conducted for honour and the glory of conquest, but served besides as a main source of gain for those who took part in it.   The wars of Rome at this period are acknowledged to be economic campaigns, contractors following the armies and buying the defeated at the auctions on the battlefield that followed upon victories.

As showing the rapacity of the Roman rich, Cicero states that the senate, composed of wealthy landed proprietors, caused the vineyards and olive-groves of Gaul to be destroyed, in order to avoid a damaging competition with the rich Roman landlords. 'The joint-stock companies, which made themselves completely masters of the commercial movement, and carried their transactions into the most distant provinces, were for a long time more powerful than the State . . . these companies permitted even statesmen and senators, who were forbidden by law to enter into commercial speculations, to participate in the enormous stock transactions of the publicans, without, on that account, compromising themselves in the eyes of the public, and without in any way openly violating the laws'—thus anticipating the Marconi scandals of our own times!

Usury was largely and openly practised, not only by bankers and publicans, but by soldiers, politicians, and philosophers.   Nitti shows that Cato, Cicero, and Seneca were extortionate usurers, Cicero, however, in spite of his amassing money, when governor of provinces refused to use his public position to exploit the dependency, although provincial governors were notorious for their extortions, and Mommsen's attacks on him are considered by many historians to be very biased.   The 'honest' Brutus, so

[1] Nitti's *Catholic Socialism.*

beloved of Shakespeare, invested his capital at Cyprus at forty per cent. 'The publicans and bankers, who formed the Roman bourgeoisie or middle class, and who possessed a large portion of the immense capital robbed from the conquered provinces, were the greatest power in Rome, and neither the hostility of the aristocracy nor the insurrections of the masses could wrench from them the monopoly of political power.' Thus, the financiers and other plutocrats were the arbiters of the senate, the dictators of peace or war, and the manipulators of the votes of even those few poor people who possessed them.

Wells comments on the introduction of money—a method of exchange which had only been in existence for a comparatively few centuries before our period. Providing a fluid medium for trade and enterprise, it had changed economic conditions profoundly. It had worked to the advantage of the rich, by giving them freedom of movement and of financial enterprise where formerly they had been tied to their estates. He speaks of a cash-and-credit-using system, which gave to the financier and the money interests a role similar to that which they play in the world of to-day.

If the Roman world was a swollen empire, built upon the foundation of the shares and profits, Mammon himself being the head corner-stone, how comes it that it finds so many defenders both ancient and modern?

Note first, that the defences are written, for the most part, by bourgeois people who have a natural liking for imperialism, and find themselves very much at home amidst the comforts that it secures them.[1]

Turn to the Roman Empire itself: one of its chief apologists is Seneca, a man of enormous wealth,[2] branded by his contemporaries as a usurer, and, in spite of his few personal wants and his puritanic life, the owner of gardens and villas, and a palace which excited even the envy of a Nero. The ideal empire, as sketched by him, was 'a single

---

[1] e.g. Friedländer, a typical modern apologist.
[2] Dill's *Roman Society*.

plan of administration for the good of the whole, in which one part must not be privileged at the expense of another, though all may claim the human right of justice whatever the provocation has been.'[1] His advice to Nero is, 'it is good to look within, and go the round of a clear conscience and afterwards to cast one's eyes on this great mass of humanity with its conflicts, its plots, its weakness, its certain fate of bringing ruin to itself and others if it should ever break our yoke and rise in revolt.'[2]

Seneca had this grandiose vision of an empire animated by good will towards the peoples it governed, but even his *ideal* was a benevolent tyranny, which in *fact* proved anything but benevolent. He was too honest not to record 'the gross luxury, treacherous and envious cruelty' that actually inspired the fashionable world of his day. 'Not even in Tacitus or Suetonius are to be found more ghastly revelations of a putrescent society.'[3]

What, then, can fairly be said for the Roman Empire in the last century B.C. or in the first century of our era? In opposition to a narrow tribalism, and self-contained nationalisms, Rome had encouraged that comparative unity of language and ideas which the Hellenizing process had begun. A bastard form of Greek culture had spread over the world after the conquests of Alexander, and in so far as this uniformity can be considered valuable, in spite of its obliterations of local customs both good and bad, Rome did bring together the peoples she had conquered by encouraging such unity.

The dominion of the empire secured for the peoples bordering on the Mediterranean a certain unity in the methods and conditions of outward existence and also a certain stability of social life. 'Throughout many provinces of the East people felt the Emperor really stood for peace; after all the dreadful storms and wars, they hailed his law as a shelter and a safeguard.'[4] This author also

---

[1] Liberty's *The Political Relations of Christ's Ministry.*   [2] Ibid.
[3] Dill's *Roman Society from Nero to Marcus Aurelius.*
[4] Harnack's *The Mission and Expansion of Christianity.*

mentions among the advantages of Roman imperialism the exceptional growth and security of international traffic, the admirable roads, the blending of nationalities, the interchange of traffic of wares and ideas, the personal intercourse, the ubiquitous merchant and soldier. If we turn to the works of Sir William Ramsay we find this evidence confirmed, and Renan sums up many of the advantages of Roman imperialism in the famous Chapter XVI of his *Apostles*. Plutarch, in his appreciation of Zeno—the philosopher under whom Alexander had studied—writes: 'He aims at inducing us, to whatever nation we belong, not to live each in his own city or district, separated off by our distinctive rights, but to think of all men as fellow-citizens and members of the same district, that so there may be one life and one order, like one herd of cattle pasturing in one meadow under a common law' (quoted by Lock in *S. Paul, The Master Builder*). Although this ideal of cosmopolitanism (an ideal which can hardly be regarded as an unmixed good) animated the ancient defenders of empire, Rome did not wage war for purposes of humanity, but for purposes of gain, and these humanitarian defences must be regarded rather as an afterthought.

Here is a very typical fancy picture from a modern apologist on the difference between the spirit of Rome and that of her rival, Carthage. 'To Rome then belonged the future. On the one hand a people of soldiers restrained by discipline, religion, and purity of manners, animated with the love of their country, surrounded by devoted allies, on the other a people of merchants with dissolute manners, unruly mercenaries, and discontented subjects.'[1]

Hilaire Belloc draws the same kind of picture, contrasting the nobility of Rome with the baseness of Carthage. He has no difficulty in showing that the Carthaginians, with their dark and inhuman religion, were uncreative, contemptuous, carriers not creators, clever negotiators, bargainers. He comments upon the excessive wealth of their great families, their government by an oligarchy which their

[1] *History of Julius Caesar*, by Napoleon III.

* B

enemies might have thought a mere plutocracy, their armies—'the vast mass of poorer members could not be armed in the service of their country, save at a wage'— their inability or want of desire to absorb or win the vast populations from which they claimed various degrees of allegiance. In spite of their splendid seamanship, which he notes, one is given the idea of a crawling, greedy, unproductive folk, abject, cruel, usurious. 'Carthage had not desire to create, but only to enjoy, therefore she left us nothing.' All this, in spite of certain exceptions such as Hannibal, is true enough, but it is when Rome is glorified as possessing most of the virtues and as the very opposite of Carthage in her aims, ideals, and accomplishments, that the picture is, to say the least of it, over-coloured. When Rome destroyed Carthage, we should be inclined to say 'Killing no murder,' but when we consider her motives that is another story.[1]

He bases his case for Roman imperialism on the fact that where Rome penetrated, there was enduring energy and creative impulse. He describes the peoples that were conquered or annexed, or who willingly submitted to the Roman yoke, as reanimated by her dominion. In fact, so splendid was their lot that it is hard to see what advantage the coming of Christendom could have brought to them. For to him the Christ and his Church, or rather the Church and her minor saint, Christ, merely intensified and extended the blessings of that divine empire.

But, in reality, the final struggle with Carthage was waged not by that earlier republican Rome of high aims and pure motives, but by a Rome which was already dominated by the financiers, inflamed by the puritan usurer Cato—a Rome which was dispossessing her yeoman class by cheap slave labour, substituting paid armies for voluntary yeoman service—a Rome in which human sacrifices were not unknown. That she was creative in comparison with Phoenicia may be true, that the peoples who

[1] Readers are referred to Hilaire Belloc's *Esto Perpetua*, and to *Europe and the Faith*, for the best defence of the empire.

followed her in North Africa created little or nothing is true, but the destroyer of Carthage and Corinth was the Rome of capitalists and masters of high finance, who destroyed the olive-groves and the vineyards of others in order to aggrandise themselves, the Rome whose own population was largely supported by doles wrung from the wretched provinces. That many peoples were ready to make alliance with her,[1] and that many nations sought incorporation into the empire is further proof of her dominance by powerful, plutocratic, and corrupt men, for it was not the poor but the rich governing classes that wished for incorporation, that they might the better subdue and loot their own workers. Rich versus poor was the real struggle even in those days.

True, the Roman rule was not all to the bad, and I do not desire to minimize the good that the empire incidentally brought about. The fate of the workers in the Near East must have been almost indescribable under such a ruler as Mithridates, but the enormous revenues which Rome subsequently took from Asia Minor do not suggest an idealistic motive for the occupation of that province.

As to Rome's creative energy, at this particular period of her history, the aqueducts and other constructive works, the remains of which are nowadays very naturally admired, were built by hordes of slaves, the human property of contractors who tendered for the jobs with the plutocratic government.

There was a certain dilettante interest in works of art diffused among the cultured classes, 'but the exercise of native art retrograded rather than advanced.' The Romans were content to gush about the works of others. 'Where they could plunder or purchase, instead of creating for themselves, they did so.'[2]

True from the reign of Nero onward (A.D. 54) humaner

---

[1] The only free people who wanted Rome's friendship were the Jews, under the Maccabees, and their information about her was based on an ideal picture of her earlier history which did not correspond to the actual facts.

[2] Mommsen, *History of Rome*, vol. iv.

sentiments were beginning to obtain concerning the poor and the slave (cf. the writings of Seneca and others), and legislation began to give the workers and slaves some sort of protection, but yet Lecky and Dill who record such mitigations, draw a dark picture of the close of the old era and the beginning of our own, and so the somewhat laboured defences of empire which we have mentioned would hardly appeal to the slave and the down-trodden 'free' workers either in Rome or in the provinces. Even Mr. McCabe [1] fully admits that a single frontier war might yield as many as 100,000 slaves, and speaks of a Rome in which rich men could live luxuriously on the produce of estates or mines which they had never seen, worked by thousands of slaves. But much of the work, he urges, was done by free workers, of whom there were at least 400,000 among the million citizens of Rome. So far from its being true, as he alleges, that 'they had a remarkably easy life,' their wages, even when they could get work, and were not supported by insufficient doles, were forced down to nearly starvation level by the competition of slave labour.

Friedländer, whose tendency is to defend the system or to minimize its horrors, describes the miserable existence of these 'free' labourers. He pictures Rome as an over-swollen, over-rich city with great destitution. [2] Some of the poor were not so unfortunate, but he says 'vast numbers were destitute and the doles of free bread only just kept them alive.' He describes the dark, low-ceilinged hovels in which they lived, if indeed they had not been evicted and had not to find shelter under steps or under archways. He pictures the 'home' with cold hearth, a broken jug, a mat, a little straw, insufficient dress and food—their drink vinegar wine, their fare black bread, beans, onions, or garlic, with a very occasional feast of pig's or sheep's head. As to the cruelty, every one seems to think that normally the cruelties on the modern slave plantation were worse. But Lecky notes their exposure to wild beasts,

[1] *The Church and the People.*
[2] *Roman Life and Manners under the Early Empire.*

and says 'they were often mutilated with atrocious cruelty, they were tortured on the slightest suspicion, they were crucified for the most trivial offences. If a master were murdered all his slaves were tortured, if the perpetrator remained undiscovered all his slaves were put to death, and Tacitus relates a case in which no fewer than four hundred suffered for a single undiscovered criminal,' although this custom was later abolished. A slave is cruci- fied for stealing a quail. Another is thrown to feed the fishes for having broken a vase.[1] I quote from this famous rationalist, for McCabe tries to suggest that the accounts are often the exaggerations of biased Christian writers. If these cases are exceptional, and meet with the indignation of a Tacitus and a Juvenal, still a society in which they were possible would need a lot of whitewashing. Mr. Belloc suggests that satirists who record such atrocities serve to prove the existence of a sane society invigorated by a healthy fury of self-criticism, but the workers of that period might be excused if they looked on things from a rather different angle.

But, after all, says Mr. McCabe, the workers had baths, free bread, and no end of amusements, 'there was the great circus . . . where, on more than a hundred days a year, he could enjoy, without payment, the finest chariot-races and the rarest entertainments that the whole world of his time afforded. In another part of Rome was the amphi- theatre (the Coliseum), where equally without payment 90,000 Romans witnessed the combats of beasts and gladiators.' A pretty picture! But the author forgets to mention that the shows were recruited from the slave class, and those of the working-class who had fallen on evil times. 'Of the poisonous character of these performances there can be no doubt.' The foulest tales were staged, and wretched victims condemned to death were foully murdered in the course of the play. Slaves were compelled to take part in the basest and most vicious scenes which were acted, not in play but in reality, before ferocious and vice-ridden

[1] Cf. Lecky's *Rise and Influence of Rationalism.*

audiences.   H. G. Wells calls the gladiatorial shows the organization of 'murder as a sport,' and his short account is fully substantiated by reference to the best historians. The gladiators were at first prisoners of war, Britons, Moors, Scythians, Negroes, etc., but, later, criminals were employed, and by such employment at least escaped the vivisecting tables at Alexandria.   'But as the profits of this sort of business grew and the demand for victims increased, ordinary slaves were sold to the trainers of gladiators, and any slave who had aroused his owner's spite, might find himself in an establishment for the training of gladiators . . . gladiators who objected to fight for any reason were driven on by whips and hot irons.' [1]   It is only fair to show that the gladiatorial shows aroused a certain amount of protest among the educated classes.

If this is how they treated human beings, the suffering of the beasts can hardly be imagined.

Little wonder that the Roman workers felt they were nearing the end of an age and longed for some life beyond the grave where their wrongs might be righted.

[1] *Outline of History.*

CHAPTER II

Mommsen shows how the earlier Roman commonwealth had been planned as an urban community, which through its free burgess body, gave to itself rulers and laws. Around it was a group of free communities, the Italian confederacy, sharing its life and fortunes, with an outer ring of allies, 'free' Greek Communes, barbaric cities and principalities, which were at first rather superintended than dominioned by Rome. 'But now the holder of sovereign power was either a single despot or close oligarchy of rank or riches. The magistrates were mere creatures of the rich. The burgesses had lost their power. The urban community had broken down through its unnatural enlargement, and the Italian confederacy had been merged in the urban community. The body of extra-Italian allies was speedily being converted into a body of subjects. As time went on the rule of the capitalists and financiers ultimately gave place to the despot Kaiser, if indeed they did not often rule alongside of him, or even sometimes dominate him.'[1]

Rome, says Döllinger, had thus become a crushing machine, imposing an iron yoke of domination on all the nations of the world.

The bitter lot of the slaves and 'free' workers of this greedy empire was intensified by contrast with the heartless extravagancies of the plutocracy. Seneca's diatribes against his fellow rich fitted ill with his own luxuries, and his much vaunted simplicity of life, mentioned earlier, hardly squares with the fact of his five hundred tables of sandalwood with ivory legs, his intrigues, flatteries and vices. (Dio Cassius, quoted by Hausrath.) But see

[1] *History of Rome*, vol. iv.

Seneca's good influence on the youthful Nero, page 8 of this book.

Among the more ostentatious and vulgar of the ultra-rich were freedmen who had bought themselves out of slavery, annexed wealth by ugly means and climbed into the highest places in the State; men like Pallas, who, as minister of finance, had amassed a fortune of sixty millions in fourteen years, Gabinius, who brought home from his consulate in Syria a fortune of three and a half millions. The excesses of such emperors as Nero or Caligula, who is said to have spent on one occasion a hundred thousand pounds in twenty-four hours, can hardly be exaggerated, but the private citizen who gave three hundred thousand pounds for a vase, four thousand for a table, or forty thousand for a Babylonian carpet, had little to learn even from Nero. (Cf. Dill.) It can hardly have been pleasant for the underfed workers to contemplate the money spent by the younger Claudius Etruscus on his private swimming-bath, with its dome of rich mosaic and its streams gushing from silver pipes into silver basins, the quarries of Numidia and Synnas contributing their richly coloured marbles to its sumptuous construction.

There is an amusing and typical picture of the doings of the new rich quoted from Petronius by Dill. An upstart freedman, whose master had left him a fortune, invests it partly in trading ships. He lost some half a million in a single storm, and gaily buys more vessels, and from that date everything prospers. He becomes fabulously rich; many of his estates he has never set eyes on. A banquet at his ostentatious villa is in progress. The bald old gentleman is discovered in a red tunic, his hands plastered with rings, playing at ball. Soon he is carried into the hall with attendant slaves, to a burst of orchestral music. Not feeling hungry, he first indulges in a game of draughts. The meal is a series of surprises, one dish represents the twelve signs of the Zodiac, another is a boar with baskets of sweetmeats hanging from its tusks. A hunter pierces its side and there appears a flight of thrushes. Towards the end the ceiling opens and there descends a figure bearing all manner of sweets. A long variety show was given, with acrobats and dancers and performing dwarfs.

At some of the dinner parties, napkins were dispensed with when the rose-scented finger-bowls appeared, as the napkins were beautiful slave boys, in whose hair the guests would dry their hands. The expenses of banquets were increased by the growing custom of giving presents to the guests—a few slaves or camels, musical instruments, weapons. On one feast, rather an exception even in Rome, sixty-four thousand pounds was spent. Friedländer, the apologist of this kind of thing, suggests that, after all, we have our freak dinners, and the object at these banquets was notoriety rather more often than guzzling. The gentleman who purchases a fish for five thousand sestertia only does so for the glory of giving a dish too dear even for the emperor. He admits that authors of the period speak of wines in which pearls have been dissolved, baths of costly scents and asses' milk, mules shod in gold and silver. There are many who would tell us all this was good for trade. Friedländer thinks the following menu exceptional: oysters, mussels, urchins, thrush on asparagus, fatted hen, ragout of oysters, fish with beccaficoes, loin of doe, wild boar, game pie, sow's udder, pig's head, fricassee of fish, two kinds of duck, hares, roasted game, meal pudding and dessert. He admits that the banquets of a later time may, with all the foreign dishes, have become more elaborate. This is fully confirmed in Gilman's *Rome*. After a description of an elaborate first course of twenty to thirty light dishes, he says that for the second course the whole world was laid under contribution and gives a much longer list of dishes than the above. There would sometimes be moving walls of painted panels suitable to each course as it appeared. The emetics to cause sickness at half-time in order to induce a second appetite have often been described.

The dressing-room of a lady of fashion contained the scents, unguents, rouge, powder puffs, scented soaps, and the hundred other fancy articles that we associate with to-day. These pampered women would reckon one another up by the question: 'How many slaves does she keep?'— and their slave girls were thrashed for the offences of sneezing, whispering, or coughing, and subjected to every indignity, while their lords and masters delighted in such sayings as: 'A man is worth just as much as he possesses,' and exhorted one another to buy in the cheapest market and sell in the dearest.

The reckless extravagancies of the plutocracy were not confined to Rome and the country houses of Italy. The great commercial centres, health resorts, watering-places, and other pleasure cities of the empire followed the lead of Rome in these matters, and indeed the Romans owed their corruption partly to the incorporation of so many Oriental peoples within the empire, kings and upstart plutocracies of the Orient vying with Rome in the vulgar magnificence of their cities and the extravagances of their private expenditure.

Of course, there were many rich people who disapproved of these vulgarities, and many kind and generous folk who, in spite of their wealth and position, lived an unostentatious life, friendly with their dependants, and disgusted at the follies of their contemporaries. The number of such families was probably on the increase, and this was markedly the case in the time of the Antonines. Extravagance and luxury are evil things, but they generally come in for a considerable amount of denunciation. It would be interesting if the moralists would sometimes turn from the subject of how wealth is spent to the more profitable inquiry as to how it is acquired. To this inquiry I will now turn.

CHAPTER III

HOW WEALTH WAS ACQUIRED

WEALTH, unfortunately, does not come down like manna from above, but comes up from the workers below. I have already mentioned the huge slave-run Italian estates of the capitalists, the directorships, the holding of shares in distant mines and other financial ventures, but we shall now consider some of what Dill calls 'the endless opportunities for self-enrichment in the administration of the provinces.' There is a passage in Pelham's *Outline of Roman History* where he says that the wealth drawn from the provinces by the State was, after all, trifling compared with that which flowed into the pockets of individual citizens. Even the smaller wars yielded a rich harvest, but 'the spoils of peace were richer than those of war and more easily won.' Many sons of the wealthy spent their energies in the civil service abroad, and, having made their pile, returned not to live a simple life upon their farms but to build themselves ostentatious houses filled with every luxury.

Mommsen's evidence is to the same effect. He speaks of the boundless extent of the mercantile emigration which tempted a great proportion of the Italian youth to spend their most vigorous years abroad.

That idealistic motives may have formed a part of the complex object of Rome in annexing a large portion of the world I do not deny, but 'the governing idea of the provincial institution was primarily financial,' and Rome was committed to a 'system of regarding the provinces chiefly from a revenue-producing point of view,'[1] but her method of extraction varied[2] in each case. Where there had been

---

[1] Rosadi, *The Trial of Jesus*. [2] Ibid.

a crushed and exploited people, she continued the tyranny in more or less degree along with the exploitation. Where some measure of freedom had formerly obtained, her administration was stern enough to produce the maximum of revenue, and light enough to avoid the expense and inconvenience of a rebellion. Sometimes she ruled directly and sometimes indirectly through native kings or native plutocratic groups. These raised a revenue large enough to pay the taxes to Rome, to pay the expenses of their own extravagant government, and to fill their own pockets.[1]

In some provinces Rome confiscated the land and worked it directly, or more often indirectly, leasing it to companies of Italian capitalists, who paid out of the huge profits of the concern a fixed yearly sum to the State. In other provinces she confiscated such lands as had formerly belonged to the native government, leaving the rest in private hands, but imposing a more or less severe tax. There were ground rents, taxes on pasture, taxes in kind on corn, oil, wine, as well as customs, port dues, frontier dues, dues on imports and exports. The cost of collection fell on the conquered peoples.

There were, in addition, all kinds of requisitions, for the people had to furnish shelter, wood, and hay to the Italians quartered on them—magistrates, civil servants, soldiers, and others. Extra supplies were commandeered in time of war, which were, in theory, paid for later, but as the assessments were made by corrupt officials without consultation with the people to whom compensation was due, and without the possibility of effective appeal, they gave opportunities for endless injustice.

Such provinces as Asia Minor, of course, yielded a rich harvest, but the fact that many districts, e.g. Britain, cost almost as much as they produced in direct revenue did not make the lot of their inhabitants any lighter.

The grossest scandal was the farming out of the taxes to private companies in all incorporated provinces (includ-

[1] Ibid.

ing Southern Palestine after A.D. 7). These companies paid a fixed sum to the State and extracted from the people extortionate amounts far exceeding that sum. 'Under all these circumstances, even a taxation, moderate in theory, might become extremely oppressive in its actual operation; and that it was so is beyond doubt, although the financial oppression which the Italian merchants and bankers exercised over the provinces was probably felt as a far heavier burden than the taxation, with all the abuse that attached to it.'[1]

Many authorities minimize the oppression of the provinces under the empire, while fully admitting their grievances under the later republic, but although the lot of the provincials was slightly better in the time of the Caesars, it was still appalling. The Italian rich continued to extract vast sums from the provinces, and the fortunes already made from these Oriental workers gave immense power to their possessors, which was wielded still further to bleed the people.

The subject of war loans and taxes has a peculiar interest for us in modern times. Mommsen notes that the employment of Rome's political ascendancy 'for the benefit of the private interest of every wealthy Roman,' rendered a usurious system of interest universal. The instance he gives is taken from a few years before Christ, but the system continued for centuries. Asia was unable to meet the war tax imposed by the Roman Government. The Roman capitalists advanced the sum required, and 'it swelled with paid and unpaid interest within fourteen years to sixfold its original amount.' Cities had to sell their public buildings, works of art and jewels, and parents their children into slavery to meet the claims of the Roman rich.

When the poor in such a province as Palestine were unable to pay their taxes, the tax collectors would advance the money on their lands, and eventually seize them in payment of the debt. When appeal was made for redress of some glaring injustice, the case came before a magistrate

[1] Mommsen, *History of Rome.*

who had often been a trafficker in taxes, or was about to be, or whose family was involved in such traffic.

The Roman state revenues in money and in kind were partly employed in doles to the Roman workers in bread and amusements to keep them quiet, partly in pensions for those members of the 'upper ten' who were fortunate enough to find themselves on the civil list, in the pay of the army, the upkeep of public buildings, new schemes of construction, salaries of ministers, magistrates, of a huge bureaucracy.

The fact is that empire always means exploitation on a large scale. 'Thinking in millions' is a most appropriate phrase for imperialists, though not quite in the sense in which Cecil Rhodes first used it. Wherever the imperial flag flies, or the imperial eagles are raised, there is freedom —freedom for the rich to exploit the poor. This is the white man's burden; and the Roman rich were ready with avidity to shoulder it. If the victims also feel it as a burden, that is because they have not appreciated the benefits of an imperialistic education.

Certain Marxists urge that the capitalist imperialism of the Roman Empire was completely different from that of modern times, e.g. Karl Kautsky, in *Foundations of Christianity*. Those who consider Kautsky a misinterpreter of *Das Kapital* agree with him here.

I have cited many authorities to show that the Roman Empire, some years before Christ, during his lifetime, and after, was a capitalist empire, based as Kautsky rightly puts it on 'expropriation of the peasant population, plundering of the colonies, slave trade, commercial wars, and national debts.' The following quotations show him to have an accurate grasp of Roman capitalistic imperialism:

'The usurious money capital of Rome also was unleashed against the provinces, in which it had every opportunity to develop its destructive power to the full, and to attain a position of importance which it did not enjoy in any other portion of the ancient world.'

'The tributes that were gathered in the Roman coffers

from the subject provinces were enormous. . . . But the ceaseless wars also cost a lot of money.'

Much of the booty from the provinces found its way directly into the pockets of the financiers; but much of it also, which went to the State, had to be used to pay the financiers who had advanced the money for the wars, and were growing enormously rich on these 'war loans.' They also gained colossal sums on their deliveries of war material to the State, much as do Krupps, Vickers Maxim, and Schneider Creusot in modern times.

'Great sums had sometimes to be advanced to the State, greater sums than any individual possessed. For this purpose, the formation of joint-stock companies was very useful. Usury is not only the earliest form of capitalistic exploitation, it is also the first function of the joint-stock companies.' Karl Kautsky then quotes Salvioli to the effect that Rome's financiers 'founded companies, corresponding to our joint-stock banks, having directors, cashiers, and other agents. Under Sulla the Asiani Company was formed with a capital that was so enormous that the company was able to lend the State twenty thousand talents, or twenty-five million dollars (five million pounds). Twelve years later it increased this loan to one hundred and twenty thousand talents. . . . Smaller resources were invested in the shares of the great companies with the result, as Polybius tells us, that the entire city [Rome] was a participant in the various financial undertakings headed by a few prominent firms. The smallest savings had their share in the enterprises of the publicans, which farmed out taxes and leased state lands, and yielded enormous profits.'

'All this [says Kautsky] sounds very modern to us, and it is an indication at least of the fact that Roman society, at the time when Christianity was being born, had advanced to the threshold of modern capitalism, and yet, the effects of this ancient capitalism were entirely different in kind from those of modern capitalism!'

He admits that modern capitalism and imperialism have the same ruthless exploitation of the people at home and the people of the dependencies abroad for its object, that both are barbarous and cruel; but there is yet an entire difference in the result, because 'modern capitalism creates a basis for an advance beyond this cruel destructive activity while ancient capitalism never could transcend that limitation.'

The motives are the same. They are equally ruthless, equally cruel, but the discovery of machinery, and the consequent vast increase of production, with again in consequence the vast opportunities of modern productive investment, give a completely different effect. He puts the crux of the matter thus:

'The accumulations made by modern capitalism, by plunder and extortion and other acts of violence, are used only in small part for purposes of consumption, are devoted chiefly to the production of new and higher means of production, thus increasing the productivity of human labour. The capitalism of the ancient world did not find the necessary preliminary condition for this task. Its influence on the mode of production was limited to a substitution of the labour of slaves for that of the free peasants, which was equivalent to a backward step economically in the most important fields of production, a decrease in the productivity of social labour, an impoverishment of society.' The gains of the financiers, officials, and small fry bourgeoisie generally, could not find an outlet in productive investment, so had to be lavished on enjoyment or on the production of new means for enjoyment 'or these gains, if we ignore those drawn from the few mining operations, might be devoted to the acquisition of property, in other words to the expropriation of free peasants and their substitution by slaves.'

'The plundering and devastation of the provinces, therefore, only served to give the financiers of Rome a means for permitting the decrease in the productivity of social labour, owing to the spread of slavery, to proceed more swiftly than might otherwise have been the case. Therefore, as a result of Rome's world dominion, the general

impoverishment of the ancient world begins to move
faster after the beginning of the Christian era than it
could otherwise have done.'

Now this is, in the main, true, but it is doubtful if Kautsky
does not rather minimize the opportunities for productive
investment in the Roman Empire. Cicero is by no means
the only authority we could quote on this subject, but the
plainest evidence may be gathered from his speech before
the senate in the year 66 B.C., and we must remember that
what is true of 66 B.C. is equally true, if not more so, of the
reigns of Augustus and Tiberius (during the Christ's lifetime) and of the early Christian era.

Cicero has been urging the continuance of the war in
Asia, admitting the vast expenses of the campaign, but at
the same time arguing that it is fully worth while from a
revenue producing point of view. A policy of the strong
arm, what we call 'firm government,' must be maintained
in the dependencies and especially in Asia, for in the case
of revenues, not only actual disaster, but the mere threat
or dread of it, affects them. Even where no actual invasion
has taken place, but the dread of such invasion is ever
present, 'flocks are abandoned, farming is given up,
sailings of merchants are cancelled. In consequence,
neither from harbour dues nor from tithes nor from the
tax on pasture lands can any revenue be maintained; it
often happens that the produce of an entire year is lost by
one rumour of danger, by one alarm of war.'

But just as we, in modern empires, do not hold on to
our dependencies only because of, or chiefly because of, their
direct revenue producing capacities, but because of their
indirect revenues from investment for powerful private
citizens of the empire, so it was, according to Cicero, in
the case of the old Roman Empire. For he continues [1]
'moreover, the property of many Roman citizens is involved,
citizens whom you, gentlemen, as becomes your wisdom,
must regard with the most careful solicitude. The publicans, most honourable and accomplished men (!!), have

[1] Cf. Dr. Grant's *The Economic Background of the Gospels.*

taken all their wealth and resources into that province; and
their property and fortunes ought, by themselves, to be the
object of your especial care.   In truth, if we have always
considered the revenues the sinews of the republic, certainly we shall be right if we call that order of men which
collects them the prop and support of all the other orders.
In the next place, clever and industrious men in all the other
orders of the State are either themselves now trading in Asia—
and you ought to show a regard for their interests in their
absence—or else have large sums invested in that province.
It will, therefore, become your humanity to protect a large
number of those citizens from misfortune; it will become
your wisdom to perceive that the misfortunes of many
citizens cannot be conceived otherwise than as misfortune
to the republic . . . for we know from experience that
when many lost great fortunes in Asia, at the beginning of
the war, *all credits failed at Rome from delay in payments.*
It is impossible for many men to lose their property and
fortunes in one city without drawing many others along
with them into the same disaster.   Therefore preserve the
republic from this misfortune!   For, believe me, as you
yourselves will see, *credit and the state of the money-market*
here at Rome, in the Forum, are inseparably bound up with
those fortunes invested in Asia.   Those fortunes cannot fall
without credit here being undermined by the same blow, and
perishing along with them.'

Dr. Grant regards this speech as 'one of the clearest
proofs of the commercial (or capitalistic) imperialism which
inspired the Roman march to world-conquest,' and notes
that this was Cicero's crowning argument for the more
vigorous prosecution of the war.   The Roman Republican
Empire, in its quick response to his pleading, '*appears*
almost in the guise of a vast commercial enterprise for the ex-
ploitation of the Near East ; a trading corporation prepared
to use force where force is required, but only as a means to an
end—greater trade and larger revenues.'

I do not, of course, mean to suggest that the opportunities
for productive investment in the old empire could for a

moment compare with the opportunities of to-day, and there can be no doubt that the Marxists are right when they insist that the modern form of capitalism and of capitalist imperialism lends itself more readily to a revolutionary transformation into a socialist structure, but I have insisted on the essential similarity in aim and, to some extent, even in structure of the ancient and modern empires, in order to show that the teachings of the Christ were given under much the same conditions as obtained in the modern world and cannot be dismissed as utterly inapplicable to it.

And, if this is the case, then it follows that what he says about usury and exploitation have a direct bearing on our own problems.

CHAPTER IV

POPULAR RELIGIONS OF THE EMPIRE

THE last years of the old era and the first years of the new were felt by all sorts and conditions of men to be the end of a world. A supreme sense of weariness dominated all classes, becoming often an acute misery among the wage-workers and slaves. A disgust at bringing children into the world increased among rich and poor. Birth-control and abortion were practised in wealthy circles, and the workers exposed and abandoned new-born children.

So dark and hopeless was the outlook that Tacitus was tempted to lose his faith in God and to despair of human nature. The rich turned to astrologers, fortune tellers, soothsayers, and magicians, and sought to drown their restlessness and disgust in alternate debauch and decadent devotions.

The poor could hardly be kept quiet by the State doles and free sports. The established religion of the gods of ancient Rome, scoffed at by the 'educated classes,' was only tolerated in the hope that it would keep the 'lower orders' in their places.

Stoicism, although it inspired certain individuals of the leisured classes with a philosophy of courage and the dignity of the soul, had no message for the workers of that under-world which it despised: in theory it related the individual to the society in which he lived, and was supposed to encourage the civic virtues, but in practice it was in-dividualistic and gave no sort of challenge to social evils, and, indeed, with its fatalistic outlook, this could hardly have been otherwise. So it encouraged men to put up with things as they were, to be passive, to endure; and when endurance was no longer possible, to commit suicide, but to do so in a leisurely and dignified fashion. We find a Stoic dwelling on the pleasing thought of how much good one might do with one's money, but the inquiry as to the source of one's income would not have been popular in Stoic circles. Stoicism, like modern Christianity, made some sort of attack upon the flesh and the devil, but none upon the world, and even the attack upon the flesh was half-hearted and sometimes consistent with a qualified approval of prostitution. Stoicism believed in the gods, but taught the one God above them all — the Lord and Artificer of the Universe, by whose breath we live — Nature, Fate, and Providence. The Stoic philosophers, as will be seen later, taught an excellent doctrine of human nature and of its original goodness in the golden age of man's innocence to which they looked back; but they had no hope of a better age to come here on earth. Undoubtedly Stoic teaching mitigated the horrors of slavery and helped the rich to a saner and more temperate life and to be more considerate to their dependants. In theory this philosophy believed in the equality of men. It possessed a literature containing many beautiful and imaginative passages, but it was, after all, as Thomas Carlyle has pointed out, a philosophy for those who were content to serve both God and Mammon. It was, in consequence, popular with the very rich, who, not unlike the pious wealthy of to-day, were relieved to think that the miseries of the poor were perhaps their own fault, or that poverty was inevitable and to be bravely borne, and that too much pity was a vice rather than a virtue.

Belief in immortality is sometimes the faith of virile people who are convinced that their activities will not be cut short by death, and who crave for some extension of personality and increased vitality beyond. But it is also the hope of the weary and disillusioned, who are content to abandon the struggle here in the hope that their wrongs will be righted hereafter. Such a hope is of great assistance to plutocratic empires, whose business it is to encourage those kinds of religion which Lenin has described as the opium of the people. It was to such religions that the Roman workers now turned, adopting with avidity certain Oriental cults with their promise of immortality, as they filtered through into the empire. We need not be surprised if Cumont, the great authority for these religions, should approve the turn the religious world of that day was taking: 'The Oriental mysteries offered their votaries radiant perspectives of eternal happiness. Thus the focus of morality was changed. The aim became to realize the sovereign good in the life hereafter instead of in this world, as the Greek philosophy had done.'

Among all these exotic worships there was one in particular which seemed to have vitality and the power of growth and endurance. This was the religion of Mithra, originally the Persian cult of a sun god. It had, with many additions, become a popular religion in Asia Minor, and from thence had spread to Rome some few years before the Christian era. Some writers date its arrival in the imperial capital rather later. It was a popular cult among dockers and wharfingers at the seaports; and in Ostia, the port of Rome, were to be found several shrines of Mithra. Rome itself possesses an immense and beautiful temple of the god. Soldiers of the Roman legions quartered in the Eastern provinces often adopted it as their faith, and, as they were continually shifting their quarters, spread it into various parts of the empire. Shrines of the god have been discovered in Britain. It was a religion peculiarly adapted to the needs of an army, making much of the heroic virtues, courage, and the like. Women were, perhaps, entirely excluded from this cult, but Cumont is uncertain of this. In any case, it was not Mithraism, but the worship of Isis, often suppressed by the Government but eventually officialized, which made a special appeal to women. Mithraism, which attempted to bridge the gulf between earth and heaven, told men of a genial god whose worship offered them release from all their gloomy forebodings, and assured them of enduring happiness beyond the grave. Its rites of initiation, fastings, scourgings, passing through fire and ice, and swords, suggested that life was a battle for the courageous, and the saviour it bade men worship was the slayer of the bull, the shedding of whose blood fructified the earth.   Its sacrament of bread and wine afforded a communion with the material things of earth, and with the being of the kindly god who was their author and the maker of all things living.   Within its oratories all were equal, although this equality was not carried beyond the sanctuary door.   Mithraism was alien to the sexual excesses of so many of the Oriental cults. In Rome itself, as earlier in Asia Minor, it was first the religion of the down-trodden, but it soon spread to the court and was taken up by the fashionable world.   It not only resembled Stoicism in the stress it laid on courage, but shared the less admirable feature of that philosophy in refusing to do battle with the world.   It offered men a life beyond, but held out no hope of a new world here below. It basked in the warmth of imperial and aristocratic favour, and the last emperor of the West and the last generation of the pagan aristocracy were its devoted adherents.   Dill speaks of the manifest support which Mithraism 'lent to growing absolutism and the worship of the Caesars.' Apparently it was destined to be *the* religion of the empire, yet it had no power of endurance.   The blood of the martyrs was not the seed of the Mithraic Church.   Immediately it was persecuted it seems obligingly to have flickered out, surviving only in certain of its more superficial aspects in the cultus of the religion that supplanted it.

About the year 51 B.C. there died, at the age of eighty-four, a philosopher named Posidonius.   Through him, to a great extent, there had come about that fusion of Oriental religions and of Greek speculation which led to cults of sun and planets, such as Mithraism, in their western form. This man, whose birthplace was about a hundred miles north of the sources of the Jordan, and therefore not very far from Galilee, was one of the great formative influences on pagan culture throughout the empire.   He was actually a contemporary of authors, who, under older pseudonyms, were reviving the Jewish faith. There are certain re-semblances between these Oriental-Roman religions, cults, and Roman philosophies, on the one hand, and that religion which helped to form the childhood of Jesus Christ, and which was the hope of the workers in Palestine. But in spite of these likenesses—the unity of the universe, the influence of demons—the differences are far more striking. In current pagan thought, events come to pass 'according to the inevitable course of things': in the Jewish faith events are shaped by the will of God and the will of men. The cultured pagan was an evolutionist, a determinist, who tended to deny evil in the world. In his religions there was no great day in the future on which God would vindi-cate himself, and in which the world would be shaped anew. To bear was to conquer one's fate. There was nothing of what George Meredith calls 'the rapture of the forward view.'

The pagan religions aimed at making men at home in the human society in which they found themselves. The religion of Palestine inspired men with the hope that it might be shattered to bits and then remoulded closer to the heart's desire. The pagan religions looked back, while the Palestinian religion looked forward.

CHAPTER V

THE JEWISH STATUS WITHIN THE EMPIRE

AFTER centuries of bondage to foreign powers, the Jews achieved political independence, about 142 B.C., and through internal corruption and dissension began to lose it again in the year 67 B.C., which saw the advent of Pompey in Palestine. There had sprung up in the period itself an intensely 'patriotic' literature which caught up and intensified the hope of a renovated earth which had inspired the prophets and other writers of the Old Testament. Men were to look forward to a golden age, after the crash of the existing empires and kingdoms. Sometimes it was pictured as the reign of a divine leader, sometimes as that of an inspired earthly leader, sometimes again as the reign of a collective people, but almost always as the reign of the Jews over the rest of the world. Palestine would become a mighty empire with the nations of the world voluntarily accepting the blessings of her rule or being crushed into submission.

As the Roman Empire increased its grip on Palestine this popular hope increased in intensity. Rich Jews of the governing class, who had allied themselves with the invaders of their country for the reasons which actuate rich men under such circumstances, had every cause to fear this fierce hope of the people, which was the very core of the ancient religion as it had developed under the prophets. The Roman conquerors had cause to fear it too. And yet the empire, instead of curbing the Jews throughout its dominions and suppressing their propaganda, actually encouraged them, allowing them their own law courts and exempting them from military service! This is the more extraordinary when we consider their

C   33

numbers and their influence. For many centuries there had been outside Palestine many more Jews than had ever lived within it. Sometimes, after a period of captivity, they had been encouraged to return, but the exiles had found themselves too comfortable in the larger world outside to become enthusiastic for a Zionist movement.

They were glad to support so patriotic a scheme with their purses rather than with their persons, and many of the poor had formed ties in the ghettoes of the commercial cities which they found it difficult to break. Hawkers and petty traders of the slums, usually, were on the way out and up to some more comfortable and remunerative position. It was not hunger for land—the Jews did not shine as agriculturists outside Palestine—but the commercial instinct which led the Jew to Greece, to Egypt, to Macedonia, to Spain, and to almost every country of the empire, and in Rome itself they had overflowed beyond their original quarter at Trastevere, and were found to the number of many thousands in every part of the city, especially in the business quarter which corresponded to the environs of the Bank of London or the Paris Bourse. The attempt of Claudius to banish them from Rome was not an unqualified success, and was quite exceptional. They were soon in favour with the Government again, and swarming all over the city. Harnack [1] shows that the Jews had become the second great power in what western writers were pleased to describe as the world, and so the dream of a Jewish empire dominating mankind was not outside the bounds of possibility.

These extra-Palestinian Jews were often immensely rich, and many a hard-pressed native government, many a political adventurer, were forced to apply to the wealthy Jewish houses of Alexandria, of Rome, of Asia Minor, as men and governments apply to the Rothschilds and other Jewish firms to-day.

With their commercial supremacy came political power, and power over the lives of men. The Jews were not

[1] *Mission and Expansion of Christianity.*

popular. Hausrath writes: 'Accustomed to cry out against oppression where they themselves were the oppressed, and ascribe to their creed an aversion due to their personality, they had no friends in the wide world but themselves, and the power of the state to which they sold themselves unconditionally.'[1]

How comes it, then, that a people so numerous, so rich, and so powerful, especially considering the fierce hope of the destruction of empires and a renovated world, which was the core of their religion, should have been not only tolerated, but encouraged by the Government?

The answer is to be found in the fact that these rich Jews, like their plutocratic compatriots in Palestine, finding themselves so comfortable in the present commercial and imperialistic world, had abandoned that ardent hope of a new world to be built on its ruins. They had 'spiritualized' away the religion of their forefathers—a process not unknown among comfortable modern pietists—and the Jewish propaganda in its new and innocuous form, with the approval of the rulers of this world, was making considerable strides throughout the empire. There was still the barrier of circumcision and the ceremonial law, but all this was kept in the background, and only brought forward, and even then in a modified form, when the would-be convert had made great strides.

Certain Jewish writings, under the name of the Sibylline Oracles, seem, at first sight, the one exception, for they do prophesy the golden age. This literature was put into the mouths of the ancient Sibyls to make it more acceptable to the Roman people, who were much attracted at this time to the Sibylline books. But the books that have come down to us are in great confusion, and their attacks on the Roman Empire are supposed by critics to be the work of Christians and not of Jews. The genuinely Jewish oracles belong to a

---

[1] For interesting accounts of Jews and Jewish propaganda in the empire, see Hausrath's "Times of the Apostles' in his *History of New Testament Times*; Renan's *The Apostles*; Harnack's *The Mission and Expansion of Christianity*, vol. i; Schürer's *History of the Jewish People*, div. ii, vol. ii.

period when the Roman Republic was still, in theory and reputation, though no longer in actual fact, just and democratic. The general destruction of the present order, and the coming of the New World, involved no direct attack on Rome, for Rome was then an ally, and not an enemy of the Jewish Free State. The golden age, in this form, was so little regarded as a menace to Rome [1] that her greatest poet accepted it and sang of its near advent. Virgil, a true nature poet, but a mild and gentlemanly citizen, living at ease among his contemporaries, takes the advent of this new world so lightly that he ascribes its coming to the messiahship of the son of his patron, a Roman politician, who, far from bringing in a golden age, was starved to death in the reign of Tiberius. According to Virgil, in the coming age the full-uddered goats will come to man of their own accord to be milked, and the lambs will stray about clothed in purple, saffron, and scarlet. This 'Swiss Family Robinson' ideal of the new world is also to be found in Philo, the plutocratic philosopher of Alexandria, whose Jewish house was a great money-lending power there, and would not wish the destruction of the empire in which he and his kind were so superlatively happy; the golden age is dished up to suit the Roman appetite. Jewish history is presented in a watered form: the strike leader and revolutionary Moses becomes, in his version, a harmless ethical teacher. Then we come to Josephus: an editor of history for imperial consumption who had vacillated between the various parties in Palestine, and eventually betrayed his country to the Roman invader. He was handsomely rewarded with lands confiscated from patriots and bestowed upon spies and traitors. In his writings, both Jewish history and Jewish religion were doctored to suit the Roman digestion, and to secure more privileges for those Jews who found themselves mentally at one with the imperial policy. It will not any longer be difficult to understand why the Jews and their religion were tolerated

[1] It is only fair to state that, owing to their spirit of independence, the Jews made bad slaves.

by the empire, and why the wiser emperors saw in them 'the surest allies of the constituted authorities.'

Even in this Grecized and attenuated form, the Jewish propaganda probably offered to the empire a religion purer than that of contemporary cults, but it was not the religion of the Kingdom of God as interpreted by Moses and the prophets, and made no attack on the system.

It is likely enough that the defenders of Nazi Germany and of British Fascism will read with delight the foregoing account of the Jews within the Roman Empire as proving what objectional persons Jews were and are, and as supporting the present persecutions. They must remember, however, that the empire only welcomed that type of Jew who was useful to it and a supporter of the *status quo*. There were pouring into Italy and the Roman provinces Jews of an opposite type, Jews who had not forgotten the ancient promise of a Kingdom of God, Jews who had become converted to the Christ and his renewal of the Ancient Hope, and his opening of the New World Order to all believers, whether Jew or Gentile. Obscure Jewish workers, converted to Christ and his resurrection message, carried the good news to all parts of the empire, and, instead of being welcomed by imperial officialdom, were persecuted and destroyed, much as modern Germany is persecuting and destroying Jewish and other Communists.

If the Jewish race have, at times, contaminated the world, it is also from that race that the hope of redemption has sprung.

PART II

THE KINGDOM OF HEAVEN

CHAPTER I

THE IDEA

IT is agreed on all sides that the Kingdom of Heaven was the main objective of the preaching of Jesus the Christ.

The message of John the Baptist as herald of the Christ had been, 'Repent ye, for the Kingdom of Heaven is at hand.'

On the arrest of John, Jesus came into Galilee, and leaving Nazareth he came and dwelt in Capernaum and 'from that time began Jesus to preach and to say "Repent ye, for the Kingdom of Heaven is at hand."' He chose certain disciples, who left their boats and followed him. 'And Jesus went about all Galilee, teaching in their synagogues the good tidings of the kingdom.' His model prayer, according to the same evangelist, contains the petition: 'Thy kingdom come, Thy will be done on earth as it is in heaven.' The Sermon on the Mount might be summed up in his phrase: 'Seek ye first the Kingdom of God and His justice and all these things shall be added unto you.' Later, 'Jesus went about all the cities and the villages (of Galilee) teaching in their synagogues and preaching the gospel of the kingdom and . . . saying the Kingdom of Heaven is at hand.' He sent out his twelve and charged them 'saying . . . as ye go, preach, saying, the Kingdom of Heaven is at hand.'

It is the same in the gospel according to Mark: 'Now after that John was delivered up, Jesus came into Galilee, preaching the gospel of God and saying, the time is fulfilled, and the Kingdom of God is at hand; Repent ye and believe in the gospel.'

Although the actual phrase is not used till later in the gospel according to Luke, the kingdom is the subject of

his first sermon at Nazareth, his preaching in their synagogues is mentioned, and that the burden of his message
was the kingdom, is made clear in a subsequent passage
where the crowd beseech him to stay with them and he
replies: 'I must preach the good tidings of the Kingdom
of God to the other cities also; for therefore was I sent.'
Again later in this gospel we find him 'going about the
cities and villages bringing the glad tidings of the kingdom,
and with him the twelve and certain others.' Later he
sends out the disciples to preach the Kingdom of God. He
tells his little band: 'Fear not, little flock, for it is your
Father's good pleasure to give you the kingdom,' and
again, although in another setting to that of the Sermon on
the Mount, he commands them: 'Seek ye His kingdom
and these things shall be added unto you.' In the Lucan
account of the Lord's Prayer some manuscripts omit 'Thy
will be done,' but all have 'Thy kingdom come.'

In the fourth gospel the mention of the kingdom is not
so frequent, but it is by no means omitted, as we may see
in chapters iii and xviii.

The Kingdom of God or of Heaven is mentioned some
hundred and fifty times by name in the New Testament, and
many more times than this, if we remember its synonyms,
such as the regeneration, the next age, the day, the city
of God, the commonwealth, the banquet.

Seeing, therefore, that the good tidings which the Lord
Jesus brought to mankind were the good tidings of the
kingdom, we must ask, at the outset, what is the Kingdom
of Heaven?

We are inclined to dismiss the unscholarly and untenable assumptions that the kingdom consists in a comfortable feeling in the individual soul between itself and
its private god, or that it is a place to which the soul soars
beyond the grave when it dies. But these misinterpretations are so popular that they will have to be corrected by
a close study of Jewish history.

There is yet one other misinterpretation which can show
a better fight, but which has equally to be corrected, namely,

the idea that the Kingdom of Heaven is identical with the Catholic Church. It seems ludicrous that modern bishops should talk of an extension of the kingdom when they really mean an extension of the area in which missionaries are at work. It is ludicrous enough when these bishops happen to be Roman Catholics, although, largely as that communion has capitulated to capitalism, it at least is an international, and is possessed of the international spirit. But when the term is used by the more imperially minded of the Anglican communion, almost as if an extension of a semi-christianized British Empire was synonymous with an extension of the Kingdom of Heaven, it is no longer ludicrous but savours of blasphemy.

Even as applied to the early Christian communities within the Catholic Church, although the phrase 'Kingdom of Heaven' was sometimes used in the sense that the early Church was the seed of that new world order, it was further defined by New Testament and post-New Testament writers; and it can be shown that the new world was conceived as still lying in the future and that the Church was considered as the organ of that brave new world, the midwife, to change our metaphor, to bring it to the birth.

Now in order to discover what the phrase actually meant in the mind of the Christ, we must first ask ourselves what it meant to the Old Testament writers, in the mind of the Apocalyptists and of John the Baptist, and how it would be understood by the hearers of our Lord. What were they expecting? How far did Jesus meet and how far did he correct that expectancy?

One cannot begin to understand the Christ's teaching, unless one has made a study of the Old Testament background which he and his hearers assume. This point is well brought out in the Report of Convocation called *The Moral Witness of the Church on Economic Subjects*. It is insisted in this document that 'Christianity inherited from the Old Testament certain social principles in part embodied in the Law and in part enforced by the prophets and moralists . . . the Lord will enter into judgment with the elders of

his people and the princes thereof; it is ye that have eaten
up the vineyard, and the spoil of the poor is in your houses;
what mean ye that ye crush my people and grind the faces
of the poor . . . the tendency of the legislation was to
raise the status of the Israelite slave to that of the hired
workman who was to be treated as a brother . . . we find
a prohibition of usury between Israelite and Israelite and
provision is taken against the permanent alienation of the
land; various enactments protect labour . . . the general
well-being is the supreme consideration restraining the
selfish acquisition of wealth. Manual labour is held in
honour; it is the necessary basis of all society.' Christianity did not take over the formal legislation of the Old
Testament, but it did inherit its moral principles which
Jesus Christ deepened and universalized.'

Dr. Gore, the editor of the *New Commentary on Holy
Scripture*, when Bishop of Oxford, wrote to the same effect:
'The Lord assumed all the Old Testament laid down . . .
the Law and the Prophets had been struggling and striving
for the establishment of a great social system on a great
moral basis. The Old Testament is full of all sorts of
social and moral doctrines, of social and individual righteousness. The Law is full of that, the Prophets are full of it.
Now do you see that every word our Lord said, he said to
people who had got all that behind them. He could assume
it all. It is the point from which he starts. Until you have
got there, you have not begun.'

The Kingdom of Heaven is a phrase which is not found
in the earlier literature, and I believe occurs for the first time
in the Book of Daniel, written about the time of the Maccabees and possibly the inspiration of their brave rebellion
against the Syrian Empire. But if the phrase itself is late,
the idea of the kingdom runs through the whole of the
ancient literature.

We shall note in our study of the Old Testament scriptures that the Kingdom of Heaven is not mainly a realm
within the individual soul, a kingdom of the domestic
virtues. That these virtues are included in its conception

goes without saying, but it is not mainly a private but a
public and political virtue that dominates the scriptures
of the Old and New Testaments, namely, the virtue of
justice or righteousness. This may seem surprising to
many of our readers who so seldom hear what St. Catherine
of Sienna called 'Holy Justice' preached from our pulpits.
To-day you will generally have to go to secular platforms
to hear this virtue mentioned. But it is this same justice
that shouts at the reader through all the sacred literature,
and it is to be the mainspring of the world for which the
writers were looking.

There are in the Old Testament nearly two hundred
references to being just and to justice, either under the
translation 'justice' or 'righteousness,' and in the New
Testament there are over a hundred references to this
same virtue. Mercy, mercifulness, compassion, pity, are
mentioned in the New Testament less than fifty or about
fifty times. Love or charity which, of course, sums up all
these virtues, including justice and pity, is mentioned in
the New Testament about one hundred and fifty times.
But we must remember the love commanded by Jesus and
his apostles is not the sentimental and emotional love so
often preached in the modern and perhaps sometimes in
the medieval pulpits, although the schoolmen set their
faces against neurotic emotionalism as did the great and
true mystics, e.g. St. Theresa, but that great love for the
Christ and his cause which demands all, and which the
many waters cannot quench, neither the floods drown.

The Hebrew words generally translated 'righteous' and
'righteousness,' but sometimes 'just' and 'justice' are
translated in the Septuagint by 'δίκαιος' and 'δικαιοσύνη,'
and in the Latin Vulgate by 'justus,' 'justitia.' Frederick
Verinder [1] gives many instances of this virtue of *justitia*
from the Law and the Prophets. It is against God's will
that you should cheat or defraud your neighbour by injustice, by false weights and measures,[2] by perverting

---

[1] *My Neighbour's Landmark.*
[2] Deuteronomy xxv. 13–16.

judgment against the poor and defenceless:[1] 'Thus saith the Lord; execute judgment and justice and deliver the spoiled out of the hand of the oppressor, and do no wrong, do no violence to the stranger, the fatherless, nor the widow, neither shed innocent blood in this place. . . . Woe unto him that buildeth his house by injustice and his rooms by wrong;[2] that useth his neighbour's service without wages, and giveth him not for his work; that saith, I will build me a large house and wide chambers, and cutteth him out windows, and it is panelled with cedar and painted with vermilion. Shalt thou reign because thou strivest to excel in cedar? Did not thy father eat and drink and do judgment and justice, and then it was well with him? He judged the cause of the poor and needy, then it was well with him; was this not to know Me? But thine eyes and thy heart are not but for thy dishonest gain (R.V.M.) and for to shed innocent blood and for oppression and violence to do it.'[3]

God himself is called Justice, without inequity, so that the conception of justice is the foundation of human law. 'That which is altogether just shalt thou follow that thou mayest live and inherit the land which the Lord thy God giveth thee.'

Nor were justice and judgment a mere matter of law courts. 'They that fear the Lord shall find judgment and shall kindle justice as a light.' This justice secured to the workers, as we shall subsequently see, the land as their right; Hebrew shall lend Hebrew, because of this fundamental justice to his brother, without grudging and without interest, the precept being extended by Jesus later to all mankind, for all men are our brothers.

Clive Binyon, the brother of the famous poet, had shown, in a little book on social righteousness in Old and New Testaments, that judgment throughout the Bible means social judgment, merciful and just administration of the law, especially in favour of the workers, the poor, the widow,

[1] Leviticus xix. 15, 35–7.   [2] R.V., by injustice.
[3] Jeremiah xxii. 3, 13–17.

the fatherless, and the foreigner. Having made this clear it is now possible to give a sketch of the history of this people as regards the idea of the Kingdom of Heaven.

The Hebrews, a branch of the Semitic race, were as a nation of no great antiquity as compared with the civilizations of Egypt or Babylonia, which again had behind them the Sumerian civilization. Their written records date back only to about 800 B.C., although they embody much ancient oral tradition and folk-lore. The Bible is a library of books containing history, poetry, legend, and its contents are of very varying value.

With the vexed question of inspiration and revelation we are not here concerned, except in so far as it may be noted that we believe this literature to contain a revelation from God and to be inspired by Him, not in the sense of being dictated by Him through absolutely correct recording but lifeless instruments, but through the mediumship and personalities of men inspired, quickened in greater or lesser degree by His spirit. The records are coloured by their individual personalities and judgments. But God does, nevertheless, speak through them to mankind, as, although in tones less clear, He speaks through the prophets of all the great religions from the dawn of history.

The Hebrew story suggests that the original home of the human race was in the neighbourhood of the Tigris and Euphrates; and describes their own stock as coming from Babylonia. There were from earliest times continual Semitic migrations into Egypt and Syria.

The Hebrews were possibly a people of the Arabian highlands, a district with rich soil, abounding with corn and grapes, with fruitful orchards and vegetable gardens, they increased in numbers and overflowed into other lands.

The Old Testament begins with an account of the creation of the world, the beginnings of mankind, their 'fall' from some original state of innocence. It is possible, as thought the Stoics and early Christian philosophers, that there had been an early communal state of innocence, unconscious, simple, unreflective, and that mankind 'fell'

from this period of 'innocence' into self-conscious individualism, where they began to have a knowledge of good
and evil, passed from the light into the darkness of greed,
individual and group selfishness, war, competition, strife,
and that the destiny of the race was, as taught the early
Church and the Communists of to-day, to win back the
communal society on a higher level.

This world commonwealth, which will be supremely
valued and maintained by collective effort, will consist of
alert and generous people, welding themselves into a class-
less society with infinite varieties within the common whole.
A commonwealth called in the Old and the New Testaments
the Kingdom of Heaven.

The 'fall,' regarded sectionally and in itself, was an evil,
but regarded from another angle, in that it was to lead on
to a kingdom of grace consciously maintained and valued
above all else—the pearl of price—was a good thing.   So
that certain of the schoolmen can speak of *felix culpa*, the
happy sin that led to the coming of the Redeemer who was
to bring us out on to a higher level of being.   Cf. Communist thinkers of our own day on capitalism.

Regarded sectionally and cut off from the whole process
of development the 'fall' was an evil thing.   Regarded
as part of the process a comparative good.   If mankind
could have had the imagination to see where all those other
paths led, the paths of selfishness, of domination, of greed,
of capitalist imperialism, of sin in all its branches, the
temptation to try out all these false avenues could have
been avoided and the higher rungs of the ladder reached
without the miseries that ensued upon these experiences.
Men ought, like Christ, who experienced certain temptations to travel the dark paths of attaining the goal, to have
rejected them, but they either did not or could not.   Hence
the path they have actually travelled.

CHAPTER II

IT may, therefore, be that the parables of Adam and Eve and of their fall contain in very primitive form a valuable account of an early experience of the race, and certain modern anthropologists would suggest that there has been such a 'time of man's innocence.' We do not wish to dwell too long on this possible explanation of the primitive stories nor to insist upon their correctness, but before we reject the suggestions contained in the folk-lore of the Hebrew or other races, we must remember that modern science often has a way of confirming what seems to us childish and absurd.

The Book of Genesis also records the flood and the fate of the iniquitous cities of the plain. We cannot comment on these stories, except to notice that, although there are many points of comparison between these tales and the literature of other peoples, there is running through them a distinctly ethical strain, which, although not entirely absent in other literatures, is more clearly marked in the Biblical accounts.

We would also point out, in passing, F. D. Maurice's interpretation of the building of the Tower of Babel,[1] as an attempt by men to build a society apart from the righteous God and in terror of Him. It was to be a society such as those founded by the great Asiatic imperial tyrannies, centred in the worship of brute force and animal powers, whose cruel purposes were to be frustrated by such means as human wit and strength could devise. There were to be many such attempts to build the polity of mankind apart from God, in societies involving exploitation and cruelty, such as those founded by the great River empires,

[1] *Patriarchs and Law Givers.*

but all alike ending in babel, confusion, and destruction. But the Hebrew polity was to be builded in protest against all such tyrannies.

We must deal at greater length with the story of the patriarch Abraham to whom was made the promise: 'In thee and in thy seed shall all the families of the earth be blessed.' The story of Abraham is of the utmost importance in Jewish and later in Christian literature, for it is the story of one who obeyed the voice of the righteous God in the spirit of those who can say, 'yea, though He slay me, yet will I trust Him.' In the Epistle to the Hebrews he is described as one who wandered forth, not knowing *whither* he went, but in faith, travelling onward, for he looked for a city which hath foundations, whose maker and builder is God. Both Old and New Testaments insist that because of his fervent faith maintained against all odds, 'in thee and in thy seed shall all the families of the earth be blessed.'

In some dim fashion Abraham saw that the Hebrews were to be separated from among men, not for some greedy pharisaic election, some private privilege against the rest of mankind, but as a holy nation, elect and precious, as God's pioneers and lightbearers for all mankind. Jesus can therefore say that Abraham rejoiced to see his day and he saw it and was glad: and St. Paul, interpreter of the Christ, alludes to the patriarch shepherd as to the father, not only of the Jew, but of all in every nation, of whatever race, who have the faith of Abraham, who are willing to do the will of God, and to co-operate with Him in establishing His international reign among men.

What, then, is this faith of Abraham, and in what is it seen? It is seen in Abraham's wandering forth, not knowing whither he went; in his brief sojourn in Egypt, his adventures in the land of Canaan, the quarrel with Lot, the division of camping-grounds between them, the birth of Ishmael, the flight from Sodom, the birth of Isaac the child of promise, when Sarah was past child-bearing and he himself impotent and as good as dead. Isaac was the only hope, for through him should come the people who should one day be formed into God's elect nation, with their poets and prophets and resolute leaders, and ultimately the Christ the redeemer of the race.

Abraham had hoped against hope, had hoped on when hope was gone, and his faith was justified by the birth of Isaac. Suddenly he heard a Voice: 'Take now thy son, thine only son Isaac, which thou lovest, and get thee into the land of Moriah, and to a mountain which I will tell thee of, and offer him there for a burnt offering.' Was this the voice of God or of Satan? But amid the confusion and darkness Abraham distinguished God's voice and obeyed. He rose up early, saddled his ass, took his young men and Isaac his son, clave the wood for the burnt offering and went unto the place that God had appointed him. Isaac with the wood upon his shoulder, and his father with the fire and the knife, journeyed together, and Isaac spake unto Abraham his father and said: 'My father.' And Abraham said: 'Here I am, my son.' Isaac said, 'Behold the fire and the wood but where is the lamb?' And Abraham answered: 'God will provide the lamb.'

The place is reached, the altar built, the wood laid in order, and Isaac bound upon the altar. And Abraham stretched forth his hand and took the knife to slay his son; and behold the voice of an angel calling to Abraham to stay his hand. 'Slay not thy son, neither do thou anything to him, for now I know that thou fearest God, seeing that thou hast not withheld thy son, thine only son, from Me.'

Abraham sees the ram caught in a thicket by the horns, and sacrifices the ram. The voice of God is heard again: saying, 'By Myself have I sworn, because thou hast done this thing, and hast not withheld thy son, thine only son, that in blessing I will bless thee, and in multiplying I will multiply thy seed as the stars of the heaven and the sand which is by the seashore, and thy seed shall possess the gate of his enemies, and in thy seed shall all the nations of the earth be blessed.'

The next great moment in the history is the story of Joseph, betrayed and sold, but destined to become great among the Egyptians: and this brings us to the period of the Hebrew sojourn in the delta of the Nile.

How long the Hebrews dwelt in prosperity under the rule of the conquering Hyksos dynasty is uncertain, but the date of 1600 B.C. is sometimes given for the expulsion of the Hyksos from Egypt, and it is probable that with the return to power of a genuine Egyptian line of kings there was an 'Egypt for the Egyptians' movement. This would account for the oppression of the Hebrews, and their being put to forced labour, for these Semitic settlers in the Delta might prove dangerous if they became the allies of an invading power, and there were at this time wars and rumours of war: labour was needed for the immense military and architectural adventures of the period. It was wise, then, to use the Hebrews, grown strong in late years in numbers, in the structural work, compelling them to leave their pastoral life for slave labour in the brickfields. Measures were taken to restrict their numbers and crush their proud spirit: taskmasters were set over them who lashed them to their work, but the night is darkest before dawn.

CHAPTER III

THE BIRTH OF A NATION

THE period of slavery may have lasted some hundreds of years or only a few decades: however this may be, the accounts in the Old Testament are too vivid for us to doubt that it was under the leadership of an actually historic character, Moses, round whose name cluster many legends, that Israel made its escape into the deserts.

The story of Moses as a babe hidden by his mother in the bulrushes and discovered by the Egyptian princess may be legend or history, but it is very likely that she adopted him and brought him up at court, and that he became learned in all the wisdom of the Egyptians. But 'it came to pass in those days when Moses was grown, that he went out unto his brethren and looked on their burdens, and spied an Egyptian smiting an Hebrew, one of his brethren. And he looked this way and that way, and when he saw that there was no man, he slew the Egyptian and hid him in the sand.' The miseries of his people might easily have been stifled in his mind by the allurements and luxuries of the court, but the attractions of a 'career' and the possibilities of advancement in the imperial favour counts with him not at all when the spirit of God had run through him like a fire of indignation on beholding the desolation of his people.

But the slaves were terrified, and when Moses interfered in a quarrel between two of them, they cried: 'Who made thee a prince and a judge over us?' Would he kill them as he had killed the Egyptian? His action reached the ears of Pharaoh who sought to slay him, and he fled from the face of Pharaoh and dwelt in the land of Midian. He lived there many years as a shepherd, and married one of

53

the daughters of the land. Under a new king, the children of Israel still sighed by reason of the bondage 'and God heard their groaning, and God remembered His covenant with Abraham, with Isaac and with Jacob; He looked upon their miseries, and determined to deliver them by the hand of Moses. Out of the burning bush He spoke and said: "I have surely seen the affliction of My people and have heard their cry by reason of their taskmasters; for I know their sorrows; and I am come down to deliver them out of the hand of the Egyptians, and to bring them up out of that land unto a good land and a large, unto a land flowing with milk and honey . . . come now, therefore, and I will send thee unto Pharaoh, that thou mayest bring forth My people, the children of Israel, out of Egypt."'

Moses drew back appalled by the difficulties of the task; against him would be arrayed all the forces of a colossal empire, and the terror and indifference of the very people he was commanded to rescue. 'They hearkened not unto Moses for anguish of spirit and for cruel bondage.' But just as Abraham had hoped on when hope was gone, so did Moses; and the spirit of God drove him forward till he had accomplished his work, and had led his people from the land of their bondage into the deserts beyond the Red Sea.

The imperial pursuers were destroyed by their riches. Their horses and their chariots availed them nothing, for the weight of their chariots dragged them down to the bottom of the waters.

The end of this agitator, who has not inaptly been described as the leader of a brickmakers' strike, was a lonely death in a foreign land, 'and no man knoweth his sepulchre to this day.' But Jewish historians have always attributed the birth of the nation to him, and looked back upon him as the great lover of liberty. Henry George concludes his sketch of Moses as follows: 'While the tombs of the Pharaohs mock the vanity that reared them, the name of the Hebrew who, revolting from their tyranny, strove for the elevation of his fellow-men is yet a beacon light to the world.'

A considerable period must be assigned to the wanderings in the deserts; again and again the people, tested by great privations and disasters, turned back in their minds to the fleshpots of Egypt. Better a tyranny under which, at least, they were fed, than starvation and uncertainty. Moses again and again recalls them to repentance, and encourages them to endure. By bitter experience they were hardened, and made courageous by the loyalties of their leaders, and began to be welded into a people destined to conquer the Promised Land.

Of the Ten Commandments and the giving of the Law, we shall speak in a later section; sufficient here to say that although much of the Law may have been of later development, there is no reason to suppose that it was not Mosaic in spirit, and that he may not actually have given them a framework of it. As legislator he had not only the learning of the Egyptian court, but the experience of imperial tyranny; his creative genius inspired by Jehovah,[1] would have foreseen the kind of social legislation which would ensure to the people their liberties. He warned them against the idolatries of the Bull, of the Baals and Nature gods, leading to brute force, sexual looseness, and apathetic laxity.

The last moments of Moses as recorded in the Book of Deuteronomy are magnificent drama. He was never to enter the Promised Land but saw it from Mount Horeb. Perhaps the New Testament writers read into that drama a completer vision of the Christ and his kingdom on earth than is justified by the text, but the Old Testament story itself suggests that God had promised to his servant Moses that a prophet should be raised up like unto him, and the Promised Land which Moses saw from afar was a land not only flowing with the good material things of life, but also inspired by the justice and mercy of Jehovah Himself,

---

[1] We have used the form familiar to the Bible reading public, although scholars would no doubt prefer 'Jahve' or 'Yahve.'

and therefore the Kingdom of Heaven in inception; for
Moses, like Abraham, looked for a city which hath foundations whose maker and builder is God.

Joshua and other natural leaders were the actual champions of the people in the period which preluded the time
of 'the Judges,' and began the conquest of Canaan, which
was a protracted task, with many alarms and retreats.
They by no means always remembered that the Lord their
God was a jealous god, but often mingled with the peoples
of the land, and with mixed marriages came mixed loyalties
and the confusion of idolatries. No doubt this driving
out of the peoples was a fierce and brutal thing, but the
Hebrews regarded themselves as God's scourges, and their
finest spirits who urged this ruthlessness also warned them
that the same fate awaited them if they practised the same
iniquities.

It was not mere economic hunger for new lands that
urged them forward, although the economic element was
a real factor in the situation; they were the ministers of
God's vengeance upon corrupt and cruel peoples as will
be shown in a later chapter.

Later we shall have something to say about the prophet
Samuel, but here we may notice the idylls of certain characters, foreign to the people of Israel, who willingly or
unwillingly furthered the cause of God and the kingdom.
There are the stories of Balaam, of Jael the Kenite, of
Rahab the harlot, and the romance of Ruth the Moabite
maiden.

The desert wanderings were nearing their end and the
children of Israel found themselves at last in a comparatively fertile territory east of the Jordan. Their advance
had been opposed by various chieftains, but they had
managed to subdue them; and they found themselves
safely encamped in the plains of Moab, almost opposite
to the town of Jericho. Balak, king of Moab, in desperation, sent messengers to a famous prophet Balaam, who
dwelt in a village on the banks of the Euphrates, imploring
him to come with all haste and pronounce a curse on the

advancing armies of the Hebrews. He sent again and again, for although the seer was willing enough to come, something, which he believed to be the voice of God, prevented him. At last he went and Balak believed that the spell would be pronounced over his enemies and that Israel would be thereby doomed. But as the seer journeyed an angel stood in the way and his beast, more psychic than the rider, refused to move. Balaam urged him on, and at last the ass spoke. That the dumb beast had seen what was withheld from the master and appealed in some way to him, perhaps by his very refusal to budge, is likely enough. 'The dumb ass rebuked the madness of the prophet.'

Balak builds the altar of sacrifice and offers the bullocks and the rams. Balaam, with the accustomed arts of the diviner, is about to pronounce the curse when again the voice of God speaks to him in the depths of his being and bids him bless and not curse, for this people is the people of divine destiny and they shall prosper and multiply. Here again is the old refrain recalling God's words to Abraham about his seed which should be as the stars of heaven in number and the sand by the seashore in multitude. To Balaam there comes the vision of a Messianic king and a world-wide kingdom to be established through this people he had been called to ruin; 'the vision of a divine kingdom, of a society in which God shall really be the King, in which all ranks and orders shall be subjected to Him and witnesses of His presence.'[1] For Balaam saw Israel abiding in his tents according to his tribes; and the spirit of God came upon him and he took up his parable, and said: 'How goodly are thy tents, O Jacob, and thy tabernacles, O Israel; as the valleys are they spread forth, as gardens by the river's side, as the trees of aloes which the Lord hath planted, and as cedar trees beside the waters. He shall pour the waters out of the bucket and his seed shall be in many waters, and his king shall be higher than Agag and his kingdom shall be exalted.'

[1] Maurice, *Patriarchs and Lawgivers*, page 231.

God had brought Israel out of Egypt, and He had the strength of an unicorn and shall eat up his enemies.

Balak's anger was kindled against the prophet who, before he returned to his own people, gave voice to the vision of a distant time; 'I shall see him, but not now; I shall behold him, but not nigh; there shall come a star out of Jacob, and a sceptre shall rise out of Israel and shall smite the corners of Moab and destroy all the children of Sheth. Edom shall be a possession; Seir also shall be a possession for his enemies; and Israel shall do valiantly. Out of Jacob shall come he that shall have dominion, and shall destroy him that remaineth of the city.' Doom is pronounced on the Amalekites and the Kenites. 'Alas, who shall live when God doeth this?'

The writer of this story does not hesitate to proclaim that the pagan and foreigner, Balaam, is inspired by the God of Israel. Whatever be the date of the romance of Balaam, the Hebrews were beginning to believe in a universal God who could inspire not only Israelites, but other peoples who listened to his voice and obeyed him.

We have mentioned Jael and note that her act of treachery, although it forwarded the cause of Israel, seemed to be below even the morality of those brutal times. Arabs and Hebrews alike would have been shocked at so base a betrayal of the laws of hospitality. But setting aside the immorality of the deed we may include it as another instance of a foreigner who recognized in the Hebrews the destined people of God. The act gave rise to the magnificent poem of triumph sung by Deborah the prophetess. The confederacy of Northern Canaanites had 'mightily oppressed' the Israelites. Jabin with his chariots of iron had kept them in subjection. Sisera, Jabin's general, was prompt to subdue any rising on the part of the oppressed people. Deborah, prophetess and mighty leader of the Hebrews, summoned the tribes to battle, and Barak, her lieutenant, equipped and trained a band of ten thousand warriors. In a daring onslaught they threw the cavalry of Sisera into confusion. 'A sudden storm caused the river to rise and overflow its banks. The horses and chariots impeded by the marshy ground were swept away by the swollen stream, and the discomfiture of the Canaanites was complete. Sisera himself fled from the field, and sought refuge in the camp of the friendly Kenites, but was treacherously slain by Jael, the wife of Heber, the Kenite chief, as he lay fast asleep and weary on the floor of her tent.'[1]

Ottley believes that the splendid ode in the fifth chapter of Judges which commemorates the triumph of Barak's army is one of the most ancient fragments of Hebrew literature, and bears every mark of being the work of a contemporary poet. 'It is evidently a product of the newly-kindled spirit of patriotism and religious fervour which impelled six of the tribes to unite in striking a blow on behalf of religious freedom.'

Deborah the poetess bitterly laments the cowardice and apathy which restrained certain tribes from sharing the peril and glory of the contest. It has been said of this ode that 'its verses go tumbling on, foaming like the waves of the Kishon upon whose banks the victory was won.'

'The kings came and fought, then fought the kings of Canaan in Taanach by the waters of Megiddo; they took no gain of money. They fought from Heaven; the stars in their courses fought against Sisera. The river of Kishon swept them away, that ancient river, the river Kishon. O my soul, thou hast trodden down strength.' Then comes the praise of Jael, the wife of Heber the Kenite, and the lament of the mother of Sisera, who cried through the lattice: 'Why is his chariot so long in coming, why tarry the wheels of his chariots? . . . So let all Thine enemies perish, O Lord; but let them that love Thee be as the sun when he goeth forth.'

When at last Jordan is crossed, and at the blast of the trumpet the walls of Jericho fall, we are given the romance

[1] Ottley, *History of the Hebrews*, page 108.

of Rahab the harlot, the foreigner who had her house on
the walls of the city and who had hidden the Hebrew spies
at the peril of her own life. She was accepted into the
comity of Israel and became the ancestress of David and
of the Christ. She may thus be considered as one of
those who had believed in the divine destiny of the
Hebrews.

There may here be mentioned another ancestress of
David and of the Christ, namely Ruth, the Moabite, who,
when bereaved of her husband, banished herself from
her native land, and accompanied Naomi, her Jewish
mother-in-law, when returning to Bethlehem of Judah. The
poem in which Ruth cries to Naomi: 'Entreat me not to
leave thee, to return from following after thee; for whither
thou goest I will go, and where thou lodgest I will lodge;
thy people my people, thy God my God . . . death alone
parts me and thee,' has become an immortal ode to the
memory of the Moabite, who came to Bethlehem in the
beginning of the barley harvest and became the wife of
Boaz, the farmer and owner of the field in which she
gleaned. So Ruth, foreigner, heretic, and peasant became
the great-grandmother of David, the poet and pastoral
king of Israel. . . .

The Judges were heroes who arose in the anarchic and
confused times of the conquest, and may be considered as
precursors of the Prophets, for they not only were leaders of
the people in battle, but recalled them to the pure worship
of Jehovah, and to the morality which was its outcome
when the tribes had mingled with the heathen 'and learned
their ways.' We may say with the writer of the Epistle
to the Hebrews, 'the time would fail me to tell of Gedeon
and Barak and of Samson and of Jephthae,' of Othniel, of
Ehud and Shamgar, and of Abimelech, the son of Gideon.

But it may be noted about this latter that he attempted
to found a monarchy, and in this connection there may be
remembered Jotham's parable of the trees who went forth
to anoint a king over them. Abimelech perished miser-
ably at the siege of the town of Thebez. After his fall,

the tribes relapsed 'into a state of social disorganization and religious degeneracy.'

The Philistines, a people of such low culture that their name has become a byword even to the twentieth century,[1] were originally a seafaring people who may have had their first home in the island of Crete. Later they migrated possibly from the coastline of the Egyptian delta to the maritime plain of Palestine. They seem to have been settled on the coastline either just before the invasion of Canaan by the Hebrews or very soon afterwards, and they pushed their conquests as far north as Gaza. They occupied five important strongholds, and are soon found in collision with the oncoming Hebrew tribes. Samson, a man of heroic valour and superhuman strength, did something to keep them in check, and the manner of his death, 'involving as it did a wholesale destruction of his inveterate foes, won him an honourable place among the ancient worthies of Israel.' Ottley sums up the period of the Judges as an age of iron, in which rude violence, treacherous dealing, murder, and robbery, were scarcely regarded as crimes, and even human sacrifice was within the range of possibility. But Israel's contact with the civilization of Canaan developed in it the trading instinct, widened the horizon of knowledge, and even gave some impetus to art.

In this period, although the Hebrews still worshipped Jehovah, they tended to identify Him with the various local baals, and it was not until the reign and reforms of Josiah that the symbols and altars of Canaanitish idolatry were finally abolished.

It is noteworthy that the Ark of the Covenant, given to them by Moses in the wilderness as a symbol of the spirituality of their worship, was used in a battle against the Philistines as a superstitious fetish. They bring it

[1] Cf. Matthew Arnold, *Culture and Anarchy* (1869), who adopted it from the term applied by German students to the townspeople, 'the outsiders'; probably first used after a 'town and gown' row at Jena in 1689, when the university preacher took for his text, 'The Philistines be upon thee.'

from Shiloh in the desperation of their defeat, 'that it may come among us, and save us out of the hand of our enemies.' The result of this was a more disastrous defeat with thousands of Israelites slain, and among them Hophni and Phineas, the iniquitous sons of Eli. The Ark of God is captured, and the Hebrews become the dispirited and disarmed slaves of the Philistines.

There follows the story of the adventures of the Ark, and the trouble it wrought among their enemies, who eventually send it back over the northern frontier.

CHAPTER IV

REPUBLIC OR MONARCHY, AND THE SCHISM

SAMUEL may be regarded as either the last of the Judges or the first of the Prophets. In this time of defeat and disruption he arose as the undoubted leader of Israel, and summoned the people to put away their strange gods, and to renew their ancient covenant. It is remarkable that he, like Isaac, was born when Hannah was past the time of child-bearing, when all hope seemed to be gone. He stirred up the people to enthusiastic resistance, and the repulse of the Philistines which he managed to accomplish was indeed an amazing performance when we consider the abject condition to which the Hebrews had been reduced. Great as was the victory, this pirate people, though no longer dominant, was still unsubdued until the time of the first kings.

Now the people demanded a king to reign over them, that they might be as the rest of the nations, and the demand was not without its justification, for the rule of the champions and natural leaders had been fitful and spasmodic, and a more organized and persistent resistance was necessary if their surrounding enemies were to be finally subjugated.

But Samuel, as the Scripture tells us, inspired by Jehovah, gives the sound republican reasons against kingship. Most critics consider the accounts as confused and contradictory at this point; God is angry with the people for their demand, which is represented as an act of disbelief in Himself, and yet God allows Samuel to bow to the wishes of the people and to anoint Saul to rule over them. But there is really no contradiction here, for neither in the

63

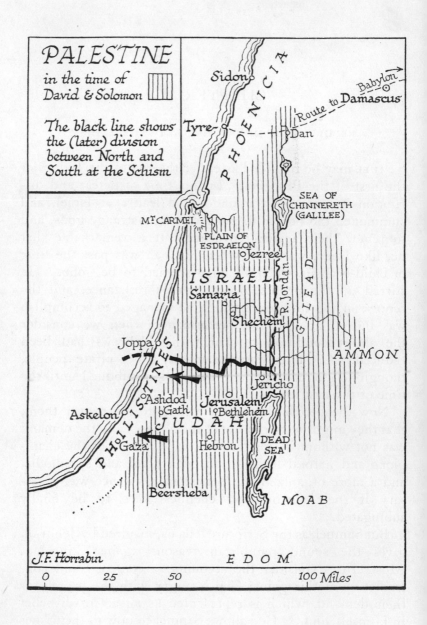

PALESTINE

in the time of
David & Solomon

The black line shows
the (later) division
between North and
South at the Schism

Sidon

PHOENICIA

Route to Damascus

Babylon

Tyre

Dan

SEA OF
CHINNERETH
(GALILEE)

M.ͭ CARMEL

PLAIN OF
ESDRAELON

Jezreel

ISRAEL

R. Jordan

GILEAD

Samaria

Shechem

AMMON

Joppa

PHILISTINES

Jericho

Askelon

Ashdod
Gath

Jerusalem
Bethlehem

JUDAH

Gaza

Hebron

DEAD
SEA

Beersheba

MOAB

J.F.Horrabin

E D O M

0   25   50   100 Miles

Old Testament nor the New does God force the wills of his people. He warns them of the consequences of their folly, but if they persist they must learn those consequences by their own bitter experience. Samuel is, therefore, to yield to them, but at the same time to say unto them: 'They have not rejected thee, but they have rejected Me, that I should not reign over them.' From the time of their coming out of Egypt 'they have forsaken Me and served other gods. Hearken unto their words, howbeit yet protest solemnly unto them and show them the manner of the king that shall reign over them. And Samuel told all the words of the Lord unto the people that had asked of him a king. And he said, 'This will be the manner of the king that shall reign over you; he shall take your sons and appoint them for himself, for his chariots and to be his horsemen, and some shall run before his chariots. And he will appoint him captains over thousands and over fifties and he will set them to ear his ground and to reap his harvest, and to make his instruments of war . . . and will take your daughters to be confectioners and cooks and bakers, and he will take your fields and your vineyards, even the best of them and give them to his servants . . . and he will take your men-servants and your maid-servants and your goodliest young men and put them to his work. He will take the tenth of your sheep and ye shall be his servants. And ye shall cry out in that day because of the king which ye shall have chosen you and the Lord will not hear you in that day.'

The subsequent history will show how completely this warning was fulfilled. It was to some extent true even of David, the ideal king; the warning was tragically confirmed in Solomon his son, and in many a monarch of the North and of the South in after years.

Before commenting on the lives of Saul and David, something should be said of the nature of the monarchy in Palestine. Many authorities deny that the kings were democratically elected, but in this they appear to be incorrect. Many of them, although anointed by prophets in obedience

D

to the voice of God, were at the same time chosen by the people. Saul was anointed by the inspired Samuel, but this choice is afterwards confirmed. 'Then said Samuel to the people, Come, and let us go to Gilgal, and renew the kingdom there. And all the people went to Gilgal; and there they made Saul king before the Lord, in Gilgal.'[1] David was the choice of the nobles and leading men, but was certainly approved and acclaimed by the popular voice. Solomon, who was not David's eldest son, but the son of his favourite, Bathsheba, was nominated by David for the succession, and was greeted by the acclamations of the populace. The successions were generally, though not always, through the royal lineage.

Much later in the history of Palestine, when an attempt was being made to put a foreigner on the throne, 'the people of the land' appoint Josiah, when only a child: or to take an earlier instance, i.e. the case of Rehoboam: 'All Israel were come to Shechem to make him king.'[2] We might also mention the popular election of Ahaziah, son of Jehoram, in Jersualem; of Uzziah; of Jehoahaz, son of Josiah.

In this connection, something should be said of the reign of Josiah. At the reading of the renewed Covenant, 'a vast concourse of people was assembled in the Temple Court,' and after a sacrifice had been made to the Lord, there was a kind of ritual dance by the whole procession, nobles, priests, prophets, and populace. 'It was a great day—the birthday of constitutionalism in Jerusalem; and the form of city law was found neither in priestly instruction nor royal ordinance, but in the solemn agreement of all classes of the free people in the presence of their God.'[3]

This digression has been useful as showing that even if Samuel's out and out republicanism was more in accordance with the ultimate ideal of the Kingdom of God, the monarchy was never in intention, and seldom in fact, to

---

[1] 1 Samuel xi. 14, 15. [2] 1 Kings xii. 1.
[3] J. C. Todd, *Politics and Religion in Ancient Israel*, page 221.

take the pattern of the cruel overlordships of the great River empires.

The first years of Saul's reign were marked by considerable victories and the exploits of the king and Jonathan his son read like some Homeric epic, but his disobedience to the voice of God leads to his rejection and the secret anointing of David. We must mention the stories of David and Goliath, of Saul's melancholy, the prelude to madness, and of David's charming him back to sanity by his music. David's growing popularity is expressed in the people's shout, 'Saul has slain his thousands but David his tens of thousands.' Saul naturally becomes a prey to jealousy, and his rival flees to Ramah. David, in danger of his life, gathers to himself in the cave of Adullam his own clan and many desperate men, outlaws, debtors, bandits, all who had grievances against the reigning monarch. There follow the stories of David among the Philistines, of his romantic friendship with Jonathan, of Saul's sense of impending doom and his consultation with the witch of Endor who summons from the grave the ghost of Samuel. Saul is defeated by the Philistines; Jonathan his son is killed; there is the splendid loyalty of the king's armour-bearer followed by Saul's honourable suicide.

David in those latter days had still loved Saul, and could sing of Saul and Jonathan: 'They were lovely and pleasant in their lives, and in their death they were not divided.' He was content to remember the genuine and brave leader of Israel before jealousy and madness had descended upon him, to remember the days when the people had said: 'Is Saul also among the prophets?'

David was a noble soldier, a great poet, and, for the first few years of his reign, a shepherd king, not unlike the natural leaders who had preceded the monarchy. He was no mean statesman and by adventurous soldiery and clever statecraft brought great prosperity to Israel. He united the tribes for the first time into a solid nation, and extended the borders of his kingdom right up to the Euphrates, and southward to the borders of Egypt, and gave the nation

their necessary seaboard on the Mediterranean. He made
Jerusalem his capital, brought thither the Ark as centre of
the national worship, and planned the Temple. He was
loyal to the faith of Jehovah unmingled with foreign cults.
His close alliance with the Phoenician city of Tyre and
with its wise and enterprising King Hiram is evidence of
his statesmanship, and he did not, like so many of the
kings that followed him, allow himself to be corrupted by
the bestial and avaricious cults of the Powers to which he
was allied. He did everything he could to atone for his
crime against Uriah and the taking of Bathsheba to wife;
if he was great in his sins, his repentances were deep and
open. There is no reason to doubt that many of the
psalms were by his hand, and the fact that the whole psalter
is attributed to David is evidence of his popularity with
later ages. 'He was a man of strong passions and of strong
virtues, a national hero indeed; and it is most human and
natural that later years should idealize him, soften or forget
his faults, and exalt his virtues, till at last he became the
pattern for a still greater king of their noblest visions, a
son of David who should at last establish an everlasting
Kingdom amongst men.'[1]

The last years of King David's reign do not, however,
bear out this idealized picture of the Messianic monarch;
a harem is, in any case, an expensive luxury, and David's
favourites were by no means always chosen from the people
of Israel. Some of these would introduce foreign ways,
and we hear in David's latter years of houses of cedar
and palaces of ivory. The transition, therefore, from the
pastoral simplicity of Israel's first kings to the capitalism
and exploitation of Solomon's reign is not so startling as
might at first be supposed.

Solomon, son of David by Bathsheba (about 970 B.C.),
determined to bring his kingdom into line with the great
empires of the world; his wisdom was not the deeper
wisdom of the prophets, but a practical insight into the
management of men and of affairs, and even of this type

[1] T. C. Fry, *Old Testament History*, page 100.

of wisdom Solomon did not possess over much, or, if he ever had it, he lost it as his reign advanced. David had at least risen from the people: Solomon was born in the purple. In accordance with his imperial ambitions, he consummated a marriage with the daughter of Pharaoh, and this act brought him in touch with the old and luxurious civilization of Egypt. In order to equip his capital with magnificent public buildings, he hired Phoenician architects, who constructed palaces for himself and his Egyptian queen and a temple of such magnificence as the rustic Hebrews had never seen. This building was constructed by foreign labour, and although it became the nucleus of a public worship, it was, in fact, but the king's private chapel, and was not indeed free of heathen symbols.

His numerous wives and concubines and his enormous court *entourage* 'necessitated a luxurious daily provision,' and this was maintained by forced levies, not only upon conquered peoples, but upon the Israelites themselves. He did indeed manage to consolidate the kingdom, welding together its disorganized tribal divisions into some sort of unity; but because that unity was not willing, not spontaneous, but achieved by the methods of an Oriental despotism, it was short-lived. 'More than any other Jewish king he realized the importance of foreign alliances which were closely connected with his commercial policy.' A lucrative trade was developed in gold, spices, sandalwood, apes, ivory, and peacocks. The Ophir trade must have been connected with South Arabia, hence the visit of the Queen of Sheba. Great wealth and poverty, the gulf between rich and poor, and growing discontent, marked the progress of this disastrous reign. The exploitation of the people became an established fact. 'His reign came to be idealized, but his policy was clearly economically and socially unsound, and could only lead to ruin.' His introduction of horses and chariots was looked on with suspicion by the old-fashioned Jews, who regarded the horse as an emblem of pride and luxury. The horse was always deemed the instrument of war, not of peace. He

established a fleet of trading vessels on the Red Sea manned
by Phoenician sailors.[1]

We have said that the tribal unity that he achieved was
short-lived. The growing opposition to the exploitation
involved in his extravagant building, the expenses of his
harem, and the other luxuries of his reign was not unnatural. 'Semitic dislike to centralization, resentment of
taxation, and offended religious feeling, combined to lay
on the people's loyalty to the central authority a greater
strain than it could bear. The institution of the kingdom
had changed the whole basis of the national life. The
'elders' and local leaders administered a law which all
men recognized, and remained responsible to the community
with which they were in close contact. The hereditary
king governed by his own will, and was responsible to no
one. His officials and the new men who carried on the
increasing trade were equally remote from contact with
and responsibility to the community. The new relations
with the outside world into which the nation was carried
implied a certain change in religious attitude. The older
system had an ethical basis, and the new kingdom as yet
had none.'[2]

Naturally enough, the prophetic party drifted into
opposition; and the growth of plutocratic imperialism, the
grinding of the poor, the departure from the ancient justice
and simplicity, the riding rough-shod over tribal law and
custom, culminated in a revolution which rent the country
in twain. As so often in history, the rebels were the true
constitutionalists, in the sense that they were loyal to custom
law against which the king himself had been in rebellion.
Significant parallels may be found in the history of medieval
Europe, and the scholastic doctrine of the people's right,
not only to elect, but in extreme instances to dethrone the
monarch, when his rule had become tyrannous and un-

---

[1] Most of this information has been taken from Hastings's *Dictionary of
the Bible*, vol. i.

[2] *The People of the Book*, Chap. **IV**, 'The History of Israel,' by Adam
C. Welch.

bearable, and a violation of constitutional and custom law.

On the death of Solomon, his son, Rehoboam, a man 'ample in foolishness and lacking in understanding,' seems to have been proclaimed king in the South without opposition, but, wanting to test the loyalty of the northern tribes, he proceeded to Shechem to have his kingship confirmed at that ancient shrine. Ahijah, prophet of the Lord at Shiloh, urged Jeroboam, an Ephraimitish officer, to revolt. Jeroboam, with a mass of the people, met Rehoboam at Shechem and persuaded them to demand lighter taxation and the cessation of oppressions as the price of their allegiance. The foolish king, who had at first consulted old and wise counsellors, ultimately listened to youthful hotheads and replied: 'My father chastised you with whips, but I will chastise you with scorpions.' And this is met with the prompt rebel watchword, 'To your tents, O Israel.' The ten tribes chose Jeroboam as their king, and the South had no power to quell the revolution. North and South were never again united.

There was intermittent war between the northern and southern kingdoms, carried on by Rehoboam and his successors, but the South was never able to win the allegiance of the northern tribes, either by diplomacy or compulsion. Judah was left small and enfeebled by the schism, and was further weakened by the invasion of Shishak, King of Egypt, possibly encouraged by Jeroboam, who had made an alliance with the Egyptians, who now plundered Jerusalem and the temple treasure.

Southern history, for the time being, becomes uneventful. The northern tribes, politically and economically strong, at first flourished under the rule of Jeroboam. This monarch stood for the elective and democratic principle against the hereditary kingship of the South, but he soon introduced the very evils, or many of them, against which his original protest was made. He exalted Dan and Beth-el, the ancient shrines of tribal worship, but he set up in them images of Jehovah in the form of a bull, and this bull-worship was always a cultus which glorified brute force against a more ethical religious system. 'The real offence of this schismatic worship in the eyes of the prophets lay in its reactionary character. . . . The establishment of the bull-worship was specially disastrous; and involved a practical abandonment of the Mosaic ideal; the simple and imageless service of Jehovah was debased to the level of a heathen ceremony,' and Jeroboam became in tradition 'the man who made Israel to sin.' More than one prophet denounced his apostasy, and foretold the doom of his house. It is significant that the history of the northern kingdom is marked by a series of revolutions, while in Judah the regular succession of Davidic kings was almost uninterrupted till the Captivity.

It is true, however, that we have scanty material wherewith to form a judgment of the character of Jeroboam; and although disaster fell upon his son, he himself reigned for twenty-two years and died peacefully in his bed.

Jeroboam's heir was murdered within two years of his coming to the throne by Baasha, who seized power; but his reign was short and his support of the bull-worship of his predecessors was denounced by one of the prophets who foretold disaster. Elah, his son, reigned in his stead, but in two years met the just reward of his dissolute life at the hands of a conspirator, Zimri, who was one of his officers. He seized the throne, but himself perished within a week in the flames of his palace, and Tibni, another pretender, was as speedily dispatched. Omri, the next northern king, was a man to be reckoned with. His power was so great that the land of Israel became known to the Assyrians as the land of Omri. He made his capital Samaria, which now becomes of great importance. It was nearer the seaboard and this helped to develop trade with Phoenicia.

There followed great military successes against the Moabites, who from now onwards for the next forty years became tributary to Israel. Assyria begins to be troublesome to Syria and perhaps to Israel. It is even possible that Omri had to buy off the Assyrians by paying tribute. By the organization of a powerful army Omri was able to reduce Moab to vassalage, and also to pacify the surrounding country. He secured an armed peace such as there had not been since the days of Solomon.

His greatest battles were fought against the Syrians, but although his wars were in the main successful, he was forced to cede to them certain important cities, and to give them trading quarters in his metropolis. Omri may be considered as the cleverest and most successful ruler in the North since the schism. He died peacefully after reigning about fifteen years.

* D

CHAPTER V

THE ECONOMICS OF MOSES

IT is impossible to deal with the reign of the son of Omri, Ahab, without treating at some length the social and economic conditions of the people both under the first kings and under the divided monarchy. And to this end we must consider the Mosaic legislation, and ask how far it had been carried into effect after the conquest of Palestine by the Hebrew people.

Hebrew tradition assigns to Moses the development of the idea of the one God, the Lord our Righteousness, the God of Social Justice: this righteous God gives through Moses his servant the Ten Commandments, or Ten Words, to the people in the desert, and indeed, according to tradition, the whole of the social, economic, sanitary, and ceremonial legislation. That there are various strata of the Law is a commonplace of modern criticism, but our Lord, his disciples, and all his contemporaries would regard the various strata as all of a piece, and I am inclined to think that the social and economic law attributed to Moses may be much more homogeneous and due to the inspiration of this great 'praiser of equality' (Philo) than is generally supposed.

We have seen that the conquest of Canaan was very gradual, but as certain tribes got possession of tracts of land what was the condition of its tenure? We may date the Trans-Jordanic conquests as well before 1250 B.C., the reign of Saul about 1020 B.C., David 1000 B.C., and Solomon about 970 B.C. The disruption of the kingdom may have been about 935 B.C. Now by the end of Solomon's reign all the tribes would have been in possession of the various districts assigned to them, and the tenure of these lands, according to the Mosaic tradition, was in this manner. The earth was the Lord's and the fullness thereof:

74

God was the ultimate landlord, but 'the earth had He given to the children of men.' The Mosaic legislation did not provide for peasant proprietorship, but for the parcelling out of the land among the tribes, each tribe again dividing it among its families. The families were not absolute owners, but something more like tenant holders under their tribe. The size of the holdings was from sixteen to twenty-five acres. Although the eldest son would succeed to the headship of the family, there was no primogeniture in the sense of sole ownership by the son; but he would be the guardian of the rights of the whole family, and the land would remain the family possession.

Landlordism was strictly prohibited; the land was, under God, to belong to groups of peasants who worked it, and they were not to be exploited by means of rent or of interest. There is indeed no provision made for a landlord class or for *rentiers*. The Levites were indeed the only tribe that were not allotted land, except a certain amount of pasturage for their cattle. They were mingled among the rest of the tribes, and were supported by them by means of tithe: but they were by no means a *rentier* class, for they had to render service in return for their support. What would have been their original rights in the land were compensated by the tithe in return for services rendered to the community, for 'they were not only the national clergy—sacrificing, absolving, and blessing—but also the teachers of religion and law, administrators of justice, the medical officers of health and sanitary inspectors, charged with the duties of inspecting, isolating, and (after recovery) disinfecting persons suffering from certain contagious diseases, of disinfecting unclean garments and bedding, of inspecting, cleansing, or, if need be, demolishing infected dwellings; and so on. This mixture of sacred and secular functions is characteristic of a theory of government which, recognizing no king but God, could draw no hard-and-fast line between the service of God and the service of humanity.' [1]

[1] Frederick Verinder, *My Neighbour's Landmark.*

The last of the Ten Commandments, 'Thou shalt not covet thy neighbour's house,' etc., so often quoted as a rebuke to those who would break up the huge landed estates, seen in reference to this distribution of the land among peasant communes, certainly gives no support to landlordism, but sternly challenges it.

Hebrew legislation was realistic in that it recognized an avaricious strain in human nature, and made every possible provision against the growth of these large estates, and the eviction of the working peasant from his holding and his home. In the first place, both the Law and the Prophets continually denounced as deadly sin the removal of a neighbour's landmark. The key passage [1] on the subject: 'Thou shalt not remove thy neighbour's landmark, which they of old time have set in thine inheritance, which thou shalt inherit in the land that the Lord thy God giveth thee to possess it,' may be more forcibly rendered: 'Thou shalt not set back thy neighbour's boundary.' This would apply both to the narrowing of the family plot, or tampering with the boundaries of the communal land. 'Under the old Hebrew system of the cultivation in common of the village land, the boundaries of the plots may have been indicated, as at the present day, by a furrow double in width to the ordinary one,' each end being marked by a boundary stone. 'The form of land grabbing by setting back a neighbour's boundary line must have been common in Old Testament times, to judge by the frequent references to, and condemnation of, the practice.' [2]

The law of the landmark was frequently disregarded in spite of denunciations of the land grabber by the prophets. However stringent the law of the boundary or landmark, there will always be greedy people, longing to become rich without working, who will be on the look out to evade the law and seize upon their neighbour's holdings. They will either annex the land by violence or by cunning. But the easiest method of annexation in such a community as

---

[1] Deuteronomy xix. 14.

[2] Hastings's *Small Dictionary of the Bible*, 'Landmarks.'

that of the Hebrews was by money lending and mortgage. The richer peasants and nobles would be inclined to lend money to a family in difficulties at as high a rate of interest as they could get; and if they were fortunate enough to be able to do this on a large scale, they might live as wealthy people on the interest of the loans. The Law, therefore, forestalled this by strictly forbidding all usury. Usury meant, as it did in the English dictionaries till quite recently, the charging of any increase. A penny increase was just as much usury as ten or a hundred per cent. All interest whether in money or in kind was strictly forbidden by the Law, which, by the way, Jesus said he had come to fulfil. But the anti-usury laws were often broken by the more powerful sections of the community and such reformers as Nehemiah rebuked the rich for this robbery of the poor and demanded restoration, not only of land, but of goods. But even where money or tools or capital in one form or another was lent to the small holder without interest, it was lent on the security of the holding, and often where the worker was unable to repay the debt, he was sold up and evicted.[1]

In view of the fact that the taking of interest bites into the life of the poor man and devours him, it is significant that the term for usury in Hebrew actually means 'biting.' The prohibition of usury in money or in kind will be found in Exodus, Deuteronomy, and Leviticus. Denunciations of the practice may be found in Nehemiah, Ezekiel, Isaiah, Jeremiah, in Psalms, and in the Proverbs.

I have suggested that Moses may actually have been the author of the land legislation, though not, of course, in its detail, but he would have seen, and made some provision against the large landed estates of Egypt; equally would he have foreseen the necessity of providing against the taking of interest, having had experience of the Egyptian practice of loans that sometimes rose to a hundred per cent.

We shall presently deal at some length with the periodic

[1] Cf. my pamphlet *The Law and the Prophets*, published by the Catholic Crusade.

re-distribution of land, or the law of Jubilee, but first we must mention the Sabbatical Year; it not only made provision for those who actually had become poor by the loss of their lands, but released them from their debts to the usurer. In this year there was also a manumission of all Hebrew bond-servants. There were certain instances in which the Law did allow for bond-slavery within the nation, but this was not to be perpetual, and was cut short by the provisions of the Sabbatical or seventh year. For these reasons, this year was often called the year of Release.

It has a curious parallel in the Sabbath, or seventh day of rest: you have in Hebrew legislation these humane provisions of the seventh day, the seventh year fallow, and the seven-times-seventh year, which is the year of Jubilee, the great half-century return of the land to the people.

The Sabbath is based on the necessity for leisure, not only for man, but for beasts; and the foreigner among them is not forgotten. The Sabbatical Year is based on this same necessity for leisure; it was to be a year of rest, but not of idleness, twelve months of recreation, or more precisely re-creation. 'It was only agricultural labour that was forbidden—ploughing, sowing, reaping, pruning, vintage. Other occupations were undoubtedly permitted, but the leisure from the ordinary work of the farm and vineyard was used at least in part, for educational ends.' Great educational meetings were held to hear the reading of the Law and to pursue its study.[1] As we are beginning to see, this study of the Law was not the learning by rote of barren rules, or of how one may go to heaven when one dies; a future existence beyond death was not its objective. 'The future life to which the Law points as the result and the reward of right doing is the ideal life of a free and industrious commonwealth, in which every citizen, secure in the enjoyment of the produce of his labour, surrounded by stalwart sons and comely daughters, sits under his own

[1] Deuteronomy xxxi. 10–13; Nehemiah viii. 16–18; cf. also Josephus's *Antiquities*, iv, 8.

vine and his own fig tree, none daring to make him afraid.'[1]

How liberal an education this year of study would give can be seen when we consider that the Law contained the biographies of national heroes, the history of the nation, the ceremonial of the sacrifice, liturgical studies, social, sanitary, and economic regulations. It was based on one's duty to God and one's duty to one's neighbour.

But the principal feature of the year of Release was that the land was to lie fallow;[2] such produce as the earth naturally brought forth from cornfields, vineyards, and olive-yards was to be common property; this legislation would obviously advantage the poor.

There are in the Law two apparently contradictory statements about poverty; the one is that there shall be no poor among you, and the other that the poor shall never cease out of the land. There is, however, no real contradiction, for had they really kept the whole law, there would have been no poor man among them; poverty arose because they broke the land and usury laws, poverty might be occasioned by an individual being lazy, in which case he was breaking the law of the fourth commandment. But as, one way or other, there were poor men among them the same writer says: 'The poor shall never cease out of the land.' Now the context shows that this does not mean that there must always be rich and poor and that it is God's will, but that the poor shall not be starved out or cease to exist by the niggardliness of their neighbours; hence the fallow year with its provision for the poor, and the periodic return of the land to families who had fallen on evil days and had lost it. It is, indeed, in connection with the fallow year that the statement is made, and the writer says that

---

[1] Verinder, *My Neighbour's Landmark.*

[2] A periodic fallow year is an ancient custom of many nations, and a conservative commentary suggests that its communal sharing of produce is the survival of an earlier communism. There may possibly have been a storage of grain in communal or tribal granaries to provide tenant farmers with a supply of food for the seventh year. Hastings's *Large Dictionary of the Bible* remarks that the fallow year is still observed in Palestine and Syria.

you are not to be ungenerous to the poor man just because
you are on the edge of the seventh year in which he can
get communal relief.

There is yet one more point to notice about the fallow
year: it was a period in which the land itself was released
and allowed to rest and to recuperate its energy.   Such
periodic fallows are common to many nations, and existed
in this country till recent times.

Now we can deal with the Jubilee year, which was
either the seven-times-seven, or forty-ninth year of release,
or actually the fiftieth year.   It would occur at least once
in the lifetime of almost every Hebrew; in this year the
original equal division of land was restored.   Whatever
inequalities may have crept in through the improvidence
of the actual holders or the rapacity of their oppressors,
were now redressed.   'It shall be a Jubilee to you, and ye
shall return every man unto his own possession, every man
unto his own family.'   As we have shown, the Hebrew
could not own his land outright, nor sell it away from his
children.   'At the end of every fifty years all the leases
fell in simultaneously, and a fresh distribution in equal
shares is made.'   The Hebrew, therefore, could not sell
the ownership of the land, but only the 'fag-end' of the
lease to the next year of Jubilee.   Josephus makes it quite
clear that the out-going tenant who had acquired the land
from the family whose inheritance it was, should not
receive a penny compensation for the land itself, which
he had seized or acquired, yet shall receive compensation
for any agricultural improvements which he himself has
in the meanwhile made.[1]   A difference was even made
between agricultural cottages, which were the necessary
homes of the people who tilled the soil, and town houses.
In this year of liberty, the cottage goes back with the land
to the original working family, while the town house does
not automatically return, but must be redeemed, if bought
back at all, within a year of the transfer.

Lest it be thought that we are relying merely on the

[1] *Antiquities*, III, xii, 283–4.

evidence of socialists and land-restorers, I will here quote a conventional and conservative authority, Eadie's *Dictionary of the Bible* (Feasts): 'The remarkable feature of this festival was that it restored individuals, families, and communities, as far as possible, to the same situation that they occupied at the beginning of the fifty years. All servants of Hebrew origin were set free; all pledges were given up, and inheritances which had been alienated, no matter how often, or for what cause, came back to the hands of the original proprietors (except houses in walled towns). . . . And as the effect of the year of Jubilee was known and anticipated, the business of society was conducted with reference to that period, and, of course, no hardship or injustice was occasioned.'

Dummelow's *Commentary* identifies Jubilee with the Acceptable Year, and praises its provision as 'putting a check upon ambition and covetousness, preventing the acquisition of huge estates, and adjusting the distribution of wealth in the various classes of the community.' The year of Jubilee was thus 'the new birth of the whole nation.'

There is a certain type of critic who tries to belittle the land legislation of the Old Testament, and especially the return of their holdings to the people in the year of Jubilee. This kind of person obviously knows little of economic history in general, or of Jewish history in particular. Actually the custom of a periodic redistribution of land is a commonplace of agricultural history: evidence of this will be found in Sir Henry Maine's *Village Communities*, in histories of the Russian *mir*, and in Penty's description of land-holding in India.

Now as to Palestine, there is an interesting paragraph in Keim's *Jesus of Nazara* (vol. i, page 351), which refers to Hillel's crafty evasion of this law on behalf of his wealthy friends. 'His relaxations of the Law are not unobjectionable; the reservation of the right to claim the payment of debts in spite of the year of Jubilee is a crafty compromise.' Hausrath, however, refers this evasion to the release granted to debtors every seventh year, and says: 'Hillel thus practically abolished the year of Release.' But if Keim is correct the year of Jubilee must have been operating even in the time of our Lord.

The *Jewish Encyclopaedia* holds that it was from time to time in operation, here following the Jewish historian Josephus, who makes no question of it. Ewald writes: 'On a close inspection, nothing is more certain than that the idea of the Jubilee is the last ring of a chain which only contains in it the necessary conclusion, and that the history of the Jubilee, in spite of its at first seemingly strange aspect, was once for centuries a reality in the national life of Israel.' Driver is equally convinced, and says: 'It is impossible to think that (as has sometimes been supposed) the institution of the Jubilee is a mere paper law, a theoretical completion of the system of sevens; at least as far as concerns the land (for the periodical redistribution of which there are analogies in other nations), it must date from ancient times in Israel.' [1]

The Hebrew families would have all received their possessions towards the end of Solomon's reign, and therefore the land system as described above should have been in full operation about the year 930 B.C. Now this is roughly the date of the schism of North and South, and the kingdom of Israel was established in protest against the corruption of Solomon and his successors, and especially against the economic oppression that prevailed in Judah. In spite of certain brutish rulers that followed Jeroboam, the North would probably have been careful to retain its Mosaic land customs intact for at least fifty years, and Ahab's murder of Naboth and acquisition of his holding, with which we shall presently deal, was probably the first encroachment upon the landed rights of the peasants. It is possible that Elijah's protest and his powerful personality may have stayed the northern landslide, and it must be remembered that he was followed by an equally resolute prophet, Elisha. If, therefore, there is no record of a general return of the land to the people about the time of Ahab, it may have been because only slight encroach-

[1] *Literature of the Old Testament*, seventh edition, page 57.

ments had been made on their lands, or because Ahab and Jezebel and their immediate successors would have the utmost contempt for the law of Jubilee. It is certainly true that in spite of the protests of these two powerful prophets, the economic conditions of Israel, a little later in its history, went from bad to worse, as we shall see when we deal with the reign of Jeroboam II, who came to the throne in the year 782 B.C., when Amos the southern prophet utters his warning, chiefly in the North, against the social injustices which will eventually bring Israel to its doom.

So corrupt were these northern conditions that there was no possibility of a Jubilee restoration of land at any period from the reign of Jeroboam II to the annihilation of the northern kingdom in 722 B.C. If, therefore, there had been a serious landslide in the northern kingdom which the Jubilee return of the land to the people would have righted, there was no proof that the Law was not meant to be carried into effect, but all the evidence points to the fact that it was evaded and flouted by a succession of evil rulers.

The history of Judah divides itself into two main periods, the first being the three hundred and thirty-three years from Rehoboam and the schism in 930 B.C. to the Fall of Jerusalem and the Exile in 597 B.C. Rehoboam, who had threatened to chastise his people with scorpions, may have been terrified into good behaviour by the revolt, but the taxation must have been heavy to pay for the civil war, and for the defence against the Egyptian invasion, and have fallen as usual largely upon the peasants. Whether this meant the mortgaging of lands and consequent evictions we are not told. There followed the two years' reign of his son, and then two long reigns, first of his grandson Assa (forty-three years), and then of Jehosaphat (twenty-five years), both of them periods in which we are told the Law was observed. It is quite possible that a Jubilee restoration of land may have occurred during this period of seventy years, but no mention is made of it.

A certain type of 'higher' critic argues that omission of

record must mean non-observance, and, indeed, that, as there are no records of periodic distribution until after the Exile, the Jubilee enactments were unknown until then, being created by the later prophets.   This line of argument we venture to consider untenable, and if applied to the medieval history of Europe it would yield extraordinary and altogether misleading results.   These same critics have argued that the Feast of the Passover was not Mosaic, and was not observed for centuries, but it seems to us that they have been completely refuted as to this latter contention by A. C. Hervey, Bishop of Bath and Wells.[1] He demonstrates that several Passovers are actually mentioned, where they are of importance as marking some reformation period, or as being celebrated with especial splendour, and rightly suggests that they might not have been recorded at all if it had not been for these particular circumstances. It is absurd to argue for their non-existence through omission of record.   'For example, thirty-eight years of the forty passed in the wilderness have absolutely no events assigned to them.   They are a blank.   The first thirty years also of Saul's reign are passed over in almost complete silence.   The long reign of Uzziah—fifty-two years —occupies four verses in 2 Kings.'   If, then, we had not had specific records of certain celebrations of the Passover and hints of others, 'it would have been a very precarious conclusion from the silence of Scripture that no celebration of the Passover had taken place.'

We may apply this argument to the land restorations of the year of Jubilee; the silence of Scripture by no means proves that such periodic redistributions did not take place. They would obviously not have taken place in the reign of Athaliah, daughter of Ahab and Jezebel, when Jezebel was dominant in the southern as well as the northern kingdom.   But it is just possible that the succeeding king, Joash (Jehoash), may have remedied this, although the records are silent on the point.   The Jubilee that should next have

---

[1] *The Books of Chronicle in relation to the Books of Pentateuch and the Higher Criticism.*

occurred in Amaziah's reign may well have been neglected. We shall deal with the long reign of Uzziah when we come to consider the Prophets. No land restoration is in the least likely during that period, nor in the following reigns of Jotham or of Ahaz, but there may have been a Jubilee in the reign of Hezekiah (thirty-two years) from 727 B.C. to 695 B.C. He might almost be described as a Christian before Christ; his reign was a time of great economic reformation. He was followed by Manasseh, who came to the throne when he was twelve years old, and seems to have ruled for fifty-two years. He indulged in sinister idolatries and child sacrifices, and a Jubilee restoration of land is unthinkable in that period. There followed the short and evil reign of Amon, which ended abruptly with the rebellion of the people and the enthronement of the boy king, Josiah, in 639 B.C. In 621 B.C., probably, was made the discovery of the Book of the Law, and its popular observance, and this may well have been accompanied by land restoration. According to Jewish tradition, the first Jubilee restoration (Talmud) occurred in 1207: other periodic restorations are mentioned, and an important one coincides with this reforming period. After the death of the good king came the deluge of puppet monarchs, with social injustice and idolatry rampant, ending with the fall of Jerusalem in 597 B.C. and the Babylonish captivity. Some of those not taken captive fly in terror to Egypt, accompanied by the prophet Jeremiah; Ezekiel accompanies the captives to Babylon, and there, towards the end of the period, paints a picture of an ideal kingdom as it might be on the return of the people to their own land, repentant and resolved to live justly with one another. 'It shall come to pass that ye shall divide it by lot for an inheritance unto you, and to the aliens that sojourn among you; they shall be unto you as the home-born among the children of Israel, they shall have an inheritance among you with the tribes of Israel.'[1] This kingdom of righteousness which shall once more flourish on the return of the exiles is also

[1] Ezekiel xlvii. 22.

described in the sixty-first chapter of Isaiah (if indeed this be by the hand of the deutero-Isaiah), where he speaks of the Jubilee year, or 'Acceptable year of the Lord,' when the returning captives shall build the old wastes and raise up the former desolations. He proclaims liberty to the captives and the opening of the prison to them that are bound.

There is, it is true, no direct evidence of the Jubilee being observed, either before or after the Exile, but the above considerations do suggest it was no mere idealistic legislation but was at least meant to be carried into effect.

Whether or no the Nehemiah reforms after the Exile, with which we shall subsequently deal, or the Maccabean land restoration, coincided with the actual years of Jubilee, they may be regarded as belated jubilees.

Now there is another type of critic who belittles the Jubilee land restoration for reasons precisely opposite to those given by people who treat the regulations of the fiftieth year as a 'scrap of paper.' These writers assert that, of course, there were such restorations of land among the Jewish people, but that there was nothing inspired about the Bible provisions, as periodic redistribution of land is a common feature of the history of other nations. They, indeed, seek to belittle the God-directed legislation of the Hebrews by comparing it at almost every point with the secular laws found in such codes as those of Manu and Hammurabi. In so far as such codes are humane and based on considerations of justice between man and man, we hold them to be divinely inspired and not 'merely' secular. That they were so inspired by a sense of justice is undoubtedly true, but their likenesses to the laws of Moses, although they certainly exist, have been grossly exaggerated in order to belittle the latter. But before comparing the Mosaic Law with that of other primitive peoples, it will be wise to summarize the remainder of the scriptural legislation. We have already dealt fully with the provisions for the Sabbatical fallow year and the Jubilee year of land restoration. We have mentioned the laws against usury or interest and the laws relating to slavery. Something more should, perhaps, be said about these latter. Slavery was the blot on the life of all these ancient Eastern peoples, not excluding that of the Hebrews. And although it has been contended that the lot of the slave was nothing like so tragic as it was in the Roman Empire or in the Southern States of America of modern times, yet it must have been hard enough, when we remember that even in the Mosaic legislation the master might flog his slave ferociously without the latter having any right of redress; in fact, even if the slave were to die under the lash, the master could escape scot-free, provided that two days or more elapsed between the flogging and its consequence.

It is true that the Law counselled mercy to the bondservant; he was to be treated as the hired servant, but there was not much protection in this pious counsel if the master were a bully or a sadist.

Up to a point, then, the lot of the slave in Palestine was not much better, if any, than his lot in any Eastern country, but in spite of this, there were important differences which were all in favour of the Hebrew legislation.

Although the Jews were permitted to have foreign slaves, they were forbidden to return a fugitive slave to his owner. They were, in fact, to allow him to choose his quarters within their gates and to treat him well. Again, although they might even take to themselves slaves of their own people, men or women who for debt or some other misfortune had sold themselves into bondage, yet these could only remain slaves for six years and were to be set free in the Sabbatical Year of Release.

If the slave of his own free choice wished to remain in the service of the family, this was allowed and the choice certified by boring through his ear against the door.

Women slaves were often the concubines of the master, but they could and often did marry into the family. Further, it must be noted that when the Sabbatical Year coincided with the Acceptable Year of Jubilee, the slave who was released would not only regain his political and bodily freedom, but also his economic liberty, for his peasant holding would then be restored to him.

If a Hebrew fell on poverty he might sell his children into bondage, but not to foreigners, which probably means not even outside his own tribe, and this would ensure their regaining their liberty in so many years.

There are merciful laws about the right of the poor to glean, the kindly treatment of wage servants, the provision of cities of refuge, where those fleeing from 'justice' would be safe; about the restoring of pledges at sundown; the pledge often being the tools by which a man earned his livelihood. Their judges were to take no bribes, were to give just and merciful judgment and to be no respecters of persons. The law was to be weighted in favour of the poor, not in favour of the rich.

There were laws against bird's-nesting and against muzzling the ox that treadeth out the corn. Generally it may be said that the Law was a protection of the weak against the strong.

The Deuteronomic Code was an attempt not merely to give the nation a code of rules with penalties attached, but to appeal to their hearts and consciences to keep them in the spirit of mercy, justice, and neighbourliness. They were to be written on the tablet of the heart. This old covenant reminds us of the words of Jesus where he appeals to his hearers, saying: 'Judge ye in yourselves what is right.' God, through his servant Moses, appeals to his people 'for this commandment which I command thee this day, it is not hidden from thee, neither is it far off. It is not in heaven, that thou shouldest say, who shall go up for us to heaven, and bring it unto us that we may hear it and do it; neither is it beyond the sea, that thou shouldest say, who shall go over the sea for us and bring it unto us, that we may hear it and do it. But the word is very nigh thee, in thy mouth and in thy heart, that thou mayest do it.'

It may strike the student as strange and unreal that a law book, whether it be the Book of the Covenant embedded in Exodus, or passages from which I have quoted in

Deuteronomy, should make this appeal to the heart of the people, seeing that it contains such edicts as we have quoted about the flogging of slaves or the *lex talionis* (eye for eye). But it must be remembered that even these harsh laws were an advance on, and modification of, earlier savageries.

And now at last having dealt with the Mosaic legislation in some fullness as it affects social ethics, we are in a position to compare it with the written laws and customs of other and earlier civilizations.

We have already remarked on those writers who contend that the laws of Moses cannot be considered as inspired by God, as parallels to them may be found in the primitive custom law of other nations. If God be the God of all the earth, we should be astonished to find that in these other legislations there was no good thing, but we nevertheless shall find that the Mosaic Code suggests an advance on earlier law and a progressive revelation of God to man.

The laws as laid down in the Bible are in very distinct contrast to the laws and customs of the Egyptians, as they would have been seen in operation by Moses, to the laws of the Phoenicians and to the Canaanites who were a branch of the Phoenician race, whom the Hebrews were commanded to drive out before them.

They were equally in contrast to the practices of the later Assyrian and Babylonish empires. But whether or no there existed a just primitive custom law, first traditional, oral, uncodified, and later, written and codified, a law common to all mankind, or at least to a common ancestry of Babylonians and Hebrews, is another question, and our examination of certain primitive codes may suggest some such thing.

A word or so may first be said about the laws of Manu, before consideration of the legislation which may have more immediately affected Hebrew tradition. The principles of Brahmanic social justice may be found in the laws of Manu. The Brahmans are to use sweet and gentle speech, are not to injure any living creature; they are to be liberal and generous, and to show mercy and to give employment to those in need. There is, however, 'no question of social equality in the laws of Manu. The ancient Hindu lawgiver is under the influence of the idea of caste, of class difference, and of inequality existing among men. . . . Manu is firmly convinced that not all men have been created in the image of God.'

Ideas of inequality are still deeply rooted in the hearts of millions of people, but nowhere has this idea been so deeply rooted as in India, 'the classic soil of caste and class.'

This inequality 'to which Manu ascribes Divine origin, is complete; physically, morally, socially, and economically . . . thus the doctrine of Manu, which frequently breathes a spirit of love and of tenderness for the weak and the lowly, is nevertheless an insolent theocracy and an oppressive monarchy, based upon the idea of the Divine right of the rulers and the obedience and servitude of the labouring classes and the slaves as ordained by God Himself.'

The lower orders are the contemptibles according to his laws, even when they had been freed from slavery; they are still and for ever incapable of equality, mental or moral, with their lords and masters.

Buddha, contemporary with Pythagoras and Confucius, with Nehemiah and Ezra (the Nehemiah reforms were in 444 B.C.), protested against this inhuman doctrine. He declared the spiritual equality of all men and so did much to undermine the teachings of Hinduism. But unfortunately this world of sense and materiality was in his doctrine of no account, and although he was filled with a profound pity for suffering, he did nothing to advance the political and economic equality of mankind. 'Preaching the benefits of the renunciation of the world, and of abnegation, he had no room for any ideas of economic equality or inequality.' The craving for life and happiness was to be entirely and utterly renounced.

The contrast is obvious between these life-denying ordinances, with their theology of the benevolent despot and the consequent gulf between man and man, and the

Mosaic theology of the God whose Word is among men and in them, the life-accepting attitude of the Hebrews, their democratic institutions, their passion for liberty and equality. They look for the good life of the coming world order not in asceticism and renunciation, but in fruitfulness and every material blessing; although these, indeed, are always the outcome of obedience to the just God, Who bestows upon men every spiritual, mental, and material gift.

And now we should turn to legislation much nearer to that of the Hebrews, namely, the Code of Hammurabi. This monarch was the sixth of a Babylonian dynasty founded about the middle of the third millennium.[1] He reigned about 2285 B.C. and succeeded in freeing his territory from the Elamite yoke: he was able to amalgamate north and south Babylonia, and to extend his dominions as far west as Canaan. He then proceeded to establish 'the heart of the land in righteousness.' He seems to have held monotheistic ideals, and it is noteworthy that Abraham was a contemporary, and came from Ur of the Chaldees, a city mentioned in the prologue of the Code. There may have been to some extent a common origin for this Babylonian tradition and Abrahamic and Mosaic ideals.

It is very difficult to judge from the fragments of the Code which we possess what were the exact conditions of land tenure in ancient Babylonia: some hints are given of primitive tribal communism, but large encroachments on this must have been made by the time of the Code, for it contained regulations about landlords, their rents, and their rights. S. A. Cook, who has written on the laws of Hammurabi, believes that in primitive times land was held in Babylonia communally, as in the Mosaic dispensation, but by the period of the Code, 'had long been either private property or under the control of superior authorities.'

---

[1] Hammurabi may be identical with Amraphel, King of Shinar, who extended his sway over Canaan (Genesis xiv). The origin and date of the dynasty and of the code are only conjectural.

There are, however, imprecations against removers of land-marks, but whether these were made against ancient communal or recently acquired landlord rights is uncertain; but Hammurabi orders the restitution of land to a certain family, for its title is ancient. Land is not to be alienated from a given family except with the consent of all its members.

In primitive times, before the Code, there are traces of a periodic distribution of land among the people by a council. Land is allotted to officers of the Crown in return for services rendered. These officers include the police and tax-gatherers; and when away on duty their estates can be cultivated by others, but if alienated during their absence they must be returned. Only if an officer let his land go to waste would it be confiscated. We may compare the laws relating to the Levites in the Mosaic Code; there were also provisions made in Palestine for Crown lands and estates of royal officers. On the whole it may be said that the land laws of Moses resembled the primitive Babylonian customs rather than the arrangements of the Code. In Babylonia of the Code there were instances of farmers hiring land and paying their rent to the landlords in kind. There are fields of partnership where landlord and tenant have equal shares. Vegetable and fruit garden-ing was a key industry, but oftentimes the cultivator of these plots was not the owner, but was obliged to pay rent to the lord. It may be noted in passing that in Egypt, where usury flourished, bodily distraint was forbidden under the Code of Bocchoris.

The Babylonian Code protects the wife or child who has been sold for debt, for in the fourth year the purchaser must give them their freedom. The Code contrasts un-favourably with Mosaic legislation in respect of interest; usury is approved, although there are certain mitigations in favour of debtors. If a man in debt experienced a bad year through drought or flood he is exempted from paying his interest for that particular year. But if a tenant had been obliged to borrow from a moneylender, in the time of harvest, he must pay part of his crop as the usual rent to the landlord and part of the crop to the moneylender. One wonders what was left to the wretched tenant after these double payments.

Although the Babylonian Code contrasts favourably with that of Moses in respect of wife or child sold into slavery (a fourth year as against a seventh year of release) yet a Babylonian could sell his slave to pay his own debt, and in that case there was no redress for the slave: it will be remembered that in the Mosaic Code there was no permanent slavery for a native, and no interest was allowed between Hebrew and fellow-Hebrew.

The Code of Hammurabi, as described in a book by R. Francis Harper, divides the people into classes. First come the householders, property-owners, the wealthy and upper class, the gentlemen. Secondly, there were the poor men, retainers, or serfs, who stand midway between the leisured class and the slaves. Harper suggests that they might be described as freemen, but is not certain that they can own property. The third class consists of the slaves. There is also a salariat, or bureaucracy, as described above. The laws relating to fugitive slaves were extremely harsh. The death penalty was inflicted upon the householder who sheltered a fugitive slave and refused to hand him over at the command of the constable. The man who found such a slave in the open country, and drove him back to his owner, was entitled to a reward. Laws relating to fugitive slaves were practically the same everywhere, with the notable exception of the Mosaic Code, which as we have seen protected these wretched people. The Code of Hammurabi, unlike that of Moses, 'lays itself out to advance industrial conditions,' such as would encourage the growth of a wealthy class, and the consequent enslavement of the workers.

CHAPTER VI

THE ECONOMICS OF IDOLATRY

WHILE the legislation of Palestine is a real advance on the Indian and even on the early Babylonian Code, this latter, although it showed a decline from earlier and more primitive traditions, contained much that is commendable.

But when we come to compare the Mosaic Laws with those of the later River empires, such as Egypt, Assyria, and the second Babylonian Empire; these laws, although they contained certain blemishes, are as light to darkness. They are also in vivid contrast to the approved customs of the peoples whom the Hebrews were commanded to drive out before them.

We shall now proceed to examine the theology of these peoples and its economic consequences, as a necessary prelude to the times of Ahab and Jezebel and to the protest of the prophet Elijah.

People may ask: Was it the idolatries which Elijah attacked or the economic corruptions, such as the seizing of the poor man's vineyard? But the question suggests a confusion in the minds of those who put it, and a study of the gods whom Ahab and his consort worshipped will soon show that such worships were bound to find their expression in acts of tyranny and injustice.

There is a passage in the Book of Wisdom which may well form the text for this whole section. 'For those ancient inhabitants of the Holy Land, whom thou didst abhor, because they did works hateful to thee by their sorceries and wicked sacrifices, and those merciless murderers of their own children and eaters of men's bowels and devourers of blood from the midst of consecration and those parents sacrificing with their own hands helpless souls,

94

it was thy will to destroy by the hands of our parents that the land which of all is most dear to thee might receive a worthy colony of the children of God.' The same chapter describes the process of dispossessing them as slow, in order that they might have time for repentance; upon such of them as should repent God will have mercy. This is a different point of view from that of the earlier books of the Old Testament which insist on the destruction of these Canaanitish peoples.

The inhabitants of Canaan included Hittites, Hivites, Amorites, Perizzites, Amalakites, Midianites, the Philistines, who seem some of them to have been already settled in Canaan, but who grew into a formidable power a little later, and the Canaanites, who are mentioned as a separate people.

Nothing certain is known of the Hivites. The Canaanites and Amorites dwelt in southern Palestine, the Canaanites inhabiting the lowlands, and the Amorites the uplands.

Now who were the Canaanites?

They were probably a later wave of the Amorite invasion, and they appeared to have given their name to the country before 1400 B.C. They were either identical or closely connected with the Phoenicians, and, indeed, Phoenician seems to have been their Greek and Canaanite their Semitic name. It is noteworthy that the terms Phoenician and Canaanite alike are synonymous with traders, and the Phoenicians are known to have been the great commercialists of the ancient world.

It is a fairy tale, as has been shown above, that represents the inhabitants of Canaan as primitive tribes, living lives of ideal simplicity. These peoples were more probably the decadent descendants of highly complicated and corrupt civilizations, with their iniquitous inequalities, sexual aberrations, and cruel customs. The Hebrews descending upon their lands and driving them out, sometimes with the cruel slaughter of whole families, may be regarded as God's scourges, just as in later times the River empires, themselves depraved, were used by God as agents to bring Israel to repentance.

The Hebrews were at least coming into Palestine with a robust ideal of public life and with just and generous laws. There is, of course, another side to the picture; for instance, Deborah's praise of the action of Jael, which seems to outrage all Eastern laws of hospitality; and at first sight we might also quote the wholesale massacre of the people of Laish, a people 'quiet and secure.' But Laish was a Sidonian city of inordinate wealth and luxury and it may have only met the fate it deserved.

The Hebrew god has been described as the champion of the simple nomadic communist tradition, as against Baal, who stood for luxurious commercialism based on private property. The Canaanitish theology was the worship of the baals. This worship 'was denounced, not merely as apostasy, but because of its impurity and its sanguinary rites. When the Jehovah worship tended to approximate to the worship of the baals, it was proclaimed by the prophets as no less offensive to him than idolatry.'[1] Loisy writes in his *Religion of Israel*: 'The worship of Canaan was a low polytheism which concealed only superficially a basis of animism and fetishism, the inheritance from old times, and perhaps also in part from the shadowy peoples who had lived in the country before the Canaanites possessed it . . . the baals were almost always kindly and did not grudge the fruits of the earth.' He adds, rather naïvely: 'Nevertheless, the sacrifice of new-born children was frequent, and probably did not cause the least repugnance.' It involved then these hideous child sacrifices and also prostitution.

Max Beer tells us a little more about the Canaanite god, Baal: 'Like the Greek Dionysus, or Bacchus, he was the religious symbol of the germinating powers of nature, the god of a country flowing with milk and honey, and corn and wine. He made men, animals, and plants fruitful: he represents the mystery of generation: his consecrated

[1] F. A. Foakes-Jackson.

mountain tops and altars became noisy public places, his sacrifices became luxurious banquets, his sacred groves became sheltered nooks for the sensual embraces of the sexes. In the eyes of the prophets, the service of Baal was vain fornication and whoredom.' [1]

These baals, or lords of the land, were sometimes sculptured in the form of bulls and calves. It is not clear if this worship of the bull in Canaan was borrowed from Egypt, though it must be remembered that the Egyptian Empire had overrun Canaan, and exercised a suzerainty over it about the time of the Hebrew invasion; but bull worship may have been indigenous in that territory.

It will be remembered that Jeroboam had set himself up as monarch of the North, and this king corrupted the worship of Jehovah by making graven images of him in the form of a bull. In later times Jeroboam II also favoured this cultus which was denounced by the prophets of his day. Bull worship was the essence of the northern schism, the cultus not only of both Jeroboams, but of Ahab and Jezebel. It was the worship of force and brutalism, to which Jezebel added the cultus of Astarte, and of other Phoenician gods and goddesses.

Foakes-Jackson contrasts the narrow but lofty morality of the Hebrew religion with the nature worship of the Canaanites, which 'encouraged some of the foulest acts of brutality and vice.' These baal worships were not only found in the northern kingdom, but introduced into the Temple by Solomon, and later were encouraged by Athaliah, the daughter of Jezebel, who attained ascendancy in the South.

The worship of Astarte was connected with a cult of sexual love and voluptuousness, and seems, like the cultus of the baals, to have involved child sacrifices. She appears as the goddess of fertility, productiveness, and love, on the one hand, and of war, death, and decay on the other; a personification of the earth as it passes through the summer and winter seasons. The nature-worships, both

---

[1] *Social Struggles of Antiquity*, page 22.

E

of Astarte and the baals, had many beautiful features; but when we consider their darker aspects, male and female prostitution and holocausts of children sacrificed upon their altars, we realize that it was impossible for the prophets of the Lord God, Jehovah, not to do all in their power to destroy them.

CHAPTER VII

TWO GREAT PROPHETS

A LITTLE over half a century had passed since the rebellion
fanned by a prophet of God against the luxuries and oppressions of Solomon's court, the rebellion which had rent in
twain the kingdom, and put Jeroboam on the throne in the
North. It had been a half-century of storm and anarchy in
Israel, civil war within, and the constant pressure of foreign
kingdoms and empires from without. The long reign of
Omri had, however, done much to restore order and to
extend the boundaries of the northern kingdom. During
his time there had loomed on the political horizon the
growing empire of Assyria, but the more immediate danger
came from the Syrians, although they presented, for the
time, an obstacle to the Assyrian menace; and Omri and
later Ahab, his son, were occupied in keeping the kingdom
of Syria in check by a series of alliances against it. Ahab
inherited much of the skill and courage of his father and
was, in many ways, a wise and reasonable ruler, but his
marriage with Jezebel and his introduction into the kingdom of her gods ultimately spelt the ruin of his house.
He reigned from about 875 to 853 B.C.

His marriage with the Phoenician princess was in the
nature of a political alliance with Phoenicia against the
Syrians, and was also effected for purposes of commercial
development. But Jezebel was a powerful and unscrupulous Oriental who dominated her husband, and introduced
into Israel that contempt of the rights of the poor which
ran directly counter to the Mosaic tradition. She was the
daughter of a priest of a Phoenician baal, the god of gain
and commerce, and Josephus says this priest served Astarte,
goddess of sexual lusts. Her father became king of
Phoenicia by murdering the reigning monarch.

The luxury of Ahab's reign may be seen in the ivory palace that he built in his capital, Samaria, the remains of which have been recently excavated. The king built Jezebel an expensive temple dedicated to her gods, and she brought nearly a thousand Phoenician priests to serve the foreign cults in the city. Ahab tried to combine the worship of these baals with the worship of Jehovah. His wife believed in no such compromise, and was for driving out the worship of the god of the Hebrews altogether: she attempted to kill his prophets, who were only saved by the intervention of one of them, Obadiah, who hid his comrades in caves, and supplied them with food.

Suddenly there appears upon the scene a stormy figure, dressed in skins, the embodiment of the terror and loneliness of the desert. His name is Elijah, or 'Jehovah is God.' He meets Ahab face to face, charges him with apostasy, threatens his country with a terrible famine, and disappears before the outraged king can seize him.

There follows the story of the priests of the foreign cult on the top of Mount Carmel, who were challenged by Elijah to a trial which should prove whether Baal or Jehovah was the true god. They called on their god all the day long, and in their desperation cut themselves about with knives, but 'there was neither voice, nor any to answer, nor any that regarded.' Then came down the fire from heaven that consumed the sacrifice that Elijah made to his God, and all the people cried out, saying: 'Jehovah, He is God; Jehovah, He is God.' A terrible massacre of the false prophets at the command of Elijah now takes place. Jezebel swears vengeance upon the prophet of God and is determined to kill him.

Exhausted by the fight, Elijah flies to the desert and asks God to take his life; then comes the storm and the whirlwind, but after these a still small voice: and he hears God speaking, encouraging him to take heart and renew the battle, as there is great work for him still to do. He is to be the revolutionary instrument for the overthrow of two dynasties, and to anoint Hazael to be king over Syria and

Jehu to be king over Israel. And Elisha, the young ploughman, was to be anointed as Elijah's servitor and successor. 'And it shall come to pass that he that escapeth the sword of Hazael shall Jehu slay; and him that escapeth from the sword of Jehu shall Elisha slay.'

Elijah believed that he was alone in his fight against overwhelming odds, but he was told that there were ready to rally to him seven thousand in Israel, all the knees which have not bowed unto Baal, and every mouth which hath not kissed him.

His strength returns to him, and he obeys the commands of God.

The years pass, and once more Ahab and Elijah are found in conflict, and the battle rages round the peasant called Naboth. No doubt the growing plutocracy, both North and South since the time of the wealthy Solomon, had been irked and hindered by what they would consider to be absurd and antiquated land restrictions of the Mosaic Law. In the South considerable inroads upon the peasants' holdings may already have been made; the same process may have been begun, although more warily, in the northern kingdom. It is, however, possible that the peasants of Israel had managed with the help of the prophets to maintain their rights: now, in any case, the battle is joined over the small plot of ground known as Naboth's vineyard.

Ahab had a summer residence in Jezreel; it would be surrounded by park-lands and gardens, but it lacked a herb garden, and how could one possibly be happy or content without a herb garden? Just over against the palace was the holding of the poor man, Naboth, a working peasant, a nobody.

Ahab must acquire this holding for his herb garden, and was ready to buy the fellow out, or offer him a piece of land somewhere else, but the obstinate churl clung to his home and the inheritance of his fathers. They had lived there long before Ahab's palace had ever been dreamed of. Why should he be turned out of his old home?

Ahab was disgusted at this unreasonable opposition, but

shrugged his shoulders and was about to abandon his project. Jezebel noticed that the king had lost his appetite and couldn't eat his dinner. She asked him what on earth was the matter, and was highly amused when she heard what it was all about. Was he really the ruler of Israel, and yet unable to settle a little affair of that sort? The queen took the matter in hand, and got Naboth falsely accused of blasphemy, and effected the judicial murder of the man and his sons.

'And the word of the Lord came to Elijah the Tishbite, saying, Arise, go down to meet Ahab, king of Israel, which is in Samaria: behold, he is in the vineyard of Naboth, whither he has gone down to possess it. And thou shalt speak unto him, saying, Thus saith the Lord, Hast thou killed, and also taken possession? And thou shalt speak unto him, saying, Thus saith the Lord, In the place where the dogs licked the blood of Naboth shall dogs lick thy blood, even thine. And Ahab said to Elijah, Hast thou found me, O mine enemy? And he answered, I have found thee: because thou hast sold thyself to work evil in the sight of the Lord.'

Elijah then foretells the evil which God will bring upon him and his posterity. 'And of Jezebel also spake the Lord, saying, The dogs shall eat Jezebel by the wall of Jezreel. Him that dieth of Ahab in the city the dogs shall eat; and him that dieth in the fields the fowls of the air eat.'

Ahab was terror-stricken and repentant, and for a while the doom was stayed; but in the war that followed soon after between Syria and Israel, in spite of the king's extraordinary courage, he was mortally wounded at Ramoth-Gilead, and died on his way to Samaria. Panic seized his army and they were scattered.

Ahaziah, his son, reigned in his stead, and followed in the evil steps of his father and mother; he worshipped their gods and relied on Beelzebub, the god of flies, turning aside from the Lord God, Jehovah. He was injured by a fall from the palace window, and Elijah once more appears and tells him of his inevitable death.

The scriptural tradition tells of Elijah's ascent into heaven in a chariot of fire, and whether or no the fiery prophet saw death, he had won for himself a deathless fame.

We shall see later that the Jewish nation awaited the return to earth of this challenger of kings and champion of the rights of the poor, as the herald of the Messiah and his New World Order. Jesus, the Messiah, sees in the coming of John the Baptist the return of Elijah, and in the supreme moment of his transfiguration, companions with Moses, the rebel leader, and Elijah, the avenger of the poor man's liberties.

Elisha, whom Elijah had been inspired to anoint as his successor, and whom he had taken from the plough, had asked his beloved master that he should pray for him that he might have his same fiery spirit and have it more abundantly. He had asked a hard thing, but if he had the eager vision wherewith he should be able to see the fiery chariots and horsemen who should uplift Elijah into heaven then he would know that God had granted his prayer.

When the moment of his testing comes, he proves worthy; his eyes are opened and he sees the chariots; indeed, probably, in that moment, understands that the giantesque man who is being exalted to the heavens has himself been both chariots and horsemen to Israel. Elisha, therefore, with the inspiration of that vision cries: 'My father, my father, the chariots of Israel and the horsemen thereof,' and goes forward to begin his work.

Through the next fifty years he is the soul of affairs in his country, and has far-reaching influence beyond its borders. He is the mainstay of northern Palestine through the reigns of four kings, the upsetter of a dynasty and the inciter to sedition. Once, when the odds seemed overwhelmingly against him, and he is as calm as ice, his companions are given to see around him the fire chariots and the hosts of heaven.

It is difficult to describe the personality and work of this most elusive of the prophets; the immense range of his activities, extending over half a century, their amazing variety; his intimate and delicate tenderness, his fierce political incursions, his encouragement to patriotic battles, his sympathy with powerful foreigners when they were in trouble, even where these were the enemies of his country, his insight into the international situation, his conviction that God had raised up the Syrians and their brutal rulers to be the scourge of his own country with its deeper guilt and hypocrisies, these seemingly contradictory things are hard to weave into a consistent pattern.

The difficulty is well illustrated by the contradictory pictures which historians have drawn concerning this farmer prophet, 'the gentle Elisha,' 'the quiet farmer, careless of wealth and indifferent to court favour, kindly on the whole and peaceful.'

The *Small Dictionary of the Bible* contrasts him with the flint-like Elijah who won his victories with hard blows. Elisha is 'a gentler and more gracious man . . . who gains his ends by diplomacy.' Although he has his fiercer moments 'like that of the Prophet of Nazareth, his ministry breathes a spirit of gracious, soothing, holy beneficence.' Yet Professor Cornill describes this gentle and soothing prophet as 'a conspirator, a revolutionist, and agitator.' And the amazing thing is that all these descriptions are, in a manner, right.

Ottley points to Elisha as the successful military adviser of his people. Their 'successes were in great measure due to the influence of Elisha, whose patriotic energy and foresight made him the mainstay of his country during this period of misery and depression.' Renan in his *History of the People of Israel* speaks of him and of his predecessor as disastrous revolutionaries whose interference in public affairs was as great a hindrance to 'progress' as was, in his time, the influence of the prophets in North Africa to the advancement of French arms and aggrandisement in that territory; a check to what he calls the French cause of civilization of the natives and liberal progress. This is what Rauschenbusch says of Elisha: 'Some of the prophets would get short shrift in a European state as religious demagogues. The overthrow of the dynasty of Omri in the northern kingdom was the result of a conspiracy between the prophetic party under Elisha and General Jehu, and resulted in a massacre so fearful that it staggered even the Oriental political conscience.'

A later Jewish writer, Jesus, son of Sirach, in Ecclesiasticus, thus describes the gentle Elisha: 'Elijah it was who was wrapt in a tempest, and Elisha was filled with his spirit; and in all his days he was not moved by the fear of any ruler, and no one brought him into subjection.'[1]

Now these seem most contradictory and irreconcilable estimates of the prophet, but those who are intimate with anarchists and revolutionists of our own day will be struck with their gentleness and consideration, their intimate concern with the individual, the feminine qualities of sympathy, combined with a ruthless ferocity, in what they consider the public cause. George Adam Smith, the classic writer of the prophets, has caught something of this, and reconciles the two sides of the prophet's character, when he writes: 'Elisha's greatness lies in his combination of the care of souls with political insight and vigilance in the national interest.'

So we find Elisha sweetening the waters for a commune of prophets, coming to the help of the prophet's widow who was threatened by her relentless creditors; saving the workman's axe from the water, turning poisoned food into wholesome; by his influence on the king, through the mediumship of his servant, restoring her allotment and home to the Shunamite woman; multiplying bread to the hungry, obtaining food and freedom for the poor Syrian troops whom he had trapped. One can picture his delicate concern for his Shunamite hostess, his raising of her only son to life. Now and again, this sweetness is marred by some outburst of rage, as when he curses the louts who jeer at him for his baldness, and by other incidents. He encourages an alliance of North and South against the Moabites, who sacrificed children to their god, Chemosh.

[1] Third century B.C., Greek translation.

*E

But his vengeance upon them could hardly be defended by the rules of honourable warfare, laid down in the Mosaic legislation.

The story of Elisha's healing of Naaman, the enemy general, is too well known to be repeated; but it will be remembered that this act of the divinely inspired prophet is referred to with admiration by Christ, and is met with anything but admiration by his jingo crowd of hearers at Nazareth.

The prophet's strategy in the war that follows with Syria is both wise and generous.

The lives of Elijah and Elisha prove conclusively that the earlier prophets at least were not only concerned with the domestic virtues but were political leaders of extraordinary force and sagacity in both national and international affairs.

We might give many more instances of this in the case of Elisha. At the end of his long and active service, when he lies dying, the king, who has come to him for political and military advice, weeps for his departing; for he sees in him, as he had seen in Elijah, the departing of one who had been his country's strength, and more, indeed, than all its materials for battle, more than all its chariots and horsemen.

CHAPTER VIII

SOCIAL AND POLITICAL CONDITIONS IN THE TIME OF AMOS, HOSEA, AND MICAH

ELISHA had passed away, but, in spite of his power and his protest against iniquities, there was no root and branch repentance in the northern kingdom.

It is not likely that the seizing of Naboth's vineyard was a solitary act; it was the glaring example, and possibly the first, of such robberies of the poor man's land. Elijah's denunciation may have been effective for the moment in staying the landslide, but the sons of Ahab, when they came to the throne, were imbued with the spirit of their mother; and both they and their courtiers would have little respect for the Mosaic land laws or the rights of the people. Of Jehu's social and economic policy we know practically nothing, but although he cleared out the Phoenician baals and restored the worship of Jehovah under the form of the bull-calf, we do not know if that worship was the cult of the God who protected the poor man from landlordism and usury. The only suggestion that we have in the Biblical record that he cared about the poor man's land was his killing of Ahab's son in vengeance for the blood of Naboth, and his casting of the dead body into Naboth's plot of ground, and his murder of the queen-mother and the hurling of her corpse on to the same fated spot. But, on the other hand, the book of the Kings records that this usurper 'took no heed to walk in the law of the Lord God of Israel with all his heart; for he departed not from the sins of Jeroboam, which made Israel to sin.'

Whatever may or may not have been the social policy of Jehu and his two successors, economic conditions in the time of Jeroboam II, the last of the Jehu dynasty,

were in flagrant contradiction to the social laws of
Moses.

A monied class, distinct from the old shepherd and
agricultural class, was being rapidly formed. The capitalists lent money to the poor husbandmen, and seized their
lands when they were unable to repay the loans. The
prophets of this period were the champions of the Lord God,
Jehovah, Who had never been the God of a commercial
people. To exact interest on money lent, or to seize the
lands of the working peasantry, 'was in Jehovah's eyes
an unpardonable oppression of the poor.' Whether this
oppression was encouraged under the cult of the foreign
baals, or the native baals of Israel, or whether it flourished,
as afterwards it did, under the nominal worship of Jehovah,
it was equally opposed and execrated by the prophets.

In the time of Jeroboam II in the North, and Uzziah in
the South, there was an enormous increase of wealth and
prosperity. The alliance of Israel and Judah for purposes
of defence, the expansion of both kingdoms on the defeat
of Syria to boundaries such as there had never been since
the times of David and Solomon,[1] the restoration of peace,
contributed to the material splendours of Palestine. To the
north, Damascus may even have been included for a time
within these boundaries; with Philistine cities once more
reduced to the position of tributaries, a gate was open to
the commerce of the Red Sea. It was an era of vigorous
shipbuilding. 'Wealth increased greatly, and palaces which
to the simple Israelites seemed vast were reared on
every hand. Every document of the time speaks of the
erection of buildings or palaces. . . . Wealth, however,
was not evenly distributed. The palaces were for a
comparatively small minority. The poor, while they saw
prosperity increasing around them, were daily becoming
poorer.'[2]

The wars between North and South, complicated by
political alliances for purposes of defence against foreign

---

[1] See map giving these boundaries, page 64.
[2] Hastings's *Small Dictionary of the Bible*.

invaders, had stimulated the growth of urban populations at the expense of the old village life. The demands of kings and their courts, their wives and concubines, the growth of a middle class and its commercial rapacity, its exploitation of an urban proletariat, had involved the ever-deepening gulf between rich and poor which would have gone on unnoticed and unchecked but for the appearance of political agitators who insisted on calling themselves the prophets of the Lord God, and on challenging and disturbing the vested interests of the wealthy classes.

As to the southern kingdom, the three reigns of Rehoboam, Asa, and Jehoshaphat covered a period of about eighty years. The last two kings had done much to reform the Temple worship, but we have no knowledge of social conditions during this time. Now Ahab and Jezebel had a daughter named Athaliah, whom they married to Jehoram, son and successor to Jehoshaphat. Here and there, prophetic voices were loud against this alliance, for it was a reunion through fear and not through friendship, and prophets foresaw that the poison of the house of Ahab would filter into the South, as indeed it did; for the king of Judah 'walked in the way of the kings of Israel, as did the house of Ahab; for the daughter of Ahab was his wife: and he did evil in the sight of the Lord.'

The southern kingdom had become even more commercialized than in the times of Solomon by the policy of Jehoshaphat the king's father. 'Through the conquest, or vassalage, of Edom the door was opened to the commerce of the gulf of Elath. The port of Akaba or Ezion-Geber, long disused, was once more alive with shipbuilders and sailors,' but this enterprise somehow or other seems to have failed. The conquest of Moab and Ammon and others besides would also make for outward prosperity. Jehoshaphat appointed judges throughout his kingdom and urged them to judge righteously.[1]

We have before suggested that idolatries and injustices were invariably bound up together, although the removal

[1] Chronicles.

of the idols did not always mean the uprooting of economic evil. Dark idolatries had eaten like a cancer into the heart of the southern kingdom in the reigns of Solomon and his immediate successors. The true worshippers of the Lord had continually to battle 'against the Canaanite and Phoenician polytheism which had taken possession of the court of Judah. . . . It almost seemed as if there was something in the old heathen origin of Jerusalem which rendered its soil congenial to the revival of those old heathen impurities. It was like a seething cauldron, of mingled blood and froth, whose scum is therein, and whose scum is not gone out of it.' Not only the Temple itself was polluted, but 'Mount Olivet was covered with heathen sanctuaries, monumental stones, and pillars of Baal. Wooden statues of Astarte under the sacred trees, huge images of Moloch appeared at every turn in the walks around Jerusalem. The valley of Hinnom, now received that dreadful association of sacrificial fires and gloomy superstition which it never lost. The royal gardens at Tophet were used for the same purpose. The holocausts of human beings, and especially of children, and their agonized cries became associated with this Hinnom or Gehenna, which in its turn becomes a synonym for the terrors of hell. The Holy City, centuries after, is called Sodom. So might it have been named in the days of Rehoboam and Abijah.'[1]

Dean Stanley points out that in the struggle between the holy and unholy Jerusalem, two powerful princesses, each of foreign extraction, Maacah and Athaliah, are the champions of these devilries. The former had become queen-mother in the reign of her son, Abijah, and her influence continued into that of Asa, her grandson. But Asa broke her power at last, removed her from her office, and destroyed the obscene images which disfigured Jerusalem: the covenant with the true God was renewed, and may have included not only the destruction of cruel and licentious rites, but the much more difficult attempt to return to the social and economic conditions of their fore-

---

[1] Stanley, *History of the Jewish Church*, vol. ii, pp. 335 ff.

fathers. Jehoshaphat continued what Asa had begun, and inaugurated regular judicial and educational functions founded on 'the Book of the Law.'

The fatal flaw in the policy of Jehoshaphat was that he had allowed an alliance in marriage between his son, Jehoram, and Athaliah. In this woman 'the fierce determined energy which ran through the Phoenician princes and princesses of that generation, Jezebel, Dido, Pygmalion, was fully developed. Already in her husband's reign the worship of Baal was restored; and when the tidings reached Jerusalem of the overthrow of her father's house, of the end of her mother, and of the fall of her ancestral religion in Samaria, instead of daunting her resolute spirit, it moved her to a still grander effort.' She becomes the murderess of all the seed royal excepting the baby, Joash, who was hidden in an inner chamber of the Temple, and herself seizes the throne. The worship of the Phoenician gods, 'uprooted by Jehu in Samaria, sprang up in Jerusalem with renewed vigour, as if in its native soil. The adherents of Baal, exiled from the northern kingdom, no doubt took refuge in the South.' Some of the stones of the Temple itself were removed to build the heathen sanctuaries which rose within the sacred precincts, with their altars and images, and relays of pagan priests. As economic abominations had followed in the wake of the Phoenician cults in the North, so would they follow in the southern kingdom, for Athaliah would be as contemptuous of the ancient rights of the workers as had been Jezebel her mother.

We have no time to tell the full story of the counter-revolution which, engineered by Jehoida the priest, dragged the foreign queen from the throne of David and acclaimed Joash, the boy who sprang from the loins of David, as king in her stead. Athaliah had cried: 'Treason! Treason!' but her cries were stifled and she was destroyed: and all the people clapped their hands and shouted: 'God save the king.'

It might have been expected that social reforms of a drastic nature would have followed the new régime, but beyond the repair of the Temple, and the renewal of its worship, little seems to have been accomplished in this direction.

On Jehoida's death, the wealthy aristocracy resolved to supplant the influence of the priests as the power behind the throne. Again the sinister cults crept back, a fitting symbol of the ambitions of this plutocracy, who can only have been growing rich at the expense of the poor. One man stood out against the cruelties and obscenities of the cultus, and was martyred as the reward of his brave remonstrance. This was the prophet Zechariah, who as our Lord exclaimed to the Pharisees was murdered by them between the temple and the altar.

The blood of Zechariah was avenged within a year. The king of Syria plundered Jerusalem, and Joash had to buy him off by a large tribute of the Temple and palace treasures. Humiliated and broken, Joash took to his bed, and some of his household conspired against him, and slew the sick man, and Amaziah, his son, reigned in his stead. He punishes the murderers of his father, makes a successful war upon Edom, but is defeated in his battle against Israel. After his victory over Edom, he brought back with him Idumean images, which he set up in the Temple, and one of the prophets foretold his destruction for this act of apostasy. This came to pass, for a conspiracy was formed against him, and after a reign of twenty-nine years he was murdered, and Uzziah (Azariah), his son, was acclaimed king by the popular choice.

Uzziah was a powerful and energetic monarch who extended the borders of his kingdom to the Red Sea, and Judah, under his rule, recalls the reign of Jehoshaphat in wealth and prosperity. He was, however, proud and presumptuous, and towards the end of his long reign of half a century attempted to usurp the office of the priesthood, and was visited with leprosy as a punishment of his audacity. From that time onwards he dragged on a miserable existence in seclusion, a kind of living death, while Jotham, his son, exercised the regency for his father.

Under Jotham foreign superstitions increased, and the worship of Jehovah Himself was corrupted by the abominable cruelties practised by the wealthy worshippers. Ahaz, who succeeded his father, was perhaps the worst of all the princes of the house of David. His foreign policy was disastrous. Terrified at the combined attack of Israel and Syria upon his kingdom, and the hostility of the Edomites and Philistines, he committed the futility of appealing for help to the ruthless empire of Assyria. It was true that Judah was always the cock-pit of warring powers, and it was a tremendous temptation to her at one time to call in Egypt, and at another time Assyria, to help her. But her prophets, more far-seeing than her kings, warned her of the dangers of this course. Assyria, as they had foreseen, having subdued Damascus and later Israel, proceeded to undermine the independence of Judah. To obtain relief from his immediate enemies, Syria and Israel, Ahaz had sacrificed the independence of his country.

Ahaz re-established the worship of Moloch on Mount Olivet and in the Valley of Hinnom, and many children, including one of his own sons, were sacrificed to the demon god: the Temple itself was filled with idols hardly less sinister. For this apostasy God cut him off in the prime of his life, and Hezekiah his son reigned in his stead.

'A state of long continued hostilities had produced its usual economic effects; the free practice of agriculture had given way before the exigencies of military organization; the insecurity of life in unwalled villages, and the stern pressure of poverty, had fostered the growth of cities; the simple manners and customs of a pastoral community had gradually been replaced by the habits of town life, with its sharp contrasts between wealth and poverty, its vices and luxuries, its artificial wants, its deterioration of character. The change from agriculture to mercantile and civil pursuits was obviously fraught with moral danger.'[1]

George Adam Smith speaks of the closer intercourse of

[1] Ottley, *History of the Hebrews*, page 184.

foreign nations and their cults, the temptations of rapid wealth, and the dangers of an equally increasing poverty. 'Cruelty multiplied with refinement. The upper classes were lifted away from feeling the real woes of the people. There was a well-fed and sanguine patriotism, but at the expense of indifference to social sin and want. Moreover the opening of new avenues to trade and commerce led to the rise of a mercantile community, tainted with the characteristic vices of a middle class; the passion for quickly making money, unscrupulous greed, dishonest trading, and callous harshness in the exaction of debt. The gulf between rich and poor grew daily wider, while the inveterate curse of Oriental life, corruption and partiality in the administration of justice, aggravated the burdens of the oppressed and helpless classes.'

The position of Israel and Judah, if they had formed a united Palestine, would have been difficult enough in face of the warring empires; but this very geographical position, if it had indeed remained loyal to the laws of Moses, would have made it a light to lighten the nations, an example of a Kingdom of God in miniature, which might indeed have been crushed out of existence by ruthless empires, but would at least have appealed to all that was best and most inspired in the peoples of those empires, and the other peoples around them, and might even have rallied those peoples into a democratic league and covenant against these unscrupulous oppressions. If such a miniature Kingdom of God on earth had gone under before rapacious invaders, its light would have been quenched in honour and glory. It might have even succeeded and survived, and in any case the policy of fear and apostasy, followed by both Israel and Judah, led those kingdoms swiftly and inevitably to destruction.

CHAPTER IX

THE TRUMPET SOUNDS IN THE COUNTRYSIDE

AMOS, HOSEA, AND MICAH

AMOS, yeoman farmer, cattle dealer, and dresser of figs, visiting urban markets, teeming with buyers and bargainers, stands amazed at the complete abandonment of the hardier and simpler life of his fathers, horrorstruck at the deep gulf between class and class. He is driven on by the spirit of God to expose the hypocrisy of the national life cloaking itself under the form of a zealous worship of the Lord Jehovah.

He suddenly appears at the sanctuary of Bethel at the height of a great religious feast. It may have been an armistice celebration on the conclusion of the war.

Abruptly he breaks in upon their religious revelries, like a death's-head at the feast. The people and their rulers were priding themselves on their recent victories and their national security. Was not Israel now the leading power between the Nile and the Euphrates? Had they not a right to be complacent about their prosperity, their wealth? 'There were palaces of ivory in Samaria then, and houses of hewn stone without number, castles and forts, horses and chariots, power and pomp, splendour and riches, wherever one might turn. The rich lay on couches of ivory with damask cushions; daily they slew a fatted calf, drank the most costly wines and anointed themselves with precious oils. All in all, it was a period in which to live was a joy. Accordingly, the feast was celebrated with unwonted splendour, and unnumbered sacrifices were offered. Men lived in the consciousness that God was on their side.'

The prophet's words at first met with no opposition, for

he began with a denunciation of the crimes of the Syrians, of the Philistines, Tyrians, Edomites, Ammonites, and Moabites. Now he comes nearer home, and pronounces judgment upon the southern kingdom, 'because they have despised the law of the Lord, and have not kept His commandments'; their life is a lie, and God 'will send a fire upon Judah, and it shall devour the palaces of Jerusalem.' Then only he launches his attack on Israel itself, 'because they have sold the righteous for silver, and the poor for a pair of shoes.' He denounces their sexual immoralities, their drunkenness, and their exploitation of the needy. Had not God brought them up out of the land of Egypt and led them through the wilderness to possess the land wherein they dwell? He had raised up his prophets, but they had stifled their voices. They had been his people, chosen out to serve him; 'you only have I known of all the families of the earth; therefore I will punish you for all your iniquities.' . . . 'I will smite the winter house with the summer house; and the houses of ivory shall perish and the great houses shall have an end, saith the Lord.'

He thunders against the rich women, 'cows of Bashan,' who share in the drunken revelries of their lords. 'Ye kine which oppress the poor, which crush the needy, which say to their masters, bring and let us drink. The Lord God hath sworn, by His holiness, that, lo, the days shall come upon you that He will take you away with hooks and your posterity with fishhooks.' Offer your thanksgiving sacrifices day and night, multiply them, for that pleases you, ye children of Israel; that is easy enough. I have sent famines and the drought upon you but you learn nothing. 'I have overthrown some of you, as God overthrew Sodom and Gomorrah, and ye were as a firebrand plucked from the burning, yet have ye not returned unto Me.'

And the ruling classes and the people who slavishly fawned upon them listened with amazement to this sedition-monger and disturber of the peace. In the midst of their joy and prosperity, what is this that he is raving about?

'The virgin of Israel is fallen, she shall no more rise.

She is forsaken in her land. There is none to raise her up.'

With his threats he mingles imploring counsel and promises of God's forgiveness if they will even at this last moment repent; but they would not hearken.

'You pray for "the Day of the Lord," but for you the Day of the Lord will be darkness and not light: "even very dark and no brightness in it." '

We shall find in Isaiah this same note about the Day. The term is important for us because it is a synonym for the Kingdom of Heaven. It runs through the Old and New Testament scriptures alike. Almost in the precise words of the southern prophet also is the next passage. 'I hate, I despise your feast days, and I will not smell in your solemn assemblies.' Your multitudinous sacrifices will be rejected. 'Take away from me the noise of thy songs; for I will not hear the melody of thy viols. But let judgment run down as waters, and righteousness as a mighty stream. Have ye offered unto me sacrifices and offerings in the wilderness forty years, O house of Israel? But ye have borne the tabernacle of your Moloch and Chiun, your images, the star of your god which ye made to yourselves. Therefore will I cause you to go into captivity beyond Damascus, saith the Lord, whose name is the God of Hosts.' Again he chastises them for their palaces and riches and their rejoicings in things which are worthless, the things of naught. 'Behold, I will raise up against you a nation, O House of Israel, saith the Lord God of Hosts, and they shall afflict you from the entering in of Hemath unto the river of the wilderness.'

Amaziah, court chaplain to Jeroboam (and prime minister?), complains to the king, saying: 'Amos has conspired against thee in the midst of the house of Israel; the land is not able to bear all his words. For thus Amos saith, Jeroboam shall die by the sword and Israel shall surely be led away captive out of their own land.'

The sleek priest of Bethel then urges the prophet to return to his own country and prophesy there as much as he likes, for this prophesying at Bethel is an unbearable interference, 'for it is the king's chapel and it is the king's court.' But Amos answers him that he is no professional prophet, nor does he belong to the school of prophets; he is just a herdman and gatherer of sycomore fruit, and God had commanded him to prophesy unto Israel. Undaunted, he turns upon the priest for his conduct, and says: 'Thy wife shall be an harlot in the city, and thy sons and thy daughters shall fall by the sword, and thy land shall be divided by line; and thou shalt die in a polluted land; and Israel shall surely go into captivity.'

Again he turns to the buyers and sellers in the sacred market, 'who swallow up the needy, even to make the poor of the land to fail.' He taunts them for their impatience for the ending of the Sabbath that they may renew their commerce, trading in false coinage, and falsifying the balances, 'that we may buy the poor for silver and the needy for a pair of shoes, yea and sell them the refuse of the wheat . . . shall not the land tremble for this and every one mourn that dwelleth therein?' God will turn their feasts into mourning, and their songs into lamentation. They shall wander from sea to sea, and from the north even to the east, they shall run to and fro to seek the word of the Lord and shall not find it. They shall be slain with the sword and none shall escape. 'Though they dig into hell thence shall mine hand take them; though they climb up to heaven, thence will I bring them down.'

Amos, afterwards writing down his prophecies, in his short epilogue ends with a note of hope.

If in their exile the people repent, the tabernacle of David shall once more be raised up out of its ruins, and the land shall be so fruitful 'that the plowman shall overtake the reaper and the treader of grapes him that soweth seed, and the mountains shall drop sweet wine and all the hills shall melt. And I will bring again the captivity of my people Israel, and they shall build the waste cities and inhabit them; they shall plant vineyards and drink the wine thereof; they shall also make gardens and eat the fruit of them. And I will plant them upon their own land.'

Within a few years there arose another prophet, Hosea, the last of the prophets of the northern kingdom; he begins to speak while Jeroboam is still on the throne, he continues during the years of anarchy and confusion that follow, in that time when Israel, like a snared and terrified bird, dashes for help towards the North and towards the South, sometimes towards Syria and then towards Egypt, for a deliverance that never comes. What Amos saw was coming true, and God lets the kingdom rock like an over-loaded cart. Nobody and nothing is safe; bandits infest the land, and even threaten the ill-gotten gains of the oppressors. Taxation becomes heavier and heavier to pay the tributes to Assyria, and attempts to get free of her, aided by this or that ally, are ruthlessly crushed. Upstart king after king is murdered, and the people turn a deaf ear to the pleadings of this gentler prophet. He perceives that the disunion of North and South, and this habit of coquetting first with one foreign nation and then with another, must bring both kingdoms to ruin. The priests and prophets are eaten up with corruption, and are making a living out of the sins of the people; the pilgrimages of the people are accursed, the shrines are scenes of abominable acts where the women prostitute themselves to Astarte, and the priests commit fornication with harlots.

The prophet mingles his terrible warnings with loving kindness; his writing is full of the poetry of the countryside he loves. George Adam Smith points out that he is the most spiritual of all the prophets and at the same time the most political. The heavy dews, the night winds, laden with the air of the mountains, the scent of Lebanon, the cottage life in valley and field, the smoke from the chimney, the chaff from the threshing floor, the doves startled on their towers, the fowler and his net, the breaking up of the fallow ground, the harrowing of the clods, the work of the reapers, teams of oxen climbing the steep roads, all these find a place in his poetry.

His home life was unhappy: his wife deserts him and becomes a harlot, but he loves her still, and takes her back and forgives her. He turns the story of his private misery into a parable of God's love for his people, their harlotry, and God's willingness to forgive them; surely the disasters that were already falling upon the nation must lead her back to her husband and her God.

But neither the threatenings of Amos nor the pleadings of Hosea have any effect upon a nation doomed to destruction. 'The unthinking mass of the people, led by worthless kings, false prophets, corrupt statesmen, and unscrupulous priests, was irrevocably doomed.'[1] The Assyrian army, the instrument of God's wrath, was already at the gates, and within thirteen years of Hosea's prophecies, the kingdom of Israel was destroyed.

Shortly before the disappearance of Israel as a nation there arose another prophet from the countryside whose name was Micah. He lived in the Shephalah or Lowlands of Judah, about a day's journey from Jerusalem. His home was not far from the Philistine border, and from his native hills, about a thousand feet above sea-level, he could see the Mediterranean. Unlike the country of Amos, which was bare and desolate, Micah's surroundings were fertile cornfields, vineyards, rich pasture, and olive groves, a land of villages with no towns of any size.

But many caravan routes converged in his neighbourhood, so that through converse with the traders of the commercial world, he would be in touch with the life of the great cities and especially of Jerusalem.

He prophesied some years after Hosea and was contemporary with the urban prophet Isaiah and probably they were in touch with one another. He raises his voice against the sins of the North and of the South, of Samaria and of Jerusalem. He well illustrates the simplicity and directness of Hebrew prophecy. For Israel the sands were

[1] Ottley, *History of the Hebrews*, page 188.

running out and he was the last to foretell its speedy and inevitable destruction.

'Will the Lord be pleased with thousands of rams or with thousands of rivers of oil? Shall I give my first-born for my transgression or the fruit of my body for the sin of my soul? He hath shown thee, O man, what is good; and what doth the Lord require of thee but to do justly and to love mercy and to walk humbly with thy God?'

The words of our Lord about the weightier matters of the Law, his words about justice and mercy, were those of this simple peasant. All this he translated into a direct attack upon the nobles who were exploiting the poor in town and country.

'The rising buildings and the growing magnificence of Jerusalem spoke to him of the grinding down of the poor by which the wealth needed for such works had been obtained.'[1]

The ruling classes had grown fat at the expense of the peasants. In contempt of the Mosaic Law they had become great landowners, squeezing the small holders out of existence. Like the hypocrites of the North whom Amos had denounced, these leading families and the clergy who flattered them pretended to rely on God to cover their robberies, making their religion a cloak for their crimes. The prophets, salaried by the rich, speak smooth words to their masters and were execrated by this bold prophet who suddenly appeared in the capital to pronounce their fate. The magistrates abhor justice and pervert all equity. They build up Zion with blood and Jerusalem with iniquity. The heads thereof judge for reward and the priests thereof teach for hire, and the prophets thereof divine for money, yet will they lean upon the Lord and say: 'Is not the Lord among us. None evil can come upon us.' Like Amos before him he includes in his denunciation those who trade by means of crooked balances and bags of deceitful weights. In the midst of Jerusalem he leaves no stone unturned to

[1] Hastings's *Small Dictionary of the Bible.*

bring home his appeal. 'I will wail and howl. I will go stripped and naked. I will make a wailing like the dragons and a mourning as the owls. For the wound is incurable.'

'Woe to them that devise iniquity and work evil upon their beds; when the morning is light, they practise it, because it is in the power of their hand. They covet fields and take them by violence and houses and take them away. So they oppress a man and his house, even a man and his heritage . . . therefore shall Zion for your sake be plowed as a field, and Jerusalem shall become heaps and the mountain of the house as the high places of the forests.'

Professor Cornill thus sums up Micah: 'His straightforward and lively sense of justice suffered itself to be neither silenced nor repressed. A moral indignation truly awe inspiring overpowers him at what he sees and experiences, especially the sins of the nobility of Jerusalem, those unscrupulous blood-suckers and the despoilers of the people, who stopped at nothing if they had but the power, are so atrocious that they can only be atoned for by the destruction of Jerusalem.'

The story of Micah, unlike that of the prophets of Samaria, has a happy ending. We shall deal in a later section with the reforms of good King Hezekiah, brought about by the influence of the peasant prophet and the aristocratic Isaiah. A century later, when Jeremiah was in danger of his life from priests and false prophets infuriated by his words, he is saved by an appeal made by the better of the nobility and people to the case of Micah whose life had been spared by the king, when his wealthy accusers had clamoured for his blood.

There are among modern critics many who deny that the hope of a Messianic restoration and a new world of justice and plenty could have formed any part of the message of these early prophets. They dismiss as later additions all such references in Micah, as in Amos and Hosea before him. After careful examination of their arguments we find them singularly inconclusive.

In any case our main object in tracing the development of the idea of the Kingdom of Heaven through Jewish history, is to discover what was in the mind of our Lord and his contemporaries in this matter, and we assert with confidence that Jesus would neither have the time nor the curiosity to inquire whether there were two Isaiahs or a hundred, or whether the Messianic references in Amos, Hosea, and Micah were or were not forgeries or at the least additions of a later date. That the writings of these earlier prophets may be treated as a whole seems to us incontestable, but we may frankly admit that in historic criticism we believe that poetic imagination is a safer guide than mere erudition.

There is only this reservation to be made; namely, that the 'higher' criticism has done inestimable service to truth, in that it has broken down the notion that the scriptures must be regarded as sacrosanct and that in their interpretation there must not be employed the usual processes of reasoning, except where such processes can be used to establish 'orthodox conclusions.'

We demand more not less daring imagination and note that modern criticism is fearlessly beginning to contradict some earlier assumptions of the 'higher' critics.

There is really no reason, therefore, to suppose that the passage we have quoted from Amos about the good time coming is not genuine. In Hosea the same note is struck: 'I will heal their backsliding, I will love them freely, for mine anger is turned away from him. I will be as the dew unto Israel; he shall grow as the lily and cast forth his roots like Lebanon.' The most famous passage is, however, in Micah, about the mountain of the house of the Lord exalted above the hills unto which all people shall flow: 'And many nations shall come and say, Come and let us go up to the mountain of the Lord and to the house of the God of Jacob; and He will teach us His ways and we will walk in His paths: for the law shall go forth of Zion, and the word of the Lord from Jerusalem. And He shall judge among many people, and rebuke strong nations from afar off; and they shall beat their swords into plowshares and their spears into pruninghooks: nation shall not lift up a sword against nation, neither shall they learn war any more.   But they shall sit every man under his vine and under his fig tree; and none shall make them afraid; for the mouth of the Lord of Hosts hath spoken it.'

CHAPTER X

ISAIAH

ISAIAH, whose prophecies cover a period of some fifty years, and who opened his campaign in the last year of Uzziah, king of Judah, and continued it through the reigns of Jotham, Ahaz, and Hezekiah, was probably an aristocrat and was, by birth and education, in striking contrast to the peasant prophets we have been describing.

He was a statesman with a world vision and an accurate knowledge of the movements of nations and empires and their rival policies. It is not necessary to believe, with some writers, that he obtained his information of the state of the countryside from his contemporary Micah, although he probably knew of his work, and indeed Micah might well have been in communication with him and possibly may have read his earlier writings. His book opens with a vision of the fate of the South, a fate which might be, and which was for a time, averted by the partial repentance of Judah.

He would not only be well informed about the state of things at his own doors, but it was likely that the oppressors in Jerusalem were, in some cases, the selfsame people who were exploiting the poor of the countryside where they would have their country residences. They would have their 'season' in town and their 'season' in the country; some of them may have been his own relations.

In his vision he sees the Lord high and lifted up with His train filling the Temple, and he contrasts the majesty of God with the meretricious exaltation of the kings and nobles on the earth who profess to worship Him. The message of this prophet of the city whom we have

125

contrasted with the prophets of the country was identical
with theirs. It teems with allusions to the political and
economic conditions of the time. His religion, like theirs,
was an interference with politics.

The very passages which, wrenched from their context,
are so dear to pietists of our day, are pregnant with
political significance. 'To what purpose is the multitude
of your sacrifices unto Me? saith the Lord'; I am 'fed up
with' the burnt offerings of rams and the fat of beasts;
'I delight not in the blood of bullocks, or of lambs, or of
he goats.' God is nauseated with their vain oblations,
their church-going, their incense offerings, their Sabbath
keeping. 'I cannot away with iniquity and the solemn
meeting.' He reminds them that the hands spread upwards in prayer are full of the blood of the poor. Therefore, 'I will hide Mine eyes from you when ye make many
prayers . . . wash you, make you clean . . . cease to
do evil; learn to do well; seek judgment [justice], relieve
the oppressed, judge the fatherless, plead for the widow.'

Why does he liken their sins to scarlet? Because they
are mingled with the blood of the poor.

'How is the faithful city become an harlot. She that
was full of judgment. Righteousness lodged in her, but
now murderers. Thy silver is become dross, thy wine
mixed with water. Thy princes are rebellious, and companions of thieves; every one loveth gifts, and followeth
after rewards; they judge not the fatherless, neither doth
the cause of the widow come unto them.'

Again, he says: 'The Lord will enter into judgment with
the elders of the people and the princes thereof; it is ye
that have eaten up the vineyard; the spoil of the poor is in
your houses: what mean ye that ye crush My people, and
grind the face of the poor?'

Once more in the poem of the vineyard, the God-planted
vineyard, which should have brought forth grapes, and
behold, it brought forth wild grapes, God says: 'I will
take away the hedge thereof and it shall be eaten up; and
I will break down the fence thereof and it shall be trodden

down and I will lay it waste; it shall not be pruned nor hoed, but there shall come up briars and thorns, and I will also command the clouds that they rain no rain upon it.' And why? 'For the vineyard of the Lord of Hosts is the House of Israel, and the men of Judah His pleasant plant; and He looked for judgment but behold oppression, for justice but behold a cry.'

'Woe unto them that join house to house; that lay field to field, till there be no room, and ye be made to dwell alone in the midst of the land. In Mine ears, saith the Lord of Hosts, of a truth, many houses shall be desolate, even great and fair without inhabitant.'

He inveighs against drunkenness and extravagance, but his fiercest indignation is reserved for 'them that decree unjust decrees, and the writers that write perverseness, to turn aside the needy from social justice and to take away the right of the poor of my people.'

They were not cursed in the days of the prophets with the modern capitalist press, but they had, as well as we, their writers that write perverseness and deal in lies.

All these warnings and denunciations are mingled with the hope of the time after the national destruction, the Messianic good time coming, when the poor shall once more own their own land and live in peace with their neighbours, the time when rulers and people shall have come to a practical repentance.

There is, for instance, the famous passage at the beginning of chapter xi about the coming forth of the rod out of the stem of Jesse. This offspring of David shall judge deep and righteous judgment and 'reprove with equity the meek of the earth, and he shall smite the earth with the rod of his mouth and with the breath of his lips shall he slay the wicked . . . the wolf also shall lie down with the lamb, and the leopard shall lie down with the kid, and the calf and the young lion and the fatling together; and a little child shall lead them . . . they shall not hurt nor destroy in all my holy mountain; for the earth shall be full of the knowledge of the Lord as the waters cover the sea.'

With this we may compare chapter xxxii, beginning, 'Behold, a king shall reign,' and ending: 'Blessed are ye which sow beside still waters, that send forth thither the feet of the ox and the ass.' He foresees captivity and banishment, but beyond it, 'thine eyes shall see the king in his beauty, they shall behold the land which is very far off.'

There are many more such passages in the later chapters, but probably they come from the pen of one who is within the Isaianic tradition and were written during the captivity.

Here we may remind ourselves that our Lord is steeped in the writings of Isaiah and would, with his contemporaries, read the book as a whole. He would probably know the writings of this prophet by heart, and over and over again quotes them, basing his Jubilee sermon at Nazareth, for instance, upon a passage about the Acceptable Year of the Lord when the land returns to the people, debtors (and political offenders?) are released, and the poor have the good news preached unto them.

Isaiah was not officially foreign minister to any of the kings of Judah, but, as has already been stated, he was an adviser on foreign affairs, although his advice was not always taken. He had a world outlook, and it was disastrous that his counsels were so often disregarded.

There had been occasional alliances of North and South Palestine, as in the time of Elisha, but these had been dictated, not by a sense of the wickedness of schism and desire for real unity, but by terror in face of foreign enemies. It was for this reason that they broke down, and Judah once more had attacked Israel in the reign of Jehoash the northern king and suffered heavy defeat at the hands of Joash of Jerusalem.

In the reign of Jotham, son of Uzziah, king of Judah, the kings of Syria and Israel combined to force Judah into a pact against Assyria. When Ahaz succeeded Jotham, these northern kingdoms of Syria and Israel, ignoring the pacts with Judah, conducted a campaign against Jerusalem and resolved to dethrone the successor of David. The people were in terror; their hearts 'shook like the trees of the forest.'   King Ahaz adopted the suicidal policy of seeking Assyrian help.   Isaiah pleaded in vain.   He had told Ahaz that he was a fool to be terrified at these two 'tails of the smoking firebrands,' foreseeing the danger was not from them, but from the mighty empire which would soon extinguish them and might well do the same to Judah if this entangling alliance were persisted in.

But once Judah had become a vassal of the Assyrians, Isaiah advised the punctual payment of the tribute and the keeping herself clear of all complicity in rebellion.   During the reigns of Ahaz and Hezekiah his advice was the same. Palestine's only chance of getting free was to remain quiet and to accept the *status quo*.   She had herself, by courting Assyrian suzerainty, made it inevitable that Judah should become the cock-pit in the wars of the wolves of Assyria and Egypt, but she would only be worsening her state by taking sides or by what must be futile and disastrous rebellions.

It would be ludicrous if it were not so pathetic that the prophet's advice as to national quietness and confidence, the non-participation in the quarrels and wars which did not concern her, should be twisted to mean the quietism of the individual soul by modern evangelicals, just as the term 'saviour' is twisted to mean the saviour of the separate soul when it means a national or international deliverer.

When Isaiah finds that his advice goes unheeded, he sets himself to build up a remnant of faithful people who, if unable to avert the coming catastrophy, will at least form the nucleus of a nation reborn in days to come.   Ahaz had sent a message to Tiglath, a message of abject submission: 'I am thy son and thy slave.'   Now he must abide by the consequences.

It is extraordinary that some historians such as Robertson Smith and Ottley should see in this wise political advice and this building up of the 'remnant,' the first conception of the Church as an organ 'for the emancipation of spiritual religion from the forms of political life . . . the prophets were, as a rule, no longer the trusted guides but

F

the antagonists of those who directed the destinies of
Judah.'

Obviously they were just as political as ever but in
opposition to the Government. Theirs was not a movement for 'spiritualizing' religion in the modern sense but
for warring against the policies of the moment. It would
be just as fantastic to say that because the left wing movement in Europe to-day holds aloof from current capitalist
policies, it is itself entirely non-political.

Before passing to the reign of the good, though sometimes feeble, Hezekiah, something must be said of the reign
of Ahaz, an almost inconceivably evil man. Jotham who
had been regent for his father Uzziah, when the latter had
been in retirement as a leper, succeeded him, but the
country under his rule went from bad to worse. The
rulers were as Sodom, the people as Gomorrah. 'The
whole head was sick and the whole heart faint.' Social
iniquity flourished.

Ahaz, his son, who succeeded him 'was himself the
centre of all the superstitious practices which prevailed in
his reign.' Soothsayers, wizards, necromancers flourished.
Every foreign nation seemed to contribute its cruel gods
to the sanctuary at Jerusalem. He even introduced a
heathen altar into the Temple in place of the high altar of
Jehovah, which had been there since the time of Solomon.
And with all this idolatry went an increasing oppression
of the people, as we may read in the pages of Isaiah.

Ahaz would seem to have died in the same year as did
his patron Tiglath Pileser, struck down in the midst of his
strength, and Judah was rid of an evil genius who came
near destroying her.

During the reign of the reforming King Hezekiah with
which we shall soon be dealing, Judah is on the verge of
yielding to the siren voice of Egypt, when Isaiah appears
dramatically in the garb of a prisoner of war, as a sign that
Assyria would descend upon them if they took this road
and they would be led away captive.

Later, when Sargon was murdered by his son Sennacherib

(705 B.C.), the little nations see their chance of freedom
in rebellion, but the prophet remains firm against all the
patriotic excitement in Jerusalem. Take no part in this
foolhardy enterprise which is bound to fail. Leave Assyria
to the vengeance of God. Give her rope enough and she
will hang herself. God plays with Assyria like a wild beast,
but will some day strike her lifeless to the earth.[1]

Hezekiah is obdurate and hearkens not to the prophet,
but throws in his lot with the rest and rebels against their
mighty oppressors, backed by Ethiopia (Abyssinia) and
Egypt. Sennacherib approaches with a mighty host and
overthrows Egypt and her allies and proceeds to overrun
Judea as Isaiah had foretold. He now prophesies that
although vast destruction is overtaking the land the capital
will remain inviolate; and amazing though it seemed the
prophecy was fulfilled and Jerusalem was saved by what
seemed to be a divine intervention.[2]

If the doom of Judah was stayed for more than a century,
it was owing to the foreign policy of the world statesman
Isaiah. For nearly half a century 'seated at the tiller he
guided by the divine compass the little ship of his fatherland
through the rocks and breakers of a wild and stormy period.'[3]

Hezekiah reigned in Judah for about thirty-two years.
He began his rule some five years before the final obliteration of Israel as a political entity. Some historians place
him later, and the invitation to Israel which we shall now

---

[1] On another occasion Isaiah seems to have urged resistance to Assyria
(chapters xxxvi and xxxvii), but this may coincide with the withdrawal of
Sennacherib's armies?

[2] Shishak, king of Egypt, spoils Solomon's temple in Rehoboam's reign;
Josiah long after is defeated and killed by Necho of Egypt (the Nekos of
Herodotus). The Assyrian came down like a wolf on the fold; and pestilence
laid low the army of Sennacherib, as both the Bible and Herodotus tell us;
the mouse in the Egyptian god's hand, which Herodotus describes, is the
signal of plague, as it was with the Philistines, when they returned the Ark
to Israel after Eli's death. A Greek geographer tells us of plague spreading
from field mice to an army in Spain; and every one knows to-day that plague
is carried by the fleas of the rat, and in America by those of the ground-
squirrel. (*The Ancient World*, Glover, chapter on Sennacherib, page 208.)

[3] Cornill.

consider is not quite incompatible with the later date, because, as Renan pointed out long ago, although the urban
populations were deported to Assyria, the people of the
land may well have remained. We are expressly told that
this was so in the case of the later deportation of the
southerners to Babylon. One of our most acute modern
critics also suggests this. The armies of the Great Eastern
empires were directed against the fenced cities rather than
against the poor cultivators of the soil, and it was probably
only the population of the cities which was deported . . .
the new inhabitants introduced by the Assyrian king were
placed in the depopulated 'Samaria and the cities thereof,'
the old village population remaining. If this was so,
there may be historical foundation for the statements of
the chronicler that Hezekiah summoned to his passover the
whole population of Israel, 'from Dan to Beersheba, from
Beersheba even to Dan,' appealing to them not to be stiff-
necked like their fathers, but by their repentance to win
the return of their land.[1] When the national life of the
northern kingdom had been destroyed, it was natural both
that the remnant left behind should turn hopefully to such
kings as Hezekiah and Josiah, and that the latter should
strive to extend their authority over them.

According to the Book of Kings, Hezekiah began his
reign before the final overthrow of Israel, but after the
first great disaster when an Assyrian emperor had attacked
both North and South, and had so far conquered as to force
both kings to become his vassals or tributaries, conquering
large territories of Israel, seizing all its trans-Jordan possessions, and deporting a mass of these populations to
Assyria. The Israelitish kings from now onwards become
mere puppets of the Assyrian Empire.

The invitation of Hezekiah which we shall now describe
may have been sent out to Israel after the final downfall
of her fenced cities and her capital or earlier, when much of
her territory had been wrenched from her, but in any case
it was a very remarkable and liberal gesture. We do not

[1] 2 Chronicles xxx. 1–11.

agree with Dr. Goudge that Hezekiah was striving to extend his authority over the schismatic North, or at least that this was his main object.[1]   As Maurice points out, 'he did not, like Rehoboam, Amaziah, or any of his predecessors, seek to recover the ten tribes to himself as part of his possession and appanage because he was the heir of David.   He did not treat them as mere rebels who, if they would not submit to him, must be left to their own courses. Nor, on the other hand, did he, like Jehoshaphat, make alliances with them in spite of their idolatries.   What he did was to claim one and all of them as children of God's covenant; as entitled to share in the feast which declared that they were delivered from Pharaoh and brought under a divine and gracious government.'[2]   All kinds of objections might have occurred to him, but 'even the divine formalities for the festival were not allowed to stand in the way.   They had not cleansed themselves.   "They ate otherwise than it was written."   Still Hezekiah prayed, "the good Lord pardon every one."   Many mocked at the invitation and would not come, but, again, many others accepted it, and in this union of North and South in the Passover feast "there was great joy in Jerusalem; for since the time of Solomon, son of David, king of Israel, there was not the like in Jerusalem."'

It was the occasion of a great turning to the Lord God of their fathers and to 'the good Knowledge of God,' and so great was the influence of this sort of unity among the Israelites that, when they returned to their own countryside they break the images in pieces and cut down the groves; as also did the southerners.

Incidentally it may be noticed that the Israelites had not all been dispossessed of their ancient holdings, at least, if the Book of Chronicles can be believed, 'then all the children of Israel returned, every man to his possession, into their own cities.'

---

[1] *The British-Israel Theory*, by Dr. Goudge, Regius Professor of Divinity, Oxford, page 4.   (Mowbray, 1933.)

[2] F. D. Maurice, Sermon 15, *Prophets and Kings*.

This was an act of unity not dictated by terror but by charity; a unity of grace.

What strikes one as extraordinary and profoundly difficult in prophetic literature is the kind of passage which seems partially fulfilled in their own times and yet looks beyond to something stupendous, to some world beyond our dreams, a thing to be planted upon this earth and yet a kingdom not of this world. A typical prophecy is that which deals with the Virgin who shall conceive and bear a son. It is not the difficulty of the 'Virgin,' for the actual word can be translated 'young woman,' or one who is yet a virgin. But Isaiah is evidently giving a sign which he believes will be fulfilled in his own time and apparently in the person of the good king Hezekiah. Yet, however great and noble this action of the king's, and however far-reaching his reforms, the sign must look for its complete fulfilment, as the New Testament writers perceive, in one far outstripping Hezekiah in divine splendour. The passage is Messianic and looks forward to the ideal Son of David, his son and also his lord.

It is difficult to determine how far Hezekiah's reforms were mainly concerned with the rooting out of the grosser idolatries and how far they included drastic social reformation.

That both prophets of his reign desired a return to the ancient justice has been abundantly shown, and the fact that Micah's life was spared would show that Hezekiah did something at least in this direction, but it is doubtful if Isaiah's vision was anything but faintly realized in him or that Jerusalem became the City State of his dreams, the city of God, in the time of the good king.

CHAPTER XI

THE RIVER EMPIRES AND THE CITY STATE

THAT Isaiah dreamed of Jerusalem as such a city of God centred in the capital, there can be no doubt. If the peasant prophets looked forward to a heavenly polity here on earth, it is in Isaiah that the dream takes shape as the perfect city, more perfect, indeed, than the Greek City States, inasmuch as they were, both in idea and in fact, founded on slavery.[1] Glorious as were Athens and Sparta their philosophers had never been able to look beyond a community of free citizens, made possible by the work of the slaves beneath, who were looked upon as tools rather than men. In Isaiah we have the ideal of a really democratic republic reformed by the common people. Athens even in her best days was 'a slave-holding aristocracy.' But Isaiah suggests that the Babylonish Jerusalem with its divisions into rich and poor, the proud and the lowly, shall be trodden under foot by the poor and by 'the steps of the needy.' It is only on the ruins of that evil polity that the new city can arise. 'In that day shall this song be sung in the land of Judah; we have a strong city, salvation will God appoint for walls and bulwarks. Open ye the gates that the righteous nation which keepeth the truth may enter in.'

It may be objected that the ideal Jerusalem was to be monarchical, but it must be remembered that even in the South with its tradition of a hereditary Davidic House there was some idea, at least, of an elective monarchy in the acclamation of the people at the king's crowning, and they had on several occasions, with the approval of the prophets, overthrown the ruling monarch if he had done evil and set up another upon the throne.

J. C. Todd writes: 'It is a natural but most serious error

[1] See Note at end of chapter.

135

to class Jerusalem with the Empires and not with the Cities. Egypt, Palestine, and Assyria are associated in our minds, while Greece and Rome fall into a different mental pigeon-hole. We conceive of Israel as being a feeble copy of its mighty neighbours on the Nile and Tigris.'[1]

This, he shows, is entirely wrong: 'In the last chapter the city of Jerusalem was reconstructed from the poems relating to its destruction. The evidence showed clearly enough that religion, nationality, and loyalty, though all present, were subordinated to civism, to the glory and pride of citizenship. The whole description might very well stand for that of a Greek city in the days of monarchy; while the passionate love for the city-state cannot be exceeded. "The perfection of beauty, the joy of the whole earth"—what more could Pericles have said of Athens?'

Jerusalem, again, is unfortunately close in idea to Athens and Rome in that they were imperialistic, having under them subject and tributary nations; but although the same ambition is found in the prophets, and occasionally even in Isaiah, for the holy city, yet there is that amazing passage which contradicts this notion of Jerusalem 'over all,' exploiting subject peoples.

'In that day shall there be an altar to the Lord in the midst of the land of Egypt . . . it shall be a sign and witness unto the Lord of Hosts in the land of Egypt; for they shall cry unto the Lord because of the oppressors, and He shall send them a saviour and a great one and He shall deliver them. And the Lord shall be known to Egypt and the Egyptians shall know the Lord in that day, and shall do sacrifice and oblation; yea, they shall vow a vow unto the Lord and perform it. And the Lord shall smite Egypt; He shall smite and heal it; and they shall return even to the Lord and He shall entreat them and He shall heal them.'

'In that day there shall be a highway out of Egypt to Assyria, and the Assyrian shall come into Egypt and the Egyptian into Assyria, and the Egyptians shall serve with

[1] *Politics and Religion in Ancient Israel.*

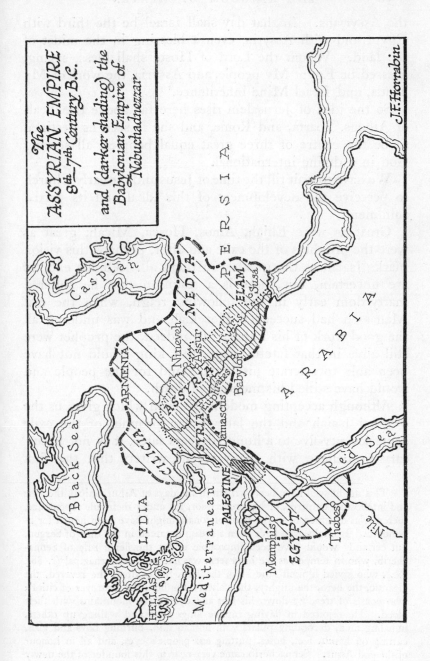

the Assyrians.   In that day shall Israel be the third with
Egypt and with Assyria, even a blessing in the midst of
the land.   Whom the Lord of Hosts shall bless, saying,
Blessed be Egypt My people, and Assyria, the work of My
hands, and Israel Mine inheritance.' [1]

So the idea of Jerusalem rises here far above the ideals
of Athens, Sparta, and Rome, and she is seen as destined
to be the centre of three great equal peoples, all serving
God in a divine international.

We have to wait till the time of Jesus and the early Church
to perceive the development of this ideal and its partial
fulfilment.

Great as were Elijah, Amos, Hosea, Micah, great as
were the prophets of the exile and after, perhaps this vision
marks Isaiah as the greatest of them all.   Of his end we
are uncertain, but there is a tradition that he suffered
martyrdom early in the following reign, when the evil
Manasseh had succeeded Hezekiah and was undoing all
the good work of his father.   If, indeed, the prophet were
still alive in that fateful reign, this king would not have
been able to tolerate his brave stand for the people and
would have stifled his message in death.

Although accepting modern criticism which gives us the
original Isaiah and the later Isaian prophet of the exile
some seventy-five to a hundred years later, it is not necessary to believe with many recent writers that the first

---

[1] This might well have been written in the days of Ashurbanipal, the wise
and intellectual emperor, or his predecessor, for under their rule repentance,
such as was dreamed of in the Book of Jonah, might have been hoped for in
Nineveh.   It might even have been a dream dreamed in the time of Sargon,
but certainly would have been impossible under the fierce rule of Sennacherib, who in temper, as we have seen, was like unto Azzurnazipal (c. 884
B.C.), who styled himself 'the king, the lord, the exalted, the revered, the
gigantic, the hero, the mighty, the stalwart, the lion, the destroyer of cities';
who boasts of treading down his foes and dyeing the mountains with their
blood.   He rejoiced in flaying captive kings alive and walling up others,
impaling men, decorating pillars with human skin, burning boys and girls,
cutting off hands, feet, noses, putting out people's eyes, and all in honour
of the god Assur.   Sennacherib came very near to this founder of the newly
constructed Assyria in cruelty. (Quoted from Dean Farrar.)

Isaiah could not and did not see in Babylon the coming power that would destroy Assyria and eventually eat up Judah.

Babylon and the district around it was already giving trouble to the Assyrians in the time of Sargon, and although he is able for the moment to put down the Babylonian rebellion (in 709 B.C.) its determined king returns immediately Sennacherib begins his reign, and it took this latter monarch many years to subdue his Babylonian subjects. Somewhere between 711 and 700 B.C. after Hezekiah had recovered from his illness, Merodach-Baladan, still king of Babylon, having heard of the miraculous power and endurance of the fortress of Jerusalem and the defeat of the Assyrians, sends envoys to Hezekiah to arrange some kind of alliance, and this gives them the opportunity of looking at the treasures of the city which the simple Hezekiah is proud to show them. Isaiah warns him that it is no longer Assyria that should be feared, but the rising power of Babylon, which will become an empire engulfing its rival and subduing Egypt.

Isaiah looks upon these ferocious empires as the scourges of God. Assyria is the rod of God's anger and the staff of his indignation to tread down hypocritical nations, as the mire of the streets. But when these proud empires have done their purifying work they too shall perish, because they have not done these things in righteous vengeance but only for their own pride and gain. They have not acknowledged the god of justice behind their victories; it is in their own strength that they boast themselves, saying: 'By the strength of my hand I have done it and by my wisdom . . . my hand hath found as a nest the riches of the people, and as one gathereth the eggs that are left, have I gathered all the earth; and there was none that moved the wing or opened the eye or peeped.'

This might well be a description of Sennacherib, who, in spite of his power and courage, was a boaster, a swaggerer; cruel, revengeful, and despotic. His own account of his exploits are in the vein of the above quotation from the prophet.

He omits all mention of the disastrous reverse, when, according to the Biblical account, 'the whole Assyrian army, gathered under the walls of Jerusalem, was stricken by the angel of the Lord who slew one hundred and eighty-five thousand Assyrian soldiers.'[1]   But it is unlikely that this type of man would record his losses and defeats.

It will be remembered that Hezekiah had thrown in his lot with many petty states who had joined the Ethiopian-Egyptian combination in opposition to Assyria, against the urgent advice of Isaiah.   This is Sennacherib's account of his exploits: 'But as for Hezekiah of Judah, who had not submitted to my yoke, forty-six of his stronghold cities and the smaller cities round about them without number, by the battering of rams and the attack of war engines(?) and by the making of breaches and the cutting through of axes, I besieged and captured.   Himself (Hezekiah), I shut up like a caged bird in Jerusalem, his royal city. Two hundred thousand, one hundred and fifty people, small and great, male and female, horses, mules, asses, camels, and sheep without number, I brought forth from their midst and reckoned as spoil . . . Hezekiah himself was overwhelmed by the fear of the brilliancy of my lordship, and the Arabians and faithful soldiers whom he had brought in to strengthen his royal city, deserted him. Thirty talents of gold, eight hundred talents of silver, precious stones . . . large lapis lazuli, couches of ivory, thrones of elephant skin and ivory . . . a heavy treasure, and his daughters, his palace women, male and female singers, to Nineveh, my lordship's city, I caused to be brought after me and he sent his ambassador to give tribute and to do homage.'

Esarhaddon, his son, was a wise emperor, forgiving, generous, religious, 'less harsh and cruel and very diplomatic.'   And Assurbanipal, his successor, was the greatest of the Assyrian emperors.   Not only was his generalship

[1] *Catholic Encyclopaedia.*

remarkable, but his learning was unsurpassed. To him we owe the magnificent library of tens of thousands of clay tablets, which in our own day are being unearthed and deciphered.

His two successors were of different metal, and under their feeble and effeminate leadership Assyria began to lose her provinces and her decline was rapid.

The last night of the siege of Nineveh was celebrated by the drunken orgies of its people given up to madness and despair. An overflow of the Tigris made easier the breach in the walls, and the last of the proud Assyrian emperors burned himself alive in his palace. Babylon was now in the ascendancy and Assyria was destroyed and its capital completely demolished.

This obliteration of Nineveh is all the more significant when we consider its size and the strength of its walls and fortifications. It has been described as the London of the ancient world, sixty miles in circumference and seven miles across. It was protected and encircled by three huge walls. One of them was a hundred feet high, and three chariots could drive abreast along its surface. Nineveh had over a million inhabitants.

The prophet Nahum speaks of God's fury against this city, as also possibly Habakkuk, although the latter's denunciation according to some scholars is applied to Babylon. Cornill, however, believes it to be directed against Nineveh. 'Woe to them that build a city with blood. The Chaldeans [Babylonians] shall destroy them.' These empires treat men not as men but 'as a harvest of fishes.' Zephaniah also denounces these ferocious empires which grind the poor and call evil good and good evil. Their goods will become a booty and their grand houses desolate. 'And He will stretch out His hand against the North and destroy Assyria and will make Nineveh a desolation and dry like a wilderness.' Alexander the Great some centuries later marched over the place where once it had been, not knowing that a world empire lay buried beneath his feet.

NOTE.—About the time of Micah and Isaiah, between the years 700 and 600 B.C., when the Hebrew prophets were denouncing the building of the great houses and palaces of Jerusalem on the blood and tears of the workers, the whole Athenian territory was in the hands of a few wealthy families, and the poorer classes were obliged to cultivate the soil for them for a mere sixth part of the produce.   If they failed to pay their dues they were liable to be sold into chattel slavery together with their wives and children.   Lands which had been their fathers' were lost to them by mortgages and usury and eviction and no slave was allowed any share in the government of Athens.   The slaves 'had no part nor share in anything.'—Warde Fowler, *The City State*.

The writings of Solon, about 600 B.C., a contemporary of Jeremiah, describe the rich as becoming richer and the poor poorer.   It was an age when aristocracy was merging into plutocracy.   Solon, the prophet of the Athenians, by his preaching of repentance, of economic and political reforms and by the legislation which put the preaching into practice, was able to restore many families to their ancient holdings and once more to raise up an independent class of workers and to safeguard them against slavery and exploitation.—Warde Fowler.

Solon was given unlimited power in Athens about 594 B.C.   The glory of Athens as a City State was mainly due to the rule and ideas of this great legislator.—Cf. Dr. Smith's *History of Greece*, pages 96 ff.

Pericles, when Athens was at its height, delivered an oration, according to Thucydides, proclaiming it a pure democracy, for 'the administration is in the hands of the many and not of the few.'   There was equal justice before the law for all, while the claims of excellence were recognized. Poverty was no bar and 'there is no exclusiveness in our public life.' A pretty enough picture, but in reality justice was not equal, and poverty plunged many into slavery.   Pericles was thinking of the Athenian citizens, a mere handful compared with the one hundred and twenty thousand slaves without human rights.   Xenophon gives a truer and more realistic picture and later Aristotle is content with the fact that slaves are mere property and what he describes as 'living implements.'   There was a movement of the dispossessed for the redistribution of the land and Aristophanes in his plays ridicules the claims of the very poor.   So frightened did the rulers become that in 401 B.C., the oath of the Heliasts contained a clause forbidding any one to put the issue of redistribution to the vote.—*Cambridge Ancient History*, vols. iv and v.

Athenian democracy has been described as 'a dictatorship of the propertied interests over the slaves.' (William Paul.)   This same writer quotes from Cleon's warning to the Athenians: 'You must remember that your empire is a tyranny exercised over unwilling subjects, who keep plotting against you . . . punish them as they deserve and give your other allies a plain example that whoever revolts, the punishment is death.'

The following dates may be of value: Solon, *c.* 640–559 B.C.   Socrates, 469–399.   Cleon, died 422.   Plato, 429–347.

CHAPTER XII

JEREMIAH AND THE DOWNFALL OF THE SOUTH

JEREMIAH, whose home was at Anathoth on the hills near Jerusalem, was probably a descendant of Moses through the high priest Abiathar, the friend of David. Abiathar had been exiled from Jerusalem by Solomon to the little plot of ground inherited from his forefathers and there the family had remained ever since. He who had done so much under David in the founding of Jerusalem was expelled from the capital. Jeremiah inherited the patriotic tradition of his mighty ancestors, but shrank from the task which even as a child was laid upon him.

His very ancestry called him to the prophetic vocation. 'Before thou camest forth out of the womb I sanctified thee and ordained thee a prophet.' Dean Stanley writes of him: 'For this desperate and solitary career there is no longer the wild and romantic energy of an Elijah, nor the royal air and majesty of an Isaiah.'

Of all the prophets Jeremiah is the most retiring, the most plaintive, the most compassed with ordinary human weaknesses. The cry which he uttered as the dark truth first broke upon his young mind was characteristic of his whole career: 'Ah! Lord, I cannot speak, I am but a child.' It is this childlike tenderness which adds force to the severity of his denunciations, to the bitterness of his grief. He was not one of the stern characters which bear without repining the necessary evils of life. He who was to be as hard as brass and strong as iron, who had to look with unmoved countenance on the downward descent of his country, yet longed that 'his head were waters and his eyes a fountain of tears that he might weep day and night for the daughter of his people.'

He longed for the solitudes of the deserts, where there was no human being nor bird of the heavens to be seen. He would fain have avoided the life of crowded cities with their sins and inhumanities. He was alone in the crowd; he had no wife to comfort or support him. He 'sits alone, crouching under his burden.' He foresaw himself unpopular, charged with the hatred of his country which he loved, hated by his fellows whom he would fain have saved. With Ibsen's *Enemy of the People*, that misunderstood and execrated patriot, he might well have cried: 'The greatest man on earth is he who stands most alone.'

Born in the closing years of the wicked king Manasseh, and as he grew up lacerated by the iniquities which continued unabated during the childhood of Josiah under the regency, he was driven forward unwillingly by the spirit of God to utter his warnings in the thirteenth year of the reign of that monarch (627 B.C.), six years before the reformation, and, as we shall see, those denunciations were continued long after that far-reaching event.

Prophecy had been stifled during the long years of Manasseh and the prophets had been put to death. There had arisen about the time of Jeremiah, the prophet Zephaniah, whose message has already been described. A little later, Nahum, writing about the year 625 B.C., tells of the impending doom of Assyria. His theme is 'the cry of distress and revenge from all the nations oppressed and downtrodden by that detestable people.' The theme of Habakkuk is the same. The Assyrian is described by the eloquent prophet as the robber who opens his jaws like hell, and 'is as insatiable as death, who devoureth all people and swalloweth down all nations.' 'He treateth men as the fishes of the sea, as creeping things that have no ruler over them. He fishes up all of them with the angle, he catches them all in his net and gathers them in his drag; therefore does he rejoice and is glad.' His destruction is inevitable.

That destruction was very close at hand, but the time was not yet. In the ninth year of the reign of King

Josiah the Jewish nation was shaken to its foundations by a Scythian invasion of Western Asia. Wild armies poured over the land towards Egypt, and although they spared the highlands of Judah and Jerusalem this onward sweep must so have terrified its inhabitants that they would now be less inclined to disregard the voice of the prophets. This chastened mood of the people would make easier the work of Josiah in his drastic reforms.

The reformation is shrouded in mystery, for it is difficult to determine whether the Book of the Law discovered in the restoration of the Temple was entirely the law of Moses, or whether it had been at least in part created by the reforming party of priests and prophets who for the moment were in agreement. There are good arguments on either side. It is certainly strange that prophets and kings of former ages would seem to have lived in complete ignorance of the fact that Moses had commanded the Hebrews to have only one centre of worship, and that all local sanctuaries with their various cults were an abomination to the Lord.

However this may be, the young king, having been stricken to the heart by the reading to him of the Book of Deuteronomy, was determined to centralize the worship of Israel and to root out all local worships. He purified the Temple of its abominable cults. No longer were heard the shrieks of children sacrificed to Moloch; no longer was there tolerated the worship of the sun-gods of Persia, the bulls of Egypt, the cruel and lustful gods and goddesses of Assyria and Phoenicia. A clean sweep was made of them all, not only in the capital, but in the provinces; and their priests were put to the sword.

The centralizing of the worship of the righteous God of the whole earth in Jerusalem, whether a new thing or the revival of ancient custom, was wise and necessary, for the multiplication of local cults had made it impossible to control and purify the worship of the Hebrews. The change that took place was, perhaps, carried through with drastic severity and unnecessary harshness. It was, for the moment at least, the more acceptable to the populace because Jerusalem had as yet been the only shrine which had never been wrecked by a foreign conqueror and, therefore, to them seemed inviolable. Had they not the high authority of Isaiah for believing that such a destruction was impossible?

It was a call to the patriotic feeling, not only of the capital, but of all Judah and of those sections of northern Israel which had not been carried away captive to Nineveh. The entire people were convened in Jerusalem and the king entered with them into a solemn league and covenant, 'both parties mutually . . . pledged themselves to acknowledge this book of the Covenant as the fundamental law of the kingdom and to observe its commandments.' Never was there so joyous a passover. It put even the glorious passover feast of Hezekiah into the shade.

'The conceptions and aims of Deuteronomy are thoroughly prophetic. It seeks to realize the hoped-for Kingdom of God as promised by the prophets. Israel is to become a holy people, governed by the will of God; and this holiness is to be manifested through worship and justice, so that man shall serve God righteously and judge his fellow-men uprightly.'[1]

So far as our study of the meaning of God's kingdom is concerned, we must concentrate our attention, not so much on the centralizing of the worship, but on the question of social justice. What did the discovery of the Law effect in this direction?

Ottley believes that Josiah attempted real social reform—such justice as is to be found in the Book of Deuteronomy, but that these reforms 'were neither deep nor permanent.' Maurice also thinks that the social reformation was only skin-deep. This would account for the attitude of Jeremiah. He admires the young king and affirms that he did judgment and justice. . . . 'The cause of the poor and needy he judged. Then was it well.'

But the prophet is not enthusiastic. He writes as if

[1] Cornill.

the reforms in social justice, whatever might be said of the thoroughness of the extirpations of idolatries, were not to be taken very seriously, and he is soon again obliged to denounce the social corruptions of the time. The Book of Deuteronomy is clear and outspoken about such sins as removing or narrowing a neighbour's landmark. Against lending at interest in money or in kind to one's fellow-countryman; for the fallow year and its common sharing; for the protection of runaway slaves. Its laws may be summed up in the command: Thou shalt love the Lord thy God with all thy heart and thy neighbour as thyself. 'It is a gospel of Jesus in anticipation. No mere outward code, but to be kept "in heart and marrow."' 'This commandment . . . is not in heaven, that thou shouldest say, who shall go up for us to heaven and bring it unto us that we may hear it and do it; but the word is very nigh thee in thy mouth and in thy heart, that thou mayest do it. . . . I have set before you life and death, blessing and cursing; therefore choose life, that thou and thy seed may live.' Cornill is here singularly obtuse. He writes: 'It [Deuteronomy] substituted for the living revelation of God in the human heart and in history, the dead letter.'

We have said that, in spite of this wonderful spirit of the law which had certainly rent the heart of Josiah and some of his subjects, the reforms were but skin-deep. This is, in fact, to put it much too mildly; Jeremiah's hopes were turned to ashes, for the reformation itself was to be poisoned by nationalistic self-righteousness, coupled with a callous disregard of the poor man's rights which was only equalled by the pharisaism of the times of Jesus and the pharisaism of that class Christianity in nineteenth-century England, unctuous and self-satisfied, while little children were being done to death in mines and factories.

Jeremiah's horror at this national apostasy which shuddered at the idols and enshrined a more subtle idolatry in the heart under the guise of a true religion is shown in such words as these: 'The word of the Lord came to Jeremiah from the Lord saying: Stand in the gate of the

Lord's house and proclaim there this word and say, Hear ye the word of the Lord all ye of Judah, that enter in at these gates to worship the Lord. Thus saith the Lord of Hosts, the God of Israel. Amend your ways and your doings, and I will cause you to dwell in this place. Trust ye not in lying words, saying, the temple of the Lord, the temple of the Lord, the temple of the Lord are these. For if ye thoroughly amend your ways and your doings; if ye thoroughly execute (social) judgment between a man and his neighbour, if ye oppress not the foreigner, the fatherless, and the widow, and shed not innocent blood in this place, neither walk after other gods to your hurt; then will I cause you to dwell in this place, in the land which I gave to your fathers, for ever and ever.'

Injustice and cruelty receive the greater denunciation, but apparently the Temple, although it had been cleansed root and branch of its more abominable idols, was again given over to a certain amount of worship of the nature baals. Again, also, 'the queen of heaven' is worshipped. But still his most serious accusation is levelled against the Temple which they have turned into 'a den of robbers.' Note that this is the identical accusation which Jesus brings some centuries later against the sanctimonious traders in his Father's house, in days when there was assuredly no outward idolatry but only the inward idolatry of Mammon.

The text of the Book of Jeremiah is in the utmost confusion, so that it is possible that what we have quoted above may belong to a different period from that which followed immediately after the Josiah reformation.

If the prophet shrank from the earlier task of denouncing his nation before the reformation, how much more hateful must it have been to him to be compelled to oppose the people after the reforms, when they had satisfied themselves that all was well with them and that they were basking in the favour of God.

Was he not a crank who could never approve anything that his people and their rulers were doing? Could he be right and all the nation wrong? Again the words of Henrik Ibsen come into one's mind, the saying about standing alone and opposing 'the damned compact majority.' God himself had formed Jeremiah in the womb to be His prophet, to set him over the nations and over the kingdoms, 'to root out, to pull down, and to destroy and to throw down, to build, and to plant.'

On the whole he heroically fulfilled his mission, but there were times when he broke out into bitterest denunciations of himself and of the burden God had put upon him. He might well have said with Hamlet: 'The times are out of joint; O cursed sprite that I was ever born to set them right.' He curses himself and the day of his birth and God replies: 'If thou becomest again Mine, thou mayest again be My servant, and if thou freest thy better self from the vile, then shalt thou still be as My mouth.' Accused of hating his country and his folk he yet 'battles with God for the salvation of his people.' In spite of their unworthiness he 'holds his fellow-countrymen lovingly in his heart and endeavours to arrest the arm of God already uplifted to deal on them the destructive blow.'

Although he execrates the idolatries of the heathen, he reminds Israel that in so far as they serve their gods in faithfulness they are dearer to God than His own chosen.

He looks forward like Isaiah to the time when the heathen nations shall be converted and take their place alongside Israel in the Kingdom of God. For every man is born a child of God, and here he anticipates with Isaiah the teaching of Jesus.

Calvinists and other rigorous predestinarians have argued otherwise. They assert that all are not God's children. They tell us that some are the children of the Devil—that God elects some to salvation and others to damnation. They quote Jeremiah as supporting this doctrine, by his parable of the Potter and his Clay.

If, however, the story be read as a whole, it gives no foundation for this doctrine. The prophet evidently is thinking of the clay as living matter which can comply with, or resist, the will of the potter. He concludes his story with an appeal to the nation, i.e. to the clay, to repent, an appeal entirely inconsistent with the idea that they, or any portion of them, have been inexorably destined to damnation.

Of the later years of Josiah we know nothing, but we may assume that after the fall of Assyria they were comparatively peaceful. Just on the verge of the crash the Egyptian Pharaoh thought he might secure for himself a portion of the dying empire's heritage. Josiah foolishly joined in this adventure, again could not resist meddling in foreign affairs, opposed Necho of Egypt and was defeated and killed at Megiddo. Jeremiah had consistently opposed this meddling in foreign affairs, as had Isaiah, 'in quietness and confidence shall be thy strength.' Jehoiakim, his son, now ruled as a vassal of Egypt. He did evil like Manasseh and persecuted the prophets. Jeremiah boldly announced that the inviolable Temple and city would be utterly destroyed if rulers and people did not repent. His death was demanded by a furious mob and he was only just saved from this fate.

The Babylonians were now inheritors of the lands and spoils of Assyria. Egypt tried its power against the new imperialism, but was defeated at Carchemish. At about this time Jeremiah was commanded by God to write the words of his prophecies and collect them into a book, which was read to the king. Jehoiakim in fury caused the book to be cut to pieces, for the prophet had perceived in the Babylonian advance the cup of the wrath of God which all nations including the chosen people were to drink to the dregs. Again Jeremiah barely escaped arrest and death. The king would not listen to the prophet's counsel to bow his neck to the new yoke, but rebelled against Babylon and died in that rebellion, and his son Jehoiakim was carried away captive to Babylon, with ten thousand of his people, the aristocracy and ruling classes and probably many of the artisan population. Only the poorest were left. Nebuchadnezzar 'set the third son of Josiah, Zedekiah, as vassal king over this decimated and enfeebled people' (597 B.C.). Zedekiah held Jeremiah in honour and befriended him, but, in spite of this friendship, would not listen to his warnings and, with his people, rebelled against Babylon.

The Egyptians poured into the holy city to help their Hebrew allies, and for the moment Jerusalem was saved. The rejoicing knew no bounds. It looked as if the prophet's gloomy warnings were to be falsified, and his unpopularity was increased by the stand he now took against the wealthy classes who were guilty of a disgraceful act of breach of faith. The Hebrew slave had a right to freedom after six years' bondage. This law had been more honoured in the breach than in the observance; but the necessities of the defence had suggested to the owners that they might advantageously set their slaves at liberty in order that they should more valiantly fight for the defence of Jerusalem. Now that all danger had passed, they compelled them to return to servitude and broke faith with them. Jeremiah thundered against this betrayal, and the ruling classes saw to it that he was arrested as he was about to set out for Anathoth, pretending that he was in league with the Babylonian enemy and a traitor to his country. He was flogged and imprisoned.

His prophecy as to the fate of Jerusalem was, however soon to be fulfilled. Despite a courageous and heroic defence it was finally captured in the summer of 586 B.C. Zedekiah was blinded and carried away captive to Babylon, and all his children had previously been murdered in his sight. Both Jerusalem and the holy temple were plundered and utterly destroyed with fire, and all but a few poor folk, vine-dressers and agriculturists, were taken away to Babylon. Godaliah who had delivered the Book of Deuteronomy to Josiah, and was the friend and protector of Jeremiah, was appointed governor of the city under Nebuchadnezzar.

The governor was, however, in his turn slain by a group of fanatical patriots and the perpetrators of the deed fled to Egypt forcing the aged prophet to go with them. In that foreign land where he still bravely maintained the faith of God against his people, he, according to tradition, was stoned to death by an infuriated mob.

Thus 'undismayed and dauntless, he fell in his harness, a soldier of the truth. He had become as an iron wall and as pillars of brass against the whole land. He had loved his people with a love that the many waters could not quench, they had struggled against him, but not overcome him. He fell as a hero, as a conqueror.'[1]

The South, like the North, had gone into captivity. They were silent and subdued. 'By the waters of Babylon we sat down and wept, when we remembered thee, O Sion, as for our harps we hanged them up, upon the trees that are therein. How shall we sing the Lord's song in a strange land.'

[1] Cornill.

CHAPTER XIII

THE BABYLONIAN EXILE AND ITS PROPHETS

The Babylonian exile may be reckoned as lasting for seventy years if we date it from the first deportation (606), or as fifty years if dated from the fall of Jerusalem and the second deportation. The prophets of this period were Ezekiel and the second Isaiah. Ezekiel was very young when he was carried away to Babylon in the year 597. He began to prophesy by the banks of one of the many canals which connected the Tigris with the Euphrates. His first visions concerned the destruction of Jerusalem. Their announcement was received with derision, but the prophet was vindicated some years later when the disastrous news at last filtered through.

The Jews were filled with despair, but the prophet met their mood not with bitter denunciation or scornful contempt for their earlier attitude towards himself, but with a message of hope and encouragement. God, for their sins, had indeed trampled them under foot; they had become 'a prey and a derision to the heathen,' but if they turned from bloodshed and cruelty, the land that was desolate should become like the garden of Eden.

Ezekiel now became certain of the return of the exiles to their own land and the rebuilding of the glorious temple, an earnest and sacrament of a yet more glorious kingdom of God. They should be governed by a prince of the house of David—himself a forerunner of that tender shepherd king whom the prophet but dimly foresaw, the Messiah who should reign in love and righteousness over the whole earth.

It might seem impossible that this dead and defeated people, lost and forgotten among strangers, should spring to life again, and the prophet could hardly have arrived at this conviction had it not been for the vision in the valley of the dry bones.

The valley that he saw was full of bones and they were very dry. And God said unto him: 'Son of man, can these bones live, and I answered, O Lord God, Thou knowest.' He is told to call upon these bones that they may hear the word of the Lord that breath may enter them, that sinews and flesh and skin may come upon them. And the bones reshaped themselves and took on form and sinews and skin and flesh, but as yet there was no sign of breath in them. And God said unto him: 'Prophesy unto the wind, prophesy, Son of man, and say to the wind, Thus saith the Lord God, come from the four winds, O breath, and breathe upon these slain that they may live . . . and they lived, and stood up upon their feet an exceeding great army.' These bones were the whole house of Israel, who had become dried up and their hope lost. But to these men, long lost and dead, God speaks through his prophet, saying: 'Behold, I will open your graves . . . and shall put My spirit in you and ye shall live and I shall place you in your own land.'

I have spoken of Ezekiel's conviction of the resurrection to life again of the group of exiles and of their return to Palestine. But he must sometimes have faltered when faced with a certain mood of despondency and fatalism in the exiles. This unhealthy spirit was shown in such sayings as: 'The fathers have eaten sour grapes, and the children's teeth are set on edge.' These degenerates would quote the second commandment about God visiting the sins of the fathers upon the children unto the third and fourth generation, in excuse for lethargy and fatalism.

Ezekiel was foremost among the prophets to expose the falsity of this interpretation. In spite of the hereditary tendency that seems to drag a family down into gulfs of evil, or to urge it upwards, each soul has its own responsibility. The modern English poet Henley re-echoes Ezekiel when he sings:

It matters not how straight the gate,
How charged with punishments the scroll;
I am the Master of my Fate,
I am the Captain of my Soul.

God speaks to his prophet: 'Behold, all souls are Mine;
as the soul of the father, so also the soul of the son is Mine:
the soul that sinneth, it shall die, but if a man be just,
and do that which is lawful and right . . . and hath not
oppressed any, but hath restored to the debtor his pledge,
hath spoiled none by violence, hath given his bread to the
hungry and hath covered the naked with a garment; he
that hath not given forth upon usury, neither hath taken
any increase, that hath withdrawn his hand from iniquity,
hath executed true judgment between man and man . . .
he is just, he shall surely live.'

He urges that no man shall be punished for the iniquities
of his father, and sums up his argument which has become
so familiar to the worshippers in the Church of England:
'When the wicked man turneth away from his wickedness
that he hath committed, and doeth that which is lawful
and right, he shall save his soul alive.'

Ezekiel died in exile, probably before the return to
Jerusalem; tradition shows his tomb in the neighbourhood
of Bagdad.

Modern scholars hold that the last twenty-six chapters
of the Book of Isaiah are by another hand, and date them
about one hundred and fifty years from the time of the
first writer who bears that name. Some critics even hold
that there were seven Isaiahs—a rather absurd assumption.

Frederick Denison Maurice, a profound student of the
prophets, and especially of the Book of Isaiah, writing at a
time when critics were beginning to put forward the new
theories, stoutly maintains the traditional position, and his
arguments, although they may not convince the twentieth
century, are nevertheless worth considering. We have
here no opportunity to deal with them, but they may be
found in the seventeenth and eighteenth sermons in his
Prophets and Kings. It must, however, be admitted that

the references to Cyrus in Isaiah, chapters xliv and xlv, seem to put Maurice's arguments out of court.

As our object here is mainly to recapture the teaching about the Kingdom of Heaven which our Lord would have received in boyhood, it does not much matter whether there were one or many Isaiahs. In any case, both in the earlier and later portions of the Isaiah writings there are warnings against idolatry and oppression and the inevitable destruction and exile which must follow them: there are also messages of hope and assurance to a people repentant, that they shall most certainly be replanted in their own land.

The 'second' Isaiah opens with the famous passage describing the exaltation of the valleys and the bringing low of the mountains, crooked paths made straight and rough places smooth; a passage which is used in the New Testament to describe the mission of John the Baptist as herald of the Lord Jesus Christ. The writer has here in mind the necessary preparation for the bringing in upon the earth of the Kingdom of Heaven. The Messiah is set forth as the righteous judge of all the nations, who shall bring forth the prisoners from the prison and open the eyes of the blind.

The most startling passage in this work is his reference to Cyrus, emperor of Persia; the prophet not only sees in him the conqueror of Babylon, a forecast which any wise statesman might have made, but the anointed of God, the Lord's chosen. He speaks of him almost in terms of the Messiah, an extraordinary conception for a Jew, considering the prejudice in which all foreigners were held. Here he speaks in the liberal spirit of the first Isaiah who had boldly prophesied that Egypt and Assyria should one day be the equals of Palestine in the all-embracing Kingdom of God. He is inspired to see in Cyrus the Lord's shepherd to perform all his pleasure and to restore the exiles to their own land. 'He shall build my city, and he shall let go my captives, not for price nor reward.'

CHAPTER XIV

THE RETURN OF THE EXILES AND THE NEHEMIAH REFORMS

I HAVE spoken of the misery of the exiles on their arrival in the Babylonian Empire; many sank into despondency and inertia; many are lost to view in the mazes of the great cities built on the banks of numberless canals. There were futile risings against their conquerors which seem to have been cruelly suppressed, but on the whole the captives were well treated and enjoyed many liberties; they were, in some cases, allowed their own colonies ruled by Jewish officers; they practised their ancient customs and their religious worship. Divorced from Palestine and its centre the Temple, Babylon may have been the first home of the Jewish synagogue used as a school and a church.

There were, however, a great many of the exiles who settled down comfortably in the empire, and who by trade and money-lending became rich and powerful. Some of these fell away from their religion altogether, others adopted religious opinions by no means consistent with the Mosaic Dispensation. This may account for the fact that of the multitudes carried into captivity comparatively few availed themselves for the permission of Cyrus to return to their own land.

Although the Persian emperor himself encouraged the rebuilding of the Temple, the repatriated Jews first began to build up their own ruined homes; a little later the Altar of Sacrifice was raised; and a great harvest festival was held. About two years passed before the foundation-stone of the Temple was laid; but the building was almost immediately abandoned by reason of the quarrel with the Samaritans. Samaria had been colonized by Assyrians who had intermarried with the native population. The Samaritans would generously have helped with the rebuilding of the Temple at Jerusalem, but their offer was indignantly refused by the people of Judah; hence there arose so strong an opposition to the whole project that it was relinquished.

For sixteen years the people were sunk in listlessness, their work upon a soil, never fertile in the best of seasons, was feeble and unproductive. Their meagre returns may have been subjected to foreign taxation. Sometimes they were ravaged by famines and harassed by surrounding enemies. But at last they were aroused from their lethargy by the trumpet call of the prophet Haggai (c. 520 B.C.). 'Thus speaketh the Lord of Hosts, saying, This people say, The time is not come, the time that the Lord's house should be built . . . is it time for you, O ye, to dwell in your cieled houses, and this house lie waste?'

Under the influence of Haggai and the more youthful Zechariah this work was now renewed, and the new Temple was actually dedicated in 516 B.C. in the time of Zerubbabel, who, by appointment of the Persian emperor, was viceroy of Judea.

High hopes had been raised by this son of the house of David. He had even been hailed by the prophet Haggai as the coming Messiah, and a golden crown had been given him by the Jews who remained in Babylon. But although he laid the foundation of the new Temple in December 520 B.C. and seems to have, after the hindrances we have mentioned, completed it with the permission of the emperor Darius and the State aid of the empire in 515 B.C., yet he appears to have been a feeble and second-rate sort of person, and to have effected no drastic reformation.

We learn something of economic and social conditions in Judea in this hundred years' period from the pages of Zechariah. The people do not seem to have been reinstated in their ancient holdings, for the prophet has still to look forward to a day when this shall happen. Some evidence may also be gleaned from Malachi,[1] who still is

---

[1] I am aware that some authors place the Book of Malachi some fourteen or more years after the 444 B.C. land reforms. If their theory be right

obliged to denounce the mixed marriages, and urges the people to remember the ancient statutes and judgments, lest the terrible day of the Lord come upon them. Every man deals treacherously against his brother, profaning the covenant of his fathers. How can the ancient and pleasant years return, when the land is full of 'adulterers, false-swearers, oppressors of wage-workers, and of widows, orphans, and foreigners?'

Even when the Temple is once more in being as the centre of the nation's life, its priests are arrogant and avaricious. The nobles were lacking in patriotism or in any public spirit. They were too busy fleecing the workers to care whether the walls of their city are rebuilt or not. They have no care for the public defences.

It is noteworthy that when at last the building of the defences began, the empire was urged to put a stop to it, because if the annals of the Jews were examined it would be found that they had been always a sturdy independent people, rebellious and a constant danger to the surrounding empires.

Cornill gives a vivid picture of the sickly state of things during this period, which applies especially to the first half-century after the return.

'What change had taken place? None. The Persians had taken the place of Babylonians, but the gentile power remained as formidable as ever. Returned to the old land of their fathers, they had to struggle hard for existence; the conditions of life were extremely meagre; only a very small part of Jerusalem had been rebuilt, a wretched unfortified country town with an indigent population.'

When at last Nehemiah arrives on the scene he finds the country in a disastrous state. Ezra had brought back with him the law which dealt with land and usury and slavery, but had apparently been refused a hearing. This

---

the reforms must have been but skin-deep, which is not evidenced in the scriptural record. Besides this, Malachi, which means in Hebrew the messenger, may not have been a proper name at all. The Targum identifies him with Ezra, a position supported later by the Vulgate.

is not surprising, if we read the description given by the new governor, of the existing state of things. The walls of the city were broken down and the gates derelict. Many of the people who were still in possession of their ancient plots (or had been given back their lands after the return) had been obliged to mortgage their fields, their vineyards, and their very cottages. Many, apparently with no land, had no means of buying corn or the various necessities. Many who were feeling the pinch of heavy taxation had borrowed money upon the security of their holdings wherewith to meet these oppressive demands. After all, they pleaded, we are of the same blood as the class that oppress us. Our children are of the selfsame blood. Yet we are obliged to let our sons and our daughters become bondsmen to these people. 'Neither is it in our power to help it, for other people have our fields and our vineyards.'

Nehemiah is furious when he hears of their misery and of the way they are being treated. He goes to the members of the leading families and contends with them, saying: 'You exact interest, every one of his brother.' His pleading with the ruling families does not seem to have had much effect, so he calls a great meeting against them. In the presence of the masses he arraigns the ruling class, and says: 'We after our ability have redeemed our brethren, the Jews, which were sold unto the heathen; and would ye even sell your brethren and should they be sold unto us?' The lords and ladies were very uncomfortable, and could find nothing to say. So he says to them: 'The thing that ye do is not good; ought ye not to walk in the fear of our God, because of the reproach of the heathen? I pray you let us leave off this usury. Restore, I pray you, to them, even this day, their fields, their vineyards, their oliveyards, and their houses, and also a hundredth part of the money and of the corn, of the wine and of the oil that ye exact of them.'

Whether through fear of the masses, or through fear of the law with a governor backing it and determined to enforce it, the ruling classes were brought to their senses and said: 'We will restore them, and will require nothing of them.'

Nehemiah was wise. He knew that these iniquities might very well be again established. He therefore did what Ezra had wanted to do and had been prevented from doing. While the people were in the right mood, he held another mass meeting, and Ezra, his friend, was at last given his chance. Surrounded by many of the leaders he stood up in this huge assembly and read them the laws, and among them, therefore, the law of the Jubilee. A solemn oath and covenant was made by the nation that they would abide by these statutes, and an historical sketch of the nation was made in which they were reminded how the land was originally given them according to their portions, and how all went well with them, and how they had abundance, till they rebelled against the statutes of God, and slew the prophets which testified against them.

Many other things besides he told them and caused them to do, regarding ceremonies and the like. He bade them put away their heathen wives, and made them draw aloof from the ideals and customs of neighbouring nations.

Cornill and many other critics speak of the harshness and narrowness of these reforms and of the law as henceforward observed, but even he was compelled to write as follows: 'One hundred and twenty-five years after Ezra, Alexander the Great destroyed the Persian Empire and made the Greeks the sovereign people of the Eastern world. Through this a profound transformation was begun, which spread with startling rapidity and irresistible might, and led finally to the denationalizing of the East. . . . Greece destroyed the nationalities of the East by amalgamating them with itself and conquering them inwardly. Only one Eastern nation withstood the process of dissolution, yea, more, absorbed into itself the good of Hellenism and thus enriched and strengthened its own existence; and that was the Jewish. If it were able to do this, it was because

G

Ezra and Nehemiah had rendered it hard as steel and strong as iron.' [1]

The dominion of the Persian Empire over Palestine persisted for more than a hundred years after the Nehemiah reforms. Persian rule was humane compared with that of the Assyrians and the Babylonians. The Assyrian Empire had exercised over its dependencies a tyranny more ruthless than even that of Babylon. The Persian religion and philosophies were much more reasonable and humane than that of the preceding empires with their gods of lust and blood, and their consequent avarice and brutalities.

The policy of wholesale deportations was rare and there was very little interference with native religions. The Persians seemed to have encouraged the worship of Jehovah and the Mosaic economy, for so long as the Jews were allowed to retain their lands unhampered by usurious credits and to practise the ancient worship, they were unlikely to interest themselves in world politics and intrigue. Ezra and Nehemiah were, as we have seen, supported by the empire and, in consequence, discouraged revolts. The leader, chosen by the Persians to organize the return of the exiles to their native land, had been a son of the house of David, as was also Zerubbabel. The latter who, as has been said, was offered a golden crown by the Jews may have entertained dreams of an independent Palestine. For this reason the Persians were compelled to adopt a less liberal policy; the Davidic line was henceforth discouraged, and the priestly caste now became paramount as ministers of a Persian satrap. In spite of all this the empire still saw the value of an independent Palestine as a buffer state between themselves and Egypt that was soon again to become troublesome.

How far the enlightened religion of Persia influenced the development of Jewish philosophy is still a vexed question, but there can be no doubt that there was some infiltration, conscious or unconscious, of Persian ideas. There was much in common between the monotheism of Zoroaster

[1] Cornill, *The Prophets*.

and of the Jews and many other similarities between these two religions. This fact and the mild rule of the empire would tend to make the Jewish people more amenable to Persian ideas, and it is noteworthy that the conception of a future life becomes developed about this period as does the idea of Satan; the demonology and angelology of the later Jewish religion seem also to date from these times.

We so often hear of the Medes and Persians. They were of the same stock, but the former had conquered the Persians, and it was not until the middle of the sixth century that Cyrus, who encouraged the Jewish return, threw off their yoke.

Even under the comparatively mild rule of the Persians there was considerable misery owing to famines resulting from bad seasons, plagues of locusts and other causes, as is witnessed by the Books of Ecclesiastes and Joel.

About this time the high priesthood became hereditary, and there was every kind of intrigue within the Sacerdotal family to secure the office; also the Scribes first come into prominence, they were voluntary interpreters of the Law or Torah. They received no pay for their work, which included teaching and the pronouncement of legal judgments. There were among them many men of noble character, but they tended as a class to become arid and without understanding. Towards the end of this period the Sanhedrim, the famous council of Jewish Elders, became powerful; it was an aristocratic body formed on a Hellenic model.

The Persians were defeated at the battle of Issus by Alexander in 333 B.C. Ten years afterwards Alexander died, and his empire was divided among his generals, and for a short time Judea was included within the dominions of the satrap of Syria, but in 320 B.C., Ptolemy Lagi invaded and annexed Syria and obtained possession of Jerusalem by a mean stratagem, and for nearly a century the Jews remained subject to Egypt. Ptolemy II was a particularly enlightened emperor, and it is remarkable that, so great was his interest in the literature and arts of the Jews, that he encouraged the making of the Septuagint version of the Old Testament which loomed so large in the history of the New Testament.

This century, under the mild suzerainty of Egypt, was, perhaps, the happiest period enjoyed by the Jews since the loss of their independence.

CHAPTER XV

'PALESTINA IRRIDENTA'

DANIEL AND THE MACCABEES

IN the year 203 B.C. Egypt finally lost control of Palestine when Antiochus invaded Judea and captured Jerusalem and Palestine was incorporated in the kingdom of the Seleucidae.

The Jews, who at first welcomed this change of rulers, subsequently found themselves in a worse condition.

Soon after consolidating his kingdom Antiochus was engaged in a struggle with Rome which ended in his overwhelming defeat at Magnesia in Asia Minor (190 B.C.). The gulf now deepens between the two factions in Palestine, the pro-Syrian Hellenizing Jews and the Patriotic Party, a schism which later on was to result in Rome's conquest of Palestine.

The accession of Antiochus Epiphanes in 175 B.C., brought matters to a head. He deprived the patriotic high priest Onias of his office in favour of the Hellenizing Jason, who went so far as to establish a Greek gymnasium in Jerusalem and sent sums of money to Tyre for the cultus of Hercules. The strife between the Palestinian parties became so acute that Antiochus was obliged to interfere.

There had been a stubborn resistance in Jerusalem to this effort to obliterate their religion and customs, but it was not until the Syrians attempted to compel the Jews at Modin to sacrifice to the heathen gods, that Mattathias, a priest of this small town west of the capital, struck down the presiding officer and escaped to the hills with his five sons and a resolute band of followers. 'Whosoever is zealous of the law and maintaineth the covenant, let him follow me.'

165

Later, one of his sons, Judas 'the Hammerer,'[1] reached Jerusalem and succeeded in cleansing the Temple from heathen pollution; he then made preparation for the Feast of Dedication. A small band of resolute men thus won both religious and political freedom in the face of a mighty empire. This was made possible in part because of their supreme courage, and in part because the Syrians were beset by powerful enemies and weakened by internal divisions. Judas, having occupied the capital, ultimately gained complete independence for his nation and sought to confirm it by an alliance with Rome which was still a republic and was considered to be a champion of liberty.

Judas Maccabaeus was an unrivalled leader in the arts of guerrilla warfare. After many decisive victories he fell at the battle of Elasa against enormous odds in 161 B.C. For further information about his campaigns we may turn to the Book of the prophet Zechariah, and notably to such passages as are contained in chapters ix, 13–17, and ix, 9–12; the former which speaks of 'the sons of Greece' may well refer to the Hellenistic empire of the Syrians; the latter's 'Behold thy King cometh unto thee; he is just, and having salvation; lowly, and riding upon an ass, and upon a colt the foal of an ass' may have been written in the year of peace which followed the decisive victory of Judas in the summer of 164 B.C.; the prophet here looks forward to the Messianic era of justice and peace.

This picture of a peaceful Messiah is also given in the much earlier writings of the prophet Micah, and later again in the writings of Enoch. The Feast of Dedication, established by Judas in the month of December as a Messianic festival, becomes important in New Testament literature, for our Lord attended this winter feast, and was there found in controversy with the Pharisees on this very question of his Messianic claim.

On the death of Judas, the Jewish cause was in the

---

[1] All this line of rulers belonged to the Hasmonean family, although they are popularly called the Maccabees. Strictly speaking only Judas should be so called, as Maccabee really means 'the Hammerer.'

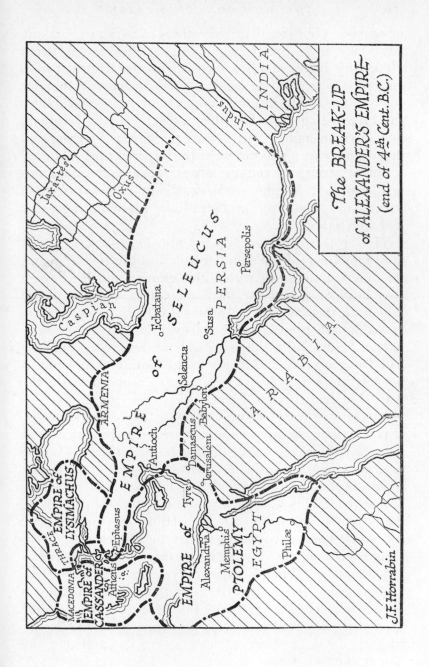

The BREAK-UP
of ALEXANDER'S EMPIRE
(end of 4th Cent. B.C.)

INDIA

Jaxartes

Oxus

Indus

EMPIRE of SELEUCUS

PERSIA

Persepolis

Caspian

Ecbatana

Susa

ARMENIA

Seleucia

ARABIA

Antioch

MACEDONIA
THRACE
EMPIRE of
LYSIMACHUS
EMPIRE of
CASSANDER
Athens
Ephesus

Damascus
Tyre
Babylon
Jerusalem

EMPIRE of
PTOLEMY

Alexandria
Memphis

EGYPT

Philae

J.F. Horrabin

utmost peril, but Jonathan his brother (160–142 B.C.), taking advantage of a Syrian withdrawal, rallies the scattered Nationalist forces, and becomes so powerful that the Syrian empire is compelled to make a treaty in terms favourable to the Jews. During the five years of peace that follow, the Hellenizing Jews lose their power. Later Jonathan, now become high priest, defeats the Syrian governor and determines entirely to throw off the imperial rule. He was a subtle strategist and came near to accomplishing his ambition; but Tryphon, who was now emperor, feigned friendship with him, entrapped him by subterfuge, and had him murdered.

His brother Simon succeeded him (142–135 B.C.) and once more revived the failing fortunes of the Jews. Again the internal divisions within the empire and its foreign complications favour the fortunes of the Nationalists and Simon is thereby able to achieve a brief independence, and although he was treacherously murdered by his son-in-law, he died with this independence secured. His rule had brought peace and plenty to the land, and his acquisition of the port of Joppa gave his nation an outlet to the sea. He died a national hero.

In the first year of the leadership of John Hyrcanus, (135-105 B.C.) the Syrian emperor besieged Jerusalem, and his onslaught was so successful that John was forced to come to terms with him, but on the death of this overlord Hyrcanus recaptured independence with the support of Rome. He now extended his boundaries almost to the ancient limits; the peasants were restored to their lands, and the economic and social laws of Moses were strictly observed.

The sect of the Pharisees at this juncture becomes prominent, and John is on friendly terms with them, but later he seems to have quarrelled with them and become a Sadducee. The significance of this great ruler will become apparent when we discuss his influence upon the group, who in New Testament times, were looking for the redemption of Israel.

On the death of John Hyrcanus, Aristobulus I succeeded

him and extended the boundaries of Palestine still further, but it was only under Alexander Jannaeus, his successor, that they reached the full limits of the ancient kingdom of David and Solomon. These military triumphs, however, offended the Pharisees and led to dissensions, and in the end to civil war. A scandalous situation now arose in which the Nationalist party was actually led by a Syrian general. Alexander was defeated, but the Nationalists, fearing the overlordship of a foreign prince, reverted to his leadership.

On the death of Alexander in 76 B.C. the Pharisees were in the ascendancy, and they enforced the laws of Moses according to their own rigid and lifeless interpretation of them. The strife between the Pharisees and Sadducees became so embittered and so weakened the Jewish State that it ultimately led to its downfall.

The two sons of Alexandra, widow of Alexander Jannaeus and successor to the throne, were in deadly antagonism, and, in consequence of a battle which took place between them, the elder, Hyrcanus, was defeated and retired into private life. At this point the sinister figure of Antipater, the Idumean, appears on the scene and persuades Hyrcanus to resume the struggle. The Roman general, Pompey, seizes this opportunity to interfere in Jewish affairs, sides with Hyrcanus, and besieges Jerusalem which, after a desperate struggle, falls into his hands. Twelve thousand Jews are slaughtered, and Judea was added to the Roman province of Syria, while the rest of Palestine was made tributary to the Roman Empire.

The Book of the prophet Daniel is the only strictly apocalyptic work which is included in the Old Testament canon, and was one of the last to receive canonical recognition. It was not written by the Daniel of the Ezekiel period, but by a writer who took his name in the period just before the Maccabean revolution, and may have been written in encouragement of this movement.

The theme of this work was the tyrannous sway of four great empires: the Babylonian, the Median, the Persian, and the Grecian which were all to be destroyed by the Almighty

* G

God who would then establish the fifth empire, the Kingdom of Heaven, upon earth. The author knows nothing of that fifth and more terrible dominion, the Roman Empire, which arises after his time, and so the fourth beast of Daniel becomes in the literature of our Lord's time the Roman tyranny, and it is so interpreted by the immediate followers of Jesus. How had this transference of thought come about? How had people come to think of Rome as a 'beast, dreadful and terrible, and strong exceeding,' with 'great iron teeth,' devouring and breaking in pieces and stamping down the residue (of the peoples) with the feet of it: Rome, the one-time ally of free states, whose proud boast had been that she had liberated peoples?

But for all her boasting, those days of liberation, if ever they had been, were long past. Warde Fowler in his *City States* tells the story how 'Rome, herself a city state, ceased at last to be one . . . in the vast reach of her endeavour to deprive all others of their autonomous life, she too lost the genius of the polis.' Expansion abroad and exploitation at home generally go hand in hand, for imperialism and Mammon are bedfellows, so we are not surprised to read of the Rome of about a century before Christ: 'The period (from about 202 to 146 B.C.) tells of a hard, ungracious expansion abroad, and of a slow destruction, by the usury and greed of the rich, of the free agricultural population of home.' [1]

Klausner has made a close study of social and economic conditions in Palestine just before and during the lifetime of Jesus. Although the land in Galilee still for the most part belonged to the peasants, not much of it remained to them in Judea. In the South there were certain large estates called *Latifundia*, worked by slaves and by free labour cheapened by slave competition. These *Latifundia* were modelled on the large estates so common in Italy where the people had long since lost their lands, and were later to prove one of the causes of the downfall of the Roman Empire. In Palestine they were owned by companies of

[1] Wells, *Outline of History*, Chap. XXVII.

wealthy Jews and Romans. We find rich Jewish bankers, who did business not with the dinar only, but with the talent (worth about seven hundred or more pounds). These bankers were not only occupied with the lucrative business of exchange, but 'acted as moneylenders to the small holder, the shopkeeper, the corn merchant, and the caravan master.'

The ruling class in Jerusalem, then, 'were not only important, but wealthy people.' Klausner mentions many of these by name and quotes the Talmud for evidence of their vast wealth which reached fabulous proportions. Even by the end of the Maccabean and the beginning of the Herodian period the number of noted wealthy men whom Herod accused of rebellion, and whose possessions he confiscated, reached many scores. The women of Jerusalem, as in the times of the prophets who had denounced them, were especially luxurious. 'The source of such wealth was most probably commerce, but it was just as probably acquired through the gradual accumulation by the wealthier peasant class of the small holdings of the poorer peasants in payments of debts.'

So we have the usual round of a luxurious court, expensive wars in consequence, heavy taxation, falling for the most part on the poorer classes. The workers are therefore obliged to apply to the richer peasants, their own brethren, who flout the ancient laws of Moses and lend to them at crushing rates of interest and evict them from their holdings when they are unable to pay. The Jubilee year of restoration is utterly disregarded, and hence, in the time of the appearance of Jesus Christ, we have the excesses of riches and poverty, the great gulf fixed between the rich and the poor.

CHAPTER XVI

THE APOCALYPTIC LITERATURE

WE have traced the decline and fall of the Maccabean world into an apostasy so grave and subtle—all the more subtle because it took place under the guise of the correct and meticulous worship of the true God—that the Jewish nation had now fallen into a condition so corrupt that there could be no hope of salvation except it were by fire.

We have already given evidence of the dark social conditions of this period, and we shall quote further proof of this decadence from the apocalyptic literature, which looks forward to an inevitable doom, and to the coming down from Heaven of a wholly new order.

The Old Testament, as we have it now, was closed about two hundred years before Christ came. The Jews had only come to believe in a future life a little before that time. The Sadducees were conservative in religious matters and still did not believe. The belief in the future had come about in connection with the belief in the kingdom. The earlier Old Testament writers, just as much as the later, believed in the kingdom to come, but they looked on it as a glorious future for the nation, and for all Jews, or, at least, all righteous Jews, who should be alive when it came. But, as it delayed and delayed, and as misfortunes were heaped upon Palestine, Jews were driven to the belief that just men and women who had given their lives for their country, and for righteousness' sake, could not go down finally into the dust, but that God was just, and when the revolution came, 'would raise them up to live on the earth, and to be partakers of the glorious Golden Age.' [1]

The Sadducean plutocrats, who were quite at home in the present age, had no use for a revolution, and therefore

[1] Archdeacon Charles. *Between the Testaments.*

had no use for a resurrection.   The doctrine of the resurrection was therefore 'political.'   That may explain why the people rioted when the hope of a resurrection was called in question.   Crowds do not often riot over a point of abstract theology.   Even in the East they riot about politics, or about a practical religion which is mixed up with politics.

Within the Old Testament canon, and among the latest additions to it, are to be found apocalyptic books—notably the Book of Daniel, but most of the apocalyptic literature lies between the close of the Old Testament and the fall of Jerusalem in A.D. 70, or just a little beyond that date. This literature deals with what is called eschatology, which means a study of the last things, or, the things beyond. It deals, that is, with the Millennium, or Golden Age, and some, as has been said, deals with the dimly conceived Everlasting Age, beyond the Golden Age, in which all who have suffered for justice will enjoy the God of Justice and His world, in which community and justice will be established for ever.   These books are called 'Apocalyptic,' because 'apocalypse' is a word meaning unveiling, manifesting, revealing, and this literature 'reveals' the Coming World.

Most modern writers are so far agreed, but some speak of this world beyond the Golden Age as being immaterial, formless, bodyless.   This conception is unproved.   It does not seem to ring true to Jewish modes of thought. The Jewish authors who write of this 'future beyond the future,' are naturally vague and a little incoherent, for they are attempting to describe the indescribable; but, as many Christians believe in a golden age here on earth, and an eternal world of justice beyond this golden age, which men shall enjoy in the fullness of their manhood, i.e. in something corresponding to the body that now is, in a transformed body, and with outward expression, it does not seem improbable that these old writers thought the same, especially when we remember that the doctrine of a *bodily* resurrection was, it is generally admitted, taken over from

Judaism and is peculiarly Jewish. Unless, therefore, new evidence is brought forward in disproof of this, we may take it that at the time of our Lord, and especially in Galilee, which was probably the home of most of the apocalyptic writing, and especially among the 'common people,' this 'future beyond the future,' so far as it was held at all, was not thought of as entirely 'spiritual.'[1]

Unfortunately, here in England, the study of these eschatological writers has been popularized by Archdeacon Charles, who has devoted a lifetime to the subject and has published the only cheap book available upon it, *Between the Old and New Testaments*.

We owe him a great debt of gratitude for his translations of apocalyptic writers not only for their own worth, but because a reference to them will largely upset Archdeacon Charles's own conclusions as set down in the little book. The author is obsessed with the 'blessed hope of immortality,' and writes of the eschatology between the Old and New Testaments, as if the discovery of individual existence beyond death was its main contribution to thought. True, he opposes Harnach's grotesque statement that the apocalyptic hope was 'an evil inheritance which the Christians took over from the Jews,' and shows, as against Schweitzer and Tyrrell, that the apocalyptic writings are sometimes as much inspired by the fire of justice and comradeship as are the writings of the prophets themselves. But his horror of the 'material' life leads him to under-value the work of the prophets, who, he laments, looked for a materialization of the Kingdom of God, and to find in the apocalyptic writers an abandonment of this hope of material expression in favour of 'pure spirit'[2] an abandonment that exists rather

---

[1] Cf. Tyrrell's *Christianity at the Cross Roads*, pages 73 ff., 8, 207, splendid passages on spirit and matter. (Longmans 1909.)

[2] e.g. an amazing passage, pages 20–21, where he charges the prophets with caring more about things than persons. This statement would make Frederick Denison Maurice turn in his grave, and shows a complete misunderstanding of the prophetic literature of the Old Testament. Maurice's *Prophets and Kings* should be studied in correction. It is one of the best books ever written on the Old Testament. Cf. the first chapter of Rauschenbusch's *Christianity and the Social Crisis* and the works of Adam Smith.

in the desires of Archdeacon Charles than in the writings themselves.

Charles writes of the period from about 100 B.C. onwards: 'At this period the earth had come to be regarded as wholly unfit for this (coming) Kingdom, and thus new conceptions of the Kingdom arose, and it was taught by many that the Messianic Kingdom was to be merely of temporary duration and that the goal of the risen righteous was to be—not this temporary Kingdom or Millennium—but Heaven itself.' There are many passages in the little book in similar strain, and, considering current ideas of 'Heaven,' they are misleading. The reader may easily overlook two small passages which do go far to correct the modern pietistic conception of 'Heaven,' and do give a more accurate description of it as it existed in the hopes of these ancient writers. He says that in the New Testament, the 'Kingdom of God' is sometimes 'used eschatologically,' and that in this sense, 'it signifies the divine community in which the will of God will be perfectly realized,' and again he says: 'In true religion unlimited individualism is an impossibility. The individual can only attain to his highest in the life of the community, alike here and hereafter.'

These passages should be read in connection with the author's correction of Dalman, and incidentally of Moffatt and of all who would interpret the Kingdom of Heaven as meaning the rule of God rather than the divinely inspired community who accept His rule. Charles points out that Dalman himself concedes in one passage that at least in a secondary sense 'for Him (Christ) the sovereignty of God meant the divine power which from the present onwards . . . effectuates the renovation of the world into whose domain mankind will one day enter.'

Charles does, therefore, in spite of the stress he lays on the individual future life, insist on the apocalyptic idea of the coming kingdom as being social or 'political,' and as founded in divine justice and comradeship among men. It is only when he contrasts the earlier Old Testament 'kingdom,' as a natural though inspired blossoming of this very earth that now is, into a fruitful commonwealth of justice, with the later 'kingdom' of the apocalyptists, that I would suggest his case is unproven. For he writes of this 'future beyond the future' as though the apocalyptic authors had abandoned all hope of this earth or of any possible renovation of it, and as though, in desperation at the complete evil of earth, they had become what Tyrrell would approvingly call 'other worldly,' and could only dream of its destruction by fire and its replacement by 'heaven.' He seems to forget that, according to his own quotations, this ultimate heaven is not the heaven of the modern pietists, but 'a new Heaven and *a new earth*'; on the 'purely spiritual theory,' it should have been a new heaven, but here we have the *expression of materialization* of the new heaven in 'a new earth,' and it is to be noted that this 'new earth' comes down among men.

Now, it is the comfortable, the compromisers, the people who are doing very nicely upon this earth and 'making their bit' out of the present system who fix their hopes on 'heaven,' and not the people who are in desperate revolt against the present order as were the apocalyptists against the world of their day. The fact that they saw that the contemporary society was so devilish that 'reform' was no longer to be looked for, does not prove them 'other worldly,' but rather the reverse. It is only the revolutionists of to-day who can understand revolutionists of yesterday, and further, it is the religious revolutionists of the present who hold the key to unlock the minds of the religious revolutionists of the past. A syndicalist or an anarchist with a touch of the poet in him might well disagree with 'progress,' with ideas of a society slowly and benignly broadening down 'from precedent to precedent.' He despairs of the present 'world,' of the present order of things, of the present damnable age. He refuses to join existing political parties. He refuses to patch up the present world. He loathes social reformers. He is a pessimist, but because he is an optimist, because that very passion for justice and comradeship which has led him to despair of the present world, and to wish to see it blown sky high or destroyed by fire—that very passion has created in the depth of his being the vision of a new heaven and a new earth wherein dwelleth righteousness. He is a visionary with an undying hope. Here is the key to all this violent apocalyptic talk of conflagration and despair.

There is not a shred of evidence that the apocalyptists hated the earth itself, hated the sunsets, hated trees and flowers, hated the vine and cornfield; indeed the evidence is all to the contrary, as may be seen in the Psalms of Solomon, in references to the birds and their carefree life, and to the brilliantly coloured wild flowers of the countryside. What they hated was not the earth, but the world; not the world that God had made, but that which man had marred.

Reformists are people who dislike the present system but do not dislike it so sharply or intensely as to see a great gulf set between the present world and the future, the age that now is and the age that is to come: with them the one can bridge over into the other without horror, without destruction: in them is no passion of hate, nor indeed of love. Revolutionists, that is, revolutionists of a certain sort, hate 'this present world,' the age that now is: they see clearly there must be a crash, a complete break, a gulf, that no petty social reforms and patchings can breach: they believe in the *pirasmos*, the fiery trials and in a completely new heaven and new earth beyond them: a new heaven that is a new spiritual outlook, a new set of the will; blossoming into new earthly conditions.

Revolutionists of a definitely Christian type long passionately for this coming world to be set up here on earth, but if this earth were to dissolve into gas, or to be annihilated, their passionate longing looks beyond it to some dimly conceived world in which the things they count on as eternal would still have their fulfilment. This may be 'other-worldliness,' but I hardly think this is what Father Tyrrell means by it when he pictures the 'earth scorning' attitude of certain apocalyptic writers. When he attacks a certain type of German and English critic who would make of Jesus a bourgeois professor of ethics, a progressive, a not too violent Labour leader, he is on safe ground, but the contrast he makes between this and other-worldliness fails to appreciate the revolutionary-poetic strain in eschatology. If he had remembered his Shelley, Swinburne, Walt Whitman, he might have given us a more accurate reading of apocalyptic literature.

This is well brought out in Burkitt's *Jewish and Christian Apocalypses*, a reprint of which is badly needed. He shows that it was the hope of a future age, in which justice should triumph, that preserved the Jewish nation from getting swallowed up in the all-prevailing Hellenism with its vulgar and decadent ideas and its hopelessness.

It is the fashion to attribute all Jewish developments to conscious borrowings from pagan sources or to the unconscious infiltration of foreign ideas: the burning of the world by fire is a case in point, but Burkitt contrasts the Stoic conflagration which 'merely started everything over again,' to the consuming of the present order of things by which the kingdom of justice should be brought in. 'Surely God [they thought] will soon, very soon, arise to avenge His own and bring in His Kingdom that will last for ever.' This was the 'struggle of ideas between Jewish religion and Greek civilization . . . the expectation of the Kingdom of God and the belief of its coming is imminent.'

The Kingdom of God—that is the central idea. It is the New Age, the new state of things that will come about when the great agony has ended by God's victorious intervention on behalf of His saints, when He comes, or sends His representative to set the world free.

PART III

THE ADVENT OF THE MESSIAH

A SYNOPSIS AND CHRONOLOGY OF THE LIFE AND TIMES OF JESUS

B.C.

5   Jesus the Christ born.

4   Death of Herod the Great. His sons Antipas, Philip, and Archelaus inherit.

2   Jesus three years old. Sepphoris, his mother's birthplace, is destroyed after a cruelly suppressed rebellion. Later rebuilt with population friendly to Rome.

A.D.
6   Jesus ten years old. Archelaus is deposed on petition from the Jews, and Judea, Idumea, and Samaria are placed under Roman procurators, while the power of the southern native government is much increased.

6–7   Census of Quirinius. Rising of Judas of Galilee.

7–8   Palestine again in ferment.

8–9   Jesus is twelve and visits Temple; might see victims of Roman suppression on the crosses that lined the roadway.

14   Tiberius succeeds Augustus as emperor. Jesus is eighteen.

23   Herod Antipas, marriage with Herodias? Jesus is twenty-seven.

25   John the Baptist begins his mission. Jesus twenty-nine.

26   Pontius Pilate procurator. Jesus leaves the carpenter's shop at Nazareth and joins the Baptist.

A.D.
26 (*cont.*)

Late Feb.   Is baptized at age of twenty-nine (or thirty?).

Early Mar.   Fasting and temptations. Some of John's
followers become his disciples; accompany
him to Cana of Galilee; the Marriage Feast.
A few days in Capernaum with his mother,
his brethren, and some disciples. Attends
Passover. The Southern Ministry; expulsion of the profiteers from the Temple, and
incident of Nicodemus; leaves Jerusalem
and conducts a special mission in the Jordan
valley, near the Springs where John was
baptizing; a crisis. Mission in Jerusalem
and the southern country lasted till about the
end of the year.

27   Makes for Galilee via Samaria; talked with the
Jan.   woman at the well. (If we take 'there are
yet four months and then cometh harvest'
literally, we may place this incident in January, and the wheat harvest would be in April.)

Jan.–Mar.   Short tour in Galilee; good reception, as the
Galileans had heard him at the previous
passover and were inclined to accept his
teaching. Comes again to Cana where he
had made the water wine; noblemen from
Capernaum appeals on behalf of his son, who
is healed at a distance.

Early Mar.   'After these things,' i.e. after completing his
tour in Galilee, Jesus attends a feast at
Jerusalem; Purim probably, but many make
it Pentecost some two months later, and some
prefer the Passover, reading with certain
manuscripts *the* feast.
The Baptist had just attacked Herod Antipas
and had been arrested.

A.D.
27 (*cont.*)

Mar.   The campaign in Galilee.

(later)   Jesus, threatened with death, is driven from
              Jerusalem. Daringly opens his campaign in
              Galilee, in spite of the arrest of his comrade
              John by the Herodians who ruled that territory.
              Tour, during which he preaches at his native
              Nazareth on the Year of Liberty; success,
              until he claims it for the foreigners; his
              fellow-townsmen attempt to kill him. Makes
              Capernaum his headquarters; chooses some
              disciples; healings, including Peter's mother-
              in-law, crowds, popularity.
              A tour, with sermons in the Galilean synagogues
              on the New World Order (Mark i. 14, 15,
              and 39).

From   The Six Scandals as given in Mark:
Spring   1. Touching the leper.
to end   2. Man forgiving sins.
of year   3. Feeding with disreputables.
                  4. Defending disciples who refused to keep
                     certain fasts.
                  5. Shocking the Lord's Day Observance
                     Society. (Spring. Note the standing crops.)
                  6. Healing the paralysed man on Sabbath in
                     Synagogue.
              Pharisees report to the Herodian authorities,
              being determined to destroy him.
              Result:
                  (*a*) Change of tactics; after spending night on
                     mountain in prayer, withdraws to the lake-
                     side, with boat ready.
                  (*b*) Special training of selected disciples to
                     carry on in event of his destruction.
                  (*c*) Parabolic teaching to attract the eager and
                     elude police spies. See later.

A.D.
27 (*cont.*)

(*d*) Attempts at secrecy; enjoins silence on those healed. What you are now taught in secret to be later proclaimed publicly.

Centurion's servant healed; increasing popularity. Another crisis caused by appearance of members of Southern executive; his mother had warned him. Jesus goes to the border town of Nain, and a little later receives a message from the Baptist in prison. Meal in Capernaum; harlot supplies courtesies which Pharisee hosts had neglected. Tour, financed by Mary Magdalene and a lady of Herod's court.

Parables as part of the new tactics:
The sower.
Wheat and tares.
Seed growing secretly.
Mustard seed.
Leaven.
Buried treasure.
Pearl of great price.
Dragnet.

Growing fame but growing opposition, and therefore sails across lake to safety zone; a mental cure, but swine destroyed; obliged by pig owners to leave. Recrosses to danger zone on Galilean lake-side; cure of leading man's daughter may give breathing space. Nazareth visited (cf. Mark; but Luke, probably rightly, puts visit earlier).

The Sermon on the Mount, in the hills, some time in the summer of A.D. 27 but the month impossible to fix.

28
Jan., Feb., and Mar.

Sends out six couples on tour. John the Baptist murdered. The mission extended; Herod hears and trembles; government crisis. Disciples report to their master on

A.D. 28 (*cont.*)	success of their independent tour; Jesus takes them into safety zone for rest and quiet, but crowds anticipate them and he teaches them.
April	And supplies them with food: the feeding of the five thousand. (Passover time John vi. 4, 'green grass' Mark vi. 39.) Crowd want to make Jesus a Nationalist king; at last gets free of them. Disciples have taken the boat and set sail for danger side. Storm. Jesus walks on the water. All land on plain of Gennesaret. Disciples must identify themselves completely with him— eat his flesh and drink his blood—a hard saying; some desert, but the twelve refuse to leave him. Dangerous crisis. Local Pharisees in collusion with some from Jerusalem challenge him. *The unwashen hands*; a revolutionary pronouncement about foods.
May–Aug.	Danger acute, Jesus has to go into exile to the north-west above Galilee, to districts of Tyre and Sidon, a pagan region. Incident of the Greek-speaking woman. Jesus is absent from Galilee some months; circuitous route back by River Leontes and sources of Jordan. At last reaches Caesarea Philippi; work on pagan side of lake: healing, crowds, and popularity. (Four thousand fed? Probably a duplicate account of former feeding.)
Sept.	Recross to Galilee (coasts of Dalmanutha. Magdala?). Crisis. Pharisees demand a sign. Jesus once more takes flight across the lake at Bethsaida Julias, heals a blind man. Jesus asks the crucial question; Peter and disciples acclaim him the Messiah.

A.D.
28 (*cont.*) Jesus tells them his objective is Jerusalem: not victory but death. Peter shocked but rebuked as Satan.

The transfiguration in presence of his three intimates. On descending from the Mount a healing.

No further ministry in Galilee, but passes through it incognito. Capernaum incident of the tax collector and the fishing to pay tax. Quarrel among disciples. Little child in midst. *En route* for Jerusalem, incident of the Samaritan village which will not receive them; disciples furious, but rebuked.

More warnings about exceeding danger of the adventure. Incident of the ten lepers (probably occurs here).

Oct.   The Feast of Tabernacles. Harvest festival after the vintage. Jesus delays, but ultimately 'appears in the midst of the feast.'

Teaches boldly in spite of threats; attempt to kill him by stoning.

The woman taken in adultery. The man born blind.

Further attempts to destroy him. October attempt fails and Jesus escapes beyond Jordan.

Oct. or   The mission of the thirty-five couples to prepare
early Nov.   for his next attempt on the capital: highly successful.

The story of the Good Samaritan.

On way back to Jerusalem Jesus stays with Martha and Mary at Bethany. The better dish.

Dec.   The Winter Feast. Dedication. Last days of the festival, Solomon's porch. 'I and my father are one.' Attempt again to kill by stoning, but he escapes.

A.D.
29

Makes his headquarters at Bathabara in Perea.

Crowds and many conversions. Specimens of teaching (cf. Luke xi).

Breakfast with a Pharisee. His host is shocked, but Jesus vehemently rebukes him and his class; calls them murderers, vipers, whited graves: denounces them in presence of thousands. 'Not peace but a sword.' His comment of the slaughtered Galileans and the tragedy of the Tower of Siloam.

Rebukes the covetousness of a smallowner.

The Kulak farmer whose life will be required of him.

Teaching and healing in a Perean synagogue on a Sabbath: fierce controversy.

A message from Bethany about dangerous illness of Lazarus. In spite of the danger, after hesitation, goes into Judea and disciples bravely accompany him.

The raising of Lazarus.

Hurried meeting of the Cabinet. 'If we let this man be.' Caiaphas presides and urges his death; all agree. Jesus retires to a small village (Ephraim), but later crosses over Jordan to Perea and resumes his mission there.

Went on his way through cities and villages teaching and journeying to Jerusalem.

Pharisees of Perea warn him to get out, for Herod will kill him. 'Go and tell that fox.'

A meal with a Pharisee on the Sabbath. The man with the dropsy. All scramble for the best seats.

The story of the great supper.

Great crowds follow him towards Jerusalem: again warns them of the terrific dangers. Pharisees sneer because the 'riffraff' follow

him.   Parables on the march in answer to
them:

> The lost sheep.
> The lost coin.
> The lost son.

Then tells the story of the wily steward: 'Dives
and Lazarus.'

Incident of the rich young man.

The story of the ten lepers (probably dis-
placed).

Again warns disciples behold we go up; death
will follow.

Pharisees taunt him: When is this kingdom
of yours coming? His answer: As the
lightning shineth. It is already amongst
you.

The parable of the Pharisee and the publican.

Fords of the Jordan. Pharisees challenge
Jesus about divorce, possibly at the very
spot where the Baptist had been arrested
for rebuking the king for his divorce and
adulterous marriage.

Children brought by mothers for his blessing,
but disciples discourage. 'Suffer the little
children.'

Along the road towards Jericho; the rich young
man.

General comment on riches.

The work or maintenance parable.

'For the kingdom . . . is like unto a man, a
householder which went out early into his
vineyard.'

Two of his most intimate disciples demand
special power and position in the coming
World Order. The rebuke of Jesus (Matt.
xx. 20 ff. Mark x. 35 ff. Luke xxii. 24 ff).

Arrival at Jericho. Blind Bartimaeus. Dis-

A.D. 29 (*cont.*)	ciples try to stifle, but Jesus encourages and heals him. The rich tax collector. Zaccheus (Luke xix). In correction of the idea that the New World Order must come immediately on his entry into Jerusalem, Jesus tells the story of the nobleman and the talents delivered to his stewards. (Archelaus?)
Sun. Mar. 13	The triumphal entry into Jerusalem. A pause made on Mount of Olives. Jesus weeps over the holy city. Reaches the Temple and observes all the trafficking and marketing in court of foreigners. Retires to Bethany for the night.
Mon. Mar. 14	Expulsion of profiteers from Temple courts: indignation of authorities. The children applaud him as their parents had on the Sunday; Jesus refuses to silence them.
Tues. Mar. 15	Jesus teaching in Temple. Challenge from magistrates about his authority. Jesus counters it with a reference to the murdered John. Turns the attack on them with the story of the two sons. 'I go, sir, and went not.' The disreputables go into the kingdom before you. The story of the vineyard. God will destroy those wicked husbandmen and give the vineyard to others. Foreigners encouraged and so the Greeks ask for an audience.

The trap about the tribute to the empire eluded. The common people were delighted (Luke xx. 26, cf. a little later Mark xii. 37).

The Sadducees now take up the attack on the question of the Resurrection in the New World Order.

The good scribe. 'Not far from the Kingdom

A.D.
29 (*cont.*)

of God.' No man after this dared to ask him any more questions. Jesus again takes the offensive. The question of the Christ and David's son. Final attack on the Pharisees; devourers of widows' houses.

A climax; at this dangerous moment Jesus lingers to watch the beggared woman put her mite into the alms chest. For all they did cast in of their abundance but she of her want. 'Even all her living.'

Leaves Jerusalem, never again to teach in its temple or in its streets.

Tues.
evening [?]

Crosses brook Kedron and pauses on Mount of Olives. The long (Parousian) discourse on the doom of Jerusalem, the judgment of the nations, and the dawning of the coming World.

Wed.,
Mar. 16

A meal in the house of Simon the leper. Martha and Mary present. Mary Magdalene's lavish act. Disciples shocked and Judas disgusted: determines to turn informer.

Thurs.
afternoon,
Mar. 17

A cabinet meeting. The Sanhedrim determined to destroy Jesus, but dilemma: popularity, so must be in absence of multitude. Judas gains admittance and solves the problem: he will lead them to the hiding-place that night: the thirty pieces of silver.

Jesus sends a couple of disciples to a friendly hostelry in the city to arrange the passover meal.

Thurs.,
6 p.m.

The Last Supper. Judas goes out to betray his master and 'it was night.'

Having sung the Hallel they depart and cross the Kedron to the dark thickets of Gethsemane. He places an outer guard of eight

WOMAN ANOINS JESUS

A.D.
29 (*cont.*)

and an inner guard of three and goes beyond them to be alone.

The Agony and the sleeping disciples.

The Betrayal and arrest.

Thurs.
night.

Preliminary inquiry before Annas. Very late. The native trial with Caiaphas presiding; charge of blasphemy. The sentence of 'guilty': but not carried out as they wished to put responsibility on imperial government. Peter's denial, during native trial. Judas commits suicide.

Fri.,
Mar. 18,
about
6 a.m.

The Imperial trial begins before the procurator Pilate.

Political charges:
  Perverting the nation.
  Forbidding the tribute.
  Majestas, i.e. High Treason.

The answer of Jesus puzzles his judge. Pilate comes forth and pronounces the sentence: 'Not guilty.'

The charges reiterated: a dangerous agitator, stirring up the people from North to South.

Pilate, shifting the responsibility, sends him for trial to Herod Antipas.

Fri.,
7 a.m.[?]

Before Herod. Accusations, but Herod refuses to pronounce sentence, mocks Jesus and returns him to Pilate.

Pilate soon again pronounces 'Not guilty,' but allows him to be scourged.

Crowds shout: 'Not this man but Barabbas.'

Fri.,
8 a.m.[?]

Warning from Claudia, Pilate's wife.

Pilate more anxious to release him but urban crowds, stirred by authorities, cry: 'Crucify him.'

A.D.   Turning point which changes Pilate's mind.
29 (*cont.*)   'If thou release this man thou art not Caesar's
                friend.'
                After appealing once more to the multitude,
                'Behold your King,' and their cry, 'We have
                no king but Caesar,' Pilate washes his hands
                of the whole matter and delivers Jesus to be
                crucified.

Fri.,
8.30 a.m.[?]   The Via Dolorosa.
9 a.m.–   Jesus upon the cross.
3 p.m.   The Seven Words.

Sun.,   The Resurrection.
Mar. 20

Thurs.,   The Ascension.
April 28

Whit-   The birthday of the Christian Church.
Sunday or
Pentecost,
May 8

NOTE.—Jesus the Christ was born in 5 or 4 B.C., but we still
have no notion of the month of his birth.   Some place it in
August.   There is no authority, as has been pointed out in
my text, for December 25.   All the dates in this Chronology
are, of course, only approximate.

CHAPTER I

THE GOSPEL MATERIAL

A FAVOURITE complaint of the modern preacher is that people no longer read their Bibles; but the reason is obvious. They have been taught by the Victorian pulpit to regard them as infallible oracles, criticism of which would land you in hell. This immoral teaching produced dull and unintelligent acceptance on the part of the conventional sheep, and a furious revolt on the part of the 'rationalist' goats. The 'rationalists' hit out blindly and were almost as uncritical in their attack as were the conventionalists in their defence. The last half-century or thereabouts, has, however, seen the rise of a real scientific and historical method in New Testament research and interpretation. Out of a welter of criticism, speculative theories, and contradictions, certain results have emerged which are more or less assured.[1]

·   ·   ·   ·   ·   ·

The good news (gospel), brought by Jesus the leader, spread by word of mouth, largely as a workshop movement, from group to group throughout the Mediterranean world. The leaders were fishermen, tax collectors, tentmakers, labourers, and many of them had been companions of the carpenter.

[1] Students wishing to follow this up and unable to devote long years to the mass of critical books on the New Testament, should read the excellent summaries of the arguments of various critics given in Sanday's *The Life of Christ in Recent Research* and Schweitzer's *Quest of the Historic Jesus* (transl.). They might also study Moffatt's *The Historical New Testament* and more recently Streeter's *The Four Gospels*. Among useful pamphlets are *The First Draft of St. Luke's Gospel*, Vincent Taylor (S.P.C.K.), and *Q. The Earliest Gospel?* Albert Peel (Publishers: Teachers and Taught). These are, of course, an arbitrary selection from a vast literature on this subject.

He had not written down his gospel, but had proclaimed and taught, and had instructed his followers to proclaim and to teach. He had wished them to gather together a living community [1] out of every nation, which should come safe through 'the tribulation,' and be the nucleus of the divine international.

Thousands were converted at Pentecost at Jerusalem, and these thousands had no Christian Bible. Hundreds of thousands sprang up in little Christian communities throughout the empire, and these communities were for a considerable time without Christian writings, and the first written documents which they received from their leaders were letters penned to meet some special occasion.

Our four gospels were an afterthought: the first was written about thirty to forty years after the day of Pentecost, and the last about the close of the century. Two of them (Mark and John) deal with only one to three years of the founder's life: the other two deal also with the same period, but preface it with an account of the birth and childhood, and all give a few lines to the ministry of the forerunner.

The whole of the gospel teaching could be read out slowly in a few hours, and would occupy only a few columns of a modern newspaper.

Matthew, Mark, and Luke are called the Synoptics from a Greek word meaning 'seeing together,' because they are much alike and are constructed on much the same principle: the fourth gospel comes later and will be dealt with separately.

The gospels are not biographies, but sketches of certain salient points in the life and ministry of the Lord, recorded

---

[1] A writer tends to form a following of isolated students, and not a closely knit community of enthusiasts. The founder was not primarily a philosopher, nor was his message directed primarily to students and highbrows. A living human community is perhaps formed best by the fire and enthusiasm of human speech and conversation, although the written record comes in subsequently as an aid to memory.

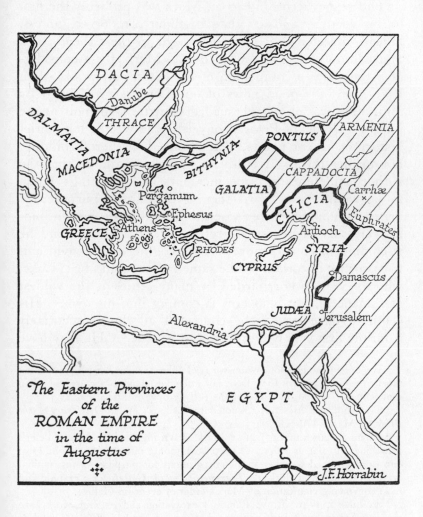

The Eastern Provinces of the ROMAN EMPIRE in the time of Augustus

J.F. Horrabin

in writing as aids to memory for those who had already been fully instructed by word of mouth in the 'Good News.'[1]

The gospel according to St. Mark was probably the first to be written, and its date is about A.D. 60–5, unless, indeed, Streeter and others are right in their theory of a first edition of Luke c. A.D. 56–8. Mark, for a considerable time, was a companion of St. Peter, and would often have heard the good news of our Lord as proclaimed by him. He was at last persuaded to write a memoir at the request of some of Peter's converts, who wished for a brief history of salient points, Peter himself neither forbidding nor urging this.[2] A study of this gospel shows that the author sometimes groups incidents and teachings much as he would have heard them grouped for purposes of instruction in St. Peter's sermons, although his chronological order of events is probably very accurate,[3] and he is coming more and more to be recognized as a vivid and trustworthy historian. The same may be said of St. Luke, who for years was regarded by many critics as the wildest of romancers, but who now is coming into his own. His claim to have traced the course of all things accurately from the first is now discovered to be true.[4] He may have

---

[1] We are in the position, when we read these sketches, of people reading short notes of a lecture they have not attended, though 'lecture' is a bad simile for the burning message of the early propagandists.

[2] Cf. Clement of Alexandria, quoted in Hastings's *Small Dictionary of the Bible* on Mark's Gospel.

[3] Papias (about A.D. 140) gives Mark as writing his gospel from Peter's preaching, but not in order. This probably only refers to the teachings of our Lord grouped together in Peter's sermons for purposes of instruction. Students should read Burkitt's *Transmission of the Gospels* for a graphic and most convincing vindication of Mark's order of events in Galilee.

[4] St. Luke i. 1–4. R. V. Ramsay's excavation and research work have corroborated many of Luke's disputed statements, and his *Was Christ born in Bethlehem?* contains not only a vindication of many historical allusions in the Infancy narrative, but of the sequence of events in the later ministry as recorded only by St. Luke. Harnack, at one time very sceptical about St. Luke as historian, has recently written a brilliant defence of the Lucan authorship of both Acts and the Gospel, and argues for an early date and general accuracy.

written a first edition of his gospel[1] about the same time as St. Mark, or even a little earlier, mainly from traditions which he himself collected in the course of his travels in Palestine—'some oral, some possibly already written down' —but the gospel, as we now have it, is generally dated between A.D. 70 and 80, embodying a considerable amount of Mark, a second written source, and his own collected traditions. The Lucan material, therefore, which is not found in Mark, is coming to be regarded as at least of equal value with the Marcan narrative. Mark deals mainly with the propaganda in Galilee, and Luke adds to this a considerable propaganda up and down south Palestine and a district beyond Jordan.

The gospel according to St. Matthew, as we have it, is not the original. Matthew, the apostle, wrote some account of the life of our Lord, probably in Aramaic, containing a great many discourses and perhaps some account of events. The editor of the present Greek work, like St. Luke,[2] embodies part of Mark, and draws on other sources, including the original Matthew, but his order of events is generally not as good as either that of Mark or Luke.

Until some years ago I should have used the fourth gospel only as an early Catholic commentary of the highest authority on the mind of our Lord, but recent researches, which will be found ably summarized in Scott Holland's posthumous work,[3] together with studies made by Edwin A. Abbott[4] and Dr. Latimer Jackson in his last book on this gospel, have convinced me that its historicity and even its chronological order of events cannot be ignored.[5]

---

[1] Cf. Streeter (*Hibbert Journal*, October 1921), whose article is a most important contribution to New Testament criticism. Canon Streeter does not claim to have proved the first Lucan Gospel theory, but his arguments are extraordinarily cogent and render it highly probable.

[2] St. Luke and the present St. Matthew not only both embody Mark, but draw on a second source or sources (generally called 'Q,' from German *quelle*, a source) common to them both. Each, in addition to this, have their own peculiar matter.

[3] Scott Holland relies largely on Richmond's *Gospel of the Rejection*.

[4] *The Fourfold Gospel.*

[5] A reviewer in *The Nation* refused to treat the author of a work dealing

That the fourth gospel is not always entirely accurate in its record of events is evidenced by the fact that the author has, at least on one occasion, to correct his own narrative, and it is inconceivable that Jesus, John the Baptist, and many other characters of the story, should have spoken not only in precisely the same style, but have done their thinking in exactly the same mould.

After the fall of Jerusalem, John, in extreme old age, or a disciple of John writing from the apostle's own sketches, published the fourth gospel. Other gospels, including Mark and Luke and perhaps Matthew, had been in circulation for many years. If he were to write another gospel it would be unnecessary to embody material already familiar to the Christian communities, except in such instances where he considered the former writers had been mistaken in their facts, or had been misunderstood by their readers, or in which he had seen a further meaning than that which they had already recorded. For the rest he mentions the imprisonment of the Baptist, but, apparently wishing to correct a wrong impression given by the other three writers, inserts before this imprisonment the following matter. A deputation to the Baptist from the authorities; the generous insistence of the Baptist on the greatness of Jesus; the attachment of some of John's disciples to Jesus with his full approval; the wedding feast at Cana (which, I shall suggest, was preliminary to the full Galilean ministry), the expulsion of profiteers from the Temple at the Passover of the year A.D. 26, and its consequences; a preliminary southern mission; disputes between the followers of Jesus and those of the Baptist, to the dismay of that leader; a Pharisee threat, in consequence of which Jesus terminates the southern mission and goes North into Galilee via Samaria; the incidental but important conversation with a woman of that country and his arrival in Galilee, probably linking up at this point with the synoptic narrative.

Any one who tries to defend this Johannine narrative

with the life of Christ seriously, because he had made use of the fourth gospel.

as giving the actual words of Jesus and the Baptist, has possibly not appreciated the spontaneity and freshness of Jesus, and certainly not appreciated the extraordinarily vivid and entirely distinct personality of the Baptist as drawn by Matthew and Luke.

When we remember that historians of that period were accustomed to invent speeches and attribute them to the people they portrayed, that no dishonesty was intended, and that it was the accepted custom, we shall not be surprised if the sacred writers adopt the customary method, nor depreciate their story on this account. We can only wonder that the authors of Mark and Luke seem to anticipate what are often held to be more modern and scientific methods, and to give something nearly approaching the very words of Jesus.

Nevertheless, the writer of the fourth gospel does portray, though through the rather ponderous medium of a later and more controversial age, a real element in our Lord's character which was not so obvious in the narrative of the earlier writers; and indeed on occasion passages in this gospel seem to stand out in such high relief that they almost compel us to believe them the original words of Jesus.

Perhaps Gilbert Chesterton had such instances in mind, as well as innumerable sayings of the Christ in the Synoptists, when he wrote in that masterpiece, *The Everlasting Man*: 'Even in this matter of mere literary style, if we suppose ourselves thus sufficiently detached to look at it in that light, there is a curious quality to which no critic seems to have done justice. It had, among other things, a singular air of piling tower upon tower by the use of the *a fortiori*; making a pagoda of degrees like the seven heavens. I have already noticed that almost inverted imaginative vision which pictured the impossible penance of the Cities of the Plain. There is perhaps nothing so perfect in all language or literature as the use of these three degrees in the parable of the lilies of the field, in which he seems first to take one small flower in his hand and notes its simplicity and even its impotence; then suddenly expands it in

flamboyant colours, into all the palaces and pavilions full of
a great name in national legend and national glory, and then,
by yet a third overturn, shrivels it to nothing once more
by a gesture as if throwing it away . . . "and if God so
clothes the grass that to-day is and to-morrow is cast into
the oven, how much more . . ."

'Merely in a literary sense it would be more of a masterpiece than most of the masterpieces in the libraries, yet it
seems to have been uttered almost at random while a man
might pull a flower.   But merely in a literary sense also,
this use of the comparative in several degrees has about it
a quality which seems to me to hint of much higher things
than the modern suggestion of the simple teaching of
pastoral or communal ethics.   There is nothing that really
indicates a subtle and in the true sense a superior mind so
much as this power of comparing a lower thing with a
higher, and yet that higher with a higher still; of thinking
on three planes at once . . . these far-flung comparisons
are nowhere so common as in the gospels, and to me they
suggest something very vast . . . so a thing solitary and
solid, with the added dimensions of depth and height, might
tower over the flat creatures living only on a plain.'

But putting aside the fourth gospel, the Jesus of Mark
'is at home in those poor, windowless Syrian hovels, in
which a housewife must light a candle in the daytime in
order to seek for her lost piece of silver; he is acquainted
with the secrets of the bakehouse, of the gardener, and the
builder, and with things which the higher classes never see
—as "the good measure pressed down and running over"
of the cornchandler; the rotten leaking wine-skin of the
winedealer; the patchwork of the peasant woman; the
brutal manners of the upper servants towards the lower;
and a hundred other features of a similar kind, are inter-
woven by him into his parables.   Reminiscences even of
his special handicraft have been found, it is believed, in his
sayings.   The parable of the splinter and the beam is said
to recall the carpenter's shop; the uneven foundation of the
houses, the building yard; the cubit which is added, the

workshop; the distinction in the appearance of green and dry wood, the drying shed; but from the pregnancy of expression peculiar to him it would be possible to find similar evidence for every other handicraft.' [1]

Or turn to Matthew. Think of the little natural touches in the recorded talk of Jesus about the brilliantly coloured wild flowers round Capernaum compared with the gorgeous clothing of imperial Solomon; the observations about seed time and harvest and the secretly growing corn; vines, granaries, boats, nets, sunsets, fig trees, the leaven at baking time, the pressing debts of poor folk. Batiffol gives a good summary of these intimate touches in his *Credibility of the Gospels*; and Headlam sums up: 'There is not a false note in the harmony, not a figure taken from a foreign medium.' [2]

Now turn to Luke: not only do you find there the life and bustle of Jerusalem and of its temple mart, long since past away, but in the early section there is the account of Zachary in the Temple, the poor man's offering of the turtle doves, and a hundred other intimate local touches.

If these accounts were invented in a century which had and could have no knowledge of the domestic and ritual life of Palestine long after the Christians had abandoned its capital and when, in fact, its capital had been reduced to ashes; when, moreover, the Jewish element in the growing Christian communities had been obliterated by the Gentile influx; if this is really so, and these accounts are forged by foreigners who had no interest in or knowledge of the intimacies of the Jewish period, how extraordinary would be the vivid and life-like touches, what consummate artistry and skill these forgers exhibit in hiding their traces and convincing their readers of their honesty and genuineness.

There is one other little piece of evidence worth adding here. According to the earliest tradition, Mark's gospel

[1] Hausrath, *The Times of Jesus*, vol. ii, page 131.
[2] *Life and Teaching of Jesus.*

* H

is an account of Jesus as seen by Peter:[1] 'Well, have you noted that this very book contains a most full and particular account of the shabby way in which Peter himself behaved towards Christ at the moment when he ought to have been specially faithful? Perhaps this has astonished me more than anything. A man tells the whole of that shameful story deliberately, about himself! And a proud, impulsive man, too, as anybody can see with half an eye. I think this incident is almost more surprising than any of the miraculous feats that Christ himself is said to have achieved.'[2]

Enough has been said to show the authenticity of these documents, and to show that they were inspired by an extraordinary personality.

[1] Almost incredible as it may seem Professor Bruce Scott Easton, whose Form Criticism in his *Christ and the Gospels* will be reviewed in Appendix V, attributes Mark's Gospel to Pauline influence, against all internal and external evidence.

[2] Barton, *Philosophy of the Gospels.*

CHAPTER II

PERSONALITY AND ORIGINALITY

AMONG all those writers who deny the historicity of Jesus there exists a common prejudice which leads them to belittle the personal factor in history. They minimize to the utmost the personalities of founders of religious and political movements, assigning sometimes to collective movements, sometimes to what they are pleased to call 'the forces of history,' what others would assign to great and original personalities. That dialectical materialism will account for strong tendencies in history, that the economic factor has been largely ignored by historians, that group movements of unknown men have often thrown up the necessary leader, I am not concerned to deny; but when it is argued that such a man as Lenin was merely the product of certain economic and political forces or merely a character 'thrown up' by his environment, the pendulum is swinging much too far the other way. Lenin was much more than all this. He was a striking and creative personality who largely shaped and directed the movement which had undoubtedly helped to form him. History can more accurately be said to consist of the interplay of the non-personal environment and the great personal genius.

It is the fashion for communist writers to reduce almost to nothing the influence of such men as Cromwell and Napoleon, to portray these giants as pygmies. One may legitimately hold that their influence was good or evil, but it is ridiculous to under-rate that creative force and to ignore it as non-existent. Napoleon may have been a good or a bad ruler, but to depict him as a statesman whose influence did not, in fact, largely reshape the map of Europe is mere childishness.

Evelyn Underhill makes a valuable contribution to the subject of personality down the ages in *Man and the Supernatural*. She writes: 'Secular history too shows us again and again sanctions and imperatives which we cannot class as natural, emerging, and exercising a determining influence on human affairs. It shows us the face of the world and the destiny of nations sharply changed by the action of minds and wills that moved to and fro between natural and supernatural regard; or obeyed an insistent push that seemed entirely unrelated to the practical needs or advantages of men. Again and again it suggests that the life of man only exhibits its full meaning, its specific character, in so far as some degree of this twofoldness appears in him; that he must partake of eternity as well as of time. History shows us successive events contributing to the creation of heroic personalities, and the building up of rich characters which seem to exceed what nature could either produce or require, as St. Joan of Arc transcends the political scene which conditioned her career. It shows us great and daring thinkers emerging within an uncomprehending and often censorious society and making gifts to it; patient scientists who reap no personal advantage from the corner of the universe they unveil; great men of action who behave from within history upon heroic levels, and thus witnessing to attractions and obligations beyond the level of the natural world. Plato and Marcus Aurelius, Pasteur and Darwin, Lincoln and Livingstone—all these manifest within history the supernatural life. It shows us, too, man's fever of creation harnessed to the service of music and plastic art. . . . History gets its real character from the often abrupt and inexplicable appearance of such particular individuals and unique actions and events; persons, actions, and events which seem to contribute to no utilitarian purpose, and seem to require for their explanation something other than the unpacking of the world's portmanteau. . . . History shows us a succession which is naturally conditioned, and yet is ever open to invasion from another order; a scene within which Personality—

that more than natural thing—first emerges and becomes pregnant.'

Now there is another point which would worry me if I were a Marxian trying to write a history of Christian origins.

When someone quite outside our traditions comes fresh to the gospels he is at once struck with the impression of an overwhelming personality. This personality is not a cheap consistency. It is full of the contradictions of an elemental genius, full of contradiction and yet an extraordinary unity. That it can be the forgery of one writer is practically impossible. That it can be a composite forgery would be a miracle before which the miracle of the Resurrection pales into insignificance.

Now many a volume has been written about the personality of Jesus and about his influence on century after century of mankind. Let me take one illustration only, and that from a modern artist, who will hardly be accused of staleness or conventionality. Oscar Wilde writes: 'Nor is it merely that we can discern in Christ the close union of personality with perfection which forms the real distinction between the classical and romantic movement in life, but the very basis of his nature was the same as that of the nature of the artist—an intense and flamelike imagination. He realized in the entire sphere of human relations that imaginative sympathy which in the sphere of art is the sole secret of creation. He understood the leprosy of the leper, the darkness of the blind, the fierce misery of those who live for pleasure, the strange poverty of the rich . . . Christ's place, indeed, is with the poets. His whole conception of humanity sprang right out of the imagination, and can only be realized by it . . . more than any one else in history he wakes in us that temper of wonder to which romance appeals. There is still something to me almost incredible in the idea of a young Galilean peasant imagining that he could bear on his own shoulders the burden of the entire world: all that he has done and suffered, and all that was yet to be done and suffered . . . not merely imagining this, but actually achieving it, so that at the present moment all who come in contact with his personality, even though they may neither bow to his altar nor kneel before his priest, in some way find that the ugliness of their sin is taken away, and the beauty of their sorrow revealed to them. . . . But his entire life is also the most wonderful of poems. For pity and terror there is nothing in the entire cycle of Greek tragedy to touch it.' [1]

Something should here be said about the originality of Jesus. J. M. Robertson (whose theories will be fully discussed in Appendix I) devotes pages of his various works in trying to prove that so far from having a human personality Jesus is a lay figure into whose mouth is put teachings and sayings every one of which can be paralleled from some Jewish or pagan sage. So far as the parallels are concerned, Mr. Robertson's task is more or less easy. C. G. Montefiore, the Jewish liberal theologian, whose knowledge of Hebrew thought is profound, in his *The Religious Teaching of Jesus*, gives us many of these parallels. But this author, less prejudiced than the mythicists, admits that the emphasis is different and that the honours are mostly with Jesus. He allows his vigour and originality. It has often been noticed by critics, both modernists and orthodox, that Jesus seems to surprise and sometimes to amaze his reporters. 'Jesus above the heads of his reporters' is a common saying, and a careful perusal of the Synoptists confirms this impression. I have before me, as I write, a short and very unusual account of the impression of Christ put into the mouth of a young Roman philosopher by J. E. Barton, who published it in the *Optimist* some years ago. 'This Christ,' he writes, 'to begin with, is quite a unique person. His behaviour and his teaching are all of a piece—unconventional in the most astonishing way. He is several times mentioned as speaking like one with authority, and not as the scribes. This precisely explains what I mean. All his utterances seem to come direct from himself. He teaches, not as a pedagogue who has received an academic training, but as

[1] *De Profundis*, pages 71 ff.

an original genius who attaches no importance whatever to rules and precedents for their own sake. How the scribes must have detested him. They are always trying to catch him tripping in small technical points (the only sort of points by the by that they understand), and if he cured somebody, or plucked corn on their solemn day, they are overjoyed; just as our own pedantic art critics delight to point out small solecisms in the technique of some really vital piece of work, and fancy that by doing so they are disposing of the artist himself. The poor creatures quite fail to perceive their own irrelevancy. Christ, on all these occasions, points out calmly that rules, like everything else, are meant to serve useful purposes, and not to frustrate them—an obvious statement, but one which pedants in all ages have hated like poison.'

This point is also well made by Dr. F. C. Burkitt in that wonderful book of his, *Gospel History and its Transmission*. Dr. Burkitt is as daring a critic as could be found, and he cannot be accused of having any particular axe to grind in the matter of gospel criticism. He writes: 'The real cause of quarrel between our Lord and the Scribes seems to me to be that it was a quarrel between erudition and intuition, between traditionalism and originality. With us the word 'originality' tends to be used for mere cleverness, but in its true sense it is the very word for the great characteristic of our Lord's teaching, especially as compared with the principles of the Scribes. It was, in fact, so original as to be superficially inconsistent. The tradition of the Elders (said he) is inconsistent with the word of God; well then, the tradition of the Elders must go. But in the matter of Divorce it is the law of Moses itself that was given for the hardness of men's hearts; well, then, the law of Moses must go. In the matter of the Sabbath, it is the very law of God which God Himself has kept from the beginning that comes in conflict with duties of kindness and beneficence. Well, then, even the law of God is to be broken, as David did. What did all this mean but that the supreme sanction lay not in a code or set of rules, however promulgated, but in an enlightened conscience, a mind really in harmony with the mind of the Father in Heaven?'

Bishop Headlam of Gloucester in his recent *Life and Teaching of Jesus Christ* admits that Jesus was by no means unique in the sense of appearing *in vacuo* with no mental antecedents. He speaks of the great movement which culminated in him, but for all that there is the impress of the original mind. 'I would suggest to you that there is a homogeneity and consistency about the life and teaching, which we cannot but look upon as a strong proof of authenticity; and the teaching bears the impress of a single mind. I do not mean to say that that would be true of everything in the gospels . . . what I do mean is that the teaching of Jesus as contained in the gospels is not a collection of different opinions held by various individuals during a period of from fifty to seventy years, but a homogeneous whole coming from one teacher of intense spiritual power.'

I venture to sum up the question of originality in words which I have written elsewhere. 'The mark of originality is not to think, say, or do something entirely new and alien, but to have the power of distilling a food from a poison; of taking in from the world around all that is vital and of rejecting the rest as refuse; and finally, of giving out to the world what has been made in one's inner self a fulgent conviction, in such a way that when a man presents his gospel, people exclaim: "Never man spake as this man." This is the originality we claim for genius. We are perfectly aware that Shakespeare borrowed some of his thoughts and all of his stories from other dramatists, but somehow or other in the process he breathed into them the breath of life. The same is true of Handel, of Beethoven, of Bach, and of other original composers. So you may parallel this or that thought or saying of the Christ from this or that philosopher; but somehow or other Christ breathed into them the breath of life and the Christian religion struck upon the conscience of the world as a vast out-pouring of the Holy Spirit.'

CHAPTER III

THE RIVAL INTERPRETATIONS OF THE NATIONAL LITERATURE

I HAVE often spoken disparagingly of pietism, and contrasted it with true piety, but readers may wish for a clearer definition.

By pietism we mean the religion taught as Christianity by many 'Catholics,' Eastern, Roman, and Anglican, by most Protestant Anglicans and Nonconformists, namely, the personal love of Jesus, the supreme importance of the domestic virtues, the concentration by the individual on the building up of his own soul,[1] and the permanence of the individual soul beyond the grave.   I hope to show in the course of this *Life of Jesus* that he deprecated the personal love of himself, and was continually warning people against it, in so far as it was divorced from a passion for the coming of his kingdom, or the love of one's neighbour.   He appreciated the domestic virtues, but taught that unless a man related his family to some wider family he would lose the way of life, that although urging the upbuilding of the soul for common wealth, he hated the concentration by the individual on his own soul, and that though accepting, he was not primarily interested in the mere permanence of

---

[1] Pietists who preach the value of this concentration would say: 'Save your soul from sin,' but others, becoming less numerous, say: 'Save your soul from punishment—by accepting salvation.'   Both schools preach an egocentric religion.   The Eastern Orthodox Churches are generally as pietistic as the Western.   A good example may be found in Mr. Charles Roden Buxton's *In a Russian Village* (Labour Publishing Co., 2s. 6d.).   A Russian priest is urging the author, a Quaker, to save his own soul, but the author replies that one cannot always be worrying about one's own soul.
Priest. It is the business of religion to save people's souls.
Author. I think it is the business of religion to save humanity, and people should think about that, not about their own souls.
Priest. No; you are wrong.   It is the only thing that matters.   If each man thinks about saving his own soul, then humanity as a whole will be saved.

the individual soul after death. He was interested in quality rather than quantity: he put the stress on how you live, rather than how long you live.

It may be objected that if Jesus believed in the 'future life,' the domestic virtues, and the upbuilding of the individual soul, and that it is only a question of his concentrating upon them, the difference between himself and the pietist is slight. Now the difference is by no means merely a question of the stress, as we shall find in the more detailed examination of his teaching, but I should like to say here and now that were it only a question of stress the difference between Jesus and the pietists might still be so profound as to be unbridgeable. The balance is all-important. The modern Pharisees tell us that to neglect family prayers, or to break your fast before Communion, is wicked, though admitting, if pressed, that 'to sell the needy for a pair of shoes' should, where possible, be avoided. The ancient Pharisees told us that to touch a leper or to walk over a grave was a crime, but admitted, when pressed, that to devour widows' houses should where possible be avoided. If you want to test the fairness of the statement, listen to the sermons of the Pharisees, 'Catholic' and Protestant, ancient and modern, and mark where they lay the stress. Mark what subjects they choose, mark what rouses them to passionate protest, mark in their debates and private conversation what interests them most. They have mixed their ingredients in the wrong proportion. They have forgotten what any doctor or chemist could have told them: that a medicine so mixed will kill your patient instead of curing him. The pietist who puts 'Thou shalt not touch a leper,' or 'Thou shalt not break thy fast,' or 'Thou shalt not do this or that on the Sabbath,' or 'Thou shalt not forget thy family prayers,' before mercy and justice, or even on a par with them, is, we shall find, denounced by Jesus as a murderer of the human soul. He has turned a healing medicine into a destroying poison. He has ignored 'the weightier matters of the Law.' To the pietist, immersed in questions of the Law, Jesus flings this accusation: 'Moses gave you the Law, and yet none of you keep it.'[1]

That Jesus put the good news of the Kingdom of Heaven above the interests of the pietists is evident, not only from the fact that the Evangelists introduce his whole mission as the preaching of the Kingdom of God, but even from his choice of material from the old literature. A man may be known by his choice of books and by his use of the books once chosen. The extraordinary thing is that the minds of both Jesus and the Pharisees were saturated with the selfsame literature. Both appealed to Moses, the Law, and the Prophets: yet from this same source they drew antagonistic religions at death grips with each other.

Moses, to whom Jesus continually appealed, calls up in his mind the champion of the oppressed. Moses, to whom the Pharisees continually appealed, called up in their minds the legalists who took of the blood and put it 'upon the great toes of their right feet.'[2]

The Law, to which Jesus continually appealed, called up such visions as the year of liberty, in which the poor were to come by their own, and the bastilles[3] were to be taken. The Law, to which the Pharisees continually appealed, called up such visions as 'all fowls that creep going upon all fours, shall be an abomination unto you.'[4]

The Prophets, to whom Jesus continually appealed, brought to his mind the age-long battle against the exploiters of God's poor, and the dawning conviction that foreign nations might be the first to enter into the Commonwealth. The Prophets, to whose memory the Pharisees erected expensive cenotaphs, brought to their minds problems as urgent as the precise dimensions of the belly of the whale.

Moses, Law, and Prophets, for most of the Pharisees, were summed up in the meticulous observance of the thousand and one rules. Moses, Law, and Prophets, were summed up for Jesus in the love of God and the love of neighbour.[5]

---

[1] St. John vii. 19.   [2] Leviticus viii. 24.   [3] St. Luke iv. 18.
[4] Leviticus xi. 20.   [5] St. Matthew xxii. 40.

The Pharisees looked forward to the Kingdom of God, to a reign of God over Jews, freed at last from pagan interference, and converted to the observance of these rules.

Jesus looked forward to the Kingdom of God, to the kingdom of justice and comradeship as pictured in Moses, the Law, and the Prophets.

A complete conversion of the mind of the nation from the rigorous to the realist conception of the Commonwealth was the immediate necessity of the moment, and would involve a most searching national repentance. This policy of reversal will first find a voice in the preaching of John the Baptist, and crowds will flock to his baptism.

Whatever else was surging through the mind of Jesus, the absolute necessity of such a national repentance must for years have been with him a burning conviction. The advent of John, therefore, involves his abandoning of the workshop in the North, his joining the Baptist in the wilderness, his acceptance of his proclamation. This acceptance was sealed by the baptism of Jesus in the River Jordan.

Now, surely, he will immediately join forces with John and commence his public work, but 'immediately the spirit drives him,' not into the public arena, but into the desert. Why?

For the answer to this we must retrace our steps and consider the mental and spiritual atmosphere of the nation at the time of our Lord's birth, and, in particular, the convictions of a certain Jewish group among whom he was brought up.

CHAPTER IV

THE REDEMPTIONISTS

HEROD's bloodstained reign was drawing to a close when, one day, to his pretentious temple, blazing with gold and marble, there came a peasant family to present their first-born to God, and to obtain his release from the clerical duties of the sanctuary that he might serve in some secular calling in the larger world outside. By law the first-born son was claimed for priestly service, and the fee for his release was about a pound sterling.[1] Almost their last penny had gone in paying this, and they had nothing left over for the usual gift of the lamb, and had to content themselves with 'the poor man's offering.'

Mary, the young mother, might have been troubled at this, but trouble gave place to wonder when old Simeon took her child in his arms, and, convinced that he held to his bosom the longed-for Deliverer, exclaimed: 'At last, Lord, Thou art releasing Thy slave in peace, according to Thy word: for mine eyes have seen Thy salvation, which Thou hast made ready before the face of all peoples, a light to enlighten the nations, and the glory of Thy people Israel.'

Out of his age-long experience, he warns the maiden in her sanguine youth that her son, who is set for the fall of the mighty and the uprising of the meek, cannot come into his own without a sore conflict, for he shall be a battle-standard which shall be execrated, and the sword of that conflict shall pierce through her very heart that the thoughts of many hearts may be unmasked. Anna, knowing that the prayers of her long vigil have at last been answered, and that the dawn has come, bears the glad news to all them that looked for the redemption of their country.

They were looking for 'the redemption' of the country:

---

[1] Money throughout this book will be reckoned roughly according to its purchasing power at the present moment.

Joseph of Arimathaea for the Kingdom of God: Zacharias and Elizabeth for deliverance out of the hand of their enemies: and Simeon and Anna for the consolation of Israel, which they sometimes speak of as salvation before the face of all peoples. These phrases have been tortured out of their original meanings by the pietists: 'redemption' is the buying back out of slavery into that primal freedom that God intended for the man or the nation: 'the Kingdom of God' would be understood by the people of that day to be the golden age of their hopes into which men should be redeemed, when they had been delivered out of the hands of their enemies: consolation means the coming alongside to help, and suggests the Leader who should arise to lift them out of their miseries, and inspire them to establish the new age: 'salvation' means deliverance, and the saving health that should obtain in that divine commonwealth. The controversy as to whether these terms are spiritual or material begs the question. They are both, for they are sacramental. That is, that at the high-water mark of their meaning they imply a change of spirit, of will, of outlook, expressing itself inevitably in changed material conditions. They are the well-defined phrases of the Apocalyptic Hope [1] that was current in those days.

In the grave of Herod's murderous reign this patriot hope might well have been buried, but there remained a little group without a name—a group so insignificant that the great political and religious parties of the day would refuse to acknowledge its existence, and the life of the group was nourished by some secret hope that seemed inextinguishable. Swinburne might almost have been thinking of them when he sang:

> We are they that have to cope,
> With time till time retire,
> We live on hopeless hope,
> We feed on tears and fire,
> Time, foot by foot, gives back before our sheer desire. [2]

---

[1] Apocalyptic Hope. See F. H. Wood's *The Hope of Israel*, Chap. V.

[2] Swinburne's 'Marching Song' (*Songs before Sunrise*).

Liberty hard won is precious, but liberty lost after hard-won victory is in the memory more precious still. This alone will explain the unconquerable spirit of Simeon and Anna, whose extreme age is stressed in both scripture and tradition; these centenarians [1] were leaders of the little company who still looked for the redemption of Palestine, and beyond that to some dimly conceived community of mankind.

Extraordinarily bitter must their memories have been. Born into a Palestine which had at last achieved that independence begun for it under the strokes of Judas the Hammerer, they had shared that economic prosperity which came through the restoration of the land to the workers for, 'then did they till their ground in peace, and the earth gave her increase, and the trees of the field their fruit. The ancient men sat all in the streets, communing together of good things, and the young men put on their glorious and warlike apparel. . . . Every man sat under his vine and his fig tree, and there was none to fray them.' [2]

But, while yet children they had seen their country defeated by the Egyptians, and although Palestine was left a certain independence, it was not to see peace. The growing corruption led to fierce factions and to a six years' civil war, in which possibly Anna's husband was among the fifty thousand slain. Simeon would almost certainly have been called to the front in the civil wars, and perhaps was not demobilized before the war against the Greek cities in Palestine increased the miseries of the impoverished countryside.

[1] Simeon's age in early tradition is given as well over a hundred, and Anna, about thirteen when she married (the customary age), after seven years of married life, had been eight-four years a widow. Her age would therefore be about one hundred and four.—Luke ii. 36–7.

[2] I Maccabees xiv. 8 ff. The author is describing the reign of Simon, when 'the Jewish State reached its greatest prosperity.'—Hastings's *Small Dictionary of the Bible*. Palestine had acquired a seaboard and had extended into northern Galilee. It now had its own coinage. These conditions would still obtain in the long and prosperous reign of Alexander Jannaeus, 104–78 B.C. It was in this reign that Anna was married and after a few years widowed.

There was only a few years' breathing space before a fresh outburst of civil war, and it was not long before the fierce internal feuds induced a rich Jewish faction to call in the Roman Republic, and it was soon found to have been an easier thing to call the Romans in than to drive them out, for the republic was already at heart an empire and, like all empires, it was inspired by 'the white man's burden' of bestowing 'kultur' upon 'the natives,' while extracting from them the uttermost farthing.[1] Sometimes a great disaster pulls a nation together and helps it to get free of its corruptions, but Palestine was fast becoming a carcass from which the principle of life and cohesion had departed. The governing classes were either cynical plutocrats in comfortable alliance with the intruders, or almost equally wealthy pietists preaching rigorism instead of righteousness as the salvation of the people, feigning to share the popular hatred of the empire while they exploited the poor.

The small, but growing, militant party were as complacently blind to the national injustice and corruption as were the parties we have mentioned: they were out for the same rigorism as the pietists, and would have thrust out the imperial intruder in order that Palestine might itself become a world empire. It was not from any such parties that these irredentist leaders could have drawn their inspiration. From what well-spring was their hope refreshed?

There must have been moments when the infidel seemed to have triumphed, and God to have abandoned his world for ever. In such moments they would turn to the little group, which they themselves had helped to create, to Elizabeth and Zacharias in the hill country of Galilee, to Joseph in Arimathaea, to many another, and the ardent comradeship of such as these would rekindle in them the passionate hope, that they would not taste of death before they had seen the Lord's Christ.

---

[1] It was 'morally' impossible for the empire to withdraw; such a withdrawal would only have meant that the half-civilized natives would have been at each other's throats! Compare India and Ireland.

But, above all, in moments of darkness, would they turn to Mary, the darling of that little company, the patriot maid of Galilee, whom they themselves had likely enough nurtured in the temple buildings, teaching her her letters, nourishing her on the old patriotic scriptures. As she grew up her single-mindedness and flaming faith would uphold them. When every patriot mother in Israel was praying that she might be worthy to bring forth the Lord's Christ, surely the eager heart of Mary, aflame with God's justice and God's love, would draw him down from the heavens that he might reign as the leader of mankind on the earth.

So when they saw Mary and her babe in the temple courts, they knew that they might sing their *Nunc dimittis*, for the day of the Lord was at hand.

CHAPTER V

MARY

From time to time a new star appears for a while in the sky, or some conjunction of planets [1] gives the appearance of a blazing star. Sometimes a thousand years or more will pass before the singular phenomenon is repeated. It was probably some such phenomenon that foreign astrologers observed, rising in the east, about 6 or 5 B.C.,[2] and so strange to them was its appearance, that they were convinced that it heralded the birth of a mighty king, perhaps the mightiest of all, the universally expected [3] deliverer of mankind. Perceiving that it rose in the Sign of the Zodiac that influenced the Jewish nation, they set out for the Jewish capital. They made for the royal palace, naturally expecting that the new-born king would there be found. Herod, terrified [4] as ever about his throne,

[1] The famous astronomer and astrologer, Kepler, observed in 1605 that a conjunction of Saturn, Jupiter, and Mars was followed by the appearance of a new and brilliant star, and calculated that a similar conjunction of these planets would have occurred in 6 B.C. His theory was that either this conjunction of planets, or the appearance of a similar star after it, would be the star of Matthew ii. 2. As the story deals with the visit of astrologers and contains several astrological terms, I have consulted an astrologer as to their interpretation, without committing myself as to the truth or falsehood of a science about which I know very little.

[2] 6 or 5 B.C. 'The calculation of our Christian era, due to Dionysius Exiguus, in the sixth century, is obviously wrong by several years.'—Hastings's *Small Dictionary of the Bible.* Hence we are now obliged to make the seemingly absurd statement that Christ was born in the year 6 or 5 'before Christ' or 'B.C.'

[3] It was not only the Jews who were looking for a deliverer and a golden age, but also some other peoples. For good accounts of this expectation cf. Renan, and also many references in Osborne Ward's *The Ancient Lowly* (Kerr & Co., Chicago).

[4] About this time, according to Josephus (*Antiquities*, xvii, 2, 4), Herod was troubled by a prophecy that the power should pass away from him and his family, and he murdered many of his own household whom he thought might be plotting against him. There is some evidence that the Bethlehem

inquired of his counsellors what city, in their tradition, was
to be the birthplace of their deliverer king. Hearing that
it was the neighbouring town of Bethlehem, he directed
his foreign visitors to the place, asking them to return with
the news that he might also come and do homage, though
secretly resolved to destroy this claimant to the throne.

And when they were come into the house,[1] they saw the
young child with Mary, his mother, and fell down and worshipped him: and when they had opened their treasures
they presented unto him gifts: gold and frankincense
and myrrh.

Mary, turning things over and over again in her mind,
would be struck by the contrast between that earlier visit
of the shepherds from the hills and this visit of richly-
clad foreigners. She had heard talk of royal blood in the
family, of a descent from David, but then, after all, David
had been a poor shepherd.

The beautiful story of the shepherds is a household
treasure, but there are about it points of importance to
be noted. In that country infested with bandits and wild
beasts the shepherds were armed, and a particularly alert

---

massacre was mentioned in a pagan source (Ramsay, *Was Christ born in
Bethlehem?*), and, in any case, it was a likely enough occurrence considering
the suspicious and murderous habits of Herod.

[1] The child was born in a tavern stable because there was no room in the
inn. Bethlehem was crowded because people had been compelled to return
to it for the imperial enrolment for purposes of future taxation, which was
carried out according to households and tribal descent, so that Jews originally
belonging to Bethlehem had to register there. Recent discoveries have established the fact of such periodic enrolments in the eastern provinces of the
empire, and this event must not be confused with the A.D. 6–7 census and
valuation of Palestine mentioned by Josephus, which was carried out according to the Roman method (cf. Ramsay, *Was Christ born in Bethlehem?*
for full discussion of this and of the Quirinius controversy). The crowd
would soon disperse, and Joseph and Mary would easily find a house if they
had decided to settle there. The presentation in the temple would occur
some forty days after the birth, and the visit of the astrologers, if historical,
must be dated after the presentation. The accounts of Luke and Matthew
are perhaps irreconcilable, but the Lucan narrative often runs on, and yet
expects the readers to understand a hiatus, sometimes of many years. But
the language of Luke ii. 39 is certainly difficult to reconcile with the Matthew
tory.

and courageous body; the story suggests that they were on the look out for the deliverer, and it would, indeed, be tidings of great joy that the angels brought them. The translation of the angelic message so well known in Anglican churches: 'Peace on earth, good will toward men,' is beautiful but possibly not accurate; we must prefer the Vulgate's 'Peace on earth among men of good will,' and it was our own St. Thomas of Canterbury who insisted in that sermon of his, just before the men of bad will murdered him, that there can be no peace on this earth unless it is built upon the sure foundation of good will among men.

The shepherds hastened to Bethlehem, 'and found Mary, and Joseph, and the babe lying in a manger,' and departed spreading the good news abroad.

Perhaps her little boy, born on that crowded day in Bethlehem in the outhouse of a tavern, outcast at his birth, would not only gather together the outcast, but all men, in all classes, who worship the divine justice. Was he, perhaps, as Simeon had hinted, to be not only the deliverer of her country but a leader of the nations? What a glorious future. But what was this sword that should pierce through her own heart? Mary trudging, a few days later, through the desert sands on their way to Egypt began to understand; for 'the powers that be' had already commenced that long warfare against her child which only ended with his murder.

Herod, who had lost his clue to the child's identity by the failure of the astrologers to return, was resolved to destroy the babes of Bethlehem, hence this flight with Jesus into that country which had so often harboured the outlaws of Palestine.

On the death of the king, Joseph returned to Palestine with the young child and his mother, but finding that the empire had placed Archelaus, a man as murderous as his father, Herod, upon the southern throne, he abandoned his lately-formed intention of settling in Bethlehem, and returned north to Galilee, which was under a different administration. They settled at Nazareth, not many miles distant from Sepphoris, which, according to an early tradition, was Mary's birthplace. Here, in Galilee, the child grew and waxed sturdy in spirit, filled with wisdom, and the gracefulness of God was upon him.

Jewish parents had much to do with the education of their children, and the first years of the child were particularly influenced by the mother. This is naturally the case in all countries, but especially was this so in Palestine, where the mother began teaching her children about the history of the country as early as the age of three or four.

Mary's eager heart had been inflamed by the fiery and independent spirit of her Galilee, and beyond the education which it could afford had, if tradition be true, been nurtured for some years in the temple precincts where she, the child of the Redemptionist group, would have come under the influence of Simeon and Anna, those aged patriots who had seen the good old days, and who would never tire of telling her of that glorious age of national justice and independence.

Mary, then, would not only have taught her boy those rudimentary lessons of freedom [1] which every Galilean mother imparted to her children, but would have been able, through that further education obtained at the temple in the environment of that alert group, to pass on to her boy such Mosaic teaching as the land for the workers,[2] and the anti-usury law, the words of those fiery revolutionaries the prophets, the story of the winning of national independence and of its loss through internal corruption and external conquest. That this is no mere fanciful conjecture of what Mary might have thought and imparted to Jesus can fortunately be shown, because we possess the record of what she was actually thinking and desiring at about the

[1] Even before they attended the synagogue schools at about the age of five, Galilean children were taught by their parents, 'Thou shalt love the Lord thy God with all thy heart,' the deliverance from slavery in Egypt, psalms dealing with the praise of God among 'all peoples,' the 'lifting) the simple out of the dust to set him with the princes,' hatred of idolatry and the corruptions that accompanied it, etc. Cf. Edersheim, *Sketches of Jewish Social Life*, and Stapfer, *Palestine in the Time of Christ*.

[2] Land for the workers. Cf. Leviticus xxv.

age of fifteen when she was with child. In her *Magnificat*,[1] which has often been described as the *Marseillaise* of the Christian movement, she exults in the God of freedom, who drags down the ruling classes from their thrones and raises them of low degree, who fills the hungry with good things, and drives the rich starving away.

That this revolutionary song should be sung by smug and well-fed congregations of our ruling classes and their dupes among the poor affords a curious study in psychology. The irony of it surpasses the irony of military bands of Europe playing the *Marseillaise* to assemblies of royalties and multi-millionaires. The great god Dope fulfils himself in many ways.

Bouck White,[2] in *The Call of the Carpenter*, devotes a chapter to Mary and pictures the character of the mother from the general outlook and even the watchwords of her son, of James, of John the Baptist, all of whom tradition says she had helped to educate.

The general teaching of the Baptist is described as valleys exalted and hills brought low; our Lord's continually recurring watchword is: The last shall be first and the first last; and James, in his epistle, proclaims, Let the brother of low degree rejoice in that he is exalted: and the rich in

---

[1] Those who see in the *Magnificat* a mere copy of Hannah's song (1 Samuel ii) would make Shakespeare a mere copyist from the mediocre dramatists from whom he borrowed his plots. Some critics have suggested that the song was not Mary's but Elizabeth's, and there is support for this in some Latin manuscripts, but 'Mary' is the reading of all the Greek manuscripts and of the majority of Latin manuscripts, and the song is more appropriate to her than to Elizabeth.

[2] Bouck White's *Call of the Carpenter* (Doubleday Page & Co., New York) is a lively and original story of our Lord's life, often discounted, because he omitted to give his authorities. His political and economic backgrounds are, as a fact, extraordinarily accurate. Unfortunately, he accepts as true the spiteful invention of the later Jews with regard to Christ's birth. He pictures our Lord as making an immediate and frontal attack on the Roman Empire, and this is not substantiated by the gospel records. His chapter on a personal god is crude, and his account of St. Paul and the early Church grotesque. I would, however, like to pay my debt of honour to this fresh and vigorous writer from whom I have learnt much, and to recommend him to the study of my readers.

that he is made low. The likeness of these ideas is certainly remarkable; and if Mary, who sang the fall of the mighty and the rise of the meek, had really had some share in the education of all three the origin of their ideas is indisputable.

The gospel shows that the Baptist was a kinsman of Jesus, that his parents were well stricken in years. What more likely than that the Baptist should, as a boy, have been in and out of the house at Nazareth, and that after the death of his parents he should have been educated by Mary, as indeed the early Church believed. James, first bishop of Jerusalem and author of the epistle, was, according to reliable critics, either brother or half-brother of Jesus, and therefore would have shared in the influence of Mary. If, then, Mary had influenced James and John, how much more will she have influenced her own well-beloved son: old enough to teach him, she was yet young enough to be his companion and comrade.

Elizabeth had called her blessed among women: blessed, not because by some accident or by some arbitrary choice of a capricious God she had borne the divine leader, but because she 'believed.' She believed the things the Redemptionist group believed, shared their passionate hopes for the nation and for mankind, and was convinced that God would lead the oppressed out of their Egypts into the fair country of justice and goodwill. Mary was blessed because she was foremost among those who had heard the word of God and had kept it, and keeping it became the mother of the divine word incarnate[1] among men.

---

[1] The problem of the virgin birth will be considered in Appendix III.

CHAPTER VI

EARLIEST YEARS AND EDUCATION OF JESUS

SIR WILLIAM RAMSAY says that the one educational aim of the Roman Empire seems to have been to prevent the mass of the people from thinking too much, and for this end it provided them with abundant and cheap amusements. The education of the Greek cities was little better. It was 'narrow in its conception, shallow, and unreal in its character, and destitute of any vivifying and invigorating ideal.' This lack of true education was one of the chief reasons that led to the decay and death of the Graeco-Roman world, and into that mental destruction Galilee, and indeed the whole of Palestine, would have been drawn, for the Herods, servile agents of the imperial policy, knew well how to use professional athletics as chloroform to the mind.

But the Jews, who had very nearly been Hellenized out of existence in the old days before the Maccabean revolt, had learnt their lesson and were determined to resist the foreign narcotic. The pride with which the Jew looked down on the Gentile was not entirely due to bigotry: 'Its strength lay in this, that the Jews stood both morally and intellectually on a far higher level than the Gentile. . . . The Hebrew nation was at that time the most highly educated people in the world.' [1]

If the Jews knew little of physical science or of the fine arts, they were familiar from early childhood with the writings of their great patriots and poets, with a national literature which is among the most heroic of all times.

A Galilean boy would especially respond to the call of this literature, for, in spite of a mingling of races [2] in his

---

[1] Cf. Ramsay, *The Education of Christ*, pages 59 ff. (Hodder & Stoughton.)
[2] Cf. Adam Smith, 'Galilee' in *Historical Geography of the Holy Land*; Hausrath, *Time of Jesus*, vol. i, page 10; Stanley, *Sinai and Palestine*, chapter on 'Galilee.'

province—a mingling which is not altogether a disadvantage—the Galileans were sturdy patriots, as volcanic as their mountains, a people of poetic imagination, lovers of liberty and mentally alert.

Of this 'chivalrous and gallant race' was the boy Jesus, and its lively spirit he shared. Educated at first by his mother, and then at the village school, he would have learned about that liberation from Egyptian bondage which was the birth of his country; the sanity and justice of the Law and the fiery righteousness of the Prophets became a part of him. From early childhood he would repeat 'the prayer'[1] to the God of his fathers: 'Who will bring the redeemer . . . to the God who supports the fallen, sets the captive at liberty, heals the sick, restores the dead, has mercy on the good foreigner . . . and humbles tyrants. . . . Sound the great trumpet to announce our freedom, and set up a standard to collect our captives . . . for Thy liberation do we hope daily.'

If every Galilean child was nourished on the Law and the Prophets, and on the hope expressed in this daily prayer, how much more would these things mean to a boy brought up in the eager spirit of Mary's *Magnificat*? And whose own soul was beginning to reach out to heights far beyond her grasp. The national literature and the national longing, already coming to life for him in the teaching of his mother, would blaze into meaning in the clear and vivid light of his own genius, as day by day 'the child grew and waxed strong in spirit, filled with wisdom, and the grace of God was upon him.'

We have evidence of what Jewish mothers were teaching their children from the age of three onwards, and at the age of five or six children would begin to go to the synagogue schools. Before this schooling he would have learned, as we have seen from his mother, the worship of the one God who had liberated them from the bondage of Egypt, and who had lifted the poor out of the dust and made them the equal of princes; God was high and exalted

---

[1] Schürer, *The Shemoneh Esreh*, div. ii, vol. ii, page 85.

I

and yet humbled Himself to care about the needy. If they followed His commandments, and were just and merciful, the land would yield her increase and there would be abundance for all.

A little later than the time of Jesus, and probably during his childhood, Jewish children would possess little parchment scrolls on which certain of these portions of scripture would be written. In addition to these every synagogue would possess in its chest a portion of the laws of Moses and one or two of the prophetic writings. Jesus, therefore, when he went to school at Nazareth would not only begin to be taught the Law and the Prophets, but would have access to these common scrolls. On his visits to Capernaum he would be allowed to read from the richer assortment of parchment scrolls to be found in the synagogues of the larger cities. There would be one other means of access to Jewish literature at the boy's disposal, and that would be the communal scrolls of the group to which he belonged. Various groups throughout Palestine had such collections and the Redemptionist group would certainly have their own selection from the scriptures. Their particular scrolls would, therefore, contain the literature on which their outlook was nourished; the social laws of Moses, the protests of the prophets, the international hope of Isaiah, the teaching about the Holy Remnant and Malachi's insistence upon justice to the workers as a preparation for the Messianic coming. All these things would, therefore, have formed part of the literary education of Jesus as a child.

Incidents in the life and the laws of the national hero and liberator, Moses, the poetic insight of the psalms, the righteous anger, the justice, and the pity of the prophets, things slurred over by the conventional and dry-as-dust rigorists of his day, would light up in his mind into amazing significance; and the national hope, already widened in some dim way in the large imagination of the prophets, would become for him a definite conviction of a glorious future for all the nations of the earth.

But what should he know about the nations of the earth,

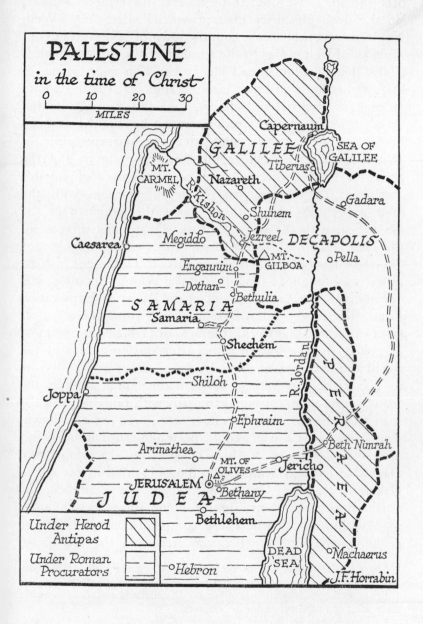

PALESTINE

in the time of Christ

0   10   20   30
MILES

CAPERNAUM

GALILEE

SEA OF
GALILEE

MT.
CARMEL

Nazareth

Tiberias

R. Kishon

Gadara

Shunem

DECAPOLIS

Caesarea

Megiddo

Jezreel

MT.
GILBOA

Pella

Enganium

Dothan

Bethulia

SAMARIA

Samaria

Shechem

R. Jordan

P
E
R
E
A

Joppa

Shiloh

Ephraim

Arimathea

Beth Nimrah

MT. OF
OLIVES

Jericho

JERUSALEM

Bethany

JUDEA

Bethlehem

Under Herod
Antipas

Under Roman
Procurators

DEAD
SEA

Machaerus

Hebron

J.F. Horrabin

brought up, as we used to be told, in the remote country, 'in the deep obscurity of a provincial village'?[1]   Well, Nazareth was probably a country town of several thousand souls and by climbing to the summit of the hill to which it clings there would spread out before him a panorama of his own nation's history: innumerable battlefields, scenes of many a victory and defeat, and the ground of that successful struggle for freedom waged by the Maccabean heroes.   'There is Naboth's vineyard and the place of Jehu's revenge upon Jezebel; there is Shunem and the house of Elisha; there Carmel and the place of Elijah's sacrifice.   To the east the Valley of Jordan, with the long range of Gilead; to the west the radiance of the Great Sea, with the ships of Tarshish and the promise of the Isles.   You see thirty miles in three directions.'[2]

Galilee has been called a map of Old Testament history, but it was far more than this.   As Walter Besant points out in his lecture [3] on the work of the Palestine Exploration Fund, it is anything but obscure.   Far from being cut off from the rest of the world, the hills of Galilee might almost be called an observation ground for the kingdoms of the world and the glory of them.   'Across Esdraelon, opposite to Nazareth, there emerged from the Samarian hills the road to Jerusalem, thronged annually with pilgrims, and the road from Egypt with its merchants going up and down. The Midianite caravans could be watched for miles going up from the fords of Jordan, and the caravans from Damascus wound round the foot of the hill on which Nazareth stands.   Or if the village boys climbed the northern edge of their humble home, there was another road within sight, where the companies were still more brilliant—the highway between Acre and the Decapolis,

---

[1] Farrar, *The Life of Christ*, vol. i, Chap. V, on the boyhood of Jesus. The author was wrong on this point, but the whole chapter forms a useful criticism on the apocryphal tales of our Lord's childhood and contains a vivid description of a cottage interior in Nazareth.

[2] Adam Smith's *Historical Geography of the Holy Land*, page 433. (Fourth edition, Hodder & Stoughton.)

[3] Adam Smith, ibid., page 432.

along which legions marched, and princes swept with their retinues, and all sorts of travellers from all countries went to and fro. The Roman ranks, the Roman eagles, the wealth of noblemen's litters and equipages cannot have been strange to the eyes of the boys of Nazareth, especially after their twelfth year, when they went up to Jerusalem, or visited with their fathers famous Rabbis, who came down from Jerusalem, peripatetic among the provinces. Nor can it have been the eye only which was stirred. For all the rumour of the empire entered Palestine close to Nazareth—the news from Rome, about the emperor's health, about the changing influence of the great statesman, about the prospects at the court of Herod, about Caesar's last order concerning the tribute, or whether the policy of the procurator would be sustained. Many Galilean families must have had relations at Rome: Jews would come back to this countryside to tell of the life of the world's capital. Moreover, the scandals of the Herods buzzed up and down these roads: pedlars carried them, and the travelling Rabbis would moralize upon them. The customs, too, of the neighbouring Gentiles—their loose living, their sensuous worship, their absorption in business, the hopelessness of the inscriptions on their tombs, multitudes of which were readable (as some still are) on the roads round Galilee—all this would furnish endless talk in Nazareth, both among men and boys.'[1]

The Old Testament is not a book but a national library. It contains every kind of literature, law, poetry, history, folklore, and as Jesus grew he would draw more and more nourishment from this manifold source, and would also likely enough be reading the modern literature of his day, the works of all those contemporary patriots inspired by the hope of the new world. It is inconceivable that the Redemptionist group should not have been steeped in this popular literature. As we see in his after life, the very

---

[1] Adam Smith, *Historical Geography of the Holy Land,* pages 433 ff. I have made a long extract because the point raised is of paramount importance and the description could hardly be bettered.

same books, which meant to the learned professors and scribes and copyists of Jerusalem little more than a code of rules and regulations, leapt into life for him, and every page becomes ablaze with immense significance.

Great as would be the influence of books upon him greater still would have been the influence of the hills and the shining lake and the teeming life of man pouring through his Galilee and surging all around him. Galilee at that time was peopled by three million souls, and from his own hills he could see two cities with populations of about fifteen thousand folk.[1]

Walt Whitman sings of the child who goes forth day by day and all that he sees becomes part of him. So would it be with Jesus. The steep street of Nazareth would become part of him, the synagogue with its painted portico,[2] his fellow-children with their games and make-believe of funerals and weddings, the baking walls decked with the scarlet of the pomegranates, the vineyards with their luscious grapes, the olive groves carpeted with red and purple anemones,[3] the slow flight of flamingoes, the intense brilliance of the little birds of paradise, the mountains of Gilboa, the busy lake at his feet and the blue Mediterranean in the distance, the hum and stir of insects on the long summer days, when the sun was too hot for games, and the children would lie dreaming in the shade of the sycamores, the excursions to the lake, the lazy movement of the waters, the gleam of the nets, the leap of the fishes, the sails, red, orange, and blue in the sun, his own gay clothes, and his comrades' red turbans, bright tunics of silk or homespun with many coloured girdles, with outer jackets of white or blue,[4] the boisterous games, the ringing laughter—all these things became a part of him. His home would be simple enough, with the doves sunning themselves on the

---

[1] Adam Smith, *Historical Geography of the Holy Land*, section on 'Galilee.' Also Stapfer.

[2] Renan's *Life of Jesus* has vivid descriptions of the scenery and life of Nazareth.

[3] The 'lilies of the field' of the Sermon on the Mount.

[4] Farrar, *Life of Christ*, vol. i. (Cassell, tenth edition.)

white roofs and the vines wreathing about them. The mats, or carpets, are laid loose along the walls: shoes and sandals are taken off at the threshold; from the centre hangs a lamp which forms the only ornament of the room: in some recess in the wall is placed the wooden chest, painted with bright colours which contains the books or other possessions of the family: on a ledge that runs round the wall, within easy reach, are neatly rolled up the gay coloured quilts, and on the same ledge are ranged the earthen vessels for daily use: near the doors stand the large common water jars of red clay with a few twigs and green leaves—often of aromatic shrubs—thrust into their orifices to keep the water cool. At meal times a painted stool is placed in the centre of the apartment, a large tray is put upon it, and in the middle of the tray stands the dish of rice and meat, or líbban, or stewed fruit, from which all helped themselves in common.[1] Such was the scene which he would remember in after years when he had left the hill town and busy, commercial Capernaum, the fishing centre on the lake-side, had become his home.

The carpenter's shed would be built on to the cottage and would contain a bench, a stack of various woods, a chest, baskets, and tools hung on the walls, saws, planes, hammers, and pincers. There the child would watch the making of rough furniture, wooden bowls, measures, sandals, coffins, and, above all, the ploughs and yokes for the work of the countryside.

His relations, who seem to have owned farms of some thirty or forty acres which they worked themselves,[2] would come to the shop about the repairs to their ploughs or other implements, and the boy would listen to their talk about the hard times. The heavy taxation that was put upon them by the native government and the threat of new taxation

---

[1] Cf. Farrar, *Life of Christ*.

[2] These small farms descended from father to son and such holdings were in the possession of the grandsons of Jesus' brother or half-brother. For the evidence, cf. Keim, transl , vol. ii, *Jesus of Nazara*, page 31. (Williams & Norgate, 1876.)

from overseas: the hawkers would come with their goods from Capernaum or Sepphoris, the provincial capital, and there would be gossip about the doings of the court and rumours of discontent and of a possible rising of the people against the conquerors, for Judas, the republican agitator, was stumping the country and the towns were seething with the spirit of rebellion.[1] Mary would find it harder and harder to keep the home together, and the boy would have among his friends boys and girls from families poorer than his own. There would be talk of the hard times in the South, of religious hypocrites who ground the faces of the poor, of men, who, while they led the prayers, were quietly increasing their grip on the people's little holdings and cottages, of the lands of the workers passing into the hands of large companies or absentee shareholders to be worked in once free Palestine by slaves or underpaid labourers. There would be the visits to Sepphoris with messages to his mother's family and for some of the shopping that could not be done in Nazareth, and he would find the provincial capital not only the head-quarters of the foreign king who had been forced upon them, but headquarters also of the republican movement, that 'Palestine for the Jews' movement, with its fierce outcry against foreign masters. 'No master but God' was one of the popular watchwords.

So with the bright strands of gorgeously coloured nature, of sunrise and sunset across the hills, of glittering caval-cades, and the gallant show along the trade roads, and of all that colour and movement that would thrill the soul of the boy, there would mingle those dark strands, and the news of things sinister and foreboding would begin to disturb his mind, and these also would become part of him. The iron had begun to enter into his soul.

Then one day, when Jesus was about twelve years old, the eventful year in the history of every Jewish boy, there came upon Nazareth, like a thunderclap, the news that the rebellion had begun, the people of the capital were up in

[1] About A.D. 6, when Jesus would be about eleven or twelve years old.

arms, recruits from the villages were urgently needed for the republican forces. Day by day news of the battle would come to them. The children, watching from the summit of the hill, would witness the swift march of the Roman reinforcements. One day, hopes would run high, the next would bring rumours of defeat: confused and varying reports would fill the countryside, and at last the blow fell, and all the gaiety and laughter of the early years were blotted out as the boy Jesus watched the devastating columns of smoke and flame and saw the burning of Sepphoris[1] by the imperial forces. That scene must also have entered into his soul, and the smoking ruins of his mother's birthplace may well, in after years, have wrung from him the cry: 'I am come to cast fire upon the earth, and how I wish it were already kindled.'[2]

Mary did not believe that a parrot's sphere was the cage or a woman's sphere was the home—not, at least, in the sense in which the phrase is thrown out by the anti-feminists of our day. She believed that in order to create a good home full of life and interest, your imagination must go beyond the home, and you must take an interest in the doings of the world outside. This is suggested by the fact that although it was not the least necessary for women to accompany their husbands to the feasts, Mary went up to the capital with Joseph. The holiday did her good, and it was cheering to see her friends in the South again, and good to keep in touch with Judean comrades of the Redemptionist movement, to share its enthusiasms and to have one's hopes revived. How desperately in need of revival they were was evident in that hideous forest of crosses, each with its human load, which crowded the countryside, striking terror into the hearts of the children and crushing the hopes of the people of Galilee. There hung the victims of the late disaster, such of them as had not been slain in battle or sold for slaves by the merciless conquerors.

[1] Hausrath, *The Time of Jesus*, transl., vol. ii, pages 79 ff.
[2] See Moffatt's translation, *The Historical New Testament*. Luke xii. 49.

*I

This year Jesus was twelve years old and was to make his first journey to Jerusalem with his parents; and the outset of the adventure was darkened by those murder trees; but a boy's moods are like mercury, and this was the eventful year when the earlier lesson books were cast aside and one might dig deeper into the national lore, if one could only make time, for now a boy was apprenticed to his father's trade. Thoroughly to master that fascinating craft which he had watched day by day and sometimes been allowed to help in as a child—that opened out a whole new world. At the age of twelve some of his comrades had joined the army, and although eighteen was the normal age for marriage, boys sometimes married as early as twelve. One was counted 'grown up' at last. So in spite of those crosses the boy's hopes ran high as his people joined the brightly clothed crowd and took to the pilgrim track. He looked back on all the good times they had had at home; to the winter feasts, when all the cottages had been illuminated; the feast of the freedom won for them by the lion-hearted Maccabeans, to the merry-making in spring time, the feast of Palestine's deliverance through Esther, to that festival of Purim, 'with its good cheer and boisterous enjoyments,' to the Easter rejoicings for the nation's birthday from bondage, to harvest home, to the camping out in the leafy booths at the Feast of Tabernacles, with its 'longing for the better harvest of a renewed world.'

But these pleasant memories paled in the excitement of this first adventure from home and in anticipation of the first sight of the capital and its glories. Nazareth is eighty miles, as the crow flies, from Jerusalem, but it would take them three or four days to do the journey, even by the direct route through Samaria, along the well-paved Roman road, through the old tribal territories of Manasseh and Ephraim. 'Leaving the garland of hills which encircled the little town (of Nazareth) in a manner compared by Saint Jerome to the petals of an opening rose, they would descend the narrow flower-bordered limestone path into the great plain of Jezreel,' the battlefield of Palestine.

Here Deborah had routed the hosts of Jabin and Sisera, Gideon had defeated the Midianites, and Saul had made his last stand against the Philistines. As they neared the mountains they would sing the marching song, 'I will lift up mine eyes unto the hills, from whence cometh my help. My help cometh even from the Lord, who hath made heaven and earth.'

It was nearing the end of March and 'the edges of the vast cornfields on either side of the road through the vast plain would be woven, like the high priests' robes, with the blue and purple and scarlet of innumerable flowers. Over the streams of that ancient river, the River Kishon, past Shunem, recalling memories of Elisha, as it lay nestling on the southern slopes of Little Hermon, past royal Jezreel, with the sculptured sarcophagi, that alone bore witness to its departed splendour, past the picturesque outline of bare and dewless Gilboa, past sandy Taanach . . . past Megiddo, where he might . . . have seen the helmets and broadswords and eagles of the Roman legions, the road would lie to Engannîm, where, beside the fountain, and amid the shady and lovely gardens which still mark the spot, they would probably have halted for their first night's rest.' Next day they would begin to ascend the mountains of Manesseh, and winding through the rich fig yards and olive groves that fill the valleys round El Jîb, they would leave upon the right the hills . . . that formed the 'crown of pride' of Samaria. 'The second night would be spent in the valley between Ebal and Gerizim, not far from the ancient Shechem, and the third day's march would bring them past Shiloh and Gibea, with its memories of the first king, to Beeroth.

'Up the hills and down the valleys and across the plains they had sung their marching songs, their psalms of ascent: I was glad when they said unto me, we will go unto the house of the Lord, our feet shall stand in thy gates, O Jerusalem. Jerusalem is built as a city that is at unity in itself, for thither the tribes go up, even the tribes of the Lord.' There were songs of hope, songs of defiance, and songs of deliverance, as they moved through these memories of their nation's passionate triumphs and defeats, and nature itself sang back to them the very themes they were chanting, until they caught the first glimpse of their beloved city with its gleaming walls, and the high towering golden roofed temple. Many thousands converging upon the same road would have joined them now and the whole company would burst into song: 'They that put their trust in the Lord shall be even as the Mount Zion, which may not be removed, but standeth fast forever, the hills stand around Jerusalem, even so standeth the Lord round about His people from this time forth for evermore.'

But the song that took his heart by storm, the favourite of that never-to-be-forgotten journey, would likely be the one they now raised, 'When the Lord turned again the captivity of Sion, then were we like unto them that dream: then was our mouth filled with laughter and our tongue with joy. Turn our captivity, O Lord, as the rivers in the south. They that sow in tears shall reap in joy.'

Tears and captivity were now the fate of his country, and with the joys of this pilgrimage there had mingled bitterness and questionings. As the caravan had crossed the more barren and sinister scenery there had been gloomy undertones beneath the notes of praise. Were these people of the South who boasted of their holiness and their minute knowledge of religion really so pious as they made out? Was the holy city, the very home of God, become a place of pedantry, and of littleness of mind?

Yet his mother had told him about the desperate battles that these men of the South had fought against the foreign empire. She had told him how, when he was a baby, she had seen the roads about Jerusalem lined with those same gibbets that had darkened the first day of their march. Rome had devoured its thousands of southern victims. For all their boasting and exclusiveness, these southerners were brave, but why did they despise his beloved Galilee? There was something arid and sinister about them, like the arid land through which they had travelled. Was not the free spirit of the northern hills more pleasing to God than this keep - myself - to - myself temper of the South? And the learned doctors of the law, the ruling classes, the higher clergy, the university professors; his people had told him how these, who should have been the leaders, had failed the people and sided with the tyrants. How could that be? The boy was troubled. What a heap of questions there would be to ask the professors in the lecture-rooms of the Temple or under the colonnade, if only they would give him the chance.

Would they, these masters in Israel, be able to give him the answer?

CHAPTER VII

THE DIVINE TRUANT

A boy in Palestine develops early, and at twelve years old
will have the wisdom of young manhood, and the intuitive
genius of Jesus, nourished by the teaching of his patriot
mother, and by the tumultuous issues of the time, would
be quick to perceive and hungry for some solution of the
conflicting problems that crowded in upon him.

Reaching Judea, the Galilean family would find itself
in territory dominioned more directly by Rome. Shortly
after the birth of Jesus, Herod the Great had died, leaving
a will that divided his estates among his three sons;[1]
Antipas having Galilee and Perea, Philip having lands on
the north and eastern sides of the lake, and Archelaus
receiving Judea with its capital, Samaria, and other southern
territories. Herod Archelaus had met with Jewish opposition from the first, and the native ruling classes found
themselves on this occasion allied with the common people
in their determination to get rid of him. Their first
embassy to Rome had failed in this object, and the Kaiser[2]
Augustus had confirmed the will of the older Herod, but
the ferocity of the young ruler and his many crimes created
such unrest that a second Jewish deputation met with better
success, and about Jesus' second birthday news had reached
Nazareth that Herod Archelaus was deposed, and that his
master, Augustus, had incorporated the South into his
Syrian province, a Roman procurator being appointed
for Judea.

Quirinius, the governor of Syria, was a malignant and

---

[1] For a good account of the Herods, cf. Hausrath, *Time of Jesus*.
[2] I need hardly remind my readers that the Caesars might be more accurately described as the Kaisers.

avaricious man, who had risen from the people and deserted them, and the new procurator of Judea was responsible to him. Both governors and procurators of the empire looked upon their posts as means of lining their pockets, and eventually returned to Rome rich with the spoils of office.

Economic conditions were bad enough in Galilee, with its highway rates, house tax, excise, market tax, poll tax, salt tax, crown tax, and tolls,[1] but Herod Antipas, foreigner though he was, respected the Jewish prejudice thus far, that he did not raise revenue from the land, or, at least, not directly. In the South, however, the incorporation of the land into the Roman province introduced this threat of direct land taxation, in addition to the many already existing burdens. Apparently only the crown-lands of Archelaus passed directly to the empire, but the threatened tax would lie heavy upon the lands of the Roman joint stock companies and of the rich Jews who were eating up the holdings of the poor, though these sharks were clever enough to see that the extra tax would ultimately fall upon the workers. The blow would fall heaviest upon the small holdings of the poor. These, in consequence, would be rapidly sold up, and would pass into the clutches of the native ruling classes and plutocratic aliens.

So the native rich had everything to gain by supporting the new Roman policy; not only in that they secured the comfortable appointments from the imperial government, but because they were now able to acquire land on easy terms.

There was a further consideration. When Archelaus had been deposed and a procurator appointed, instead of weakening it actually strengthened the southern native government, the Sanhedrim; for the empire's policy was to rule through rich natives, so long as these were able to keep the people in order. Now the Sanhedrim was composed of Sadducees and Pharisees. In numbers the former were perhaps slightly in a majority, but the influence

[1] Hausrath, *Time of Jesus*.

of the Pharisees was very great, and, many think, paramount. The Sadducees were largely the landed plutocracy of Judea; from their ranks the empire chose the
bishops and higher clergy, so that the established Church
should be in subservience to the State. The high priest
was at the time of Jesus' visit to Jerusalem the notorious
Annas, powerful, greedy, and an unscrupulous profiteer;
by virtue of his office he was prime minister, and he with
others of the clergy was a large shareholder in the temple
markets, bank, and stalls.

It was puzzling enough to the mind of the boy Jesus,
when he had discovered that the higher clergy and the
Sadducean rich, so far from sharing the popular hope,
poured scorn on the people's longing for a golden age,
and were hand in glove with the foreign conquerors; but
current suspicion of the Pharisees, those pious leaders of the
people, would seem to him almost incredible. That they
should be plotting to mortgage the lands of the defenceless,
while they lifted up their hands in prayer; how could such
things be? How could those who were said to believe in
the golden age be the first to contradict its most sacred
principles? Then there were those disturbing rumours
that they were not to be trusted: that they would betray
the popular cause: that they themselves were almost as
friendly with their imperialist conquerors as were the
Sadducees; that their religion began and ended with dead
formalisms. Well, at last he was to see for himself. There
must be some among the learned men whom he was now
to hear who would be inspired with the love of God and
the ancient justice.

As they entered the crowded streets of Jerusalem these
problems were put aside, and the boy quickly found himself absorbed in a moving kaleidoscope of colour. His
people were anxious to get away to their lodging outside
the city, but they yielded to his eagerness to have a glimpse
of the market broadway, and Mary was able to make her
purchases before they reached their resting place. They
had done the last stage of their journey very early in the

morning, and a few hours' walking had brought them to
Jerusalem, so that the wholesalers were still busy bargaining for goods which they would sell to the retailers later
in the day.   Shops, booths, and tables on each side of the
wide street were loaded with wares of every conceivable
kind: fish from Jesus' own northern lake, cakes of figs
and raisins, ornaments of all kinds, fruit and vegetables,
meat, cloth, sandals, scarves, stalls heaped with scrap-iron
and various metals, and squeezing between these a huckster
is crying up some medicine or other, and a huge water
melon cut into slices attracts a thirsty little crowd.   Here
is a man crying his grape syrup; yonder another recom-
mends his Egyptian lentils of prime quality; a third has
cumin for sale and turns a pepper mill.   Where the
space in front of the houses is unoccupied, those artisans,
whose work permits of it, have turned the street into a
workshop, and are so industrious that even if some great
Rabbi should pass by, they would not interrupt their business
to rise.   Here a shoemaker is fitting the uppers to the sole
of a sandal; there a tailor is trimming a prayer-cloak with
fine fringes; yonder an armourer is hammering at the handle
of a sword of Syrian steel.   The market grows busier still.
Buyers, sellers, and onlookers crowd in from all the gates.
At the lower corner by the market-place, in the very centre
of the town, stand the cunning donkey-drivers; one of them
has the luck to be hired to move a bed and other household
furniture, together with the indispensable flutes, over to
Bethany, against an approaching wedding.   This is a
group of men who let no one pass by without giving him
some satirical comment.   A grave, abstracted man, who
looks ill, hastens past.   'The gentleman has certainly had
a bad dream,' says one of the donkey-drivers; 'to which
of the twenty-four interpreters does he mean to go?'
A barber elbows through the crowd.   'Good morning,
sir surgeon,' they call to him.   'How's trade?'   'A
hundred cuppings a penny,' cries he.   A fat scribe with a
copper face pushes an old woman rather roughly out of his
way.   'How red you are, old man,' she screams; 'you

are either a winebibber or some pawnbroker or pig-
breeder.'[1]

The sun grows fiercer as the day advances. The family
from Nazareth are tired and hungry. In the street of
the woolcombers there is a house by which are some great
jugs standing out in the sun. There is wine in them for
the heat to ferment. They turn into this hostelry, and
ask the landlord for a dish of locusts baked with flour, or
with honey or perhaps salt, and their meal is washed
down with the wine of the country or cider or Median beer;
but the inn is so crowded with pilgrims that they are glad
after this short rest to be out in the open again. Often
the boy would catch glimpses of the dominating Temple.
Against some of its huge walls the scaffolding was still
erected, and the workmen were busy upon it. Coming
nearer, Jesus could see the huge blocks of masonry, coloured
marbles, and other stone. All the morning he had seen
stone-cutters, masons, carpenters, about the city, looking
well fed and in great good humour with themselves. They
were skilled men, highly paid by Herod. Jerusalem had
been recently paved with white marble by workmen of
this type.

At last they leave the city for their rough lodging among
the hills, and that night, perhaps, the dreams of the boy
are full of crowds and golden-domed buildings and march-
ings and scribes and Pharisees, and Herod's secret spies
that he had been told about by people in the inn. To-
morrow the Temple and the great service and what new
adventures?

The family from Nazareth were now ascending towards
the vast Temple, which could hold within its borders over
two hundred thousand people. 'The mount itself seemed
like an island, abruptly rising from out deep valleys surrounded by a sea of walls, palaces, streets, and houses, and
crowned by a mass of snowy marble and glittering gold

[1] Frank Delitzch, *Jewish Artisan Life*, page 43. (Unit Library,
1902.) My description of the broadway is based on this remarkable
booklet.

rising terrace above terrace . . . at its north - western angle, and connected with it, frowned the castle of Antonia, held by the Roman garrison. The lofty walls were pierced by massive gates'—the unused gate on the north, the Susa gate on the east, the 'weasel' gates, which led by tunnels from the suburb of the priests, and the four gates on the west. Within the gates ran the immense colonnades with their benches. There was the twofold double colonnade with a wide space between, and beyond the eastern colonnade Jesus saw the huge pinnacle from which a priest at dawn would announce 'the earliest streak of day.' Below the pinnacle 'the Kedron valley yawned 450 feet beneath.'[1] Soon they would find themselves in the courts where the native parliament sat. Passing out of these colonnades they entered the vast court of the foreigners. On three sides of it ran a double, and on the fourth a triple, colonnade of brilliantly shining white marble with elaborate cedar roofs and coloured stone pavements, and Jesus would now find himself in the temple market held within this court, and would see the taverns or booths with the tables of the money-changers and the benches of those who trafficked in oxen and lambs and doves. There was a noise and a crying of beasts and men, of sellers and buyers, and a rolling and clinking of money, and he would wonder at the jostling and bargaining, and the unscrupulous advantage taken of the poor pilgrims. Near by were the brokers who exchanged the money of travellers of every quarter of the globe into the sacred coin of the Temple, in which alone they might trade, and making a handsome profit out of the transaction.[2] The court was reeking with the stench of cattle, and the wrangling and screaming of buyers and sellers made it almost impossible to hear oneself speak. There was a poor man looking miserable. The Temple rate collectors had ordered him to give up his outer garment because he had no money to pay the sacred tax, and the term allowed was long overdue. Jesus turned

---

[1] Edersheim, *Life and Times of Jesus.*
[2] Keim, *Jesus of Nazara,* vol. v, pages 116 ff.

aside, sick with disappointment. The problems of yesterday were crowding upon him again with a vengeance, and
as they left the noisy court and passed beyond the notices
warning the foreigners that they must not come farther on
pain of death, they climbed the steps leading to the terrace
which was bounded by the wall of the Temple buildings
proper. Now the splendour of the Beautiful Gate failed to
arouse his interest. Up more steps they trudged, the climb
seemed never-ending, and his eyes grew tired of the glitter
of Corinthian brass and coloured marbles.

It was difficult to reconcile the sights he had just
witnessed, the fleecing of the workers, the rumour that
the clergy were financially implicated, the spirit of greed,
and even these pretentious vulgarian buildings of the
Herods—for, after all, were they really beautiful?—with
the meaning of the feast, with the coming out into freedom
from Egyptian bondage and the expectation of a righteous
world. But when the flame leaped high upon the great
altar of burnt sacrifice, and they all began to pray, while
the priest brought the incense before God within the
sanctuary, something of the old enthusiasm may have come
back to him.[1]

The actual meal eaten with his own folk had been
wonderful. They had brought back the lamb consecrated
and slain in the Temple, and it had been roasted in their
lodging. Joseph had blessed the first cup of red wine,
saying: 'Blessed art Thou, Jehovah, our God, Who hast
created the fruit of the vine.' They were seated on a
thick carpet. Jesus asked Joseph the question, now
become a ritual: 'What meanest thou by this sacrifice?'
The reply was: 'This is the passover of the Lord which
we eat, because the Lord passed over the houses of our
fathers in Egypt,' and, as they partook of the bitter herbs,
he added: 'We eat these because the Egyptians made
the life of our fathers bitter in Egypt.'[2] Then came the
eating of unleavened bread, and Joseph exhorted them to

---

[1] Weiss, *Life of Christ*, vol. i, page 275.
[2] Stapfer, *Palestine*, 'The Feasts,' pages 441 ff.

praise God, 'Who has brought us out of darkness into light: out of bondage into liberty.' Then there arose the song: 'He taketh up the simple out of the dust, and lifteth the poor out of the mire, that He may set him with the princes.' And again they sang: 'When Israel came out of Egypt,' reminding Jesus of the thrill of those songs of freedom on the march.

Then another blessing, again speaking of the redemption of their people from the Egyptian tyrants, and the second cup was drunk in common. So the ritual meal went on until, after the lamb was consumed, it closed with the last draught of wine and the singing of that group of songs opening once more with 'When Israel came out of Egypt,' and including the song of fruitfulness: 'Blessed is he that cometh in the name of the Lord.' And to Jesus, as he joined in the singing, remembering the plight of his fellow-countrymen in the South, now robbed of their little holdings, that song that they were singing, 'the earth hath He given to the children of men,' would be charged with defiant thought.

So the seven days of that memorable first visit flew by, and soon they would be returning home. He had been impressed by that later function of the festival, the offering to God the first fruit of harvest; to him it would suggest the harvest of the good time coming when men would live in comradeship with one another, and the earth would yield abundantly her increase.

The caravans had started on the home journey, but it was not till the evening of the first day that Joseph and Mary began to be anxious about their boy. They had missed him some hours before, but had supposed him to be with some group of their kinsfolk or with his friends. There were so many returning that he was sure to be in one or other of the companies of pilgrims. But the search proved fruitless, and they had to return. Three days were spent looking for him, and at last they came upon him in the cloisters, or perhaps in the Hall of the Hewn Stones, in the threefold ring of scholars seated upon the ground, listening to the learned professors as they expounded the law of God. He was all ears to hear, and as he listened it came upon him that his mother's suspicions and all the talk he had heard about these 'leaders,' these 'masters in Israel,' was the stark truth. It was the final disillusionment.

We know the kind of things they discoursed on, these sapless university professors, with what George Meredith would have called their 'damned punctilio.' Was their theme, this April morning, the Sabbath, and did Jesus want to hear how God had given it for man, for his freedom and leisure, and for the worship of the God of liberty and the study of their country's past? What he actually heard was a disquisition on whether a man with a wooden leg might or might not go out on Saturday, for unless he unscrewed his leg and left it at home he would incur the grave displeasure of God for carrying a burden.[1]   Or was this morning's discourse devoted to that favourite question: 'Which is the greatest commandment of the Law?'—that law which, with their infinite precision, they had divided up into 248 affirmative precepts and 365 negative precepts.[2] The lecturer might assure his hearers that the greatest of them all was the one that dealt with the exact pattern and correct length of the fringes and phylacteries. 'He who diligently observes it is regarded in the same light as if he had kept the whole Law.' How these learned people scorned 'the outsiders,' the common people, who could hardly hope for salvation, for they were ignorant and, therefore, accursed.[3]

One can well imagine the piercing questions which the boy Jesus would put, when question time came—questions exceedingly awkward to answer. 'And all who heard him were amazed at his intelligence and replies.' But now his people saw him, and 'they were astonished; and his mother said to him: "Child, why have you treated us in this way?

---

[1] Conrad Noel, *The Day of the Sun*.   (David Nutt.)   Out of print.
[2] Farrar, *Life of Christ*, vol. ii, page 239.
[3] Edersheim, *Life and Times of Jesus*, vol. ii, pages 290 ff.

Your father and I have been hunting for you everywhere, sorrowing."' But he answered them: 'Why so anxious? Why this search? Didn't you understand that I was certain to come home, because I was apprenticed to my father's trade!' [1]

[1] The more traditional 'About my Father's business,' may be right, but the Greek sentence bears either interpretation.

CHAPTER VIII

EARLY MANHOOD

'AND he went down with them, and came to Nazareth, and was subject unto them: but his mother kept all these sayings in her heart. And Jesus kept on increasing in wisdom and stature, and in favour with God and man.'[1] Jesus settled down to the carpentering as apprentice to Joseph, and became a craftsman, who, judging by the many allusions he made to his work in after years, delighted in handling his materials and in turning out well-made goods.

He lived the life of a working man, and his after-mission, as we have seen, betrays a knowledge of its hardships and an intimacy which could only have been gained by actual experience.

Joseph seems to have died before the mission of Jesus commenced, and Jesus the carpenter became the main support of the household at Nazareth. We have seen how various was the work of the carpenter's shed, and the work of the village craftsman would be a great education for what he was afterwards to undertake. News of the big world would filter into the shop. When he was about fifteen, he would hear of Tiberius, who was afterwards to become emperor, receiving authority over the provinces. And when he was about eighteen the great Augustus Caesar died, and Tiberius, at fifty-six, ascended the throne. It was thought that the new emperor would not long escape the plots that surrounded him, and ambitious men began to dream dreams of becoming emperor. Tiberius disappointed their hopes, and reigned for twenty-three years. Philo wrote a flattering verdict of his reign, and some historians speak of the peace and good administration of

[1] Luke ii. 51–2.

248

the provinces in his time; but these estimates are fictitious. Galilee is referred to as a hive of rich honey, but Galilee was, in fact, a busy hive from which 'almost all the honey was extracted as soon as produced.' Fishermen and land-workers were alike bled almost to death, not only by the taxes already mentioned, but by super-taxes to meet the cost of every kind of extravagant enterprise; in the South it was unlikely that a peasant yeomanry any longer existed.

Tiberius recognized that legates and procurators would always amass whatever they could, and his only solution of the difficulty was to favour long appointments in place of the continual changes that had taken place. Perhaps, he argued, a governor of a province, once he has collected sufficient to become a plutocrat, will not afterwards be so rapacious. He told the story of the wounded traveller in illustration of this cynical point of view. A passer-by, taking pity on the wounded man, offers to drive the flies from his wounds, but the sufferer implores him not to, as these insects are already satiated, whilst the advent of a fresh batch, who would certainly come, would only mean that the blood-sucking process would begin all over again, 'a frightful picture of the condition of the tortured provinces.' [1]

All this affected the life of the family at Nazareth, and Jesus was receiving his education in a hard school.

How could he honour his king, the crafty and avaricious Herod Antipas, with his eighty thousand pounds a year, wrung chiefly from the labourers, who had to be content in consequence with some twenty pounds annually, and from the diminishing peasant holders of the hillsides round Nazareth? How could he respect a king who, to satisfy his extravagant lusts, squandered sums far beyond this income, and tried to make good by levying extra taxes on the already maddened workers? In accordance with the 'gentlemanly' tastes of the period, the king 'loved to reverse the order of nature; turning the sea into dry land for the purposes of a banquet and enjoying spring in winter,

[1] Hausrath, *Times of Jesus*, vol. ii, page 89.

the north in the south, regardless of the cost.'[1] To please
his Roman masters, and to flatter them, he lavished money
squeezed from the people on the building of vulgar ostentatious cities in the heathen fashion, named after the
emperor, or some princess, and introduced amphitheatres
with their blood sports and immoral dramas, and revelled
in freak banquets and every kind of luxury.

Sejanus, the emperor's closest adviser, was certainly no
friend to the provincial poor, and under his powerful
influence, things went from bad to worse. It was owing
to him, and not really to the legate of Syria, that the
notorious Caiaphas was appointed as high priest, and held
office from A.D. 18 to A.D. 36.

There were other landmarks in the early manhood of
Jesus, such as the banishment of the Jews from Rome,
which happened in his twenty-fifth year. Many of these
were press-ganged into the military expedition against the
Sardinian robbers, but as the Jews had been before exempted from serving, on account of their religious customs,
these men mutinied and refused to fight. To their credit,
as we have shown, the Jewish workers were often too
independent to make good soldiers for imperial projects,
and for the same reason they made bad and intractable
slaves. The upshot of it was that many had to be repatriated, and this would likely bring some few of them
back to Galilee and to the neighbourhood of Nazareth,
and from them Jesus would learn something of the life
of Rome, and of its slums and palaces. Many of these
Roman Jews returned to Jerusalem, and seemed to have
had a synagogue of their own there, which is called in
the New Testament the synagogue of the Libertines or
freed Jews.

In the year A.D. 23, when Jesus was about twenty-seven,
the son of Tiberius, who had been named as the next
emperor, died, and this encouraged fresh speculations and
sinister ambitions of numerous adventurers, who were in
the running for the supreme command. Ever since the

---

[1] Hausrath, *Times of Jesus*, vol. ii, page 64.

accession of Tiberius, things had been in an unsettled condition. His own claim to the throne had not gone undisputed. There were the mutinies of A.D. 14, the conspiracy of A.D. 16, and now again, and from this time onwards, 'his court was distracted by palace intrigues and feuds, and even his closest adviser, the ambitious and unscrupulous Sejanus, proved faithless and unworthy.' [1]

I have laid stress upon these ambitions and unsettlements, because if even Herod Antipas had hopes of the imperial throne, it cannot have been entirely outside the ken of the keen and imaginative spirit of Jesus that to a man of adventure, a man of genius, however obscure his origin or environment, there might one day come the chance of seizing power and dominating 'all the kingdoms of the world.' All this will be discussed when we deal with the Temptation. It will be impossible to understand his life and its special temptations and achievements, unless my readers will patiently study these backgrounds of his own manhood with the long vista of possibilities that they were opening out for him.

It was an atmosphere of plots and counter-plots on the part of the ruling classes that surrounded Jesus, and the spirit of the 'upper classes' was, to some extent, reflected among the workers. Had the poison gone too far? Was it possible that someone should arise to rescue them from corruptions which threatened to destroy them? Where was the redeemer of Israel? Why did he tarry? Had God forgotten Palestine and altogether forsaken mankind?

Normally, at about the age of eighteen years, the Galilean young men married. How, then, was it that Jesus of Nazareth, the most human of our race, who, as the New Testament insists, had all our bodily passions, yet without sin,[2] never married?

The fact that most modern 'Christians' burke this question, and will be scandalized at its being raised, is one of the many reasons for recovering the true picture of Jesus as presented in the Gospels, those first records of the

---

[1] Pelham, *Outlines of Roman History*, page 435.   [2] Hebrews iv. 15.

Christian community, and as supported by the orthodox [1] theology of that community from the beginning. No one dares, in the face of the New Testament evidence, to describe him as a woman-hater: neither was he indifferent to women, for the Christian community, with its vivid memories of the real Jesus, was able to fight successfully the speculative prudes [2] who would have made him the mere ghost of a man lacking all virile capacity, without bodily parts or passions.

He did not despise marriage: he blessed the marriage feast of Cana, he speaks of the love of man and woman as divine, and places the true marriage union above even the obligation to parents. On one occasion his disciples interpret him as despising marriage and its offspring, and he deliberately blesses children in correction of this misinterpretation. [3]

He champions women, and has many women followers; his close and unconventional friendships with women, often even with harlots, [4] scandalize his opponents. Why, then, did he not marry?

When the times are out of joint, and the daily life of men has been forced into unnatural and abnormal channels, he who knows himself 'born to set things right' is driven from the normal path in order that he may create a normal world for his fellows. Though farming be the normal life of the yeoman, when abnormal vices threaten the country's life, he leaves his plough to save his country: the lover leaves his lass to join up in some battle of the oppressed. The golden age was ahead but could not be brought into being without a terrific struggle and in-

---

[1] The *conventional* pietist theology of to-day must not be confused with *orthodox* theology, i.e. the theology accepted and developed by the historic Christian body from the beginning.

[2] They came to be called 'Docetists,' i.e. those who held that Jesus was a phantom and no true man, only having the *appearance* of man.

[3] 'Whom God hath joined together,' i.e. the love of God. According to Catholic theology the ministers of marriage are not the priests but the contracting parties.

[4] e.g. his friendship with the Magdalene and with publicans and 'sinners,' which term in the language and thought of his day generally meant harlots.

conceivable sacrifices. That this was the motive for his sacrifice of that love of woman which leads to marriage, home, and children is evident from his own poignant saying—there are some that have made themselves eunuchs for the Kingdom of Heaven's sake.[1]

If then he early felt driven to give himself to some colossal enterprise, as yet but dimly conceived in his mind, why was it that the years passed and still found him at the carpenter's bench? This, if not an insoluble problem, is at least one that has never yet been solved. One feels convinced of the psychological fitness of these long years of waiting, especially in face of the dynamic force of the public ministry into which he is at last driven, but if any one had asked him at the age of twenty-seven or twenty-eight why he had not yet taken the field, I think he would have found it hard to give a completely satisfactory answer to his questioner, or perhaps even to himself. Those questionings 'if Thou be the Son of God' of a later period do suggest an internal conflict and hesitation that probably were present in these years of waiting; he may well have thought that if the hour had not yet struck for some titanic public struggle, still there was something of leaven and of healing in the work of the craftsman honestly done, the making of a plough, the sailing of a boat, the mending of a net.

Before the new world could be brought into being he was convinced that someone must emerge, who would aim at an entire change in the national outlook; the axe must be laid to the root of the tree; an attack on the avarice and pride and those other lusts which were ruining private and public life must at all costs be made. Of this he was convinced, but he was not convinced that God was urging him to do this preliminary work. There was forming in him the conviction of a life and mission infinitely more constructive and creative than the work of the ancient prophets, and yet the emergence of a new prophet calling the people to repentance was as absolutely necessary as

[1] Matthew xix. 12.

the clearing of forest lands before they can be sown and become fruitful. Where was this prophet to be found? From what group would he come?

Not from the Essenes, who, giving up the struggle as hopeless, had retired into the wild country and formed communal groups for prayer and purification. They could, at any rate, save their own souls, yet how could one do this unless one took 'the whole heaviness of this wrong world's weight' upon one? It was not in isolation from the shiftless miserable bulk of mankind that the prophets had lived and done their work. The Essenes did not believe in the golden age ahead; it was for that age that the prophets had died.

What hope was there from government circles in the South, from the Sadducees, rich landlords, and cynical speculators, or from their prime minister, Caiaphas, appointed by imperial foreigners to do their ugly work for them? These folk believed in no resurrection of the nation, nor of the righteous dead to share in the triumph of the good time coming.

We have already spoken of his disillusionment about those other members of the southern government, the Pharisees, whose hypocritical pretences in the matter of the golden age were even more dangerous than the cynicism of the Sadducees. What prophet could arise from such a party?

There was, indeed, that small but growing group among them, sincere enough and gaining in power, who later became known as the Zealots, but their jingo imperialism and colossal self-satisfaction gave no hope that they would either repent themselves or urge the necessity of national humility.

The only hope lay in that little Redemptionist group, scattered up and down the country; as yet they had not found a voice. Would it be from their ranks that the prophet would arise?

CHAPTER IX

THOSE few people who were aware of the existence of the Redemptionist group would be inclined to lay stress on the smallness of their numbers, their exclusiveness, the absence of big names among their leaders and their waiting policy. It was all very well for them to say that their hour had not yet come, but would it ever come? There was so much devotion, so much eager expectation, but where were the practical results? It was all very well to criticize the Pharisees, whether activist or fatalist, to dissociate themselves from the 'save your own souls' Essenes, to pour scorn upon the plutocratic Sadducees, but what practical good were they doing themselves? What influence had they upon the nation?

Suddenly the criticism was silenced, for the Redemptionists had found their spokesman, and a voice was heard above that wilderness of counter-cries and delusion, proclaiming that the New World was thundering at their doors, and calling upon men so completely to revolutionize their lives and their outlook that they might seize upon it and make it their own, lest they be ground to powder in the coming destruction.

Who was this herald of the dawn?

In the days of Herod the Great two prominent members of the Redemptionist group in the South were the priest Zacharias and his wife Elizabeth. They had dreamed in their youth that if ever they had a son they would dedicate him to the movement, but the years passed and they were getting old and Elizabeth was barren. They had long ago given up the dream, and Zacharias seems to have become despondent and to have settled down into the routine of his temple duties. But one day the honour of offering the incense in the sanctuary came to him, and as the smoke of the incense curled heavenwards, his heart leapt up with it in ardent longing for the coming of the good world. Was God's arm shortened? Why could not the freedom and prosperity of a hundred years ago—of the reign of John Hyrcanus, when it was still true to say that every man lived under his own vine and his own fig-tree, the reign of which the good old Anna and Simeon were always talking—be restored? True he could not now have a son whom he could name after that patriot king, and as that bitter thought once more threatened to darken his hope he is suddenly aware of God's messenger, who said to him: Fear not, Zacharias; for your prayer is heard; and your wife Elizabeth shall bare you a son, and you shall call his name John. Don't be downhearted, for you will have joy and gladness; and many shall rejoice at his birth. For he shall be great in God's sight, and shall drink neither wine nor strong drink; and he shall be filled with the spirit even from his mother's womb. And many of the children of Israel shall he turn to the Lord thy God. And he shall go before him in the spirit and power of Elijah, to turn the hearts of the fathers to the children, and the disobedient to the wisdom of the just; to make ready a people prepared for the Lord. [1] But dark despondency still held down the spirit of Zacharias and he would not give himself to this hope. He asks for some conventional sign and the immediate reply is a sign arising out of the very nature of his own inner state. Just as his soul was paralysed by hopelessness, so now this inner constriction suddenly affects his speech and he becomes dumb; that dumbness can only be removed when belief returns with the fulfilment of the angel's promise in the birth of the child.

But Elizabeth conceived. She has never shared his despondency. She rejoices, and in her buoyant faith is the first to recognize that the baby of her young cousin Mary, will be the Messiah. Mary, who is pregnant, stays with her till the Baptist is born. The neighbours say

[1] See Luke i.

the child should be called after his father, but Elizabeth, filled with the hope of the restoration of the glories of John's reign, wants him called John. So they appeal to Zacharias, who writes now in his recovered joy and belief: 'His name *is* John.' And at once that inward renewal and its definite expression in the writing affects his speech, removing the inhibition, and his mouth was opened and his tongue loosed, and he spake praising God: because in the coming of this child, He had visited and redeemed His people, as He had promised by the prophets, that Palestine should be freed from her enemies and serve God without terror, in justice and singleness of heart, 'and thou child, shalt be called the prophet of the highest,' the herald of the coming Lord and of his commonwealth. Their sins shall be purged away in God's mercy; the dayspring from on high shall visit them, to give light to them that sit in darkness and in the shadow of death, to guide their feet into the way of peace.[1]

The child John grew and waxed strong in spirit. Luke speaks of him as being in the desert until his mission began, but a good tradition that his people moved North, and that for a time he was the playmate of Jesus and shared in the teaching Mary gave, must not lightly be dismissed; Luke may only mean that he went for some considerable time into the wild country in preparation for his work.

What had he been thinking and doing all these years? There are no records: we can only tell by his after-teaching. Whether he had been brought up with Jesus or not, they had both come to the same conclusion. On the surface this conclusion might be confused with that of the fatalist Pharisees, namely, that all the miseries that had come upon the nation through foreign conquest were deserved because the people had broken God's laws, but beneath the surface these conclusions were worlds asunder, for by 'God's law' the Pharisees meant a merciless legalism while John meant the eternal justice and humanity of the good God.

On the appointment of Pontius Pilate a crisis was

[1] See Luke ii.

K

reached. We have before noted the exhaustion of the people by relentless taxes, the appointment of 'provincial governors greedy of gold and reckless of right,'[1] and the conversion of the national government itself, both religious and secular, into a political cat's-paw of the imperial tyrants. But in the year A.D. 26 came Pontius Pilate who, in spite of the praise of the Roman historian Tacitus and all Renan's attempts at whitewashing, went beyond any of his predecessors in his almost unrelieved reign of blundering and cruelty.

The ferocity of the new governor and the consequent fury of the national opposition stir John to break the silence of years and wring from him the call to repentance. John hated the extortion and oppression of the Roman rule, because he hated extortion and oppression; but to his horror he had found them in the very heart of his own nation.   He had marked the avarice and usury of the pious and 'patriotic' leaders, who devoured the holdings of the poor: he had seen the people doped by their fellow-countrymen into acquiescence with corruption at home so long as they might shout against the extortionate foreigner. But how could avarice cast out avarice, or as Jesus was to say later: how can Satan cast out Satan? John, the patriot, loved his nation so much that he would rather have seen it ruined than flourishing upon a lie;[2] the lie must be exposed at all costs, the cancer cut out.   So, and so alone, could the prophecy of the Redemptionist group be fulfilled that the people of Palestine should be saved from their enemies, and from the hand of all that hate them, that they might serve God in holiness and justice all the days of their life.

Some time during the winter months of A.D. 25–6, the voice of this rugged prophet[3] was heard in the wild country

---

[1] Keim, *Jesus of Nazara*, vol. i, pages 305 ff.

[2] Cf. Ibsen, *Enemy of the People.*

[3] A prophet is not some magician who can foretell, or boasts that he can foretell the future, but some moral genius who dares to look the present in the face, to pierce beneath the surface and lay bare the roots and causes of things, and from this deep insight with the present, foresees its inevitable outcome in the future.

of southern Palestine, crying: 'Repent ye, for the Kingdom of Heaven is at hand.' And there went out unto him all the country of Judea, and all they of Jerusalem; and they were baptized of him in the River Jordan, confessing their sins.

It was no reed shaken by every gust of popular opinion, no court preacher immaculately dressed and living on the fat of the land, that had drawn[1] them out into the wilderness. Dressed in coarse clothing with a leather girdle about his loins, and nourished on such scanty fare as he found to hand, he seemed to them to have been nurtured by those elemental forces of mountain and desert among which he moved.

Why did the proclamation of the Kingdom of Heaven attract crowds, and what would they understand by it? Although the term itself is scarcely found in the Old Testament, and is not even the most common term for the New World in the Utopian literature of that day, all the critical historians who write of this period, opposed as they are on so many questions, are agreed that the term would call up in the mind of John's hearers the idea of that divine commonwealth with which they were perfectly familiar, and which, indeed, is the foundation of their religion as found in the Old Testament and as developed in their later literature. Schweitzer[2] thinks that the idea had for a time died down among the people, but even he admits it to be present, though dormant, and to have been aroused into flame again by the new prophet. He would be the first to admit that John, though creative, did not create an entirely new conception among the people, while Schürer, with most authorities, holds that 'the Messianic idea never quite died out, at least not in its more general form, of the hope of a better future for the nation. In any case, it was again very active in the last century before Christ, and especially in the time of Christ, as the course of the gospel

[1] Cf. Luke vii. 23–4.
[2] Schweitzer. Cf. Prologue for description of this writer and his *Quest of the Historic Jesus*.

history shows. It therefore appears as thoroughly alive among the people, without Jesus doing anything to revive it.'[1]

In our own days constructive thinkers in all countries and the more alive among the people look forward to a golden age, but interpret it in most varying ways. Some conceive it as the guild state, others as communism, others again as a distributivist community, others again as state socialism, yet all believe it will be brought about here on earth. In the same way the Jews of Palestine, both the thinkers and the common people, with the exception of the Sadducees and perhaps the Essenes, looked forward to a golden age but interpreted it in varying ways. Some conceived it as a docile age upon which a benevolent God imposed His rule, others as a creative age of God-inspired people; some as a free Palestine dominating subservient peoples, others as a free Palestine attracting to its rule willing tributaries; some as an age ruled over by a Messiah from the clouds, others by a God-inspired Messiah arising from human-kind, others again as a community doing God's will without the intervention of any Messiah: yet all believed it would be brought about here on earth.

Jesus later claims John the Baptist as the last and greatest of the prophets,[2] in that he recalled the people to the deepest and most vivid conception of the coming commonwealth as found in prophetic lore. In contrast with the rigorous and petty scribism of his day, John appeals to the eternal righteousness of those old messengers of God whom the nation had murdered.

Now, while some are preaching the complacent doctrine that God will in due time bring in the golden age without

[1] Schürer, *The Jewish People*, div. ii, vol. ii, page 136. *Religious Development between the Old and the New Testament* (Home University Library) should also be carefully studied.

[2] Scott Holland's attempt (in his posthumous work on the fourth gospel) to belittle John in order to heighten the majesty of the Christ is neither good history nor does it really do honour to our Lord, who himself exalted the Baptist and gave him the utmost importance. 'The least in the Kingdom of Heaven' follows on extreme praise of his imprisoned comrade.

any change on their part, and others that He only delays till the nation observes the thousand and one regulations which they are pleased to call His laws, John the realist lays bare the deep-lying causes of their misfortunes. The nation must repent, there must be a complete change of mind and heart and will, a rebirth of outlook, a root-and-branch renunciation of the ugly thing that masqueraded as religion in their day and a return to the ancient justice.

What was it that drew these vast crowds into the wilderness? The bulk of them came because of their hope of deliverance from the Romans, the wrathful destruction of their enemies, the dominance of a triumphant Palestine in that new world which the prophet was said to be announcing.[1] Some of the Pharisee rulers would be genuinely with the people in this hope; others, if they were to retain their hold, must seem to approve, though somehow or other they would have to square their approval with their secret treaties with the conquerors. Such few of the Sadducees as came, rejecting as they did the idea of a golden age, must have thought it politic to be there as spies of what might prove a dangerous movement; and as to baptism,[2] the ceremony would, perhaps, be a mere form, and involve them in nothing.

But once in the wilderness, the crowds and their rulers were met, not by some comforting assurance of speedy triumph, but by a series of blows, under which many of them reeled with amazement, for to the crowds that went out to be baptized of him—and especially to their rulers [3] —John thundered, 'Ye offspring of vipers, who hath warned you to flee from the wrath to come?' They would

---

[1] Such an announcement always drew its crowd, as witness the movements of Judas of Galilee, Theudas, Bar-Cochba, and others. Perhaps this John was the Messiah himself, or at least his eagerly expected forerunner.

[2] Baptism was practised among the Jews of a later generation, and probably in John's day, as part of the formal and ceremonial admission of proselytes. It does not seem to have had much moral significance. John's baptism must not be confused with the frequent 'washings' current among the Essenes.

[3] Cf. Matthew iii. 7 ff. Cf. Luke iii. 7 ff.

often have seen the grass and thistle of the desert blazing
for miles, and sometimes the brushwood of the Jordan
valley was deliberately cleared in this way, and scorpions
and vipers would scuttle away before the wrath of smoke
and flame.   The ruling classes would be infuriated at this
thrust of the prophet, for the priestly prime minister and his
kinsmen were often charged with a whispering like the hiss-
ing of vipers, in reference to their private influence on the
judges, whereby they perverted the course of justice, and
to other of their secret political and ecclesiastical deals.[1]

The easy notion current among many that 'the wrath
to come' was to be poured out upon the foreign nations,
while they, the aristocracy of Abraham, secure in their
Jewish birthright, would escape the judgment, would prove
their death-trap.   This complacent optimism was boldly
challenged: 'Bring forth, therefore, fruits worthy of repentance, and begin not to say within yourselves, We have
Abraham to our father; for I say unto you that God is able
of these stones to raise up children unto Abraham.   And
even now is the axe also laid unto the root of the trees:
every tree, therefore, that bringeth not forth good fruit is
hewn down, and cast into the fire.' [2]

Although the Pharisees had had a considerable following
among the people, and it had been a shallow Pharisaic
view of the new world that had drawn the multitude into
the wilderness, there must have been beneath the surface
of the people's complacence a certain uneasiness, some
stirrings of discontent with their rulers and with themselves.
This smouldering discontent blazed into real repentance
at the call of the prophet, and wrung from them the cry,
What, then, must we do?

His answers were blunt and practical, reminding them
of Elijah, that prophet of the ancient justice, who had
denounced the mighty for robbing the poor man of his
holding, and who had called the whole nation back to
realities.

[1] Edersheim, *Life and Times of Jesus,* vol. i, pages 263 ff.
[2] Luke iii. 8, 9.

In that crowd there were many who were wearing the overcoat[1] of the 'comfortable classes' above the coat generally worn, while some were without even necessary clothing. Many were amply provisioned, others were without food. So to their 'What, then, must we do?' he replied: 'He that hath two coats, let him impart to him that hath none: and he that hath food, let him do likewise.'

Then there were the tax-gatherers, who asked for his baptism. The system of farming out the taxes afforded ample opportunity for extortion and robbery, not only among the absentee shareholders, but among the smaller people, the actual collectors who worked for them. When they said to him: 'Master, what shall we do?' he replied: 'Extort no more than that which is appointed you.' There were soldiers in that crowd, possibly imperial infantry on the march or perhaps some native troop employed by Herod. These were quartered upon the peasantry and, not satisfied with their rations or army pay, would eat the people out of house and home. They were notorious for their pillaging of the natives with violence, and for cheating by blackmailing on false accusation. To their 'And we, what shall we do?' he replies: 'Extort by threats from no one, neither blackmail by false charges, and let your rations suffice.'[2]

Of course, these are merely a few examples of his dealing with various sections of what must have been an enormous crowd, but the writers chose them to show the practical repentance demanded by him. Some modern Socialists, misled by misinterpretations of the pietists and by blind prejudice, make light of this counsel of John, as they do of the counsels of Jesus after him, for how ridiculous to

[1] Cf. Gould, *St. Mark*, page 107. (T. & T. Clark, 1912.)

[2] Note carefully the Greek of this passage and cf. Farrar, *St. Luke*, page 88. (Cambridge University Press, 1890.) Some pietists have had the affrontery to use this text as an argument that Jesus (!) forbids workmen to ask for an advance in wages. The Greek word is apparently not 'wages,' but 'soldiers' rations': the Greek word 'content' is not 'contentment in the mind,' but a word meaning to avail or suffice. As given in our text above, the translation, though free, is very accurate. The 'violence to no man' of the Authorized Version refers really to forcible pillaging and, of course, has no reference to warfare.

attempt to solve the social question by personal generosity and private almsgiving! This, then, is the end of all John's talk about a new world—the present system tempered by a great deal of individual brotherly kindness.

Such an interpretation, however, is a complete travesty of the proclamation of John the Baptist. The party to which a child is going is not the frock in which it goes, but the frock is a preparation for the party. The new world for which John was seeking to prepare the people did not consist in mere acts of generosity and kindness, but they were absolutely essential as a preparation for the coming of that world. People say, What are John and Jesus to us now? What can men or gods of thousands of years ago matter to the present generation? But if Socialists or trades unionists, reformists or revolutionists, are attempting to get their new world without such a repentance among the nations and individuals of our day as John preached, it will be a damnable failure.

That this preaching in the desert was what is called eschatological—that is, was the proclamation of a new era arising out of the ruins of the existing system—is, as has been shown, a commonplace of contemporary scholarship, and both the pietists who preach a parody of the old religion and the agnostics who airily reject it, must alike abandon their ignorant contempt of history; they must be prepared to do some hard mental work, and to abandon their prejudices.

John's preaching of the naked truth wedged its way into that crowd, dividing those, who had some sincerity left, from the hopelessly corrupt. If John's preaching had been a mere preaching of personal kindliness, the government would have let it alone. Even if it had been merely the urging of the rich to share to some extent with the poor, it would not much have mattered. But the urging of such acts as the preparation for the coming of a world where the first should be last and the last first, of a world which could only be established on the ruins of the present order in which they were so deeply and guiltily involved, this terrified the native government, both North and South; and Herod, noting the rapid growth of the movement, and furious, not only at the attack on his personal morality, but also on his many political misdeeds,[1] arrested and silenced the prophet.

The popular movement started by John was so mighty that even the arrest of the leader could not entirely crush it. Herod still dreaded it,[2] as did the rulers of Jerusalem.[3] We find traces of the Baptist's movement in distant Asia Minor a long time after,[4] and even Josephus, who always tries to minimize [5] revolutionary tendencies among the Jews, is obliged to emphasize the dimensions and importance of this movement.

He even records [6] that his fellow-countrymen believed that the disaster a few years later, Herod's defeat and the destruction of his army by the Arabs, was God's retribution for his murder of the prophet.

At last the coming kingdom had been announced in the new way which was, as all fresh and living things are, the ancient way, the way of the prophets of old. Probably John did not conceive of the new world as a commonwealth of nations. Possibly he did not conceive of its God as writing His law in men's hearts and their very nature. He may have thought of a distant God dominating men with His rules and commands and of a dominant Israel, ordering subject nations, but, at least, the commands of this God were just and loving and reasonable, and the commands of imperial Palestine ruling the nations in His name would be just and beneficial, and acceptable to the subject peoples. The dominance of Palestine in the coming era was not to

---

[1] Luke iii. 19: '. . . and for all the evil things which Herod had done.' Cf. Josephus, *Antiquities*, XVIII, ch. v, sec. 2: 'Herod who feared lest the great influence John had over the people might put it into his power and inclination to raise rebellion.'

[2] Mark vi. 16.

[3] Matthew xxi. 26.

[4] Acts xviii. 25 and xix. 3.

[5] In order to persuade his Roman imperialistic friends that the Jewish people were on the whole docile and law abiding.

[6] Josephus, *Antiquities*, XVIII, ch. v, sec. 2.

*K

be for gain but for service. Of the nature of the coming world he did not profess to have a clear conception, except that he denounced current notions of it and proclaimed the only kind of repentance that could make the nation worthy of it. Without such a repentance, it could not come, or if it came, it would grind the chosen people, who fondly imagined themselves to have the sole monopoly of it, to powder. Beyond this he claimed to know nothing but this—he would never give up preaching. He did not claim to be the Messiah of the kingdom. He did not claim even to be its expected prophet.[1] He did not claim anything, except certainty of the truth of his message, being driven on by the God of his fathers. There would arise one mightier than himself, who would know the very secrets of the new world; this leader and lord of men must come, and perhaps was even now in their midst.

At last, then, there had rung out in Palestine the longed-for voice long expected by the little Redemptionist group, and this 'back to realities' movement of John the Baptist drew not only men and women from the South and midlands, but many a northerner—peasant holders from mountains, craftsmen, fishermen from the Galilean lake, and among them there came the carpenter of Nazareth, who, year by year, had waited for this note to be struck, hoping against hope for such a moment. Now his tools were thrown down and his decision was made. 'It came to pass in those days that Jesus came from Nazareth of Galilee and was baptized of John in the Jordan.'

In contrast to the modern watered conception of Jesus, the 'Gentle Jesu, meek and mild,'[2] there stands out the Church's conception of the real historical Jesus, as suggested in her choice of a lesson at Christmastide with which she introduces his birth. 'Every battle of the warrior is with confused noise, and garments rolled in blood.' The

---

[1] John i. 20 ff.

[2] 'Gentle Jesu.' I shall deal in a later section with the apparent paradox of his anger and his love: whether rightly or wrongly the Baptist did not expect a mild Messiah.

modern pietist would expect Isaiah to continue: 'But this shall be with mildness and genteel moderation,' but he actually proceeds to something more terrific than confusion, blood, and noise: 'But this shall be with burning and with fuel of fire,[1] for unto us a child is born.' So also John the leveller is convinced that his own method will be like water compared to the fire of the coming leader. The water of his baptism was the outward sign of that necessary cleaning of the people's mind and will, to prepare them for the flaming gospel of the Christ. 'I indeed baptize you with water; but there cometh he that is mightier than I, the latchet of whose shoes I am not worthy to unloose; he shall baptize you with the wind and the fire:[2] whose winnowing fan is in his hand, thoroughly to cleanse his threshing floor, and to gather the wheat into his granary; but the chaff he will burn up with unquenchable fire.'

When Jesus came to be baptized, John 'would have hindered him, saying, I have need to be baptized of thee, and comest thou to me?'

The fourth gospel makes the Baptist say: 'I knew him not,' but St. Luke says they were cousins, and there is the tradition of their being early playmates. The accounts may be contrary, but there is no need to assume this. It is quite possible that the child John may have made a long stay in the North with his cousins or even have lived with them for some time; in fact, we know the tremendous respect John's mother had for her younger cousin Mary, and how the whole group to which they both belonged had looked to Mary's child for future leadership.[3] What more likely than that the two families should have been in close touch; then, as the years went on, they seem to have

---

[1] Isaiah ix. 5.

[2] It is difficult to translate the gospels into vivid English which will convey the actual sense to modern readers. 'Wind' is not satisfactory, but the 'Holy Ghost' has become a conventionalized phrase, further still from the original meaning. The 'Divine Wind' or the 'breath of God' perhaps is better. The Baptist then in the wild country would be thinking of the ways of God in terms of tempest and flame.

[3] Luke i and ii.

gone their separate ways, and latterly John had by some inner drive of the spirit sought the desert solitude, as the prophets before him, in preparation for his work. He may have loved Jesus as a boy and often wondered whether there was not some tremendous destiny in store for him, but could this carpenter's son, working away quietly at his craft, be the long-expected God-filled leader of the new world that was coming?

Often in a flash the truth rushes in, and when he saw him come and felt the old conviction of his own inferiority, and looked upon that face which was so often to appeal to men with intense and healing potency, the truth would suddenly burst upon him that this was the Messiah.

The humility of Jesus, the greater undergoing the baptism of the less, would not diminish, but enormously increase, the baptizer's conviction of his dignity. The courtesy and mutual respect of these two leaders of men shines through all the stories. Jesus replies to John's hesitation to baptize him: 'Suffer it now, for thus it becometh us to fulfil all justice.'[1]

> Pride juggles with her toppling towers,
> They strike the sun and cease,
> But the firm feet of humility,
> They grip the ground like trees.[2]

The new leader was determined not to take the field before he had completely identified himself with this movement. This was to be his starting-point. Without this he would not have come forward. He had waited for it all these years. Now at last, after the ground-work had been laid in this root-and-branch repentance, the new creative movement can come into being. On no other foundation could it be laid.

---

[1] The Greek word δικαιοσύνη means 'justice,' and is translated always in Latin by 'Justitia.' It has a richer meaning than mere justice alone, and the Authorized Version 'righteousness' would be a good translation, except that like so many other 'religious' terms, it has come to mean so little, or even to have a perverted and artificial meaning.

[2] From Gilbert K. Chesterton's *Ballad of the White Horse.*

In going into the Jordan and allowing the Baptist to pour over him the waters,[1] he allied himself with the justice, the comradeship, the courage, the purity of the prophets and martyrs of the past, fulfilled and consummated in this last voice crying in the wilderness. The new world was to go deeper and wider than this. It was to be so far deeper and higher and broader than the conception of the Baptist that the least in the Kingdom of Heaven would be greater than John, and yet without this daring and profound preparation, the new world would have been inconceivable. The eternal foundations had once more, and more thoroughly than ever before, been laid bare.

'And straightway coming up out of the water,' Jesus, illuminated in the light of this act of humility, in the deliberate identification of himself with all the living past, 'saw the heavens rent asunder and the spirit as a dove descending upon him: and a voice came out of the heavens: "Thou art My beloved son, in thee I am well pleased."'

---

[1] Or immerse him: it is uncertain whether the person was dipped under or stood in the stream and had water poured over him.

CHAPTER X

INTO THE DESERT

WE have seen that Jesus, though familiar with current literature, had drawn only sparingly from it for his own mental development, and had found nourishment for his mind chiefly in Moses, the Law, and the Prophets. We have seen, moreover, that his use of these was highly selective; his spirit instinctively seized upon the more vivid and generous conceptions in them, and he may even in his youth have sometimes found himself rejecting, or at least going behind, the thought of the greatest of these teachers of the old covenant—as he certainly did in his maturity.

John the Baptist was, in any case, the voice of the past, and the voice of all that was most living in that past. He was recalling the nation to all that was most fundamental in the ancient conception of the Kingdom of Heaven. The fact that Jesus took up the phrase from John's lips, submitted himself to John's baptism, is found continually referring to the ancient tradition, makes it impossible to regard him as a mere innovator, separating himself from the ancient conception of the kingdom, and using its terms in a completely different sense: but the fact that he found himself questioning even the greatest leaders of the past, deepening and widening their outlook, and challenging Moses himself, must have forced upon him the most disturbing problem of the nature of his own personality. Who then am I, who, child of the past, am yet its master?

The greater the man, the greater that paradox within him of humility and confidence. Jesus had neither the bombastic self-assurance of the fool who steps in where angels fear to tread, nor that false humility of a Hamlet that paralyses leadership. There often comes to a man in the moment of some daringly generous acknowledgment

of another man's work and personality, a stupendous conviction about his own. John was come in the way of
justice reviving the ancient realities of the Kingdom of
Heaven, to this extent anticipating the work of Jesus.
Jesus does not resent this, nor allow himself to be over-
critical because John's way of putting things would be
cruder than his own. He generously and completely
recognizes the validity of John's work, submitting himself
to his baptism as would any other mere disciple, for thus it
became him to commit himself to the whole revival of the
old justice;[1] thus Jesus, creator of the future, submits
to John, restorer of the past. In the daring humility of
that act there breaks in upon him the answer to that oft-
recurring problem about his own work and person: 'Thou
art My beloved son in whom I am well pleased.' Thou art
that very leader through the tribulation into the new world.

If he had felt himself to be another John, at the same
point of view, but more eloquent and better equipped for
the task, the spirit would have driven him into the public
arena; but if this overwhelming conviction were true,
what then? Immediately the spirit drives him from the
haunts of men to consider whether it was indeed a reality,
and to face the future which it involved.

Often after the sudden conviction comes the reaction,
and so it happened with Jesus. At the moment of baptism
he had been certain he had heard the very voice of God,
but again in the wilderness doubts crowd in upon him.
'Am I, in reality, this son of God, this greater than all the
prophets? Is it the evil or the good in me, the illusion or
the reality, that insists that I am greater than John? Is
it the voice of God or the voice of the Devil that tells me
that I am the representative of the race who has grasped
the meaning of the kingdom more fully than John, and
made it my own more completely than any other man?
Is it of its own very nature so completely mine that before
time was I had somehow to do with it in the mind of God,
and was destined to be not only its child but its master?'

[1] Matthew iii–xv.

People are often tempted through their good instincts as well as through their bad, so that it is difficult to see whether it be God or Devil tempting. The Devil appears as God's angel using the very words of Scripture to support his suggestions. The temptation within the temptations was to think that it was God and not Satan who suggested: 'If thou be the Son of God.' [1]

In considering the key temptations one by one, we shall find that they were temptations, not only to convince his crowd or to bring in the kingdom a certain way, but to do certain daring acts, which, in the natural course of events, would mean destruction, but which, if he were really the Son of God, would supernaturally be turned into victory. The temptation was to accept current and conventional views of the Son of God, and of what was expected of him as Messiah. 'Unless I am able "to bring off" these amazing victories expected of me how can I ever convince myself, let alone my crowd, that I am in reality the Messiah about whom we have been taught from our youth up?'

Of course these expectations varied, including magnificent acts of patriotism in the spirit of their ancient heroes, and trivial imitations of certain historic deeds that once had glowed with meaning. The great leaders had wished to see their people free and powerful and crowned with plenty. The waters of Jordan had divided that they might escape into freedom, the walls of Jericho had fallen that they might establish their power and enter into a land of plenty. Certain 'messiahs' nearly contemporary with Jesus, giving themselves out as sons of God and the saviours of their country, no doubt honestly wished to free their people, and to see them established in power and prosperity, but the futility of their actions suggests that their conceptions of power and freedom were futile. They were,

[1] Accounts of the temptations must have come from our Lord himself, who after the fight had been won would clearly see that it was the Devil and not God that suggested certain things to him: but the fact that the temptations came through the very words of scripture suggests that he might well have mistaken them for the voice of God at the time and that no small part of the struggle was in deciding whether they were of God or Satan.

after all, mere copyists, and the copyist almost always copies wrongly, because he has lost the urge and meaning of the original deed. One such, in complete misunderstanding of the purpose for which the waters of Jordan divided, and thinking of God as the divine conjurer, went to infinite pains to get his crowd across Jordan and argued with them that, as he was the true messiah, God was bound at his word to divide the waters of the river so that they could return on dry land.[1] Another took a great crowd out into the country and commanded the walls of Jerusalem (their own capital!) to fall. There was not only something radically wrong with their ideas of liberty and power, but with their ideas of God. God does not act in this way, and it is not surprising that these honest dupes of convention should have gone down in history as false messiahs. It was not thus that Jesus was tempted, in spite of the general pietist interpretation of the temptations which would seem to put him on a level with these deluded claimants.[2]

It is worth noting that only two temptations are prefaced with 'If thou be the Son of God,' namely, the suggestion that he should turn stones into bread, and the suggestion that he should cast himself down from the pinnacle. Now I hope to show that these temptations were not trivial but magnificent, that they were concerned with what was greatest, and not what was meanest in the current expectation of the nature of the Messiah and of the nature of his kingdom.

The refusal to accept the role suggested to him (by God or Satan?) might well have seemed to him a refusal of the one possible test of his capacity to lead and of his divine vocation to the leadership.

[1] The Romans seem to have taken advantage of this elaborate delay to fall upon them and to destroy them.

[2] The pietist would, of course, reply that Jesus resisted the temptations, but our point is that dividing the waters, falling from pinnacles without hurt, and demolishing walls are miracles, purposeless except as proving he was the Divine Leader, and are not temptations that would be likely to appeal to a great nature. On the other hand, if they made no appeal to him there was no temptation.

CHAPTER XI

THE FIRST TWO TEMPTATIONS

THE mind of Jesus was so concentrated upon the terrific problems of the coming commonwealth and his relation to it that he forgot to take food.[1] He wandered[2] about the desert torn by conflicting thoughts. There had been the flash of intuition at the baptism followed by the natural reaction, but during this long conflict of the desert his spirit was winning through to a more reasoned conviction of his leadership. After his forty days' fast the strife left him exhausted, the body reasserting its claims —'he was afterwards a-hungered.'

To the imaginative mind of Jesus, his own hunger would inevitably call up a picture of his hungry people, starved by the conditions that the conquering foreigner imposed and the exactions of the native governing class. The food problem was ever with them and from the years of his boyhood the spectre of want had increasingly haunted him. It had threatened his own home and the homes

---

[1] Forgot to take food, or, as in the case of so many great leaders, deliberately fasted, in order that his body should not interfere with his spirit in this great mental conflict.

[2] If St. Luke's vivid Greek phrasing is here correct, cf. Liberty, *The Political Relations of Christ's Ministry*, page 48, though with this author I prefer Matthew's account of the temptations. Luke, the careful historian, is often to be preferred to Matthew, but Luke is a Greek and would be unfamiliar with the intensely national and patriotic problems raised in the temptations, problems which would be fully appreciated by the Jewish Matthew, whose account forms the basis of our present edition of the gospel that bears his name. Matthew's sequence of the three temptations is more convincing than that of Luke. This point is fully dealt with by Stephen Liberty, and his book was the first, so far as I know, to give an intelligible account of the temptations, and forms the basis of my further researches on the subject. Students should secure this work, but should be aware of Liberty's pro-Roman Empire bias, and in the light of the evidence against the empire given earlier will be in a position to discount it.

of his peasant kinsmen. He had seen the bankruptcy of many a family: the merciless creditor, the threat of the bailiffs; poor debtors sold into slavery; countless evictions; the grip of the money-lender drawing tighter and tighter; the worker driven from the soil; banks of exchange flourishing; speculators multiplying their capital five-fold and ten-fold; in a word, 'the material ruin which Rome and her vassals had brought upon the land.' [1] If he was, indeed, the Son of God, who was to inaugurate the golden age, he must give his people plenty. It was to be a kingdom of fruitfulness. This was what was expected of the Messiah; this was what a real Messiah, filled with passionate love for his people, was bound to achieve. 'If thou be the Son of God, command that these stones be made bread,' turn your creative energies to the task of converting these barren stony lands into fields of corn.

It is a common heresy of the 'religious' to belittle the mind at the expense of the heart, and to preach Jesus as the sacred heart, forgetting that he is also the sacred mind, the sacred imagination, and the sacred will. Sentimentalism seeks thus to magnify Jesus, but only succeeds in making him a holy weakling. There were in reality immeasurable possibilities in him. He could have turned his energies into this or that channel; whether he could, by a sudden effort, have miraculously changed stones to bread, or whether he would have done this by concentrating his mind on the problem of production by anticipating the discoveries of modern chemical science, does not much signify; the temptation was to be absorbed in the problem of supplies, and to bank his energies up into that particular channel, for, however great his human genius, however great his reserve of force, he was subject to limitations. He suffered hunger, and he suffered exhaustion.[2] He could at the outset of his public life choose an avenue for

---

[1] Hausrath, *Time of Jesus*, vol. i, page 189.
[2] Mark v. 30. Luke viii. 46. He perceived that virtue had gone out of him. The word virtue means strength. The acts of healing cost him much. 'He felt that his strength had been drawn from him.'

his energy; he could *not* act in every direction at the same moment. His resources were huge, but like other men he had to harbour them and concentrate his energy if he were to do his work in the world.

But what better channel for his energy could there be than solving the food problem, relieving want, proving his leadership to himself and his people by being the bringer of plenty? What more human, what more divine could there be than such a course? Moreover, it fulfilled the expectations of both scribes and people; it was in the line of the ancient Messianic hope.

But terrible as was the problem of food and the material pressure, he had been convinced that John had struck the right note in his 'axe-to-the-root' campaign. The country must be brought back to realities. No mere tinkering with the food problem would do that; no mere policy of social reform. As a disciple wrote years after—the Kingdom of God is not food and drink, but justice and peace and the divine spirit of comradeship.[1] Neither happiness nor peace nor splendid life could be secured simply by increasing the food supply. It was not that the coming commonwealth had nothing to do with material needs nor the bodies of men. It was to have its tangible expression in these things. All these material things would be added to a world of comrades who had learned the secret of the kingdom, but flesh and blood [2] can neither create nor inherit the Kingdom of God. It does not consist in what is, in our day, miscalled charity, nor in higher wages nor in clever schemes for improving the food supply,

---

[1] Romans xiv. 17. 'Righteousness,' i.e. justice. Joy in the Holy Ghost, i.e. such joy as is described in Acts iv. 31-2, when a group lived in the joy of the Holy Ghost: all filled with the Spirit, i.e. the spirit of love and justice and comradeship which inspired them to a generous communal life, like the life of God himself.

[2] 1 Corinthians xv. 50. St. Paul fervently believed that men and women, with all that is essential to their full human personality, would inherit the kingdom, but the merely fleshly and lumpish and material could neither give the urge and energy to storm the kingdom nor find any place within it. He preached the resurrection of the body, but of the body transmuted by the spirit, by the imagination and the will.

or the supply of houses, or clothing. There must be an entire change of outlook, a fresh imagination, a new set of the collective will. 'Man shall not live by bread alone, but by every word that proceedeth out of the mouth of God.' What are these words of God that will transform the world?

God spake unto the fathers by the prophets. Jesus was thinking of those burning words of justice and liberty and equity that had poured forth from the men of old time and from his great comrade John. It was such words as these that exhilarated the people and inspired them. They alone could bring life and renovation. The right spirit must be renewed in the nation. Thus and thus only could the new world be established. Besides this shallowness of merely trying to get surface things right, there was a practical consideration that had to be taken into account. What would be the good of increasing the food supply, so long as imperial Rome were left in possession? Increasing taxation would absorb all the benefits of an increased production. And, after all, was the Messiah really the bringer of plenty? Would he not inevitably fail to give his people that, if he did not remember that other thing they expected, and perhaps rightly expected, of him? Did not their national history demand of him that he should bring them liberty, and if he could do that, would not plenty follow in its train? Liberty was surely one of those burning words that had always proceeded out of the mouth of God. To get rid of the tyrant empire and to establish his people in freedom—that was surely the role of the Son of God. To save his people from their enemies and from the hands of all that hate them— this must be his first task. Then would the land yield her increase and God, even their own God, would bless them.

Was he in reality the Son of God? Then he must bring plenty and liberty. But the order of the two must be reversed; as, indeed, it was reversed in the clearest patriotic thought of the past. His own insight had convinced him that the poverty that oppressed his people was an effect rather than a cause, and that the cause lay largely in the Roman occupation.[1] How then must he act, if this burden of Roman oppression was to be lifted from Palestine?

Action of some sort there must certainly be. Of that he was convinced. He was not now, nor ever subsequently, attracted by the majority Pharisee policy of inaction. Such a policy was never even a temptation to him. But there was a minority of the Pharisees who diverged from the main body in that they believed that the coming of the kingdom could be hastened by bold action. This minority may have been a closely knit party, but consisted, more probably, of various groups and individuals drawn together into a people's front by a common hatred of Rome. In after years they became known as the Zealots. Although Josephus calls them the fourth party (Sadducees, Essenes, Pharisees, Zealots) they were really Pharisee in outlook, being zealous for the Law, hating the Romans because they interfered with its punctilious observance. This revolutionary party drew its adherents largely from Galilee, and with the Galilean love of freedom had a larger conception of the Law. They valued not only the ceremonial detail, but traditions of liberty and prosperity inherited from Maccabean times and from a further past.

'They consistently put their faith in practice by professing republican views and declaring themselves implacably

---

[1] Roman occupation: the Romans after conquering Palestine tried the experiment at first of administering the land, not indeed by native kings (as Masefield imagines in his drama *Good Friday*), but by Orientals, the Idumean Herods, whom in their ignorance of Jewish psychology, they supposed would be acceptable to the native population. The Herods governed so atrociously in the South that at last the native ruling classes, supported actively or passively by the people, petitioned for their removal and for more direct Roman administration; hence the procurators in Judea in our Lord's day. This, curiously enough, actually strengthened the Jewish rich as we shall see later. After the defeat of A.D. 70, the Romans, finding that the Jewish governing classes, though willing enough to support their policy of extortion, had not in fact been able to keep 'law and order,' assumed complete control and, 'took away their place and nation.' The government of Palestine was subject to the government of the Roman province of Syria.

hostile to royalty at home and the Romans abroad.'[1] Even Josephus, who disliked everybody who opposed his Roman patrons, has to admit that they drew to themselves all lovers of liberty.[2] 'They agree with the opinions of the Pharisees, but they are distinguished by an unshakeable devotion to liberty, holding that God alone is ruler and Lord. They consider it a trifling matter to endure extraordinary deaths and the tortures of relatives and dear ones, in their refusal to address any mortal as "Lord." And since multitudes have witnessed their immovable courage under such circumstances, I do not dwell upon it in detail. For I am not afraid that anything related of them should be disbelieved, but, on the contrary, I fear lest the narrative may do less than justice to their contempt in enduring the misery of pain.'

All their fierce patriotic hopes clustered round the Temple as the concrete embodiment of the new world freed from Roman dominion: they were a veritable temple party, who recalled to one's mind the people who were rebuked by Jeremiah for crying: 'The Temple of the Lord, the Temple of the Lord, the Temple of the Lord are these.'[3]

Now if Jesus was, as Messiah, to hurl back the Roman Power, this party with its extreme faith and splendid audacity, must inevitably have appealed to him. In its growing popularity lay the hope of the future. Surely, if he were the Messiah, he must climb to the summit of the temple party, attain the pinnacle of nationalist fame,[4] and lead his people in a desperate throw for freedom.

Now the programme of the revolutionists was not to lie

---

[1] Stapfer, page 76.

[2] Josephus, *Antiquities*, xviii, 1, 6. For Zealots, cf. articles in *Encyclopaedia of Religion and Ethics*, and Kirslopp Lake and Foakes Jackson's *Prolegomena*.

[3] Jeremiah vii. 4. Cf. the early Christians who probably adapted a current Jewish phrase to Christian use, 'Ye are the temple of the living God' (2 Corinthians vi. 16), showing that 'the temple' sometimes means a group of living people.

[4] Pinnacle of temple. Cf. our sayings 'the top of the tree' and 'the pinnacle of fame.'

in wait for the Kingdom of God, as did the fatalist [1] Pharisees, who waited for its coming by a miraculous act of God as of some *Deus ex machina*, but to force it into being by an apparently suidical act. They, the few, but of desperate and impregnable faith, would cast themselves down against the 'living walls of Rome.' Were there not abundant examples in their history that a small band, absolutely trusting in God, could vanquish hosts of evil? God was bound to turn this certain defeat, as it would appear to the wordly-wise, into victory, for had he not promised to give his angels charge over the righteous lest they be dashed to pieces? [2]

In the rebellion of A.D. 68–9 the revolutionary party, persisting in that programme which had been so tempting to Jesus in the wilderness, made the 'reckless and desperate experiment by which the Zealots meant to settle for ever the question whether Jehovah of Whom they boasted was or was not on a par with the Bels and Nebos ridiculed by their prophets as unable to defend their worshippers or their shrines, and carried into captivity with the nations who served them.' [3]

Here in the wilderness,[4] allured by the fascination of this audacious policy, Jesus had foreseen its inevitable

[1] The majority of the Pharisees were pacifists in policy, though not in principle.

[2] Cf. Liberty, *The Political Relations of Christ's Ministry*. The author's treatment of this second temptation should be carefully studied. His treatment of the first is interesting but not so convincing.

[3] Margoliouth, quoted by Liberty, *The Political Relations of Christ's Ministry*, page 67.

[4] It is just possible that although the scene of the first temptation was laid in the wilderness, the second may actually have been laid in the holy city itself on the occasion of his preliminary southern ministry. He may well have climbed to the summit of the Temple and may even have experienced that common form of vertigo, the desire to cast oneself down from a height, and the whole incident would have suggested to him the climbing to the leadership of the nationalist party and the suicidal attempt against Rome. Considering his popularity with the crowd after the expulsion of the traffickers from the Temple Court he might almost be considered as their uncrowned king, but 'he did not trust himself to them.' Should this theory be correct the third temptation would have taken place on some mountain top to which he climbed on his way from Jerusalem to Galilee.

failure.[1] When a month or so later he finds himself the
hero of a patriot crowd in Jerusalem, and later still in
Galilee is actually urged to become the Nationalist leader,
he is able, by the fact of his having already faced and fought
it in the wilderness, to reject this policy as both false and
futile.[2]

Over and over again, he warns his countrymen that it
is the road to national ruin.[3]

What right had he to assume that if he, as pinnacle and
leader of a nation in arms, were to cast himself down
upon the Roman forces, God was bound to give him the
victory? Every right, according to the very words of
the scriptures.

Had God not divided the waters, and overwhelmed
their enemies with the sea? Had He not led them with
a cloud, and all the night through with a light of fire?
He clave the hard rocks in the wilderness and the waters
gushed out like rivers. Many a time He had helped them
against overwhelming odds, and made the multitude of
their enemies like unto a wheel and as the stubble before
the wind, like as the fire that burneth up the wood and as
the flame that consumeth the mountains. Was it not the
very devil of doubt that thought not of His hand, and of the
day when He delivered them from the hand of the enemy?
Would not He give His angels charge of the nation and its
leader in so divine an adventure, for 'in their hands they
shall bear thee up, lest at any time thou dash thy foot
against a stone'?

And yet, was this not, after all, the shallow Pharisee
way of reading the nation's past? His countrymen
prided themselves on being children of Abraham, the

---

[1] That last desperate challenge of the Zealots ended in complete and
final disaster. The Palestinian rebellion of A.D. 68–70 resulted in the destruction of the Temple, the centre round which all their hopes had clustered,
and their capital was made a heap of ashes. The later rising under Bar-
Cochbar was but the final flicker of the dying Nationalist embers, and those
three years of sanguinary struggle ruined and depopulated Palestine.

[2] Cf. John iii. 26 and vi. 15.

[3] e.g. Luke xiii and Luke xxiii. 28 ff.

favoured of the most high God. But this same God who had given them countless victories was not bound by their demand nor boundaried by the national ambition. His own inheritance had provoked Him to wrath, so that He had delivered their power into captivity and their beauty into the enemy's hand. Supposing God forsook them and allowed them to bring upon themselves the final disaster? There would flash through the mind of Jesus that ancient national tragedy when his people had thought to force the hand of God by bringing the ark, His dwelling place, into the battle against the Philistines, so that the enemies were afraid, for they said: 'God is come into the camp.' But that day ended in a disaster so tremendous that the patriot mother who had just brought forth a son, the greatest joy of any Jewish woman, answered not the women who announced the birth, neither did she regard it, and dying in misery she named the child Ichabod ('The glory is departed'), because the ark of God was taken, and God had abandoned his people. Would not this final throw against the Romans end in a like disaster?

Yet he may have reasoned in his mind—what right have I to assume that such an effort must end in failure? Are not the revolutionary party, in their opposition to our conquerors, striving to establish that Messianic liberty that must be dear to the heart of God? Has He not covenanted to help them to right that suffer wrong? Is He not bound to help us? Is not this the bargain between ourselves and the most High? If we make trial of the Lord God He will not fail us.

Our God is the Lord who brought the water forth out of the stony rock, and fed us with quails in the desert: is His arm shortened that He will not give us the victory over our enemies? We must make trial of Him, and He will not fail us. But there have been victories more disastrous than defeats. Will the Lord be with us or not in such an adventure? We may fight, making trial of the Lord our God, demanding His help as our covenanted right. He may seem to keep His part of the bargain: we may succeed in what will appear to be a God-given victory, but while the fruit of that triumph is still in our mouths the heavy wrath of God may come upon us. Might not such a victory of our nation be a curse and not a blessing to mankind, and its fruits be a moral pestilence which would destroy not only our tributaries, but our own tribes, so that the last state of our nation will be worse than the first? There are writings without number in our national scriptures so that the mind is tossed to and fro among them, but it comes to its anchorage at last in this, it is written: 'Thou shalt not make trial of the Lord thy God.' [1]

In order thoroughly to understand the second and third temptations and how the mind of Jesus was led from one to the other, it will be necessary to go deeper into the Jewish politics of the day. Why should Jesus have thought that a Jewish victory over the Roman Empire might be a curse rather than a blessing?

A revolutionary movement attracts various types of men to its standard.[2] The bandit or plunderer is always present, taking advantage of the confusion of the times to line his own pockets and to exploit the movement for his

---

[1] 'The *locus classicus* for this sin is Exodus xvii. 7. In demanding water in the wilderness they were "trying" their God: they put Him to a test of their own devising—if this thing came about, they would believe in His protecting presence; if not, it was not true that He was their God. Similarly Psalm lxxviii. 18 of a later test . . . this, then, is the subtle disloyalty connoted by "tempting of God." It may wear the cloak of exuberant faith . . . but it is really arrogant and wilful with its sceptical implication that, if God does not come up to the human test, He is no God. It was, as Judith says, "putting God to the test, setting themselves above Him" (Judith viii. 12), wanting to know what He will or will not do. . . . Devising tests for the Almighty, then, "asking for signs" of His protecting power, any action designed to "force His hand" (the irreverence of the phrase is apposite!), with the *arrière pensée* that if He fails the discredit is upon Him this was the approved meaning of "tempting God" among the Jews.'—*The Political Relations of Christ's Ministry*, by Stephen Liberty, pages 65 ff.

[2] As indeed is true of constitutional parties, who uphold the *status quo*, which is sometimes not unfairly described as legalized robbery. In any case, such political parties attract to their standard a far larger number of bandits than do revolutionary movements; albeit, these bandits are garbed in top-hats and frock coats. They join forces with these parties to protect and to increase their private gains, and admit it quite blatantly.

own purposes. He, like Raisuli in modern times and Robin Hood of old, may have some crude political outlook beyond the merely personal outlook of loot and burglary, but if he robs the rich to help the poor he generally helps himself even more liberally in the process. During the revolutionary turmoil in Russia there was a great deal of private looting, and there were even instances of groups of bandits seizing a town and holding it to ransom and dominating its inhabitants with unbelievable ferocity. These people were called Bolsheviks by the European Press, and were glad enough to cloak themselves under that designation. The Moscow Government, when it had established itself, shot private looters and suppressed the bandit groups.[1] The constitutional government of Spain in its fight against Fascist rebels is faced with the same problem. This 'robber' element has been very evident in the anarchic turmoil of Balkan politics of modern times, and was, of course, a factor in the French Revolution. That it has to be taken into account when writing of the Jewish movement is evident not only from the writings of Josephus, who would be inclined to exaggerate it, but from the allusions of New Testament writers and of other historians.[2] Jesus might have allied himself with the revolutionary movement in spite of its bandit element, for this element is seldom really dominant except in the imagination of middle-class historians.

What really united the more serious types of the movement was that general contempt of the foreigner which was common to most Palestine Jews, and which was fanned into a flame of resistance by his actual presence and domination in their land. Jesus might possibly have allied himself with a movement against the Roman as tyrant, but could have no sympathy with the actual movement against the

---

[1] We are not here concerned with the charge of the ordinary Press that the Bolshevik policy is in itself robbery. Whether the commandeering of private property for public ends be right or wrong, it is on an entirely different moral level from the lootings by individuals and groups for private ends—lootings which the Bolshevik Government have sternly suppressed.

[2] John xviii. 40; cf. Luke xxii. 52.

Roman as foreigner. Supposing a nation devil-ridden by avarice were to be victorious, would it not be a substitution for the Roman demon of dominion of a Jewish devil seven-fold more powerful? In the revolutionary group would, no doubt, be some who would be Sinn Feiners rather than imperialists, but what a Sinn Fein was theirs! They wanted a 'splendid isolation,' because the rest of mankind was worthless. Just as individuals cannot save their own souls so long as they concentrate merely upon their separate salvation, so nations must wither and perish if they withdraw into themselves alone, refusing a wider and more generous outlook. 'Ourselves' is the true translation of 'Sinn Fein,' but 'Ourselves Alone' is the more fitting description of a section, not only in Ireland, but in most nationalist movements, who concentrate only on national independence and forget that interdependence which is its complement.

But the majority of the revolutionists were not really Jewish Nationalists but Jewish Imperialists. Some of them thought of the coming kingdom as a revival of the age of Solomon, and of the Messiah as 'an Oriental despot who creates an empire on the corpses of his vanquished foes.' [1] The Day of Judgment was still, for many of them, a Day of Judgment on a heathen world. These people who prided themselves on having Abraham as their father looked forward to an all-Jewish state,[2] exploiting the nations of the world, its conquered tributaries.

Others, as apocalyptic literature abundantly testifies,[3] still imperialist rather than nationalist in aim, conceived of the Jewish nation as a benevolent despotism ruling subject nations for their good. The policies of these various sections would be present in the mind of Jesus,

---

[1] Cf. Latimer Jackson, *The Eschatology of Jesus*, page 126.

[2] Including perhaps such foreigners as had submitted to circumcision.

[3] Much of the apocalyptic literature seems to go beyond this, and very nearly to attain the international outlook, but the psalms of Solomon and some other writings seem to suggest the benevolent despotism. Readers are warned against the travesty of apocalyptic literature given by Miss Dougall in *The Lord of Thought*. (Student Christian Movement, 1922.)

and all but the last he would have no difficulty in rejecting.

But what *Kultur* had these benevolent imperialists to bestow upon mankind? The Kingdom of Heaven was not, in their intention, a kingdom of naturalness, humanity, spontaneity, for the nations. It was a kingdom for the middle aged, the mentally muscle-bound rather than for little children; the child would not accept it gladly; the *Kultur* they would have given mankind was 'a fearful burden which a spurious legalism had laid upon the shoulders of the people. . . . Nothing was left to free personality, everything was placed under the bondage of the letter. The Israelite, zealous for the law, was obliged at every impulse and movement to ask himself, What is commanded? At every step, at the work of his calling, at prayer, at meals, at home and abroad, from early morning till late in the evening, from youth to old age, the dead, the deadening formula followed him.'[1]

Could the imposition of such a *Kultur* upon mankind, either by arms or by argument, be other than a curse?

[1] Schürer, *The Jewish People*, div. II, vol. ii, page 125.

CHAPTER XII

THE THIRD TEMPTATION

IT was inevitable that once Jesus had seen the hollowness of the programme suggested by the second temptation he should sooner or later abandon the whole idea of nationalist dominion with which it was essentially bound up. But the mind in rejecting a certain policy does not for the moment perceive all its implications. His struggle in the wilderness had already brought him to the certainty that liberty is more important than provender, and that the liberty preached by the Jewish revolutionary party was the Puritans' liberty—that is, liberty to impose on others a 'rigorist culture.' Must he not then abandon the conventional role of the 'Son of God,' the programme expected of a Messiah by his nationalist contemporaries?

Here in the rank swamps [1] of the desert both mind and body are oppressed and circumscribed. The Galileans loved the heights. Jesus had been brought up in a hill country and in after life, faced with tremendous issues, a climb in the mountains brings him vigour and assurance; there he could walk and talk with God; they seemed to transfigure him. 'I will lift up mine eyes unto the hills, from whence cometh my help.'

As he climbs into that free world of the hills he seems to be climbing out of the small world of Palestinian politics,

---

[1] 'Desert' or 'wilderness' calls up in the mind great stretches of sand, but the region near the Dead Sea, technically known among the Jews as 'The Wilderness,' is described by Adam Smith, in spite of fertile patches, as 'stretches of sour soil, the unhealthy jungle, the obtrusive marl, and to parched hillsides out of reach of the valley of the Jordan, which trails and winds like an enormous green serpent, more forbidding in its rankness than any open water could be, however foul or broken.'—*Historical Geography*, page 484.

with its attempt to force God's hand, its bargainings, its parochial self-satisfaction, its Pharisaic sneer at all that is not Israel. Moses from the summit, that now loomed above him, must have had a great outlook on things, and a national poet had sung: 'Ask of Me and I shall give thee the heathen for thine inheritance, and the uttermost parts of the earth for thy possessions.' [1] But Moses, after all, had wanted to annex these lands for the benefit of his own folk. Surely God's scheme of things is larger than this? The winds from far lands that beat about him as he climbed, and the mountain earth beneath his feet warmed by the universal sun, proclaimed a bigger world than Palestine. And suddenly, from the top of that exceeding high mountain, there bursts upon him a vision of the kingdoms of the world and the glory of them. He sees one at least of the great trade routes that cut through Palestine, linking up Europe with the desert people of the East, and perhaps the route that connects Egypt with Asia. He sees the caravans of many nations crawling along the roads beneath him—a Roman legion or the troops of Herod, that Edomite servant of Rome.

He would see from that height those foreign cities which Rome had planted in and around conquered Palestine. If he could not actually see, with the bodily eye, the Mediterranean, his mind's eye would travel there and his imagination would call up what he would often in reality have beheld—the Roman navy and the merchant vessels of many nations. All this would form a vision of that huge western empire embracing a multitude of nations and peoples and languages. Saturated as his mind was with the literature of his nation, the great empires of the past, which had so often threatened the national existence, would be present to his imagination. The very mountain on which he stood had seen the rise and fall of mighty empires, the Egyptian, the Assyrian, the Babylonian, the Persian, and the colossal empire of Alexander, with its nearly three thousand miles' stretch and its thrust on India. Eastward lay the desert

[1] Quoted by Liberty, *The Political Relations of Christ's Ministry*, page 69.

lands of Arab peoples, and beyond, those vast Parthian hordes, who were so constant a threat to Palestine and to the Roman Empire.

The nationalist-imperialist temple party, with their narrow Pharisaic *Kultur*, were hopeless; God could not wish the divine leader to ally himself with, or to lead, such a party. If he wanted all men in his kingdom, why not separate himself entirely from the national movement, both active and passive, and soaring above the narrower ideal of a merely Jewish empire, suggested by the pinnacle of the Temple, make a bid for the lordship of the whole world?

The more liberal Jews dispersed throughout the empire had thrown aside the narrower ideal of an all-Jewish state. This larger extra-Palestinian Judaism was a mighty force in the world; there were vast numbers of Jews among the Eastern peoples. This wider Judaism could easily have become the second great political force in the world of that day: why not the first? These Jews of the Western dispersion were 'broad-minded' people who had given up many of the customs of their forefathers, and were able to get on with the Gentile world in which they moved. They still had their own quarters in every city, but had sometimes burst the bounds of their ghettoes and, as in the case of Rome, were to be found everywhere. They looked with a more tolerant eye upon foreign civilization and had some idea of compromise. They represented their religion in a more liberal guise, and were certainly winning proselytes. Of course, many Jews of the ghettoes resisted this liberalizing tendency, but still they were not able to stem the tide. Might it not be possible to learn something from this widely dispersed liberalism, which was, in any case, infinitely to be preferred to the dead rigorism of the Palestinian movement. Might not an appeal to this wider Judaism, that discarded the 'provincialism of Palestine,' give him his opportunity?

But, after all, the larger Jewish movement had its limitations. For all its liberalism and compromise, it really despised the foreigner and found itself unable to break

L

away from certain useless, or comparatively useless, taboos. By insisting on circumcision it proved less attractive to men than to women; while relaxing much of the Jewish rule it still imposed enough of it to hinder large numbers from joining. If that rule still had life and meaning, well and good; but if it had lost its significance, at least, as believed and preached by liberal Jews, why ruin his chance of converting mankind by the imposition of this curtailed rule on would-be converts?

He had definitely rejected the leaven of the Pharisees, and was not this liberal movement, after all, a merely diluted Pharisaism? The Herods had none of these scruples, their leaven was of a very different kind. Did not the Herodian policy suggest an eminently successful way of gaining the lordship of the whole world?

The horizon widens. He has cast aside the nationalist dream. He has reviewed and rejected the project of leading that more liberal Jewish dispersion. Is he not called by God to the lordship of existing kingdoms and empires, welding them into a mighty whole and dominating them for their good?

By capturing the existing governmental machineries would he not also capture the allegiance of the peoples? If Rome had succeeded, to some extent, in mingling the peoples of the Mediterranean world, destroying frontiers, removing barriers of race and speech, and overcoming those prejudices of the mind and spirit which divide mankind— if Rome had done this in spite of her but thinly-concealed object of exploitation, how much better would he be able to weld the world together for the purpose of bringing mankind that peace it so much needed? Could not a benevolent overlord, rejecting the greed and avarice of both Gentile and Jewish imperialism, secure for the nations the freedom and plenty which were their God-given right?

Would not the capture of existing machineries secure for him the allegiance of the common man, who only longed for peace and security? After all, why make too great a demand on human nature at the first? Why not win the world by satisfying its age-long needs? Were they not anxious about what they should eat and what they should drink and wherewithal they should be clothed? After all these things the nations were seeking, and surely with reason after ages of internecine wars. Why not satisfy their immediate needs, and once having won their loyalty begin to teach them those deeper principles which the cares of hunger and bondage must for the present obscure?

What were the chances of success?

In a political world order, established and permanent, a mighty genius like Jesus of Galilee might just possibly have won his way to leadership, but in the confusion and instability of the world of his day, the rise and fall of states and empires, the insecurity of the Roman Empire itself, much less forcible personalities than his were making a by no means hopeless bid for lordship.

The amazing exploits of Alexander the Great, the building and the break-up of his far-flung empire, were in men's memories. How many since his time had climbed exceeding high mountains and dominated worlds?

The 'republic' of Rome, swollen into an empire, had been recently fighting for its very existence. The last century had been strewn with the names of dictators, who had had their hour or so upon the stage, blazing like meteors across the political skies: Pompey, Caesar, Cassius, Antony, and many another. The emperorship was but a new experiment, and even Augustus was but the first citizen of the 'republic,' and his reign, apparently so secure, was in reality shaken with war and intrigue. So far from being a stable and hereditary office, it was not until forty years after Christ's death that serious efforts were made to regularize it. Tiberius was now over sixty years of age, and speculation as to a successor was in all men's mouths. There were many claimants to the imperial purple, some from the most unlikely quarters. Subsequent history justified the passing temptation of Jesus and the dream of the Herods, in so far as Tiberius himself was murdered, and not one of the six succeeding emperors died a natural death, and in no case did a son succeed his father. So great was the chance of this imperial lordship for any man of enterprise that within half a century it was secured by a plebeian 'outsider.'

Westward lay the kingdoms of the Mediterranean and that imperialism which had absorbed them, with all its possibilities for Jesus. But turning to the east, from that high mountain top, his mind embraced the desert kingdoms and the Parthian dominions beyond. Here lay possibilities almost as tempting.

That these dreams of vast dominion, either Western or Eastern or both in combination, were by no means merely dreams, but intensely practical politics is seen in the policy of the Herodian House.

The Herods were past-masters at playing off one Power against another, and their intrigues, now with the East, now with the West, mark the policy alike of Antipater, Herod the Great, Antipas, and, in later times, Herod Agrippa.

Now Agrippa (10 B.C.–A.D. 44) was the supreme example of Herodian statecraft, and his accession to power within a few years of Christ's death, and the events that followed it, show how well within the possibilities was this gaining of the Lordship of the world by the game of 'The Balance of Power' so dear to the hearts of our contemporary statesmen. Agrippa, grandson of Herod the Great, brought up with his sister Herodias at the imperial court, playmate of future emperors, and as a young man having such enormous influence as to arouse the suspicions of the Roman aristocracy, regained all the Jewish territories of his grandfather and reigned as king over the whole of Palestine by favour of the Western empire. He was the first of his house to pose as a true-born Jew,[1] gaining the support of the Pharisee section of the ruling classes, which was then uppermost, while retaining the support of Rome, their supposed enemy. His attempt

---

[1] The redeeming feature about Herodias was that she preferred banishment with her husband to the wealth and security offered her by the emperor.

to fortify the larger Jerusalem of his day in such a way as to make it impregnable against the most powerful attack was represented by his political enemies as being a threat to his masters, the Western powers, rather than a defence against the East. So unbounded was his ambition that, after the example of his Roman master, he wished to bestride the world as a god: the tragic sequel is to be found in the pages of the New Testament.[1] His crafty audacities at last roused the suspicions of the Western empire, and the fact that her minister had found him in conference with potentates who held the keys of the Farther East lent colour to her fears.[2] Never again did Rome try the experiment of a Jewish kingship; she was not prepared to take the risks.

Jesus, in after years, shows himself not unaware of this 'leaven of the Herods.' If they, by questionable means, could come so near to obtain a world objective, could not he, with genius incomparably greater than theirs, have attained the same goal?

'All the kingdoms of the world and their glory.' To grasp the significance of this, the mind had to think imperially, but that was not all. He must over and over again have considered the burning question of his times: Gentile versus Jewish culture, the breadth and tolerance of Hellenism over against the senseless narrowness of the Jewish patriots. The mind, in revolt against that self-satisfied parochial 'culture' of his own nation, would swing round to a not unfriendly survey of Gentile civilization and its ideals.

Over a century before his time the battle between the two ideals had been fought out in the rising of the Maccabees to cleanse Palestine from foreign contamination, and at first the national victory had seemed to restore the ancient justice, but how soon the eternal things had been forgotten; and now what remained but dead and senseless

---

[1] Acts xii. 21 ff. Cf. Josephus, who, however, gave a rather different account of his as swift and tragic end.

[2] The 'conference' at Tiberias comprised Antiochus of Commagene, Sampsiceramus of Emesa, Cotys of Lesser Armenia, Polemon of Pontus, and Herod of Chalcis.

rules which fettered the Jews themselves, and which they wished to impose as fetters upon all mankind? Was not the wider culture of the foreigner infinitely preferable to this Jewish mind in chains? He would remember the discussions in the workshop of Nazareth, where the building of the magnificent new town of Tiberias, not many miles below them on the lake shores, had been a burning topic among his friends and customers. It was only completed about four years since. Erected on the site of an ancient graveyard, and designed entirely on 'Greek' models, its building had aroused such a fury of opposition that 'Herod was obliged to use force to people it with any but the lowest of the nation.'

There were many cities like Tiberias in and around Palestine. There was Bethsaida Julias, named like Tiberias, in honour of the Roman masters of the land; Sepphoris had been rebuilt on foreign models, and the huge modern port of Caesarea, besides those purely Greek towns of the Decapolis.

Even the magnificent temple at Jerusalem was built in the foreign style.[1] All ambitious young men among the Jews would learn Greek and the richer classes furthered the infiltration of foreign customs.

'In this temper of the governing class it is easy to see how great would be the influence of the Greek-speaking people settled in Palestine. All the higher civilization, all the art, all the science, lay with them. They were the intermediaries between the Jews and the rest of the cultivated world.' [1]

Thus once more Palestine was becoming rapidly foreignized, in the matter of cities, architecture, and indeed of language, literature, science, and the arts. Herod's (the Great) ambition 'led him to foster the liberal arts and culture, but any form of culture than that of Greece was scarcely recognized by the world of that day . . . the culture which he sought to spread throughout his land was essentially Greek and pagan.' The theatre at Jerusalem

[1] Mahaffy, *Progress of Hellenism*, page 129.

and the amphitheatre near it were regarded with horror by old-fashioned Jews, but the 'young bloods' of the time were forsaking the old ways and flocking to it. And, after all, was not this infiltration of foreign ideas to some extent a healthy offset against the ignorant parochialism of the narrower patriots? Such thoughts would likely enough be present to Jesus, attracted by this prospect of the kingdoms of the world and their allegiance. If his religion was not to be confined to the Jew only, was not some alliance with this larger world and spirit possible?

How attractive was this dream of an overlordship which would break up the ancient prejudices, boundaries, separations, and fuse all nations into one undifferentiated whole? A common language, a common rule, a common culture, 'a common ground on which Roman and Jew, Macedonian and Syrian, could meet and hold intercourse.' [1] Why not aim at a universal empire, mightier than the Alexandrian, mightier than the Roman, in which under the rule of a strong man there should be neither Greek nor Jew, barbarian nor Scythian? This had been the dream of Xenophon, the dream of the more idealistic defenders of the Roman Empire. And, after all, were not the Herods, if one looked at the rosier side of their ambition, doing much to make that dream a reality?

Although the mind of Jesus might, for the moment, in its revolt against a bigoted nationalism be attracted by Hellenistic culture and the possibilities of moulding it to his purposes, he would soon have reflected that avarice and empire were historically bound together; and perhaps such a connection is not accidental but essential, for avarice invariably collects and does not create. Avarice always considers that man's life consists in the abundance of the things which he possesses; privately it collects and amasses money and art treasures; publicly, it collects and amasses peoples and nations and cities, extracting from them the uttermost farthing. Besides, although Greek culture was infinitely preferable to that of the Jewish pedants, could it

[1] Mahaffy, *Progress of Hellenism*, page 136.

really be compared with that deeper Jewish culture with which the Redemptionist group and his mother would have familiarized him?

As Jesus looked across the world from that mountain top and saw the dim outlines of cities with which he was familiar, and which had always filled him with an instinctive disgust, he began to perceive that their building was 'mortal sin of stone.'[1]

If then the fruits of empire were evil, was there something essentially unnatural and satanic in the imperial ambition? For freedom is the natural inheritance of the individual soul, and it is natural to man to live in groups and nations, and he finds in such a life his joyous expression. Now empire is seen, at least, to have crushed this spontaneous life, but it professed to intermingle groups and make men one, and this comradeship of mankind was also according to human instinct. It had, however, failed to carry out its pretensions, not only because its advocates were greedy men, but because its attempt to bind men and nations in one, not by internal fusion, but by external domination, was essentially inhuman.

At all costs one must worship God and do him service, but what is the nature of God? If God be the thundering Jupiter of the pagans, or the alien Jehovah of current Jewish thought, then he is truly represented by the divine emperor exercising lordship over all the kingdoms; but Jesus was convinced that God was not like that. He called Him the father of the human family, and His Messiah the servant of mankind.

To rule mankind as benevolent tyrant was now clearly seen by our Lord to be a rejection of the will of God who does not impose His sway upon unwilling peoples or force them into submission for their good. If Jesus were truly

---

[1] Huysman, *The Cathedral*, contrasting Gothic with Roman Renaissance, page 105 (transl.). (Kegan Paul, 1898.) Cf. Ruskin on the 'accursed architecture' of a people who harked back to the Roman period for their inspiration. *Stones of Venice*, vol. ii, Chap. VI.

the Son of God, his Messiahship must not be a benevolent despotism; he must not rule men in majestic aloofness, but must become their commander through having learned to be their minister.

And even if a good despotism had been the divine method of governing mankind, what methods had to be used if one were to climb to such a world-leadership? Political cunning, crafty alliances, callousness to human suffering, lying subterfuges—the leaven of the Herods which we have already described.

Not only the long and mudstained climb to the summit, the Herodian way,[1] by which one might gain the whole world, but lose one's own soul and find oneself a soulless despot, possessing all power, but with the will to use it benevolently for ever gone—not only this sinister method of obtaining power, but the power itself when obtained is seen by Jesus to be a falling down and a worshipping of Satan. With vehemence he rejects it with the words: 'Get thee hence, Satan; for it is written, Thou shalt worship the Lord thy God, and Him only shalt thou serve.'

---

[1] By worldly alliances, hypocritical friendships with men in high places, marriages not for love but for policy, countless intrigues, compromises with injustice and bestiality, possibly even inhuman crime.

*L

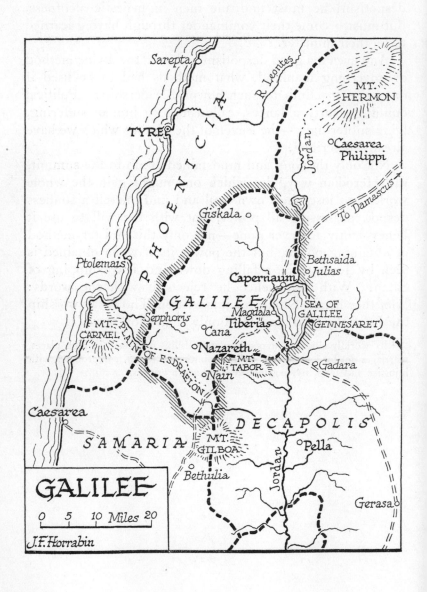

Sarepta

R. Leontes

MT. HERMON

TYRE

PHOENICIA

Caesarea Philippi

To Damascus

Jordan

Giskala

Ptolemais

Bethsaida Julias

Capernaum

GALILEE

Sepphoris

Magdala

Tiberias

SEA OF GALILEE (GENNESARET)

MT. CARMEL

PLAIN OF ESDRAELON

Cana

Nazareth

MT. TABOR

Nain

Gadara

Caesarea

DECAPOLIS

SAMARIA

MT. GILBOA

Pella

Jordan

Bethulia

Gerasa

GALILEE

0   5   10 Miles 20

J.F. Horrabin

CHAPTER XIII

THE GALILEAN PROLOGUE

ACCORDING to the fourth gospel Jesus rejoined the Baptist after his experiences in the desert, and was present when the Pharisaic element in the southern government caused a deputation [1] to be sent to John challenging his whole position. This deputation would naturally wish to discredit his work, and would hope to draw from him some political admission which might form the basis for an arrest.

The object of the government deputation was not mere curiosity but to secure incriminating evidence against the Baptist. This is probable when we consider the abuse that he hurled at them or at their adherents and their hostile attitude at a later period.[2] The deputation returned for the moment baffled. They had failed to secure the needed evidence, for John neither claimed to be the coming Lord, nor did he even put himself forward as one of his forerunners. He was anxious to turn the searchlight of

[1] John i. 19: 'the Jews sent,' used in the fourth gospel 'to denote the theocracy in its opposition to Christ's claims, especially as represented by the Sanhedrim.' *Century Bible*, St. John, page 123. The deputation seems to have been composed of priests and Levites, although these were sent at the instigation of the Pharisees. Most of the priests, and especially the 'higher clergy,' were Sadducees, but there were also Pharisees within their ranks.

[2] Cf. Mark xi. 27–33 and ix. 11–13. These passages seem to suggest that the scribes had a hand with the northern government of Herod in his death. The 'authority' incident of Mark xi shows that the Government definitely opposed him, which is not astonishing, for, cf. Matthew iii. 7, where John denounces the Government, or the two parties chiefly represented in the Government, as 'off-spring of vipers.' The Herodians who stood for the Hellenizing of Palestine hated scribism. The scribes or 'the learned,' the interpreters of the Law, of the Scriptures, were generally Pharisees, but occasionally Sadducees. They were chiefly found in the South, and especially at Jerusalem, but even when in Galilee and Perea, their headquarters were Jerusalem and their support was the southern government. Cf. Schürer, *The Scribes*, div. II, vol. i, page 11.

inquiry from his person to his message. He was content to be but a voice crying in the wilderness, if only people were arrested by the burden of that cry. For the rest, he was convinced that in the person of one who stood among them, and whom he had so recently baptized, was the leader that the nation was expecting.

He even pointed some of his followers away from himself to that overmastering personality. He was content to lose his own following: 'He must increase, and I must decrease.' This stupendous humility marks John as a great man willing to be himself obliterated, so long as the cause marches on.

Who were these followers of the Baptist?

They were fishermen from the Lake of Galilee. According to the Synoptists it might have been supposed that Jesus suddenly called certain fishermen to leave their boats and follow him without any previous knowledge of them. Here the fourth gospel seems to supply a necessary link. It was in the crowd who surrounded the Baptist that Jesus first came to know them.

They were Galileans who owned their boats in partnership, and may have belonged to a boatman's guild [1] or some such association. They had either permanent or occasional hired labourers under them. Some people have suggested that, because they owned their boats and employed hired labour, they were not of the working class. It might as well be argued that the guildsmen of the Middle Ages working at a craft were not working class, because they worked for the public and for themselves instead of for a private master, or that the modern blacksmith, because he is not employed by some firm or private individual, is not a working man. And as to the labourers under them, the miner of to-day has labourers under him; the same is true of carpenters, masons, and other high-grade labour.

---

[1] Boatmen's guilds. Cf. Delitzsch, *Jewish Artisan Life*, page 28 (although he does not consider them to have been guilds in the strict sense), but cf. also Osborne Ward, *The Ancient Lowly*, vol. ii, page 164.

The new movement found its support, not at first in the slums of overgrown cities, but amongst this type of intelligent and skilled worker. They were comparatively poor men,[1] their earnings reduced by various imposts and excessive taxation, but they were not like the abjectly poor of the modern slum. There is an impression in some quarters that Jesus blessed extreme poverty. There is no evidence that either John or Jesus did anything of the sort. They neither looked for nor obtained their first recruits from the very poor. Their first converts were recruited from that type of workman nearest to the highest grades of labour in our own time, from the skilled class that supplies the revolutionary movements of to-day with the largest percentage of adherents.

These boatmen disciples of the Baptist were freer than the slaves and the hired proletariat, in that they could choose their own time for work and had greater freedom of movement. Their calling not only included the actual fishing on the lake, but the marketing of their hauls, locally at Capernaum but also at Tarachea, the centre of the dried fish trade at the extreme south of the lake; they may have hawked their fish among the villages of the thickly populated Jordan basin,[2] and even sold it to the Tyrian dealers in the fish-market at Jerusalem.[3] The fiery independence of the Galilean fisher-folk may be gauged by the fact that, some years after, they formed the backbone of the rebel movement which actually captured, and

---

[1] Students who support the present system have attempted to deny the poverty of these fishers, but Delitzsch, *Jewish Artisan Life*, page 33, shows that the fisheries were open, save that the sinking of creels was forbidden because it hindered navigation; with that sole restriction every one might try his luck with net or hook, and therefore 'this fishing was not a lucrative business.'

[2] The Jordan runs through a valley which stretches sometimes half a mile across. The villages are on the ridge of the hills on either side, and the inhabitants come down to work in the valley.

[3] Stapfer, page 50. John the fisherman perhaps had access with his fish to the servants' hall at the palace of the high priest. For servants' hall cf. Weiss, *Life of Christ*, vol. i, page 366 (John xviii. 15).

for a considerable time managed to hold, the fashionable city of Tiberias.[1]

It is not surprising, then, that the four men who were first attracted to this new leader, the carpenter of Galilee, were of this sturdy stock. Two at least of them are mentioned as disciples of John in his daring adventure. He it was who first roused their curiosity concerning Jesus as the coming leader.[2]

The first of these, Andrew, bore a Greek name, and was the friend of the cosmopolitan Philip. He is consulted in emergencies.[3] He shows initiative and good judgment. His mate John[4] was equally curious about Jesus, and alert to find out all about him. This disciple, 'whom Jesus loved,' seems to have been of a fiery and turbulent disposition; he has to be rebuked when he wants to call down fire from heaven upon opponents;[5] he and his brother James are called by Jesus 'the sons of tumult.'[6] The modern portraiture of John as a tame sentimentalist is as much akin to the real man as their parody of love is to that large virtue which the many waters cannot quench.

These two comrades followed Jesus and found his

---

[1] Delitzsch, *Jewish Artisan Life*, page 34.

[2] Whether John the Baptist called Jesus 'the Lamb of God,' or the first disciples called him at the very outset 'the Christ,' is doubtful. John the Evangelist, writing in extreme old age, or some disciple transcribing the memories of the aged fisherman, may have heightened the colouring of the whole incident. But it is not inconceivable that the Baptist and some of his followers may have had this dawning conviction of Jesus as the inspired leader they expected: that his subsequent actions, which 'scandalized' and horrified the religious and political world of his day, shook their confidence in their earlier conviction (Matthew xi. 2–6, cf. John vi. 66–7), so that Jesus, when he had taught them how different was the real Messiah from the Messiah of conventional expectation, had once more to draw from them a recognition of him as their only possible leader and lord of the coming world.

[3] John vi. 8 and xii. 22. An early tradition says that Andrew was killed by being bound to a cross, and that he bravely taught the people for two days from his cross.

[4] Most critics, with considerable probability, suppose that John the Evangelist is meant. Cf. the commentaries.

[5] Fire from Heaven (Luke ix. 54).

[6] Sons of tumult or uproar (Mark iii. 17). Cf. Gould's *Commentary on St. Mark*, page 57. James, his brother, was probably still in Galilee with the nets.

lodging, perhaps in one of the temporary booths which were sometimes set up in times of pilgrimage. There they stayed with him, for it was getting late. Andrew soon finds his brother Simon and tells him of his extraordinary experience. He then brings him to Jesus. Simon, who eventually becomes the leader of the propagandists of Jesus, is another of the eager independent boatmen. This 'son of the dove' is afterwards to be the rock man.[1] He is described as daring and impulsive.

Next day they set out walking for Galilee, where Andrew [2] finds his other comrade Philip. Philip's name, like his friend's, is Greek, and although, like Andrew and Peter, a native of Capernaum(?), he is living in the paganized Bethsaida.[3] Bethsaida (Fisherholm) had once been a little Jewish fishing town, with a track down to the beach, from which it was, curiously enough, some little distance. Now it had been rebuilt as one of the fashionable watering-places of the empire, and dedicated by one of the Herods to the empress. No strict Jew would live there, and it argued a considerable amount of unconventionality and independence for a fisher family, not actually natives of the place, to move there. Philip is the disciple to whom, in after years, the Greeks apply when they want to see Jesus. He is eager, like Andrew, to spread the news, and searches out Nathanael, a native of the hill village Cana,[4] which they have now reached. Nathanael [5] seems to have been a peasant holder, and, like many such yeoman lovers of their

---

[1] Farrar, *Life of Christ* (tenth edition), vol. i, page 147.

[2] Some think the 'he' refers to Jesus, others to Peter, but it probably refers to Andrew.

[3] The conjecture that there was a second town of this name, beside the famous watering-place, is apparently without foundation. Abbott translates John i. 44: 'Philip was domiciled at Bethsaida, a native of the city of Andrew and Peter.'

[4] The supposition that the whole party was still south of the lake, and that Nathanael was merely resting by the way under a fig-tree, is very unlikely. The expression 'under the fig' seems to have been a term denoting the possession of one's own plot of land.

[5] Nathanael, probably the son of Talmai, i.e. Bar-Talmai or Bartholomew; cf. the pairing of Bartholomew and Philip in the Synoptic lists.

native soil, a single-minded patriot.[1]   It was curious, this friendship between the more liberal-minded fishermen and the peasant, but they had this much in common, their love of the old political writings and their hope for a new world.[2]

'On the third day'[3] there was a marriage in Nathanael's village, Cana, a few miles over the hills from Nazareth, and apparently on the road to the lake.   Jesus and his new friends were invited, and his mother was there.   Probably it was the marriage of some peasant kinsmen.[4]   In these eastern marriages the bride is heralded by torchlights, with songs and dances, and the music of the drum and flute to the bridegroom's home.   In the little procession of friends there would be those who distributed nuts to the children, and oil and wine to their elders; some bore myrtle branches and some bore flowers.   The 'ritual' which actually declared the couple man and wife was not uttered in any public place of worship, but in the new home, and only took a few moments.   After certain legal transactions, there came a ceremonial washing of hands and a blessing. Then began the festival meal, with its sacred cup of wine. After this ceremonial drinking, the wine flowed freely, and the food was abundant.   There was the usual joking and merry-making, and they were not likely to forget their old saying: 'Without wine there is no joy.'   To those who had just left the company of the stern and ascetic preacher in the wilderness the scene must have presented an amazing contrast, and they may have wondered what their new leader would make of it all.

At that moment Mary is anxious, for the wine has run

[1] Cf. John i. 47.

[2] Cf. John i. 45.

[3] The southern region of Jordan was a three days' march from Cana, so this reference may be to the third day of their march, and, in that case, I have placed the region of John's activity too far north; but if the text is studied carefully this raises several difficulties, and I think it probably means the third day from their return to Galilee.

[4] Mary seems in a position of some authority, and gives instructions to the servants.   The Greek is 'ministers,' or 'people who served,' not slaves or even paid servants, so it was not a wealthy household, but possibly the farmstead of some fairly well-to-do peasant.

short, and mentions it to Jesus. He answers: 'Woman,[1]
is it any concern of ours? Mine hour is not yet come.'[2]
He had intended, first to preach his good news of the coming
commonwealth, and then to put forth his energy so that
men might have a foretaste of its abundant life; but in
response to the distress of these homely people and his
mother's appeal, he renews the supplies with such excellent
wine[3] that the chairman[4] chaffs the husband with the
words: 'Everyman serves the good wine first, and when
people have got drunk[5] he serves the poorer wine. Thou
hast kept the good wine until now!'

There are many passages of the gospel which show our
Lord as the teacher of moderation in both food and fermented drink, but in face of his own deliberate contrast
of himself with the abstainer John, the charge against him
of wine-bibbing, his gift of wine at the Last Supper, and the
above incident, the attempt of some moderns to portray
him as a total abstainer is a grotesque and dishonest misstatement. If these people really think that Jesus turned

---

[1] The Greek means literally 'woman,' but there is no disrespect in it
(cf. commentaries generally), cf. John xix. 26, and xx. 13. Greek literally
'what is it to thee or to me?' She does not take it as anything like a rebuke,
for she at once assumes that he will somehow or other put things right, and
bids those serving to do whatever he tells them.

[2] 'Mine hour.' Various attempts have been made to insert the Cana
incident into the framework of the synoptic narrative, but unsuccessfully.
I think that if the fourth gospel story is to be taken seriously, this incident
must be preliminary to the Galilean campaign. It should be dated about
spring A.D. 26, followed by the Passover visit and a preliminary southern
ministry of some months: only after this would come John's imprisonment
and the opening of the Galilean ministry. If this interpretation is correct,
'Mine hour,' etc. would mean that he purposed first to proclaim his good
news in Galilee, and to let the healing and other fruitful signs flow out of
this general ministry in illustration of the fruitful and life-giving nature of
the new world he proclaimed. But as we shall see, he over and over again
turned aside from his intended programme in response to some human appeal.

[3] Six water-pots containing two or three firkins each, i.e. about 130 gallons
in all, or more than 1,000 pints.

[4] Chairman of the table; probably not, as some critics say, as a hired waiter,
for note his bearing and conversation. Moffatt translates 'chairman of the
table,' i.e. some guest chosen to preside.

[5] Moffatt's translation, cf. Greek Lexicon, μεθύσκομαι, to be drunken
with wine.

the water into something like lemonade, they ought to have the honesty to translate 'Be not drunk with wine, wherein is excess,' as 'Be not drunk with lemonade, wherein is excess.' The word for wine is precisely the same here as in the Pauline passage. If οἶνος, wine, throughout the New Testament means unfermented grape-juice, how can St. Paul warn us not to get drunk on it, and how can the 'ruler of the feast' describe it as the liquor which makes men intoxicated?

It is remarkable that the writer of the fourth gospel, whose declared object is to relate such 'signs' as should convince people that Jesus is the Messiah, the Son of God, and that believing they might have life in his name,[1] should give as the first of these 'signs' this kindly act of supplying a village feast with merry wine.

It is also important to notice that the word used is not 'miracle' but 'sign.' The miracle is a thing to arouse astonishment and stupefaction; the sign, as used in the Gospels, is an act *significant* of the life and fruitfulness of the new world.

[1] John xx. 30.

CHAPTER XIV

A SOUTHERN MINISTRY INTERRUPTED BY A SHORT VISIT TO GALILEE

THREE or four of the newly-found comrades of Jesus, who lived at Capernaum, would, no doubt, be going home after the marriage in the hill village, and would persuade Jesus to go with them as there were still a few days before Passover at Jerusalem, at which he wished to be present. The fact that his mother and his brethren went with them may suggest that Jesus already thought of Capernaum as a possible headquarters for his Galilean propaganda, and Mary would be anxious to see it before they abandoned Nazareth.

Jesus now went to Jerusalem for the Passover, in late March or early April of this year A.D. 26,[1] and he found in the outer court of the Temple, the court of the foreigners, a market[2] of oxen and sheep and doves, and outdoor banks for foreign exchange. 'Among the litter that strewed the court were pieces of rope, cast-off tethers and baggage cords, and, snatching up a handful of these and plaiting them into a scourge,'[3] he drove them all out of the

---

[1] The question of chronology is very complicated, owing to the various changes in the calendar and in methods of reckoning time, but it seems probable that Jesus, after a ministry of three years, was crucified in A.D. 29.

[2] The fourth gospel gives the expulsion of the traders at the outset of Jesus' ministry, while the Synoptists place it at the end, but there may well have been two such expulsions, considering that this marketing within the Temple precincts was probably illegal, and that the act would be enthusiastically supported by thousands of pilgrims. Salmon, who is intensely critical and by no means a blind supporter of the fourth gospel, thinks that the repetition of this expulsion is quite possible, and that 'there is thus no harmonistic difficulty in reconciling John and Mark.' (*Human Element in the Gospels*, Murray, 1907, page 434.)

[3] It was no mere symbolic whip that he held aloft, but an actual scourge made of thick cords, being the same word as is translated 'ropes' in Acts xxvii. 32.

Temple, together with the sheep and the oxen,[1] and scattered the coins of the money-changers and upset their tables, and said to the dealers in doves: 'Take these things away.   Make not my Father's House a market-place.'

Whether Jesus on this occasion forcibly expelled the drovers, as well as their beasts, is disputed; but, by those who accept the story of the fourth gospel, it cannot be in dispute that he here used methods other than those of suasion; for, in any case, he did not gently persuade the money-changers to replace the coins into their bags and withdraw, nor suavely argue with the dove - sellers.   It cannot be disputed that, a few days before his crucifixion, at the climax of his mission, he indignantly threw out the traders, and did not politely argue them out.   We are therefore driven to the conclusion that 'the Method of the Cross' included the forceful method of that same 'Holy Week,' or, at least, did not contradict it.   Renan's alternative that Jesus lost his temper and behaved in a very undignified and unchristlike manner, will hardly commend itself to Christians or to any one who has made a close study of his character.   Those who nowadays describe the expulsion from the Temple as the act of one too isolated above human nature to be moved with indignation, as a mere ceremonial act carefully conceived and calmly executed, in actuality deny the manhood of Jesus and the gospel record, or believe only in an attenuated manhood, which has no place for righteous indignation, and are

---

[1] Some translate: 'He drove them all, sheep and oxen together, out of the Temple,' but whether the Greek can bear this interpretation is doubtful. Farrar considers that the phrase must refer to the drovers as well as to their beasts (*Life of Christ*, vol. i, page 187).   The *Century Bible Commentary*, although passivist in outlook, and thinking it was beneath the dignity of Jesus to strike a blow, is nevertheless constrained to write as follows: 'Taking the law into his own hands, he put a stop to the unholy traffic, overturning the money-tables, driving out before him both men (as the Greek implies) and sheep and oxen'; while Peake's *Commentary* is doubtful, saying: 'Notice especially the driving out of the cattle and (?) their attendants.'   I had some correspondence with Stephen Liberty whose book *Political Relations* we have often quoted.   Although a pacifist, he is convinced that the Greek words must include the driving out of the men as well as of their beasts.

incapable of appreciating the nuances of great and vivid literature.

But why this indignation? The huge outer court of the Temple into which the markets had overflowed from the slopes outside was the court of the nations. Foreign proselytes and foreign visitors, who were sympathetic and wished, as far as possible, to join in the worship, were not allowed into the strictly Jewish precincts within, and therefore this court afforded them the only opportunity for temple worship. Their worship was being made impossible by the loud bargaining round the market stalls, the cries of hucksters, the bleating of sheep and the lowing of oxen, and the confusion was added to by the court having become a noisy thoroughfare from one congested trading district to another. Jesus, jealous for the rights of the foreigner, was determined that his father's house should once more be a house of prayer for all nations.[1] This is suggested by Mark's insistence on the fact that not only the profiteering sellers, but the noisy buyers, are cast out, as also the porters, and would explain the reference of the fourth gospel to the house of merchandise. That it was not only the noise and confusion of the market that Jesus objected to, but the avaricious and usurious nature of that market, as will be seen when we come to consider the second expulsion, with his fiery denunciation of the market profiteers as a den of robbers.

The expulsion of the traders [2] from the court of the

---

[1] Speaker's *Commentary* on Mark xi. 17. Cf. Gould on same passage: 'It was the court of the Gentiles, which they thought just good enough for these debased uses.'

[2] In consequence of the expulsion of the traders, the Government (for that would seem to be the meaning of John's expression 'the Jews') demanded some sign from Heaven to prove his right to take the law into his own hands in this summary fashion. He answered: 'Destroy this temple, and in three days I will raise it up.' The opponents answered: 'Forty and six years has this temple taken to build, and is still building, and will you raise it up in three days?' But the writer thinks Jesus meant the temple of his body raised from death, after the crucifixion. I do not deal with the incident in my text, because, after reading about a dozen of the best interpretations and advancing several of my own, I am still dissatisfied. He may have meant that they

nations was enormously popular among the hundreds of
thousands of pilgrims, most of whom would have been,
at one time or another, the victims of their exactions. It
is therefore not astonishing that masses of people were
ready to accept him as their leader, but with his penetrating
insight into the minds and motives of the people around
him he discounted this sudden allegiance, and 'did not
trust himself unto them.' But among those attracted to
his leadership was Nicodemus, a member of the Government. He was elderly, well-to-do, cautious,[1] visiting
Jesus under cover of the darkness. He did not openly
identify himself with the new propaganda until after the
death of Christ, but he was fair and open-minded, and when
in October of the year 28 the Government met and decided
to destroy Jesus, he protested that, according to the Jewish
law, one ought not to condemn a man unheard. He was
absent from the subsequent trial of Jesus in the spring of
the following year, but he came forward boldly with another
rich man after Christ's death to do his body royal service.
Curious to know more about the Galilean and his new
movement, this 'teacher of Israel,' this member of the most
influential party in the Government, now seeks out Jesus,

were bringing the Temple and all it stood for to rapid and inevitable ruin,
but that in an incredibly short time he would have built up a living compact human movement, with himself as its centre and inspiration. This did
actually happen, and the risen Jesus was the centre of the temple not made
with hands—the new movement in the world; but it is unlikely he should
have thought or spoken of his own destruction thus early. So difficult is it to
fix the chronology of the gospel events that Farrar gives the forty-sixth year
of building as 29, or better 28, Edersheim as 27, while Ramsay gives it as 26.
Maclean prefers 27.

[1] Elderly (John iii. 4), wealthy (John xix. 39). Some writers think he
was sent as a delegate from the Government. They take the Greek, 'a
man from the Pharisees,' in that sense. They suggest that the members of
the Executive wanted to make up their minds about the new prophet. But
it is more likely that, as on a later occasion they had taken the expulsion of the
traders, in whose business so many of them were involved, as a declaration of
war against themselves, and we shall see them, apparently, in a very short
time, moving against Jesus. The whole 'field' of the incident is that
Nicodemus was an exception to the rest, but too cautious to come in
the day.

perhaps among the thick groves of the hill slopes, where the leader would, with his followers, spend the night, or possibly in some guest chamber within the city. To most of the Executive, the recent assault on their vested interests by a Galilean workman had seemed an insufferable impertinence; to Nicodemus it seemed a sign from heaven, for must not the Government be purged of its avarice if, after the downfall of the Roman Empire, it was to be entrusted by God with the domination of mankind? How could the Kingdom of God be inaugurated except by a nation cleansed from such corruptions? This rather unimaginative person, with his professorial type of mind, had at last reached the conclusion that the new era which he expected, dominated by the Jewish race, captained by a Jewish Empire, must be built on principles of fairness and generosity and purity, but nothing short of a complete change of outlook, a new birth, the freshness and spontaneity of a child's vision and wonder, could give to this weary middle-aged official a perception of that new world of Jesus to be built on the living impulses of men. Nicodemus doubted if a man, getting old, fixed, and bound in a routine of thought, could enter a second time into his mother's womb and begin all over again. Jesus answers: Unless a man can shake himself free of the old conventions, the dusty traditions of the universities, second-rate contemporary thought; unless he can be born of the running waters and the untrammelled breezes,[1] he cannot enter the Kingdom of God.

Nicodemus seems, at least, to have reached the position which had attracted Jesus, but which he had eventually

[1] The Greek word translated 'spirit' means either breeze or spirit. Probably there was in our Lord's conversation, as was customary, a play on these two meanings. Verses 11 to 21 are possibly the comment of the author of the gospel, revealing the mind of Jesus at a later stage, but can hardly be the actual words of Jesus as spoken at this moment, unless we are to make havoc of the vivid and convincing development of the story as given in the Synoptists, where he does not force his claims, but leaves his followers gradually to become convinced for themselves, that conviction at last finding a voice in the confession of Peter. That most wonderful and subtle of all dramas is ruined by this presentation, if we take it too literally.

rejected: the conception of a Jewish kingdom, cleansed indeed of its more obvious injustices, strait-jacketing mankind with its excellent rules and regulations. What he failed to see was that it was to be an international commonwealth built upon the eternal impulses of the whole human race. That is why later we find Jesus describing his kingdom as a kingdom which could be entered only by those who had become as little children. It was a gay and genial new world, to be won indeed after much tribulation, but a world natural to men, tired of artificiality and routine, born again into their true and living heritage. This new birth is not a portentous, *un*natural birth. If the doctrine which is the foundation of this gospel is true; if the Word that was with God and was God is creator of men; if his life is the light of men; those who entertained his light, those who did not refuse to be penetrated by his life, became what they were meant to be; they fulfilled the purpose of Him who called them into existence.

Leaving Jerusalem Jesus now continues his mission in the Jordan valley where his disciples baptize many converts; the preaching of their master is so successful that he would have continued there but for two reasons which convinced him that it would be wise to go on to Galilee. The first was that jealousies had arisen among the followers of the Baptist which the prophet rebuked, but was not perhaps entirely able to subdue; the second was the attitude of the Pharisees. Much as they feared the Baptist, they had for a time hesitated to play into the hands of their Herodian opponents by condemning him, as is suggested by the words 'you were willing for a season to rejoice in his light,' spoken in Jerusalem in the spring of the following year (John v. 35). Later their hatred of John overcame their dislike of these semi-pagans, and they are found in collusion with them against the Baptist, as afterwards against Jesus himself.

For these reasons, therefore, he leaves the basin of the river and takes the Samaritan route to the North. Entering a certain city where the famous well of Jacob was situated, he rests by the well and asks a woman to give him a drink.

She is astonished, as the Jews have no dealings with the Samaritans. But he, ignoring this, speaks to her of the living water which will be in men as a well of water springing up into eternal life. From his knowledge of her inmost secrets, she perceives that he is a prophet, and therefore feels that he would be able to solve the riddle of the rival worships at Jerusalem and Samaria. Where ought one really to worship God? He replies: 'Woman, believe me, the hour cometh when ye shall neither in this mountain, nor yet at Jerusalem, worship the Father. Ye worship ye know not what; we know what we worship, for salvation is of the Jews. But the hour cometh, and now is, when the true worshippers shall worship the Father in spirit and in truth; for the Father seeketh such to worship Him. God is a Spirit and they that worship Him must worship Him in spirit and in truth.'[1]

The universal fatherhood of God is unknown to the Jews of that epoch, and the Samaritans are even vaguer about it. But the time is coming, and is to be ushered in by Jesus, when all shall be able to perceive Him as their father and as the universal spirit, and in that time all these senseless separations will be done away.

His disciples were amazed to find him in conversation with a woman, and, more than this, a Samaritan woman. The response of this despised person, in spite of her immoralities and her separatist nationality, shows Jesus that the fields are already ripening for a great and universal harvest. Many of the Samaritans, moved by the tale of the woman, believed on him and besought him to stay with them, but after two days' rest and preaching, he pursues his journey to Galilee.

Jesus comes to the village of Cana again where he had turned the water into wine, and a certain nobleman from Capernaum visits him there, appealing to him to come down to the coast town and heal his son. Jesus said to him 'Go thy way; thy son liveth.' The nobleman had great faith and went home convinced that he would find his son alive

[1] John iv. 21–4.

and well, and found, when he reached Capernaum, that it was even as the Master had said.

Now this would have seemed the very moment for Jesus to open his campaign in Galilee, but perhaps because he did not entirely despair of the capital, he goes south again to Jerusalem and attends the spring feast of Purim, a little feast of liberty which was held yearly in the month of March to commemorate the escape of the Jewish nation from the plot of Haman the Persian governor, in the year 473 B.C., to kill every Jew throughout the Persian Empire, which at that time was dominant over Palestine. This Nazi mass murder had been averted and Purim was kept annually with feasting and with merry-making and giving of presents, and later with religious ceremonies. It would be a festival dear to Jesus, the lover of liberty, and so, although not a 'feast of obligation,' he would be glad to attend it.

As he entered the city he saw the pool of Bethesda with its five porches under the shelter of which there were many sick persons, lame, crippled, blind, and infirm who were waiting for the 'troubling of the waters.' It was supposed that an angel from time to time went down into the pool and stirred its waters, and that whoever entered them first was made whole. There may have been a periodic vortex in the pool which would have had healing qualities. Jesus observed a cripple lying in one of the porches and spoke to him. The man had often lain there, but had no one to lift him and dip him in the water after it stirred, so one of the others always got into it before him. He had been crippled for nearly forty years, and Jesus had compassion on him and asked him if he wanted to be made whole. Seeing his faith he said to him: 'Arise, take up thy mat and walk.' And it was the Sabbath day.

When they saw a man carrying a burden on the Sabbath, the religious people were shocked, for this was no sudden accident which required immediate attention, but a chronic illness of many years' standing. Could not the Galilean up-start have waited a few hours and respected the Sabbath?

The cripple could not at the moment identify his helper, but later Jesus met him in the Temple, and said unto him: 'Behold, thou art made whole: sin no more, lest a worse thing befall thee.' His paralysis, like that of the man let down on the mattress through the roof, seems to have been caused by some sexual sin.

The man, then, being a simple fellow, told the religious leaders who it was who had cured him, and they attempted to kill Jesus for breaking the Sabbath. Confronted by his accusers Jesus makes his case much worse by what they considered a most blasphemous claim; for he said: 'My Father worketh even until now, and I work.'

The Jewish world thought of God as putting forth His energy by creating the world in six days, and then as enjoying the Sabbath rest. Jesus thought of His energy as continuous, as was also His rest; there were two aspects of the one consistent Being, and although normally Jesus would respect the Sabbath as affording rest and refreshment to the children of men, he would claim that human need must take precedence of religious law. As, therefore, his Father was continually creating and recreating, so he must put forward his energy to recreate and heal, even on the Sabbath. Had Jesus not said on an earlier occasion, 'The Sabbath was made for man, and not man for the Sabbath'? This attack on conventional theology and claim to be one with his Father enraged the religious world; for had he not made himself 'equal with God'? The very same conflict arose some months later at the winter feast of dedication when he spoke of himself as one with his Father.

But on both occasions the words of Jesus fall on deaf ears; at the spring feast his opponents are the more infuriated because he claims that, having the energy of his Father, he will raise from death unto life those who accept his good news and become his followers.

There is in this discourse a significant reference to John, so recently murdered. Jesus reminds them that the Baptist bore witness to him; the now silenced prophet had certainly spoken of him as one standing among them 'mightier than I, whose shoe latchets I am not worthy to unloose,' but the reference here is confusing, as later in this gospel Jesus himself charges them with the rejection of the Baptist, and this is supported by synoptic evidence, while here Jesus is recorded as saying: 'He was the lamp that burneth and shineth: and ye were willing to rejoice for a season in his light. Much as the Pharisees feared the Baptist, they seem for a time to have hesitated to play into the hands of the Herodians by condemning him; later, their hatred of John overcame their dislike of their semi-pagans, and they are found in collusion with them against the Baptist, as afterwards against Jesus himself.

There is one paragraph which is so often misquoted that its real meaning should be considered. We are told by a certain type of fundamentalist that Jesus commands us to 'search the scriptures,' and Bible societies often preface their editions of the Old and New Testaments with this text. But it is not without an element of humour that even if we take this gospel as an actual record of the words of Jesus, it is, at least, doubtful if he ever gave such advice. In point of fact he seems to have said almost the opposite. In effect, he twits his opponents with always having their noses glued to the written text of the scripture instead of abandoning the written and dead words of a book for the living personality who was among them to give them life.

'Ye search the scriptures, for in them ye *think* ye have the words of eternal life, but ye will not come unto me.' Their scriptural researches are barren, because they never lead them to an appreciation of the living present nor to one who stands among them, an unnoticed and despised working man from Galilee who is, nevertheless, one with God and possesses the key to life.

The 'living past' is a phrase with which we have recently been made familiar, and it is a good phrase, and many people believe in the 'living future,' but it is rare to find anybody who believes in the 'living present' or who so passes through things temporal as not to lose the things eternal.

But the religious world is generally the last coterie in which this is appreciated, and they turned from what seemed to them outrageous blasphemies with scornful indignation and with murder in their hearts. They would neither listen to the witness of John, nor were they capable of perceiving the witness of the works which Jesus did; works of mercy and of liberation.

Jesus, in spite of his taunt at their dry erudition and continual searching of the scriptures, was himself a profound student of the written word. He therefore now refers them to their great leader Moses who testified of him. But this would appear to them lunacy; once more the holy city rejects its liberator and Jesus is cast out.

CHAPTER XV

THE FIRST TWO SCANDALS

ABOUT this time John the Baptist had made an attack on Herod Antipas for his adulterous marriage with Herodias, his brother Philip's wife. This union had been effected, not only through motives of lust or of true affection, but for political reasons. Herodias was powerful at the imperial court, and just as Herod had before married the daughter of Aretas, in order to gain the alliance with the trans-Jordanic Arab tribes, so now he wished to gain the support of the Roman imperial power by the new alliance. The Baptist denounces him for this adulterous union, and for 'all the other evil things that Herod had done,' for instance, for his extortions and cruelties.

John's audacity had led to his arrest in which the southern government seems to have had a hand, although it was actually effected by the Galilean government of Herod, and probably at the instigation of Herodias who seems to have been the Lady Macbeth of the piece.

It is natural that students of the gospels should try to harmonize the various accounts and to make from this piecing together a complete picture of what happened. To this method there can be no objection; in fact, it is inevitable; but the harmony is often attempted too soon, and the individual contributions to the picture are not sufficiently appreciated nor their differences of method the one from the other sufficiently noted. This hurried work is a method inherited from the bad old days when the Bible was looked upon as written by God with the authors of each book treated as so many pens used in the process. It is a legacy from the days of the theory of

318

mechanical inspiration. All great literature is inspired, and the gospels are at the high-water mark of inspiration, but Christendom teaches with a sanity which will appeal to ordinary folk that such inspiration does not destroy but heightens the personality of the writers.

Before, therefore, we try to get some general impression of the Galilean mission, we shall consider its opening phases, as given by the three Synoptists, separately.

We shall begin with the gospel according to St. Mark, which, it will be remembered, is a compression of material gathered from the account of Christ's work as arranged by Peter.

The salient points in Peter's story of the opening of the campaign in Galilee, are that it began at the time of the Baptist's imprisonment, that it was a campaign for God's good news of the kingdom, which was announced to be quite near, that people must repent and believe in the kingdom. This implies at least a short tour; he calls four fishermen, he teaches in the synagogue at Capernaum on the Sabbath, and heals a man mentally diseased; all are amazed, and people say a new teaching! With authority he commands even the unclean spirits and they obey him. His fame spreads through Galilee. They enter the house where Peter and Andrew live, as also James and John, and there are indications that Jesus lodged there and made it his headquarters. Peter's mother-in-law who lives with them is ill; Jesus heals her and she is able to do the work of the house again and to get them a meal. That evening crowds of invalids come and he heals them. Masses of people were gathered round the door. Next morning before daybreak he gets up and goes off into the wild country to be quiet, and there prays; but Peter and the others follow him and tell him that crowds seek him. But he says: 'Let us go elsewhere into the next towns, that I may preach there also, for to this end came I forth.' So he tours Galilee preaching the good news of the approaching age, in the synagogues, and healing mental cases.

Now Peter in his teaching about the Galilean ministry

seems to have grouped together six incidents which were, perhaps, spread over the first year. In any case, they all happened before the first 'police crisis,' of which we shall speak later, and all led up to it.

There was, for instance, that first incident of the leper who came in complete faith that Jesus could cure him. It was embarrassing, because this man had no right to approach any human being or mix with men. He was polluted, and the law was rightly strict about separation. Jesus was anxious not unnecessarily to scandalize the authorities and come in collision with the law. He was not an anarchist. He showed no contempt for good laws, nor did he suggest that law in itself was an evil thing. But in spite of this he allows the man's approach and converses with him, and in that is already a law-breaker. From the man's intense faith and entreaty he turns not away: 'If thou wilt, thou canst make me clean.' Moved with compassion, he violates the law, stretches forth his hand and touches him saying: 'I will; be thou clean,' and straightway the leprosy departed from him. Jesus had broken the letter of the law, but to fulfil its spirit, for the Mosaic law was a set of humane and merciful provisions for mankind. But the religious world of that day would seize upon the fact that God's law had been violated.

Jesus insists that the leper should report himself to the sanitary authorities and comply with their requirements, and urges him not to publish his cure, as he was anxious lest the works of healing should overshadow the actual propaganda. Taken in conjunction with the preaching of justice and the new world, these acts were significant of its health and fruitfulness, but alone they might seem merely wonder works, and attract just any one who wanted doctoring and not doctrine.

Owing to the fact that the patient disobeyed and blazed the news abroad Jesus was compelled to alter his plan, so that he 'could no more openly enter into the city, but was without in desert places; and they came to him from every quarter.'

After an interval he is back again in Capernaum at his headquarters, in Peter's house, and at once a crowd collects, so dense a throng that it not only filled the room but the courtyard. He preached the word to them. There was a man suffering from paralysis who, with his friends, was determined to get to Jesus as the only chance of being cured; but the door was completely blocked. His friends who carried him on a mattress were not dismayed; using the outer stairs of the low-built house they lifted him on to the flat roof and, removing a few tiles or cutting through a thin partition, lowered him into the room at the feet of Jesus. The story suggests great faith on the part of the patient and his determined friends, and faith did not perhaps mean belief in the powers of the Master divorced from his character and propaganda, but faith in the whole personality and the ardent convictions of Jesus and all that he was bound up with.

Now at first sight this cure may seem to contradict the assertion that Jesus never worked miracles to stagger people into believing. The incident is often explained as follows: sin is more deadly than disease; wishing to read the sufferer and the crowd this lesson, Jesus at first ignores the paralysis and the need of cure and says: 'Son, cheer up, thy sins be forgiven thee.' Some Pharisees present, probably on the watch, at once object: 'This man blasphemeth; who can forgive sins but God alone?' Their notion of forgiveness was as formal and mechanical as the rest of their outlook. Jesus replies in effect by saying: Well, if you do not believe I can do something spiritually amazing which you cannot see, I will do something materially amazing which you can and shall see. So that seeing beyond question I have the power to do something tangible and evident, you may believe I have that other power also.

Now, I believe this is altogether a false rendering of the incident. To the scribe and Pharisee notion of a formal and mechanical forgiveness he opposed a generous human conception. Very likely in derivation 'forgiveness' has

M

nothing to do with 'forthgiving,' but that the two ideas
are identical in Christ's conception there can be no doubt.
He believed that the Son of Man must always be generously
giving himself forth in service and understanding to his
fellows. That was the true character of the representative
man, the true character of men as conceived by God in
their making. It was not the prerogative of God only,
but of men, as children of God, to give themselves, therefore
to forgive, to understand, to be generous, and in the power
of that generosity, that love and understanding, to meet
the failures, the sinners, the diseased, along the road and
to heal them.

Now much of paralysis is caused by sin. Sins of the
flesh often result in paralysis; sometimes it is the sins of
the fathers leaving their mark upon the bodies of the
children; sometimes a man's own indulgencies. In this
case the words 'thy sins be forgiven thee,' show where
the origin of the disease lay. It had been some repeated
sin of the flesh, drink, or sexual excess or the like that
had resulted in this paralysis. Paralysis often vanishes
as suddenly as it appears.

This man had had no sufficient reason in his life to
check his self-indulgence, nothing sufficiently powerful to
lift him out of himself and his flesh. He had given way
to temptations, until paralysis had seized him and stricken
him down.

But he had heard of the new preacher, and of his joyous
message. It was the new hope, giving a new motive,
and for the first time making life worth while. If only
he could get close to this Jesus of Galilee who had such
power, he would understand; if any one could put him
right it would be Jesus. His friends also were taken with
the new prophet, and believed in him and in his good news,
so they were determined to give the sick man this last
chance.

This faith in the new prophet and his work put him in
the right mind for a cure. The cause of the disease not
being physical the healer would apply himself to the mind

of the patient rather than the body. Jesus understood the ardent longing, the complete and generous faith, of the sufferer. There was something in the man's attitude, in his determination, that would appeal to him. This man would use his new life for the kingdom. He had wrecked his body, but now he wanted back his lease of life and strength, not for the private sins of his flesh, but for the public service of the new hope. Hence, 'Child, be of good cheer, thy sins be forgiven thee.'

Immediately the man would feel the life coursing through his whole being, affecting spirit, mind, and body, and even as he lay there the paralysis would lift from him. It was not that Jesus said to his opponents, I will show you a staggering miracle, and then perhaps you will also believe I have the power of forgiving sins, but the proof that I have been able as man to heal this man's soul is shown in the fact that the illness which was conditioned by the sick state of the soul is gone. 'Take up thy mattress and go thy way to thy house,' and 'he arose, took up the mattress and went forth before them all; insomuch that they were all amazed, and glorified God, who had given such power unto men.'

It is curious how little there is in the Old Testament about human forgiveness. There are only about three references to it, and it was easy for the Pharisees and their scribes, the official religionists of the day, to overlook or deny it. The astonishment of his own disciples at the liberality of the good news of Jesus on this point will be remembered; not till seven times, which seemed even to Peter an extravagance, but until seventy times seven. Man, as has well been said, must always be the priest in absolution.

It is an exaggeration or a misstatement to say that God forgives before the sinner repents, but the least sign of repentance is met by the Father, and should be met by His children, with forgiveness, when the prodigal is yet a great way off. It is the law of generosity in God's dealings with men, and in man's relation with his fellow-men.

But the official religious mind is disgusted at this new attitude and certain of these critics sat there and reasoned in their hearts, 'why doth this man thus speak blasphemies, who can forgive sins but God only?' It is significant that Luke, whose order of events is generally accurate, suggests that even thus early it was not merely a local Galilean opposition, but that there were with the local Pharisees others of that school from Jerusalem on the watch to trap him and thwart his work.

Although his works of healing are themselves propaganda, for they were actually, and would by the people be understood to be, an inthrust of the coming world of sanity, health, and fruitfulness; yet he was above all, anxious that this side of his work should not swamp the more definite deliverance of the good news. They accepted the kingdom, but still had much to learn about its nature. Many things in their minds had to be corrected. He had said sometime before this, when there seemed a real danger of the acts of healing becoming too popular and excluding the giving of the word of God, that it was for this propaganda of God that he was sent: 'For this therefore came I forth.'

We now find him preaching to the crowds on the ample spaces of the lake-side, and no doubt glad to be within hail of the boat, in view of the growing opposition. He would take no unnecessary risks of his work being broken before he had secured their full understanding. Somewhere, not far from where he taught, perhaps within earshot, sat Levi, the toll-gatherer, 'at the receipt of customs.'

The Jews regarded, and not unnaturally, these customs officers as a criminal race. Matthew was of the lowest class of tax-gatherer, for the 'small' officer was he who himself stood at the receipt of custom, while the 'great' officer was the local man who employed him and remitted the dues to the financial company.[1] It is possible that

---

[1] The imperial government required large sums from the conquered provinces, but did not collect them directly. The business of collecting the revenue was farmed out to firms of tax-gatherers, and these firms undertook

in Christ's time the imperial government had in the case of Judea ceased to employ the Roman financial companies, and that the big collectors were appointed in the country itself by the native administration. These would, however, still employ a series of underlings, who would have opportunities for extortion and oppression which they actually used, as there is ample evidence; and even the gospels furnish proof, for the Baptist has to warn them to exact no more than is appointed them. The fact that Matthew was probably in the employ of some official not directly responsible to Rome, but to the Herodian administration, would not make him any the less unpopular. All alike were regarded as licensed robbers, as wild beasts in human shape, and if the pagan world so regarded them, how much more would a Jew, for the publicans were traitors, helping to 'bleed' their fellow-countrymen in the interests of the conqueror. Herod himself had to remit enormous sums to Rome, and considering the reckless

to render a fixed sum annually to the exchequer. Should the province yield less, the deficiency must be made good; if it yielded more the excess went to the company. 'Since only wealthy men durst run the risk, the business was in the hands of wealthy capitalists of the equestrian order. It was their interest to extort the utmost from their provinces. They did not conduct the business directly but employed agents to collect the revenue from the various districts.' (Smith, *The Days of His Flesh*, page 123.) These underlings, or sometimes even a third class of petty officials employed by them in their turn, are the publicans of our gospels. 'They carried on the rapacious work, bearing the brunt of the popular odium, while their superiors waxed fat securely in the distant capital and were belauded as "an ornament of the State, a bulwark of the Republic." ' (Cicero, quoted in *The Days of his Flesh*.)

These petty officials are again divided into two classes, the tax-gatherer proper, who collected ground tax, income tax, and poll tax; and the customs house officer in charge of the *douane*; he was more bitterly hated than the income-tax collector, for he might, and often did, 'inflict much greater hardship upon the poor people . . . there was tax and duty upon all imports and exports; on all that was bought and sold; bridge money, road money, harbour dues, town dues.' There were imposts on almost every conceivable thing: 'axles, wheels, pack animals, pedestrians, roads, highways; on admission to markets; on carriers, bridges, ships, and quays; on crossing dams, on licences —in short, on such a variety of objects, that even the research of modern scholars has not been able to identify all the names.' (Edersheim, *Life and Times of Jesus*, vol. i, page 516.)

luxury of his court, the expenditure for which had to be got somehow from the workers, it is possible that taxation in Galilee may have been even heavier than in the South. Herod's ambition to be regarded as half Jew by no means deceived the Galileans, who perceived him to be a foreigner, and who, in spite of the fact that they were themselves laxer and more liberal than their southern neighbours, must have been shocked at his pagan disregard of Jewish sentiment, and his introduction of heathen customs.

The fact that the 'common people' heard Jesus gladly was galling to the Pharisees, whose estimate of the masses will be dealt with later; and the more liberal Galileans who followed him, and from whom he sprang, were regarded with contempt by the stricter Jews, but the Pharisees would at least have believed that a teacher who professed to be a prophet of God would have joined with them, and indeed with these not over strict common folk of Galilee, in unsparing condemnation of Matthew the publican.

Jesus who denounces rapacity will soon be found companioning with these outcast extortioners. Was he a 'friend of every country but his own'? By what strange and obstinate perversity did he open out towards these 'untouchables'? It could not even be his absurd love of the worker, his sentimental liking for the poor, for here he was befriending their natural enemies. And although Matthew was not a rich man compared with the exploiters above him, still, he would be very comfortably circumstanced in comparison with the fruit-growers, and perhaps even the boatmen of the district. True, to follow Jesus it was demanded of him that he should abandon his profession, a severer demand than that of the sterner John, who bid the tax-gatherers not abandon their calling, but not to extort more than was due. But the 'religious' world of that day did not, with few exceptions, believe the conversion of a publican was possible and refused to mix with such outcasts nor did they entertain any hope of them.

Now Jesus penetrated below the surface of their trade. He saw men not just in the lump, but individually; and he refused to regard any class as beyond hope. What angered him was hypocrisy and smugness; the holy people who feared defilement if they should even speak to the toll collector, were themselves 'devouring widows' houses,' and were full of extortion and excess. Christ springs to the defence of the publicans, as against such censors as these; at least, the very fact that they did not pretend was in their favour; there was some possibility there.

Matthew the publican—it is he himself, in his gospel, who uses the humiliating name—sitting at the customs house by the lake at the entrance into Capernaum, would have to levy a toll on all the caravans of 'the great white road,' the 'way of the sea,' that artery of commerce between East and West. He would have to examine the baggage of the travellers arriving by boat, and the produce of the lake brought in by the fishing smacks, and the produce of the fields brought to market at Capernaum; also the loads brought out from the city by marketers and other buyers. Perhaps he had sold up some fisherman and his family, or some poor peasant. It was an unpleasant business but one must live.

The personality of St. Matthew presents us with a difficult problem. If he had been from the beginning merely a loose-living unpatriotic Jew with no interest in the national records, slightly contemptuous of the Mosaic legislation and the writings of the prophets, his taking service as a customs house officer in the employment of the pagan Herodians would be understandable. But his gospel, although it gladly lays stress on 'Galilee of the Nations,' and on such of our Lord's sayings as include all types of foreigners in the wide sweep of the kingdom, and in this respect is as internationalist as that of the Greek-speaking St. Luke, is steeped in reverence for the Law and the Prophets and for the patriotic traditions of his race.

All this concern with the national history may, of course, have been acquired by Levi after his conversion, but it is much more likely that as a boy he had loved the Jewish scriptures and looked forward to the coming of the Messiah.

What had happened that should have driven him to abandon his hope and to become a traitor to his country? It is significant that the gospel according to Matthew gives in much more detail and with more emphasis our Lord's bitter invective against the Pharisees. Matthew, I imagine, was not himself by nature a strong or creative leader. He had looked, perhaps, in earlier years to the sect of the Pharisees or the party of the Zealots for the leadership which he lacked, but had turned in disgust from the prevarications and hypocrisies of the first and from the crude and exclusive nationalism of the second. He had obviously not come across the Redemptionist group with their saner patriotism, their conviction of the need of a deep national repentance and their wider aspirations. He had turned in despair, had given up his faith and found in the comfortable and secure position of a *douanier* an apparent solution of his difficulties. In the companionship of a class whom the 'religious world' excluded from their company he had found good fellowship and friendships preferable to those of the Puritans. But down in the depths of his heart he must sometimes have felt a misery which it was difficult to stifle; he was a man who had lost his way and for him there seemed no hope and no future.

But of late months, on the wide quayside, there had been gathered crowds attracted by the words of one whom they hailed as a new prophet. Matthew would have listened to him from his seat at the customs, and have become more and more aware of something titanic and original in this teacher and in his burning message. Here was the very thing that the publican had longed for and not been able to create. Life might once more be worth living if he could become a disciple of this man. But Jesus of Nazareth would never stop to take notice of Levi the Outcast; the thing was inconceivable.

And then the miracle happened and the dream came true: 'And as Jesus passed forth from thence he saw a man, named Matthew, sitting at the receipt of customs; and he saith unto him, Follow me. And he arose and followed him.'

CHAPTER XVI

THE CULMINATING SCANDALS

JESUS knew that the calling of Matthew would further infuriate the 'good,' and place him for ever outside their consideration as a prophet. He took that risk, or rather certainty; he had no use for the self-styled 'just,' the rigorist authorities, the 'good.' He had come to call the 'sinners,' that was his answer to the critics when they observed that he called this rank outsider to be his follower, an officer in his new army of *sans-culottes*.

Matthew gave a supper party, a social; and invited other customs house officers, the riff-raff, harlots, and other soiled and wretched outsiders; and the 'people who count' tried to upset the new disciples and questioned them: 'Why eateth your master with publicans and sinners?' To missionize them is bad enough, as expressing hope in them; but to share a meal with them, to put himself on their level is to put himself quite outside the pale.

When Jesus heard it, he said unto them: 'They that are whole do not need the doctor, but the sick. I am not come to call the just but sinners.'[1]

Very soon the pious and propertied brought a new count against this impostor. It was on the question of the stated fasts. Perhaps it would put doubts in the minds of some of his new followers and divide them. The disciples of John and the Pharisees used to keep the stated fasts twice a week. These were not enjoined in Mosaic Law but were a later rule: like the Law generally, they had become a meaningless piece of rigorism, a burden on men's shoulders. Jesus probably kept the recognized fast, and may have been fasting on the day of his Eucharist. A new-fangled custom had arisen by his time for strict religious folk to observe

[1] 'To repentance.' This is left out in the best manuscripts.

two fasts weekly, Monday and Thursday; a custom to which Jesus would certainly be opposed. The freshness and realism of Jesus blow like the south wind through all moth-eaten formalism: 'Can the children of the bride-chamber fast while the bridegroom is with them?'

True, he has not come in contempt of the laws, but they have emptied law of its meaning and imposed a thousand new and burdensome regulations. He will squeeze out, and use, every ounce of meaning in the Law: all the real meaning and force of law for man shall be kept, but certain things must go, when they have become useless; for though this is a revival it is also the inauguration of a new dispensation, and you cannot stitch a patch of unfulled rag on an old cloak. When the patch gets wet it will shrink and tear the rotten stuff, making a worse rent. It is like putting new wine into old skins; the new wine will ferment and burst the unsupple skins, and wine and skins will both be lost.

In the gospel according to Luke, and only there, our Lord adds: 'And no man having drunk old wine desireth new: for he saith, the old is good.' This may be St. Luke's own comment, for doctors enjoy their glass of old wine and recommend a matured vintage to their patients. If the remark were really uttered by our Lord, it may be slightly ironical, like his 'that seeing they may see and not perceive,' and in that case the allusion would be to the conservatism of his less sympathetic hearers. It is, of course, possible that it may be actually a concession to that conservatism,[1] a sympathetic understanding of their slowness in grasping the new idea; he must not be too impatient with them, but must give them time to let the new wine of his gospel mature.

Some commentators have suggested that St. Luke merely collected any saying of our Lord on the subject of wine, but the Beloved Physician was not so unintelligent as that. The only other possibility is that it was, indeed, a saying of Jesus, but a piece of irony directed against himself. It is just the kind of thing you will find in Henrik Ibsen or

[1] Cf. David Smith, *The Days of His Flesh*.

Bernard Shaw, a witty comment, not on the authenticity of his teaching, but on the inadequacy of his illustration.

The rigorism of the religious world culminated in their observance of the Sabbath and the extreme importance they attached to it; and it is, therefore, the fifth and sixth of the scandals which Mark groups together that brought things to a crisis. Jesus had flouted the Law in touching the leper, had claimed for man the power to heal sin, had companioned with the 'untouchables,' had defended his followers when they had ignored the formal fasts, had become the hero of the common people and taught them to look with contempt upon the hypocrisies and greed of their political and religious leaders.

'And it came to pass that he went through the corn-fields on the Sabbath day, and his disciples began as they went to pluck the ears of corn.' St. Luke adds: 'And did eat, rubbing them in their hands.' And the Pharisees said unto him: 'Behold, why do they, on the Sabbath day, that which is not lawful?'

Now the religious world was not content with the laws of Moses as they stood, strict as those laws were as regards the Saturday rest. The Old Testament visits with death the Sabbath breaker: any one for instance found guilty of even gathering a few sticks to light a fire was to be stoned to death. Reaping and threshing were, of course, forbidden, but the Sabbath as other Jewish holy days, or holidays, were mostly feasts and times of rejoicing; days on which thou shalt rejoice, thou and thy household, 'this day is holy unto the Lord your God; mourn not nor weep . . . and all the people went their way to make great mirth.'[1]

This, then, was the idea of a holy day among the Jews of an earlier time, and the Sabbath, which, by the way, dates back much earlier than the recorded history of the Jews and is found among other nations, was based by the Hebrews on the parable in Genesis about God's work and rest, and upon the fact that on that day Jehovah had

[1] Nehemiah viii. 9–12.

declared Himself the enemy of tyrants and had effected the nation's deliverance from the bondage of the Egyptian Empire. They, then, under his command, devoted that day to rest and remembrance and to the worship of the God of liberty; and the study of their national and political history, and to works of mercy. The Law was savage as regards work on that day, to safeguard the poor, and to safeguard the joy and rest of the holiday. Pleasure was not forbidden. The Sabbath might be taken by a reader of the Old Testament as made for God, for His worship, but also equally well for man, as our Lord insists: 'The Sabbath was made for man and not man for the Sabbath.' But certainly they had made it of null effect by their traditions. They had laid it down that to pluck the ears was a kind of reaping and to rub them threshing. This seems extravagant, but is common sense itself as compared with some of the current interpretations.[1]

---

[1] There were thirty-nine principal prohibitions and a multitude of derivatives. Farrar gives an example of the persistence of these artificialities among the Jews. Abarbanel relates that when in 1492 the Jews were expelled from Spain and were forbidden to enter the city of Fez lest they should cause a famine, they lived on grass—yet even in this state religiously avoided the violation of their Sabbath by plucking the grass with their hands. To avoid this they took the much more laborious method of grovelling on their knees and cropping it with their teeth. Now these derivatives included the most absurd regulations. Among certain of the scribes it was argued that a woman must not look in a mirror on the day, for fear she should discover a grey hair among her locks and be tempted to pull it out: the extraction would be labour. To kill a flea was a criminal offence. One extreme school forbade movement of any kind, walking, talking, or even eating, though many still had their feasts on that day, but they had to be cold, as cooking was forbidden, but sometimes the difficulty was overcome by curious devices. A false tooth must not be worn: that was carrying a burden, a thing forbidden by the Law. A person suffering from lumbago must not rub the afflicted part. A tailor must not go out with his needle pinned on him on Friday towards even, lest he break the Law by carrying his burden on the holy day. It applied even to animals: a cock might not have a ribbon tied on its leg. Everything must rest, said the strict school of Shammai, even lifeless things: a lamp kindled on Friday must rest by being extinguished before the Saturday. The thing became so intolerable that the Mishnic Tractates include one devoted to legal evasions, of extraordinary puerility: e.g. a Sabbath journey is 2,000 cubits from one's house, but if on Friday a man deposited food for two meals it became his house and he might go on another 2,000 cubits

When the Pharisees object to this violation of the Sab-bath, he retorts: 'Have ye never heard what David did, when he had need and was hungry, he, and they that were with him? How he went into the house of God, when Abiather [1] was high priest, and did eat the shew-bread, which it is not lawful to eat save for the priests, and gave also to them that were with him?' [2]

The shew-bread was arranged in two piles, each con-taining six cakes, and would form a good meal for the royal law-breaker and his followers. The Lucan version, 'Have ye not read so much as this?' brings out the taunting nature of the challenge—you, so careful of every upstroke and comma of the scriptures, conveniently overlook whole passages which do not suit your purpose! Their hero David had courageously violated the Law on the plea of necessity with the sanction of the high priest, and Jesus approves his action.

The Pharisees are scandalized, for it would seem to them almost as presumptuous an attitude as would be the defence of breaking into the tabernacle and eating the hosts on the plea of hunger. True enough, the shew-bread was not supposed to contain the Real Presence, but it was among the most holy offerings of the Lord and was actually called the 'Bread of the Presence.'

His conclusion that the Sabbath was made for man and not man for the Sabbath, 'therefore the son of man is Lord even of the Sabbath,' is again a defence of the rights of

(about five-eighths of a mile). Narrow streets could become a private house by extending a beam across or a wire or rope along them; this by a legal fiction made them one house, so that anything done that might be done in a house might be done in the whole street.

For the whole subject cf. my *Day of the Sun*, which also discusses the medieval and modern Sabbath, and shows the extreme persistence of Sabbatarianism among Christians of many ages.

[1] Luke omits Abiather, and if Jesus mentions him his memory had failed him, as Abiather was not high priest at the time: but the insertion may be due to a copyist.

[2] Luke (Codex Bezae) inserts after vi. 4: 'The same day, having seen a man work on the Sabbath, he saith to him, Man, if thou knowest what thou doest, blessed art thou, but if thou knowest not, thou art accursed and a transgressor of the Law.'

man, as was his claiming for mankind the power to forgive sins.

The ultimate scandal is also concerned with the Sabbath. He had been teaching in the synagogue, and there was among his hearers a man with an atrophied hand. His opponents, knowing Jesus to be a Sabbath breaker, are on the watch. Telling the man to stand forth, he challenges them by asking if they hold it lawful to do a good action on the Sabbath day, and they are silent. 'And when he had looked round about on them with anger,'[1] being shocked at their hardness of heart, he tells the man to stretch out his hand and makes it whole. The Pharisees, driven to desperation, determine to destroy him.[2]

But how could they, seeing that they have no executive authority in the North? They are, therefore, obliged to appeal to their scornful opponents, the Herodians, and report him to the "Scotland Yard" at Capernaum.

---

[1] Some say Jesus, always mild and peace loving, never exhibited the slightest signs of anger. The above is among the many incidents which refutes this reading of his character.

[2] 'And they were filled with madness and communed what they might do with Jesus.' (Luke vi. 11.)

CHAPTER XVII

THE HERODIAN VIGILANCE JUSTIFIED

THIS appeal to the Herodian authorities was in fact extraordinary; for the Pharisees were horrified at the customs which the Herods were introducing into the land: the amphitheatres, the temples, the baths, the heathen games. Herod Antipas was contemptuous of the puritanism of the Pharisees; there was bitter opposition between the two, and yet their determination to destroy Jesus overbore their prejudice and drove them to this strange proceeding.

But if these six scandals against Pharisaic morality would have been anything but scandalous to the Herodians, what chance was there of securing government support in this effort to destroy Jesus? If we had only St. Mark's opening before us, the question would be a complete enigma. This much the Herodians [1] knew; namely that John the Baptist had been a disturber of the peace, and that Jesus had been in alliance with him, that at the moment of his friend's arrest he had returned to Galilee, and might be supposed to be carrying on the Baptist's agitation. But was there any definite proof to support this proposition? What was the nature of the Kingdom of Heaven which the new prophet was proclaiming?

If it was merely a system which would abolish puritan

---

[1] 'These supporters of the Herods were opposed to any dangerous manifestation which might shake the position of that dynasty. For such half-native rulers were only tolerated by the Romans as the best means of keeping order among a turbulent people. In particular any Messianic movement was dreaded by these courtiers. It would not only cause disturbances, but it seemed to reflect upon the lawfulness of the Herodian rule . . . they were glad to have the support of "the earnest and fanatical people." So this unholy alliance was formed.'—Headlam, *Life and Teaching of Jesus Christ*, page 199.

taboos, so much the better; but was it? Did not the
Baptist's teaching suggest something less innocent than
this? To solve the problem we must now turn to the
gospels of Matthew and Luke for an account of the first
year's propaganda in Galilee. We have already dealt
with their fuller accounts of John's mission and its
dangerous political content. We must now consider the
Sermon on the Mount as recorded by St. Matthew; here
we shall find a description in some detail of the nature
of the coming commonwealth, of the type of persons who
will enjoy it, and of those who will be refused admittance
and treated as *emigrés* and outcasts. This done we shall
turn to St. Luke and give an account of our Lord's visit
to Nazareth, where he addressed his fellow-townsmen on
the subject of the Acceptable Year. Both these accounts
of the teaching given during his first year's mission in
Galilee will afford ample evidence of the wisdom of the
Pharisaic report to the authorities at Capernaum, and of
the reason for the government treating the matter sufficiently
seriously to keep Jesus under observation.

It is, of course, possible that the Sermon on the Mount[1]
was delivered after the crisis, and that he retired into the
hills with certain chosen disciples in order to give them more
intensive instruction to prepare them to carry on his work
in the event of the coalition of Pharisees and Herodians
being successful and leading to his immediate destruction.
True, the instruction in the hills was not given exclusively
to these few followers, for he exclaimed: 'He who has ears
to hear, let him hear,' and St. Matthew tells us of crowds of
people who made a fringe round the disciples and listened
eagerly.

[1] Dr. Gore, who has written a useful short life called *Jesus of Nazareth*,
and given us many other valuable books, has written an unfortunate earlier
work on the Sermon on the Mount. He describes our Lord as going into
the hills to avoid the crowd, a description not borne out by the text, and
interprets the sermon as giving a new set of regulations which it is practically
impossible for men to follow. Jesus heaps difficult rules upon them, in order
to show them that they cannot, without the help of his grace, obey them.
This will be seen by reference to the text to be a very perverted account of
the sermon.

But even if this was so, the hill teaching would be an example of what he had been proclaiming before the report to the authorities, and, therefore, the exact sequence does not greatly matter.

Critics have often described the Sermon on the Mount as St. Matthew's collection given on various occasions and in separate localities, but there is no real reason for this assumption; and it is more probable, as has recently been suggested, that it was a kind of 'summer school' which may have lasted for several days.

And seeing the multitude, he went up into the mountain: and when he had sat down his disciples came unto him: and he opened his mouth, and taught them, saying:

'Blessed are the spirited poor: for theirs is the Kingdom of Heaven.' Poor in spirit does not mean poor spirited, but can best be paraphrased as above: it is the eager and intelligent poor, those fishermen, craftsmen, and peasants who were alive to his message, who were seizing hold upon the idea of the coming commonwealth and would hasten its advent.

'Blessed are those that mourn: for they shall be comforted.' This probably refers to those who lament the tragedies of the present system.

'Blessed are the meek: for they shall inherit the earth.' It is not the skies that these people will inherit, but the earth: but the meek in our modern sense are unlikely either now or in the future to own the earth. The term really means generous or reasonable,[1] and a modern critic [2] translates it as 'good in team work with others.' It is the alert and generous who work not one against the other but in co-operation, who will inherit the earth.

'Blessed are they who hunger and thirst after righteousness: for they shall be filled.' Righteousness has already been explained as meaning justice: it may mean more than this, but it certainly means this much, both in its Hebrew and Greek forms.

[1] Aristotle.   [2] Du Bose.

'Blessed are the merciful: for they shall obtain mercy.'

'Blessed are the pure in heart: for they shall see God.' Pure in heart does not refer so much to sexual purity, although it includes this, but to single-mindedness in all things. The Christ's beatitudes do not only include material blessings, but the spiritual perception of God.

'Blessed are the peace-makers: for they shall be called the sons of God.' Peace-makers as against those that are contentious and quarrelsome.

'Blessed are they that have been persecuted for righteousness' sake: for theirs is the Kingdom of Heaven.' Those who have been martyred in the cause of justice hold already in their hearts the righteous commonwealth which they will soon inherit.

'Blessed are ye when men shall reproach you, and persecute you falsely, for my sake. Rejoice, and be exceeding glad: for great is your reward in (the coming commonwealth of) heaven: for so persecuted they the prophets which were before you.'

The beatitudes according to St. Luke are given a little differently and quite certainly after the crisis. It has been supposed that Luke gives them in their harsher and more original form, but it is likely enough that the Lord would many times repeat these blessings in slightly varying words.

The chief difference between Matthew and Luke is that the latter author quotes Jesus as contrasting the blessings on the eager and generous seekers after the kingdom with the doom that awaits the callous rich and the scorners of that brave new world.

'But woe unto you that are rich; for ye have received your consolation.' They had received their 'good things,' their clothing of purple and fine linen, and their sumptuous daily fare.[1]

'Woe unto you, ye that are full now; for ye shall hunger.' We may compare with this his mother's joy, when God is

---

[1] Cf. the parable of Dives and Lazarus.

sending the rich empty away and filling the hungry with good things.

'Woe unto you, ye that laugh now; for ye shall mourn and weep.' This may refer to their enjoyment of idle and luxurious pleasures or to their scornful laughter at the idea of a coming world in which the first shall be last and the last first.

'Woe unto you, when all men shall speak well of you: for in the same manner did their fathers to the false prophets.' The false prophets were those who found it paid them to toady to the rich and throw in their lot with them.

The eager-hearted listeners are the mental descendants of that living group 'The Holy Remnant,' which in times of decay kept the nation alive: they are the salt whose cleansing power runs through Palestine. But if the salt should lose its pungency, what hope is there for Israel? Even this living group, this last hope of national redemption, will then be trodden under foot of men as a heap of worthless rubbish.

'Ye are the light of the world. A city set on a hill cannot be hid. Neither do men light a lamp and put it under the basket measure but on the stand: and it shineth unto all that are in the house, even so let your light shine before men that they may see your good works, and glorify your Father which is in Heaven.'

People accuse me of being a lawbreaker, because I have pierced beneath the dead letter to the living meaning as did the prophets. 'Think not that I came to destroy the law or the prophets; I came not to destroy but to fulfil. For verily I say unto you, till heaven and earth pass away, one iota or upstroke shall in no wise pass away from the law till all things be accomplished.'

Accused of law breaking he yet exhorts them to keep the least of the commandments, if, indeed, they keep them in their spirit and original intention. For I say unto you that except your sense of justice shall exceed that of the scribes and Pharisees ye shall in no wise enter into the divine commonwealth.

In order to show them that he did not mean by keeping every upstroke of the Law a meticulous observance of sanitary or ceremonial regulations, he now gives certain illustrations which are all humanitarian.

He first speaks about killing and by the context it is obvious that he is not speaking of slaughter in battle but of private murder. He refers to the ancient law of an eye for an eye and a tooth for a tooth: this law was in reality a humane modification of a more ancient vendetta which went on piling up revenge against your enemy.

Jesus further modifies the ancient law or actually abrogates it. 'I say unto you that ye resist not the evil man, but whosoever shall smite thee on thy right cheek turn to him the other also, and if any man will sue thee at the law and take away thy coat let him have thy cloak also.' If a civil or military officer compels you to go a mile, you should willingly go two.

Turning the other cheek is a counsel which has often been hotly challenged, and once more, it all depends upon the spirit in which the action is done. If a boy refuses to hit back through being a little coward, turning the other cheek obviously becomes a contemptible action. It is sometimes also necessary to hit back if your motive is to suppress a man who has been a bully and has made himself a nuisance to the whole neighbourhood; when persuasion has been tried and has failed. The counsel of Jesus about non-resistance was given to a very quarrelsome people, always taking provocation on the slightest offence, and always up in arms to defend their rights or their supposed rights. Turning the other cheek is not only often heroic but immensely sensible. It means greater courage than hitting back, it involves generosity and self-restraint. If done in this heroic spirit the enemy has sometimes been converted into a lifelong friend.

After showing that it is not enough to avoid the actual sin of murder, but that all murderous thoughts and hatreds are destructive to the soul, he goes on to show that the ancient law, spiritually discerned, does not only condemn adultery as ordinarily understood, but that there are adulteries of the heart and desire.[1]

He reminds them that the ancient law forbade them to break their oaths or to falsify them; this may refer to oaths taken in a court of law, but covers the common practice in the East of swearing on every occasion by God or some sacred thing, about the soundness of the material you are selling or in concluding a bargain. Buyers and sellers exonerate themselves from the sin of dishonesty if they have not used an oath; whereas the Mosaic Law holds them to their oaths, our Lord exclaims: I say unto you, swear not at all, neither by God's heavens nor by any sacred thing: let your assertions be unsupported by oaths, so that your simple yea, yea, and nay, nay, be taken as the statement of an honest man who can be absolutely relied upon.

Again he insists on strictly honest relations with your neighbour. When you give alms do not make a flourish about it, or as we now say don't publish it in the newspapers. He seems to suggest, in using the term righteousness, that your almsgiving is a bare act of justice to your poorer brethren. 'Take heed that ye do not your righteousness before men to be seen of them.' Jesus and his followers held that riches were the wealth gained at the expense of the workers and that almsgiving was the act of restoring to them what they themselves had produced.[2] When, therefore, you give alms, 'let not thy left hand know what thy right hand doeth.' Even if the above interpretation of almsgiving is questioned, Jesus would still have insisted that it must be done quietly and without ostentation.

As to private prayer, let it, above all, be private, and not as the prayers of the 'religious world' who love to make a great show of their prayers and to feel by their much praying immeasurably superior to their neighbours. 'And in praying use not vain repetitions' as the heathen do. We must notice the word 'vain,' for he does not here forbid

---

[1] The whole subject of our Lord's teaching on divorce and sexual morality will be dealt with in a later chapter.
[2] See Chapter XXVI, 'The Mammon of Injustice.'

any kind of repetition. A child may use repetitions when demanding sweets or jam of its mother; these are often annoying, but by no means vain or useless, as the child generally succeeds in getting what it wants. Our Lord himself apparently noticed this, as we may see in his parable of the importunate widow and the judge. Idle repetitions refer more probably to purely mechanical demands or to such devices as the prayer-wheel of the Buddhist. Your Father already knows your needs, let therefore your prayers be short and to the point. 'After this manner, therefore, pray ye,' and Jesus then goes on to give them the Pater Noster as their model.

We must notice first of all that it is 'Our Father,' not 'My Father,' and that all through it is not 'me' but 'us,' not individualistic but collective; the needs and difficulties of the group are in contemplation. The name of God means the personality of God, and first of all we pray that the Divine Being may be reverenced, but His name can only be hallowed by hastening the coming of the divine commonwealth, according to His will. It must be noticed that the words 'as in heaven, so on earth' govern not only the doing of the divine will, but also the coming of the divine kingdom; so that we are to pray, not that we should go to heaven when we die, but that heaven should be established on earth while we live.

The next petition is concerned with the food supply for our neighbours and for ourselves: 'daily bread' may be translated as 'food for the coming day.'[1] Some, shocked at so material a request, have tried to spiritualize this into sustenance for our souls, but this is not an allowable interpretation.

'And forgive us our debts, as we also have forgiven our debtors.' It must be noted that the request is conditioned by our forgiveness of others; God will *not* forgive us unless we forgive them.

'And bring us not into temptation, but deliver us from the evil one.' This prayer may have special reference to

---

[1] R.V., margin.

the doom and disasters which are immediately to precede the Messianic age; when men's hearts will fail them from fear and many, unable to endure, will betray the Christ. Bring us not into this terrible disaster, lest we fail Thee; deliver us from the satanic power.[1]

The Master's last instance of the spiritual interpretation or development of the old tradition is concerned with fasting. We have already shown that although he defended his disciples in their non-observance of novel Pharisaic fasts, he probably fasted himself, and here distinctly contemplates the continuance of the practice by Christians. But fasts must be observed in the right spirit.

Fasting has been practised in all times and in almost all religions. It has proved itself of inestimable value in the development of the soul. When some great mental or spiritual adventure is on foot, people have trained and prepared themselves for it by days and days of abstinence from food and sometimes from drink. By abstinence money is often saved to be given to the needy and destitute. But fasting, like everything else, is often abused; and it is against such abuses that Jesus warns his followers. As in the case of almsgiving and prayer, let your fasting be done quietly and without showiness and fuss. St. Francis de Sales says that it is better to take a little food if otherwise you would shame your kind host and make every one at table feel uncomfortable. If by your abstinence from food you are feeding your self-satisfaction and priggishness, it is better not to fast at all. Therefore, 'when thou fastest, anoint thy head, and wash thy face; that thou be not seen of men to fast, but of thy Father which is in secret; and thy Father, which seeth in secret, shall recompense thee.'

Just as earlier in his discourse he dealt with private

---

[1] The doxology, 'For Thine is the Kingdom . . .', is probably an early Catholic addition as it is not found in Luke or in the best manuscripts of Matthew. It is curious that Protestant churches invariably use it, although they base themselves on scripture and reject the authority of the Church; no concluding phrase, however, could have greater power or beauty.

killing and demanded of the new group who were to form
the nucleus of the divine commonwealth that they should
not bear malice against their brethren, and that no sacrifice
at the altar would be accepted until they had put themselves right with their neighbours, so now he sums it
all up: 'Ye have heard that it was said, Thou shalt love
thy neighbour, and hate thine enemy; but I say unto you,
Love your enemies, and pray for them that persecute you;
that ye may be sons of your Father which is in heaven: for
He maketh His sun to shine on the evil and the good, and
sendeth rain on the just and the unjust.   Ye therefore shall
be perfect, as your heavenly Father is perfect.'   This,
then, is to be the spirit of the new group and of the New
World Order which they are seeking.

There is much in the above which would be offensive
to the Herodian government, and Herod's secret service
men might see in the teaching on divorce a criticism of
their king, remembering the conflict between the Baptist
and Herod on his remarriage.

Our Lord's instructions on the use of material things
would also be taken as challenge to the 'powers that be,'
for they had certainly been all too successful in laying up
for themselves treasures on earth where moth and rust
corrupt [1] and where thieves break through and steal.   The
followers of Jesus are ordered to lay up for themselves
treasures in the coming commonwealth, such treasures as
neither moth nor rust could corrupt, nor thieves steal.
He gives examples and tells them not to be over-anxious
about food or clothing or shelter.   You cannot serve God
and money.   The carefree birds neither reap nor sow nor
store up in barns, and yet the generous Father feeds them:
'Are ye not of more value than they?'   And as to clothing,
the brilliantly coloured anemones are more gorgeously
clothed than even the luxurious Solomon; God will provide
for His children.   Do not, therefore, worry about food

---

[1] Where food is hoarded it decays; where by reason of excessive possessions
clothes are stored the moth eats them away: the same is true of many metals
when hoarded.

or clothes or shelter, for after all these things the pagan nations seek. First things first: put in the forefront of your minds and lives God's commonwealth and found it upon His justice and all these material things will be added unto you.

A very usual interpretation is that if an individual submits to Jesus, however poor he may be, he will be abundantly provided with all the necessaries of life. This does actually happen in the case of some, but our Lord does not promise his followers a room at Brown's or the Waldorf Astoria.

No doubt in many cases the man or woman who follows God absolutely, who perhaps has been dismissed from some big draper's shop for telling the truth to a customer, when questioned as to the quality of the goods, may find other employment or may be supplied by his comrades with 'bread sufficient for the day.' But many instances could be quoted to the contrary, such as that recorded by Alexander Irvine in one of his early books, where an old 'down and out' comes forward out of the darkness and a policeman asks him: 'Who are you?' The old man answers: 'A friend of God.' The constable replies: 'Is that how God treats his friends?' The old man was joyous and satisfied; God was really his friend, but God had not satisfied him with bread.

Jesus warns a certain scribe who is anxious to follow him that foxes have holes and the birds of the air have nests, but the Son of Man hath not where to lay his head. To another would-be follower he says, in effect, who marches with me marches with the hangman's noose round his neck.[1]

At first glance our Lord's answer to Peter's 'We have left all and followed thee, what shall we have?' may seem to contradict this, for according to St. Luke he promises his followers 'a hundredfold now in this time, houses, and brethren, and sisters and mothers, and children and lands, with persecutions: and in the age to come eternal life.' It would, however, be a very unimaginative critic who would interpret the promise literally; it would be a little

---

[1] 'Let him take up his cross.' (Mark viii. 34.)

embarrassing to have so large an addition to your family, even if you had a hundred houses to lodge them in. The obvious meaning is that to the man who abandons cares and riches and luxuries, or who gives up his all to follow the Christ and the cause, wide avenues are opened up; closer friendships and a whole world of mental and spiritual possessions.

The promise that all material necessities will be abundantly provided to those who sought God's kingdom and his justice was not, in fact, given to individuals as such, but to individuals in a company which was already becoming the nucleus of the new world. If they were to establish the divine commonwealth on the foundation of God's justice, if a world of men were to spring up in which greed had given place to generosity and domination to service, in which men co-operated to produce, instead of competing to destroy, all things would be added to them.

Many people dismiss Jesus and his message as outmoded in our days. But if it was true that the world could be abundantly provided in his times with all necessary goods, if only men would reconstruct it on the rock of God's eternal will, it is surely a thousand times truer to-day, when harvests of fish are thrown back into the sea, when thousands of bags of coffee are sunk, when acres on acres of corn are wantonly destroyed or burned as engine fuel, because men obstinately persist in the capitalist-imperialist system of production for the profit of a few, and turn their backs on God's co-operative commonwealth and its principle of production for the use of all. Under modern conditions the earth has become so prolific that if mankind were to take the Sermon on the Mount seriously, the wants of every nation, and of all its citizens, could be abundantly secured.

This, then, is the kernel of Christianity, and not every one that saith unto Jesus: 'Lord, Lord,' will enter into the Kingdom of Heaven; this commonwealth of spiritual buoyancy and material plenty is reserved for those who 'do the will of my Father which is in heaven.'

'Every one, therefore, which heareth these words of

mine, and doeth them, shall be likened unto a wise man, which built his house upon the rock: and the rain descended and floods came, and the winds blew, and beat upon that house, and it fell not, for it was founded upon the rock. And every one that heareth these words of mine, and doeth them not, shall be likened unto a foolish man, which built his house upon the sand: and the rain descended, and the floods came, and the winds blew, and smote upon that house; and it fell, and great was the fall thereof.' [1]

[1] Matthew vii. 24–7.

CHAPTER XVIII

THE DRAMA DEVELOPS

BEFORE Jesus sends out his twelve disciples on their tour through Galilee, he instructs them again in a second series of teachings on a tableland among the hills. The opening beatitudes of this second 'summer school,' if indeed it be such, have already been dealt with. It only remains to comment on one other peculiarity of this Lucan account.

In the Matthean Sermon on the Mount, our Lord urges them to 'give to him that asketh of thee, and from him that would borrow of thee, turn not thou away.' In the instructions given by St. Luke this command is developed fully.

Many commentators water down the teaching on loaning and the *New Commentary* curiously enough entirely ignores it; but Jesus is explicit on the subject. He commands them to 'lend, hoping for nothing again.'[1] Some have said that this is merely an instruction to give liberally, not caring whether or no the money is returned. But the Greek word is definitely 'loan,' not 'give,' and as Jesus emphatically states that he is come to fulfil the Law and the

[1] 'Lend hoping for nothing again,' is the A.V. translation, and is supported by the Vulgate. The R.V. has 'Lend never despairing' and in the margin 'some ancient authorities read "despairing of no man."' 'Never despairing,' i.e. 'without anxiety about the result' (Alford) is the rendering given in the Alexandrine, Vatican, Bezae, and other manuscripts. Another reading found in some versions is 'causing no one to despair,' i.e. refusing no one (Alford). Whether 'despairing of no one' or 'hoping for nothing again' be the correct reading, the context given in my text shows that a loan on interest is in our Lord's mind. Either he means 'loan hoping for no interest' or 'loan believing that the creditor will pay you back your capital.' We are giving one instance of 100 per cent per annum, but if this were not in the mind of Jesus, he would still have been correct in stating that sinners lend to sinners, hoping for as much again; as the creditor who lends hopes, by interest, within a few years to double his capital, and still ultimately get the loan repaid.

Prophets, and both Law and Prophets are full of the prohibition of all interest in money or kind, it would have been strange, to say the least of it, if our Lord had not repeated the ancient command.

It is said that this was not the type of instruction that he would have given to simple fisherfolk and peasants. Critics should be more careful of their context. Fisherfolk might, it is true, have no temptation in this direction, but Klausner has conclusively shown that there was in that day a class of richer peasant, whom we should in our own times call the Kulak or 'hard fist,' who was in the habit of lending at interest to his poorer neighbours and evicting them when they could not pay him, and this in direct contradiction of the Mosaic Law. Besides all this, among the audience, we are distinctly told, were not only the simple folk of the countryside, but a great multitude of people from Trans-Jordan, from the pagan cities of the Decapolis, from the sophisticated Syrophoenician district, from Jerusalem which had become riddled with capitalists waxing fat at the expense of the workers, and from the Idumean province south of the capital. He had also among his audience publicans such as Levi, who were in the habit of loaning at interest.

It is highly significant that not only at Rome, but in the provinces, usury had become a scandal of the first magnitude; so much so that laws had to be enacted limiting it at this time, or a little later, to twelve per cent. These laws were, however, more honoured in the breach than in the observance; forty per cent and even seventy was often charged.

There is at least one instance where the creditors were so grasping that they were demanding a hundred per cent on their loan. This was the case, some three-quarters of a century before Christ, when the banking firm of Rabirius and Co.[1] were charging Ptolemy of Egypt 100 per cent on the enormous sums they lent him. In the sequel to that particular story, the bankers and smaller investors

[1] Cf. Kautsky, *Foundations of Christianity*, page 105.

lost everything, but it is a significant commentary on the Christ's shrewd saying in his Sermon on the tableland to the effect that sinners lend to sinners hoping to receive as much again. The bankers in this case expected to receive as much again every year. The rates of interest charged were, indeed, so excessive that they remind one of the loans of the modern usurers who demand of the poor the most exorbitant returns. The private moneylender in India and in the East generally might also be quoted as an instance of ruinous exactions.

So far, then, from its being unlikely that Jesus would deal with the subject, it was almost impossible for him, in the presence of moneylending farmers and a corrupt cosmopolitan audience, to ignore what was a burning topic of the day.

There is one other instance of his teaching given as part of that first year's Galilean propaganda which we must deal with as likely to be considered by the Herodian administration as subversive and politically dangerous. We refer to the first and, indeed, the only address that he was ever allowed to give in his native town of Nazareth.

St. Luke gives the fullest account and puts it very early in the Galilean ministry, but there does seem to have been a preliminary tour and certain healings before the visit to Nazareth. Capernaum apparently had already been made the general headquarters of the movement. Luke may have got the information from accurate traditions picked up in Palestine; Mark puts the incident later, and Matthew puts it after the Sermon on the Mount and many other incidents, and does not give the content of the sermon, but only their astonishment at his wisdom, considering that he was only the carpenter's son, that his family were well known to them and just working-class folk. Jesus might well exclaim, a prophet is not without honour, save in his own country and among his own kinsmen.

It is noteworthy that Luke had Mark before him when he wrote and yet ignores his order of events. It is, therefore, likely that Luke's own order and account of the incident is the more correct considering that he is so careful an historian.

We may take it then that Jesus came back to his native town, and there was allowed to preach in the synagogue.[1] Being handed a scroll of the prophet Isaiah he deliberately chose a certain passage and, as was the custom, commented upon it.

The passage was the famous quotation concerning the Acceptable Year: it was a passage filled with Messianic significance and charged with hope about the good time coming. The Acceptable Year was either the seventh year fallow when the whole community were to share the fruits of the earth in common, when all debts were to be cancelled and there was to be a general amnesty; or more probably the year of Jubilee when, in addition to these generous enactments in favour of the workers and the peasants, the land was to be returned to the original families who held it. This would, indeed, be good news for the poor and by no means an acceptable year for the wealthy, whether they were rich Jews or Herodians.

'The spirit of the Lord is upon me, because he anointed me to preach good tidings to the poor: he hath sent me to proclaim release to the captives, and recovering of sight to the blind, to set at liberty them that are bruised, to proclaim the Acceptable Year of the Lord. And he closed the book, and gave it back to the attendant, and sat down; and the eyes of all in the synagogue were fastened on him. And he began to say unto them, To-day hath this Scripture been fulfilled in your ears.' To-day is a new order of society being proclaimed; and all the congregation wondered at the words of grace which proceeded out of his mouth. They were astonished that a son of the carpenter who made their ploughs and benches should speak with such authority; astonished but a little sceptical. He says, therefore, 'doubtless ye will say unto me this parable, Physician, heal thyself: whatsoever we have heard done at Capernaum, do also here in thine own country.'

[1] Cf. Luke iv for the whole incident.

So far they had listened to him with a certain amount of admiration; they welcomed the proclamation of the new society if it were to be a good time for their own nation, but now their attitude suddenly changes, and it is with indignation that they hear the conclusion of his sermon, for Jesus continues: 'But of a truth I say unto you, There were many widows in Israel in the days of Elijah, when the heaven was shut up three years and six months, when there came a great famine over all the land; and unto none of them was Elijah sent, but only to Zarephath, in the land of Sidon, unto a woman that was a widow. And there were many lepers in Israel in the time of Elisha the prophet; and none of them was cleansed, but only Naaman the Syrian.'

They were all filled with wrath in the synagogue as they heard this pronouncement in favour of foreigners; their jingo nationalist spirit was aroused, and in consequence they rose up and cast him forth out of his native town and led him to the brow of the hill, up which their city climbed, that they might throw him down headlong; but, calmly passing through the midst of them, Jesus went his way.

Although the contents of these three proclamations, the Sermons on the Mount and on the tableland and that at Nazareth, would infuriate the Jewish religionists, there was much in them to make the Herodian government uneasy and to put it on its guard. Hence the justification of the report to the Capernaum authorities.

Jesus, in consequence of the combined opposition of the Pharisees and Herodians, now to some extent changes his tactics and exercises a certain amount of caution. He immediately 'withdrew' to the lake-side and ordered a fishing-boat to wait on him because of the crowds that thronged him, but also quite possibly in order to effect an escape to the opposite shore, where he would be safe from arrest by the secret service men of Herod Antipas; for he would be in the territory of Herod Philip, a mild and gentle ruler, who would have no quarrel with him.

The crowds were immense, and he again healed many who were afflicted with bodily and mental ailments, and tried to silence the mentally diseased when they proclaimed his Messianic mission, calling him the Son of God; the claim to Messiahship would certainly have hastened his arrest.

Arrest, however, was not in fact immediately attempted, so Jesus now climbs up into the hills to pray all night and to be alone with God. There in the silence he is thinking out a new plan of campaign, for, in spite of all the dangers, his word must, somehow or other, take root in the people's wills and minds. The people are beginning to look to him for a lead, as sheep to a shepherd.

Suppose the authorities should succeed in destroying him, what would happen to this confused and scattered people? There in the quiet hills he discovers the plan which will ensure the continuance of the propaganda. The disciples, who have already had their marching orders in the summer school instructions, are now assembled, and from them he chooses twelve [1] that they might be his intimately instructed friends, and that he might send them forth to preach the kingdom and to heal. Before they actually begin their tour they are accidentally, if anything in this world is accidental, to witness a scene which should have changed their whole outlook, for on entering Capernaum, the Roman centurion in charge of the city sends the elders of the synagogue, asking Jesus to heal his servant who was dangerously ill. The Roman officer was a pious man who had much sympathy with the Jewish nation, and had built them a synagogue. Jesus set out towards the man's house, but was met by friends of the centurion with the message: 'Lord, I am not worthy that thou shouldest

---

[1] Their names were: Simon Peter and Andrew his brother; John and James his brother; Philip and Bartholomew (Nathanael); Matthew (Levi) and Thomas; James, the son of Alphaeus (Alphaeus and Cleophas are synonymous) and Thaddaeus (identical with Lebbaeus and with Judas son of James); Simon the Zealot (Canaanite is synonymous with Zealot) and Judas Iscariot, who turned traitor. Iscariot means the man of Kerioth, a town in the south of Judea. Judas was the only apostle who was not a Galilean. Peter is generally the spokesman, *primus inter pares*, and, with James and John, is the intimate of the Master.

N

come unto my roof: speak the word only and my servant shall be healed.' Being himself an officer with authority, accustomed to order his soldiers about, he did not wish to give Jesus, or the crowds, the impression that he was *ordering* him to do this; he would not trouble the Master, but confidently believed that Jesus had the power to cure his servant by merely speaking the word of healing. This amazing faith so impressed Jesus that he exclaimed: 'I have not found so great faith, no, not in Israel.' It is then that he makes the pronouncement, startling and heretical to his Jewish hearers: 'I say unto you, that many shall come from the east and the west, and shall sit down with Abraham, and Isaac, and Jacob, in the kingdom of heaven; but the sons of the kingdom shall be cast forth into the outer darkness: there shall be the weeping and gnashing of teeth.'

This saying became the battle-cry of the early Church in its controversy with the Judaizing brethren for the inclusion of foreigners on terms of equality.

The centurion had not believed in vain, for they that were sent returned to the house and found the servant healed of his disease.

Jesus now goes home. But the crowds are so great that he and his disciples cannot even get a meal; people are thronging about him, beseeching him to cure them. He heals many and casts the demons out of those mentally diseased. His friends warn him of the danger of this renewed public mission and tell him he must be mad. The danger is indeed imminent, for there now appear on the scene scribes from Jerusalem who accuse him not of being mad but bad, saying: 'He hath Beelzebub, and, By the prince of the devils casteth he out devils.' But Jesus immediately answered: 'How can Satan cast out Satan?' and gives poignant illustrations of the absurdity of this charge. It was not only absurd but blasphemous. It was the unforgivable sin.

This blasphemy against the Holy Spirit which can never be forgiven, neither in this present age or order of things, nor in the age to come, has puzzled theologians and ordinary readers of the Bible for centuries. The Christ says nothing whatsoever about the ultimate fate of those guilty, but the sin, whatever its character, seems so grave and so deeply rooted, that not only during the present disorders, but in the coming commonwealth, God himself cannot cure it nor forgive it. Every other vice can be healed and absolved, even the crimes against men and women and against the Messiah himself, the Representative Man, but this sin against the very spirit, this black depth of iniquity at the root of certain people's nature, which calls evil good and good evil is almost impossible to root out and forgive.

A man's nature has become so warped that there is no place for him in the new world nor would he understand it. He will be its most implacable enemy, he will be among the *emigrés* cast out and bitter, where there shall be weeping and gnashing of teeth.

It was because of this fierce conflict with the Pharisees, who at Jerusalem were possibly members of the southern executive, that his mother and his brethren tried to see him, to warn him of the danger he was in. 'And they say unto him, Behold, thy mother and thy brethren without seek for thee. And he answereth them, and saith, Who is my mother and my brethren? And looking round on them which sat round about him, he saith, Behold, my mother and my brethren! For whosoever shall do the will of God, the same is my brother, and sister, and mother.'[1]

His mother was naturally anxious for his personal safety, but he seems to have been impatient of her solicitude. We have shown that she had seen in her son the Messiah who would put down the mighty from their seats and would champion them of low degree, but she was only now beginning to understand that the sword must pierce through her own heart also. The sword's point was indeed at her heart when she perceived the enmity which her son was arousing, and the danger of his destruction.

[1] Mark iii. 32–5.

He would naturally include his mother among those who did the will of God: she was normally pre-eminent among such, but her mother love and care for his bodily safety got in the way and, for the moment, he felt it a hindrance to his work. At a later stage a woman was to cry out: 'Blessed is the womb that bear thee and the paps which thou hast sucked.' He immediately replies: 'Yes, indeed, but,[1] blessed are they that hear the word of God and keep it.' He by no means denies the blessedness of his mother, but that blessedness depended not on God's 'capricious' choice of her as mother of the Messiah, or on the mere fact of her having borne such a son, but on her own eager heart, her purity, her single-mindedness, on all those virtues which had drawn God down to earth from heaven. Our Lord's attitude to his mother when she comes to warn him reminds us of that earlier incident at Cana, when the wine supply had run short; although for the moment he seemed to ignore her, she knows him so well that she is quite sure that he will do what she asks, and therefore says to the servants: 'Whatsoever he saith unto you, do it.' It is remarkable that here again he seems, after all, to have taken her advice, for he either goes South on the same day to the border town of Nain, where within an hour or so he could cross into safety, or teaches the crowds from a boat which could soon be sailed across the lake to the territory of Herod Philip.

It is really impossible to say for certain whether Luke's order of events is to be preferred to Mark's, but assuming that St. Luke was compelled to insert into the Markan narrative certain information which later he himself had come by, we will deal with the incident at Nain, and what follows it in his story, here.

Jesus, going southward to this border town, is met at its entrance by the funeral procession of a young man. The mother, disconsolate, is weeping by the bier. Jesus

[1] Alford's translation; Calvinists and some others think that they are honouring God by referring His acts to His own Capricious Will, and not to His Will or Reason conditioned by human response.

stops and has compassion on her grief; he raises the dead
and restores the only son to his mother. The crowds are
amazed and there is great commotion and excitement. His
fame grows apace, and John the Baptist in his fortress
prison further south at Machaerus hears rumours of these
things. His disciples were still at large and were allowed
access to him in the prison, and he sends them to Jesus,
with the pathetic question: 'Art thou he that should come,
or look we for another?'

It was perhaps more than a year since his arrest and his
recognition of Jesus as one greater than himself, and the
commencement of the fiery and consuming mission of the
prophet of Galilee. Amazing rumours were being spread
about his personality and propaganda, but how much was
idle gossip and how much was truth? If indeed this was
the Messiah of his dreams, why had no rescue of himself
been effected? Here he was, month by month, languishing
in jail, and when the new prophet came South, and the
rumours grew more and more insistent, perhaps a ray of
hope lit up the dark prison and he sends the messengers
with that question, the answer to which would be the turning point for him. What, then, would matter imprisonment or torture, life or death, if the leader of his dreams
had really come?

The reply that Jesus sends back to the imprisoned Baptist
is of a realistic nature. It would certainly not have convinced the 'religious' world, but it would reassure the
prisoner, for it would tell him that just such a Messiah as
he had been announcing was among them. For 'in that
hour he cured many of diseases and plagues and evil spirits;
and on many that were blind he bestowed sight. And
he answered and said unto them, Go your way, and tell
John what things ye have seen and heard; the blind receive
their sight, the lame walk, the lepers are cleansed, and the
deaf hear, the dead are raised up, the poor have good
tidings preached to them. And blessed is he, whosoever
shall find none occasion of stumbling in me.'[1]

[1] Luke vii. 21-3 (R.V.)

This warning not to be scandalized which runs through all his teaching, for 'scandalized' is a closer translation of the Greek word than the Authorized 'offended,' was very necessary in case many should fall away, shocked at so unconventional a gospel.

When the messengers had gone, he begins to appraise John as the daring and rugged herald of the new world. 'What went ye out into the wilderness to behold? A reed shaken with the wind? But what went ye out to see? A man clothed in soft raiment? Behold, they which are gorgeously apparelled, and live delicately, are in kings' courts. But what went ye out to see? A prophet? Yea, I say unto you, and much more than a prophet. This is he of whom it is written, behold, I send my messenger before thy face, who shall prepare thy way before thee. I say unto you, Among them that are born of women there is none greater than John.' [1]

There follows a difficult passage where Jesus adds: 'Yet he that is but little in the kingdom of God is greater than he.' The Baptist was of a truth more heroic than many privileged children of the new world, but just as Abraham, Moses, Elijah, Isaiah, and the rest of the prophets of the older dispensation were, in the sequence of time, outside the new order of things, so the Baptist remained on the threshold of that new world and did not actually experience its joys. He was the necessary link between the old and the new. In that world beyond the grave he might be counted, as might Abraham, far greater in spiritual stature than some of his contemporaries who were privileged to enter the kingdom itself.

Perhaps our Lord's next words will explain this. John came neither eating meat nor drinking wine, the necessary ascetic forerunner of that world of grace and gaiety, but the Son of Man came eating and drinking. Although that kingdom must be entered with hardship and difficulty, and must be maintained by heroic discipline, yet the least within it were 'at ease in Sion' as none of its forerunners

[1] Luke vii. 24–8.

could be. They had tasted of its fullness and were satisfied.

As to the Pharisees they rejected the severe preparation of the Baptist and the joyous kingdom alike. Jesus says they are like sulky children in the market-place, who will not join in the games of their playmates, who say let's play at funerals or let's have a game of marriages. Jesus would often have stopped to watch these games, and as a boy joined in them himself. The cry 'We have piped unto you and ye would not dance: we have wailed unto you and ye did not weep,' fell on deaf ears. We may notice the homeliness of his illustrations and their lasting freshness and poignancy.

Soon after this a Pharisee asks him to a meal, possibly at Nain, but more probably at Capernaum. He must not be confused with Simon the leper of the later story. This Pharisee may have had some slight reverence for Jesus, or may have invited him merely out of curiosity; this is suggested by his lack of courtesy in not giving the kiss nor washing the feet of his guest. These courtesies were, however, not always given.

There was present a prostitute, 'a woman in the city, a sinner,' who had apparently come in with his disciples. She brings an alabaster flask of ointment and begins to wet his feet with her tears and wipe them with the hair of her head (only the harlots wore their hair loose) and kissed his feet and anointed them with the ointment which was always carried by such women. His puritan host was naturally shocked and said to himself: 'This man, if he were a prophet, would have perceived who and what manner of woman this is which toucheth him, that she is a sinner.' Jesus said unto Simon: 'Seest thou this woman? I entered into thine house, thou gavest me no water for my feet; but she hath wetted my feet with her tears, and wiped them with her hair. Thou gavest me no kiss; but she, since the time I came in, hath not ceased to kiss my feet. My head with oil thou didst not anoint; but she hath anointed my feet with ointment. Wherefore I say unto thee, Her sins, which are many, are forgiven; for she loves much: but to whom little is forgiven, the same loveth little. And he said unto her, Thy sins are forgiven. And they that sat at meat with him began to say within themselves, Who is this that even forgiveth sins? And he said unto the woman, Thy faith hath saved thee; go in peace.' [1]

It is remarkable that in our Lord's later comment on John the Baptist [2] he insists that publicans and harlots accepted the new evangel while it was rejected by the 'religious.' There follows the story of the woman who was a harlot and after this incident there comes the mention of a tour through all Galilee conducted by Jesus and his disciples.

This tour was financed among others by Mary of Magdala, out of whom he had cast seven demons. It is difficult to avoid the conclusion that this Mary was identical with the prostitute of the previous story.

We are not given any details of this circuit of Galilee, but it was made possible by the donations of the Magdalene and by Joanna, the wife of Chuza, an official at the court of Herod, and by certain other women. It was brave of this bourgeois lady to associate herself with a former prostitute and to break her connection with the royal court; and it is noteworthy that people of every rank and station joined the new movement, and not only the working classes, although these latter would of course be in the vast majority, for it seems always to have been 'the common people who heard him gladly.'

It is not always explicitly stated, but it is assumed, that the harlots on being converted to Jesus and his movement left their ghastly trade, as had Matthew the *douanier*, who left all to follow the Master.

Jesus now returns again to the seaside by Capernaum and begins to teach in parables.

---

[1] Luke vii. 44–50.   [2] Matthew xxi. 32.

CHAPTER XIX

PARABLES AND MIGHTY WORKS IN GALILEE

JESUS had been ready for all emergencies and had, therefore, prepared his disciples to act alone in the event of his being put out of action. Finding that no arrest was attempted he had conducted a tour with the twelve, probably with the idea of allowing them to gain experience with him which would prove invaluable in their Galilean mission undertaken independently of their leader at a later stage.

St. Mark gives the teaching in parables as begun somewhat later in the ministry, but we shall here follow the Lucan order.

All three Synoptists place the story of the sower first among the parables, for Jesus would naturally warn the apostles he had chosen to carry on his campaign that their propaganda would not meet with the entire success they hoped for. The seed would fall in many cases on the hard road, that is, many who heard would be scornful or indifferent. Sometimes it would fall on stony ground, where the surface soil would be rich, but it would soon strike the rock and wither away, because there was no subsoil. Other seed falls among thorns and the thorns spring up and choke it. Avarice and worldliness are the prickly brambles which strangle the desire for the new world of fraternity, equality, and generosity. Snobbery and the love of position and riches will again get hold of many who have been attracted to the new teaching. The success of the propaganda will meet with many checks, but some seed will fall on good ground and will spring up and yield an abundant harvest.

When the eager and more intimate of his followers asked him in private to explain the parable of the sower, he said: 'Unto you it is given to know the mysteries of the Kingdom of God; but to the rest in parables: that seeing they

may not see, and hearing they may not understand.'
St. Mark's version adds: 'Lest at any time they should be
converted and their sins should be forgiven them,' while
St. Matthew gives this addition as a quotation from Isaiah
in a somewhat fuller context.

Teaching by parables was common enough in the East,
the story so given would arouse the interest of those who
were eager for more knowledge; and the Master here
explicitly states that this was his main reason for adopting
it: it is only to such as these that the mysteries of the new
world are to be revealed, and not to the apathetic nor to
the antagonistic. It is, however, possible that as towards
the end of his ministry they sent forth *agents provocateurs*
to catch him in his talk, to have matter on which to arrest
him, and as already both the governments of the North and
the South were alarmed at his propaganda, he may have had
a second reason for wrapping up his meaning in parabolic
form. It was important that dangerous teachings about
a new system which should bring the existing order to
sudden desolation should be expressed in guarded metaphor.

It must not, however, be supposed that these mysteries
of the New World Order are a secret theosophic doctrine
only for a few highly trained initiates. For he goes on most
emphatically to repudiate this esoteric mistake. His gospel
is not for some little coterie of intellectuals, but for all
mankind, for as many as 'have ears to hear.' For a candle
is not to be put under a bed where no one can see it, but
to give light to the whole household. For the moment,
things must be in secret, because of the police agents
who will destroy him and his propaganda alike; they are
only kept hidden that they may be preserved and afterwards revealed to all the world, 'for there is nothing hid
that shall not be manifested; neither was anything secret,
but that it should come abroad.' In another place he
says that what is now kept secret shall one day be shouted
from the house-tops. It is, indeed, a gospel for all who have
ears to hear, but, 'take heed how ye hear; for with what
measure ye mete, it shall be measured to you again.' To

those who hear truly 'shall more be given,' and now he concludes this exposition with the words so abominably misinterpreted and abused by supporters of the system which he came to destroy: 'For he that hath, to him shall be given; and he that hath not, from him shall be taken even that which he hath.' His plain and unvarnished meaning is that to the eager-minded who are alert to learn the mysteries of the new world whose values are in direct opposition to money - grubbing and domination, more knowledge shall be given; while those who do not want to learn about God's coming order of justice and generosity, from them shall be taken even that little knowledge which they have. To interpret this as meaning that he that has money and advantages shall be allowed with God's approval to amass a fortune at the expense of his less fortunate fellow-men, is just such an example of not taking heed how ye hear, but hearing and misinterpreting to your own damnation.

This maxim is again used as the concluding words of the parable of the talents and again abused by many modern interpreters.

The missioners must not, however, be over anxious about immediate results, for much of the work would at first appear fruitless, and yet would eventually produce a good crop. It is like the seed which is sown and the farmer goes his way and forgets all about it, but there it is, germinating secretly in the earth without his help and when the time is ripe he puts in the sickle, for the harvest is come.

Jesus, in order to get in close touch with his hearers, or because he really found great difficulty in expressing the idea of the Kingdom of God in striking analogies, now seems to hesitate and says: 'Whereunto shall we liken the Kingdom of God, or with what comparison shall we compare it?' How shall I bring it home to you? Perhaps this is a good illustration. It is like a grain of mustard seed which when it is sown is less than all the seeds, but when it is grown it becometh the greatest of all herbs, and a mighty tree so that the birds come and lodge among its branches.

People sometimes take this parable as illustrating the slow growth of the kingdom, and defend, by reference to it, the doctrine of the 'inevitability of gradualness,' but although the mustard seed in northern climes is of slow growth, in Palestine and on warmer soils its growth is amazingly swift. The parable would, therefore, suggest that instead of expecting thousands or even millions of years to pass before the world could look for the consummation of the new world order, we were to expect its advent in the near future. The same suggestion is made in the parable of the leaven which a woman took and hid in three measures of meal. Leaven by no means works slowly, but swiftly and with turbulence. The idea here would bring to the mind not slow evolution but revolution.

We must now deal with the parable of the wheat and tares, which Matthew alone records and places immediately after that of the sower. This story has been the occasion of sharp controversy down the ages. The enemy sows tares among the corn; some are eager to root them up immediately upon their appearing, but this is folly, because in rooting up the tares some of the good wheat would be rooted up along with the rubbish. Let both grow together till the harvest, when the good can be separated from the bad and the whole crop garnered.

Now Jesus does not say that the field is the Church, or new community of his followers, but the whole world as at present organized. In it are the children of light, those who are as the salt to season it and as the city set on a hill. But they are inclined to condemn and to root up before the time is ripe. He is not here directly concerned with the discipline of the Catholic Church or the question how far the ecclesia can or should allow evil members to remain within it, and so to corrupt the good. In fact, he explicitly orders the contrary policy, for he says, as recorded in the same gospel of Matthew, that if a brother in the beloved community sins against you, you are first to remonstrate with him alone, but if that fails, to do so in the presence of one or two fellow-members, and again in the last resort tell it unto the Church or the whole community, and if he refuses to hear the Church, to excommunicate him until he repents. How soon the parable was applied to the Church, rather than to the world, is uncertain, but such an application was natural, for its members are inclined to judge one another too hastily and too harshly and excommunication should only be applied as a final measure. New ideas are often at once dismissed as shocking and heretical; here again patient and sympathetic examination is essential unless the good be rooted up along with the bad. In the earliest Church there would seem to have been a group who advocated that there should be no forgiveness for mortal sin, but it was surely under the guidance of the spirit that more lenient counsels began to prevail. Laxity is dangerous, but bigotry and intolerance are still more dangerous.

If, however, our Lord's original object in giving the parable was not to anticipate these troubles, but to instruct his little ecclesia in dealing with the world in which they moved, his meaning would seem to be that they must not be too ready to call down fire from heaven upon their opponents.

There were occasions on which he himself bitterly condemns the Pharisees for their worldliness and hypocrisy, but he had the more right to utter such condemnations, because of his deep discernment of human character. He knew 'what was in man,' in a degree which was not true of his followers before their baptism with the spirit, and was not even true of their judgments even after that greater enlightenment. There were occasions on which after long deliberation condemnation had to be given against those outside the ranks of the Church, but this condemnation was not to be made with harshness and smug self-satisfaction. The Church could sometimes learn from the world, as indeed it did in later days, when St. Augustine called Plato a Christian before Christ, and when St. Thomas Aquinas incorporated the thought of Aristotle into the Catholic Philosophy. The history of the Catholic Church has been a strange mixture of liberal thought and extreme intolerance; and its liberality is as well instanced by the above as its intolerance is by the Spanish Inquisition against the Jews and heretics.

Again, God's commonwealth is like a drag-net that was cast into the sea, and gathered of every kind, which, when it was filled, they drew up on the beach; and they sat down, and gathered the good into vessels, but the bad they cast away. So shall it be at the consummation of the age; the angels shall come forth, and sever the wicked from among the righteous, and shall cast them into the furnace of fire: there shall be the weeping and the gnashing of teeth. It will be noticed that this parable is identical in teaching with that of the wheat and tares. The propaganda for the new world is broadcast and will attract both the just and the unjust, the worthy and the worthless, but it is only at the consummation of the age that the true citizens of the new world will inherit it, and that those who have only pretended to believe in it, or have joined the little company which forms its nucleus for unworthy motives, will be expelled and will find themselves outside its borders and refused its privileges.

It will be remembered that this expulsion and the misery that followed it is the comment of Jesus on the unfaithfulness of many of the Jewish religious leaders as contrasted with the faith of the foreign centurion. The furnace of fire and the misery of the excluded brought to its climax, as we have seen, the parable of the wheat and the tares: 'There shall be the weeping and the gnashing of teeth,' is the refrain that runs through his teaching.

This, then, is the fate of all those who join the movement and use it hypocritically for their own ends, who undermine and sabotage, or through cowardice or apathy betray it.

In the parables of the wheat and the tares and the drag-net we are told that at the consummation of the age the Father or the Son of Man shall send forth His angels to separate the good from the bad, so that men who have loved God and justice will shine forth in the new world and the traitors will be destroyed. Although Jesus certainly believed in angels, and we believe with Milton that 'millions of spiritual creatures walk the earth unseen,' it is possible that the ministry of angels is effected through the agency of man. Our Lord clearly held that certain actions, which he describes as being 'from Heaven,' are nevertheless made effectual through the actions of inspired men; when, using Oriental imagery, he sees Satan 'as lightning fall from Heaven,' this vision is the result of the preaching of his very human disciples: they are his angels or messengers (the Greek word ἄγγελος means also messenger or agent) who have achieved this end. His meaning may therefore be that, although men are to 'judge nothing before the time,' they will be used under his guidance at the end of the age to consummate the divine commonwealth.

He concludes his cycle of Galilean parables with two little jewels: the one of the man who found the treasure hidden in the field and sold all that he had to buy the field; the other of the merchant who beggared himself to obtain the pearl of great price.

It is remarkable that many of these Galilean parables are incompatible with the Pacifist assumption that the Kingdom of Heaven is not to come with upheaval and violence, but with gentle and almost imperceptible growth, and that its advent is to be delayed until the last impenitent rich man or the last abject poor man is converted. The stories of the wheat and tares and of the drag-net have both of them a catastrophic ending, while those of the mustard seed and of the leaven will not, as we have shown, bear the ordinary interpretation of slow and gentle development. The fact is rather that our Lord's interpretation of the kingdom and its coming seems to follow the true evolutionary process in the natural world. Just as the slow and gradual trickle of a small stream of water in the cliffs results in the sudden thunder of the landslide, so shall the quiet years of preparation result in the sudden cataclysm which ushers in the new world.

Darwin himself admitted that other scientific theories

must be taken into account besides his theory of natural selection, and of late years the theory of 'mutation' or 'leap' has become generally accepted in the scientific world; this again implies slow growth, but also the sudden leap into the new species. Karl Marx, even in his time, knew something of these facts and applied them to the history of human society; and the Russian Communist philosophers of to-day, with all the advantages of the latest scientific discoveries at their disposal, have been able to elaborate the theory of quiet growth and revolutionary change. As Julius Hecker writes in *Moscow Dialogues*: 'The "leap," or "mutation" as it is called in biology, is a very important fact in the evolutionary process, for upon it is based the teaching of the necessity of revolution, i.e. of a sudden change from one state to another, when the slow preparatory quantitative or qualitative changes have been fulfilled. Thus "revolution" is a dialectic necessity and a part of the evolutionary process.'

The theory of 'mutation,' one form of which is called 'Emergent Evolution,' must not, of course, be pressed to cover all the facts either in chemistry or biology or, indeed, in the history of human society, but its truth must never be forgotten, and it seems to have been fully recognized by the Christ in his teaching.

Passages which at first sight would seem to run counter to this doctrine such as the oft-quoted, 'The Kingdom of God is within you,' will be dealt with as they occur.

That the situation was dangerous is not only suggested by his method of concealing his meaning from his opponents in parables, but by his crossing the lake on that same evening. How urgent this crossing was is suggested by Mark's words: 'They take him with them, even as he was, in the boat.' Other fishing-boats set out with them. Suddenly the calm surface of the lake is lashed into fury and huge waves threaten to submerge the boat; the other fishing craft probably put back to harbour. Jesus, utterly exhausted by the long day's work, by the enormous energy put forth in teaching and healing, and by the pressure of the crowds, sleeps peacefully in the stern: 'And they awake him, and say unto him, Master, carest thou not that we perish? And he awoke, and rebuked the wind, and said unto the sea, Peace, be still. And the wind ceased, and there was a great calm. And he said unto them, Why are ye fearful? have ye not yet faith? And they feared exceedingly, and said one to another, Who then is this, that even the wind and the sea obey him?'[1]

Sceptics will dismiss a story like this as incredible, and the modernists reject or explain away the miraculous, but to-day it may well be that we are obliged to out-modern the modernists. Mental and spiritual healing are coming to be recognized by the medical profession as a legitimate method of dealing with disease, and what would in the old days be called miraculous is nowadays coming to be considered strictly scientific.

It is important to notice that our Lord's 'miracles' are hardly ever so described in the New Testament; the 'miracle' is a thing to cause wonder, and the Victorians used to assume that our Lord worked miracles in order to trick people out of their unbelief. They were left gaping and gasping at his prodigies and were forced to the conclusion that they must love both himself and his goodly commonwealth if he could smash the laws of nature so effectively.

Now this is precisely the opposite of what is recorded in the gospels. Far from doing miracles in Nazareth because of their unbelief or to force them into acceptance of his plans, 'he could do no mighty works there because of their unbelief.' When the sceptical Pharisees demanded a sign, he refused their scoffing request. It was in answer to belief or faith, and not to unbelief, that Jesus was able to work his miracles.

The gospel story, then, does not depend for its value upon the gospel miracles; and it is, of course, possible that the miraculous element may have been exaggerated in the minds of the writers or in the tradition that they had handed down; or that here in this incident the storm may have

[1] Mark iv. 37–41.

subsided almost as rapidly as it had arisen, but it is, we conceive, likely enough that things happened as the narrators have recorded them. All that we would insist upon is the foolishness of ruling out the miraculous on some *a priorist* ground.

I can well remember in my early days that the fast of forty days and forty nights was considered 'miraculous,' and on these grounds dismissed as incredible by sceptics. I have myself recently met a lady who was so weak as to be almost unable to talk at the beginning of a thirty days' fast, and who came out of it vigorous and an attractive conversationalist. I was at the same time told by an intimate friend that she had met another lady who had been at death's door, and had undergone a fast of a hundred and twenty-seven days and was walking about the garden and entertaining everybody at the end of the period.

In 1935 photographs were taken and published in the *Illustrated London News* of experiments in fire-walking in which men and women traversed with bare feet a burning track of charcoal before an audience, including doctors and scientists. They had previously been examined and their feet had not been prepared in any way and were again examined at the end of the trial and their feet found to be absolutely unscathed.

These cases of fasting and fire-walking, then, prove the 'miraculous' powers of men, and as to control over nature modern science treats as commonplaces what would formerly have been dismissed as impossible.

The sea of Galilee was six miles across and the winds were contrary. They would have been delayed by the storm so they may not have reached the opposite shore until dawn. Jesus and his disciples were in need of rest, but once more he was called upon to put forth his energy in reply to tragic need.

They landed at Gergesa, the modern village called by the Arabs of to-day Gersa or Kersa. Matthew is probably accurate here as he would know the lake intimately; but Mark and Luke, who call it the country of the Gadarenes, may also be correct, as the important town of Gadara may have given its name to the whole district. Gadara was some six miles farther inland, and Geraza was a very large city, situated thirty miles from the scene of landing. Kersa was on the coast opposite to Capernaum, and was in a wild district near which were caves in the rock and steep cliffs. These were used as tombs, and were inhabited by lunatics who were in those days driven forth from all human dwellings and compelled to fend for themselves as best they could.

It was one of these who met Jesus as he landed. He had the usual strength of the madman, and although he had often been bound he had as often broken the strongest chains and got free. In his misery he would cry out and wound himself with stones. The demon-possessed recognized Jesus as the Messiah, addressing him as the Son of the Most High, and doing him reverence and beseeching him not to hurt him; for Jesus was ordering the demon to come out of the man. The Master addresses him and asks him his name, for this is essential, in order to try to recall such mentally afflicted people to themselves, their own personality and their responsibility. But the man cried out: 'My name is Legion, for we are many.' He would be familiar with the Roman Legions, and felt that he had lost his own identity among a host of demons who had taken possession of the house of his soul.

In the violent struggles of the lunatic which brought the scene to a climax a herd of swine took fright and rushed down the steep cliff and were drowned in the sea.

Whether the demons actually entered the animals or not is uncertain, and the fact of demon-possession will also be questioned. But to suggest, as did Thomas Huxley, that there was any cruelty in the drowning of the pigs, is to be hypocritical when we consider that in a few weeks, or perhaps even days, they would have been marketed in the neighbouring luxury town of Gadara and killed for the table. They were regarded by their owners and breeders as mere property and with Jesus human rights always took

precedence of vested interests; although we are not surprised that the property owners besought him to leave their
coast. His presence never seemed to be good for trade.

As for the lunatic, the storm in his soul had been subdued
and there was a great calm. He doubtless felt utterly
dependent on his healer and besought him to let him come
with him in the boat, but Jesus did not allow this, because
he wished him to stand on his own feet; so he was told to
go into the city and publish his cure among his friends,
telling them all what great things God had done for him.

Certain spiritual healers counsel their patients after a
cure to keep secret about it, as the cure would be the more
effective, and they have sometimes interpreted the gospels
as giving the same advice, but although in Galilee Jesus
advises secrecy, he here orders publicity. We conclude,
therefore, that there must be some other reason. These
contrasted counsels suggest that he wished for secrecy and
caution within the danger zone, but outside that area no
such precaution was necessary.

He sets sail and lands once more near Capernaum and
crowds immediately begin to gather. Out of the throng
there appears one of the rulers of the synagogue, Jairus by
name, and he falls down and beseeches him to come and
heal his daughter who is at the point of death. He would
often have heard Jesus in the synagogue, and have known
of his wonderful powers as a healer. The healing of the
servant of the centurion, the officer who had built their
house of worship, would be fresh in his memory.

While Jesus was on the way to the house, and a great
multitude followed him, a woman with an issue of blood
which had troubled her for twelve years, touched his
garment, hoping to escape notice, believing that if she
could but touch the hem of his clothes she would be made
whole. This was her last chance as she, like some modern
patients, 'had suffered many things of many physicians
and had spent all that she had, and was nothing better but
rather grew worse.' Luke the physician considered her
incurable, but, 'straightway the fountain of her blood was

dried up; and she felt in her body that she was healed of her plague.'

Considering the nature of her disease, she would want at all costs to avoid publicity, but Jesus, perceiving that energy had gone out of him, turned round to his disciples and asked them who had touched him. They replied that in a multitude of that size it would be wellnigh impossible to say who had done so, and they thought it absurd that Jesus should ask who touched him. 'And he looked round about to see her that had done this thing. But the woman, fearing and trembling, knowing what had been done to her, came and fell down before him, and told him all the truth. And he said unto her, Daughter, thy faith hath made thee whole; go in peace, and be whole of thy plague.'[1]

While he is speaking, a message comes that the ruler's daughter is dead, so why trouble the Master. But Jesus, ignoring this, turns to Jairus, and says: 'Fear not, only believe.' He enters the house taking with him only his three intimates, Peter, James, and John; and annoyed at the tumult made by the professional wailers and others, he turns to them, saying: 'The child is not dead but sleepeth. And they laughed him to scorn.' Turning every one out of the room except the parents, and taking the child by the hand he said unto her: 'Talitha Cumi,' which means 'My little child, arise.' Straightway the damsel rose up and walked; for she was twelve years old. Mark alone gives the very Aramaic phrase with which Jesus aroused the little girl—a vivid memory of Peter's story. And they were amazed with a great amazement, but here, back once more in the danger zone, he enjoins strict secrecy, and with his usual common sense, 'commanded that something be given her to eat.' Although Matthew and Luke believe that the child was dead, it must be remembered that Peter was an eye-witness, and that there is no necessary suggestion of this in his story as set down by Mark.[2]

[1] Mark v. 25 ff.

[2] According to St. Mark, Jesus now visits Nazareth, but we have preferred Luke's record in this respect, and have already dealt with his expulsion from his native town.

CHAPTER XX

DARKNESS AND A GLIMPSE OF THE DAWN

EARLIER we have recorded the instructions given to the twelve preparatory to their mission: and have explained why it was delayed. How much more would they be able, after these varied experiences with their Master, to go forth independently of him throughout the cities and villages of Galilee.

So now he sends them out in couples to preach the divine commonwealth, giving them power to cure both mental and physical diseases, and commanding them that they should take nothing for their journey except a staff, no bread, no knapsack, no money in their girdles, no boots but only sandals, and they were not to carry a change of the homespun tunic. They were to travel as light as did their followers, the early Franciscans. They were not to be fussy about accommodation, but 'wheresoever ye enter into a house, there abide until ye depart thence.' And whatsoever place was inhospitable and would neither welcome them nor listen to their news, 'as ye go forth thence, shake off the dust that is under your feet for a testimony unto them.'[1] This was a common symbolic act of repudiation in the East.

In St. Matthew's record the above charge to the apostles is given immediately after Jesus had chosen them, and is much expanded. Our Lord, for instance, adds: 'Behold I send you forth as sheep in the midst of wolves, be ye wise as serpents and harmless as doves.' What follows may be a collection of warnings given to the disciples at various

---

[1] St. Matthew's account adds a severer condemnation which appears also in Mark, but is omitted in the R.V.: 'Verily I say unto you that it shall be more tolerable for the land of Sodom and Gomorrah in the day of judgment, than for that city.'

374

times, and especially towards the end of his life; for he prepares them for a time when they shall be arrested and scourged and brought for trial not only into native, but into imperial, courts. 'Before governors and kings shall ye be brought,' for a testimony both to Jews and Gentiles.

They were not to be over anxious about preparing an elaborate defence, 'for it shall be given you in that hour what ye shall speak. For it is not ye that speak, but the spirit of your Father that speaketh in you.'

The Evangelists must not expect any better treatment than their Master; they also will be blackened with the name of Beelzebub, but in spite of revilings and persecutions they must proclaim boldly from the housetop and to all the world what has been told them in secret. He speaks of a crisis so intense that families will not only be rent asunder, but will give information the one against the other, brother against brother, parents against children, children against parents, which will lead to their deaths: 'But when they persecute you in this city, flee into the next: for verily I say unto you, Ye shall not have gone through the cities of Israel till the Son of Man be come.'

This evidently does not refer to the coming of the Son of Man at the consummation of the age, but either to some great success of his mission (cf. 'I saw Satan as lightning fall from Heaven,' the victorious result of the mission of the Seventy) or to the first harvest of his followers in Jerusalem, when after his resurrection and ascension thousands are added to his community.

In the course of these warnings Jesus says: 'Be not afraid of them which kill the body, but are not able to kill the soul; but rather fear him which is able to destroy both soul and body in hell.' [1] It is unfortunate that the Greek word Ψυχή means either 'life' or 'soul,' but it is confusing to translate it as do the Authorized and the Revised Versions: 'soul' in verse 28 and 'life' in verse 39. Their translation of the former, 'be not afraid of them which kill the body, but are not able to kill the soul,' is obviously

[1] Matthew x. 28.

better than 'are not able to kill the life,' but, in that case, our Lord goes on to say: 'He that findeth his soul shall lose it.' It is true that 'Safety First' is not always a trustworthy motto, either as applied to the spirit or the body. Caution is necessary, but the mountaineer who is nervous about his safety, and has no audacity, may, in his over anxiety, lose his life. So with the soul-savers, if they concentrate on saving their own souls, not willing to risk them for the Christ and his brave new world, they will inevitably lose them. Revivalists should consider St. Paul's words: 'I could wish that even I myself were accursed from Christ for my brethren's sake.'[1] In that desire to lose his own soul for the sake of his brethren, he found it unto life eternal.

Before leaving the subject of this longer version of the charge it must be noted that Jesus, who is so gentle that he will not break the bruised reed, is also the prophet of a terrible gospel which will divide families to the point of their destroying each other. He has come to cast fire on the earth and the sooner it is kindled the better: 'Think not that I came to send peace on the earth; I came not to send peace, but a sword.' Mercy and terror are two facets of the one personality, and the method of the cross must be reconciled with the method of the sword, if we are to read aright the character of God and of His Christ.

It seems evident that only the earlier portion of this charge can apply to the immediate Galilean mission. The disciples are sent forth to preach the good news of the approaching kingdom, to anoint and heal the sick; success attends their efforts, but the wide publicity resulting from this tour reaches the ears of Herod Antipas who takes alarm at this subversive movement.

The king had but recently, much against his better judgment, murdered John the Baptist, and here was John the Baptist all over again. This deed had been engineered by Herodias, the Baptist's implacable enemy. It was on the occasion of Herod's birthday when he had asked the notables of the court to a banquet and Salome had

[1] Romans ix. 3.

pleased him immensely by her dancing. Rashly he had promised the girl anything she should ask for, even to the half of his kingdom. She went at once to her mother, whose influence over her, as over the king, was sinister, to ask what she should demand of him. The queen seized her chance: 'Ask for the head of John the Baptist.' Salome returns to the banquet and demands the murder of the prophet. The king was very sorry, but for his oath's sake, and for fear of them who feasted with him—they were, perhaps, of the queen's party and would be glad to see the prisoner out of the way—he consents. 'And there was brought unto the damsel the head of John the Baptist in a charger.'

Herod is haunted by his act and like Macbeth cannot rest. Is this rebel movement, indeed, indestructible, and has John arisen from the dead to confront his royal murderer?

This terror of the king would likely enough lead to a new and more dangerous political crisis, and the disciples were at the moment without their leader, as Jesus had left them to carry on this adventure without him.

When the disciples report to their leader on the success of their first independent tour, they would probably tell him of the danger arising from the suspicions of Antipas.

Jesus, understanding this, and the immediate necessity of rest, both for himself and his disciples after their strenuous adventures, counsels withdrawal into some district of quiet safety. This was the more necessary as multitudes were again beginning to throng him so closely that he had no opportunity for a meal. Accordingly they set sail across the lake, landing probably near the head to the north-east, for the very crowds that they were anxious to escape, perceiving the direction they were taking, ran round the bend of the lake and met them when they reached the shore. Jesus, seeing their eagerness, not only for healing but for instruction, began to teach them about the divine commonwealth,[1] and they listened with such enthusiasm that the

[1] Luke ix. 11.

day wore on and on until they were exhausted for want of food.

The disciples suggested the dismissal of the crowd that they might go into the cities and villages to purchase provisions. But Jesus said they need not depart; 'give ye them to eat.' The disciples are astonished; are they to go into Bethsaida and buy enough to provision the great multitude? The five loaves and the few small fishes that they had would certainly not meet the need. But Jesus commanded them to bring the scanty provisions to him and to make the crowd sit down upon the grass in orderly companies, 'and they sat down in ranks by hundreds and by fifties.' The sacramental nature of the meal that follows suggests his last Supper and 'the action of the Mass.' Looking up to Heaven, he blesses the bread, breaks it, and gives it to the disciples to distribute among the multitude; they become the deacons of this sacramental rite. The whole crowd are fed in such abundance that they were able to collect of the fragments that remained twelve baskets full. And immediately he constrained his disciples to get into the fishing-boat and cross over to the western shore, while he attempts to send the multitude away.

All four records give the numbers as about five thousand, and even if this is an exaggeration a large multitude seems to have been fed. We have noticed the sacramental character of the meal, and just as in the case of the Blessed Sacrament itself, it seems to be a foretaste and first fruit of the new world which the Christ had come to proclaim, with its fruitfulness and abundance for all mankind. Is it too fanciful to suggest that, in the orderly grouping of the crowd upon the grass insisted on by the gospel narrators, we have a picture of an ordered society in which men will no longer grasp for themselves, and trample on each other in their competition for food, but in their obedience to the bountiful Father and in their production and distribution of the generous fruits of the earth will find that there is abundance for all mankind?

We have said enough about the nature of the miraculous

to remind our readers that it is unwise to give a summary
dismissal of all these nature 'miracles' as antecedently
impossible.

This sacramental feeding of the people seems in direct
contrast with his refusal to feed them in the temptation to
turn stones into bread which prefaces his ministry.[1]   But
there is really no contradiction, for in the first instance he
refuses to be the 'bringer of plenty' to an unawakened
people, while in the second he supplies with plenty those
who are hungering and thirsting after righteousness.

When Jesus attempted to dismiss the crowd considerable
difficulties arose, for they acclaimed him as the 'prophet
that should come into the world,' and attempted to crown
him as their king.   That they were eager to learn about his
kingdom we have already recorded, but they were very
far from a full understanding of its nature.   Even if his
inner band of disciples could fail to grasp its deeper significance after intensive instruction, is it likely that these sheep
without a shepherd upon whom he had compassion would
more quickly have understood his teaching?   When a little
later he tells his intimate followers that they cannot tread
in his steps or obtain the new world unless they are prepared to eat his flesh and drink his blood, that is completely
to identify themselves with him and to risk their very life
and soul, many of them turned back scandalized and
disillusioned.[2]   How could he, then, trust himself to this
multitude who, replenished with the miraculously given
food and flushed with a passing enthusiasm, wished to
make him their king that he might lead them against the
conquering empire of Rome?

You throng me, not because you really understand the
significance of the communal feeding, as sign and presage
of the swiftly dawning age: when you were lifted into the
proper spirit, you came to me hungering for a new world
order, and forgetful of the meat that perished.   I was
able to feed you, and you sat down to that common meal

[1] See Chapter XI, 'The First Two Temptations.'
[2] John vi. 53.

in orderly co-operation and companionship. But you are now only thinking of the material loaves and fishes. The kingship you tried to force upon me has in it too much of the spirit of this world of corruption. So Jesus disperses the crowd and once more climbs up into a mountain to be alone and to pray.

CHAPTER XXI

AN EXILE FROM GALILEE

THE disciples meanwhile are having difficulties with the fishing-boat. The wind is against them and they are making no progress. Suddenly they see walking on the water what seems to them an apparition of their Master. They are terrified, but he comes into the boat and re-assures them, saying: 'Cheer up. It is I. Don't be afraid.' Their troubles are at an end,[1] and they beach about sunrise on their own native side, the shore of the plain of Gennesaret.

As they moored the boat the people immediately began to gather again and throng around him imploring him to heal their sick. There was thus the usual publicity and danger. He once more visits some cities and villages of the district, but this mission is abruptly terminated by the arrival of scribes and Pharisees from Jerusalem who enter into controversy with them.

These incursions of opponents from the South are significant as proving that Jerusalem was fully aware of his dangerous propaganda and so suggest that the fourth gospel must be taken seriously. What more natural than an arrival of the southern Pharisees, if they had just been in violent conflict with him at Jerusalem during the spring feast and were determined to take his life?

The dispute of the embittered Pharisees is concerned with the washing of hands. They evidently mean to pick a quarrel with him and they challenge him in these words: 'Why do thy disciples transgress the tradition of the elders? For they wash not their hands when they eat bread.'

[1] Matthew alone records Peter's impulsive act of walking on the water to meet his Lord and his sinking because of failure of faith; Jesus raises him and they climb into the boat together.

St. Mark now contemptuously comments on the customs of the Pharisees, on their continual hand washings, the cleansing of cups and pots and of brass vessels and a thousand and one petty details which they hold to be of supreme religious importance. Jesus counters their challenge by saying, Ye reject the commandments of God, that ye may keep your own tradition. For Moses commanded you to honour your parents and to support them, but you evade this by mean trickery, by calling a thing 'corban,' that is, by dedicating to the service of God what should go to the support of your father and mother. They ear-marked these religious gifts as inalienable, and yet sometimes used them to their own advantage. But in any case Jesus was indignant at their evasion of the natural law by a supposed religious obligation. 'He implies clearly that natural duties and responsibilities have the first claim: the man who stints himself to give his children a good education is doing his duty better than the man who stints his children's education in order to subscribe largely to church or chapel, even though the subscription is called "Peter's Pence" or by any equivalent name.'[1]

Having dealt with his immediate accusers, he called all the people to him and said: 'Hearken unto me every one of you and understand: there is nothing from without a man, that entering into him can defile him; but the things that come out of him, those are they that defile him.' When they had reached home, his disciples told him that the Pharisees had been scandalized by his pronouncement; it was, indeed, a revolutionary saying, for it sweeps away the whole Mosaic Law regarding food.[2] It was not only

[1] *New Commentary on Holy Scripture*, edited by Charles Gore, page 74.

[2] 'Making all meats clean.' Note that this is only found in Mark, the Peter Gospel, and compare Peter's vision at Joppa of the sheet containing all manner of meats and the voice saying: 'What God hath cleansed, call not thou common.' St. Paul later bases his whole case as against the Judaising Christians on this interpretation of Jesus and his attitude to foreigners. They were to be admitted on equal terms with Jews and were not to be troubled with observance of the Mosaic regulations regarding food. Cf. 'Eat such things as are set before you,' Luke x. 8.

the Pharisees, but his own disciples, who were shocked at
their Master's pronouncement, and it was not till after
his death and resurrection that they began to understand
the vital importance of this teaching.

Crisis after crisis there had been in his ministry; he had
several times come into conflict with the Galilean and
southern governments; and this last combat had been so
serious that, although he had no fears for his own safety,
like a wise general, he was compelled to retreat in order
that his plans should not be brought to ruin. True, there
was no formal sentence of exile against him, for it was not
his exile, but his destruction on which the authorities were
determined. Flight was, therefore, self-imposed and he
sought safety to the north of Galilee.

From thence he arose and went into the borders of Tyre
and Sidon. Now as later he might utter the plaintive cry:
'The foxes have holes and the birds of the air have nests,
but the Son of Man hath not where to lay his head.' The
march with the disciples begun on that day would have
been between twenty and twenty-five miles, and the town
eventually reached may have been the Jewish Giskala,
which was now in Phoenician territory.

To the vine-clad heights of the city the road led through
magnificent hills and valleys. 'He entered into a house
and would have no man know it,' for he must have been
exhausted with the long march and the recent conflicts;
rest and quiet were essential, if he were to think out that
new plan of campaign which recent circumstances had
forced upon him. 'But he could not be hid. Straightway
a woman, whose little daughter had an unclean spirit, having
heard of him, came and fell down at his feet. Now the
woman was a Greek, a Syrophoenician by race.' She is
also called a Canaanite, because the Phoenicians were often
described as the descendants of the people of Canaan; but
they had been Hellenized, Greek culture had penetrated
throughout Syria, of which Phoenicia was a district, and
the woman was Greek both in speech and in nimbleness
of wit.

The disciples, knowing that their master was travelling incognito and wishing to avoid publicity, would have sent the woman away, and Jesus does not appear to have been over anxious to help her. It was not only that he was exhausted and needed his remaining energy for concentration on new tactics, but that he passionately desired to build up his own followers, the seed and remnant of his own nation, so that through the holy nation redemption should spread throughout the world. He was perplexed and silent, but the foreign woman kept on beseeching him to heal her daughter. To her entreaties he answered: 'Let the children first be filled,' and adds, with gentle irony and perhaps with a smile: 'It is not meet to take the children's bread and to cast it to the dogs.' The quick-witted mother at once caps this with the reply: 'Yea, Lord, even the puppies eat of the crumbs which fall from their master's table.' Jesus, filled with admiration at the persistency of the woman, said unto her: 'O! woman, great is thy faith; be it done unto thee even as thou wilt.' And her daughter was healed from that hour.

The cure would create excitement in the district, and many would have crowded about him, bringing with them their sick for healing. Jesus, therefore, is compelled to leave the city and takes the road to Tyre, about twenty-three miles to the north-west, and would probably find a lodging there in one of its narrow winding streets. Tyre was still the capital of Phoenicia, but, although of considerable age, was not the ancient city of that name, the ruins of which lay close by along the seashore, some of them under water. It had been a city of great palaces and public buildings, columns and other fragments of which Jesus may have seen beneath the blue sea. The Phoenicians, in spite of their Semitic origin, were the great maritime people of the ancient world, and Tyre, the Queen of Commerce, had sent forth her ships along the Mediterranean and into many waters. She was, indeed, as Isaiah calls her, the merchant city, the mart of nations. Ezekiel catalogues her multitudinous crafts and commerces; firs

for planks, cedars for masts, oaks for the making of oars;
ivory from the islands, linen from Egypt to be worked up
into coloured sails and flags; blue and purple cloths for
awnings, tin from the mines of far Britain; mules and horses
from Armenia, wines and wool from Damascus; from the
Greek mainland slaves and silver, from the gulf of Persia
ivory tusks and ebony, from surrounding Syria emeralds,
coral, agate, and other precious stones, broidered purple
work and fine linen; from Arabia wrought iron and
spices; from Palestine wheat, honey, oil, and balsam;
Indian gold and jewels, Arabian goats, rams, and
lambs.

Tyre was still the richest commercial city of Phoenicia,
and its factories were famous all over the Mediterranean
world; many of them being devoted to the working up
of the silk and other cloths dyed in the beautiful purple
obtained from the shellfish found in the waters beneath
the rocky promontory.

The persistence of Tyre is extraordinary; over and over
again destroyed, it was as many times rebuilt. Hundreds
of years later Jerome describes it as still the richest commercial centre of the empire, and mentions its mar-
vellous factory of purple cloth as again the foremost
in the world. It is still to-day a city of considerable
importance.

Jesus would have appreciated the beauty of that city,
which an old poet describes as sea and land mingled: 'The
sailor furrows the sea with his oar, as the ploughman the
soil; the lowing of oxen and the song of birds answer the
deep roar of the main.'

He would now take the sea road to the even more ancient
city of Sidon, which had, before Tyre, been the capital of
Phoenicia; there he would spend at least a night, for they
would have covered another twenty-four miles. He may
well have broken the journey at Sarepta, where Elijah
had stayed during the famine, and it would have recalled
to him his own address in the synagogue of Nazareth
which had raised such a tumult among his countrymen

o

when he told them that God had sent his prophet not
to succour any Jewish woman but the foreign widow of
Sarepta.

He now at last commences the long and circuitous
journey home 'through the deep gorges of the rushing and
beautiful Leontes, and would see the great mountain ranges
to the north'; finally they would reach Caesarea Philippi,
or Paneas (the modern Banias). The whole of this district was fertilized by the many sources of the Jordan, and
was rich in wheat, barley, maize, and other crops. Keim
describes its hedges of olives and stretches of luxuriant
pastures: 'In summer the whole district is a sea of flowers
from which the bees gather a rich harvest. The Jordan,
here only twenty paces wide, and the many nameless sources
and brooks which are collected in its channel, sportively
dash their clear sparkling waters into foam among islands
and rocks. A thicket of oaks, terebinths, Sindian trees,
and bushes alive with all kinds of birds, surround the foot-
hills of Hermon, whose snow-capped summit arises above
bald and broken walls of rock.'

The journey was evidently made in summer, as at no
other time of year was it possible, and Jesus may have
lingered with his disciples for weeks or even months in
these northern territories and in the Decapolis. Probably
he was away from Galilee from May until autumn.

At Caesarea Jesus would have noticed the mysterious
rocky grotto of the pastoral god Pan, and the popular cult
of this Greek deity. Nearby was the town of Daphne, the
ancient Dan, sometimes called Laish, a corrupt pleasure
city, 'quiet and secure,' which the ancient Israelites had
destroyed. Here had been carried on a cultus of the calf
for hundreds of years, and Josephus mentions it as still
active at the period with which we are dealing.

Passing farther south through the Decapolitan district
he would still be on pagan soil and among the shrines of
Zeus, Astarte, and Athene, of Artemis, Hercules, Dionysus,
Demeter, and other Greek divinities.

The cities of the Decapolis were not under the rule of

Herod Philip, but were more or less autonomous Greek cities, subject only to an ultimate suzerainty of the Roman governor of Syria. This district was not strictly confined to ten Greek cities, but may have been considered by the gospel writers to have included the cities in league with them. The district would cover a great depth of territory inland and much of the eastern coast of the lake.

Passing among these pagan cities with idolatrous cults, it is remarkable that Jesus utters against them no word of condemnation. What other Jewish teacher would not have been filled with indignation at these heathen shrines? He seems to have reserved his anger for the idolatries of his own countrymen. They would be surprised and scandalized at the making of graven images and at bowing down before them, and would indignantly have repudiated the charge of idolatry, but Jesus rebukes them for the idolatries of the heart, covetousness, pride, and other deadly lusts. Perhaps if he had been conducting a preaching mission in these foreign territories, he would have denounced the idols and the cruelties and impurities which were the expression of these cults, but there is no evidence of much teaching on the east bank of the lake, although there are healings, and possibly the second feeding of a great multitude.[1]

The record is confused, but they seem to have taken their own boat laid up at Bethsaida Julius during the summer months, to have coasted along the eastern banks and finally to have crossed into Galilee and landed at Dalmanutha (Magadan or Magdala), possibly a suburb of Tiberias.

But the long absence from Galilee has not allayed the opposition of his enemies, for as soon as Jesus and his disciples have landed the Pharisees 'come forth,' demanding

[1] It is likely, however, that the miracle of the four thousand is a duplicate of the earlier sacramental feeding as recorded by all four evangelists. That this event was supposed to occur on the east side is evident by their crossing over the lake afterwards, and by the comment of Matthew: 'And they glorified the God of Israel.'—Matthew xv. 31.

of him a sign from heaven. Ironically he taunted them
with being good weather prophets, but how was it they
could not discern the catastrophic signs of the times? They
wanted him to do some astounding miracle, but no sign
should be given them save the sign of the prophet
Jonah.

The contention was so sharp that Jesus had once more
to take flight; the journey across the lake into safety was
hurried, and they had no time to provision the boat. The
disciples discovered that they had no food and were dis-
concerted, but Jesus rebuked them saying that their hearts
must be hardened indeed, if they did not remember the
significance of the sacramental feeding of the multitude.
They should be on their guard against the leaven of the
Pharisees. Another account says, 'the leaven of Herod.'
They misunderstood him to refer to their lack of bread.
This dense stupidity must have been galling to Jesus.
He bade them beware of the policies of the Pharisees and
Sadducees and of the Herodian house. Those doctrines
and policies we have already fully described as crafty and
worldly alliances and hypocritical compromises.

As to the lack of bread and their dullness of heart, Jesus
seems to mean that if he had been able to feed thousands
when they had been eager to listen to his doctrine of a
new world of righteousness and of plenty, how much more
could he supply the physical needs of his own intimate
followers who would be expected to have a deeper understanding of that age to come of which he was both Master
and Lord.

Eventually they land at Bethsaida Julius where he heals
the blind man. 'And he took hold of the blind man by the
hand, and brought him out of the village; and when he had
spit on his eyes, and laid his hands upon him, he asked him
Seest thou aught? And he looked up, and said, I see men;
for I behold them as trees, walking. Then again he laid
his hands upon his eyes; and he looked stedfastly, and was
restored, and saw all things clearly.'[1] This is an instance

[1] Mark viii. 22 ff.

of slow healing with material means; his earlier cures were often instantaneous.[1] Here he enjoins secrecy upon his patient, as his purpose is not a healing mission with its publicity, but the great testing of his disciples, which, if it succeeds, is to form the turning point in his life's work.

[1] Some critics have suggested that our Lord, in this later period, shows more sign of fatigue, and is obliged to perform his cures with a conscious output of energy which is lacking in the glad early days of the Galilean ministry. They give some evidence of this, but the theory may be too fanciful.

CHAPTER XXII

ACCLAIMED BY MAN AND BY GOD

PASSING rapidly northward through the towns of Bethsaida and Caesarea Philippi, Jesus halts along the road to ask his disciples that crucial question: 'Whom do men say that I am?'[1] They reply that some say John the Baptist; others Elijah, or one of the prophets.[2] This identification of Jesus in the popular mind with John the Baptist, the brave revolutionary leader, whose murder lay heavy on the conscience of the king, will no longer surprise us, for we have closely followed the social and political activities of the Christ, and have seen him driven from his country by a coalition of the governments of Galilee and Judea. Would he not also call up in the mind of the people the stormy Elijah who had rebuked Ahab and Jezebel for the murder of a peasant, and the stealing of his little plot of ground? Writers who picture Jesus as the preacher of an 'over the hills and far away' pietism, must find it embarrassing to explain such passages and a hundred others as the narrative of the gospel rushes to its tragic conclusion.

Now Jesus comes to the dramatic moment which is to show him that his followers have really grasped who he is and what tremendous role he is destined to play. Never mind what the crowd think, what is *your* conviction about me? Whom do *ye* say that I am? And Peter, spokesman for the rest, immediately answers: 'Thou art the Christ, the Son of the living God.'[3] Jesus exclaims: 'Blessed art

[1] Matthew, or his Greek editor, has 'that I the Son of Man am'; if 'Son of Man' is a Messianic title our Lord would certainly not have put the question in this form, as his whole object was to elicit from his disciples the confession of his Messiahship.

[2] Matthew adds Jeremiah also, whose teaching on social justice has already been described.

[3] This confession is recorded in all three Synoptists, and also indeed in the fourth gospel, but in a different setting. Luke, it will be remembered,

thou, Simon Bar-Jonah: for flesh and blood hath not revealed it unto thee, but my Father which is in Heaven. And I also say unto thee, that thou art Peter, and upon this rock I will build my church; and the gates of Hades shall not prevail against thee. I will give unto thee the keys of the kingdom of heaven: and whatsoever thou shalt bind on earth shall be bound in heaven; and whatsoever thou shalt loose on earth shall be loosed in heaven.' [1]

omits the conflict with the Pharisees, the consequent exile, the return to Galilee resulting in another collision with the same opponents and another hasty retirement. He therefore records the Petrine confession, as does the fourth gospel, immediately after the feeding of the five thousand. In this latter gospel, the writer records the desertion of many disciples and our Lord's words, 'Would ye also go away? Simon Peter answered him, Lord, to whom shall we go? thou hast the words of eternal life. And we have believed and know that thou art the Holy One of God.'

[1] The authenticity of this glorification of St. Peter has been questioned; possibly Mark, Peter's spokesman, would have omitted it for the very same reason that he inserts the rebuke. If we were to question the authenticity of the events and sayings recorded only in a single Synoptist, we should have to omit the parable of the prodigal son and many other obviously genuine sayings of the Christ. The wording suggests the Aramaic, and seems to be of primitive origin. If the saying is genuine, which we believe, it is our Lord's penetrating discernment of Peter's rock nature, for, although he fails his master and denies him with curses, our Lord has really read his character aright as the sequel shows, for Peter becomes spokesman and prince of the community at Jerusalem, in Palestine, at Antioch, and at Rome, although these two latter churches are built upon St. Peter and St. Paul as equals.

The Roman Church was actually founded by obscure working-class propagandists, and was later consolidated by the two great apostles, although it is possible that Peter was labouring in Rome before the arrival of Paul. We know of no church founded by St. Peter alone, but of many founded by St. Paul and some, perhaps in Asia Minor, by St. John. No one would wish to underrate St. Peter's great work of evangelization, but Jesus, in praising him, is obviously not praising all the successors of Peter and Paul at Antioch or Rome. It would be about as accurate to claim this as to claim that when he called Peter 'Satan,' the Master was conferring that title on all the Roman pontiffs down the ages. Even Roman Catholic historians have painted Caesar Borgia in satanic colours, and other popes before him; the papacy has produced both its sinners and its saints. The tenor of our Lord's words refer to St. Peter alone and do not confer upon Roman officialdom either a guarantee of personal purity or of teaching authority. The commentaries of the early Catholic Fathers make this clear. The authority of the keys, the authority to bind and loose, is a rabbinical expression, and while conferred on St. Peter at this point is, after the resurrection

Jesus has at last drawn from them the confession that they themselves are convinced that he is, indeed, the Lord and Master of the coming world. Immediately he feels it possible to initiate them into a more tragic phase of his mission. He now takes them aside and warns them that the conventional idea of the Messiah, a Messiah all the way and everywhere victorious, is doomed to disappointment. 'From that time forth began Jesus to show unto his disciples how that he must go unto Jerusalem and suffer many things of the elders and chief priests and scribes and be killed, and the third day be raised up.' [1] Mark adds: 'And he spake that saying openly,' that is, for the first time boldly and definitely.

So astounded are they at this prophecy of failure and destruction, that they hardly hear, and certainly do not understand, his saying about the resurrection. Peter rebukes his Master sharply, and the Christ's reply is extraordinary: 'Get thee behind me, Satan; thou art a stumbling block unto me; for thou mindest not the things of God, but the things of men.' [2]

Jesus now calls the people unto him, with his disciples, and gives to them all the counsel he had originally given to the twelve; if any man will come after me, let him deny himself and take up his cross daily and follow me; for whosoever will save his soul [3] shall lose it, and whosoever shall lose his soul for my sake and the gospel's (the good news of the divine commonwealth), the same shall save it. For what shall it profit a man if he gain the whole world and lose himself or be cast away?

given to the whole company of about one hundred and twenty in the upper room at Jerusalem; that is, not only to St. Peter, not even only to the eleven, but to the Catholic Church in embryo. It is a magisterial authority not necessarily implying the infallibility of St. Peter, or of his successors, or indeed of the Church.

[1] Later, on the road to Jerusalem, Jesus again warns his disciples in almost the same words, except that he adds that the Jewish authorities will deliver him to the foreign power, and the foreigner shall mock and scourge and crucify him, and the third day he shall be raised up.—Matt. xx. 17–19.

[2] Peter himself, in his great humility, must have told Mark of this rebuke.

[3] Cf. page 375 f.

Unfortunately the 'cross' has become conventionalized, but he is here warning them that by joining him in this adventure they are not only endangering their lives, but their reputations; by identifying themselves with one who is shortly to be condemned as a blasphemer and a criminal, they will be disgraced by the religious and political world as outcasts from decent society. But what does it matter if men *are* ashamed of you? What *does* matter is that the Son of Man shall not be ashamed of you and cast you out when he comes in glory. 'Verily I say unto you, There be some of them that stand here, which shall in no wise taste of death, till they see the Son of man coming in his kingdom.' The Christ here is again referring, not to the final consummation of the age, but to its inthrust with power in the birth of the new community after the resurrection.

What reaction in the minds of the disciples would be caused by this astounding announcement of a defeated Messiah, who yet was to come in power, we do not know; but during the week that followed their thoughts must have been in a tumult. Peter, James, and John, his three intimates, would have been making serious readjustments, and their partial recovery of faith is now strengthened on the summit of the high mountain up which Jesus had led them. Here he is transfigured before them, and his face did shine as the sun, and his raiment was white as the light. There talked with him Moses and Elijah, who spake of his death at Jerusalem. The disciples were heavy with sleep, but when they were fully awake they were amazed to see the three mysterious beings, Jesus, Moses, and Elijah. Was their leader then equal with Moses, the giver of the Law, and Elijah, the Alpha and Omega of the prophets? Peter makes a confused suggestion that they should set up three tents, canopies of equal dignity for these mighty leaders, as this would surely be a better Feast of Tabernacles than that which they would soon be keeping at Jerusalem.

At this very moment God reveals to them that Jesus transcends the Law and the Prophets. Out of the
*O

overshadowing cloud there comes a voice, saying, 'This is My beloved Son, hear ye him.' Terrified, they fell upon their faces, and when they lifted up their eyes they saw no man but Jesus, alone, transformed, supreme.

During the descent he charges them to keep quiet about the vision until the Son of Man is risen from the dead. They question among themselves what this rising can mean, as they still refuse to accept in their minds the idea of defeat. Then again, must not Elijah first come, and Jesus answered them: Elijah has indeed come and revived the message of the prophets. The religious world has rejected and murdered him, and it will be just the same with me. Then they understood that he spake of John the Baptist.

They now rejoin the main body of the disciples, who have been taunted by the scribes for being unable to heal a lunatic. The crowds were amazed at the radiant countenance of the Master, who immediately takes charge of the situation and restores speech, hearing, and sanity to the afflicted boy. The father had approached Jesus in despair at the failure of his followers, with the appeal: Lord, if thou canst do anything, have compassion on us and help us. 'If thou canst!' Jesus replied, Why, anything is possible to him that believes. The father of the child cried out and said with tears, Lord, I believe, help thou my unbelief. 'Then came the disciples to Jesus apart, and said, Why could not we cast it out? And he saith unto them, Because of your little faith: for verily I say unto you, If ye have faith as a grain of mustard seed ye shall say unto this mountain, Remove hence to yonder place; and it shall remove; and nothing shall be impossible unto you.' [1]

We must not take this too literally, but must allow for Oriental imagery; it is, however, worth recording that a lady who had been impressed by this story, prayed hard one night that the hill in front of her bedroom window should vanish before morning. In the morning she jumped out of bed, ran to the window and exclaimed, There it is

---

[1] Matthew xvii. 19–21. Some manuscripts insert: 'But this kind goeth not out save by prayer and fasting.'

still, I knew it would be! Her faith was of such a quality that it would hardly have moved a molehill much less a mountain.

Leaving the regions of Caesarea Philippi, they pass through Galilee, and in view of the danger of arrest, 'he would not that any man should know it.' Again he insisted on the fact that the Son of Man was to be betrayed and killed, but would rise the third day.

Jesus had been so long away from his headquarters in Capernaum that when he reached that city a tax collector approached Peter, saying, 'Doth not your Master pay the tribute?' Peter, not wishing to be at loggerheads with the authorities, unthinkingly answers: Yes. When he entered the house Jesus meets him with these words: 'What thinkest thou, Simon? Of whom do the kings of the earth take custom or tribute? Of their own sons or of foreigners? Peter saith unto him, Of foreigners. Jesus saith unto him, Then are the sons free.' Morally, there is not the slightest reason why we, the children of the New World Order, should pay any tribute to an exploiting empire or its Herodian cat's-paw. But the last thing we want is that the officials should detain us in Galilee on some trumpery charge; so do a little fishing and raise the money to pay our tax.[1]

Before leaving Peter's house, Jesus is disturbed by a quarrel that had arisen among the disciples on their march as to who should be the greatest in the coming kingdom. In spite of all his warnings, they evidently still clung to the idea of an immediately victorious Messiah and were anxious as to the order in which their names would appear

---

[1] This incident is given in Matthew alone, probably the original Matthew and not the later Greek editor as the author; a customs house officer would be especially interested in all questions of taxation. Most commentaries take the 'tribute' to be the temple tax, arguing, quite correctly, that it was a denarius: in Galilee, however, the Herodian tribute was also sometimes reckoned in denarii. Our Lord's comment on the whole situation is clear as daylight if the Herodian tax is in question, while the modern exegetists are confused and involved in their explanations of the Christ's words as a result of taking it to be the temple tax.

in the Honours List of the new régime.   Jesus took a little
boy, possibly a son of Peter, and set him in the midst,
saying, Unless you get a complete change of outlook, and
become like little children, you will have no place in the
new world order.   Your minds are set, middle aged, blind
to new ideas.   You must be as fresh and humble and
receptive as little children.

Perhaps a contemptuous glance or a shrug of the
shoulders suggested to Jesus that they were none too ready
to learn from this boy, for he adds: 'Whosoever shall receive one of such children in my name, receiveth me; and
whosoever shall receive me, receiveth not me, but Him
that sent me.'

This has its effect on the mind of John, for he feels
uneasy about their treatment of one who was exorcising in
the spirit of Jesus, but who had refused to follow them.
They had rebuked this man.   John doubts, now, whether
they had done rightly.   Jesus says, Forbid him not for it is
not likely that any one, who can heal in my name, would
lightly speak evil of me, for he that is not against us is for
us.   People like this exorcist are but children in the cause
who have a long way still to travel, but whosoever shall
scandalize such little ones who believe in me, it would be
better for him that a millstone were hanged about his neck,
and that he were cast into the sea.[1]   The world is full of
such scandalous unkindnesses, but woe unto him through
whom they come.   As for you, you pride yourself on the
fullness of your capacities; your two hands, your two feet,
your two eyes, and yet you have scandalized that exorcist
not so fully equipped.   Better for you to enter maimed
and humbled into life than, in the pride of your full capacity,
to be cast into hell.   I chose you to be the salt of the earth,
but if the salt hath lost its pungency, wherewith shall it
be salted?   By your quarrels and your condemnations you

---

[1] Note here again the gentleness of our Lord towards the immature and
his sternness towards the 'mature,' who were so ready to condemn the
former.   The millstone around the neck and the hell of fire ill accord with
pacifist assumptions.

have lost the savour of the gospel; have salt in yourselves, and have peace one with another.

Perhaps at this point should be recorded the incident of the ten lepers. Jesus was travelling in a district somewhere between Galilee and Samaria and there met these ten men who were lepers. He was not afraid to approach them, and cared nothing for the regulations against touching them. At their earnest request he healed them and told them to go and show themselves to the sanitary authorities, the priests, that they might pronounce them clean and fit to mix with ordinary people. They went as he commanded, but only one of them had the grace to turn back and thank his healer. Jesus says, Were there not ten cleansed, but where are the nine? Not one of them has thanked me excepting this foreigner, and he is a Samaritan. He alone has given glory to God who has healed him.

There are, then, Samaritans who put to shame, by their attitude, the righteous and self-contented Jews who are only too ready to condemn them.

If this is the place to record the incident, it becomes all the more significant that the disciples should be so furious with the Samaritan village which denied him hospitality, and would go far to explain why the Master refuses to regard the whole of the Samaritan district as hopeless.

CHAPTER XXIII

THE HARVEST FESTIVAL IN JERUSALEM

GALILEE had now become impossible for Jesus, and members of his family were taunting him [1] that he dare not go up to Jerusalem for the October feast. It is all very well your proclaiming your kingdom here in provincial Galilee, but so great a prophet as you should really have an international audience in the metropolis. Surely you are not afraid, even if they did expel you last spring. 'Manifest thyself to the world.'

Jesus had already determined on this very course, not because of their taunts, but because 'the days were well-nigh come that he should be received up, so he stedfastly set his face to go to Jerusalem, but he would have no man know it.' Especially was he anxious that his sceptical family should not know his plans: 'Go ye up unto the feast: I go not up yet unto this feast.' What were his chances of success in the capital? He had trained his small band of followers intensively, showing the nature of the new world, the spirit that animated its members, especially its leaders, insisting that the Son of Man would almost inevitably be rejected, and that only out of defeat would the victory be snatched. But had they yet understood? Were his fellow-travellers to be a compact and convinced band? If ever he had entertained that delusion it was at once to be shattered. At the very outset of the adventure they showed the old spirit of intolerance. He decided on the Samaritan route, which was both shorter and also avoided the trans-Jordan territory of Herod. He therefore sent his messengers to prepare for his reception in Samaritan villages. On his arrival at the first of these his plan is checked by their refusal to give him hospitality.

[1] See John vii. 3 and Luke ix. 51 for this conflation.

398

James and John, 'the Sons of Thunder,' are furious and ask: 'Lord, wilt thou that we bid fire to come down from Heaven and consume them?' But Jesus turned and rebuked them,[1] and they went to another village.

In our Lord's charge, some time before, to his twelve apostles he had said that it would be more tolerable for Sodom and Gomorrah in the day of judgment than for those Palestinian cities and villages that rejected the gospel of the new world which they were bringing them, and this fierce note is again struck in his charge to the seventy disciples which will be recorded somewhat later. How can we reconcile the militant activism of such passages, with the pacifist rebuke to the 'Sons of Thunder'? The fate of those who deliberately reject the Messiah and his fair world is inevitable, but to call down fire from Heaven upon an alien village which had never seen him nor had any opportunity of considering his gospel, is quite another matter. The new world order and its rejection is not here in question, but the trifling prejudice of Samaritans against giving free passage to Jews through their territory.

Other Samaritan villages do not seem to have shared this prejudice, for Jesus apparently still took the short route and reached the capital about the middle of the Feast of Tabernacles. There was much discussion as to whether he would make his appearance or not. Some believed him to be a charlatan, others a good man, but none dared talk openly about him for fear of the authorities. When eventually Jesus makes himself known he begins once more to teach openly and speaks so convincingly that people say, Where does this fellow get his learning, for he has certainly had no university education?

He refers to the conflict regarding his healing on the Sabbath, which had arisen during his last visit in the spring; they had attempted to kill him for his alleged

---

[1] Some ancient manuscripts add: '. . . and said, Ye know not what manner of spirit ye are of.' Some, but fewer, add also: 'For the Son of man came not to destroy men's lives, but to save them.' These may well have been Jesus's words and are certainly in the vein of his teaching.

breach of the Mosaic Law, but he argued that if Moses had approved of circumcision on the Sabbath, how much more would he have welcomed actual healing? The crowd remember that the rulers had tried to kill him. Why, then, did they not now at once arrest him? Is it because they themselves are divided, and that some of them are secretly convinced of his claims?

Jesus now proclaims that he is working not on his own initiative, but on that of the Father. Many of the multitude, though probably a minority, believed on him, and in order to stay this growing movement in Jerusalem the magistrates now once more order his arrest, but this attempt fails, for 'his hour was not yet come.'

His next words mystify his hearers, for he speaks of his going into some region where they cannot follow him; perhaps he means he will go far afield and teach the Jews dispersed amongst the Greek-speaking world.

On the last and greatest day of the feast, Jesus cried: 'If any man thirst, let him come unto me and drink. He that believeth on me, as the Scripture hath said, out of his belly shall flow rivers of living water.' Moved by these words many argued that this was, indeed, the prophet; others even spoke of him as the Christ; others again doubted, for surely the Messiah was not to arise out of Galilee. Even the police sent to arrest him did not carry out their orders, as they found that they were in sympathy with his cause, and the magistrates taunted them with being followers of this Galilean pretender. Then Nicodemus, a member of the Government, and a disciple in secret, now speaks out bravely: 'Doth our law judge a man, except it first hear from himself and know what he doeth?' Your minds are closed against him and ye refuse to give him a fair hearing. They answered: 'Art thou also of Galilee? Search and see that out of Galilee ariseth no prophet.'[1]

---

[1] Here is bracketed in the R.V. of the fourth gospel the story of the woman taken in adultery. It was probably not in the original text, but may well have been a genuine tradition of the Lord's teaching, so we record it.

The next day the Pharisees bring a woman to him in the Temple courts and, in the presence of the crowd, accuse her of adultery; they evidently wish to make it a test case, for if Jesus refuses to condemn her, he will, indeed, be proved a lawbreaker and an impostor. When they charge her and demand his condemnation he remains silent and writes in the dust; they keep on clamouring that she should be stoned to death, and at last he raises himself up and says: 'He that is without sin among you, let him first cast a stone at her.' Her would-be judges are for once dumbfounded, and shamefacedly go out one by one. Jesus and the woman are left alone. The silence is at last broken and he says: 'Woman, where are they? Did no man condemn thee?' To which she replied: 'No man, Lord.' And Jesus said: 'Neither do I condemn thee: go thy way; from henceforth sin no more.'

The climax is reached when Jesus said to those Jews who were beginning to be attracted to him: 'Ye shall know the truth, and the truth shall make you free.' Their recently found faith was immediately shaken, for they reply: 'We be Abraham's seed, and have never yet been in bondage to any man; how saith thou, Ye shall be made free?' The controversy reminds us of John the Baptist's answer to those Jews who were relying on their physical descent from Abraham: 'God is able of these stones to raise up children unto Abraham.' Jesus was thinking, as was his predecessor, of the mental and not of the fleshly ancestry. The descendants of Abraham are all those who have the free spirit of Abraham and do the will of Abraham's God. That free and generous spirit is natural to mankind: it is the spirit of the Son of Man, of representative man, who abides in the house of men's souls for ever, while the devil is an intruder.[1] Freedom is your natural heritage, but ye have thrown it away and become the bond-servants of sin; technically, you are Abraham's seed, 'yet ye seek to kill me, because my word hath not free course in you.' There follows the awful condemnation of this highly religious

[1] John viii. 34–6.

coterie, the very chosen people of God: 'Ye are of your father the devil, and the lusts of your father it is your will to do.'

They are by nature children of the God of truth, but they were so twisted and perverted, that all unconsciously they had become the children of Satan.   They now accuse him of being a Samaritan heretic and of being demon-possessed.   Jesus refutes them and they are further mystified when he makes what seems to them the impudent assertion: 'If a man keep my word, he shall never see death.' This is to them conclusive that he was a demon-ridden impostor and a lunatic.   But he keeps on asserting that if he was making these stupendous claims to glorify himself they would be justified in their indignation, but he was being driven on by the spirit of God and was convinced that in the real world, the world where time was illusory, he was one with the past and with the future, for 'your father Abraham rejoiced to see my day, and he saw it and was glad.'   To their dull and literal minds this seemed insanity; how could he who was well under fifty years old have seen Abraham?   But Jesus replies: 'Verily, verily, I say unto you, before Abraham was, I am.'

There have been moments when poets, prophets, and men of genius have known themselves to be before all time sharing in the timeless nature of God and the unerring mouthpiece of his message to the world.

His hearers, not being poets, took up stones to cast at him, but Jesus hid himself and went out of the Temple.

If Jesus had only been considering his own safety, he would naturally have left Jerusalem as soon as possible, but as he passed by he noticed a man blind from his birth. His disciples, brought up in the tradition that all disease was a penalty for sin, ask him: 'Rabbi, who did sin, this man, or his parents, that he should be born blind?'   Jesus knew that certain afflictions were caused by the sins of the flesh, such as the paralysis of the man whose faith he had awakened in Galilee and whose sins he had forgiven.   But he now corrects the pernicious doctrine that all disease is punishment, and declares that this unfortunate man was innocent, and that his blindness was due to some other cause; in any case it was to result in the restoration of his physical eyesight and in the reception of mental and spiritual illumination which, perhaps, he could never have come by but for his blindness. Jesus, therefore, answered: 'Neither did this man sin, nor his parents; but that the works of God should be made manifest in him.' He spat on the ground and made clay of the spittle and anointed the blind man's eyes. He was then told to wash in the pool of Siloam and he 'went away therefore and washed, and came seeing.' The cure resulted in a long and bitter controversy with the authorities, and the people were bewildered, some doubting and many being convinced that this was the work of a great prophet.

The conflict is graphically described by St. John, and is among the greatest passages in literature. It is very possibly a close record of this dramatic moment and of the *ipsissima verba* of the Christ. The 'Jews' try in every way to discredit the cure, and when at last they are forced to acknowledge it, denounce Jesus once more as a lawbreaker, for it had been done on the Sabbath day. They threatened with expulsion from the synagogue, any person who acknowledges him to be the Messiah. They bully the man himself and urge him to denounce his healer as a sinner. He quickly answers: 'Whether he be a sinner, I know not: one thing I know, that, whereas I was blind, now I see.' The authorities excommunicate him, but Jesus draws from him a confession of faith, and welcomes him into the community of the children of light. 'For judgment came I into this world, that they which see not may see; and that they which see may become blind. Those of the Pharisees which were with him heard these things, and said unto him: Are we also blind? Jesus said unto them, If ye were blind, ye would have no sin; but now ye say, We see: Your sin remaineth.'

This man recognized the ideal shepherd,[1] and would

[1] John x. 1 ff.

understand him when he pronounced that all that had come before him, that is, all that were claiming to be shepherds and leaders were merely trading on the people and exploiting them for their own ends: they were but 'thieves and robbers.'[1] The true shepherd anticipates the time when not only these obscure common people whom the Pharisees so ruthlessly expelled should be gathered into the one fold, but when the depressed and 'untouchables,' the foreigners of many nations shall pour into the new community and 'they shall become one fold, one shepherd.'

When the hour comes he would, of his own free will, be prepared to lay down his life and, through that death, would come the triumph of his cause. It seemed almost inevitable that he should be judicially murdered in Jerusalem, but he was to make further demands upon the mind of the holy city and to give its citizens a last chance. For the moment he must escape beyond Jordan and rally his followers that they might carry on an intensive propaganda in preparation for his next appearance in the capital. Either now, or earlier on his way through Samaria a man declares himself as ready to follow him wherever he may go, but Jesus warns the would-be disciple that he would be following an exile, outcast and hunted down. He urges many to follow him, but they must count the cost. One such was prepared to do so, but asks leave first to go and bury his father and is met with: Let the dead bury their dead: go thou and preach the New World Order. Nothing must stand in the way: there is not even time to go home and say good-bye to one's parents: 'No man, having put his hand to the plough, and looking back, is fit for the kingdom of God.'

Jesus now appoints some thirty-five couples[2] to prepare the cities and villages through which he was to pass to the capital. The harvest is plenteous but the labourers are few; pray God that their numbers may be increased. These missioners are sent forth in the midst of dangers, as sheep among wolves. His commission to the seventy is

[1] John x. 1 ff.   [2] Luke x. 1 ff.

more or less a repetition of his earlier commission to the
twelve; they are to heal the sick and announce the divine
commonwealth. That they will sometimes be marching
through Gentile territory is suggested by the words: 'Eat
such things as are set before you.' Once more he denounces a terrible doom upon those cities which will not
accept the Messiah and his cause.

This mission through towns and villages may have taken
a couple of months, but it was highly successful, for the
seventy returned with joy and report the acceptance of
their message, and not only physical, but mental cures;
for, 'Lord, even the demons are subject unto us in thy
name.' Our Lord sees in this success a veritable downfall of Satan, but bids the missioners rejoice, not so much
on account of the mental cures, but because their names
are enrolled as members of the divine commonwealth.
Jesus glorifies his Father because He has revealed His
secrets not to the learned and intellectual world, but to
simple common folk. It is these innocent people who
are beginning to see the fulfilment of the ancient hope
for which prophets and kings of old had longed. St.
Luke now records a saying of the Christ which will be
found in a different setting in the gospel according to St.
Matthew and this saying may be considered as the high
watermark of the Messianic claim of Jesus as unfolded in
the Synoptists; it reminds us strongly of his utterances in
the fourth gospel: 'All things have been delivered unto me
of my Father: and no one knoweth who the Son is, save
the Father; and who the Father is, save the Son, and he
to whomsoever the Son willeth to reveal Him.'[1] This
saying might well be compared with the pronouncement
that Jesus is soon to make at the winter feast in the
capital, to which he travels in a mood of exultation and
joy caused by the success of his evangelists along the
road.

Perhaps he had just left Jericho when a lawyer accosted
him with the eager question as to what he should do to

[1] Luke x. 22; cf. Matthew xi. 27.

inherit eternal life.[1] Jesus here, as so often, adopts the Socratic method and draws from the questioner himself the answer to his problem: in the love of God and the love of his neighbour lies the true life. But then, who is one's neighbour? The answer to that is to be found in the parable of the good Samaritan. It was not the lawyer's own kindred, not the Jewish religious world, that acted in a neighbourly fashion to the victim of the highway robbers, but the unexpected Samaritan, the religious outcast.

The lonely robber - infested road from Jerusalem to Jericho was unsafe for travellers unless they joined themselves to some caravan or other. A certain man found himself on this rocky road alone and defenceless and was held up by robbers. They stripped him of his clothes and all that he had and beat him and left him half dead. And by chance a certain priest passed that way and saw him, but thought it was no affair of his and hurried by on the other side. Perhaps he was intent on saying his breviary.

Another devout man intimately connected with the Temple and with religious education came along and looked on him and decided on non-intervention. But a certain outsider, a Samaritan, came along and when he saw him he had compassion on him; rendered first aid, put him on his own mule, and brought him to an inn where he arranged for the host to look after him, paying for him and promising when he returned to be responsible for any further expenses.

Which now thinkest thou, of these three men, was neighbour to the victim of the robbers? And the lawyer said, He that showed mercy on him. Then Jesus said unto him, Go and do thou likewise.

[1] Eternal life, or life abundant, is a synonym for the overmastering life of the divine commonwealth.

CHAPTER XXIV

THE WINTER FEAST

At Bethany, on the Mount of Olives, the last halt on the road to Jerusalem, Jesus stays for a meal with Martha and Mary who keep house for their brother Lazarus. Mary had a deep insight into the Lord's message and plans and sat at his feet eager to hear him. Martha also loved him, but was too interested in his physical needs. She was 'distracted with much serving.' She complains that her sister is not helping, and that she is left to prepare the meal alone. Perhaps she was, equally with Mary, wanting to listen, but the meal must be prepared. The Master answered and said, Martha, Martha, thou art worried about preparing an elaborate meal, but one dish [1] is all I need. Mary has chosen the best dish which shall not be taken away from her.

Jesus reaches Jerusalem for the winter feast. This festival of Dedication [2] had been established by the Maccabees about a century before to commemorate the liberation of their country. In the large open space of Solomon's Porch the Jews throng around him and try to draw from him an open declaration of his claim to Messiahship. He appeals to his divine works, but these are nothing to them. When further he declares himself one with the Father, they take up stones to kill him. Jesus answered them: 'Many good works have I showed you from the Father;

---

[1] Both Moffatt and the *New Commentary* suggest that the one dish is meant and Moffatt translates 'Mary has chosen the best dish.' This is probably correct, but the ordinary translation: 'One thing is needful,' has the advantage of leaving it an open question whether it refers to the propaganda or the meal. It is not usually remembered that the Church has, perhaps rightly, canonized Martha as well as Mary.

[2] This feast apparently began on 25th December, our present Christmas day, and continued into January.

for which of those works do ye stone me? The Jews answered him, For a good work we stone thee not, but for blasphemy; and because that thou, being a man, makest thyself God.'

The reply of Jesus to this accusation is astonishing. He does not say, 'But I *am* God, while you are mere men,' which is the answer conventional Christians would have expected, but, 'Is it not written in your law, I said, Ye are gods?' He not only identifies himself with the human race, but here declares that race divine. If therefore the men of old time with a divinely inspired message are lawfully to be called gods, how much more has he the right to call himself by the more modest title of 'Son of God,' he whom the Father has sanctified and sent into the world. But they remained implacably hostile and 'sought again to take him; and he went forth out of their hand.'

Jesus once more crosses the Jordan, and in its wide basin, where John used to baptize, or in some hill village above it on the farther side, he dwells for a time with his disciples. The valley would remind them of those enthusiastic days when they had dedicated themselves to him and his movement, 'and many believed on him there.'

Jesus is now in Perea on the other side of the Jordan, which at the present day is not so thickly populated. At that time, however, there seems to have been not only hill villages on the trans-Jordan banks, but a considerable population of cities and villages for many miles eastward before you reach the Arabian desert.[1]

Jesus had one day been praying and his disciples asked him how they should pray; he replies with the Pater Noster as the best model for all prayer.[2] He advises them to be

---

[1] This is substantiated by a friend of mine who often flies over the Jordan to his work north-eastward near Bagdad, and by travellers on horseback who describe innumerable remains of a Graeco-Roman civilization. This explains St. Luke's account of crowds thronging Jesus in the trans-Jordan territory. Cf. St. Luke xiii. 22. Many modern critics discredit the Lucan story of a Perean ministry, but their arguments seem to me entirely unconvincing.

[2] We have already dealt with the Lord's Prayer in Matthew's earlier order.

urgent in their prayers, to besiege the Father in heaven with their requests and gives as examples the man who knocks up his friend at midnight asking for food: even if the friend is too sleepy to rouse himself, he will at last be persuaded to respond because of the man's persistence. 'Ask, and it shall be given you; seek, and ye shall find; knock, and it shall be opened unto you. For every one that asketh receiveth, and he that seeketh findeth; and to him that knocketh it shall be opened.' It would be a very unnatural father who in response to his child's demands for a loaf, should give him a stone, or for an egg should give him a scorpion. 'If ye then, being evil, know how to give good gifts unto your children, how much more shall your heavenly Father give the Holy Spirit to them that ask Him?'

Somewhat later, but with the same moral, comes the parable of the importunate widow who wore down the bad judge by her repeated demands for justice; if the unjust judge yielded at last, how much more will the just and beneficent Father yield to the demands of His children? Jesus does not, therefore, mean that any demand, however often it may be made, will be granted, for here he explicitly says it is the demand for the Holy Spirit, and subsequently adds that prayer must always be made *in his name* by which he means in accordance with his will and personality; but an urgent faith, if governed by this qualification, will remove mountains.

Certain incidents and teaching which follow in St. Luke's gospel have already been dealt with in an earlier section of this work, but we must notice the parable of the empty spring-cleaned house into which seven other demons worse than the first find an easy entrance, because the house-holder has forgotten to fill the house of his soul with an effectual army of good thoughts and good works.

One day great crowds gathered round Jesus and he told them that the times were evil because every one was on the look out for signs and miracles; they would not believe in his gospel unless he were willing to support it by stupendous wonders, but for his part he would give them no sign, but the sign of the prophet Jonah. The prophet's convincing teaching had converted the almost unconvertible and utterly corrupt metropolis, Nineveh. The men of Nineveh would stand up in the coming day of judgment and condemn 'this generation,' for a greater than Jonah had pleaded with them, and they were turning a deaf ear to his pleadings. 'The queen of the south shall rise up in the judgment with the men of this generation and shall condemn them; for she came from the ends of the earth to hear the wisdom of Solomon; and behold, a greater than Solomon is here.'

The above passage is hall-marked with authenticity, for second-century Christians would have been much more likely to present the risen Lord as a wonder-worker, and if it be objected that he did sometimes work amazing miracles, the answer has already been given, that he never worked them in order to stun the spectators into belief.

As he was speaking a Pharisee asks him to breakfast, for although Jesus was merely a Galilean workman, with the crowds he was the lion of the moment, and the Pharisee's curiosity had been aroused. But this pious man was shocked at what he considered the uncouth behaviour of his guest, and his disregard of ceremonial custom—for he had not washed before the meal. Jesus noticed his disgust and answers in a passage which reminds us of his earlier conflict with the same type of men, the conflict which had driven him into exile. With great indignation he charges the Pharisees with cleansing the outside of the cup and the platter, while their inward hearts are full of extortion and exploitation; if instead of grasping from the people they were in the habit of giving to them from generous impulse all things would be clean unto them.

It was natural after this violent provocation that 'when he was come out from thence, the scribes and the Pharisees began to press upon him vehemently, and to provoke him to speak of many things; laying wait for him, to catch something out of his mouth.'

There follows a considerable amount of teaching on which we have already commented when dealing with the Sermon on the Mount, and with our Lord's charge to the twelve; but here he expands his teaching, reiterating his warning that the good news of the coming age will divide families to the extreme point of their delivering one another to death, and he insists that he is come to cast fire on the earth, and that he is glad that it is already kindled. 'But I have a baptism to be baptized with,' and he feels 'cabined, cribbed, confined' until he has been to this fiery baptism of death. He is not come to bring peace, but rather division; or, as Matthew says earlier, 'not to send peace, but a sword.' Here, again, Jesus, who will not break the bruised reed, forewarns them that the genial world of peace and happiness can only be reached through the flame and the sword.

Here we must consider his answer to some who told him about the slaughter of the Galileans by Pilate and the tragedy of the Tower of Siloam. Pilate was a cruel and provocative procurator and certain Galileans had risen in revolt against him. Jesus considers this rebellion a blunder of the greatest magnitude, and when commenting on it adds: 'Except ye repent, ye shall all likewise perish.' Revivalists have interpreted repentance in the modern sense and the word 'perish' as meaning punishment in a future hell. The whole incident has, therefore, become meaningless.

Jesus considered all such rebellions as almost criminal follies from the point of view of policy; and perhaps as wrongly motived from the point of view of morals. The first business of the nation was 'repentance,' that is, an entire change of mind and outlook. All these revolts he regarded as Satan casting out Satan, because the people were only anxious to overthrow the Roman yoke that they might fasten upon mankind a yoke just as oppressive. The same thing might be said about the incident of the Tower of Siloam. The Roman authority had begun to build a water tower to bring a good supply of water to the capital.

It was not too wisely arranged, for this interference with Jerusalem would be regarded as an interference with native religious custom. But it was foolish of the crowd to riot as they seem to have done. While the tower was in process of construction, the people massed in the street and attempted to hinder the work, and were by the Roman soldiery pressed back against the bricks and the tower fell, killing some eighteen of the crowd. In all such cases it was wiser to 'make friends with thine adversary whilst thou art in the way with him.' Some day when the people had learned to hunger and thirst after the new world of righteousness, and to welcome into its fold all the children of men, then would be the time to cast out the oppressor within their gates, and to establish with the help of many peoples the divine commonwealth which would finally supplant all imperial tyrannies. Meanwhile one must wait.

Unless, therefore, the nation repents and achieves a new outlook, its fate will be that of the barren fig-tree planted in a vineyard, which had been dug round about and manured for three years,[1] and had borne no fruit. Why waste time on it any longer? Cut it down. 'Why doth it also cumber the ground?' But the vinedresser pleads with the owner to give it a last chance. So Jesus has preached to the nation these three years, but the preaching has been almost fruitless; a few months remain in which this barren people may yet bear fruit.

The synagogues of Galilee had long since been closed to Jesus, but it is still possible for him to teach in the synagogues of Perea. One Sabbath day his attention is arrested by a woman bent double with rheumatism (?); she had been a sufferer for eighteen years and the Master immediately determined to cure her. What better day could there be than the Sabbath for this good work? Disease to Jesus seemed satanic, and he would fight the devil on God's day. But the ruler of the synagogue who

---

[1] Many critics reject the theory of a three years' ministry, basing the arguments mainly on Mark, but this story suggests a three years' mission now drawing to its close.

witnessed the cure, was horrified and rebuked Jesus and his patient with pious platitudes. The Master indignantly replies that they are in the habit of loosing their live-stock for water on the Sabbath day, 'Ought not this woman, being a daughter of Abraham, whom Satan hath bound, lo, these eighteen years, to have been loosed from this bond on the day of the Sabbath?' His opponents for the time being are silent and ashamed, but all the multitude glorified God.

It was, perhaps, at this moment that Jesus received an urgent message from Martha and Mary to come to Bethany as their brother Lazarus was dangerously ill; it was the Mary who anointed the Lord with ointment and wiped his feet with her hair. The evangelist adds that Jesus loves the family at Bethany intensely, and yet lingers two days longer in Perea before making a move. Was this hesitation due to the conflict in his mind between the appeal of the desperate need of the individual, and the claims of the world plan and of the strategy that was necessary to preserve it? Although there was a certain danger from Herod, he was gaining adherents daily in Perea, who going up with him to Jerusalem would later constitute a valuable bodyguard for his defence. The disciples understood the immediate danger of crossing into Judea where the authorities had but recently attempted to kill their Master. In spite of the danger Jesus determines to go. The disciples decide to go with him, although such an adventure seems to them to involve certain death.

It was only on the fourth day that Martha, distracted with anguish, sees her helper coming and meets him along the road with the reproach upon her lips: 'Lord, if thou hadst been here, my brother had not died.' But quickly she adds: 'But I know that even now, whatsoever thou wilt ask of God, God will give it thee.' Jesus assures her that her brother shall rise again, but such an assurance does little to comfort her: for she believes that her brother will arise in the resurrection at the last day. Her heart springs into life once more when she heard the Master in triumph exclaim: 'I am the resurrection and the life: he that believeth

on me, though he were dead, yet shall he live: and whosoever liveth and believeth in me shall never die. Believest
thou this?' Immediately the answer comes: 'Yea, Lord:
I believe that thou art the Christ, the Son of God, which
should come into the world.'

She now goes quietly to her sister and tells her that
Jesus has at last come, and is asking for her. He is led
by the sisters and the Jews who accompany them into the
village, and his spirit is grieved at the sight of their grief.
They lead him to the tomb and moved with deep sorrow
'Jesus wept.' When he commands them to remove the
stone Martha once more doubts, for must not the corpse by
now be decaying? Jesus reassures her and the stone is
removed and he cries with a loud voice: 'Lazarus, come
forth.' The dead man lived again, and the grave clothes
in which he had been wrapped, were unwound, and once
more he saw the light of day.[1]

Some of the onlookers were convinced and believed in
Jesus, whilst others went and reported the matter to the
Pharisees. There was a hurried meeting of the cabinet,

---

[1] We have already suggested that the miraculous element in the gospels
cannot be ruled out as antecedently impossible, nor should we reject off-
hand the stories of restoration to life. The daughter of Jairus may have
been roused from a trance or raised from death; but a Synoptist author
definitely speaks of the funeral procession at Nain, and the raising on that
occasion of the widow's son. If we accept the possibility of this, why should
we hesitate to accept the Johannine story of the raising of Lazarus? Here
there is not only the difficulty of a body corrupting for three days in the
tomb, but also the more serious difficulty of the omission of this key incident
in the Synoptic narrative, for this is a turning point in the drama, the drawing
of Jesus back into that very danger zone from which he had so recently
escaped with a price on his head. If, however, the Master could have
raised the body of Lazarus from death, he could surely have preserved it
from corruption. And as to the omission of the incident from other accounts,
there is a tradition that Lazarus was to become so active in the Master's
service that he suffered martyrdom. The Provençal story of his death at
Marseilles may be a legend, but it is almost impossible to believe that he
would not have become a missionary, and that he could have escaped a
martyr's end. Now if this is so, may it not be that the Synoptists, writing
while he was still alive, would not wish to draw too much attention to his
activities; both because they would have been cut short by the authorities,
and for the avoidance of a superstitious worship of the man himself. These
arguments may not be convincing but they are at least worth considering.

who were more than ever disturbed at the extraordinary
activities of Jesus, and the response of the crowds. If
they let this man alone, the Roman Empire, convinced
that they are unable to preserve law and order, will come
and take away their position as a ruling class and destroy
the last vestiges of their nationality. How modern this all
sounds. The British Empire, like the Roman, has experi-
mented in its colonial administration with many different
types of government, ranging from direct rule as in Kenya
to native administration as in northern Nigeria.

Caiaphas, who was that year archbishop and prime
minister, was especially urgent that they should take immediate action, for was it not expedient that one man should
die rather than the whole nation perish? In his tragic
ignorance he did not perceive that he was dealing with
the very saviour of his nation and of all mankind; nor
did he know that this man was indestructible, that Jesus,
the Christ, must, through life or through death, become
Salvator Mundi. 'So from that day forth they took counsel
that they might put him to death.'

Jesus could no more openly teach in Judea, but for a
time hid himself in the secluded village of Ephraim, near
to the wilderness; and it was only later that he was able
secretly to cross the Jordan with his disciples and once more
resume his Perean mission.

He is still determined to make Jerusalem his objective,
and to reach the capital with the mass of pilgrims who will
be marching to the coming Passover. It is of the utmost
importance that he should carry on an intensive propaganda in Perea so that as many as possible of the Galileans
and Pereans shall have heard his message and been converted before they accompany him to the feast. Time
presses, he has only a month or two left, so 'he went on his
way through cities and villages, teaching and journeying
on unto Jerusalem.' His theme is as ever the coming
commonwealth; and he illustrates it once again with the
stories of the mustard seed and the leaven. One of the
crowd asks him, Lord, are they few that will escape and

come through the impending catastrophe into the kingdom? Jesus refuses to satisfy the curiosity of his questioner, but bids all to strive that they may enter in through the narrow gate; it is no broad, easy road, but one which demands energy and sacrifice; and the mere fact of having been close to him in the throng and having heard him speak, will be no guarantee of safety; moreover it is the very people that think themselves secure and pride themselves on their ancestry who will find themselves outcast from the common-wealth of Abraham, Isaac, and Jacob and all the prophets.

This doctrine is, as usual, particularly offensive to the local Pharisees, who think it high time to get him out of the district; so they suggest, probably with some truth, that he is in danger from Antipas: 'Get thee out, and go hence: for Herod would fain kill thee.' Jesus shows no particular respect for royalty and replies: 'Go and say to that fox, Behold, I cast out devils and perform cures to-day and to-morrow, and the third day I am perfected. How-beit, I must go on my way to-day and to-morrow and the day following; for it cannot be that a prophet perish out of Jerusalem.' Jesus is not to be intimidated by this threat, but will continue his teaching through the densely populated district, in spite of the danger from the anti-clerical Herod [1] and his clerical allies. Besides, he ironically adds, I am surely safe in this district; it is only the holy city that murders its prophets; it is there that the tragedy will find its end. 'Jerusalem, Jerusalem, which killeth the prophets, and stoneth them that are sent unto thee! how often would I have gathered thy children together, even as a hen gathereth her own brood under her wings, and ye would not! Behold, your house is left unto you desolate; and I say unto you, Ye shall not see me, until ye shall say, Blessed is he that cometh in the name of the Lord.' [2]

One day he is invited by a Pharisee to a meal on the Sabbath, and offends his host by healing a man afflicted

---

[1] Herod Antipas was not only Tetrarch of Galilee but also of Perea.

[2] This prophecy was actually fulfilled when the crowds welcomed him into Jerusalem with these very words.

with the dropsy, and again contrasts the contemptuous attitude of the religious world towards human need with their solicitude even on the holy day for their own property. If his host is scandalized, still more scandalized is Jesus when he notices how the guests scramble for the best places at the dinner table, and he gives them the very practical advice to choose less honourable places, and wait until one or other is invited to sit near the top of the table. 'For every one that exalteth himself shall be humbled; and he that humbleth himself, shall be exalted.'

When you are giving a dinner party it is better not to ask your richer neighbours who will have to return the invitation; why not invite the poor, the maimed, the lame, the blind, who cannot give you a grand spread in return, and whom your hospitality will really be helping? When the day comes when these people will enter into their kingdom, they will recompense you. The same moral is given in the parable of the unjust steward, on which we shall soon be commenting.

Meanwhile it is noteworthy that the teaching of Jesus is much more self-regarding than the teaching of most of the Oriental religions. In these the self is obliterated and Nirvana is reached by self-annihilation, or by the ego being swallowed up in the Being of God.[1] But in the philosophy of Christ and the Catholic Church the ego loses itself in the adoration of God and the love of its neighbours, and in

[1] Edward Carpenter, however, suggests in *From Adam's Peak to Elphanta* that Nirvana does not necessarily imply self-obliteration; he writes: 'Great have been the disputes among the learned as to the meaning of the word Nirvana—whether it indicates a state of no-consciousness or a state of vastly enhanced consciousness. Probably both views have their justification: the thing does not admit of definition in the terms of ordinary language. The important thing to see and admit is that under cover of this and other similar terms there does exist a real and recognizable fact (that is, a state of consciousness in some sense), which has been experienced over and over again, and which to those who have experienced it in ever so slight a degree has appeared worthy of lifelong pursuit and devotion. It is easy, of course, to represent the thing as a mere word, a theory, a speculation of the dreamy Hindu; but people do not sacrifice their lives for empty words, nor do mere philosophical abstractions rule the destinies of continents. No, the word represents a reality, something very basic and inevitable in human nature.'

P

this very process finds itself, saves and enriches itself unto life eternal. The *as* in 'love thy neighbour as thyself' is remarkable in this connection.

We have already quoted the oft-repeated words of Jesus: 'Whosoever shall save his soul shall lose it, and whosoever shall lose his soul for my sake and the gospel shall find it unto life eternal.' The Catholic doctrine of inspiration is a development of the same idea, and directly contradicts the doctrine of the fundamentalists. They seem to teach that God uses human beings as the chess player uses his ivory pieces moving these lifeless things hither and thither across the board of life: the Catholic Church in one of its oecumenical councils condemns this theory and teaches that, in inspiration, God enriches rather than obliterates human personality.

One of the guests, on hearing of this recompense in the coming kingdom, remarks on the blessedness of the meals that will be shared together in that joyous age, but our Lord replies with the parable of the great supper, to which many are bidden and some refuse to come because they are newly married, and the wives object to being left, or because they are occupied with their newly bought property. The master of the house, being angry, tells his servants to go out into the streets and lanes of the city and to invite the poor and the maimed to the banquet; the servants do this and yet there is room. They are then told to go into the country, into the highways and hedges, and compel [1] them to come in: 'For I say unto you, That none of those men which were bidden shall taste of my supper.'

In St. Matthew's account of what seems to be the same parable, the guests who refuse the invitation slay the servants, and the host, who is described as a king, sends forth his armies 'and destroyed those murderers and burnt

---

[1] Compel them and *compelle entrare*. St. Augustine's unfortunate and quite unjustifiable use of this text has been the cause of much misery in the Christian world. He interpreted it as meaning that whole districts might be compelled by force to be baptized.

The wedding garment incident has been equally abused by Calvinists, and even by such modern writers as Schweitzer, who suggests that God, by an arbitrary decree, saves certain souls and damns others.

up their city.' Neither this nor the incident that follows is easy to reconcile with extreme pacifist assumptions. Our Lord concludes with the story of the man who appeared at the feast without a wedding garment. Some students of the times have suggested that wedding cloaks were handed to the guests at the door, but this has been disputed. If true, the guest who had come in with the crowd from the highways and hedges would prove himself an unsociable churl; but even if he had been too lazy or indifferent to tidy himself up and put on his best clothes, he would show himself utterly lacking in the spirit of comradeship and in courtesy to his host. When the king came into the banquet, he asks: 'Friend, how camest thou in hither not having a wedding garment?' If the man had been able to reply that he had nothing better than his everyday clothes to wear, the king would obviously have put him at his ease, and told him to enjoy himself with the rest. But the man remains speechless, for he knows himself to be a boorish fellow who hates good company; so his host orders them to bind him hand and foot and cast him into the dark night without, where shall be weeping and gnashing of teeth; for although the whole world is invited to the banquet, only those who arc in the spirit of comradeship are chosen.

The man's punishment is drastic, but we must allow for the heightening of the imagery in the parables and must also note that the offence against companionship is always treated as mortal sin by our Lord.

Jesus has considerable success in his preaching of the kingdom, and great crowds of the common people follow him journeying to Jerusalem; but he warns them that if they identify themselves with him they will be marching to almost certain death. Many a time he has given them this warning, but it can never be too often repeated. He now puts it in stronger terms than ever before; unless they are prepared to forsake their families and all that they have they cannot be his disciples.

Jesus was not a philosopher but an imaginative poet. He does not weave his sayings into a dull and carefully guarded consistency, but flings out a challenge here and a challenge there, leaving later generations to do the necessary work of weaving a philosophy out of his paradoxes. So here one must be prepared to hate one's father and mother, although on another occasion he teaches that hatred is so deadly a sin that even to be angry with one's brother brings one into condemnation.

Parents are often utterly selfish and make quite unjust claims on their sons and daughters. They forbid them to marry or to enter this or that profession, expecting them to remain at home and dance attendance on them. They will charge them with hatred if they dare to disobey; but if the children have their own rights how much more is this so when their whole being is inspired with the great cause and its demands upon them. Of course, children are often inconsiderate towards their parents, but this is not at the moment in the mind of the Christ. You must be prepared on occasions figuratively to hate your father and mother or you are not fit to be his disciple.

The psychologists of to-day definitely teach that there comes a time when there must be a complete break with parents, and that the adolescents must free themselves from the cloying parental affection which will otherwise smother their own personalities. They must for a time, at least, 'hate' their father and mother, in order later to re-establish right relations with them. Perhaps our Lord would not have gone quite so far as this, but it shows that so far from being outmoded and old-fashioned he anticipated modern thought in the matter of psychology, as he did in the matter of physical science.

It is a costly business this business of the Cross. What man is fool enough to begin building a tower without reckoning up the costings? For if he is unable to complete the building he will only make himself a laughing stock. Or what king is there, if he is going to declare war, will not first reckon up his forces and see if they are strong enough to meet the enemy? If not, far better to come to the best terms he can get, rather than court certain disaster.

CHAPTER XXV

PARABLES ON THE MARCH

UNDISMAYED by these warnings crowds still thronged him as he journeyed to Jerusalem, and disreputables, tax-gatherers, and harlots were eager to hear him. The Pharisees expressed their usual contempt and Jesus finds himself once more in bitter conflict with them.

It is the lost and the disreputables that attract him; they are so much more companionable than the pious.

It shows what kind of fellow this is, observed the 'Vigilance Committee.' A man may be known by the company he keeps. To preach to such people is ridiculous enough, but to 'pal up' with them and have meals in common with them long before they had been converted is evidence of his own loose living.

Jesus replies to all this with the parables of the lost sheep, the lost coin, and the lost son.

It is the lost sheep for whom the shepherd will risk his life. What matter the ninety and nine, folded and secure? It is the one poor stray that he will go over hill and dale, through fire and water to save; and what rejoicing when he brings back the poor silly thing safe and sound.

It is the little coin that has rolled into a dark corner under the wardrobe that the housewife values more than the change on the mantelpiece. How diligently she searches for it, and what a fuss she makes with her friends and neighbours over its recovery.[1]

It is the lost son whom the father loves and for whom he is inconsolable, the black sheep of the family who has

[1] It may not have been a lost coin, but a piece of silver forming part of the ten-piece necklace or bracelet given to the bride as part of the wedding dowry.

been given every chance. How his parents have scraped and saved for his education, and now he is spending half the little family fortune on prostitutes and riotous living. His 'friends' only care for him so long as they can get the price of a drink out of him; and have soon squeezed him dry. He becomes just one of the failures and ne'er-do-wells, just one of the 'undeserving poor.' At his wits' end he hires himself to a respectable farmer, who proves himself too respectable to bother his head whether the poor chap gets a meal or not: 'And he would fain have filled his belly with the husks that the swine did eat, and no man gave unto him.' It is now that he comes to his senses and realizes what a damned fool he has been; and he thinks of the poor old man at home whom he has let down so abominably. 'And when he came unto himself, he said, How many of my father's labourers have food enough and to spare, while I perish here with hunger? I will arise and go to my father.' His misery has awakened in him the deeper shame: he will tell his father that he has sinned against heaven and against him, and is not worthy to take his place as his son. Will the old man give him a job as an agricultural labourer?

But all these years the father has hoped against hope, and had always been on the look out, and when the boy was yet a great way off he saw him and was moved with compassion and ran and fell on his neck and kissed him. He sees repentance in the boy's face and cuts short his confession with an order to the servants to put out his best clothes and to prepare a good spread for him, 'for this my son was dead and is alive again; was lost and is found.'

The boy's elder brother, his hard day's work on the farm just ended, is astonished to hear sounds of music and dancing, and asks the servants what on earth it all means. He is naturally indignant at the answer he gets, and refuses to go in. His father comes out and entreats him, but he reminds him that he has always stayed at home and worked himself to the bone for the farm; there has never been a

feast for him.   But his father replies: 'Son, thou art ever
with me and all that is mine is thine.   But it was meet to
make merry and be glad; for this thy brother was dead,
and is alive again; was lost and is found.'
     God is just like this.   He is ever on the look out; he
meets the prodigal more than half-way, makes it easy for
him, and holds out a helping hand.   'There is joy in the
presence of the angels of God over one sinner that re-
penteth' more than over the respectable persons who pride
themselves that they are in need of no repentance.
     'Forgive and ye shall be forgiven.'   What exactly does
this mean?   Is it conditioned by the prior repentance of
the offender?   That the sinner should repent is evident,
but should not the injured party make the first approach?
Would it not then be far easier for the offender to admit
his fault and resolve to amend?
     This is the way of the Heavenly Father, and should be
the way of man, his child and care.   The lost sheep is not
left to find its way back to the fold alone, but the good
shepherd takes infinite risks to bring it back home.   It
is remarkable that the Christ's 'If thy brother sin against
thee' immediately follows this parable.   If he sins, you,
not he, are urged to make the first move.   You are to
go and talk it over with him, and you might then find
that there is fault on both sides; if that fails, you make
another attempt with one or two friends; and again, that
having failed, you bring the question up before the whole
community.   It is only when he refuses to hear the
community and hardens his heart against the common
judgment that he becomes for the time being an outcast,
an excommunicated person.   St. Paul, remembering the
Book of Proverbs, writes: 'If thine enemy hunger, feed
him; if he thirst, give him drink; for in so doing thou shalt
heap coals of fire upon his head.   Be not overcome of evil,
but overcome evil with good.'   The Lord said: 'Forgive
us our trespasses, as we also *have forgiven* them that
trespass against us.'
     St. Peter thought he was being extraordinarily generous

when he suggested that perhaps Jesus would demand of them the forgiveness of their brethren seven times; and there are very few people who will go to this length. He must have been staggered by the reply: 'I say not unto thee till seven times, but until seventy times seven.' Mankind is, therefore, *always* to be 'the priest in absolution.'

Repentance and confession to God and to man is insisted on over and over again in both Old and New Testaments, and neither the absolution of God nor of the community can operate where it is absent. If a man has closed the shutters of his mind against either his Father in heaven or his fellow - men, God's forgiveness is shut out. He must open the shutters if the sun of righteousness is to pour in.

We have already attempted to explain the admittedly difficult problem of the sin against the Holy Ghost which is pronounced to be unforgivable in this age and in the age to come.

But something must now be said about sins, not against the individual, but against the community. What is to be our attitude to rack-renters, extortioners, and oppressors of the poor? Are we to forgive them? Does Jesus give any ruling on this point? His violent attacks on all such people are unmistakable, and so are also his warnings about the doom that awaits them. But in his last words from the cross, 'Forgive them, O my Father, for they know not what they do,' may include in their wide and generous sweep the hypocrite and the extortioner. St. Peter charges the people and their rulers with the murder of Jesus, and yet adds: 'I wot that in ignorance ye did it.'

It is certain that a much fiercer note is struck when attacks against offenders of this class are launched, and that we must also fight them unflinchingly, but are we called upon to forgive them? If a Mussolini repents of his acts of mass murder and turns his back on all such deeds, makes such restitution as is possible and willingly undergoes severe penance, then he must be forgiven. But it is such people when they glory in their shame who make any

forgiveness impossible.   They, like Dives, have dug their
own grave and have themselves fixed the gulf.   But
Abraham in this parable begins his stern rebuke with the
gentle words: 'Son, remember.'

It has been essential to lay stress throughout this work on
the fierce and uncompromising attitude of the Christ towards the enemies of God's commonwealth, because our
sentimentalist age is inclined to ignore it; but the God of
vengeance and of wrath who casts the hypocrites out of
his kingdom is also the God who makes his sun to shine
upon the evil as well as the good, upon not only the just
but the unjust.

We are not here immediately concerned with the subject
of everlasting punishment, and Jesus says nothing very
definite about the life beyond the grave.   He urges men
to concentrate on the present time and to find the eternal
values underlying the temporal.   'Now is the accepted
time; now is the day of salvation.'   It is as if he said to
mankind, Take care of the pence of the present life, and the
pounds of the future life will take care of themselves.   Do
not be over anxious about the future; if you do God's will
now, and strive to bring down heaven upon the earth,
God will look after your souls in the world beyond the
grave.

But here and there hints may be found about the world
beyond.   It has already been pointed out that in the story
of Dives and Lazarus no suggestion is made that the
punishment of the rich man would last for ever, and in
St. Paul's epistles it is taught that there will come a time
when God will have subjected all things to Himself, and
when He will be all and in all.   Jesus himself said: 'If I be
lifted up, I will draw all men unto me.'   How else could
his victory be completed?   It would be no triumph for
Christ or for the Father if a single soul remained outside
the fellowship of heaven, cursing and unconsoled.   That
the majority of us will have to undergo a long and bitter
purgatory, a remedial cleansing or purgation, is evident
enough.   There is no support given in the New Testament
* P

for the easy gospel so dear to some modern spiritualists, that the soul passes from a life of callousness and cruelty straight to a heaven of lawn tennis and comfortable enjoyments. But a future world where men still for ever and ever resisted God would be the triumph of Satan and the defeat of God.

True, the Catholic Church has had to safeguard the doctrine of the freedom of man's will. God forces no man in this life or in a life to come to act righteously or to love Him. How could he? Who shall command the heart? But neither life nor death can entirely quench the Holy Spirit in the individual soul. At least, so it would seem, and many of the early Catholic fathers were of this opinion. After long ages the love of God will melt the hardest heart, even if it be 'so as by fire.'

There have always been within the Church teachers of the type of the Spanish Inquisitors, worthy but implacable men from the early Fathers to the good but rigorist Pusey in our own day. But the Church has never faced the subject in a universal council, nor condemned as heretics the Greek fathers and many another throughout the ages, men like Dean Stanley and Charles Kingsley and, above all, the great Frederick Denison Maurice, who have contended for the more generous and merciful view. Perhaps, after all, they are right and some day they may be canonized as leaders of orthodox catholic doctrine.

From his prison Oscar Wilde wrote,[1] and what he wrote may be applied to the prisons, to those hells which men had in his day made of earthly prisons; and to the everlasting hell of torment which men have manufactured for their fellow-men in a world beyond the grave:

> And thus we rust Life's iron chain
>   Degraded and alone:
> And some men curse, and some men weep,
>   And some men make no moan:
> But God's eternal Laws are kind
>   And break the heart of stone.

[1] *The Ballad of Reading Gaol.*

And every human heart that breaks,
  In prison-cell or yard,
Is as that broken box that gave
  Its treasure to the Lord,
And filled the unclean leper's house
  With the scent of costliest nard.

Ah! Happy they whose hearts can break
  And peace of pardon win!
How else may man make straight his plan
  And cleanse his soul from Sin?
How else but through a broken heart
  May Lord Christ enter in?

And he of the swollen purple throat,
  And the stark and staring eyes,
Waits for the holy hands that took
  The Thief to Paradise;
And a broken and a contrite heart
  The Lord will not despise.

CHAPTER XXVI

THE MAMMON OF INJUSTICE

In an earlier section we have noted the teaching of Jesus on the subject of riches and poverty. It will be found in the Sermon on the Mount, the Sermon on the Plain, and in his discourse about the Jubilee year at Nazareth. He now, towards the end of his ministry, deals more in detail with this subject.

While he was teaching the crowds about the coming age, and warning his disciples that they would be brought before native and imperial courts for advocating his cause, he is interrupted by a fatuous demand from a small holder, asking him to bid his brother divide the inheritance with him. Perhaps at any other time Jesus might have interested himself in this man's problem, or it may be that he perceived that he was wholly bent on his own private concerns. In any case, the man's mind was so occupied with his own affairs, that he had not been lifted out of himself by the Master's warnings about the new world and the dangers of its propaganda. Jesus, therefore, severely rebukes him with: 'Who made me a judge or a divider over you?' What have I to do with your petty squabbles about private property? My business is with a world where all essential property will be held in common, and there will be found to be not only enough, but plenty for all.

This seems to have been the common interpretation of the incident in the early and medieval Church, although it is often quoted by the modern Christian world in exactly the opposite sense, as if Jesus had no concern with the material things of this earth, but only with the spiritual values of a world beyond the grave. The classic example is from the *Glossa Ordinaria*, the most popular commentary of the Middle Ages; in its *Quis me constituit?* the *Glossa* interprets Jesus as meaning: I am not the God of dissension, but of peace and unity, I have come to reconcile men with the angels that the many may have one heart and one mind, so that there may be no division, but that they may have all things in common, and that no one may be in want among you. (*Ut habeant omnia communia nec sit aliquis egenus inter eos.*) He that gathereth not with me is disruptive of brotherhood and a spreader of dissension.[1]

That the early and medieval commentaries are correct is suggested by our Lord's conclusion, which is a warning against avarice; and by his immediate comment on the whole incident with the parable of the 'Kulak' farmer, who, instead of sharing his good fortune with others, hoards his produce and in high self-satisfaction pulls down his barns to build greater. But God called him nothing but a fool, for 'this night is thy life required of thee' (Greek, 'they require thy life'—R.V.M.). What good will your precious pile be to you now? Perhaps here is suggested the taking of his life by the angry peasants who will share out among themselves his hoarded gains, for again Jesus warns his hearers not to lay up for themselves treasures on earth where moth and rust eat away all that is not used but hoarded. Lay up rather treasures in the divine commonwealth.

The parable of the unjust steward which has baffled most exegetists is certainly charged with difficulties; our Lord seems to have demanded that his disciples should study the example of a rascally farm bailiff, who had been discovered by his master to have wasted his goods. The farmer told him to make up the books and hand them over as he was to consider himself dismissed. The man was smart and was determined to think out some plan by which he could feather his own nest, and secure his future; he was physically unable to dig and was ashamed to beg. He had lost the confidence of the farmer, so he would approach the tenants and 'wangle' the accounts in their favour. By so doing when the accounts were presented

---

[1] Compare the two homilies of St. Basil on the subject; St. Augustine on *Memento David*, and Eadmer in his *Life of Anselm*.

it was made to appear that one of the tenants only owed half the amount which was actually due; another was granted a rebate of twenty per cent.

Thus he gained new friends, and even the landlord [1] could not help admiring the ingenuity of the fellow. He was very much a child of his times, thoroughly conversant with all the tricks of the trade; for the children of this world are, for their own generation, more astute than the children of light. This man put the tenants in his debt so that in their gratitude they would support him in his need. So likewise, says the Christ, make to yourselves friends by means of the mammon of injustice, that when ye fail (or it fails) they (the workers to whom you have been generous), may accept you in the coming kingdom as one of themselves and receive you into habitations founded on the eternal rock and not on the shifting quicksands of this crooked generation. Jesus, of course, did not mean that they were to be as slippery as was this unjust steward, but be as alert and alive for the new world as he was for his own interests in the present age, where smartness and sharp practice are considered as good business.

If you have been unfaithful in distributing what really belongs to the workers, is it likely that they will let you share with them in the coming commonwealth, or be partakers with them in the true communal riches? For this is how 'that which is anothers' is interpreted by many of the early Fathers.

'The Pharisees, who were lovers of money, heard all these things and they scoffed at him,' and they would be no better pleased at the parable which follows.

It is the story of Dives and Lazarus, and Jesus has been called a sentimentalist for giving it. Not much scientific socialism in this parable would protest his critics, when he suggests that a rich man, simply because he is rich, will go to hell, and a poor man, simply because of his present poverty, will go to heaven. This much is true, namely

---

[1] 'The Lord commended' refers not, of course, to our Lord, but to the landlord.

that the Christ does here mention the life beyond the grave, and the future fate of those who behave in this or that way here on earth. But whether this is or is not scientific all depends on whether there is or is not a future life for the individual beyond death. It is about the only time that our Lord alludes to such a life, for 'this world and the world to come' should be translated 'this covetous epoch and the good time coming,' and his 'Kingdom of Heaven' is to be set up, as has so often been insisted in this present work, here on earth. Eternal life also is concerned with the quality of life, rather than with its quantity or persistence after death. But if there is for the individual a future life, it would be unscientific and, indeed, the most extreme folly to ignore the fact. That Christians have concentrated too much of their attention upon it we have over and over again emphasized, but to suggest that a man's conduct here will not affect the future hardly seems reasonable. It is, moreover, at least, arguable that to regard men as though they existed like summer flies, just for a moment or so, and then are extinguished, is not likely to lead to a high respect for them. One may even so out of pity do the poor devils a good turn and work for the amelioration of their hard conditions; that many atheists do so work for the benefit of mankind is beyond doubt, but whether this attitude of contemptuous pity will, in the long run, drive one to respect and reverence the rights of each personality is doubtful. The alternative, it is often assumed, is to do nothing for them here in this life, because they will automatically have a good time playing their harps above in the everlasting orchestra. But this is a false antithesis. Jesus teaches that both the oppressed manual workers and all men of goodwill must fling themselves with all their energies into the cause of a new world here on earth, and that this new world is a replica of the world as it exists in God's mind and of a fellowship beyond death. Such a faith will inspire us to ardent work for the reconstruction of human society, and will give grace and generous inspiration for the task, when we know that it is the abiding and everlasting plan of the Father and will be brought to its perfect fruition in the world beyond.

Now here in the parable of Dives and Lazarus, Dives does not go to hell because he happens to be rich, nor Lazarus to heaven because he happens to be poor. It is because the rich man has not thrown in his lot with the poor and helped to build the kingdom, because he has *trusted* in riches, i.e. enjoyed being rich at the expense of the workers and banked on the system continuing, perhaps saying in his West End club as the unemployed march by: 'Well, thank God it won't come in our time, this revolution; our generation, at least, is safe in spite of that damned agitator.' He has trusted in the vested interest and voted and worked for the party which supports them every time. That is why Dives finds himself in torment.

Dives was a rich and highly respected gentleman who enjoyed being clothed in purple and fine linen and dining sumptuously every day. It gave him a nice comfortable feeling to know that the Lazarus class existed, and to feed them with the leavings. Lady Dives often took round a basket with cold rice pudding or tapioca to the poor dear cottagers. She loved playing the Lady Bountiful and her husband would never dream of turning Lazarus from his door.

And it came to pass that the beggar died, and from a pauper's grave was carried up by the angels into Abraham's bosom. The rich man also died, 'and was buried' with the usual pomp and ceremony, and to his utter amazement found himself in the place of torment.[1] The whole thing was most extraordinary, but he would, at least, ask Abraham to order the beggar to fetch him some water to quench the intolerable thirst. But Abraham replied that it would be impossible, for 'between us and you there is a great gulf fixed.' The gulf has in this life been dug by the plutocrats who have completely separated themselves from the poor; it may have been so deeply dug as to be almost un-

---

[1] There is no suggestion here that the punishment should be everlasting. This is fully dealt with in Chapter XIV.

bridgeable in the life beyond the grave.   But the sting of
the story is in the tail.   Dives fears that his brethren,
unless they are warned, may come to the same torment.
May someone be sent to warn them?   Abraham replies
that it would be useless; they already have Moses and the
prophets; let them hear them.   If they have not listened
to them 'neither will they be persuaded though one rose
from the dead.'   Dives had, very likely, been something
like a churchwarden in his synagogue, and read the lessons
Sabbath by Sabbath: his brethren had probably also been
deeply 'religious' men.   If they had really listened to what
had been read, to such passages, for instance, as have been
quoted from the land and usury laws, and the warnings
of the prophets, they could never have become inordinately
rich.

It is, then, not merely a question of the sacred stewardship
of riches, but of how you get your riches, of whether riches
had been wrung by land-grabbing, mortgages, and usury
from the poor.

That this is the real point of the parable is suggested
by a later incident, when a member of the ruling class, a
very rich young man, came running and kneeling to
Jesus and asked 'the Good Master' what he should do to
inherit that abundance of life which he promised in the
coming kingdom.   Jesus said to him: 'Why callest thou
me good?   There is none good, save one, that is God.'
Then Jesus quotes not the duty towards God, but the duty
towards one's neighbour, duties to wife and parents and
brethren.   Do not murder, steal, defraud, or lie about them.
Of course, if the rich young man had been properly instructed in the laws of Moses, he would have understood
that one could not grow very rich without stealing from and
defrauding the poor; squeezing their very life's blood out
of them, that is, murdering them.   But it was hardly his
fault that he did not know this, considering the kind of
university education that the scribes would be giving in
that day.   So all unconscious of any wrong-doing, he
replies: 'All these things have I kept from my youth up.'

Jesus loved the eagerness of the young fellow, but perceived that he was too wrapped up in his properties and responsibilities to become a whole-hearted disciple. If you really mean to follow me in this dangerous adventure, you must travel light and unencumbered. 'Sell all that you have, give to the poor, and come, follow me.'

The test was too much for him and he went away sorrowful, for he was enormously rich.

Jesus, full of compassion and of disappointment, comments: 'How hardly shall they that have riches enter into the Kingdom of God. It is easier for a camel to enter in through a needle's eye, than for a rich man to enter into the Kingdom of God.' They that heard it, said, Well, then, if the ruling classes whom we have been taught to look up to and to respect cannot be saved, who on earth can? Jesus, in his reply, admits that it is terribly hard for God to convert the plutocrats, but it is possible to change their outlook and to bring their thoughts into line with the ideals of the divine commonwealth.

The needle's eye probably refers to the needle gate of the Temple, through which the baggage camel could just squeeze only if it were unloaded. It is as difficult for a rich man to enter into the spirit of the kingdom as for a proud man to enter into the fun of a child's game of hopscotch. The rich are so cut off from the experiences and realities of a working man's rough daily life, that they seldom are able to enter into the struggle for a better age, although a few of them, like Zaccheus and Nicodemus, take up the challenge and throw in their lot with the Master and his ideals.

The ideals are illustrated in the parable of the labourers in the vineyard, which may have been given at this point.

A certain man owned a vineyard and he went into the market-place very early one morning to hire labourers to work in it, and agreed with them for the current daily wage. At nine o'clock he went out again and got more labour at the same rate. He did likewise at later periods of the day, and just an hour before work was knocked off he found himself still short of workers if the job was to be finished that day. So back into the market-place he went, and was astonished and relieved to find there were still some men standing at the labour exchange waiting to be employed. He said to them: 'Why stand ye here all the day idle?' And they told him it was because they could get no one to employ them. Then he told them to go and work in his vineyard and whatsoever was right he would pay them. Sunset came and the labourers ceased work and the owner instructed his steward to settle up with them, beginning at the last batch and ending with the first.

To the annoyance of those who had been hard at work since sunrise, these last were paid the same wage as themselves; and they ungenerously complained. But the employer meets the complaint of their spokesman with, Friend, I do you no wrong. Did you not agree with me for the customary rate? Take that which is thine and go thy way. 'It is my will to give unto this last even as unto thee.' [1]

The employer adds that he has a right to do what he likes with his own money. This is often seized upon by the opponents of trade unions as meaning that the employing class can do just as they please with the workers; but they forget that the owner adds: 'Is thine eye evil because I am good?' He has every right to do what he likes, if what he likes is in accordance with God's law of fairness and justice. He had been generous 'unto these last,' for they had been standing all the day unemployed, not because they were lazy, but because 'no man hath hired us,' and it was ungenerous of the others to begrudge them their full day's wage. Thus Jesus elaborates the social principles of the new world.

There is another parable which is really more concerned with the eager use of such varying gifts as we may have in the service of God and our fellows. It is so often quoted as a defence of interest that it must be dealt with here. Jesus tells it because they are nearing Jerusalem, and

---

[1] Cf. Ruskin's famous work *Unto this Last*, in which is given a Christian political economy.

because they thought that on his triumphal entry the commonwealth would immediately appear.

There was a certain overlord [1] who was obliged to go to Italy in order to negotiate with the imperial authorities for a kingdom. Before he left he gave large sums of money, with which to trade, to ten of his officials. When he returned from Rome, having gained his kingdom, he demanded from each an account of their stewardship. All but one had made good use of the sums entrusted to them, and were rewarded by being given command of certain cities and territories. But the last was obliged to confess that he had done nothing with his money,[2] but had hid it in the ground. When asked for some explanation of his gross slackness, he replied that he knew the overlord to be a harsh close-fisted master, reaping where he had not sown and gathering where he had not strawed. But the lord's reply to this was very much to the point, for he said: Out of thine own mouth will I condemn thee, thou wicked servant, for you admit that you knew me to be a rascal, making profits where I had not done a stroke of work. Being that type of fellow, you ought at once, if you were not going to work and administer the money, to have invested it with the bankers that I might, in due course, have received mine own with interest.

The overlord then takes the sum of money away from him and gives it to the energetic servants who had traded successfully: 'For unto him that hath, shall be given, and from him that hath not, shall be taken away even that which he hath.'

I have already commented on this remark of the Christ in another connection, but considering the slackness of one slave and the activities of the others, it is obvious that the supporters of the present system cannot twist this into

---

[1] The overlord was probably Archelaus, who, about the time of our Lord's birth, went to Italy to obtain the kingdom of Judea and returned successful.

[2] The pound was the mina, worth, if a gold coin, about one hundred pounds. A gold talent (see Matthew's account) was worth about six thousand pounds.

meaning that if you happen to have a considerable sum of money, you have a moral right to receive more, or that if you happen to have next to nothing you can starve and be hanged to you. As the story has here been retraced it seems on reflection inconceivable that these same supporters of the present system can have the face to use it as a defence of those who live on interest and without working.

CHAPTER XXVII

WITHIN OR AMONG?

THE teaching which so completely disregarded the 'rights of property,' and extolled the rights of man was, as has been said, for the most part given in the course of the Perean ministry in the last months of the life of Jesus. It further defined the nature of the coming commonwealth, and further, therefore, enraged the Pharisees, especially as he charged them with being not only rigorists in religion but full of extortion and excess. They therefore derisively demand of him when this precious new world of his is to be expected. They themselves have long ago given up its ideals, but still gave it lip-service.

When certain Jews in Salonica in our own times were asked: 'But do you not believe in the coming of the Kingdom of God here on earth?' they replied: 'Of course we do, but we rather hope it will not come just yet.' Their business happened to be in a very flourishing condition. They were truly the mental descendants of the Pharisees of our Lord's time.

It seemed to the scornful questioners grotesque in the extreme that a Galilean agitator and his little band of supporters, peasants, fishermen, and worse than this, untouchables, should claim to be the nucleus of this coming world. But Jesus replies that the kingdom will not come by craning your necks or straining your eyes for some conventional sign from Heaven, while you fold your arms and do nothing to bring it an inch nearer, nor is it any use your saying, lo, here, or lo, there; for behold the kingdom, in my own person and in the little community around me, is already in the midst of you.

I am aware that this interpretation is controverted, and

438

that some great scholars, notably Canon Streeter, still interpret the phrase as meaning 'within you.'

That the Kingdom of Heaven cometh not with sudden catastrophe that would be manifestly observed (with observation), but invisibly within the individual heart is also the usual theme of the popular preacher and is accepted generally by the man in the street.

The Greek phrase can be interpreted 'within you' or 'among you'; but the context alone can decide, and most modern scholars consider that 'within you' is here quite inadmissible. That the older rendering has been generally abandoned by the best authorities will be seen by reference to my note below.[1]

[1] Canon Streeter, to whom we are greatly indebted on innumerable points of Biblical criticism, here strangely enough writes: 'Among you is a meaning which the Greek will not bear.' He has, I think, been misled by his pacifist sympathies, preferring to think of the reign of God as in its essence 'something invisible and internal in the hearts of men.' He shrinks from violent catastrophe, as we do, but we are living in a world of apocalyptic violence, and it is no use hiding our heads in the sands. Dr. C. F. Burkitt thus answers Streeter (*Interpreter*, July 1911): 'And as for ἐντός ὑμῶν in Luke xvii. 21 (translated by "within you" R.V. and A.V.) does not the whole context point to conceptions of overwhelming catastrophe, such as overwhelmed the contemporaries of Noah and Lot? Do not look for symptoms and indications, says our Lord to the Pharisees, they are no use; you cannot take precautions for your life. There may come times when you are longing to see some sign of the end, but you will see none. When the Son of Man comes there will be no doubt about it; it will be like the lightning. It is not a case of saying 'look here' or 'look there'; the Kingdom of God will be in your midst before you are aware of it.'
Streeter's assertion that the Greek words cannot bear the interpretation which Burkitt puts upon them is refuted by the fact that the word ἐντός is used as equivalent to 'among' by Plato, Xenophon, and Thucydides, and the following authors support Dr. Burkitt in his translation of the phrase as 'within your midst': Dean Alford, Bleek, Plummer in his commentary on St. Luke, Loisy, Bishop Headlam, A. B. Stanton, E. A. Abbott, Hausrath, Montefiore, Dean Farrar, Winstanley, David Smith in *The Days of His Flesh*, the *New Commentary* by Dr. Gore and others, and Thomas Walker in his *Jesus and Jewish Teaching*. This latter urges that the Kingdom of God is actually present in nucleus in Jesus himself and his small circle of disciples. 'Look, the Kingdom of God is in the midst of you.'
Scott, in his *The Kingdom of the Messiah*, writes as follows: 'Jesus is addressing the Pharisees and protests against their view of the kingdom as so remote and shadowy that its coming can only be determined by abstruse calculation. He declares that the great day is even now imminent, and will break on the

Now if you read St. Luke's account and the whole setting of the incident you will find that the Pharisees who asked the question were the bitter opponents of his gospel of the kingdom. That there were better Pharisees, reasonable, humane, there can be no doubt. But these questioners were very far from the kingdom. They had no kingdom of fair dealing and kindliness and justice within their hearts. St. Luke tells us so. They were scoffing at his generous gospel, because they were 'lovers of money.' They murmured and sneered because the riff-raff whom they said were accursed were following him and he accepted them. Were these the people, these dogs, these outsiders, who were going to form the nucleus of his precious kingdom and to shine forth as rulers in the good time coming, and were they, the teachers of Israel, to be thrust out? What a preposterous teaching of the Kingdom of Heaven.

Is it likely then that these Pharisees, full of contempt and bitterness, men whom Jesus is soon to call snakes, hypocrites, and whited sepulchres, men who were soon to be responsible for his judicial murder, would be told that 'the Kingdom of God is within you'?

If the question as to the coming of the kingdom had been put by the disciples of Jesus, he might have told them that the kingdom was within their hearts, for unless the new world order is held within the heart and life of many of its protagonists, how can it ever materialize in the outward world of affairs? But it was not the disciples, but their bitterest opponents who had asked it.

Over and over again they had demanded from him some startling and conventional sign. They said within themselves, this wretched working man, this pretender, this charlatan from Galilee, is, of course, unable to give us one

world suddenly, without sign or warning. Men will still be disputing about it, and straining their eyes into the distance, when lo the kingdom is in the midst of them. The saying thus expresses in vivid dramatic fashion the nearness of the kingdom and the unexpectedness of its coming. It will be here as a realized fact while it still seems to be a distant dream.'

We may conclude with the margin of the R.V., which reads: 'In the midst of you.'

of the accredited signs of the Coming. And, of course,
they were quite right. They were craning their necks
forward for the wrong kind of sign. Some astronomical
wonder, some astounding miracle, but they denied that
healing men, giving them happiness and a new outlook,
bringing them to repentance for injustice or cowardice,
was any sign at all. And again they were right if the kingdom were to be a mere triumph of beast force, of avarice,
of sanctimonious observance, of a Mammon nation, calling
itself the specially chosen of God, over the other Mammon
nations which at the moment held them down; then these
'signs' would really be the signs of its approaching victory.
These were the signs for which they were making scrupulous
and careful observation.

But if the approaching new age was to be an age of world
flung justice, of mercy, an age in which the unrepentant
'religious' and the unrepentant plutocrats were to be sent
empty away, if it were to be an age of generosity and all
the God instincts applied to the whole realm of life, then
its signs would be the kind of signs he had sent to the
imprisoned Baptist; and the sign of the prophet Jonah who
had preached repentance and release to the despised
foreigners. They were signs of a different order, signs
entirely beyond the comprehension of these unimaginative
religious worldlings.

So he replies, The Kingdom of God cometh not with this
tense straining for conventional signs, for lo the Kingdom
of God is already among you; it is thundering at your doors.
Pretenders shall say to you, Look here at this miracle, or
look there at that astounding sign; but go not after them;
they are false Messiahs.

In the coming catastrophe and in the manifestation of the
kingdom there will be no time to salvage your goods; leave
your property and flee for your lives; if your heart is still
entangled in the old system and its values, which is crashing
into ruins about your heads, in its destruction you also will
be destroyed. The disciples, terrified, asked him, Where
will be the scene of this disaster? Jesus does not reply,

'in Jerusalem,' although later he warns them that the holy city, which is to reject him and his message in favour of pretenders and Messianic conjurers, will be ruined. But at this moment he insists on the universal truth that wherever a nation has become a putrifying carcass, there will the vultures be gathered together to consume it.

Those who believe in the kingdom as within the heart and its coming as a gradual spread from heart to heart are almost always convinced that there will be nothing sudden or startling, nothing of terror, nothing ungentlemanly in its coming. Now they are very anxious to prove this from the New Testament, partly because they have the timid bourgeois mentality which cannot bear anything so unpleasant or disturbing as a crash, partly because they see the kingdom has not come in that startling way, and they want to find some theory that will save the honour of their Lord, and again because they do not feel the horror of the system under which their poorer neighbour groans. They think they do, but there is ample proof that they do not understand in the least. Therefore they say, The world is good, doubtless there are serious faults, and the whole apocalyptic assumption they dismiss as Manichean and false to the facts.

But here Christ is speaking the language of catastrophe rather than of gradualism. Can any one seriously in face of the analogies of the destroying flood and of the doom of Sodom, maintain that this passage secures unmistakedly that the kingdom is a slow and gentle influence in the heart, and that its coming will not harm a fly?

CHAPTER XXVIII

JESUS AND THE SEX PROBLEM

JESUS having completed his Perean teachings through cities and villages, proceeds on the march towards Jerusalem for the Passover. He reaches the fords of the Jordan, and is there confronted by Judean Pharisees who challenge him on the question of divorce. 'Is it lawful for a man to put away his wife for every cause?' This challenge was probably made near the very spot where the Baptist had attacked Herod Antipas for his adulterous union with Herodias, and the Pharisees may have hoped to involve Jesus in some pronouncement which would lead to his arrest and death. Although our Lord would have the episode of Herod in his mind, avoiding any particularization, he answers his opponents by a treatment of the problem of divorce in its general aspect.

According to the laws of Moses an adulterous wife and her paramour were to be put to death by stoning, burning, or strangulation. Adultery was therefore not here in question. But the Mosaic Law allowed a man to divorce a woman for any 'unseemly thing he found in her,' and on the question of this unseemly thing a violent controversy was raging among the Rabbis at that very moment.

The school of Shammai interpreted the passage as meaning actual indecency, but the looser school of Hillel which was very popular, although I should imagine not among the women folk, allowed divorce for the most trifling and absurd causes, and even surpassed America or Russia in the liberality of its interpretations. This looseness was much more serious for the women of that day than for the women of the Soviet republics, inasmuch as the latter are, at the present time, economically free and can earn their own living. But in Palestine, if a woman were divorced she was practically forced into another union, which Jesus considered was driving her to commit adultery. The followers of Hillel allowed a man to put away his wife if her cooking displeased him or if she had grown old and ugly, or (somewhat later than our Lord's time?) if the husband saw a woman who was more attractive to him. Jesus, who always championed woman's rights, asks his antagonists what Moses had commanded them, and they, thinking to score a point, replied that he had allowed a bill of divorcement. And Jesus answered and said unto them: 'For the hardness of your hearts he wrote you this precept.' Our Lord evidently did not interpret Moses in the cruel sense that Hillel put upon the passage, but agrees here with Shammai that the cause of divorcing a wife must be one that is both real and serious; and even then lays stress on the point that this was only for the hardness of men's hearts, a kind of accommodation to male psychology, but that 'in the beginning it was not so; God made them male and female. For this cause shall a man leave his father and mother and cleave to his wife and they twain shall be one flesh,' that the real abiding bond of marriage is the love and companionship of man and woman, and what 'God hath joined together, let no man put asunder.'

It can, therefore, be nothing less than adultery that would justify divorce. Whether it could be anything more serious than adultery, e.g. a bitter and permanent estrangement, incurable insanity, or the marriage of a young girl practically under duress from her parents, for the sake of a fortune, remains a burning topic of controversy even to this day. If it be said that the Holy Catholic Church has settled this matter once and for all by its strict rulings, it may be questioned whether this is actually the case.

No general council of the universal Church has ever thoroughly examined the question or pronounced upon it; but the Church has universally laid down that the ministers of marriage (i.e. the man and the woman) are the contracting parties, and not the priest who rightly blesses the marriage; so that the 'what God hath joined together' of the marriage service refers not to the blessing of the Church, but to the love and comradeship of bride and bridegroom. Supposing this love never to have existed, or to have ceased to exist after every effort has been made to maintain it, is not the marriage thereby dissolved, and ought not the Church to grant a divorce or a decree of nullity? The difficulties are great, as too easy a ruling might mean that husband and wife might fly apart on the slightest quarrel, and under our present system the question is further complicated by the economic dependence of women upon men. We would, therefore, not presume to dogmatize on the point, but would urge that Christendom should seriously review the whole matter in the light of modern Biblical criticism, in the light of common sense, and under the guidance of the Holy Spirit who has been given to guide us into all truth.

It is said by Catholic rigorists that our Lord allowed divorce under no circumstances whatever, and that the words in St. Matthew's gospel, 'save for the cause of adultery,' were a later addition. Whether the original Matthew contained them, or whether they were added by the later Greek editor, is impossible to determine, but even without these qualifying words it is obvious from the context both in Matthew and Mark that the Pharisees are referring to the passage in Deuteronomy (xxiv. 1–2) which deals not with adultery but with divorce for lesser causes. If these words are a later addition, they show the attitude of the Church on the subject, and the more liberal interpretation of some of the early Christians.

The attitude of the Catholic Church has, in fact, varied in actual practice, as may be seen by the permission of remarriage for the 'innocent party' in the East, certain annulments of marriage by the Roman Catholic Church for people with long enough purses, and the confusion of judgment at the present moment in the Anglican Communion.

A word ought to be added on the question of separation. The Church allows this where the marriage has become intolerable.   It secures or attempts to secure the economic support of the family, and is granted in the hope that some day the apparently estranged couple may come together again and make a better job of it.   This, at least, would seem its only justification as otherwise the separation order must be given merely in obedience to an arbitrary decree against divorce on the supposed authority of our Lord, or in deference to the wishes of the Catholic Church.   If in reality the marriage bond has been irreparably broken, or if such a bond never really existed, i.e. if God had never joined them, in that case it would not be an order for separation and maintenance that was needed, but an order for divorce or pronouncement of nullity.   This could only be entirely satisfactory where conditions had been so altered that the woman was, as in modern Russia, as economically free to earn her living as the man, although here again much might be said for remarriage, as that might keep the woman in the home to bring up the children.

There are cases when lifelong separation places an intolerable strain on a young woman or a man, and where it might be wiser for the Church to grant the right of re-marriage both on the lower ground that 'it is better to marry than to burn' or on the higher ground that some really lifelong comrade or mate had at last been found.

Again I would insist that these are the merest suggestions for consideration by groups of Christians, and ultimately, after due deliberation by a universal council of the Catholic Church itself.   A full and unbiased study of early and medieval patristic literature should form part of the inquiry on which the Church should base its ultimate decisions.[1]

---

[1] The Church, however, is divided, and has almost abandoned the main objective of the Gospel teaching, a New World Order.   The Roman Catholic hierarchy in Italy and Spain is openly allied with Fascism; the churches of the East are pietistic, and making no effective challenge against capitalist imperialism, while the Church of England, if she faintly stirs in her sleep, is far from being awake.   What chance, therefore, is there of a clear and alert collective mind in Christendom on points of morality, whether public or private?

Meanwhile the priest is faced by the difficult problem raised when two persons or one of them earnestly desire the Church's blessing on a remarriage.   Until the Church has reviewed the whole subject it may be impossible for the priest officially to give such a blessing, but it might be of help to the parties concerned for him to remind them that as they, *in the presence of public witnesses*, are the ministers of matrimony, marriage in a registry office is a sacrament.

We have laid stress on the public witnesses because we cannot take the individualistic view that marriage is the affair of the two parties concerned only, and not to some extent, at least, of the community also, whether the common concern be expressed in a State or in a Church.

The disciples of Jesus, noting the strictness of his attitude about divorce as against the laxity of the school of Hillel, remark naïvely that perhaps it is better in that case for a man not to marry.   The reply of Jesus is ambiguous, because we do not know if it is made in reference to what he has just said, or as a preface to the words about celibacy which immediately follow: 'All men cannot receive this saying (about divorce, which I have just given you; or about celibacy, which I am just going to give you) save those to whom it is given.'   There are some who are eunuchs through physical incapacity, and others who are physically marred by their fellows; others again have figuratively made themselves eunuchs, that is, have remained celibate, for the Kingdom of Heaven's sake.   If men are to do dangerous work for the furthering of the New World Order, if they are to risk their lives daily for the great cause, it is better to be unencumbered by wife and children.   Nor have they the right to drag these into risks and dangers, or to let them starve.[1]   His disciples seem to misunderstand the point and take their Master as advocating celibacy as a higher estate than matrimony, for this is how one may interpret their next action?

[1] Cf. Chapter VIII, 'Early Manhood,' for our Lord's possible reasons for himself remaining unmarried.

When some mothers brought young children to receive his blessing the disciples rebuked those that brought them. But Jesus by word and deed hallows for all time the human family. For, taking the children in his arms, he says: 'Suffer the little children to come unto me and forbid them not; for of such is the Kingdom of Heaven.'

CHAPTER XXIX

THE PILGRIM WAY

Jesus and his disciples and an immense crowd of pilgrims, including the mothers and the children whom he had blessed, now move forward to their appointed goal—Jerusalem.

As they approached Jericho there come to Jesus on the march James and John, the sons of Zebedee, and either themselves, or their mother on their behalf, ask him, in modern phraseology, that they should be given cabinet rank in the coming kingdom, and the rest were indignant. But Jesus called them to him and said: 'Ye know that the supposed rulers over the foreign nations exercise lordship over them, and their magnates impose imperial authority upon them. They are called "imperial benefactors." So shall it not be among you: but whosoever will be great among you shall be your minister, and whosoever will be chief among you shall be the servant of all. For even the Son of Man came not to be ministered unto but to minister, and to give his life a ransom for the many.' In the Vulgate the word 'Empire' is actually used, and I have translated benefactors as imperial benefactors because that was the actual position to which he was alluding. Statues of emperors and governors and empire builders were erected, and at their bases were inscribed the supposed benefactions to subject peoples of which they boasted. Note also the 'supposed rulers.'[1] The commentaries suggest that Christ meant that they were not really God's servants ruling legitimately, but that imperial authority is a usurpation over unwilling peoples. Christ spoke emphatically because he himself had been tempted more than once to

---

[1] Mark x. 42.

go the imperial way.[1] Peter was among the indignant disciples who were so ready to rebuke James and John for their imperialist ambitions, but it had been Peter who had urged his Leader along the same path, and had been left with the fierce rebuke: 'Get thee behind me, Satan, for thou savourest not of the things that be of God, but the things that be of men.' Scott Holland suggests that St. Peter's proposal had called up in the mind of Jesus the success and joy that awaited him if he had taken that path, that it had called up something that had more than once been a real temptation to him, and that had not been entirely eliminated from his mind in that conflict with the devil that had formed the introduction to his whole mission.

The Pilgrim Way lay through the Jordan valley to Jericho, the city of palms. Every conqueror who aimed at Jerusalem knew he must first take Jericho, and that conquest of that city was comparatively easy. Once conquered she became an important source of supply to the armies advancing on the capital. 'She has been called the key and the guardhouse of Judea; she was only the pantry. She never stood a siege and her inhabitants were always running away.'[2] Her people, weakened by the steaming heat of their climate, and in days past in close vicinity to the infamous cities of the plain, fell an easy prey to the invader.

The pilgrims would see a stately city rich in hanging gardens, palm-groves, fruits of every kind. Here were the famous baths, the theatres and the palace of Herod. It was 'the city of fragrance, the city of roses, the paradise of God.'[3] At the gates of such cities, then as now, would be seen the halt, the maimed, and the blind craving alms, and Jesus was accosted by a blind beggar named Bartimaeus, who sat by the highway and heard the tumult of the tramping

[1] Although Jesus had fought down these preliminary temptations they would seem to have appeared again from time to time, for the devil had only left him for a season.—Luke iv. 13.

[2] George Adam Smith, *Historical Geography of the Holy Land.*

[3] Farrar.

crowd. He had asked what it meant and had been told that 'Jesus of Nazareth passeth by.' Now he keeps crying out: 'Jesus, thou son of David, have mercy on me.' It was a dangerous outcry this, for it acclaimed the Messiah, and suggested a rebellion and an attempt to dethrone the Caesar. The disciples were later to make the same claim for their Master, but the time was not yet. If attention were drawn to him now the authorities might arrest their progress. They tried to silence the beggar, but Jesus stood and commanded that he should be brought unto him, and asked him: 'What wilt thou that I shall do unto thee?' and the blind man said: 'Lord, that I should receive my sight.' Jesus said unto him: 'Receive thy sight. Thy faith hath saved thee.' Immediately his sight returned unto him and he glorified God, and all the crowds, when they saw it, likewise gave praise unto God.

On they went into the city and the crowds were so great that one had to press very close to get a sight of the prophet. Now there was a rich tax collector named Zacchæus, who had been enormously moved by the teaching of Jesus and was longing to talk with him. But he could not get anywhere near him; he was very short, and could not see over the heads of the people. So he climbed like some little urchin into the branches of a sycomore tree: he did not care in his excitement if he made himself ridiculous. When Jesus came to the place he looked up and saw him and said: 'Zacchæus, make haste and come down, for I must lodge in your house to-day.' The rich man, overwhelmed with delight, hurried down and prepared to entertain him. But this was too much for many in the crowd, and they were shocked that the prophet should accept the hospitality of a man who was a sinner. Zacchæus, perceiving this, defends himself, saying, 'Lord, behold, the half of my goods I give to the poor; and if I have wrongfully exacted ought of any man, I restore fourfold.' Jesus, ignoring the scandalized crowd, accepts the defence of the chief among the publicans and tells him that in this act of generous renunciation salvation has to-day come to his household. In spite of the Jews pronouncing him denaturalized, with his birthright gone, Jesus acclaims him 'a son of Abraham.'

Note that here, in contrast to the demand upon the rich young ruler to give up all, our Lord accepts the assurance of Zacchæus that he is in the habit of renouncing, or will in future renounce, the larger part of his fortune. Zacchæus, unlike Matthew, was not a customs house officer, sitting at the *douane*, but the chief official of the Roman customs department.[1] He would have unlimited opportunities of growing exceedingly rich, and the 'this day' of the narrative suggests that now, henceforward, he would give half of his fortune to the poor, and make enormous restorations where he had abused his position to exploit any man. It is noteworthy that the Christ is willing to accept among his followers rich men such as Zacchæus, Nicodemus, and Joseph of Arimathea, without their actually beggaring themselves. They must, however, be very generous and work whole-heartedly for the New World Order.

[1] Jericho had at one time been given by Mark Antony to Cleopatra, and leased by her to Herod the Great; it was one of his favourite residences and he died there. But at the time of Zacchæus, Jericho was directly under the Romans who farmed its revenues.

CHAPTER XXX

CAVALCADE

A HALT was made at the village of Bethany, a mile or so from Jerusalem, and the Christ sent two of his disciples to a village nearby to secure an ass on which he was to make his entry. An agreement had been come to with one of his followers to supply the beast and all went according to plan. The disciples returned and Jesus, mounting the ass, prepared to make a public and ceremonial entrance into the city with his Galilean supporters.

It is sometimes pointed out that if he had wished to appear as a military conqueror he would have chosen the war horse, and that the choice of a donkey showed that he was coming in peace. This is quite a correct inference, but when it is suggested that the entrance had, therefore, no political significance we must deny the assumption.

A great multitude spread their garments in the way, and branches of the trees were strewn along his path; some went before him and some followed, crying out, Hurrah for the Son of David, Blessed is he that cometh in the name of the Lord, Hosannah in the highest. Blessed is the kingdom of our father David that cometh. Many also came out from Jerusalem to meet him and welcome him; some of the Pharisees who were among the crowd asked him to rebuke his followers for making political capital out of this procession, and acclaiming him the coming king. But Jesus refuses to restrain their enthusiasm, saying: 'If these should hold their peace, the stones would immediately cry out,' thereby identifying himself with these political claims. This was obviously high treason, but his popularity was so great that the authorities said, among themselves, the position is hopeless as 'the whole world is gone after him.' The children next day echo their parents'

cry in the Temple courts, as do boys and girls nowadays at
contested elections.   Again the authorities protest, but Jesus
welcomes the shouts of the boisterous children and will not
have them silenced.

From the village of Bethany the road climbs the Mount
of Olives, 'through green fields and under shady trees till
it suddenly sweeps round to the northward.   It is at this
angle of the road that Jerusalem, which hitherto had been
hidden by the shoulder of the hill, bursts full upon the
view.'   The Christ reins in his animal as the city of a
thousand memories now comes into sight.   Jerusalem,
seen at close quarters, did not impress him, but distance
lends enchantment to the eye, and on this early morning
its glittering magnificence thrust itself upon him in the
sunlight.

He weeps over the 'holy' city that had murdered its
prophets and was so soon, and for the same reasons, to
murder its Saviour.   Blind and misled, would they even
yet listen to his last appeal, or would they bury their heads
in the sand, refusing to see the doom that awaited their
obstinacy?   'For the days shall come upon thee, when thine
enemies shall cast up a bank about thee, and compass thee
round, and keep thee in on every side, and shall dash thee
to the ground, and thy children within thee; and they shall
not leave in thee one stone upon another; because thou
knowest not the time of thy visitation.'

'Sternly, literally, terribly, within fifty years, was that
prophecy fulfilled.   Four years before the war began, while
as yet the city was in the greatest peace and prosperity,
a melancholy maniac traversed its streets with the repeated
cry: "A voice from the east, a voice from the west, a voice
from the four winds, a voice against Jerusalem and the
holy house, a voice against the bridegrooms and the brides,
and a voice against this whole people": nor could scourgings or tortures wring from him any other words except:
"Woe! woe! to Jerusalem; woe to the city; woe to the
people; woe to the holy house!" until seven years afterwards, during the siege, he was killed by a stone from

a catapult.   His voice was but the renewed echo of the voice of prophecy.'[1]

Jesus reaches the Temple and observes with indignation the trafficking and bargaining, but resolves to do nothing till the next morning.   He retires to Bethany with his disciples for the night, and at daybreak they return to the city and he enters the Temple.   Jesus found himself in the outer court of the nations, a court in which Jews and foreigners mingled.   It had beautiful double and triple colonnades on three sides, cedar roofs, and wonderfully coloured slabs paved the floor.   The markets were established here, and as we have shown on a former occasion, roused the indignation of Jesus not only because of the exploitation of the pilgrims, but because it was an insult to the foreigners who worshipped there.

Jesus cast out all those that sold and bought, and attacked the officers in charge of the *bureaux de change*, and overturned the stools of the dove-sellers.   With anger he exclaims: 'My house shall be a house of prayer: but ye have made it a den of robbers.'   The cause of this action on the part of the meek and gentle Jesus, and its popularity with the pilgrim crowds, will be understood when we describe the situation in detail.

It was here in the outer court that were found the taverns or booths with the tables of the money-changers, the benches of the traders, of whom the sacrificial cattle and offerings, wine and oil, corn and salt and incense, were bought . . . the provisions . . . the oxen, the lambs, and the doves— the poor man's sacrifice—were here exhibited . . . the lambs were to be counted by the thousands.   There was a noise and a crying of beasts and men, of sellers and buyers, and a rolling and clinking of money . . . of traders hankering after speculation and profitable bargaining.   The brokers, who exchanged the money of the festival guests from three-quarters of the globe, current Greek, Roman, or Jewish coins, for the half-shekel, the indispensable temple tribute of two francs, were legally entitled to a considerable percentage

[1] Farrar, *The Life of Christ*, vol. ii, page 201.

for every half-shekel they exchanged, even when they gave two half-shekels for one shekel. Keim shows that the priests who had the oversight and charge of all this were not innocent of this trading, and speaks of our Lord's action as undertaken 'in a spirit of stormy zeal.' Some say this marketing only went on *outside* the outer court, but it seems obvious that it had gradually encroached upon the sacred ground itself.

Edersheim shows that the profits of the exchangers ran into many thousands of pounds; reforming Pharisees sometimes protested at the 'greed' of the merchants. A couple of pigeons sometimes ran up to fifteen shillings and threepence from their proper price, fourpence. Of course it was not the lower clergy from the provinces, but the priestly officials of the Temple, who were implicated, 'and especially the high-priestly family.' There is little doubt that the temple market was identical with what was then called the bazaars of the sons of Annas, and a light is thus thrown on the bitter economic hostility of the native judges to Jesus a few days later in the preliminary trial. From the injustice of this traffic and the greed of the priestly members of the Government, it may be seen how unpopular the market would be, and what a mass sympathy would be aroused by his action. How he would have had the crowd behind him.

Edersheim shows the immense profits made, not only on exchange, but on the sale of animals. Many bought within the market itself. Many brought animals pronounced unclean for sacrifice, and were forced to buy anew in this questionable market at high prices. Protests are quoted, and 'popular fury, three years before the destruction of Jerusalem, less than forty years later, swept down the bazaar of the family of Annas . . . on account of the sinful greed, as is expressly stated, which characterized its dealings.' Of the avarice and corruption of this infamous high-priestly family, Josephus and the Rabbis alike give a terrible picture. The son of Annas is described by Josephus as 'a great hoarder of money, very rich, and

as despoiling by open violence the common priests of
their official revenues.' The sons of these high priests
were the treasurers, their sons-in-law assistant treasurers,
and their servants beat the people with sticks. It were
easy to add from rabbinic sources repulsive details of
their luxuriousness, wastefulness, gluttony, and general
dissoluteness.

Not a stone's throw from the market did the local government sit and plan the destruction of the Galilean who had
challenged their economic corruptions and exploitations.

The action of Jesus alarmed the authorities. If they
left him alone what would become of their financial interests
in the temple trade? So, as usual, they hold a meeting at
which they deliberate how to rid the city of him, but the
popularity of his recent defiant attitude makes it impossible
for the moment to proceed against him, so that he is able
every day to teach in the Temple, and at nights to retire to
the home at Bethany which is, later in the week, to come
under such close surveillance, that he has to hide with
his disciples in the thickets of Gethsemane.

One morning before breakfast Jesus left Bethany for
Jerusalem, and being hungry and coming across a fig-tree
with leaves he hoped to find some fruit. Although the
ripening of figs was not yet, there should apparently have
been fruit sufficiently formed to satisfy his hunger, but
he finds a great show of leaves and not a single fig. He
curses the tree, for it has proved itself useless and was merely
cumbering the ground. It is always important to cut
down such trees, as they sap the nourishment from the
ground which would go to feed other plants. So, if this
incident of the parasitic tree was an actual event, there
seems nothing unreasonable in his action; in any case, he
uses it as a parable. Obviously the fig-tree represented the
nation which had once been fertile and full of sap and had
yielded her fruit abundantly, but now had become an
accursed thing. But the immediate lesson he draws from
the incident is to emphasize the necessity of faith, and, like
the most modern psychologist, tells his followers that if

* Q

they ask anything with such assurance that they believe that it is already theirs, it will be granted to them. This is the type of faith that will uproot mountains.

On the Tuesday [1] Jesus was teaching in the Temple, and his opponents demanded if he had any sort of permit for spreading his propaganda in the sacred precincts. He replied, I will tell you by what authority I do these things if you will first tell me what was John the Baptist's authority. Where did he get it? Was it from heaven or of men? This put them in an awkward position, for if they should answer 'of men,' the crowds on whom they were already losing hold would be further disillusioned, and get altogether out of hand, and might even attempt to stone them, for John was now recognized as a prophet; whereas, if they replied that his authority was from God, Jesus would immediately counter that by saying, Why did ye not then believe him? The honours were, therefore, for the moment with the prophet of Galilee, and they were silenced.

Jesus himself now turns the attack on them with the parable of the two sons who were told by their father to work in the vineyard. The first, 'fed up' with the whole business, blankly refuses, but afterwards thinks better of it and goes; the second blandly agrees, but has not the slightest intention of budging. Jesus asks: 'Whether of the twain did the will of his father?' and his critics answer: 'The first.' He then replies, The tax collectors and prostitutes, the last people in the world from whom anything can be expected, go into the Kingdom of God before you, 'for John came unto you in the way of justice and ye believed him not. But the publicans and the harlots believed him.' The Pharisees, like the second son, are full of promises, but have not the slightest intention of lifting a finger to bring the kingdom nearer.

With John the Baptist, the prophet in whose death they had been implicated, still in his mind, Jesus now tells the story of the vineyard hired out to husbandmen. When the owner sends his servants to demand the fruits thereof

---

[1] The days of the week are, of course, approximate.

they ill-treat them and beat them as the Pharisees and their predecessors had maltreated the prophets and John, the last of that great stream of inspired men. Last of all he sent his son, and the husbandmen argued among themselves, here comes the heir, let us kill him and the vineyard will be ours. The magistrates were bent on the destruction of the Son, and would bring down upon their own heads the terrible vengeance of God.

All his life Jesus had longed for the revival of his own nation, and had hoped against hope that they might fulfil the role in history for which God had created them; that they might be a light to lighten the nations, so that in Abraham and his seed should all the nations of the world be blessed. That is why he had hesitated to preach directly to foreign peoples, and had only done so on the rarest occasions. But he had often been disturbed by the possibility that his own people would not respond, and now he sees that they have become a carcass, rotten beyond all hope. As the vineyard is taken away from the wicked husbandmen, and given to others which shall render him the fruits in their seasons, so the commonwealth will be taken away from this 'chosen' people and given to peoples from every quarter of the globe who will bring forth fruits a thousandfold.

Jesus reminds them that according to their scriptures, the stone which the builders rejected became the very stone that held the whole building together. Whosoever stumbles over this stone will be shattered, but those who have dared to oppose this stone (the divine commonwealth), shall be ground to powder.

It must therefore have delighted the mind of Jesus, in the midst of all this tragic and bitter conflict with his own people, that certain foreigners, Greeks, began to show an interest in his teaching. They would have been moved by his championing of their rights to respect in the foreign court of the Temple, and his prophecy that other nations should be admitted into the divine kingdom and carry on its work. They therefore approached Philip, who came from the Greek-speaking district of Bethsaida Julias, and asked that they may be introduced to Jesus. Philip tells his friend Andrew and they bring them to the Master. This interview leads to our Lord exclaiming: 'Now is the Son of Man glorified,' and for a moment he may have seen in it an escape from the tragedy that awaited him. Might he not, after all, escape and preach his new world among the foreign nations? But he puts the thought aside, for if he were to run away from the martyrdom he would lose his power to drive home his gospel; who would believe in a runaway Messiah? So he says: 'Verily, verily, I say unto you, except a grain of wheat falleth into the earth and die, it abideth by itself alone; but if it die, it beareth much fruit.' If I cling to my life I shall lose my soul; to win the world I must stoop to conquer. Out of the death of one shall arise life for the many.

Up in Galilee in the first years his parables had been carefully veiled, but now concealment was no longer necessary, and his enemies perceived that he was speaking against them, but although they longed to arrest him they still feared the crowd.

CHAPTER XXXI

RENDER TO CAESAR

Jesus must be destroyed. Of this both Sadducees and Pharisees were convinced. Their enemies, the Herodians, must be conciliated. This was no time for quarrelling among themselves. It must be a combined attack by all who had anything to lose by the success of his teaching. Some plan must be thought out which would incriminate him with their imperial overlords or with his own following. Rapidly they constructed a plot which for its ingenuity would have been hard to beat. Their victim could hardly escape them.

By the concerted action of the Pharisees, Sadducees, and Herodians they send to Jesus 'plain-clothes detectives,' who pretend to be in sympathy with his movement,[1] and who flatter him as a brave man who fearlessly proclaims the truth at whatever cost. 'Master, we know that you teach truly and fearlessly, neither care you for any man; is it lawful to give tribute to Caesar or not? Shall we give or shall we not give?'

If he says pay the tax, he will lose his own crowd, for the people are groaning under the burden of taxation and rebelling against it. Having lost his supporters, he can at once be arrested, and although this particular charge of forbidding tribute must then be dropped, there are plenty of other counts against him. They will still have enough and more than enough to convict him as worthy of death, e.g. the threat to destroy the Temple, and, for the imperial court, his claim to the throne.

If, on the other hand, he forbids the paying of the tribute, this will be a further count against him at the trial, and

---

[1] Luke xx. 20.

although it will increase his popularity with the crowd, there will come an occasion when he can be separated from his following and they can arrest him hurriedly, perhaps at night in his hiding-place. It is a trap from which there seems no escape.

Now it was the unwritten law of the Oriental countries that no people had accepted the fact of its conquest and acknowledged its subjugation until it accepted and traded in the coin of the conqueror. The extremists were still holding out against the use of Roman coinage, because 'the use of Roman money by Jews was a recognition of Roman authority.'[1] The contemporary saying was: 'He whose coin is current is king.' Maimonides, the great Jewish legal authority of the Middle Ages, lays it down: 'Wherever the money of any king circulates, there the inhabitants recognize this king as their master.' This had been the principle of the theocracy, and, indeed, the Maccabees had issued a coinage dating from the 'liberation of Jerusalem,' a coinage still current in the time of Christ, and Bar-Cochab during the last rebellion against Rome a few years later issued a similar currency. Later, official Judaism lays down the principle that the right of issuing currency implies the authority of levying taxes and, indeed, constitutes such evidence of *de facto* government as to make it a duty absolutely to submit to it.[2] So strong was the feeling against the use of the imperial coinage that the Roman authorities had had to mint a special coinage for Palestine without the image of the emperor, and this was still current till the rebellion of A.D. 69. But so great had been the collapse of the Jewish spirit of independence among the governing classes and their followers that the native government had allowed the use of the foreign denarius with the head of Tiberius on one side and the blasphemous inscription on the reverse: 'Tiberius Caesar, the Son of the deified Augustus.' Here, then, is another example of the hypocrisy of the Pharisees, who still did

---

[1] Carey, *Synoptic Gospels*, page 263.
[2] Edersheim, *Life and Times of Jesus*, vol. ii, page 385.

lip-service to the idea of an independent Jewish kingdom, while they acquiesced in the *status quo*, traded in a blasphemous coinage, and waxed fat under the Roman régime. It was a Pharisee general who later betrayed his troops to Vespasian. They ran with the native hare and hunted with the imperial hounds.

Now Jesus, who had once said: 'Cast not your pearls before swine,' and was always ready to speak in such a language that the detectives who dogged his footsteps might 'hear and not understand, see and not perceive,' meets the plot by a brilliant counter-stroke. To a serious disciple, or even an opponent who wants to learn, he returns a serious answer, but as to the knaves who would incriminate him he answers them according to their knavery. 'Perceiving their trick,'[1] he replied with the only possible answer which would hold his crowd and give no handle to the spies. *He does not ask his supporters to produce a coin, but his opponents.* They produced the incriminating denarius, and at once he asks: 'Whose is this image and superscription?' And they say, 'Caesar's'; and by their answer have put themselves into the trap they have laid for him. 'Give back, therefore, to Caesar the things that (according to your usage and custom) are Caesar's.' They were embarrassed and silenced, not being able to 'take hold of the saying before the people.'[2] Their embarrassment was all the greater, for the onlookers knew full well that not only had they decided the question for themselves by possessing the coin and trading with it, but that it was a strict rule that, wherever else one might, if one were loose in one's allegiance to Palestine, use it, on no account was it ever to be used in the Temple precincts. For trading purposes in the Temple courts the people were forced to exchange the profane coinage for the special Temple currency. Hence the Temple bank in which the Government held controlling shares, and out of which they drew enormous profits.

[1] Moffatt's translation of Mark, or 'Noting their knavery,' Luke.
[2] Luke xx. 26.

His own followers would know full well the meaning of his command, 'and unto God the things that are God's.' They would understand him to mean 'whether you pay these taxes or no is a matter of small importance, the day is soon coming when you will be free from all such burdens. Hasten, therefore, the coming of that new woild order the children of which shall be free.' [1]

The usual interpretation of his answer is impossible. It is assumed that he seriously ordered all to pay the hated tax. If that is the correct interpretation, the critics must explain how it was that he kept his crowd to the end.[2]   The people were delighted, not disgusted, with his answer: 'and they could not take hold of his words before the people, and they marvelled at his answer and held their peace.' After this incident Mark records, 'the common people heard him gladly.' Matthew records the incident, and adds that there was a hurried sitting of the council afterwards, and they considered how to arrest him by subtlety and kill him, 'but not on a feast day, lest there be an uproar among the people.' Luke later says: 'The chief priests and scribes sought how they might kill him, for they feared the people.' Judas promises to betray him '*in the absence of the multitudes.*' [3]

How again could they bring the charge against him of forbidding to give tribute,[4] if he had ordered every one to pay it?

His own attitude can be gauged by this incident.   He would not approve of an immediate campaign against the empire, for he held with the prophets that, evil as were these bloodstained empires, they were allowed by God as His scourges to purify the nation.   It was not until the Jews had cast out their own imperial ambitions that they would be found worthy of freedom, or would be supported by

---

[1] Cf. the analogy of the tax in Matthew xvii. 25.

[2] We shall suggest that it was not the Galilean multitude who cried, 'Crucify him, crucify him.'

[3] Luke xxii. 6.

[4] Luke xxiii. 2.

God in an attempt to overthrow their oppressors. Hence his dissociation from the Zealot movement, and his approval of the preaching of John with his call to a nation-wide repentance.[1]

[1] I am not concerned in this chapter with the Pauline doctrine of the State nor with early Christian nor medieval thought about the spiritual and the temporal power. The subject is extremely complicated and may be found worked out very thoroughly in A. J. and R. W. Carlyle's *History of Medieval Political Theory*, or Gierke's *Political Theories of the Middle Age*, translated by Maitland. The theory of the Church may or may not have been a legitimate development from the teaching of the gospels, but it seemed important to subject this particular incident to scientific treatment and a minute re-examination.

CHAPTER XXXII

THE LAST ROUND

SADDUCEAN plutocrats, the landed gentry and rich aristocrats of that time, powerful members of the Government from whom the Roman imperialists chose the high priests, now approach Jesus. They believed neither in a life beyond the grave nor in the resurrection of the just to take part in the triumph of the New World Order here on earth. In fact, they were well content with this present life, as 'the highest gain, the true destiny of this existence, is to be sought in a pleasant life, in riches and honour, in the avoidance of punishment by acting justly, and by exhibiting a peaceable disposition, in leaving a posterity, and in dying without fear or hope for soul or body . . . they never warmly interested themselves in the ideal of the present life, the ideal Kingdom of God upon earth.' [1]

They sought to tie him up in a disputation in which surely they would win an easy victory over him. They put with sarcasm the following poser. Moses had decreed that if a man died childless, so great was the importance of family continuance, his brother should marry the widow in hope of offspring: 'Now there were with us seven brethren: and the first married and deceased, and having no seed left his wife unto his brother; in like manner the second also, and the third, unto the seventh. And after them all the woman died. In the resurrection, therefore, whose wife shall she be of the seven? For they all had her.'

Jesus charges this priestly party, who were supposed to know their Bibles from A to Z, with being ignorant of the scriptures and of the power of God. For in the resurrection of the dead when the new world should have dawned,

[1] Keim, *Jesus of Nazara*, vol. i, pages 360–1.

and when the dead heroes should be raised to take part in its triumph, there would be neither marrying nor giving in marriage, but mankind would be raised to the status of the angels of God and would live a transformed and angelic life.

If angels in the time of Jesus had been considered to be the sexless beings of the modern Christmas-card variety, we might hold the conventional interpretation of this passage; but it must be remembered that certain angels 'came in unto the daughters of men,' and had offspring,[1] and that somewhat later St. Paul wrote that 'for this cause ought the woman to wear power (or rather a covering) over her head, because otherwise her hair might tempt the angels.[2]

This new order of things on earth does not, therefore, seem to be entirely sexless; sex is not annihilated, but rather transmuted into some fourth dimensional experience of which we have as yet no knowledge. Some analogy might be found in the risen body of Jesus which could materialize and dematerialize at his will and could even apparently partake of earthly food.

Whatever, therefore, may be the meaning of this much disputed passage, our Lord here sides with the Pharisees in a belief in the continued life of Abraham, Isaac, and Jacob, for God says: 'I am the God of these patriarchs.' He is not the God of the dead but of the living. Jesus here definitely states his belief in the life beyond the grave, and also apparently teaches that these fathers of the race will take part in the resurrection life on this earth in which they will see of the travail of their soul and be satisfied.

We have recorded that Jesus had escaped the trap set by the coalition on the question of paying taxes to imperial Rome, and had proved himself master of the Sadducees in debate, leaving his antagonists for the moment completely baffled.

---

[1] For the Sons of God are in the Genesis legend interpreted not as human beings but as angels. Hastings, *Small Dictionary of the Bible*. Genesis vi. 2.

[2] I Cor. xi. 10. Interpreted thus by Bousset and others, though Gore's *New Testament Commentary* disputes this.

St. Mark gives the fullest and most generous account of the good scribe [1] and alone records the Master's commendation. Matthew, in his very natural hatred of the Pharisees, although he had Mark's account in front of him when he wrote, deliberately omits the praise of this man.

A certain scribe, having listened to the various debates between Jesus and the authorities, and 'knowing that he had answered them well,' now detaches himself from his own party and asks: 'What commandment is the first of all?' And Jesus, as on a former occasion, replies with the whole-hearted love of God and the whole-hearted love of one's neighbour; instead of arguing as did that other lawyer as to who is one's neighbour, this man replied: 'Master, thou hast well said, for to love the true and only God and one's neighbour as oneself is more than all burnt sacrifice, more than going to mass, more than fasting communion, more than Bible reading, more than the quiet hour, more than everything in the world.' Jesus is immensely moved and exclaims: 'Thou art not far from the Kingdom of God.

The support of this possibly powerful lawyer has it's effect, for 'no man after that durst ask him any more questions.'

Jesus again takes the offensive and asks who the Christ is, and the crowds or the Pharisees reply that he is the heir of David. How then is it that David under inspiration calls him Lord, saying, 'The Lord said unto my Lord, sit thou on my right hand, till I make thine enemies thy footstool. If David then call him Lord, how is he his son?'

Jesus does not necessarily here repudiate his Davidic origin, but makes light of it compared with his divine origin.

The cavalcade into Jerusalem had been accompanied by the welcoming shouts of the common people, who had supported him in his expulsion of their exploiters from the Temple. They had applauded his nimble escape from the

---

[1] Certain modern authors, such as Travers Herford and I. Abrahams, have written elaborate works in defence of the Pharisees, and attempt to make the good scribe typical of Pharisaic thought. Their arguments are not convincing.

coalition trap and his silencing of the authorities, both Pharisees and Sadducees, who habitually regarded them as the contemptible rabble. Here was their champion 'and the common people heard him gladly.' 'The common people,' ὁ πολὺς ὄχλος, whom Punch, in our own time, used to describe as 'the great unwashed,' were the 'Am Ha-ares' (or, Am-ha-aretz) of Palestine. They were the people who were careless of ceremonial ordinances, who did not trouble to wash their hands before meals; they had little learning and, in consequence, were spoken of as accursed.[1] Some modern critics with all the smug middle-class prejudice against the 'lower orders' will not have it that these could have been the people who, above all others, heard the Christ gladly. They contend that the 'common people' must have been the 'pious in the land.' That Jesus regarded them as truly pious is indisputable, but that the Rabbis, those righteous people who thought themselves in need of no repentance, regarded them as pious is a perversion of the truth. Rabbi Eleazar went so far as to say: 'It is lawful to stab an "Am Ha-ares" on a Day of Atonement that falls on a Sabbath' (i.e. a day of double holiness). His disciples said: 'You mean to say, to slaughter him.' He replied: 'Slaughtering requires a benediction, stabbing does not.'

How these 'common people' would have rejoiced in the final attack that Jesus now launches against their arrogant 'superiors.'

Some time before, near the Jordan fords, Jesus had told the story of the Pharisee and the publican for the benefit of those who trusted within themselves that they were righteous and despised others. Two men went into the Temple to pray, the one a Pharisee, the other a tax-gatherer. The Pharisee congratulated himself, saying, God, I thank Thee that I am not as other men are; extortioners, unjust, adulterers, or even as this miserable publican. I observe every fast day; I am scrupulous not to take a crumb before the communion; I subscribe largely to missionary societies

[1] John vii. 49.

and every Church activity, my name appears at the head of all subscription lists.

'But the publican standing afar off would not so much as lift up his eyes unto heaven, but smote upon his breast, saying, God be merciful to me a sinner.' This is the kind of man and the prayer beloved of God, for every one who exalts himself shall be abased, and he that humbleth himself shall be exalted.

Our Lord once more uses these very same words when he launches his last and most bitter attack upon the Pharisees and the legal authorities who formed part of the Government. He denounces them as hypocrites, vipers, whitewashed sepulchres which, indeed, appear beautiful without but within are full of corruption. They loved men to touch their hats to them, and to be seen walking about in their fine clothes, to be looked up to as the people who count. They devour widows' houses, lending them money at exorbitant rates, and then getting an agent to evict them from their cottages while they themselves are at church making long prayers. They are careful to pay the minutest tithes, but omit the weightier matters of the law, justice, and mercy. They have been entrusted with the keys of the Kingdom of Heaven, but lock out all who are longing to enter in by their perversion of the truth. They are scrupulous to strain out the gnat while they swallow the camel. They 'compass sea and land to make one proselyte,' and when he is become so, make him two-fold more a son of hell than themselves, not because they are eager to spread their religion, but because it is such a damnable religion that they spread. They laud up the ancient prophets to the skies and garnish their tombs, but they are in reality their murderers and 'how shall they escape the damnation of hell?'

The claimant to the coming kingdom when he was speaking of imperial conquerors talks of them as *supposed* rulers, people who are 'accounted to have the rule,' but in this long and bitter indictment of the Pharisees and their scribes there is not one word to suggest that they were not God-appointed and legitimate rulers. In fact, he says, 'the scribes and the Pharisees sit in Moses' seat: therefore whatsoever they bid you observe, that observe and do.' He is much more indignant with them for this very reason. The shepherds themselves, these divinely appointed men, had misled and befooled the people. It is they who might have taught and guided the nation into the truth, who have actually betrayed their trust and taken away the key of knowledge: they to whom had been entrusted the keys of God's own world of happiness and righteous living. There is not, perhaps, in all literature so stinging an indictment of legitimate authorities; and the fury with which they would meet such a charge is not difficult to imagine. He must be stifled and murdered before he could do any more mischief.

This, then, was the climax, the most dangerous moment in the campaign of Jesus. And yet it is at this very moment that he chooses to linger on the field of battle, although fully aware of the danger and the necessity of immediate escape, and for what reason? To watch an old widow woman putting her miserable farthing into the collecting chest, and to contrast her offering with those of the wealthy who ostentatiously threw in their gold and silver and bank-notes. Perhaps his disciples were impressed by this display of wealth, but Jesus indignantly shows them that the poor woman's offering is worth more than all the bounty of the rich heaped up together, 'for all they did cast in of their abundance; but she of her want did cast in all that she had; even all her living.'

Again he is prepared to sacrifice his own safety and his world plan for a nobody who had possibly been evicted by one of the wealthy subscribers and had, therefore, only her last coin left to give. In the same way he had neglected world statesmanship at the cries of the Greek widow and of blind Bartimaeus.

That is why Jesus is hall-marked for all time as Very God of Very God and Very Man of Very Man, because of such penetration, because in the midst of the battle for the world plan for all mankind, the statesman can turn his interest away from the world situation and become absorbed in the doings of the nobodies. It is upon the outcasts and untouchables, the unlettered and despised, that the divine commonwealth shall be built and shall blossom as the rose. Upon such as these shall the world renew its youth; upon such as these, and for such as these, destruction and a criminal's death is after all worth while. And upon this note Jesus at last left the city for Bethany, never again to teach in its Temple or in its streets.

CHAPTER XXXIII

THE JUDGMENT OF THE NATIONS

JESUS with his disciples may have crossed the brook Kedron when they looked back and called their Master's attention to the glittering domes and glistening walls of the unfinished Temple. They are awed at its magnificence, but he turns to them and says: 'Seest thou these great buildings; there shall not be left one stone upon another that shall not be thrown down.' They continue their climb and, pausing on the Mount of Olives when they are separated from the crowd of pilgrims, his more intimate followers ask him privately when all these things shall happen, and what shall be the sign of such incredible disasters. They would be immensely impressed by the grandeur of Herod's costly baroque architecture, and one can imagine their distress at the announcement of the destruction of the sacred centre of all their hopes.

The threat to destroy the Temple, although as a fact he had only foretold its destruction, was a day or so later made a major count against him at the trial and brought the Jerusalem crowd on to the side of the native government. The reasons for this were partly economic, for among that crowd were skilled artisans employed in the building operations, lodging-house keepers and provision merchants, bankers, stall-holders, and a thousand others whose interests centred around the sacred building; but largely their concern about the Temple was bound up with the genuine belief that its destruction would inevitably involve the departure of God from their midst. They did not understand that God was being driven out of Palestine not by any threatened destruction of His Temple, but by the gradual destruction of His poor.

Jesus continues the famous discourse about the end of

this age and the coming of the Son of Man in the new and divine age. There has been endless controversy as to its meaning. Many think it is not all genuine, and that on to a shorter original has been grafted other matter; some few believe that the whole matter is spurious and was a kind of loose sheet circulated by the early Christians among their members. This theory must, however, be rejected for two reasons; first, because there is no difference in style between the discourse and the rest of the Synoptic record, and second, because the whole of the record is interpenetrated with precisely the same kind of teaching as to the crash, the end, and the coming of the kingdom.

The difficulties are great, because the perspective seems to change; sometimes the end is to come within the lifetime of this generation, at others the end seems far distant—a long distance is often read into the text to save the honour or sanity of Jesus, as it is argued that the world has not come to an end and his prophecies have gone unfulfilled. Jesus himself says: 'But of that day and that hour knoweth no man, no, not the angels which are in heaven, neither the Son; but the Father.' It is on such passages as this that theologians have based the doctrine of the self-limitation of knowledge by Jesus. We prefer to think that it was not so much a deliberate self-limitation as that, in the course of his earthly career, the Master never professed or expected to know everything. By divine intuition he penetrated deeply into human character, and was able accurately to interpret the course of world events, but claimed no powers of occult prognostication.

His sure insight convinced him that all these things would come to pass within the lifetime of his hearers, even although the day and hour were unknown to him, and I would deny that his prophecies were unfulfilled. To make this clear let us recall what he actually foretold. False Christs and false prophets should arise and would deceive many. Such a one was Herod Agrippa, who allowed himself to be acclaimed as God's Messiah and, indeed, as God; another was John of Gischala, who raised a rebellion of deluded people by the pronouncement that Jerusalem could not be taken by the Romans, 'even if they had wings.' Typical of these false Messiahs, though at a somewhat later date, was Bar-Cochab, the son of a star, who awed the people by breathing out fire through his mouth and nostrils (later exposed as a conjuring trick, produced by lighted tow). This valiant pretender, after Jerusalem had been reduced to a heap of ashes, led a last attempt against the Roman Empire, but his effort ended in abject failure. The Christians, remembering the warnings of our Lord against any such nationalist risings, alone stood aloof.

Jesus tells his disciples that they would hear of wars and rumours of wars, 'nation shall rise against nation and kingdom against kingdom.' Within a few years of his death there was the Jewish-Arab war in which the youth of Palestine was conscripted for the front; there was the nationalist rebellion that preluded the fall of Jerusalem, and the last terrors of the siege revealed horrors that have never been surpassed. The earthquakes, famines, and pestilences which he foretold are in secular history recorded as actually occurring. In fact, so completely fulfilled were the prophecies of Jesus that some modern critics, who love to have it both ways, first assert that these things could never have happened, and then, overwhelmed by the evidence, say that the fact that they did happen proves conclusively that Jesus cannot have foretold these events, but that they must have been put into his mouth by forgers of a later date.

Jesus foretells that the disasters to his nation will be preluded by certain portents in the heavens, falling stars, the darkening of the sun, and the moon turned into blood;[1] the language may be figurative, but it is remarkable that world disasters are often accompanied by such omens, and

---

[1] Albert Schweitzer argues that Jesus took his imagery in this Parousian discourse from the extra-canonical apocalyptic literature. That he knew these writings we have already admitted, but his mind was steeped in the prophetic literature of the Old Testament canon; and Edgar Gibson, *The Old Testament in the New*, has traced all the imagery of this discourse to Old Testament sources.

there are records in secular history of the heavens being sensitive to the destinies of mankind. Whether all this was figurative or not, the sign of the Son of Man which shall then appear in heaven must certainly be taken as a figure. It is the ensign, the blood-red banner of man, which is to rally the elect from the four winds of heaven, and all earth-bound empires shall mourn at the appearance of the heaven-sent Kingdom of God.

But it may be objected that Jesus has not returned to earth nor has the new world come into being, and that although the first and more dreadful part of the prophecy has been fulfilled in the destruction of Jerusalem, the second part has been falsified; the joyous new world still tarries. The author of the second Petrine Epistle, writing somewhere early in the second century, tells us of many who were saying, 'Where is the promise of his coming? For, from the day that the fathers fell asleep, all things continued as they were from the beginning of the creation.' Many, in our own day, might well make the same complaint, although they could hardly object that the gospel has not been published among all nations. Actually, when our Lord said that his gospel must first be preached in all the world, he was referring to the Mediterranean world; his words do not really go beyond St. Paul's words, which distinctly assert a preaching of the gospel to all the world in his own day.[1]

If we see in the doom of Jerusalem a fulfilment of the Lord's prophecy, we may certainly also see in the resurrection and the creation of 'the new race' a coming of the Son of Man in his kingdom. That this coming was not completely fulfilled was due to the failure of the international in its compromise with the empire in the fourth century.

There have been moments in history when the Kingdom of Heaven has been thundering at our doors, when mankind at best has only feebly responded and at worst has utterly failed to seize the opportunity:

[1] Col. i. 6. Romans x. 18.

Earth might be fair and all men glad and wise,
Age after age their tragic Empires rise,
  Built while they dream, and in that dreaming weep:
  Would Man but wake from out his haunted sleep;
Earth might be fair and all men glad and wise.

The fall of Rome was one such opportunity; another was the fall of the ancient régime in France, where the revolution was but a partial response to the call of God's kingdom. Here, indeed, in France was a coming of the Son of Man, but the state of that country to-day would hardly justify us in claiming that the Kingdom of God had, in that nation, wholly come. In spite of God's judgment on Tsarist Russia, and the creation of a wonderful new world in that territory, the great response has been warped by an atheist philosophy, and fails to exhibit the full graciousness and spiritual riches that we may expect in God's completer kingdom.

Jesus ends on a note of urgency. Again and again the warning comes, Be on the alert, because suddenly the catastrophe will be upon you and will catch you unawares as in a snare. There will be no gradualism here, no time for a man to salvage his property. In illustration of this he gives certain parables with which we have already dealt and concludes with the stories of the ten virgins and the Judgment of the Nations. The former again suggests the suddenness of his coming and the folly of the five girls who were found unprepared.

This parable is a good illustration of what I have often pointed out, namely the danger of taking any of his stories as of general application. Each must be interpreted narrowly according to the one object which has called forth the illustration. Just as the parable of the unjust steward does not commend the rascality of stewards, nor the unjust judge the prejudice of judges, so here the refusal of the five wise virgins to share with the five foolish does not commend bad comradeship. This parable, as all others, is objective and realistic, and simply points out actually what certain young women would have done under the circumstances; urging everybody to be on the look out and as alert as the stupid virgins should have been.

The long discourse concludes with the great parable of the nations. In this our Lord gives his disciples a picture of the last assize at the end of the world. This has been so extravagantly misinterpreted that we must again insist that the arena is the earth and not the clouds, and that the assize takes place at every crisis of world history. It is noteworthy that here the judge is not the Father but the Son of Man, that is, Man as represented by the Messiah. Before him are gathered not all separate souls but nations composed of individuals in their corporate aspect. The judgment is on no theological issue in the abstract, but on the intensely practical issue of the corporal works of mercy. It must be remarked also that the question is not whether you personally have fed the hungry, but whether your nation has fed the hungry, clothed the naked, welcomed the foreigner, cared for the sick, and given good conditions to the prisoners. In fact, any nation that has done such things has accepted the Christ, and any nation neglecting such social duties has rejected him. It is remarkable that this is precisely the opposite to the teaching of certain evangelists of our own day, who seem to assert that your first and sole duty is consciously to surrender to Jesus, and that, as a consequence of that surrender, you may individually come to love the poor and do good to them. But this 'secondary' love of your neighbour will then be a 'command performance,' and not flow instinctively from your relation with him. All this is bad psychology.

Jesus may not here immediately be contemplating the case of nations who are secularist and atheist, as there were none such in his day; but the parable may well be applied in the spirit of his teaching to the nations of modern times, in so far as these, without conscious faith in him, have fulfilled the social conditions laid down in this parable. On the other hand are the nations who do him lip-service, but who fail to see him in the hungry and the thirsty, the outcast and the foreigner, the naked and the prisoners. On these he pronounces the judgment: 'Depart from me, ye cursed, into eternal fire,' prepared for the devil and his angels. To the others he holds out hands of welcome, saying: 'Come, ye blessed of my Father, inherit the kingdom prepared for you from the foundation of the world.'

We have already commented on the significance of the word 'eternal,' and should, therefore, interpret the judgment as meaning that the righteous nations will find their joyous place in the New World Order and inherit all its blessings, while upon the unrighteous will come extreme disaster.

Many people have been so impregnated with the individualistic virus that they are quite incapable of seeing that this parable deals with corporate bodies and not with separate souls. But history is strewn with the carcasses of unrighteous nations and both the Old and New Testaments make no question of the fact that God visits with his judgments nations as well as individuals. So steeped in this conception were the earlier prophets that Ezekiel had to make his famous protest against their extreme interpretation of history which allowed for no possibility of individual guilt. We have dealt very fully in an earlier section with his protest: 'The soul that sinneth, it shall die,' but nowadays the pendulum has swung too far the other way. As I write this, the significance of Abraham's plea for Sodom comes into my mind. Abraham had pleaded with God on behalf of the corrupt city of the plain, and had urged him to spare it if fifty righteous men were found within its borders who might have been able to leaven it with their goodness. In a descending scale he persuades Jehovah to spare it for the sake of ten; ultimately these ten could not be found and the city met its doom. Sodom, then, is an example of corporate destruction. Likewise, Jerusalem would be corporately destroyed, although some individuals within it would have been rich towards their neighbours in good works.

We may remember also the judgments on the seven churches as corporate bodies, in the revelation of St. John the Divine. The common sense of mankind has always recognized this right to deal with groups as corporations, and not only to suspend individuals but an offending group: instances of this might be cited from the annals of sport. Taken in its context, which deals with the impending doom of the Jewish nation, the communal interpretation of the parable can hardly be avoided, and this interpretation is good for all time. It comes as a searching challenge to modern nations and empires as regards their internal economy and their foreign policy.

CHAPTER XXXIV

THE SACRAMENT OF DEATH

On Wednesday[1] Jesus and his disciples were having a meal in the house of Simon, who had been a leper. He was evidently a friend of the Lazarus household, for Lazarus sat with them at the table, while Martha, characteristically, dished up the meal. Mary Magdalene, Martha's sister, took a very costly alabaster flask of ointment and anointed the head and feet of Jesus, and wiped his feet with her hair. Some of his disciples were shocked at this lavish waste, and Judas Iscariot voiced the general indignation and objected that the ointment might have been sold for over twelve pounds and the proceeds given to the poor. Whatever motive inspired the rest we are told that Judas cared nothing for the poor. Jesus rebuked their grudging spirit, and would not have her discouraged; hers was a generous and intuitive act, it was an anointing for burial, for she alone perceived the certainty of his arrest and death and nothing, therefore, at such a moment could be too extravagant a gift, and it would be remembered for all time wherever his gospel would be preached. Praising Mary, he next shows the emptiness of their argument: 'For ye have the poor with you always, and whensoever ye will ye may do them good, but me ye have not always.'

It seems incredible but there do exist people crass enough to bring this forward as evidence that Jesus contemplated and enjoyed the idea of a world in which there would always be the contrast of riches and poverty. It should be remarked that he does not say the poor ye *shall* have always with you, and he is, within a few days, to be

---

[1] The fourth gospel places this incident at the beginning of the week, and also mentions Judas as the objector and Mary as the anointer.

judicially murdered for announcing a world in which all these distinctions should be a thing of the past.

As to Judas Iscariot, the problem of his character is almost insoluble. He was the only southerner among the twelve and seems to have been a lonely, taciturn man. What had attracted him to the new movement? The fact that he was coupled with Simon the Canaanite, or Zealot, suggests that he was a nationalist revolutionary who had seen in Jesus one who would free them from the Roman yoke. His sins and shortcomings, such as avarice, may have sunk in the background in the first blaze of his enthusiasm, but as time went on he became soured and disappointed. How disgusted he must have been when Jesus, along the road, had warned them that he must travel the way of defeat and not the way of victory. Was this supposed leader a mere defeatist? Perhaps John the Evangelist, looking back after many years, may have thought that he had summed up the character of Judas from the beginning; he had never liked the fellow, as the fourth gospel clearly shows. He had charged Judas with a pretended concern with the poor, 'not because he cared for the poor, but because he held the bag.' I used to consider this a harsh judgment, but it may have been that Judas Iscariot belonged to that class of revolutionaries who cared much more for revolution in the abstract, than for the poor for whose sake revolution is worth while. Jesus was willing to sacrifice his life for a revolutionary cause, because he knew that such a cause would benefit the poor and outcast and harlots, and indeed the rich, whose souls were entangled in this present world order. Judas cared for none of these things. Did he, like the Pharisees, shrink with horror from the publicans and harlots, and was he driven, by our Lord's appreciation of Mary of Magdala and her lavish act, to desert him? But although Iscariot became the traitor, Jesus must have seen good in him or he would never have chosen him. There was in Judas the possibility of great things, although he sank to the lowest depths.

This reading of the action of Judas must, of course, be discounted if we are wrong, as so many modern critics would suggest, in identifying the woman with the alabaster box with Mary Magdalene. The fourth gospel does, however, speak of her as Mary, the sister of Martha, and this Mary as the woman out of whom seven devils were cast. It may be that Saints Mark and Matthew, as also St. Luke in the earlier story, speak of her vaguely as a certain woman in delicate reserve for her own feelings while she was still alive, whereas the fourth evangelist, writing long after her death, was able to be more explicit. We have already pointed out that the harlot, who was plying her trade in the city of Capernaum and who anointed Christ's feet at the Pharisee's breakfast party, was almost certainly Mary Magdalene of the same narrative who immediately afterwards was found financing a Galilean tour, and was described in the Lucan story as the woman out of whom Jesus had cast seven devils. Although the fathers of the East reject this identification, the Western tradition is consistent in its favour. To me it seems inconceivable that a comparatively poor family in Bethany should have in their possession a box of ointment costing about twelve pounds, or that the village store could supply such a box at a moment's notice. When we realize that these expensive flasks were part and parcel of the stock-in-trade of a prostitute, the evidence for the Western reading of the story seems overwhelming.

For Judas, then, this was the last straw. Utterly disillusioned with his Master for his favouritism towards a woman who had been a harlot he resolves to play the traitor and to betray him to the authorities. On Thursday afternoon another cabinet meeting of the Sanhedrim was held, when all the chief priests and elders, with the exception apparently of Nicodemus and Joseph, were assembled to compass the best means of destroying the Galilean impostor, but they said: 'Not on the feast day, lest there be an uproar among the people.' Incidentally this shows that Jesus, in spite of the trap laid for him by a coalition of governments, was still the hero of the populace. Judas comes to this assembly and gains admission. The difficulty which had confronted the authorities was how they might separate Jesus from the crowd and so effect an arrest. Here at last was their opportunity. Judas, for the price of a slave, for a mere thirty pieces of silver, now promises to betray his Master by leading the police officers that night to his hiding-place.[1]

Meanwhile Jesus sends two of his disciples to an hostelry in Jerusalem to arrange the room for his Passover meal. It may have been the market room of the inn and the meal had evidently been prearranged with the landlord, as it would have been impossible to procure accommodation at the last moment, considering the immense crowds of pilgrims and their demands. Likely enough the landlord was a disciple of the new movement.

It may seem strange that the Passover, which was generally celebrated on the Friday, should in this case have been anticipated by twenty-four hours, but it was a custom among the Jews to celebrate it at six o'clock on Thursday [2] when the actual feast fell on a Sabbath, when the necessary work in preparing the meal would be considered a breach of the Sabbath law, and we must remember that the feast day in that case would commence on Friday evening.

The disciples earlier would have bought the lamb and had it blessed by the priest in the Temple and carried it to the guest chamber. The floor was strewn with carpets and they prepared a table, setting out the cups of wine and bitter herbs; the lamb would have been roasted, and our Lord and the rest of his followers would have arrived about six o'clock. They reclined upon the floor, for the old custom had long since vanished of standing with staff in hand as they ate the meal in memory of their hasty flight from their

---

[1] Albert Schweitzer believes that Judas betrayed the claim of Jesus to be the Messiah, but the Synoptic story negatives this; for the crowds had proclaimed him to be the Christ in the hearing of the authorities and he had actually refused to silence them.

[2] For arguments from Jewish writers supporting this view see Warschauer's *The Historical Life of Christ*, pages 300 and 363.

oppressors in Egypt. The reclining may have signified the being at ease in Zion and the satisfaction that would be experienced in the new world of which the Passover and especially the eucharist was a foretaste.

The rite began with the blessing of the bowl of wine of which the president first drank and then passed round as a communal act. After the washing of hands bitter herbs were eaten to remind them of the bitter bondage of Egypt. Unleavened bread was eaten at the same time as a symbol of the haste with which they had escaped from the Egyptians, for there had been no opportunity to leaven the bread. This is the origin of the wafer in communion, but in the early Church the wafers were very large and were broken into small pieces for communicating the people. They were brought to the altar in baskets along with flagons of wine and fruits of the earth; and the paten held by the deacon at a modern high mass under the humeral veil is a reminiscence of the large basket for which there was no room on the altar.

Jesus and his disciples would then have sung the Hallel, which consisted of psalms commemorating the flight from bondage into liberty and the lifting of the poor out of the dust. The ceremonies continued until the roasted lamb was carved up and passed round among the guests. At some moment during the meal 'Jesus took bread and blessed, and break it, and gave to them, and said, Take; eat; This is my body.' Taking the 'cup of blessing' Jesus, 'when he had given thanks, gave it to them; and they all drank of it. And he said unto them, This is my blood of the new Covenant which is shed for many. Verily I say unto you, I will drink no more of the fruit of the vine until that day that I drink it new in the Kingdom of God.'

It is difficult to interpret the meaning of this saying about drinking in the Kingdom of God, but he may have meant that in his resurrection life he would be present with them in their common meal and their communions, and that the communal life would be the first inthrust of the kingdom. It is, of course, just possible that Jesus believed that the

New World Order would be completely manifested in a short period of time, and that in that new order of things he would share their joyous meals.

Although the question of the Real Presence belongs rather to the realm of sacramental theology than to the pages of an historical book, something about it may here be said. In his 'This is my body; this is my blood,' Jesus cannot be referring to his own material flesh; and yet we think that the Church is right in not interpreting the holy eucharist as the bare memory of a long-since dead Messiah. Just as Jesus appeared on earth in the garment of flesh, so he may well have been telling his disciples that he would convey his presence to them through the garment of bread and wine, and that whether they receive worthily or unworthily, they would actually be feeding on that Divine Reality.

There arose at this last and sacred common meal a puerile quarrel among them as to who should be the greatest; Jesus had often rebuked them for this ambitious and uncomradely spirit, and now again he has to show them by his own extraordinary act of humility how tragic are their divisions. He took a towel and knelt down and washed their feet in a basin of water and wiped them. In the deep humility of this act he once again teaches his disciples to serve one another as their Master and Lord has knelt down to serve them.

Jesus began to be exceeding sorrowful and had said to them: 'Verily, one of you shall betray me.' And it is noteworthy that not only Iscariot, but all the disciples had been uneasy and disturbed, for each one of them said: 'Lord, is it I?' Considering their quarrelsome dispositions and the divisions among them, as also the subsequent denial of Peter, they may have felt the uneasy stirrings of conscience. Peter himself indignantly denied the possibility of betraying his Lord; but Jesus said unto him: 'Verily I say unto thee, that this day, even in this night, before the cock crow twice, thou shalt deny me thrice.' But Peter spake the more vehemently, 'If I should die

with thee, I will not deny thee in any wise.' Likewise
also said they all.

It was not, however, Peter of whom Jesus was thinking,
but of that sullen disciple who had sunk to the depth of
degradation by sharing that common meal and dipping his
hand in the dish with his Master. After this act Satan
seizes upon Judas, and when Jesus exclaims: 'What thou
doest, do quickly,' Judas Iscariot goes out. And it was
night.

When Jesus had sent forth his twelve on their earlier
missions he had counselled them not to carry the usual
short sword or dagger under their cloaks, to go along their
way lightly clad and in a friendly spirit; but now in face of
the imminent danger, he tells them to be prepared: they
are to take their purses, their wallets, and to sell their cloaks
for daggers. They reply that they have among them already two short swords, and he says that will be enough.

Pacifists interpret this as though Jesus had said, 'Enough
of this folly,' and in their denseness the disciples had taken
him too literally. They argue that if he had really meant
them to be armed, two daggers would have been ridiculously
insufficient. But in view of the general practice of Oriental
governments to attempt assassination, especially where
their victim was popular and arrest was difficult, it was
ordinary common sense on the part of Jesus to give this
advice. A bodyguard of two disciples, one on each side
of him, as they left the guest-chamber and plunged into
the dark night would be a safeguard against the assassin's
dagger.

They now once more sing the Hallel and make for the
brook Kedron.

We have no room to give our Lord's long discourse at
the Last Supper, as recorded in the fourth gospel, but his
saying about the vine is of such poignant beauty that we
must quote it: 'I am the true vine, and my Father is the
husbandman. Every branch in me that beareth not fruit,
he taketh it away: and every branch that beareth fruit, he
purgeth it, that it may bear more fruit. Already ye are

clean because of the word which I have spoken unto you.
Abide in me, and I in you.   As the branch cannot bear
fruit of itself, except it abide in the vine; so neither can ye,
except ye abide in me.   I am the vine, and ye are the
branches.   He that abideth in me and I in him, the same
bears much fruit; for apart from me ye can do nothing.'

'I am the True Vine,' said our Lord, 'And Ye,
My brethren, are the Branches.' And that Vine,
Then first uplifted in its place, and hung
With its first purple grapes, since then has grown,
Until its green leaves gladden half the world,
And from its countless clusters rivers flow
For healing of the nations, and its boughs
Innumerable stretch through all the earth,
Ever increasing, ever each entwined
With each, all living from the Central Heart.
And you and I, my brethren, live and grow,
Branches of that immortal human Stem.

Measure thy life by loss instead of gain;
Not by the wine drunk, but the wine poured forth;
For love's strength standeth in love's sacrifice;
And whoso suffers most hath most to give.[1]

Across the Kedron then they hastened to the 'Garden of
Gethsemane,' a close-planted thicket of olive and other
trees which afforded an ideal hiding-place for any one who
wanted to avoid capture.   Jesus there set an outer guard
of eight of his followers, and a little farther on in the deeper
shrub an inner guard of his most intimate and trusted
friends, Peter and James and John (if even these, considering their quarrel but an hour or so ago, could be
counted on).   He himself went farther into the thicket to
be alone; they were to keep watch and sound the alarm.
And being in an agony he prayed.

Jesus must have been more alone in that hour than ever
before.   He could not rely on his disciples; Judas had
deserted to the enemy, Peter was soon to deny him, and
of the rest he felt uncertain that they had really grasped his
message to the world.   If this was true of his more im-

[1] Harriet Eleanor King, *The Sermon in the Hospital.*

mediate followers, what could be said of the vast crowd of Galilean pilgrims and of the proletarian crowds of Jerusalem? He began to be appalled and tormented with doubts, and he said: 'Father, if it be possible let this cup pass from me, nevertheless, not my will but thine be done.' He came back and found his inner guard sleeping. Did they not see the danger, could they not have kept a watch for one little hour? He especially addressed himself to Peter: 'Simon, sleepest *thou*; couldst not thou have watched with me one hour?' Again he went away and was alone, and the agony was so acute that his sweat was as drops of blood. Supposing he had failed and would be done to death with no one to carry on the message of world redemption. But he resigned all to his Father's will, and would drink this cup to the dregs. He returned and again found them all asleep: once more he went away and for the third time returned to find them sleeping, and said with bitter reproach: 'Sleep on, take your rest, no vigilance will save us now. Rise, let us be going, for the Son of Man is betrayed into the hands of wicked men,' and as he spoke he saw the lights of his enemies creeping up the dark hill, and immediately cometh Judas, one of his own twelve. And Judas kissed him.

That kiss was to be the signal to the armed guards of the Government reinforced by a Roman cohort; they evidently feared trouble and were taking no risks. There might well have been a rising among the people to rescue their hero, but they need not have feared, there was no attempt at a rescue. Jesus remarked bitterly: 'Are ye come out as against a robber, with swords and staves to take me? I was daily with you in the temple teaching, you did not dare arrest me then.' Some feeble attempt at resistance was made by one of the disciples (one account says by Peter), but Jesus said: 'Put up your sword again into its sheath; whoso takes the sword shall perish by the sword.' So they arrested him and led him over the brook and took him before Annas.

Now the pacifists make great play with this forbidding
*R

to use the sword, and with the saying: 'Whoso takes the sword,' but it is evident that a wise general who could counsel two of his followers to guard him with their daggers against the possibility of assassination would equally point out the utter folly of armed resistance on the part of one, or a feeble few, against overwhelming odds.   Whosoever took the sword on such an occasion would most certainly perish by the sword.   And why, it may be asked, were any of the disciples of a complete pacifist carrying arms at all, and that not only with his permission but at his express orders?

CHAPTER XXXV

THE TRIALS

HURRIEDLY that night in the high priest's palace, occupied by his father-in-law Annas, there was conducted a preliminary and illegal inquiry; for Annas had been deposed some years ago, and no longer held any office. Through corruption and intrigue, however, he still swayed the councils of the Sanhedrim, and Caiaphas, who seems to have been present, was under his thumb.

Meanwhile in the courtyard below Peter had with difficulty gained admittance. John had access to the precincts, probably having a standing order for the sale of his fish to the palace household; through him, Peter secured his admission from the girl who kept the gates, whose suspicions were only allayed when he deliberately denied that he was a follower of the Galilean. A cock crew, but Peter in his excitement did not hear it; it was a bitterly cold night, and Peter sat among the servants and police officers warming himself at the open fire. A maid who had been watching him narrowly denounced him to the others, saying: 'This fellow is one of them.' With increasing terror Peter vehemently denied it. An hour later one of them, perhaps a relation of the officer whose ear Peter had damaged, says: 'Surely you are a Galilean, for your accent proves it.' Then Peter began to curse and to swear, saying, I know not this man of whom you speak. And the second time a cock crew. At that very moment, Jesus, tightly bound, was being led through the courtyard from the apartments of Annas to the native hall of judgment. He has overheard Peter's repudiation of him. The Lord turned and looked upon Peter, who caught that look and understood the significance of the cock crowing; he called to mind the words of Jesus, how he had said:

'Before the cock crow twice, thou shalt deny me thrice.' And when he thought thereon, he wept.

It was not yet daybreak when they hurried their prisoner into the native court to appear before Caiaphas in his official role, sitting with the members of the Sanhedrim. This, again, was an illegal trial, not only because they all were acting as members of the prosecution rather than as impartial judges, but because 'it openly violated the Mosaic law which prohibits capital cases being tried at night.' [1] Their indecent haste was probably deliberate, as they would wish to avoid calling such members as Nicodemus and Joseph of Arimathea, who could not be relied upon to vote for this judicial murder.

In that earlier examination Annas would have wished to incriminate the prisoner and the same tactics were now employed. Considering that Jesus had been allowed no sleep and had been bullied by the police incessantly, we may, without exaggeration, say that he had been subjected to severe third degree methods.

Now the chief priests and all the council were determined to bring in the death sentence. They staged a 'frame-up,' seeking false witnesses to secure a conviction. 'According-ing to the Mosaic law no confession can dispense with the proof required from witnesses by the law. A single witness only does not suffice, whatever may be the offence or crime with which an accused may be charged. There must be two or three witnesses. This is one of the clearest texts of the law. And until their depositions were public-ally given against a man he was held to be, in the judgment of law, not merely innocent, but unaccused.' [2]

At first they tried to establish the charge that Jesus was plotting to destroy the Temple, appreciating the fact that such a plot would involve him in blasphemy, but they could not get their witnesses to agree. So they abandoned this ground and the Sadducean high priest now asks him directly if he claims to be the Messiah or not. Such a claim would be high treason, not only against the imperial overlords,

[1] Giovanni Rosadi, *The Trial of Jesus*, page 155.   [2] Ibid., page 180.

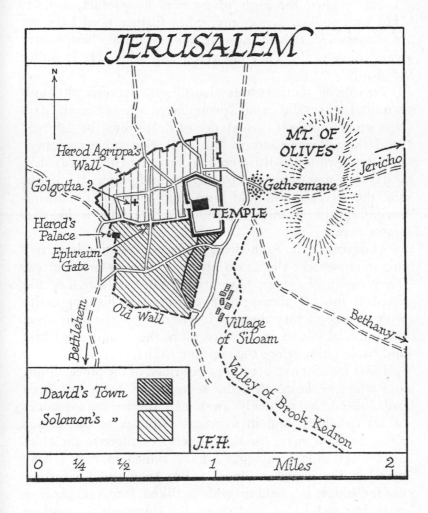

JERUSALEM

N

Herod Agrippa's
Wall

Golgotha?

Herod's
Palace

Ephraim
Gate

Bethlehem

Old Wall

MT. OF
OLIVES

Gethsemane

Jericho

TEMPLE

Village
of Siloam

Bethany

Valley of Brook Kedron

David's Town

Solomon's »

J.F.H.

| 0 | ¼ | ½ | 1 | Miles | 2 |

but against the Jewish state. There can be no doubt that his reply, 'Thou sayest,' is tantamount to a confession, and St. Mark makes it quite clear, for he records it as 'I am.' Then the high priest rent his clothes, saying: 'He hath spoken blasphemy, what further need have we of witnesses? Behold, now ye have heard his blasphemy; what think ye?' They answered and said: 'He is guilty of death.'

This death sentence was also illegal, because, although acquittal was valid when pronounced on the same day, 'the pronouncement of sentence of death must be deferred until the following day in the hope that some argument may meanwhile be discovered in favour of the accused.'[1]

Jesus is now subjected to further indignities; the police and the servants blindfold him, smite him, and taunt him, saying, Prophesy unto us, thou Christ; who is he that smote thee?

At daybreak the Sanhedrim held a consultation how they might implement the death sentence already pronounced. They could, of course, have stoned him, as later they did Stephen for blasphemy; but considering his popularity with the people they thought it wiser to put the onus upon the imperial governor, so once more they handcuffed him and hauled him before the supreme court.

Judas Iscariot had been kept informed of the proceedings, and when he heard that the sentence of death had been pronounced, he suddenly awakened to the consequences of his treachery, and in a belated attempt to put things right, brought again the thirty pieces of silver to the chief priests and elders, saying, 'I have sinned in that I have betrayed the innocent blood.' But they had no further use for Judas; he could do what he liked, it was no concern of theirs: and Judas 'cast down the thirty pieces of silver in the temple, and departed. And went and hanged himself.'[2]

[1] *Mishna,* note 8.

[2] A different account is given in St. Peter's speech (Acts i. 18), but St. Matthew's version of the story as given in the text is probably correct.

It was about six a.m. that Pilate, sitting on his judgment seat, interrogated Jesus; the charges made against the prisoner had been brought in the open space outside the praetorium, because these 'holy' accusers, who were continually straining out the gnat while they swallowed the camel, were now meticulously careful not to enter Pilate's court on the feast day, lest they should be defiled. The irony of the situation is found in the fact that they had broken the law that very night in the process of a native trial, and were now again breaking it by bringing Jesus up for trial in Passovertide, when, according to Hebrew law, no legal proceedings were permissible.

They did not ask Pilate to confirm their sentence of death on the theological charge of blasphemy, but now brought three entirely new counts against their captive; political charges which they reckoned would appeal to Pilate as procurator. 'We have found this fellow perverting the nation,' that is, attempting to stir up sedition. This charge was not accurate, because Jesus had, for reasons already explained, never made a frontal attack on Rome. The next charge was concerned with his forbidding the people to pay the imperial tribute.[1] It is true that Jesus had not actually ordered the common people to pay the tax, but had only told the Pharisees and their allies that as they were trading in the coinage of the conqueror, they should in strict logic render back to him the things that they themselves had admitted to be his. Jesus had, therefore, refused to give a ruling one way or another on this hotly disputed point.

Pilate seems to have been sensible in dismissing these two charges. Their third accusation was a charge of 'majestas,' or high treason, in that Jesus claimed to be Christ the king. Pilate takes this more seriously; here is perhaps 'matter' worthy of an inquiry and which might lead to the death sentence. So he asks the prisoner about this, and our Lord, who had been silent when accused of many other things, now speaks. But first of all he wants

[1] This has been fully dealt with in the section 'Render to Caesar.'

to know if the accusation is made by the procurator or by the native rulers. Pilate replies: 'Am I a Jew? Thine own nation and the chief priests have delivered thee unto me. What hast thou done? Are you really a claimant to the throne?' This puts Jesus in a dilemma and cannot be answered by a simple yes or no.

What follows is conventionally interpreted as meaning that our Lord only claims to be a king of some heavenly realm beyond the skies, or at most a king over the hearts and emotions of mankind. But when the crowds hailed him as Messiah on Palm Sunday they meant something very much more material than this, and Jesus had refused to rebuke them. What then does he actually mean by this claim? First of all he fully admits it, but must have mystified his cynical pagan judge by adding that his kingdom is not of this order of things, does not belong to this avaricious, bullying, fighting system. He is not concerned with the overthrow of Rome in order to set up an exploiting imperial kingdom just as pernicious as that of the Roman Empire. If my kingdom were of this type you would have found my followers armed to the teeth, but 'Now is my kingdom not from hence.' It belongs to a realm of ideas which is beyond your comprehension, or indeed that of my own nation; much work must be done, a deep change in their moral outlook effected before my kingdom can materialize among the nations. It is true, he might have added, if he had not been a consummate tactician, when it does materialize it will bring to the dust your empire and all the kingdoms of this world. But what he does add is that his kingdom is to be built not upon the lies of imperial systems or swollen nationalisms, but upon the living truth. 'To this end was I born; and for this cause came I into the world; that I should bear witness to the truth.'

It was certainly a strange and unusual claim to kingship this. The kings of this world do not generally base their claims on the fact that they are bearing witness to the truth. And yet the kingly function does not only consist in upholding just laws and defending the poor and oppressed, but in going deep down to the rock-bottom foundation of the truth. Every natural leader of mankind must be able to make good this claim or he is exposed as a false shepherd perverting his people. But if this is not usually recognized by the people themselves how much less could it be understood by the agnostic procurator? So Pilate replies: 'Truth, what is truth?' What was he to make of this fellow? There was a strange dignity about him, and as regards any immediate designs upon the empire he seemed innocent; his followers had not been found, like Barabbas, contemplating armed rebellion. Pilate therefore goes out and pronounces to the assembled Jews: 'Not guilty.'

But his infuriated accusers were determined not to be robbed of their prey. They reiterate the charge that Jesus was a dangerous agitator stirring up all Palestine from Galilee even unto this place. When Pilate understood that the man was a Galilean he grasped at the chance of shifting the responsibility of giving judgment on to Herod's shoulders, for Herod Antipas, ruler of Galilee, was in his quarters at Jerusalem at that time. So Jesus is sent to the palace of Herod, who, we are told, was glad to see him, as he had long wanted to satisfy his curiosity about this Galilean prophet who he feared might be another John the Baptist and as dangerous a disturber of the peace.

The chief priests and elders again bring their angry accusations against him, but Herod refuses to pronounce any sentence, and merely makes sport of the prisoner; in mockery he arrays him in a royal robe and sends him back to Pilate. Luke adds that Herod and Pilate were made friends that day, for formerly they were at enmity. Possibly they agreed that the prisoner was not dangerous, and, in any case, they both alike hated and despised the Jews.

Pilate once more pronounces his verdict of not guilty to the amazement and acute disappointment of the accusers. He will so far satisfy them as to scourge the prisoner and then release him; after all some prisoner or other had by custom to be released on a feast day. But the members of the Sanhedrim had made sure of the proletarian mob [1] of the city, and all who had economic interests involved in the preservation of the Temple, and in the concourse of people who attended these feasts. They had evidently told the crowd that if Jesus were to be spared the hope of their gains would be gone. The people therefore at their instigation cried: 'Not this man, but Barabbas.' Now Barabbas was a bandit chief.

At this moment there comes a warning to Pilate from his wife, Claudia, a powerful lady related to the emperor, who sent a message to her husband to do no harm to this just man, 'for I have this night suffered many things in a dream concerning him.' Claudia's intervention made Pilate all the more anxious to release Jesus. Wasted by loss of blood, wearing the purple robe and the crown of thorns with which the soldiers had crowned him, Jesus is exhibited by Pilate to the people with the words: 'Behold the man.'

To Pilate this 'Ecce Homo' meant little, and to the Jewish authorities, bent on destruction, the words mean nothing at all; but they have sounded down the ages as the penetrating truth, for here before them was the personality in whom was gathered up all that was most human and eternal in mankind.

What was the use of appealing to people such as these? On seeing Jesus the chief priests and magistrates again immediately cry out: 'Crucify him, crucify him.' Pilate

[1] It is considered by many that the crowd that cried out 'Crucify him' was the same crowd that had hailed him as Lord on Palm Sunday, but there is abundant evidence to show that the latter, composed as it was mostly of poor pilgrims, could not afford to lodge in the holy city and would, therefore, have to procure what rooms they could in Bethany and Bethphage or in the villages round about: many would camp out in the open some distance from the city. The majority of them would not be able to get into Jerusalem at that early hour in time for the trial, and those that had been able to arrive early would form a scattered outer ring round the urban Jerusalem crowd, and their protests, if they had the courage to make any, would have been drowned in the clamour of execration.

says to them, Take him out of my hands and crucify him yourselves, for my verdict is: Not guilty. For a moment the authorities play with the idea of stoning him for blasphemy, for they urge upon Pilate that they have a law, and by that law any one claiming to be the Son of God ought to die; but they soon dismissed from their minds this method of destruction and are still determined to force Pilate to take the responsibility.

The procurator is disturbed and afraid; once more he examines the prisoner, but Jesus remains silent until Pilate reminds him that he has the power to sentence or acquit him. Then Jesus says: 'Thou wouldst have no power against me, except it were given thee from above: therefore he that delivered me unto thee hath greater sin.'

This 'from above' would not convey to the mind of the procurator 'from Heaven,' but must here either mean from the emperor and the whole imperial system or from Caiaphas, for Annas and Caiaphas had Pilate in their grip as the sequel will show. Jesus clearly perceived that the Roman procurator was an underling with very little choice in the matter.

He was grateful that Pilate was trying against enormous odds to protect him, but sensed the situation accurately, for within a few moments the authorities play their trump card, which inevitably decides the fate of their victim, by crying out: 'If thou release this man, thou art not Caesar's friend; every one that maketh himself a king, speaketh against Caesar.'

When Pilate hears this cry and understands its full significance his terror of Tiberius overcomes his own prejudices. The emperor was now an old man, living in rigid seclusion on the island of Capri; his madness was increasing, he was taciturn and suspicious, many of his supposed rivals had suffered death at his hands, and the provincial governors trembled lest they should be among his victims.

Now Pilate himself had made many blunders in his administration of the 'Crown Colony of Palestine.' He had foolishly set up effigies of the emperor within the holy city. This caused a great tumult, and when the Jews appealed to him to remove these sacrilegious emblems, he threatened to slaughter them, and yielded when he found that their passive resistance could only be overcome by the murder of a mass of unarmed people. He later brought to Jerusalem a water supply and constructed a water tower, the tower of Siloam. The intention was sensible enough, for the sanitation of the city must have been unspeakable, but the project offended native tradition and he had actually raided the sacred treasury to accomplish his scheme. We have already made some mention of the riot which followed, and of the blood which Pilate mingled with the sacrifices. Knowing that Tiberius was anxious not to offend the provinces it is quite understandable, therefore, that Pilate should consider the immediate problem of his own safety and bow to the inevitable.

He decides to take one last remote chance, and appeals to the masses, considering that the spectacle of Jesus may yet move them to sympathy. Pilate therefore proclaims, 'Behold your king,' but the people, moved as we have shown by the authorities, cried out: 'Away with him, away with him. Crucify him.' Pilate said unto them: 'Shall I crucify your king?' The chief priests answered: 'We have no king but Caesar.'

With this answer not only the Sadducees but the Pharisees who still did lip-service to patriotism, once and for all abandoned the national hope and betrayed their country to the imperial conquerors in their fanatical determination to rid themselves of their redeemer.

Pilate's last gesture was characteristic of a well-intentioned but feeble judge. He took water and washed his hands before the multitude, saying: 'I am innocent of the blood of this just person; see ye to it.' And as the crowd shout, 'His blood be upon us and on our children,' he delivers Jesus to his fate.

He disclaims all responsibility, but his hands were stained with the blood of Jesus to the end of his days, and

we are reminded of the lament of that other murderer,
Macbeth, equally the victim of circumstance:

> Will all great Neptune's ocean wash this blood
> Clean from my hand?   No!   This my hand will rather
> The multitudinous seas incarnadine,
> Making the green one red.

CHAPTER XXXVI

DID CHRIST COME INTO THE WORLD TO DIE?

IF mankind had accepted the principles of Jesus and applied them to the building of the new world, would there have been any necessity for the death of Christ?

Orthodox or rather conventional Christians, for orthodoxy and conventionality are very different matters, would at once reply that it is only through the cross that we can be saved, for Christ is a propitiatory sacrifice. No lesser sacrifice than that of his only begotten son could satisfy the Father, so that Christ had inevitably to die if the world was to be redeemed.

We shall deny this doctrine in the crude form in which it is generally proposed, and much more emphatically shall we deny the doctrine of substitution. This doctrine in its starkest form suggests that the heavenly Father requires a blood sacrifice and will not be satisfied with any less perfect sacrifice than the death of his son. In consideration of that death he will be graciously content to overlook the sins of mankind, and to allow them to escape that everlasting torment which their sins merit. The son has made a sufficient sacrifice and has been substituted for other men or, at least, for a chosen few among them.

And this leads us to a consideration of the most pernicious form of the doctrine of substitution, namely, that the majority of mankind are, by the caprice and whim of an Almighty God, predestined from birth to the torments of hell, and that no thought or deed on their part can alter their doom. A few, a mere handful of the elect, are to be chosen out of the general ruin and these alone are destined to everlasting bliss. Many Protestant and some Catholic theologians, although they would deny Predestination, suggest that part of the enjoyment of the blessed will consist in contemplating the torments of the damned; it seems that St. Thomas Aquinas was among their number. This only goes to show that the most holy men may sometimes have in their composition the most unholy patches.

The term 'ransom,' in the phrase 'to give his life a ransom for many,' has been twisted into the most fantastic theological mystery. Its meaning, however, is simple and straightforward. Professor E. P. Gould [1] gives an analogy from the American Civil War where the soldiers gave their lives a ransom for their country, and remarks that every martyr's death is λύτρον ἀντὶ πολλῶν.

Professor E. F. Scott also takes the phrase in its natural sense, and objects to its being tortured by theologians into something strange and inhuman. This author connects it with the idea of Christ's coming commonwealth and says: 'When he spoke, as he does, here of the grand purpose for which he had come, he must have been thinking of this advent of the kingdom in the widest range of its significance. By his death he was to deliver men, not from one particular evil or another, but from the whole state of bondage to which they were subjected in the present age. In other words, his act of self-sacrifice was the appointed means whereby the Kingdom of God would be realized. Many were to enter into life through the death of one. . . . The apparent limitation involved in the word "many" is, indeed, perplexing; yet we can understand why Jesus chose this word in preference to any other. He did not mean that his death would only avail for a certain number, but that he would die, like the Suffering Servant, for the common deliverance. The saying, then, if we have interpreted it rightly, declares that Jesus by his own death will effect the coming of the Kingdom of God.' [2]

Jesus, therefore, through the offering of his whole life crowned by the supreme sacrifice of his death and flowering into resurrection, satisfies the Father, not because He needed

[1] *International Critical Commentary.* *St. Mark.*
[2] *The Kingdom and the Messiah*, pages 234-5.

any expiatory blood sacrifice, but because He saw in His son's act a first fruit of what He might expect from the many when they had been caught up by grace into the nature of the son, so returning to their own proper nature as originally constituted in the mind of God.

The phrase in the second of the Thirty-nine Articles of the Church of England, 'to reconcile His Father to us,' is, therefore, unfortunate, and can only escape the charge of heresy if we interpret it as meaning that God is so reconciled by being assured of our own co-operation in the abolition of sin. Jesus saves us not so much from the consequences of sin as from sin itself; the whole New Testament is witness to this doctrine.

If, then, we might have been saved by the life of Christ how was his death at that moment and in that historical situation supremely necessary, and indeed inevitable? Had men not fallen away from their original innocence into greed and strife and every dark bypath, when Christ came as fruit and crown of the race they would have accepted both him and his principles, and pressed forward to further heights of human achievement. They would have been saved by his life.

But things being as they were, and the above path being deliberately rejected, it was inevitable that corrupt rulers in high places, supported by a populace who loved to have it so, should kill him.

The death of martyrs in all ages has been the cleansing salt of the world; through these supreme heroisms men have been shocked out of their complacency; surprised and elated into newness of life. The death of Jesus was the gathering up of all these martyrdoms in a stupendous and unique act of sacrifice, and because it was a pure oblation, the oblation of the perfect Son of Man, it was bound to result in a resurrection and ascension into the inner fulcrum of God's Being from which the Christ, transformed into a higher condition of life, refreshes and recreates the world.

But supposing the Jewish nation had been converted by the life and teaching of Jesus, how could they, by the acceptance of his life and the practice of his teaching, have saved the world? We have frequently pointed out that Palestine was in a very real sense the centre of world activities; it had been 'put on the map.' Now if the Jewish nation had put their own house in order, they would have become what God had intended them to be, a light to lighten the Gentiles, and in them all nations of the world would have been blessed.

Peoples groaning under the yoke of empire, under vicious national rulers, and burdened by their own corruptions would have seen in Palestine a new hope, would have in the light of this encouragement reformed and reconstructed their own lives and the life of their nation, and would have rallied round Palestine and become the international 'Israel of God.'

It is unlikely but not impossible that such a movement would have converted the Roman Empire, but if the attempted conversion had failed it would have swept the Roman Empire off the face of the earth.

But things turned out differently, and Jesus is found on the road to Calvary.

CHAPTER XXXVII

THE VIA DOLOROSA

ABOUT nine o'clock on that Friday morning, Jesus, victim of the brutal play of the Roman soldiery, was led out of the city by the Ephraim gate towards the little hill which had the sinister form of a skull. This was the place of execution.

Weakened by the long hours of mental and physical agony he was unable to support the heavy wooden cross which the convicts themselves had to carry. Among the crowd that followed him were jeering priests and Levites, citizens of Jerusalem, and women, both from the city and the provinces, who grieved for him. Coming in from the countryside and joining in that sinister procession was one Simon of Cyrene; perhaps this man was a disciple, and would have been horrified at the turn events had taken in the night while the Master's pilgrim supporters had been bivouacked outside the city. 'Him they compelled to bear his cross.'

The faithful women included Mary, the wife of Cleophas, Salome, mother of St. John the Evangelist, and two of those who had financed his Galilean tour, Mary Magdalene, and Joanna, the wife of Chuza. Tradition has it that another brave woman named Veronica looked down from her window and saw the royal victim, his forehead covered with dust and blood, and that she came to him and wiped his brow with a towel which ever after has borne the imprint of that sacred face.

This company of women were weeping and bewailing him, but Jesus turned to them and said: 'Daughters of Jerusalem, weep not for me, but weep for yourselves and for your children. For behold, the days are coming, in which they shall say, Blessed are the barren, and the

wombs that never bear, and the breasts that never gave
suck. Then shall they begin to say to the mountains,
Fall on us; and to the hills, Cover us. For if they do these
things in the green tree, what shall be done in the dry?'

The sap in the green tree of the nation's life was running
very faintly, but soon that tree would be completely dead.
About forty years after this prophecy of Jesus' the revolt
of the Jews was met by the battering rams of the empire;
the besieged, in spite of their desperate defence, overtaken
by plague and famine, were mowed down in their hundreds
of thousands. The daughters of Jerusalem buried themselves under the hills to escape the Roman vengeance;
some went mad and fed upon their own children. The
horrors of that siege are indescribable. God's scourge
had once more fallen upon the nation, and the pagan Titus,
when congratulated on his victory, replied: 'It is not I who
have conquered. God, in His wrath against the Jews, has
made use of my arm.' [1]

As to the persons chiefly concerned in the judicial murder
of Jesus, Judas committed suicide, Pontius Pilate was
banished and came to a like end, Herod Antipas was
banished, the Emperor Tiberius, more remotely responsible,
was murdered, Caiaphas was deposed within a year of the
crucifixion, while, as for Annas, his house was a generation
later destroyed by the people, and his son 'was dragged
through the streets and scourged and beaten to his place
of murder.'

On what the Latins call Calvary, and the Jews Golgotha,
the place of the skull, were now erected the three short
crosses to which were nailed two bandit rebels with Jesus
in the midst, and 'there they crucified him.' According
to the usual custom the crime for which Jesus was sen-
tenced, that is, 'majestas,' or claiming the throne, was
posted in Latin, Greek, and Hebrew, on the cross: 'Jesus
of Nazareth, the King of the Jews.' The native authorities
protested, but Pilate stood firm, saying: 'What I have
written I have written.'

[1] *The Catholic Encyclopaedia*, article on 'Jerusalem.'

But there was to be another turn of events by which Black Friday became Good Friday, and the shameful cross became the adored crucifix.

> Faithful cross! above all other,
>   One and only noble tree!
> None in foliage, none in blossom,
>   None in fruit thy peer may be;
> Sweetest wood and sweetest iron!
>   Sweetest weight is hung on thee.

CHAPTER XXXVIII

JOURNEY'S END

Now there was in Jerusalem a guild of women who suc-
coured condemned prisoners and administered narcotic to
those about to be crucified. These mild anaesthetics
somewhat deadened the tortures of the convicts which were,
however, still excessive. Jesus was offered the wine
mingled with myrrh but would not accept it.

He had asked the Father that this cup should pass from
him, but had said: 'Nevertheless not my will, but thine
be done.' If he was to drink it, he would drink it to the
bitter dregs. He would keep full possession of his mental
powers, and so experience all that he was obliged to undergo
as a fully conscious oblation for all the sufferings and sins
of mankind. If his mind had been dulled and drugged
how could he have helped his mother or have saved the
dying robber or uttered those healing words from the cross?

Unto each man his handiwork, unto each his crown,
    The just Fate gives;
Whoso takes the world's life on him and his own lays down,
    He, dying so, lives.

Whoso bears the whole heaviness of the wronged world's weight,
    And puts it by,
It is well with him suffering, though he face man's fate;
    How should he die?

Seeing death has no part in him any more, no power
    Upon his head;
He has bought his eternity with a little hour,
    And is not dead.[1]

The people stood beholding; the soldiers mocked him,
saying: 'If thou be the king of the Jews save thyself.'

[1] Swinburne, 'Super Flumina Babylonis,' from *Songs before Sunrise*.

The dignitaries of Holy Church and others that passed by derided him, wagging their heads and saying: 'Thou that destroyest the temple and buildest it in three days, save thyself. If thou be the Son of God, come down from the cross and we will believe.'

'Seeing is believing.' But is it? If the Christ had descended from the cross they would grudgingly have admitted a marvel, but they would have been no nearer believing in Jesus and his message of world-wide resurrection. He had done his utmost to save them, but they had made it impossible. 'Save thyself,' they cried, but how can one, by saving his own skin, save his fellow-men? These learned people were desperately ignorant; they had no conception of what they were doing.

Jesus cries: 'Father, forgive them, for they know not what they do.'

One of the malefactors which were hanged with him took up the prevailing cry and in his agony appeals to Jesus, for if this fellow is really the Messiah why can't he save himself and us? The other rebukes him, saying: Dost not thou fear God, seeing that we are all alike in the same death-trap, and we indeed justly, for we were found in arms and as bandits have committed many atrocities and are now paying the penalty; but this man has done nothing amiss. And he turns his head towards Jesus, and says: 'Lord, remember me when thou comest into thy kingdom.'

The people had found it hard enough to believe in Jesus and his new world when he had been alive, and there had been some possibility of triumph, but the dying felon began to believe in the very moment of Christ's defeat and destruction. How could such a faith be nurtured in the soil of death? And was it not sheer credulity at this moment to believe that there could ever be a kingdom, a power, or a glory? What splendid credulity and how grandly it was to be justified.

If this man had all his life attended to his own affairs and his own family, and had lived on the comfortable principle

of 'safety first,' he would not have been able to build up
that generous faith. It was because he had had some dim
vision of a better order of things in his twisted and embittered soul and had risked his life for his ideal,[1] such as
it was, that he was able to see in his dying companion the
victorious Saviour of the whole world and of his own
poor soul.

And the Lord hearkens to his cry and delivers him out
of his distress: 'To-day shalt thou be with me in paradise.'
That paradise was not yet to be the complete world of God's
dreams, but it was sufficient for the dying robber, for to
be with Christ is to be in paradise.

As Jesus had concerned himself with the malefactor, so
now he concerns himself with his mother. 'Now there
stood by the cross of Jesus his mother, and his mother's
sister, Mary, the wife of Cleophas, and Mary Magdalene.'
Excepting for St. John the men seemed to have fled; and
one had betrayed him while another had denied him with
curses. Perhaps Jesus had wished them to escape that
they might carry on his campaign, or perhaps they were
cowards. As so often happens the women had proved
themselves braver than the men.

What was passing through the mind of Mary? The
night of his birth, the hopes of her Magnificat, the taking
him up to the Temple when he was twelve years old, the
years in the carpenter's shop at Nazareth? The sword
had, indeed, pierced through her heart; she had been
terrified for his safety. The people he wanted to help
had become his bitterest enemies, they had pursued him
into every province, and had been determined to murder
him. He had been impatient with her when she had
warned him of the danger. Perhaps she had sometimes
got in his way; she was proud of him and proud of his
kingly mission, but so troubled about his bodily safety.

Well, now they had their way with him and had got him

[1] It is possible that the malefactor was a common highwayman, but
equally possible that he was a fierce insurrectionist who had robbed and
pillaged as he fought.

in their clutches; it was dangerous to be found anywhere near him, but she would be by him to the last. 'Now there stood by the cross of Jesus his mother.'[1]

Jesus, world saviour and world statesman, bowed down by all the ignorance and cruelty of mankind, busies himself with his mother. What is to happen to her when he is gone? He would commit her to the care of the disciple whom he loved. And he says to Mary: 'Woman, behold thy son,' and to John: 'Behold thy mother,' and from that hour the beloved disciple took her to live with him.

She would have been with him years after in Asia Minor, and would perhaps have seen him carried away for exile and imprisonment on the island of Patmos. Was it of her or of that church which she represented that he wrote: 'And there appeared a great wonder in Heaven; a woman clothed with the sun, and the moon under her feet, and upon her head a crown of twelve stars'? In any case, she has been worshipped by hundreds of thousands in all generations as the woman who bore Jesus, who believed in him, and in the good time coming, and who stood by his cross to the last.

But not even that ray of hope that broke through the dark cloud of death at the bravery of his mother and the audacious belief of the crucified robber could lift his spirit out of the deep disgrace and the dust of death. God had forgotten him and left him to perish; his enemies had triumphed, and all hope of God's new world had been blotted out: 'And at the ninth hour Jesus cried with a loud voice, saying: Eloi, Eloi, lama sabachthani? which is, being interpreted: My God, my God, why hast thou forsaken me?'

Do the crowds deliberately misunderstand him when they cry out, This man calls upon Elijah; let us wait and see whether Elijah will come and take him. But Jesus, wearied by their cynicism, and his throat parched, says:

[1] For a wonderful picture of Mary at the cross I would recommend to my readers Charles Rann Kennedy's incomparable drama 'The Terrible Meek.'

'I thirst,' and one of the soldiers touched by his suffering
fills the sponge with vinegar and, fastening it on a reed,
gives it him to drink.   In the prelude to his ministry, after
the long fast he had been hungry, and his hunger had
included the needs of all the hungry poor; now when he
thirsted he would remember the parched and swollen
throats of the prisoners, and of all the tired and down-
trodden people of the world.   Not only of bodily hunger
and thirst would he be thinking, but of those who hunger
and thirst after justice.   Had God forgotten to be gracious?
Would they ever now be filled?

In the hour of death Jesus was filled with 'that boundless
hunger of the immortals, which only God's infinitude
supplies.'

Well, now at last it is all over.   Could the crowds hear
that almost inaudible 'It is finished'?   Was it a sigh of
relief?   Did he really feel that he had finished the work
which his Father had set him to do?   There is the satisfaction of the artist when he puts the finishing touches
to his masterpiece; there is also the cry of despair forced
from the lips of the man who sees himself cut short in his
work, and all the things he wanted to achieve incompleted.
The end is upon him and he can, at least, hand back
his sword unbroken and untarnished to God.   With this
thought he breathed out his soul to the Father in whom,
after all, he still believes.   'Father, into thy hands I commend my spirit.'

'And the veil of the temple was rent in twain from the
top to the bottom.   And when the centurion, which stood
over against him, saw that he so cried out, and gave up the
ghost, he said, Truly this man was the Son of God.'

S

CHAPTER XXXIX

THE MIGHTY RESURRECTION

OUR materials for the story of the resurrection are the gospels according to Mark and Luke, with Matthew in its Greek form and the fourth gospel as supplementary and corrective. The version of St. Mark, as we have it, unfortunately breaks off abruptly and therefore gives us the briefest account of all, but the added story may well be genuine, although omitted by certain valuable manuscripts. St. Luke must have had Mark before him when he wrote, but strangely enough omits the words of the risen Jesus telling the disciples to meet him in Galilee and substitutes for them a command that they should tarry in Jerusalem. This word 'tarry' should be translated 'take up your permanent abode,' and when we turn to Luke's second book, the Acts, he mentions there that our Lord was appearing among them for some forty days before the ascension. The disciples then would have had ample time to make the journey to Galilee, sell up their boats and fishing-tackle, and to return to the capital.

Many of the apparent discrepancies between the gospels can be reconciled as naturally as this; it must, however, be admitted that there do exist wide divergencies which are very awkward for the fundamentalists but need not greatly trouble us. They are, to say the least of it, no greater than the contradictions which may be found between various historians writing about contemporary events within a few years of their occurrence. Accounts of the battles of the Somme and of the Marne and of the naval engagement off Jutland, even when written by eye-witnesses, are quite irreconcilable. Experiments conducted by the Psychical Research Society and many of the scouting tests show the extraordinary possibilities of mal-observation.

For all this, it would be absurd to suppose that the above mentioned battles did not occur.

The account of the resurrection is difficult to reconstruct, but taking all the evidence into consideration it becomes reasonable and convincing.

A rich and influential disciple, Joseph of Arimathea, went to Pilate and begged the body of Jesus, to give him decent burial. Victims of this terrible death sometimes lingered for two or three days, unless their tortures were more speedily brought to a close by breaking the legs or piercing the heart, as was done in Jerusalem in Passover time, that the bodies should not remain on their crosses to the scandal of the faithful. Pilate granted the request, but doubted whether Jesus was already dead, but his messengers informed him that the poor victim had expired; to make doubly sure the soldiers had pierced his side with a spear, and there flowed forth blood and water.

Joseph received the sacred corpse and is joined by Nicodemus, another member of the Government who had come to Jesus by night, and the two rich men hurriedly swathe the body of their Master in linen and spices and laid it in a rock-hewn tomb, Joseph's family vault, and certain women disciples observe the place where he was laid.

Meanwhile the Jewish authorities had asked Pilate for a guard of soldiers to watch the tomb, lest the disciples should spirit the body away and pretend that their Leader had risen from the dead. The guard remained before the tomb from Good Friday afternoon until just before the dawn on Easter Sunday. Then something happened to terrify them, and they fled affrighted by an earthquake which shifted the stone from the tomb, for these stones were arranged in a groove and the disturbance of the soil would dislodge them.

Some of the women came in the early morning to complete the anointing and were amazed to find an open sepulchre, for they had been troubled as to who should move the stone for them. Among them were Mary Magdalene, Mary, the mother of James, and Salome. Some of the women entered in and saw a young man in white who told them not to be afraid, for Jesus whom they sought had risen; they were to go to the disciples and to Peter and tell them that the Master had risen and would meet them in Galilee.

Mark says that the women were so disturbed and afraid that for the moment they told no man, but according to Matthew Jesus himself appeared to them on the road and said to them: 'All hail!' and they did him reverence and clung to his feet, as if to hold him to earth, but he said to them: 'Be not afraid; go tell my brethren, that they go into Galilee, and there shall they see me.' So the women went and reported the joyful news to the disciples, but they were sceptical about it all and thought it was only the idle tale of a pack of hysterical women.

Now Mary Magdalene would seem, according to the earlier accounts, to have been foremost among the women who had seen the risen Lord, and it is difficult to reconcile the story in the fourth gospel with this. It has been suggested that she was at the tomb, but, weighed down with grief, did not hear the message of the young man and got separated from the rest on the way back to Jerusalem, and did not see the risen Lord. According to St. John she therefore came straight to himself and St. Peter, who was lodging with him, for they had not yet joined the rest who were gathering together for fear of the authorities, and told them: 'They have taken away the Lord out of the sepulchre and we know not where they have laid him.' The 'we' of this narrative suggests that the Magdalene was, as we are told by the other evangelists, not alone when she visited the tomb, but one of several women.

Hearing her story of the empty tomb Peter and John ran towards it and the younger man outran Peter, and stooping down saw dimly the linen clothes but did not go in. Simon Peter, more impulsive, entered, and, seeing the position of the grave clothes and the linen head-cloth just a few inches from them 'wrapped together in a place by itself,' was convinced that Jesus was risen from the dead.

It was the custom in the East, and I believe still is, to swathe the corpse in linen, but to leave the neck exposed, so that the cloth that surrounds the head is separated from the wrappings of the body. Now Peter, seeing that this was the precise position of affairs in the tomb, and that neither the body wrappings nor the head-dress had been disarranged, but had merely caved in, concluded that the Lord had been exhaled through the linen clothes and had risen. He saw and believed and in his delight told John, who then entered in and was also convinced. They ran back in haste to tell the rest, but Mary, wearied and slow of foot, reaches the tomb later and stooping down looks into the sepulchre. She sees two angels, one at the head and one at the foot of the place where Jesus had laid. 'And they say unto her, Woman, why weepest thou? She saith unto them, Because they have taken away my Lord and I know not where they have laid him.' Puzzled and confused, she turns round and sees Jesus himself, but mistakes him for the gardener. Jesus says to her: 'Woman, why weepest thou? whom seekest thou?' She replies: 'Sir, if thou hast borne him hence, tell me where thou hast laid him and I will take him away.' Jesus said to her: 'Mary.' She turned herself, 'and saith unto him in Hebrew, Rabboni; which is to say, Master.' Like the other women, she wanted to cling to him and never let him go; but he must not be earthbound, so Jesus says to her, Cease clinging to me.[1] I have not yet ascended to my Father, but go to my brothers and tell them, 'I am ascending to my Father and your Father, to my God and your God.'

Meanwhile the joyous drama had been moving fast. Two disciples, one of them the brother-in-law of our Lady, Cleophas, were going towards Galilee and had nearly reached Emmaus. The conversation was all about the recent tragedy and when a traveller joined them and asked them about their trouble they replied, Are you a foreigner to these parts that you do not know the things that have happened in the capital? 'And he said unto them, What

[1] Dr. Moffatt's translation.

things? And they said unto him, The things concerning Jesus of Nazareth, which was a prophet mighty in deed and word before God and all the people; and how the chief priests and our rulers delivered him up to be condemned to death and crucified him. But we trusted that it had been he which should have redeemed Israel.' They had a confused memory of words spoken long ago by Jesus about the third day, and this was actually the third day since these things were done. And then there was that tale of the women about the empty tomb and a risen Christ; what was 'one to believe? All this they told their fellow-traveller, but he replies: 'O fools, and slow of heart to believe all that the prophets have spoken. Behoved it not the Christ to suffer these things, and to enter into his glory?' He demonstrates from their own scriptures all the things that concerned himself, and as they came to the village he would have left them and pursued his journey, but they urged him to lodge with them that night and to share their meal. He consented, and when they had sat down he took bread and blessed it and break and gave it to them. In this sacramental act at long last they understood who he was, but he vanished out of their sight.

Hurriedly they changed their plans; they would abandon the journey to Galilee and would hasten back to Jerusalem to tell the rest the glad thing that had befallen them. As they went they said to each other, 'Did not our heart burn within us, while he spake to us in the way, while he opened to us the scriptures?' We ought to have known from the first that it was he. They burst in upon the rest of the disciples, but before they could get their story out the rest said unto them: 'The Lord is risen indeed, and hath appeared unto Simon.'

And as they spake these things Jesus himself stood in their midst and said, 'Peace be unto you.' But they were terrified and thought they had seen a ghost and he said to them: 'Why are ye troubled? and wherefore do reasonings arise in your heart? See my hands and my feet, that it is

I myself: Handle me and see; for a spirit hath not flesh and bones as ye see me have.'

It is evident that the four evangelists, St. Peter and St. Paul, and the early Christian Church in general, believed that Jesus Christ had risen, body, soul, and spirit, from the grave. He was no mere instance of spirit survival; that is exactly what they at first thought and were, in consequence, 'terrified and affrighted,' but he himself assures them that he is not a ghost, and bids them touch him and handle him, 'for a spirit hath not flesh and bones as I have.' He eats and drinks with them and is in every way a living human being and not a shadowy spirit from beyond.

So stupendously difficult to believe is this story that thousands of modern Christians reject it along with the majority of the more sceptical public. I myself must confess that I at one time found it impossible to believe, not only because of the contradictions in the narratives, but because of the difficulties raised in the story of a post-death personality eating and drinking. Even if the body was in some manner transformed, translated, glorified, and this we shall presently discuss, how could it feed on untransformed and ordinary material food so that it should pass out in the ordinary way as excreta? If you read the incident on the road to Emmaus you must assume that the risen Jesus was clothed in ordinary material dress. But he had not been buried in his ordinary clothes. Where did he find them or leave them? How could he have put them on and taken them off? If he vanished, as we are told, 'out of their sight' the clothes must have dematerialized also.

Now these to me are all but insuperable difficulties in the story of the empty tomb, and it would be the height of stupidity and of dishonesty not to face them. Can we believe such a story?

I have shown in an earlier section on the miraculous that nothing must be ruled out *a priori* as impossible and that we should certainly, if it had been otherwise, have ruled out as impossible the telephone, wireless, aircraft, television, and a thousand and one modern inventions which were once the wildest dreams and are now among the accepted commonplaces and realities of everyday experience. The mind staggers at the story of Christ's resurrection. And yet?

There is one small detail with which I will deal before passing to a consideration of the evidence.   It is the point concerning the stone rolled away.   I think this is often interpreted as the door of the tomb being opened in order to effect the passage of the risen Christ.   Now it is obvious that this was quite unnecessary, for the risen body could pass through walls and doors, could appear and vanish, could materialize and dematerialize.   If the stone was rolled away it was by some natural occurrence such as the earthquake, and the incident need not be associated with the passing out of the tomb of the risen Lord.

Now at last we may consider the negative evidence or what may be called evidence by means of a process of elimination.   Whatever be the contradictions in the narratives, we are convinced that the witnesses were honest men who had themselves been changed and transformed in some way, possibly by the effect on them of the incidents they relate.   If the resurrection is not a mere invention we may ask what other explanation of their belief can be given?   It is sometimes said that the disciples secretly removed the body and buried it in another tomb.   Against this assumption there is the fact that highly disciplined Roman soldiers, although for a short time they might have run away frightened by the earthquake, would soon have returned to their posts and have prevented such a removal. Besides all this the disciples' story of a risen Christ would have been false and the very vigorous and living movement of the first Christians evidently inspired with honesty and glowing with life and joy would have been founded on a lie. If one studies carefully the account of the early Church given in the Acts of the Apostles, the epistles, and early literature of the movement generally, this explanation is frankly impossible.

But if, on the other hand, the body was still in the tomb suffering disintegration and corruption the resurrection story is equally a deliberate and calculated falsehood upon which no movement, such as we have described, could have flourished. Besides, if the Christians were fabricating the resurrection story while the corpse was still in the tomb, or in some other tomb, moved there by Joseph of Arimathea with the permission of the authorities or by their orders, the tale of these turbulent disciples could have been squashed within a day or so and would certainly so have been exploded by an immediate order to exhume the body of Jesus. Why was such an order never given? Although the Talmuds mention the resurrection tales and naturally scoff at them, there is throughout the whole of Jewish literature no mention of exhumation or of any such refutation of the Christian tale.

There was at one time a theory which had a great vogue, and which was popularized by Ernest Renan, to the effect that Jesus was not really quite dead but in some kind of coma. This would discredit the honesty of the gospel narrative which we have decided to accept. But when further it is suggested that he crept out of the tomb, perhaps on the dislodging of the stone, and as a feeble convalescent led that thunderous and everspreading and irresistible movement of the first years, the interpretation must be dismissed as grotesque and much more incredible than the gospel story.

There are many other suggested interpretations which are equally unbelievable, but the difficulties of the story as given in the early Christian records still remain. One may dismiss as fantastic the explanation so far given without committing oneself to the story of the resurrection.

It is too readily assumed that an appeal to modern science would afford us no help in the matter of the resurrection of Jesus. It is true that physical science and psychology to-day have reached no very certain conclusions either in the study of life or of death; but the old belief in matter, and, therefore, in the body, as being ultimately

*S

ponderable mass, has been abandoned for a theory of sub-atoms which are not electrified matter, but are electricity itself. Gross matter is a grouping of systems of electrical monads, and of the ultimate nature of these monads no one knows anything beyond the fact that they are not what the man in the street would call matter at all. As Lord Balfour put it: 'Matter is not merely explained, but is explained away.' [1]   Now, if this be so, a resurrection body becomes much easier for thought, which is no longer compelled to conceive of a spirit attracting to itself at some future date millions of scattered atoms which have gone to build and rebuild innumerable forms of life, or of recalling from some distant grave the bones which at one time belonged to it. Granting the possibility of some kind of continuance of the personality beyond death it is not difficult to imagine that at the moment of death the spirit may be able to subtract from the body certain essential realities wherewith to clothe itself, or even to collect about its centre electrons from the surrounding world. In fact, the more fluid and subtle, the less ponderable and stationary, be the ultimate reality of matter, the easier it is to conceive of it as the expression of spirit. And, granted this much, it is possible that such a form as it is able to create for itself at the moment of, or soon after death, may not be the final form, but that as it grows in strength and precision it may in time gain a creative definiteness, a familiarity with its new conditions, which will make it possible to express itself through a more evident and glorious medium than in its enfeebled and confused first moments it was able to adopt.

Now this might seem to be mere speculation of no particular value if it were not for that long and general tradition, and that body of modern scientific experience which so singularly confirm it. The conception of a cloud-like ghost, sometimes visible, sometimes invisible, permeates all literature and all tradition. There is also the evidence of actual sensation and experience at the moment

[1] *Reflections suggested by the new Theory of Matter.*

of death, or just preceding it—the sensation of depletion
in every part of the body as of a hand being drawn out of
a glove. Clairvoyants often observe at the death moment
a luminous and cloudy outline or shape of the dying person
slowly distilled from the body. In the state of ecstasy
closely allied to death there is the same sensation of withdrawal. Again, the medium experiences coldness and
exhaustion while some portion of his or her vital being
appears to be functioning outside the body. In dreams,
especially under anaesthetics, there is the common experience of imagining one's body flying through space.

My own studies connected with the subject of the inter-
action of mind and spirit and body suggest the conclusion
that the line of demarcation between organic and inorganic
disease is purely arbitrary, and that the spirit which is now
generally admitted to be able to create stigmata or to disperse ulcers under certain conditions can be conceived as
creating and building for itself a body of some such nature
as is suggested in the New Testament and other religious
literature in such phrases as the renovated or glorified body.

Now I think that these converging lines of thought,
modern and traditional, may throw fresh light upon the
resurrection of Jesus Christ. Health, as Thomas Huxley,
following the Ancients, was always insisting, is a matter
of unity. Our bodies become diseased and corrupt when
they are held together by no central principle of the will.
It is true that you may have a grossly material and flabby-
willed person who happens to inherit from his ancestors
a splendid and athletic body; but it is just this kind of man
who goes all to pieces physically when disease gets hold
upon him; whereas in the case of the man who has made
his body, possibly not so fine a structure at the beginning,
the tense and energetic and responsive servant of his will,
that body becomes wiry and capable of almost miraculous
feats of endurance. The man in the street acknowledges
that disease and death are the wages of the more obvious
sins; but the medical scientist knows that anger and pride
will actually alter the physical tissues, and that faith and

hope and happiness are factors essential to sound health. Death would often seem to be the result of disunion and anarchy within this interdependent community which we call our body, or at least death as we generally know it—that is, death from internal corruption.

But it may be objected that so many saintly persons who would on this theory be presumably healthy are lifelong invalids, resigning themselves to 'the will of the Lord.' I am not at all sure that this is true. Our modern conception of saintliness is, perhaps, a little morbid and heretical. Are any of the saints that we find in the calendar of our prayer-book bed-ridden invalids? It is possible that the Church of Rome may not nowadays quite understand the significance of the Catholic tradition of canonization, which fortunately it adheres to loyally though somewhat blindly. Rome refuses to canonize a saint unless the working of miracles can be proved. But the best attested miracles are generally miracles of healing, as may be seen in a careful study of the Synoptics and of later Christian records. Now the healer is not the diseased and resigned invalid, but the man or woman glowing with exuberant vitality, and therefore it is more than possible that the saint, or the fully balanced and developed ideal man of the universal consciousness, is the man who can, indeed, be slain from without, but from no corruption within.

One would by no means be inclined to deny a very real measure of saintliness to the invalid, and inasmuch as the development of human character is often one-sided, a person nurtured in an age which has lost the proportion of the faith, and therefore the expectation of God as our health, may radiate grace and the saving spiritual influence from a bed of sickness, when all kinds of accidentally healthy people may be dull and unhealthy and useless at the core. But the complete and ideal saint—the 'Proper Man' of the Christian Faith—may still be as I have described him.

If we grant the foregoing as a good working hypothesis, let us carry the matter a step further. Conceive of a man inheriting from a mother blessed above women a splendid body, and from the first moments of childhood preserving his will uncorrupt, and co-operating energetically with the God of Life and Saving Health, growing in wisdom and stature as the years go by; is it not likely not only that he would radiate health and sanity and all wholesome things from the core of his being, but would be able to do so because in his case the outer was as the inner, quick and responsive, and in complete union with that inner creative personality; and should we be much astonished in such a case at such stories as the walking on the water, the transfiguration, the abstinence from food, and the swift transference from place to place? If from out our gross, misused, and corrupted bodies there comes at death an inner colony of central energies, unable through the failure of our central personalities to hold the outer together or any longer to use it, is it not conceivable that where the central principle has all along been creative and healthy and unitive, not only that such a personality could not be holden of death, not slain by internal disloyalties, but that having suffered and been slain only by external forces, it should be able to return into the outer and visible and 'material,'[1] and once more to hold it and energize it and use it in the transformed and transmuted shape that tradition describes as the Resurrection Body of Jesus? In this case the empty tomb is no longer a difficulty; it would be the tomb with its corpse that would now be scientifically unthinkable.

It may again be objected, does not such a Christ become so unlike ourselves as to be valueless? The answer is that such a Christ is infinitely more like ourselves than we ourselves are. When we sin, we are—to use a popular expression—not quite ourselves, and the state of the body that results from sin is not quite our own body. We are

---

[1] Which has been shown to be electricity, motion, or energy, i.e. in its last analysis immaterial. It is remarkable that energy (ἐνέργεια) is often found in Catholic theology as an alternative for the Word of God (Verbum Dei).

ourselves only when we become as God meant us to be. We must measure our true and enduring selves not by the base and faulty measure of the unspeakable thing which we have at present made of ourselves, but by the true and human measure of the full stature of the Christ the goal of human nature, its interpretation, and our proper man.

That the resurrection, therefore, was no mere survival of the spirit but a triumph over death of the whole personality of Jesus is highly probable. God had vindicated His son against those enemies, both theological and political, who had sought to destroy him; and it is evident that if there had been so complete a resurrection, it was much more than a resuscitation from the grave, but was rather a transformation into a new order of being, in power far transcending even those remarkable powers which Jesus had possessed in his earthly life.

These considerations will, perhaps, help us to face the difficulties presented by such incidents as the eating and drinking with his disciples and the wearing of what were apparently material clothes. It is at least possible that a being, translated into what may be called the fourth dimension, could, while partaking of food, transmute it into its essential element, its primal quality of energy, so that the difficulties connected with excreta, the passing away into the draught, might not occur. And as to clothing, it would be ridiculous to suppose that our Lord found robes and then, on vanishing, discarded them. Taking our analogy from his transforming of the food, it is more probable that this new and creative personality would assemble around it the elemental essentials of clothing to materialize and dematerialize them at will.

It is significant that, so far as I know, there is no evidence of relic worship in connection with the Christ; no reliquary containing a sacred hair or a finger joint or a thread from some post-resurrection clothing exists in any part of the world.

It is impossible, of course, to bring absolute proof of the resurrection of Jesus Christ, but we submit that we have shown it to be extremely probable. And at this point there enters another consideration. Physical scientists collect sufficient evidence from their researches to support a certain adventure of the mind; on such evidence they put forward a theory, not yet proven, but of high probability. They make a guess that such and such a thing is true and proceed with further researches on the assumption that these will confirm the hypothesis already made. If the research work fails to confirm it, the guess must be discarded, but without some such adventure of the mind, some such leap forward to a conclusion, research work would sometimes prove fruitless.

Now we have no right as Christians to give credence to the incredible; our faith must be founded on reason. But reason is a slow-footed beast and will carry us few miles along the road to ultimate reality. When reason has removed certain inhibitions and has allowed us to go forward, we must then make the venture of faith. William James gives a good example of this. He supposes that a mountain climber on a misty afternoon had got himself into difficulties on the screes; he cannot retrace his steps and regain his footing on the firm tableland, and yet below him is a sheer precipice. Just within leaping distance there seems to be firm ground, and he guesses that there is a narrow chasm, and that if he boldly makes the jump he will be saved. He is compelled to make the adventure of faith, and in a moment of time has proved what was before but merely probable.

So it was with the early Christians and so it is with us. They had considerable evidence of the resurrection; with the passage of time we have less, but we have enough to make the leap forward. They experienced in their common prayers, their common meals, their common worship, and their common life the presence of the risen Lord. We may and sometimes do actually experience this same joyous thing, so that with certainty we may proclaim to the world: 'Now is Christ risen from the dead, and become the first fruits of them that slept; for since by man came death, by man came also the resurrection from the dead.'

CHAPTER XL

THE GLORIOUS ASCENSION

For over a month the disciples were exulting in the confirmation of their hopes, evidenced by the many appearances of the risen Lord. The power of his resurrection made itself felt not only among them, but also among the spirits in purgatory, who might rightly now be described as the prisoners of hope. Even in the depths of hell and in the midst of its cleansing fires a new hope of redemption was to arise at the preaching of the Christ, and here was being fulfilled the words of the psalmist: 'If I climb up into heaven, thou art there: if I go down to hell, thou art there also.'

For the space of forty days he had spoken to his followers of matters pertaining to his divine commonwealth. Now when he was manifested among them for the last time in bodily form, they eagerly asked him if the kingdom is at once to be wrested from the Romans and restored to Israel. But he replies, It is not for you to know times or seasons, which the Father hath set within His own authority. Neither is it to be a narrow nationalistic restoration; the Kingdom of Heaven, in the words of the *Te Deum Laudamus*, is to be open to all believers. For the moment they are to wait and prepare themselves until they receive power from on high. After the outpouring of the spirit they shall be sent as his messengers not only throughout all Palestine, but throughout all the world to gather into an international fold all such as shall receive the good news. 'When he had said these things, as they were looking he was taken up; and a cloud received him out of their sight.'[1]

We have shown that there is remarkable evidence for the resurrection of Jesus Christ, but the evidence for the

[1] Acts i. 9.

528

ascension is not so abundant. Mention of his ascending is made in the last verses of the gospel of Mark, but it has been before argued that these may or may not be the original ending. It is curious that neither the gospels according to Matthew or John record this stupendous event. In the gospel according to Luke are found these words: 'And he led them out until they were over against Bethany; and he lifted up his hands and blessed them. And it came to pass, while he blessed them, he parted from them, and was carried up into heaven,' but these are not in all the manuscripts. There is also in St. Luke's second volume the undisputed passage which we have already quoted.

Now at first sight this seems very literal and materialistic, and with our modern knowledge of a more or less round earth, an account of the ascension, written in days when the earth was considered a flat place with heaven above and hell below, it might be thought that we can hardly take such an account seriously. But when one comes to think of the matter more closely it is not easy to see how the ascension could have been put in language other than this. We must, perforce, use the language of symbolism, and even nowadays when our knowledge of the earth's shape has altered it would seem absurd to abandon such metaphor. How can we do otherwise than speak of 'lifting up our hearts,' nor does the psalm 'I will lift up mine eyes unto the hills' seem ridiculous. When we meet a friend bowed down under some real or imaginary grief we do not greet him with a hearty 'cheer down, my friend,' and we still notice that the bowing down of the head or of the whole body expresses unconsciously illness or anguish, while joy and health find their expression in an upright carriage. How, therefore, could the ascension in fact or in word be described in anything but the old familiar terms?

There may be greater difficulty in accepting such a statement as 'This Jesus, which was received up from you into heaven, shall so come in like manner as ye beheld him going into heaven.' It is, of course, possible that 'in like manner' may mean in that cloud of glory, and may refer to a second coming which will be fulfilled not in a vision of the materialized Jesus, but in his appearance in a glorified humanity, of which we are told he was the first fruits. It is also possible that the passage is to be taken literally, and that we shall see him with our bodily eyes among a great company of the redeemed. In either case we believe that a cloud received him out of their sight, and that he was taken up into heaven; not, that is, into the skies, for heaven is no more beyond the clouds than it is upon the earth or under the earth. For heaven is where God is, and God is everywhere present. And yet this statement needs some qualification, for man, through greed and brutality and other sins, has almost driven God from the earth; or if not from the earth, at least from the marred and disorganized world.

In the birth of the early Christian communes we may see the re-entrance of God, His emergence once more into the arena of human affairs in the presence and power of the ascended Jesus. For, as St. Paul tells us, we are to seek those things which are above where Christ is seated on the right hand of God. There can here be no doubt of the symbolism, nor would any one take literally the collect in which we ask to be exalted unto the same place whither our Saviour Christ has gone before.

Now St. Paul gives the most rational interpretation of the ascension. In the fourth chapter of the Epistle to the Ephesians he writes in effect that this phrase, 'he ascended,' implies that he also descended into this world below. 'He that descended is the same also that ascended far above all the heavens, that he might fill all things'; or as Moffatt translates, 'to fill the universe.' The ancient special preface for the ascension, still used in the Latin rite, speaks of the ascension of Jesus into heaven 'that he might grant us the fellowship of his Godhead.'

Let us, therefore, sum up the true doctrine of the glorious ascension of our Lord and Saviour Jesus Christ. He was withdrawn from human sight into that central Energy which permeates the universe and at the same time

transcends it.   After his earthly experience he once more
becomes identified with it, but with a power and glory
gained through the things he had suffered; from this divine
fulcrum he is able to pour forth his spirit upon all flesh,
and, just in that measure to which humankind responds to
his spirit, to give them the fellowship of his Godhead and
to renew the face of the earth.

EPILOGUE

We are they that have to cope
 With time till time retire;
We live on hopeless hope,
 We feed on tears and fire;
Time, foot by foot, gives back before our sheer desire.

  · · · · ·

O nations undivided,
 O single people and free,
We dreamers, we derided,
 We mad blind men that see,
We bear you witness ere ye come that ye shall be.

  · · · · ·

The locks shall burst in sunder,
 The hinges shrieking spin,
When time, whose hand is thunder,
 Lays hand upon the pin,
And shoots the bolts reluctant, bidding all men in.

         (SWINBURNE)

THERE was one fact about the resurrection which was briefly touched upon but left for fuller treatment here in the epilogue. It is the undisputed and indisputable resurrection of the disciples of Jesus from the grave of despair to newness of life.

We left the disciples a scattered and dejected flock, their hope gone and their bones dried up. They had trusted that it had been he that should have redeemed Israel, and so firmly fixed in their minds was the idea of a triumphant Messiah that now he had been stifled and murdered there would be nothing left to live for.

All but the wildest mythicists admit as genuine the bulk of early Christian literature, including the Acts of the Apostles and the Epistles of St. Paul, and this literature is instinct with the impetuous life of the Christian communities, of a people who, whether hated or loved, were actually, by friend and foe, acknowledged to be the new race. So great was the rising flood of missionary enthusiasm that our calendar dates from the beginning of Christ's life, and this could never have been if that life had ended with the death upon the cross. Jesus would, in that case, have been remembered as perhaps the greatest of the world's heroes, but it was the impetus of the resurrection alone which can explain the dating of the new era from his birth.

The first thing that strikes the imagination in reading the Acts of the Apostles is the miraculous change in Peter; the coward denying his Lord with oaths converted into the daring spokesman, witnessing not in some far-off city but in the dread capital itself to his living Master, and defying the authorities whom he said had murdered him. When the magistrates and the populace wanted to know what this new movement signified, and would have put it down to a mere drunken outburst, he admits that they are drunk, not with wine but with the spirit. Had not Joel foretold that days would arise in which 'your young men shall see visions, and your old men shall dream dreams: Yea, and on my servants and on my handmaidens in those days will I pour forth of my spirit; and they shall prophesy.' By what power had the old dream, shattered by the crucifixion, now begun to renew the face of the earth? What power was it that drove them not only to a common worship, a common eucharist, to common meals where class was abolished and rich and poor sat down as equals, but, above all, to that communism of possessions where the principle of 'each according to his abundance to each according to his need' had become a reality?

The Roman Empire might note with disapproval early Christian attempts at communism, but it was the more direct opposition to the imperial rule that began to awaken the authorities to the dangerous revolutionary aspects of the movement. Because of this intense revolutionary zeal it might be supposed that Christians were dour and forbidding bigots; but people who got to know them at all intimately were struck with their extraordinary joyousness. One would not have been astonished if the art of a people persecuted and driven underground had been harsh and gloomy, but the remarkable thing about the paintings in the catacombs is their *naïveté* and freshness—the very intimate handling of nature, delightful scrolls and patterns of vines and pomegranates, of birds and animals.

The earliest name for their principal service was the eucharist, the giving of thanks in a joyous feast. The term is connected with a Greek word meaning pleasing, charming, graceful. There is a wonderful description of this service in Walter Pater's *Marius the Epicurean*, where, in his picture of the lyrical gaiety of the worship, he writes: 'It was a sacrifice also, in its essence—a sacrifice, it might seem, like the most primitive, natural, and enduringly significant, of old pagan sacrifices, of the simplest fruits of the earth. And in connection with this circumstance again, as in the actual stones of the building so in the rite itself, it was not so much a new matter, as a new spirit which Marius observed, moulding, informing, with a new intention, many observances which he did not witness now for the first time. Men and women came to the altar successively, in perfect order; and deposited there, below the marble lattice, their baskets filled with wheat and grapes, their incense, and oil for the lamps of the sanctuary; bread and wine especially—pure wheaten bread, and the pure white wine of the Tusculan vineyards. It was a veritable consecration, hopeful and animating, of the earth's gifts, of all that we can touch and see—of old dead and dark matter itself, somehow redeemed at last, in the midst of a jaded world that had lost the true sense of it, and in strong contrast to the wise emperor's renunciant and impassive attitude towards it. Certain portions of that bread and wine were selected by the bishop; and thereafter it was with an increasing mysticity and effusion that the rite proceeded. Like an invocation or supplication, full of a powerful *in-breathing* or *empneusis*—the antiphonal singing developed, from this point, into a kind of solemn

dialogue between the chief ministrant and the whole
assisting company:

> *'Sursum corda !*
> *Habemus ad dominum.*
> *Gratias agamus domino Deo nostro !*

'It was the service, especially, of young men, standing
there, in long ranks, arrayed in severe and simple vesture
of pure white—a service in which they would seem to be
flying for refuge (with their youth itself, as a treasure in
their hands to be preserved) to one like themselves, whom
they were also ready to worship; to worship, above all in
the way of Aurelius, by imitation and conformity to his
image. *Adoramus te Christe, quia per crucem tuam redemisti
mundum !*—they cried together. So deep was the emotion,
that at moments it seemed to Marius as if some, at least,
there present perceived the very object of all this pathetic
crying himself drawing near. Throughout the rite there
had been a growing sense and assurance of one coming—
yes! actually with them now; according to the oft-repeated
prayer or affirmation, *Dominus vobiscum !* Some at least
were quite sure of it, and the confidence of this remnant
fired the hearts, and gave meaning to the bold, ecstatic
worship of all the rest about them.'

In the Acts of the Apostles there is a picture of the first
converts which strikes the same note of joy, 'great grace
was upon them all,' and, having all things common, 'they
did take their food with gladness and singleness of heart,
praising God and having favour with all the people.'

This word 'grace' runs like a golden thread through all
their writings, occurring some two hundred times in the
New Testament alone. It signifies beauty, charm, naturalness, and reminds us of that ease and gracefulness of the
trained athlete. One of the early writers speaks of them as
living above the law, not as denying the laws or having
contempt for them, but as possessing some secret of
spontaneity. It was as if they had drunk of a hidden
well of life. Their Leader had said: 'I am come that

they might have life, and that they might have it more abundantly.'

In reading of these first communities of Jesus, we are reminded of Bernard Shaw's picture of Siegfried as a type of the healthy man rejoicing in his impulses, raised up through 'an intense and joyous vitality which is above fear, sickliness of conscience, malice, and the make-shifts and moral crutches of law and order which accompany them.' Such a character appears extraordinarily fascinating and exhilarating to our guilty and conscience-ridden generations.

Many prophets have mourned to the people, and sometimes wept, but after these necessary forerunners there seemed to have arisen One who had lured men with his shepherd's pipes and they had begun to dance. So true is this that the folk in a later age sang their creed in ballad form under the title of 'The General Dance.'

The contrast lies between a more or less ineffectual series of efforts to obey an externally imposed rule in the hope of acquiring faith, and a faith which, once it had seized hold upon them, expresses itself with joy and naturalness in good works. Among modern poets Walt Whitman has recaptured this Christian rapture, and sings, 'I give nothing as duties. What others give as duties I give as living impulses. Shall I give the heart's action as a duty?'

This triumphant gaiety was not quenched but actually nurtured by persecution. They were stoned, they were sawn asunder, were slain with the sword, they were shut up in sacks with snakes and thrown into the sea. They were tied to huge stones and cast into the rivers; crucifixion was not sufficient agony, the crucified were beaten with rods until their bowels gushed out, vinegar and salt were rubbed into their wounds; women were stripped, children enclosed in nets and exposed to the attacks of furious bulls. They were made to lie on sharp shells, tortured with pincers before being delivered to the mercy of the flames, they were broken on the wheel, they were torn in pieces by wild horses, red-hot plates were fixed to the most delicate parts of the

body, limbs were torn from them, molten lead was poured
down their backs. Women were tied to trees by one foot
and there left to perish, hanging downwards stark naked.
They were more fortunate than some of their sisters, many
of whom were dragged to the brothels to suffer shame
before being led to the stake or cast to the lions. . . .
'Christians to the panthers, virgins to the panders,' was
often the cry of the imperial mob.[1]

One of their writers had said: 'We count them happy
that endure,' and for the hope that was set before them,
the joyous re-creation of the whole earth, they endured the
cross and despised the shame; and although the fulfilment
of their hope is long delayed, out of their suffering has
sprung mirth—the wheels of St. Catherine's torture have
become the Catherine wheels of carnival. This could
hardly have happened had there not been mingled with
the bloodshed so amazing a joy and ecstasy that many a
tormentor, ordered to destroy the Christians, seeing this
rapture was himself transformed and with his new-found
comrades was in his turn willingly destroyed. The
youthful Lawrence, his body slowly burning, dies with a
jest on his lips; Perpetua, the young Roman mother, sings
through the night that preluded her torture; and the comrades of the martyrs keep the day of their torment and
death as merry birthday feasts.[2] Rome had so often been
successful in suppressing rebellions by force that it took
the imperial authorities several centuries to learn that this

---

[1] There were, of course, considerable periods in which the early communities were comparatively free from persecution, periods in which all
kinds of people joined the movement from all kinds of motives, and these
are just the times when joyous enthusiasm was less intense. When the
storms burst many of these pseudo-converts betrayed the movement and
sacrificed to the empire. It is to be noticed that it was not always the
profligate emperors who were most bitter against the Christian movement,
but indeed, such emperors as the moralist, Marcus Aurelius, whose writings
meet with phenomenal sales among pietist Christians. See Workman's
Persecution in the Early Church.

[2] G. B. Shaw, in *Androcles and the Lion,* recaptures something of their
mirth, but the extraordinary dignity which impressed the onlookers
escapes him.

rebellion could not be so suppressed, and that the blood of the martyrs was the seed of the Church.[1]

Faced, then, with this indisputable resurrection of despairing men, a resurrection out of their dead selves to serve the living God, faced with their grim courage in the moment of martyrdom, a stark determination mingled with laughter and gaiety, we may again ask what tremendous event would be sufficient to create this communal resurrection? The cause will be at least as great, nay greater, than the effect. If we were able to ask them what had given them a renewed life, they would have replied that one who was dead was alive again and would in a great chorus have thundered: 'Now is Christ risen from the dead and become the first fruits of them that slept; for since by man came death, by man came also the resurrection from the dead.'

What tragedy has for us obscured the tremendous force of this evidence for the resurrection? Why has the revolutionary zeal died down into comfortable complacency? What has stifled the laughter? The Church has capitulated to the forces of Mammon, and this capitulation was evident as early as the fourth century in the union of Church and State. Constantine's apparent act of liberation encouraged the Christians to dismiss into a world beyond the grave that divine commonwealth the hope of which had inspired them in the early years. The Church, indeed, under the persecution of Julian revived and it was owing to catholic loyalty to the old dream that Europe was reshaped into the medieval civilization out of the anarchy of the Dark Ages.

When in the Middle Ages the Church emerged from the chaos, she set herself to the task of re-thinking her philosophy and of reshaping her policy. Land and riches had been showered upon her and the estates bequeathed to

---

[1] The popular idea that by persecution you can never suppress is erroneous. Students of history will recall many instances of successful repression. Success or failure will depend on what kind of faith and what kind of people you are trying to suppress.

monasteries and other ecclesiastical bodies gave into her
keeping thousands of slaves attached to the soil. At first
they were well looked after, and there was made some
attempt at manumission. As time went on the slaves
became serfs, but this new condition did not always ensure
them a much better status. If it is hard for a rich man to
enter the Kingdom of Heaven, the same may be said of a
wealthy church; and the people were often obliged to
revolt not only against the lords secular but also against the
lords spiritual.

It must, however, be remembered that such rebellions
were in the Middle Ages inspired by the doctrines of the
medieval fathers and by the revolutionary liturgies for
Rogationtide. The doctrines of the just price and of
loaning freely, expecting no interest, also served as a defence for the working classes. The Catholic doctrine of
tyrannicide by which Christians were encouraged to de-
pose the mighty when they abused their office was also a
safeguard for the popular liberties, for this doctrine was
no mere theory in a vacuum, but was sometimes put into
effect.

The Church in the earlier medieval period was not
altogether identified with feudalism, and was often found
in revolt against it, but the feudal powers managed to
buy over Catholic officialdom, as was later the case with
the rising commercial interests which the Catholic doctors
had previously opposed and kept in check.

The last fifty years before the Reformation saw the
Church sunk in almost indescribable corruption, and although a few of the schoolmen still maintained the ancient
popular doctrines they were not able to stem the drift
towards apostasy.

The Reformation, unfortunately, instead of curbing,
actually encouraged the wealthy industrial lords, although
it must be said in their honour that the Anglican reformers
in general were an exception to this rule. Such bishops as
Latimer, and later Laud, were outspoken in their condemnation of the oppression of the workers; the same

may be said of Roman Catholic reformers, such as More
and Fisher.

It should be remembered that there were certain Christian
movements, outside the orthodox Church, which, before the
Reformation and after, maintained libertarian traditions.

In spite of the counter-reformation the Papal churches
settled down into an acquiescent lethargy, and made their
peace with the capitalist system, and the same may be said
of the Church of England and of its Puritan opponents,
whilst the Protestant churches abroad were found in close
alliance with industrial magnates. The Anglican Church
seems to have collapsed with the restoration of the monarchy
and to have reached its deepest depravity about the middle
of the Victorian era.

The Christian Socialist Revival began with Maurice,
Kingsley, and Robertson, and has ever since been carried
on by English liberal Catholics who have numbered among
their ranks many priests and laymen and some few bishops.
These people by a daring revaluation of the gospels and
of early Christian literature have attempted to shake the
churches out of their stupor. They are recalling Christian
folk to the fact that the Kingdom of God is a new world order
in deadly opposition to the prevailing economic disorders,
and to the fact that the world must be reconstructed according to the will of God, the divine justice, or perish in the
conflagration that awaits it.

The sands are running out, but there is still time for
Christendom to remember that there was once a Church
which prided itself on being the specially chosen of God,
which believed itself divine and invulnerable, and took its
ease and became gross and wicked in its self-satisfaction.
The Jewish Church and nation, for all it now counts in
the world, has perished; its heroes and prophets are forgotten—its candlestick has been removed.

The Catholic Church of the newer dispensation prides
itself on a like security. Are not her people 'the chosen
people of God,' and has not she the promise of Christ that
the gates of hell shall not prevail against her? But the

promises of God are conditional. As he brought to dust and ashes the church of the old dispensation, so will it be with the church of the new. If the salt hath lost its savour it is fit for nothing but to be cast on to the dunghill and to be trodden under foot of man.

There have been many revolutionary movements in the world before Christ and many since his coming. Men and women who have prepared for them and suffered martyrdom for their sake have shown a bravery and self-sacrifice which has been excelled by none of the Christian martyrs, but there has, perhaps, not been in the world that peculiar and delightful combination of joy and daring, of grace and audacity before or since. It is the tragedy of the Church's failure that this particular note of music has been lost to mankind. If she had remained true to her Lord and his commonwealth, men and women would not have been driven into atheism, nor would those discords of bitterness and hatred have marred the splendid achievements of the French and Russian revolutions. But in spite of these jarring notes, the miraculous uprising of the Russian peoples from bondage and despair has not only within it large elements of that early Christian renaissance, but has achieved, through the wisdom and courage of its leaders, and countless other participants, so amazing a triumph that it is a matter for shame that Christians will not generally admit its glorious record. If Russia will not, or is not for the moment, through our own sins, able to recognize God as the source and inspiration of their creative efforts, God recognizes them as among those other sheep whom his son has, and who, in so far as they are doing his will, belong to the one fold and the one shepherd.

My hope and longing is that this present book may act as a challenge and spur to Christians to believe in Christianity, that the world may experience a greater and more generous resurrection than has ever been experienced by mankind.

God give aid, for Now is the time.

THE END

APPENDIX I

Was Jesus of Nazareth an actual human personality or a myth invented by the collective imagination of the first Christians?

Most modern critics believe in his historicity, but we must examine the arguments of that learned minority who do not; we must analyse the assertions of such writers as Karl Kautsky, semi-mythicist, of Albert Kalthoff, and of the thorough-going mythicists, J. M. Robertson, W. B. Smith, George Brandes, Arthur Drews, and their populariser T. A. Jackson.

There is in all these writers an initial blunder about the term 'Son of God' which should here be noticed. Unfortunately for these theorists, the term never meant in Jewish literature 'God,' but a human being divinely inspired. The prophets who would have shrunk with horror from describing themselves as God, and whose human birth was never in question, continually gave themselves this title.

There are, in the Greek, two terms used for 'man': the first means 'man' generically, or mankind (ἄνθρωπος); the second, 'an individual man' (ἀνήρ).

These two terms are used in the Acts and in the gospels, of Jesus the Christ, and although 'man' is the more mystical of the two, it does most certainly not mean God. The same may be said of the title 'Son of Man,' so often applied to Jesus. But just as often, however, we have the individual human description, as in St. Peter's speeches in Acts—'a man approved of God.'

We have discussed the human significance of the titles 'Son of God' and 'Son of Man'; but some have further held that Jesus, in using the term 'Son of Man,' does not refer to himself, but this can hardly be upheld in face of such sayings as 'foxes have holes and the birds nests, but the Son of Man hath not where to lay his head,' or 'that

543

ye may know that the Son of Man hath authority on earth
to forgive sins.' Note the inference of the crowds who
'glorified God who had given such power unto men.'
Again he warned his followers that 'the Son of Man must
be delivered up.' There are countless other passages
which prove beyond cavil that he gave himself this title; in
Aramaic the title means simply 'Man.' It is only in a few
extra-canonical works, by no means in all, that the title
seems to be used of a cloud-man, a kind of semi-God semi-
man, but in our Lord's usage it seems always to mean
'Man' or 'Ideal and Representative Man'; Jesus, as
embodying what God intended man to be from the beginning. The mythicists cannot, therefore, claim the term as
in any sense equivalent to 'God.'

T. A. Jackson writes: 'The historical Jesus for me
represents not the beginning of the movement, but the
consummation of its defeat.' But if all mention of Jesus
as a man, all representation of him as a historic human
being must be considered to date from after that alleged
defeat, or, at least, as near the end of the process which
culminated in defeat, then we must date Acts and the
Synoptists as literary compositions of the fourth or at least
the third century. If the reference to a human founder
were incidental in the Synoptic literature and in Acts, and
showed signs of having been ingeniously inserted into an
early literature, we might avoid this conclusion, but no such
case can be made out.[1]

We presume that both Kalthoff and Jackson would date
the defeat of what they agree with us in describing as the
early Christian revolutionary movement with its hope of a
New World Order, to the compromise between the Church
and the empire in the reign of the fourth-century Constantine. At that period there occurred what Dr. Bethune
Baker of Cambridge University describes as the greatest
betrayal in the history of religion, namely, the putting off
into another world beyond the grave of the hope for the
transformation of this world which had animated practic-

[1] It might just be possible to argue the opposite, although I think not
convincingly; namely, that the 'theological' Christ had been thus super-
imposed upon the human, and that the famous Lucan passage (x. 22) was
such an insertion of a later date; but if so the forgery is very skilful as there
are no signs of dislocation in the text.

ally the whole Christian Church up to that date. It was in the fourth century, then, that in the words of Mr. Jackson: 'The movement became nobbled'—the revisionists and reactionists (the social-democrats of their day) got control of the movement, and turned its mystical revolutionary faith into a theology—a literalized, rationalized, pessimistic other-worldism.

He suggests that part of this process of reaction (which St. Paul seems to have been the last to resist) consisted in the literalization of and the humanizing of Jesus. They now tie him down to a particular date, crucify him, 'packing him off to heaven along with the revolutionary Messianic expectation.'

Thus, Jackson (and Kalthoff?) would place not only the Acts and Synoptists, but also *all* the epistles of St. Paul in the fourth century!

It will be remembered that the representative Christian writer of the second century was Irenaeus, with his graphic account of the New World Order, and that the almost equally representative Lactantius in the early years of the *fourth century* is still voicing that Christian hope of the new communal society for all mankind. It will also be remembered that Irenaeus was a pupil of Papias, and that Papias claimed to have received the tradition of a New World Order from the writer of the fourth gospel, who had, it was alleged, received it from Jesus.

It will be proved later that the rebel community looked to a rebel leader, and that the Synoptic Gospels are saturated through and through with the hope of the New World Order; so that to place them in the fourth century, when the Church had abandoned that hope, is to be guilty of gross absurdity.

There is another fact which would seem to be damning to the theory of a fictitious and non-historical Messiah. Messrs. Kalthoff and Jackson both speak of the general expectation of the Christ as though it were the expectation of a non-human figure, a 'God from Heaven.' To meet this expectation the Church created the theological Christ and only about the fourth century converted him into a human being.

Now the apocalyptic literature which lies between the close of the Old Testament canon and the first century of

T

our era is very varied; some works of that group depict
the Messiah as a semi-human, semi-divine emanation from
the heavens, but much of the literature describes him as
human, a man born of woman, and generally as a natural
descendant of David; hence the title 'Son of David' which
continually occurs as Messianic in the Old Testament,
the extra-canonical literature, and the New Testament. If
we remember rightly it is Kalthoff himself who points
out that the Jews had hailed the Persian deliverer, Cyrus,
as Messiah. They hardly conceived that emperor as a
cloud-man or demi-God!

All these controversialists who argue for the non-
historicity of Jesus admit that the figure of the Gospel
Christ was created to meet the popular Messianic expectation, but that popular expectation was in no single instance
the God-from-heaven, but always the God-inspired man
born of woman.[1] Can they quote a single instance to the
contrary? Was Judas of Galilee supposed to be a God?
or Theudas? or 'that Egyptian' who preached revolt?
Was Bar-Cochab, the last of the Jewish claimants to
Messiahship, a God or a man?

There is a passage in Justin's dialogue with Tryphon
the Jew, when the Jew explains to Justin: 'We all expect
a Messiah who will be a man born of men.'[2]

So the apriorist argument of the mythicists and fiction
school breaks down at the outset; if Jesus, fiction or fact,
claimed to be the Christ, it was a human Christ, 'born of
a woman, born under the law' that he would claim to be.

Professor Barnes, Hulsean lecturer at Cambridge University, quotes the apostolic fathers, who themselves had
known the apostles, as witnesses to our Synoptists, and
in their writings we have the selfsame tradition, quoted
either from written gospels or from a common oral source,
probably from the mouths of the apostles of Jesus them-

[1] Superficially they are able to bring Daniel's 'Son of Man' as evidence
of the semi-divine Messiah, descending from the heavens and not born of
woman: but, alas! for them, modern scientific criticism has knocked away
this support. Daniel's Messiah is now discovered to be 'Collective Israel,'
reformed and obedient to the will and purpose of God. Kalthoff can
hardly contend that reformed Jews were not human beings, born of woman,
born under the law.

[2] *Dialogue,* xlix. 1.

selves. In them we find that Christ, the Lord, our God, the Eternal Word, Creator of the World, was manifest, born of the Virgin Mary, of the race of David according to the flesh. Many of the gospel incidents of his life are given in words identical with those of the Synoptists, some in phrases practically identical. He was crucified under Pontius Pilate and rose again from the dead. These writers range from between the years A.D. 96 to 120, and so we are brought down to the epistles of St. Paul and the rest, to be dealt with later. We may, then, conclude that at the very first the Christ who preached was a divinely inspired servant of God, a man who was crucified and rose from death; very soon he was recognized as God, but without losing any of his human features, and that in consequence the myth theory may be dismissed as chimerical. In any case, the foregoing analysis of the composition and acceptation of the gospels demonstrates the absurdity of the fourth-century theory.

In Irenaeus we find the Logos incarnation as in the prologue to the fourth gospel, in Irenaeus he is also represented as a material Christ who announces the coming of a material world of goodness and plenty. Much the same doctrine appears in the epistle to Diognetus and earlier, between A.D. 100 and 117, we find the same doctrine of God and Man in Ignatius.

Once again, in reference to this extraordinary theory of a fourth-century date for the composition of the gospels, the date of their acceptance by the Church will help to fix the date of their composition. It is sometimes said that the four gospels only became accepted by the whole Church in the fourth century, and that the gospel canon was formed by order of the Emperor Constantine, but this is not so. There was a period when each of the great sees, Rome, Antioch, Caesarea, and Ephesus, had its own treasured gospel, and guarded it jealously, and each of these centres would forbid any conscious tampering with their own particular treasure, and much earlier than Constantine's recognition of the Church we find the four gospels quoted as of authority and as the inspired written word of God.

The gnostics *of the second century* appealed to the selfsame four gospels as did the Catholics, as may be seen from the writings of Irenaeus about A.D. 118. Tertullian about A.D. 210 bears witness to the fact that the Montanists also agreed with the orthodox as to the authority of the four gospels. He affirms that they were received by all the great churches of the Christian world. W. E. Barnes, in his *Canonical and Uncanonical Gospels*, quoted abundant evidence to show that the four gospels were accepted in early centuries by orthodox and unorthodox alike. 'Let it then be placed on record,' he writes, 'that at the earliest date after apostolic times (A.D. 180 and earlier) at which we have a Christian literature, wide in scope and large in bulk, and consisting chiefly of works addressed to Christians, we have overwhelming evidence that our four gospels were current from Antioch in the East to Lyons in the West, and were looked upon as the great authoritative documents of the Christian Faith.'

The formation of a canon of inspired scripture is of very gradual growth, and if they were quoted as final authorities by all in or about A.D. 180 this would argue that they must have been in existence for many decades at least before that date. It is fairly certain that Tatian in the making of his *Diatessaron*, or harmony of the gospels, used our four gospels with certain few omissions. Tatian's date is A.D. 160–80; Justin Martyr is earlier, having been Tatian's instructor. He wrote about A.D. 150. It is almost certain that Justin used our four gospels, or at any rate the Synoptists quoting rather loosely from them. That curious book, *The Shepherd of Hermas* (*c.* A.D. 140), sometimes quoted by early writers as itself inspired, alludes to four gospels known in Rome and there used. The evidence from *The Shepherd* is carefully marshalled, and Professor Barnes concludes: 'That in the time of Hermas at Rome (A.D. 140–50), then fast becoming the headquarters of Christianity, there were for Christians two, and only two, great facts, and one of these was the Church, and the other our four gospels.' The witness of Papias at about the same date to Mark and Matthew is then quoted; Papias being the disciple of Polycarp, Polycarp himself having sat at the feet of John the Evangelist. This author is writing many years ago and recent criticism would, perhaps, not allow quite so early a date for the canon.

Canon Streeter[1] argues that the three Synoptists were accepted at Rome and, therefore, probably throughout most of Christendom, Rome being the clearing-house for ideas, and the central mart of the Mediterranean world 'at any rate by the time of Justin Martyr.' He believes that 'four stages can be traced in the evolution of the Gospel Canon at Rome, originally Mark alone; by A.D. 90 Mark and Luke; after A.D. 119 the three Synoptists, and from about A.D. 170 the four.' What becomes of the reckless assertion that there is no trace of Mark or Luke before A.D. 130, even as separate authorities, and that Luke at that date was still a gospel without authority? Streeter puts Mark's date of writing about A.D. 65 and its place of composition Rome, where it would at once gain recognition and become the authoritative gospel for the West. He believes that Matthew cannot be later than A.D. 85 and might be as early as A.D. 75, while Luke, he thinks, was the accepted gospel of the great see of Antioch, founded before the Christian religion had reached Rome. As to Luke, Streeter would date his writing A.D. 80–5, and leaves the question of the place of authorship uncertain, although he inclines to Rome. It might have been written for Romans in the provinces, either at Rome or some provincial capital. This would explain its not being received at Rome before A.D. 90, as it would take a few years in that case to find its way back to the imperial capital. In any case, once we reach the date A.D. 119 or thereabouts when all the Synoptists had been recognized at Rome as canonical, no deliberate alteration in their text would any more be possible; although accidental alterations by copyists might still occur.[2]

In introducing the evidence for the reality of Jesus from the gospel records, it may be pertinent to say something of the controversy between Conybeare and Robertson. The mythicists are very angry with Dr. Conybeare, and Mr. T. A. Jackson wrote to me of the uselessness of quoting this writer as believing in the historical reality of Jesus Christ. He says, in effect, 'What are mere names to me? Dr. Conybeare cannot hold a candle to J. M. Robertson

---

[1] *The Four Gospels*, page 526.
[2] See Appendix V on 'Corruption of the Gospel Text.'

from a point of learning or of common sense.' We shall quote from the two combatants, but first of all let us show what is the particular value of F. C. Conybeare's evidence. It is remarkable, for he was not a Christian but an agnostic opponent of the Christian claims. But patent honesty as critic, and minute and scholarly research, force him to the conclusion that Jesus Christ is a real historical character.

His special field of research was early Christian history, and he had, according to Edward Clodd, again a very far from orthodox critic, a thorough knowledge of early Christian, Pagan, and Jewish manuscripts. Mr. Clodd writes in the *Literary Guide*, an agnostic journal, as follows: 'His sudden death makes a big gap in the ranks of the dwindling company of investigators into ancient documents bearing on the ever fascinating subject of Christian origin. In addition to his Armenian studies, and his studies on the Roman Empire, he published his *Myth, Magic and Morals, A Study of Christian Origins*, and a *History of New Testament Criticism* in 1910 . . . recognition of Dr. Conybeare's brilliant work came in the bestowal of honours from seats of learning in Britain, France, and Italy. In a larger world than the academic, his place among those who have done their best to deliver men from fear-begetting superstitions is secure.' (19th Feb. 1924.) Of course, if his actual arguments are weaker than those of the Right Honourable J. M. Robertson, his scholarship and academic attainments will have to be discounted.

Let us now give one or two examples of the alleged greater common sense of Mr. Robertson and compare Conybeare's answers. Mr. Robertson holds that among the evidences that Jesus was merely a sun-myth is the fact that the gospels relate that he was buried in a rock tomb. Obviously because he was Mithras, or some rock-born God of the Mithras kind. Mr. Robertson would be the first to admit that a sound rule of criticism is to prefer an explanation simple and direct to one which is both tortuous and elaborate. Dr. Conybeare pertinently remarks: 'We would like to know what other sort of burial was possible round Jerusalem where soil was so scarce that everyone was buried in a rock-tomb. Scores of such tombs remain. Are they all Mithraic?'

Mr. Robertson asks, Why was Jesus born at the winter solstice? Because he was a sun-god. Unfortunately, as Dr. Conybeare points out, the choice of the winter solstice is nowhere mentioned in the gospels, and December 25th was fixed as the date of his birth as late as A.D. 354 by the Church, and never heard of in Rome till that date and in Jerusalem till A.D. 440.

Why did Jesus choose twelve apostles? Obviously, say Mr. Robertson and the mythicists, because they were the twelve signs of the Zodiac. Whether or no the number twelve is correct, it is quite clear that on Jewish soil it would be chosen as the number of the twelve tribes of Israel. I think the mythicists are on stronger ground when they object to the mission of the seventy. That may well have been a legend, although one must not be too hasty in its rejection as Luke is being more and more recognized as a careful historian.

Jesus, say the mythicists, preached his sermon on a mount, for as a sun-god he had to take his stand 'on the pillar of the world.' Conybeare reminds them that 'in a country like Galilee, where you can barely walk a mile in any direction without climbing a hill, what could be more natural than for a narrator to frame such a setting for the teacher's discourse?'

Scholars can judge between Robertson and Conybeare as to their learning: the ordinary reader can decide for himself as to their respective sanity and common sense.

Whoever the author of the fourth gospel may be, he insists on Jesus as a human being. In spite of the heightening of his miraculous nature and his being made more like unto God, yet where the Pharisees charge him with making himself God, his reply is that their own scriptures speak of all men in similar strain, 'I have said ye are gods.'

It is a commonplace of criticism to point out that it was written deliberately to correct the errors of the Docetists who minimize the fleshly nature of Jesus and make him a man only in appearance. The fourth gospel insists that he was subject in all things to human weakness, being weary and having to rest at the well; he weeps over the dead Lazarus. The picture of his career is very like that of the Synoptists' for he is shown as a human being, attacked by and attacking his opponents on the issue of the Sabbath, of ceremonial observances, of the desecration of the Temple. He is eventually crucified and rises again. One might say that here is depicted a human being in process of becoming a god; it is impossible, so far as this account goes, to deny that Jesus has come in the flesh. But the mythicists say, exactly so; this is the latest gospel [1] and therefore lays stress on his humanity. But in that case how account for the stress laid upon his divinity. For their theory the latest gospel should be fuller of the human Christ than the earlier records. It does lay stress on that side, but also on the *Divine* side. In any case, they will have to maintain that the Synoptic Gospels show no trace of a human Messiah in order to maintain their thesis of God into Man and not Man into God. There is no trace according to them of a human Christ come in the flesh in the Synoptists, neither in Mark, nor yet in Matthew or Luke. This seems incredible, but here are the actual words of Kalthoff whom T. A. Jackson follows. Kalthoff, it is true, is not precisely mythicist, but is in agreement with them as to the Synoptists presenting a non-human Messiah. 'The real question of the historicity of Jesus is not merely whether there was a Jesus among the numerous claimants to a Messiahship in Judea, but whether we are to recognize the historical character of this Jesus in the gospels, and whether he is to be regarded as the founder of Christianity. If the whole of the older Church, including the New Testament, literature, entirely rejects the notion of a human founder of the religion, how can our theologians venture to suggest that this literature really wanted to describe such a human founder to its readers?' (page 28).

Now it is generally agreed among both orthodox and heterodox that Mark's gospel is the earliest. I need not go over the arguments as to how nearly the whole of Mark is embodied in both Matthew and Luke. It is a commonplace of criticism, and even J. M. Robertson generally accepts it, except on one occasion when it does not fit in with his theory. It must be remembered that the author does not profess to be writing a life of Jesus, but rather

---

[1] Some of the extreme mythicists are, I believe, inclined to place the fourth gospel first and the gospel according to Mark last.

short reminiscences of salient teaching. As we followed the life of Jesus we discovered, in the Gospel according to St. Mark, a human Christ, a carpenter of Galilee, well known as were his parents to the crowds. He submitted to the baptism of John with whom he was often identified. They called him a great human prophet as they listened to his teaching and witnessed his healings. Mark even records his failures to heal at Nazareth. He walks in and out among them as a man, and as a man is crucified under Pontius Pilate with the despairing cry upon his lips: 'My God, my God, why hast Thou forsaken me?'

We shall also discover that, more or less, the same human picture is drawn by the historian St. Luke and by the original St. Matthew, although the theological aspects may have become a little heightened by the later Greek editor.

Dr. Conybeare crosses swords with Mr. Robertson over his treatment of Schmiedel's *Nine Pillars*. Some of them, I think, are not very convincing, but where Schmiedel quotes Mark in the matter of the scribe coming to Jesus and saying: 'Good Master, what are the great commandments?' and our Lord replies: 'Why callest thou me good, there is none good but God,' he is on sure ground. No devout Christian would have invented such a saying, believing, as Christians do, in the sinlessness of Christ. Matthew and Luke have Mark in front of them. Luke sacrifices devotion to accuracy and keeps the saying. Matthew, however, or at least the Greek writer who edits what may be an original Matthew, is too shocked to reproduce such a passage. So we have in Matthew, 'Master, what good things shall I do to inherit eternal life? and he said unto him, Why askest thou me concerning that which is good?' This surely is remodelled. Now even Mr. Robertson is enough abreast with modern criticism to acknowledge the priority of Mark, yet here to serve his purpose he throws him over and talks of Matthew's as the original text.

He again, in the interests of his apriorist theory, belittles the significance of the Marcan story about Christ's mother and his brethren coming to restrain him, pronouncing him mad. Surely, argues Dr. Conybeare, this bears all the marks of an early and genuine tradition? But it would

*T

certainly establish the historicity of Jesus, so Robertson must needs assert that it is another late invention on a par with the absurd stories of the crucifixion and resurrection.

It is only fair to Mr. Robertson to mention one argument which has a little more weight, namely, the haziness shown by Irenaeus about the age of Jesus, and the date of his death. This early Christian writer differs from the date usually assigned for the crucifixion by twenty years, and, instead of making Christ thirty years old when he met his fate, he makes him about fifty. This is curious, but classical writers are equally vague about dates as were medieval authors also, but their faulty chronology is certainly not sufficient reason for asserting that their respective heroes were mere myths, and in the case of Irenaeus he was very likely misled by a verse in his favourite fourth gospel where the opponents of Jesus exclaim: 'Thou art not yet fifty years old and hast thou seen Abraham.' As will be seen there is here no real indication of his age except that he was not yet fifty. He might well have been much less; but the mistake of Irenaeus in face of this verse is, perhaps, not unnatural.

I will give one more example of the non-historicity school's obtuseness in criticism, this time from Kalthoff. He argues that our Lord's prophecy that he will be crucified is obviously false, as how could he possibly have had any inkling of his fate or have warned his disciples of the danger? How could he have known anything about it till it happened? This is delicious, for this selfsame author tells us the roads of Palestine were lined with hundreds of crosses on which hung victims of the Roman Empire. Jesus was, at the moment, being hunted by the native government who were acting on behalf of their masters the Romans.

It would hardly be difficult for him to predict his probable fate if the native authorities should choose to bring a charge of sedition on top of the charge of blasphemy against him and hand him over to the procurator.

These, then, are fair examples of the arguments brought by the mythicists against the historicity of Jesus.

There is one piece of testimony to the human reality of Christ which Kalthoff is himself candid enough to give. Although he is convinced of his non-historicity he admits that theological 'hypnotism,' as he is pleased to call it, 'derives a certain force from the fact that the figure of Christ in the gospels has, in spite of its predominantly superhuman character, a number of quite individual traits. Sayings of his are quoted in which we seem almost to feel the beat of his human heart; stories are told of him in which we seem to have the very man before our eyes. But this fact only proves that, as no one questions, such sayings and stories are the work of a single individual. When the early Christian literature began to ascribe individual characteristics to its figure of Christ, the greater or less intensity of these features was merely a matter of literary tendency or literary skill.' He considers that this realism no more proves the historicity of Jesus than the realism with which the character of Ruth or Jonah are drawn proves *their* historicity. He regards those two personalities as more vividly drawn than the portrait of Jesus, and yet no one for that reason considers them historical. The analogies from Ruth and Jonah have already been considered.

In dealing with the work of Karl Kautsky on the Synoptic problem[1] we shall, I fear, be travelling much of the road already explored, but Kautsky's point of view being slightly dissimilar from that of the mythicists, it is necessary to give it a separate section for consideration.

What, then, it may be asked, is the evidence which would lead Kautsky, writing in 1908, to the conclusion that the gospels, including the earliest so-called Gospel of Mark, were all written considerably after the fall of Jerusalem in A.D. 70? Mark's gospel is 'therefore the product of an evolution of legend during half a century.' Why? Because as the Jesus of Mark predicted the fall of Jerusalem it 'must already have been accomplished when the Gospel was written.' That is precisely all the evidence Kautsky can give us.

Let us examine the 'argument.' When the next world war breaks out, the prediction of those who say it must inevitably do so and that it will destroy civilization, i.e. the predictions of Ministers of the Crown and of publicists, many of them given with surprising details, will all be proved to be forgeries of a date later than the event. The

[1] *Foundations of Christianity.*

prediction of Savonarola as to the fate of Rome is a forgery because the fate that he had predicted came upon that city.[1]

If Christ prophesied what did not happen, the Kautsky type of mind puts him down as a false prophet and a charlatan. If he prophesied what did happen, then the prophecy is forgery after the event. This might be called the heads-I-win-tails-you-lose school of criticism; but, in fact, it is not a criticism at all but a complex. What Kautsky needs is a psycho-analyst.

There is, therefore, no valid argument for dating the first gospel, Mark, after A.D. 70, and if it were written before A.D. 70, there is no argument left for not putting it very early. But Kautsky cares for none of these things. In his ignorance of modern thought he asserts that 'everything apparently written by contemporaries of Jesus has been recognized as a forgery, at least, in the sense that it is the product of a later age.'

Kautsky admits the resurrection as the dominant idea of the earliest Pentecostal community, although to him it is merely an impudent invention. But here is this first community of Christians intoxicated with the belief that their Master had risen in triumph, and that he was among them as the inspiration of their new life. Has Kautsky never considered that this supposed risen Lord, this glorified Saviour whom they believed in as actually dominating them, would so absorb all their thoughts that they would feel it unnecessary any longer and indeed uninteresting to

[1] I am aware of J. M. Robertson's comments about the prophecies of Savonarola. Of course, he admits many prophecies are made which are afterwards fulfilled, but that is in the case of men who can politically discern the times! When will the rationalists learn to be rational? It is they, not we, who refuse the critical method and still look at Jesus through the tinted spectacles of the Victorian Sunday school, clinging to all the assumptions of Tennessee. The popular preachers have much to answer for. They will talk of Jesus as a great heart, a sweet sentimentalist, and never say anything about his colossal genius, his political discernment, his penetrating mind. Yet it was he who said they could read the weather signs, but would not discern the political signs. He knew 'in his bones' that Jerusalem would inevitably be destroyed if he could not turn the nation from its disastrous policy; just as Savonarola knew that the sack of Rome was inevitable, or the war prophets of our own time know that certain cities of Europe will be destroyed by poisonous gases within the next few years, if we do not discern the signs of the times and repent ourselves.

record his merely earthly life and doings? And yet we have the references to that life in the Epistles of Paul, and in St. Mark, whose date we have shown was very early. Now, according to Kautsky, as the God myth grew, there should be less and less insistence on the earthly life. Yet Luke and Matthew, which he dates absurdly late, are full of it, and even the most spiritual of all the gospels, which Kautsky dates much later still, at a time when, according to him, the God myth should entirely have drowned all necessity for a reference back to the mere humanity of the founder, is insistent on that very humanity. Not only are his human attributes here portrayed, but it is the same fourth gospel that records the conviction of the native government to the effect that 'if we let this man be' the imperial government will come and take away our political position and our nationality, if we permit this agitator to go on stirring up the people, Rome will say, we can no longer preserve 'law and order,' and will think it high time to end this experiment of Roman imperial administration through a native capitalist cabinet.

This is a curiously accurate piece of historical reflection for a late second-century forger. True, the fourth gospel does heighten the mysterious and miraculous elements; but it also contains these notes of contemporary history, and alone records the turning point in Pilate's mind, namely, that it was when the native rulers urged that if he insisted on the sentence of 'not guilty'—passed on one who was making dangerous claims to the throne—he would be considered disloyal to his master the emperor, that Pilate decided to condemn Jesus, or at least no longer to protect him against the fury of the native administration. The more closely Pilate's life and motives are studied the more does this appear to be good history.

Of course, it must be remembered that Karl Kautsky's attitude is in a sense the reverse of that of the mythicists, for where they argue from god to man he argues from man to god. Both they and he, however, are at one in pouring scorn on the gospels, and at counting them all alike to be the merest fiction. Kautsky on his theory can afford to allow that Mark, though late and fictitious, is prior to Matthew and Luke who used him in their compositions; the fourth gospel with him comes last of all.

But supposing the mind were capable of believing this forgery theory, we are face to face with another and more serious difficulty. If, as Kautsky maintains, the community of Jesus came into existence during his lifetime, in some senses predates him, and is in no sense a product of his stupendous personality, why was it necessary for that community to invent his personality at all?[1]

It was, according to Kautsky, so little sprung from him that it was able to survive his defeat, a defeat which would prove him to be a deluded dreamer or a criminal impostor. Very well then; why not drop him out of the picture altogether if it was only the idea of the international commonwealth that mattered—only that idea that kept them going? Presumably Kautsky knows nothing of apocalyptic literature, or he would have known that it was quite impossible to believe in the kingdom without believing in a Messiah at all, and that such a belief was actually common. Well, then, the obscure Jesus of Galilee having failed them, they would naturally forget him as soon as possible. He would now be only an encumbrance to their new propaganda.

And yet the whole life of the early community is admitted by Kautsky (for he accepts Acts), to be dominated by this colossal personality of the man who had completely failed them. Besides, if they were to create him at all, why not frankly create him as a sun-myth, or a Mithra Saviour? Why take all this trouble to depict him in the intimate colours of a man of Galilee? Why all this subtle detail? Why, indeed? Does not all the evidence point to a dominant personality leaving an unforgettable impress upon the early records and missionaries?

Kautsky's one chance of carrying conviction would seem to have been in admitting the titanic personality of Jesus, but still insisting that it was a composite creation of a unique school of literary artists, who had not only succeeded in creating this colossus, but had actually filled in the details of the flora and fauna of his native land, of his intimate life as a workman in Galilee, of a national life and tradition long since passed away; his only chance was to admit the genius of this band of forgers, their learning, their inimitable gift of style, their unique position in the history

[1] See Part III, Chapter II, 'Personality and Originality.'

of literature. He would have still had to slur over their object at so late a date in creating this figure at all, and would have had to persuade us that, at that late date, they would have created this very human Christ, and not a fleshless and cloudy god, but the one thing, of course, which he could not do without committing a sort of mental suicide would be to urge us to believe that they were consummate forgers, unique artists, the most intimate and delicate craftsmen, and then to turn round in a fit of silly spite and call them 'extremely ignorant men,' ladling us out 'a concoction thus brewed into a gospel,' 'ingenious contortionists,' 'men who in their ignorance set down the baldest nonsense.' The one thing he must not do, if he is still to be taken seriously, is to talk of 'the thoughtlessness and simplicity of the compilers of the Gospels.' But if the reader will turn to pages 32, 33, 361, and 397, they will find that this is precisely what Kautsky has done.[1]

Let us now examine the evidence from the epistles of Saints James, Jude, and John, Saints Peter and Paul.

J. M. Robertson holds that in the epistle of James there is not one word of specifically Christian doctrine, and save in one or two passages which are probably interpolations, no mention of Jesus. This latter statement is a pure assumption to suit his purposes as there is no sign in the passages mentioned of any tampering with the text. As to Christian doctrine, the letter was not written to establish any difficult theological dogma, but to warn the rich and hearten the poor by reminding them of the speedy coming of the new world order of the Christ, which is precisely the point of view recorded in the Synoptic Gospels. If you compare the gospel teaching about the improbability of the rich entering the coming commonwealth, the denunciation of extortionists, the story of Dives and Lazarus, with St. James's 'Away, you rich men, weep and howl for the miseries which are coming upon you'; 'Do not rich men oppress you and drag you before the magistrates,' the teaching is seen to be identical; or if you compare the Baptist's announcement of the Kingdom of God at hand and our Lord's warning that they were approaching the downfall and end of the age and the beginning of the new

[1] *Foundations of Christianity.*

era, with St. James's 'Stablish your hearts for the coming
of the Lord is at hand,' the same conclusion is reached.
The gospels report Christ as saying that oaths are not to
be used but your word is to be taken as your bond, 'but
let your communications be yea, yea and nay, nay.'   St.
James says, 'My brethren, swear not . . . but let your yea
be yea and your nay, nay.'   And yet according to J. M.
Robertson this epistle has 'not a word of specifically
Christian doctrine.'   James Adderley dates the epistle very
early, between A.D. 40–50, and gives good reasons for this
in his masterly work on the epistle.

Dr. Conybeare probably dates the epistle of Jude too
late (A.D. 90–110), but in any case the author exhorts his
converts to remember 'the words spoken before by the
apostles of our Lord Jesus Christ,' and holds that this is
not an interpolation.   The first epistle of Peter he dates
about A.D. 100 or earlier—many good critics put it much
earlier.   It testifies that 'Jesus Christ suffered in the flesh.'
The Johannine epistles are probably from the same hand
as the fourth gospel, and belong to the period A.D. 90–110.
The author insists (1 John iv. 2) as against the Docetists
that 'Jesus Christ is come in the flesh.'   In the Revelation
of John (about A.D. 93) Jesus is made to testify that he is
of the root and off-spring of David (xxii. 16).   This work
'testifies to the existence of several churches in Asia Minor
in that age, and in spite of the fanciful and oriental character
of his imagery, it is from beginning to end irreconcilable
with the supposition that its author did not believe in a
Jesus who had lived, died and was coming again to establish
the new Jerusalem on earth.' [1]

And now we are in a position to examine the epistles
of St. Paul.   The mythicists dispute the authenticity
of them all, but Kalthoff and Kautsky consider that
some, at least, of them may be genuine.   Albert Kalthoff
asserts that 'all that we find of historical character in
regard to him (Jesus) are references to his death and
resurrection.'   Kautsky claims that the epistles of St. Paul
have all been disputed, which, after all, might be said of
most historical works, both sacred and secular.   There is
still some doubt as to the epistles to Timothy and the

[1] Conybeare, *The Historical Christ*.

second to the Thessalonians, but to describe this latter as a 'brazen forgery' is either due to ignorance or gross bias. No responsible critic goes as far as this.

Kautsky repents himself as to some of the epistles and says 'a number of other epistles of St. Paul perhaps constitute the oldest literary products of Christianity, but they mention practically nothing about Jesus aside from the fact that he was crucified, and then rose again from the dead.' Now Paul expressly tells his hearers that he has little interest in the earthly or fleshly life of Jesus; so we would hardly expect in these occasional letters written to meet this particular scandal or establish that particular doctrine to find much about it. If there was, as Kautsky alleges, nothing about it, the fact would prove little. But as a fact there are just those hints and allusions and even occasional quotations which do corroborate the portrait of Jesus as drawn by the so-called forgers; and they occur not in the disputed epistles, but in those generally acknowledged to be genuine. Conybeare, the agnostic historian and critic, points out in his *Myth, Magic and Morals* why Paul's interest in the earthly life was slender, but he adds that though slender it still existed. From St. Paul we gather that Jesus was born of a woman. He was of the seed of David. He was subject to the Jewish law. His gospel was intended for the Jews first, but also for the foreigners. Paul speaks of the brethren of the Lord. He speaks of the twelve chief disciples. He says he received certain facts from those who believed before he himself did. 'The passages in which Paul insists that Jesus was crucified, died, and rose again are so numerous that they almost defy collection.' We learn further from Paul about the last supper. He mentions his stay with James, the Lord's brother. He refers to the poverty of Jesus. He reminds his Salonican hearers of the necessity of personal holiness according to the teaching of Jesus.[1] He quotes in Galatians a passage about the law which coincides closely with Christ's words in the gospels. He refers to the Lord in his teaching about marriage in 1 Corinthians x. 27. His 'eat whatever is set before you,' is identical with the command of Jesus in Luke x. 8. He says the Lord ordained that the

[1] 1 Thessalonians iv. 2.

propagandists who preached the good news might live by their preaching, and he speaks of the Lord's coming as a robber in the night; and these are the very words of the Synoptic Christ. His 'it is more blessed to give . . .' is quoted as a precept of Jesus, and, though not actually recorded in the Synoptists, can be paralleled over and over again. Compare also Paul's thought with that of the Gospels in the following: 'Not rendering evil for evil'; 'love your enemies'; 'pray for them that persecute you'; 'be not overcome of evil but overcome evil with good.' Close students of St. Paul's thought say that he, more than any others, understood the precepts of the gospel and liberated them from their narrower Jewish moorings. If, therefore, we had no Synoptic Gospels, no Johannine portraiture, we should still in the epistles of St. Paul be able to reconstruct a considerable portion of the early teaching of Jesus, and to obtain just that portrait of him that the 'forgeries' give us—and these reminiscences are of one who had lived and taught some twenty years before. But if the portrait painted so soon after is identical with the portrait as given in the Synoptic Gospels, the chief reason for pronouncing them forgeries of a later date disappears; and what becomes of Kautsky's confident assertion that 'there is practically not a single element in the Christian literature concerning Jesus that will bear the test of examination'?

The fact is that the non-historicity school are in a profound muddle about the Pauline epistles, at one moment treating them as forgeries of the second century, and at another as authentic, but riddled with interpolations. Everything that runs counter to their theory of a mythical Christ must of necessity be an interpolation or a late forgery. Why a *late* forgery we have no notion. They are in a genuine fix, as almost the whole stream of scientific criticism is inclined to date them early and countless objections are brought against a second-century date, notably the controversy between the universalizing Paul and the Judaisers, a contest which had lost its significance by the time of the second century.

As for interpolation, the passages which witness to Christ's having come in the flesh show no sign of tampering or alteration or difference in style and structure.

Paul in many of these epistles opens with the announcement that he is an apostle of the Messiah Jesus, in answer to the objection at first raised by some of the original apostles that he had not, as they, known the Christ in the flesh or been appointed by him. This again precludes a second-century date.[1]

And now we are in a position to examine in detail the arguments of Karl Kautsky and also the mythicists as regards the Talmud, Josephus, and the Roman historians. The references to Jesus in the Talmudic literature are late but significant. For, as far as I know, no one disputes their authenticity. Dr. Klausner, a non-Christian, regarded as the greatest Jewish scholar of our day, argues for the historicity of the Christ from them. The argument runs as follows. The Jewish references are bitterly hostile. They are meant to damage the Christians as much as possible. Now if Jesus had never existed, and had been but a figment of the Christian imagination, how eager they would have been to advertise the fact. And yet there is no hint of such a thing. His historical personality in this most hostile literature is never so much as questioned. The Palestinian Talmud is an encyclopaedic composition of the third century.

When we come to Josephus the case is not so clear. Kalthoff argues that the longer mention in this author is a forgery, which is possible. He goes on to doubt the shorter mention also, where Josephus speaks of James as 'the brother of Jesus, who is called Christ.' Now, says Kalthoff, Josephus, like all his Jewish contemporaries, hated the Christians, and so cannot have mentioned their claimant to Messiahship without abuse. That he would certainly not himself have admitted the claim is true enough, but that in a passing reference he must needs abuse him seems to be unconvincing. True, the name Jesus is common enough, but the particular Jesus of the gospels claimed to be Messiah and he just barely mentions the fact. If I had in passing

[1] Students who wish to go further into the question of the genuineness of the Pauline letters and their testimony to the historic Jesus, should read Conybeare's chapter on the epistles in *The Historical Christ*, and Maurice Goguel's chapter 'The Apostle Paul and the Gospel Tradition' in *Jesus the Nazarene*.

mentioned a certain person 'called Sir Roger Tichborne,' I do not think any one would of necessity think that I had thereby admitted his claim to the title.

Now as to the history of this Josephus. Born about A.D. 37–8, he probably began to write about twenty-seven years after the 'alleged' death of Jesus, dating that event for the moment according to the usually accepted chronology. He wrote in Aramaic and afterwards re-edited in Greek. It is the Greek versions which have come down to us. His chief works are *The Antiquities* and *The Jewish Wars*. He completed *The Antiquities* about the year 93. He was a precocious, and, according to himself, an amazingly clever youth of sixteen in A.D. 53. The *Jewish Wars* was an earlier work. Both the alleged references to Jesus are in *The Antiquities*. He would be about sixty-three years old when he wrote them. But the versions known to us in Greek were written much later. As to the recent controversy that has arisen over the discoveries of Slavonic versions in which there are undoubted mentions of Jesus we would offer no opinion; these references may or may not be forgeries. Dr. Robert Eisler, whose judgment is of some weight, champions them as genuine.[1] According to these Slavonic versions, Jesus was a revolutionary leader whose followers actually captured Jerusalem, or, at any rate, the Temple, and held it for some days till dislodged by the Roman forces. He was destroyed by the Roman Empire. Dr. Eisler holds that the silence of the western version can be accounted for by the 'censor's inkpot' and that the Slavonic texts, though possibly corrupted, are far less so, and do give a genuine account of the rebel leader of Galilee.

Dr. Vacher Burch writes that the references to Jesus in the Russian version are probably genuine, but were suppressed, not by Christians, but by Josephus himself in the text he wrote for western consumption. It should, however, be added that many scholars believe that Dr. Eisler has treated the text of the gospels with unjustifiable freedom, and are unconvinced by his interpretation of the newly discovered versions.

Dr. Klausner accepts the following reference to Jesus

[1] *The Messiah Jesus and John the Baptist.* Methuen. Transl. 1931.

in *The Antiquities,* all but the words given in italics. 'Now there was about this time (about the time of the rising against Pilate) Jesus, a wise man, *if it be possible to call him a man,* for he was a doer of wonderful works, a teacher of such men as received the truth with pleasure. He drew over to him both many of the Jews and many of the Gentiles. *He was the Messiah,* and when Pilate, at the suggestion of the principal men among us, had condemned him to the cross, those that loved him at the first ceased not to do so, *for he appeared to them alive again the third day as the divine prophets had foretold these and ten thousand other wonderful things concerning him,* and the race of Christians as named from him are not extinct even now.'

This may possibly have been the original Greek text, as Josephus, if he mentioned Jesus at all, would have referred to him just in this way. This is precisely his method with John the Baptist whose story he relates as that of a goodly sage, although he has to admit that he was killed by the Herodian administration for sedition. It may possibly be that this Greek text is, after all, genuine, and that some mention is made of the Christ in the Slavonic versions; but the matter must still be considered *sub judice.* It is possible that Josephus suppresses all mention of the founder of the Christian sect. As has been said above, Josephus being the slavish careerist that he was, might eliminate from his works all mention of a sect of Jews who would be unpopular with his imperial paymasters, especially if he was writing or re-writing a tendency-history to prove to them what harmless and useful people the Jews were to the imperial interests. It is significant in this connection that Josephus was actually living in Rome in A.D. 64 at the time of the fire, and must have been aware of the Christian movement in the ghettoes,[1] and of the charge against the Christians and of their terrible punishment. But he makes not the slightest mention of them. Here, then, is the silence *not of ignorance, but of deliberate and interested suppression.*

Note, then, that this voluminous history of the Jews, which shows extraordinary erudition and minute knowledge

---

[1] Kautsky, Kalthoff, Robertson, Couchoud, and Jackson all admit the existence of a Christian movement in Rome by the year A.D. 64.

of various Jewish movements, was written some sixty years after the birth of the mother church at Jerusalem, and the rapid spread of this at first Jewish Christian proletarian movement throughout the empire, and yet according to Kautsky he nowhere mentions it. Why? There is no mention of the mother church, no mention of the spread of the movement to Antioch, to Asia Minor, to Rome, although by A.D. 93 the movement had become international and a danger to the empire, of which the imperial authorities were thoroughly aware. The fact is that Josephus was commissioned to write his voluminous history of the Jews in twenty books by his wealthy Roman patron, and in consequence toned down any incident in their history which might offend his susceptibilities or those of his class. Even the rebellion was made to appear the work of a handful of fanatics and Josephus' own part in it as innocent as might be. Hence the comparative silence about a working-man of Galilee, an agitator and pretender to Messianic honours and the throne is just what might have been expected. He was bent on proving to his Roman patrons that 'Judaism is a pure doctrine, elevated in philosophy, inoffensive in policy; the Jews moderate, and, far from making common cause with sectaries, have usually been their first victims. How could they be the enemies of the Romans? They who had asked from the Romans aid and protection against the revolutionaries.' [1]

Now if Jesus really existed, and although all-important to the communities he had founded, was but an obscure rebel in the eyes of the authorities, we should expect to find but the slightest mention of him in Roman historians: just this bare mention is exactly what we do find. Pliny the Younger is, perhaps, the first Roman author to mention the name of Christ. He wrote to the Emperor Trajan in A.D. 110 for advice in dealing with the Christians in his province. They were accustomed to meet on a certain day, and to sing a hymn to Christ as though to a God—*quasi deo*. It is suggested that if Pliny had believed their Christ to have been an entirely mythical character he would not have used the expression *quasi*. Nothing much can

[1] Renan, *The Gospels*, transl. Matthieson, page 69, cf. Schürer and Batiffol, who account for his 'silence' in the same way.

be deduced from this passage either for or against the historicity of Jesus, and, in any case, he was writing only on hearsay.

The next reference to Christ occurs in the *Annals* of Tacitus composed about A.D. 115 in which he gives an account of the burning of Rome. He tells of the report that Nero had burned certain quarters of the city. 'In order to counteract the report, he accused persons who were called Christians by the people, and who were hated for their misdeeds, of the guilt, and visited the most excruciating penalties upon them. He from whom they had taken their name, Christ, had been executed in the reign of Tiberius by the procurator, Pontius Pilate.' Tacitus goes on to say that this superstition was thus for the moment put down, but that it soon rose again not only in Judea, the original home of the plague, but even in Rome itself. These people were deserving of the severest punishment, but 'there was some public sympathy for them, as it seemed they were being sacrificed not to the general weal but to the cruelty of a single man.' In the same passage Tacitus says so many things against the Christians that Kautsky is convinced that 'this testimony is not a forgery made by Christians in favour of Christians.' He is aware that its genuineness has been questioned, but thinks we must accept it. He adds, 'Suetonius, who wrote not long after Tacitus, reports in his biography a persecution of Christians, people who have embraced a new and evil superstition.' He accepts this also as genuine, adding, 'but of Jesus, Suetonius tells us nothing at all, and Tacitus does not even hand down his name. Christ, the Greek word for "the anointed," is nothing more than the Greek translation of the Hebrew word "Messiah." Concerning Christ's activities and the content of his teaching Tacitus has nothing to say. That is all that non-Christian (Pagan) sources in the first century of our era tell us about Jesus.' But this is all that we require or could expect from plutocratic Roman historians, advocates, and lawyers. Why should they trouble to inquire too closely about a contemptible proletarian movement or its originator? Why should Kautsky expect them to be minutely interested in its founder? Why does he think that the fact that they barely mention the movement at all, and are ill-informed about its secretly distributed revolutionary literature, the Synoptic Gospels and other writings, suggests that it had no founder, or that all that is said about him, in secretly circulated and unpublished literature, is forgery? It is not generally understood that the gospels, the Revelation of St. John and the like, was the literature of a revolutionary movement which could not see the light, was never published, and was difficult to ferret out, unless one were a member of a Christian congregation.

But the point is well made by Streeter in his *The Four Gospels*, by Rope's *Apostolic Age*, by Gilbert Murray and other historians. Every one admits that the persecutions and hostility first arose from the Jews, and that the Roman authorities were contemptuous of what they considered some wretched family quarrel about theology among the Jewish ghettoes; but when they became aware of the dangerous character of the Christian propaganda they proscribed the Christian communes as a sinister movement threatening the empire, without inquiring too closely into the minutiae of their teaching or into the life and purpose of their founder.

Karl Kautsky admits that the early Christian movement began in Jerusalem among the proletarians of that city, and spreading through Caesarea and Antioch, thence reached Asia Minor and eventually Rome. The Roman historians barely mention it, but Kautsky is certain of its existence and its growing power. He argues that their incuriousness about the Synoptic Christ proves he never existed. Why then does it not equally prove that the Christian movement had no existence?

But the Acts and some of the Pauline letters are too obviously genuine as Kautsky is compelled to admit. Very well, then. The Christians were not so called by themselves nor by their Jewish enemies, but were first given their name at Antioch, the third city of the empire and the trade-mart of the world, by their Pagan opponents, and this as early as about A.D. 42–3, that is, about twelve years after the crucifixion under the Procurator, which this author allows as fact.

Now it is interesting to notice that Seneca, who died in

Rome in A.D. 65, the year after the fire, makes no mention of the Christians, although he witnessed the Neronic persecution. Does that fact then prove the non-existence of the Christian movement? Why then does the omission of reference to their founder prove his non-existence?

Now once the genuineness of Acts has been admitted, as it is with certain reservations, by Kautsky, we are compelled to believe that the early Christians worshipped a man approved of God called Jesus, who had been crucified, and who they alleged had risen again from the dead, and was among them as a mighty force stirring them to a very active life, and one which was beginning to disturb the governments of the day. Suetonius, in his life of Nero, mentions the persecutions of the Christians but, as we have noticed, says nothing of their teaching or their founder. In his life of Claudius, however (c. A.D. 150), he refers in passing to the expulsion of the Jews from Rome of which there is also mention in the Acts of the Apostles. The community of Christians in Rome was largely Jewish. Maurice Goguel quotes him in *Jesus the Nazarene* as writing: 'He expelled from Rome the Jews, who under the impulsion of Christ (*impulsore Chresto*) did not cease to make tumult.'

It cannot, of course, be proved that the *Chrestus* was Jesus the Christ, but it is worth noting that the Christians at Rome were often called *Chrestianoi*. Tacitus had used the form *Chrestianos* and *Christians*, while in Acts and Peter i, an early copy of the Sinaiticus manuscript, has *Chrestianoi*. The term *Chrestianoi* is frequent in early inscriptions; so it may well have been that the early Jewish converts to Christ at Rome were expelled because they were dangerous, and were dangerous because they believed that the risen Jesus was inspiring them. This would fit perfectly the story as recorded by Suetonius.

I do not think that the authenticity of the text of Suetonius is challenged, but only the point about *Chrestus*. It is, however, otherwise with the reference in Tacitus as given above. Drews actually asserts it a forgery probably by Poggio. F. C. Conybeare, whose importance as a witness to the historicity of Jesus has been shown, reminds us that Poggio lived in the fifteenth century, whereas our oldest manuscripts of this part of the Tacitus narrative dates from the eleventh century. Conybeare writes: 'It is hardly necessary to inform an educated reader that the text of Tacitus is recognized by all competent Latin scholars to be remarkably free from interpolations . . . that Severus merely abridged his account of Nero's persecution from the narrative he found in Tacitus, an author whom he frequently copied and imitated.' Conybeare has an easy task in demolishing their assertions about the Roman historians.

In all the gospels alike, then, the early Church (according to Kalthoff and also apparently the mythicists) drew the picture of a god who had descended as god among men. You will not, therefore, be surprised to find him with certain human traits: weary, suffering, at cross purposes with his family, dying. All these human traits, says Mr. Robertson, can be paralleled in the myths of gods come down among men.

I was anxious to test my impression that there was nothing in Greek mythology which would suggest a vivid human personality such as that of Jesus in the synoptic accounts, and therefore wrote to a close student [1] of the subject, who replied: 'To the question in the form you put it, i.e. whether we get a vivid picture of a human personality in Greek stories of gods and heroes, the answer is simply No . . . there seems no real analogy between the personality of the synoptic Jesus and the Greek gods.'

There is the further difficulty that the Jews hated the Pagans so fiercely that they could not have borrowed from them, and, therefore, must themselves have had in the Old Testament gods and god-myths parallel with those of the Pagans, without any borrowing, but because of the universal myth-making tendencies of mankind.

But set against this hypothesis is the fierce monotheism of the Jews, and the fact already alluded to, that they were on the look out for a human Davidic Messiah and not a cloud-god or demi-god become man; especially was this so among the common people who were stirred to renewed expectation of a human deliverer from their miseries. We have already proved that the gospels could not have been written so late as freely to have borrowed from Pagan

[1] Mrs. John Miller to whom I am indebted for this information.

ideas, and when the Christian Church had altogether freed itself from its Jewish traditions.

Now if the Christians from the first knew that Jesus was God, they would have had no scruple in so worshipping him. Perhaps the mythicists, not knowing much about early Church history, have overlooked the very significant fact that the earliest prayers were seldom addressed to Christ.[1] There is hardly a prayer directly addressed to our Lord in the whole of the primitive Roman Mass or the oriental liturgies. The *kyries* in the eastern rites did not contain a '*Christe Eleison*,' and there were no *kyries* in the Latin rite till the fourth century.

Justin Martyr is the first Christian writer to describe a mass, but he merely gives its order and mentions prayers, but does not say to whom they are addressed. Duchesne, the best authority on early liturgies, says this omission can be made good by reading the epistle of St. Clement of Rome, an early document. He includes in his epistle the example of the kind of thing the leaders of such services were wont to say. The long prayer is addressed to Almighty God the Creator. It asks that the world may be preserved through 'His well-beloved Son Jesus Christ, by whom He has called us from darkness into light. . . . *Thy well-beloved Servant by whom Thou hast instructed, sanctified, and honoured us . . . and that all people may know that Thou art the only God, that Jesus Christ is Thy servant, and we are Thy people.*'

Now it is clear that Christ is not here God but the servant of God, divinely inspired. We are not here as far advanced as in the prologue to the fourth gospel, where the Word is with God and is God; and through the Word the world is created and this Word became flesh. I am not saying that this development from man to god is illegitimate, but I am insisting that it *was* a development and no part of the primitive evangel; or, at any rate, not till about A.D. 100, and then was very slow in finding its way to general Catholic acceptance.

[1] In the New Testament, apart from the cry of St. Stephen who saw the heavens open and Jesus as Son of Man (i.e. as MAN) sitting on the right hand of God, and cried: 'Lord Jesus, receive my spirit,' and 'Lord, lay not this sin to their charge,' *we have no instance of prayer addressed to Jesus.*

Confucius[1] was not only a philosopher, but had the profoundest respect for the Chinese gods and especially for the ancestral gods. No one denies that Confucius was a human being. He died about 470 B.C. About five hundred years after his death, a Chinese emperor visited his shrine and worshipped him. By the six century A.D. temples had been erected in his honour and his worship as a god-proper had begun.

There is now an impressive cult, consisting of music, dancing, and sacrifices. If it be objected that this cult might be parallel with saint worship, the opening hymn will settle the matter:

> Mighty art Thou, O Confucius,
> Perceiver of the future, endowed with fore-knowledge,
> Compeer of God our Father and of earth our Mother,
> Teacher of the myriad ages,
> Auspicious fulfilment of the skein on the line,
> Thy voice has a music of metal and silk,
> By Thy aid the sun and the moon run their courses,
> And the stability of the universe is preserved.

Here, then, is a striking example of man to god, not god to man, and clean contrary to the wishes of the founder himself.

But in the history of Buddhism[1] we may see the process of god-making out of human material at its strongest. Readers need hardly be reminded that, 'the whole pull of the founder's teaching and the tenets of the orthodox religion based on that teaching' are against any such deification. But the god-making instinct of mankind is too strong to be resisted. When Gautama had his vision under the tree of enlightenment he cast off for ever the gods and their salvation. Life is illusion; sense is illusion; the gods are illusion. Man by his own self must cast off the self and so attain Nirvana, escaping from the weariness of rebirth. This may not seem to us the most vital part of his philosophy, most of which is long since corrupted or forgotten; while his own character, his courtesy, his compassion, his iron self-discipline and democratic spirit are still

---

[1] I am indebted to notes supplied me by Gladys Keable for accounts of Confucius and Buddha worship.

loved and worshipped. His ethic still lives; but there is not a doubt that to himself this atheism leading to the extinction of desire was the quintessence of his teaching.

Gautama Buddha died in the fifth century B.C. By the time of the Buddhist emperor Asoka (third century B.C.) there were shrines enclosing relics of Buddha. By A.D. 100 images of Buddha had been set up. By this time he is already recognized as the incarnation of a series of former enlighteners. Now Greek and Mongolian influence appear, and there is a definite split into two sects. One remained fairly orthodox; the other worshipped Buddha as saviour and manifestation of the One Supreme Creator-God. To-day Buddha has become a manifestation of the supreme god 'Boundless Light,' and has rows of incarnations in the forms of gods and demons, both male and female.

If, therefore, Christianity borrowed from oriental sources, it would not be borrowing the idea of gods in process of becoming men, but of men in process of becoming gods.

It is, however, extremely unlikely that either Jews or Christians would have borrowed from oriental cults, seeing that they were almost too purist and exclusive in thought; and that their prophets and writers were terrified at any infiltration of foreign ideas. Albert Schweitzer, who is an expert not only on the gospel records but on oriental cults, and who is known throughout the world as a most independent critic, sums up the position as follows:[1] 'From every point of view, therefore, the contention that Christianity can be explained by being traced back to Graeco-Oriental religious thought, has to be regarded as fantasy introduced into the sphere of the comparative study of religions.'

As I was writing this analysis of the human element in the gospels, I happened to turn up an old secularist pamphlet attacking the Synoptists as frauds and forgers in the usual style, but published in the days when orthodox and un-orthodox, Christians and atheists alike believed in Matthew as the primitive gospel, so far as any atheist would admit anything as 'primitive.' It is called the *Pillars of the Church, or the Gospels and Councils*, and attempts to prove how unstable are these pillars. The joke is that in order to

[1] *Christianity and the Religions of the World.*

belittle the gospels the author shows that the whole process was from man to god, and shows it fairly conclusively; how awkward for the mythicists are these earlier attacks on the Christ. The author is, of course, wrong about the priority of Matthew as he had not the advantage of modern scientific criticism on this point, but as to the character of the Christ as portrayed in that gospel, he concludes: 'One thing is most striking and that is this; that the gospel of Matthew, claimed to be the first in order of time, and said to have been written by an apostle, so completely ignores the divinity of Jesus that it is called universally the Somatic or Unspiritual gospel; showing to demonstration that the divinity of Jesus was a subsequent development, and was no part of the creed of the apostle Matthew.'[1]

We have examined carefully the contentions of these writers who assert that Jesus the Christ never existed or that, if he did exist, practically nothing can be known of him. We have pointed out their errors in regard to the titles 'Son of God' and 'Son of Man'; we have reminded our readers that the general expectancy in Palestine and among the Jews throughout the empire, was for the coming of a divinely inspired man, and not a god‑Messiah, and that purism and exclusiveness of the Palestinian Jews at the end of the last century B.C. and the beginning of the first century A.D. would have prevented their borrowing from Pagan cults. We have noted the fantastic depreciation of personality current among the mythical school of interpreters and their over-emphasis of the non-personal collective and economic factors in history—factors which, we willingly admit, have often been altogether slighted.

We have duly exposed the errors of these writers in their assertion that the usual tendency in human thought is to convert gods into unsubstantial men, instead of men into gods; and we have noted their unscientific dating of the New Testament writings. We have reviewed their interpretation of Jewish and Roman historians, their contemptuous dismissal of the epistles as forgeries, their ignorance of the gospels and of the gospel backgrounds as political and economic history. We have brought evidence from the gospels themselves of the domestic intimacies and ritual

[1] By 'Julian,' London.   W. Stewart & Co., Farringdon Street.

customs which could hardly have been the result of second-century invention, much less of the collective imagination of the third or fourth century.

How fantastic will now appear Karl Kautsky's contention that the gospels are a mass of credulous forgeries of the second century written up by bunglers and idiots. Rather let us take Klausner's summing-up, the considered judgment of a non-Christian scholar to the effect not only that the Synoptic Gospels are early and probably genuine works, but that their contents may well count as one of the most wonderful collections of ethical teachings in the world. Klausner, like many other critics, points out that probably every other saying of the Christ can be paralleled in Jewish and other literature, but he points out also that Jesus condenses and fortifies what is best in the Talmudic and other sources and leaves the rest. The teaching, he concludes, obviously proceeds from one genuine historical character, and is throughout 'hall-marked with his personality.'

We have, therefore, held ourselves justified in coming to the conclusion that Jesus Christ existed as a real human being on the stage of history, the dominant personality, who created a movement so powerful and widespread that it began to change the face of the world.

APPENDIX II

COMMONWEALTH OR REIGN?

THERE are some critics who are of the opinion that the idea of the 'Kingdom of God' had become 'spiritualized' about the time or just before the time of Christ, and that, in consequence, the term need not necessarily have called up in the minds of its hearers a liberated Palestine or a renovated earth; but I think all these critics admit that in Galilee particularly, and, indeed, as regards the 'common people' generally, the phrase would have called up some tangible commonwealth that was coming here on this earth, and that, therefore, no teacher who used the phrase would have expected the peasants, artisans, craftsmen, to have understood anything different by it, unless he very carefully and deliberately told them in what other sense he was using it. Now John the Baptist was announcing the kingdom for which the crowd was longing, but told them that it required of them a national repentance. In doing so, he was only returning to the best tradition of the prophets. Jesus would, in like manner, explain any departure from the current popular belief in his teaching of the people, as his ministry developed.

Loisy shows that the idea was in some of the current literature expanding from a national to an *international* hope, and that some few writers were beginning to ask themselves what would happen ultimately to the individual soul, and, in consequence, to suggest a kingdom beyond the millennium, which should be everlasting. Yet Loisy writes as follows: 'But it appears certain that the people were more occupied than the books, with the expected liberator, and that for him the national independence was a matter of the first importance. The pious and righteous prince of the psalms of Solomon was acceptable to the devout, and the heavenly man of Enoch to the theologians,

576

but the first-comer who spoke about the liberty of Israel was the favourite of the populace.'[1]

Moreover, the very books in question which talk of the pious prince and the heavenly man both speak of the commonwealth as a kingdom that is coming on this earth. The Psalms of Solomon, written about 70–40 B.C., thunder against a world in which riches abound along with much evil; a world in which the proud govern and believe that their prosperity and power is to last for ever. But God is a righteous judge, and no respecter of persons. These tyrants shall be overthrown. 'Let God destroy them that work all iniquity with insolence, for a great and mighty judge is the Lord our God in justice.' Looking to that future hope the psalms continue, 'Thou wilt establish us in the time appointed, when Thou shalt succour us, and shalt have mercy on the house of Jacob, on the day wherein Thou didst promise them help.' There will be a great ingathering in that time from the east and the west and the north, and from the isles. The good shall inherit life and gladness. The authors look forward to a time of 'unexampled prosperity' in a world in which God Himself, not the Messiah, is king and judge. In this coming world the righteous live out their life and die. Beyond this golden age of God on earth, there is to be a resurrection to some world which is to be everlasting, and is to be founded in the divine justice. Dr. Latimer Jackson thinks 'it is evidently not a bodily resurrection,' but by no means proves the point. If he argues that in that far off, dimly conceived world, they shall be as the angels, we must remember that this would not prove them immaterial, for in these apocalyptic books the angels are by no means bodiless. This same author suggests that two other of these psalms must be by a different hand or that their author must come from a different school of thought, because they speak of a blessed, divinely inspired Davidic kingdom on this earth, that shall not fail, and are full of the popular hope of an inspired human Messiah; but the separate authorship is an assumption; and, in any case, the whole of this psalter rings with the hope of a just and bountiful commonwealth among the sons of men and upon this earth, with God for its ruler and

[1] *The Religion of Israel.* Chapter on 'Messianism.'

U

inspiration.   Even if one or two of the psalms look beyond
to some Utopia, it is still a Community-Utopia founded
on justice and mercy.   It must, therefore, be noted that the
idea of the kingdom of God, even in these two psalms, is
emphatically not a feeling inside the separate soul nor the
union of the individual soul with God.   These two psalms
are still concerned with community, with justice, with the
political man, with 'public affairs,' with the judgment of
nations.

Now let us turn to the Book of Enoch.   We are told
that it is really a composite work, belonging to different
periods and by different hands.   Again this statement
must be accepted with caution, for some, at least, of
the arguments brought in support are inconclusive.   But
accepting the statement provisionally, let us examine the
supposed different works that group themselves under the
one title.

In the so-called first part, the just will inherit the
commonwealth which will be established here on earth.
They will be fruitful in children and the earth will be tilled
in justice.   All nations will praise God.   The just who have
died shall rise to take part in the Golden Age, while the
wicked will be cast out into torments.

Jerusalem will be the centre of this kingdom; 'the scene,
then, of this Messianic kingdom is laid upon this earth.'
The 'next section' also places the kingdom on earth: 'I will
transform the earth and make it a blessing and cause Mine
Elect Ones to dwell upon it.'   In the 'third section' there
is a great rally of the forces of evil, but they are overthrown,
and 'God seats Himself on a throne erected in the pleasant
land, and judges.'   'An old house is folded up' and 'a new
house, greater and loftier than the first,' is established.   The
surviving heathen, converted, become God's vassals.   There
is a resurrection (of the righteous) and the new house
becomes too narrow for the transformed members of 'a
kingdom, which, established on earth, is to last for ever.'

The so-called 'fourth section,' in opposition to the
Sadducean governing classes who believe in no new world
and compromise with the imperial conquerors, looks forward to a golden age here on earth, the age of 'the Messianic
Kingdom set up by the righteous,' but, beyond this, the

writer dreams of an everlasting age prepared for all the just, who shall have 'goodness and joy and glory.' Their spirits shall not perish but 'live and rejoice and be glad.' Latimer Jackson says that this writer knows nothing of a bodily resurrection, and that these just men rise 'not with their bodies.' But there seems no clear evidence that this is the real meaning. The writer's description of that dream of good things beyond the golden age, which all admit that he believes in, is much too vague for us to affirm that he either asserts or denies material form or bodily expression to it.

It should be noted that this 'fourth section,' which is supposed to be the most 'spiritual,' is just as full of the fire of social justice as the others, and, indeed, reminds one of the justice passages in Isaiah. The writer proclaims: 'Woe unto those who build up their houses with crime, for from their foundations shall their houses be demolished, and by the sword shall they themselves fall.' Those who amass 'gold and silver shall justly and suddenly perish.' Again: 'Woe unto you who build your houses by the labour of others, every part of which is constructed with brick and with stone of crime. I tell you that you shall not obtain peace.'

It is the governing classes who do these things who will be cast down by God in the Day of his Judgment, and the just will inherit that kingdom which is to come upon the earth, and shall enjoy that everlasting community which stretches out beyond the golden age.

A study of other books of about this period, the only remaining fragments of a long-since lost literature, yields the same result, namely, the hope of a kingdom here on earth, and in one or two cases the looking forward to a new heaven and a new earth beyond, but a new earth in which the God of justice will prevail and the saints shall live in comradeship. Therefore the kingdom is invariably conceived as a political kingdom, if we are to use the term 'political' not in its journalese sense, as do most writers who deal with eschatology, but in its strict sense, as defined by English dictionaries, namely, public as distinct from private affairs.

The kingdom of God is, therefore, a world which Christ

wishes men to build up here on earth. Although it is not
to be a man-made kingdom, for it is God-planned and
God-given, yet it must be man-accepted and man-actualized
by the grace of God. No one now seriously contends that
the constant 'this world' and 'the next world' of the gospels
refers to the world in which we now live as contrasted with
a world beyond the grave, but to 'this present age' contrasted with 'the age to come.'

But among those who do believe in the coming of this
kingdom here on earth there is a serious difference of
interpretation. I am not referring to the controversy
between those who believe that the kingdom is the Church,
and those who believe that the Church was intended by
God to be the chief organ for the ushering in of that kingdom—but to the difference between those who translate
βασιλεία τοῦ θεοῦ as the reign of God and those who translate
it as the commonwealth of God. Some advocates of the
reign of God or God's sovereignty go so far as to assert
dogmatically that the phrase means this and can mean
nothing else. Only a study of the leading motifs of the
Old Testament can yield the true interpretation of the term.

The majesty of God is certainly one of those motifs,
but equally dominant is the collective ideal, 'the People of
God,' 'the Holy Nation.' It is, in fact, a commonplace of
Old Testament criticism that the 'I' of the psalmist and
prophet generally refers to the nation, to the whole people
of Israel, so much do the writers think in terms of community. Religion might be said to be summed up in the
phrases of Jeremiah and Zechariah, 'they shall be my
people and I will be their God.' There is even in Zechariah
some idea of a world-wide community beyond the narrow
bounds of Israel, 'and many nations shall join themselves to
the Lord in that day, and shall be my people, and I will
dwell in the midst of them.'

There is also the famous passage in Hosea, where the
prophet looks forward to the day when it will be said:
'I will call that my people who was not my people . . .
that in the place where it was said unto them, ye are not
my people, there shall they be called sons of the living God.'

If the main theme of Christ as given in the four gospels
be only the majesty of God, and His reign over the separate

heart, it is odd that the rock from which the New Testament was hewn is this rock of community, and, that the very first interpretation of what Jesus meant, should again be in terms of community and not merely of the individual soul. For this very passage is quoted by St. Paul (Romans ix. 25), when he speaks of the ingathering of the foreigners into the beloved community; and in the first epistle of St. Peter the faithful are addressed, not as a mere chance heap of individuals, but as 'an elect race, a royal priesthood, a holy nation, a people for God's own possession . . . which in time past were no people, but are now the people of God.'[1]

The same thought runs through the apocalyptic literature, which, although derivative and not creative, is yet full of this collective ideal. We need not study them in detail, for Christ makes little use of them compared with his use of Moses and the prophets.

I have already referred to the first interpreters of Christ's 'Kingdom of Heaven.' It is significant that St. Paul, in trying to get the idea of βασιλεία understood among his Greek-speaking converts, should not have borrowed some individualistic term from the fashionable mystery cults of the day, but should have used this very word 'commonwealth.' He speaks of foreign converts as being in past times alien from 'the commonwealth of Israel,' and goes on to show that they are now a new people, a living body, the true Israel of God, 'fellow citizens with the saints and of the household of God.'[2]

The advocates of the kingdom as reign of God in the individual heart refer us to the Greek βασιλεία, and urge that whatever it means, βασιλεία τοῦ θεοῦ will also mean. We have shown that the βασιλεία of Israel becomes the commonwealth of Israel; it is difficult to avoid the conclusion that the βασιλεία τοῦ θεοῦ becomes the commonwealth of God.

St. Paul repeatedly uses city and citizenship as synonyms of the kingdom, and describes the kingdom as the heavenly city which is free and is the mother of us all. Nor is he content that it should remain above, or that the separate soul should soar to it after death; for he, like the writer of the 'Revelation,' sees it coming down upon earth, giving to

[1] 1 Peter ii. 9, 10.   [2] Ephesians ii. 19.

the world its liberator, who shall transform all things here below.[1]

If, as is becoming more and more recognized, the common life of the first eight chapters of St. Luke's 'Acts' is a sacrament of the Kingdom of Heaven, and an inthrust of that kingdom even into the jaded and dying epoch of the empire, we should expect the kingdom as preached by Jesus to contain the idea of commonwealth. That the crowds who thronged him, the common people who heard him gladly, had this collective hope has been shown above.

We may quote here a passage from Rauschenbusch, who in a masterly summary of this 'collective hope' of the Old Testament, of the people in our Lord's time, and of the Baptist, concludes as follows:

'When Jesus used the phrase "the Kingdom of God," it inevitably invoked that whole sphere of thought in the minds of his hearers. If he did not mean by it the substance of what they meant by it, it was a mistake to use the term. If he did not mean the consummation of the theocratic hope, but merely an internal blessedness for individuals with the hope of getting to heaven, why did he use the term around which all the collective hopes clustered? In that case it was not only a misleading but a dangerous phrase. It unfettered the political hopes of the crowd; it drew down upon him the suspicion of the government; it actually lead to his death.'[2]

When, therefore, it is urged that the βασιλεία as taught by Jesus did not contain the idea of this collective hope, and that as a fact the Greek term cannot possibly bear this meaning, one is astonished at the audacity of the assertion.

V. H. Stanton, writing over forty years ago, in a period which was inclined to individualize and over-spiritualize the message of Christ, is yet convinced that both sovereignty and community are contained in the term. In the Old Testament it is a 'realm of men in which God's will would be done' (p. 218), and in the New Testament 'a society' of those whose ruling principle is love of the brethren (p. 51). Stanton's *The Jewish and the Christian Messiah* is still considered authoritative. The same conclusion is

---

[1] Philippians iii. 20; cf. Revelation xxi. 2 ff.
[2] *Christianity and the Social Crisis*, pages 57, 58.

reached in Scott's *The Kingdom and the Messiah*, perhaps the best book on the Kingdom of God. In the Old Testament conception 'a new community will be formed to inherit the new age' (p. 25). In the teaching of the Baptist it is still a collective hope, but Jesus frees the idea of all its limitations, and announces that in the 'new time that was at hand God himself would be supreme and would choose out a people to serve him.' He concludes that 'the Aramaic word, like its Greek equivalent, bore a double significance; and it was impossible to keep the two meanings strictly separate. Again and again when Jesus speaks of the coming reign of God, he appears to connect it definitely with the new community in which it will be realized' (p. 96).

W. C. Allen (*St. Matthew, Int. Crit. Comm.*) also finds in the term both sovereignty and commonwealth; A. C. Headlam (*Life and Teaching of Jesus the Christ*, 1923) gives its normal meaning as sovereignty, but finds in it also the idea of an universal people acknowledging God's rule. The nucleus of this great people is 'the little community' in the time of Jesus (pp. 250, 254, 265).

Charles (*Between the Old and New Testaments*) admits that βασιλεία often means reign, but often again 'signifies the divine community in which the will of God will be perfectly realized.' In this kingdom, 'so closely is the individual life bound up in that of the brethren that no soul can reach its consummation apart' (pp. 48, 127, 128).

I was inclined at one time to think that Canon Streeter would interpret 'kingdom' as 'The reign of God excluding the idea of commonwealth'; but on inquiry I received a letter from him assuring me that this was not his intention, and referring me to *Foundations*, page 115, where he speaks of our Lord's conception as including 'the idea of a corporate national regeneration of this earth.'

S. C. Carpenter (*Christ according to St. Luke*), Loisy (*L'Évangile et L'Église*), and many other authorities, are in emphatic agreement with this conclusion. Stephen Liberty (author of *The Political Relations of Christ's Ministry*) kindly gives me leave to quote a letter in which he concludes that in biblical Greek, and possibly in oriental Greek generally, βασιλεία has acquired a very general and concrete sense covering 'any body of people,' being

practically synonymous with 'nation' . . . 'I should think
then that "the Kingdom of God" would also suggest to a
Hellenistic mind the thought of a people doing God's will.'

Stephen Liberty refers us to Hellenistic Greek, and when
we remember that the Greek version of the Old Testament
(the Septuagint) was the popular version of our Lord's day,
was quoted even by Palestinian rabbis, and that his own
references to the Old Testament as given in the gospels
are from that version, his use of the term βασιλεία should
be discoverable by the Septuagint use of it, i.e. if we find
the idea of community is present in the Greek version
of the Old Testament, we cannot, to say the least of it,
rule it out as incompatible with the Greek of the gospels.
There are passages in the Septuagint use of βασιλεία where
reign seems the dominant thought, but the collective meaning predominates in the following and other quotations:
2 Samuel iii. 28, 'I and my kingdom are guiltless before
the Lord'; 1 Kings xxi. 7, 'Dost thou now govern the kingdom of Israel?'; Psalms lxviii. 32, 'Sing unto God, ye
kingdoms of the earth' (cf. Psalms lxxix. 6); Psalms cii. 22,
'when the people are gathered together and the kingdoms';
Daniel iv. 29, 'he walked in the palace of the kingdom of
Babylon' (cf. Daniel v. 11); Daniel v. 21, 'he knew the most
high ruled in the kingdom of men.'

It has therefore been shown not only that it is highly
probable that our Lord's use of 'the Kingdom of Heaven'
will include the idea of community, but that such an idea
is compatible with the use of the Greek phrase as current
in his times. Linguists suggest that the people who deny
this are thinking in terms of classical rather than in terms
of Hellenistic Greek—of the actual Greek current in our
Lord's day.

The ground has now been cleared for an examination of
the text of the gospels themselves, although such examination is still further complicated by many advocates of
the 'God's reign' theory, who, as regards the New Testament records, assert that βασιλεία means no longer God
reigning, but God reigning in the hearts of individuals.

After having been admonished to the effect that βασιλεία
can only mean reign and can never, under any circumstances,
mean the community accepting the reign, it is just a little

confusing to be told that, after all, it means the reign of God in the individual heart, i.e. the *acceptance* by individuals of God's reign.   If, then, they now abandon their whole argument by including human action as well as Divine within the term βασιλεία, namely, the action of the individual in accepting, why should they exclude *a community* accepting the reign?

Many of the parables of the kingdom suggest god reigning, but never God's majesty in the abstract.   The kingdom is likened to an absent ruler, but the story is concerned with the people who accept him and the people who do not. There is the lord of a vineyard, but he rules over a property where men work together, and some accept him while others reject him, and commonwealth rather than reign would seem to be the dominant thought when the kingdom is described in terms of a festal throng, a wedding feast, or some other social event.

Such passages do most certainly not suggest the reign of God in the individual heart.   This latter meaning is surely incompatible with the following citations: Mark ix. 47, 'good for thee to enter into the kingdom with one eye, rather than, etc.'; Mark x. 23, 'hard for those who have riches to enter into, etc.' (cf. Luke xviii. 24 and Matthew xix. 24); Mark xiv. 25, 'drink it new in the Kingdom of God'; Mark x. 15, 'as a little child, shall in no wise enter therein' (cf. Luke xviii. 17 and Matthew xviii. 1–4); Luke xxii. 30, 'at my table in my Kingdom'; Matthew xxi. 31, 'harlots go into the Kingdom of God before you'; Luke xiv. 15, 'shall eat bread in the Kingdom of God,' i.e. enjoy a meal or feasts in the kingdom, cf. our Lord's own words at that last social meal with his disciples about not drinking any more of the fruit of the vine (Mark xiv. 25), 'till I drink it new in the Kingdom of God.'   Matthew stresses the social character of this (xxvi. 29), 'until that day when I drink it new *with you* in my Father's Kingdom.'

Let us apply the reign of God, or the reign of God in the heart, to the following Lucan passage (xiii. 28 ff.).   'There shall be the weeping and the gnashing of teeth, when ye shall see Abraham and Isaac and Jacob and all the prophets in the reign of God within the heart, and yourselves cast out.   And they shall come from the east and west . . .

* U

and shall sit down in God's reign in the heart.' Is it not more natural to speak of sitting down and taking your ease within God's commonwealth, from which the hypocrites and the self-satisfied are excluded? (Cf. also Luke xiii. 24, 'strive to enter in by the narrow door.')

Or again, Luke xvi. 16, 'the law and the prophets were until John'; since that time the reign of God in the heart 'is preached, and every man presseth into it'; or in its more extended form in Matthew xi. 11, 12, 'but he that is least in the reign of God in the heart is greater than he'; and from the days of John the Baptist until now the reign of God in the secret places of the heart suffereth violence, and men of violence take it by assault, i.e. the eager-hearted and vehement force their way into it, or, with Luke, press their way into it. Community is surely the meaning here?

How can the reign of God within the hearts of individuals be likened to a drag-net (St. Matthew) gathering good and bad people? At the end of the epoch the bad people are cast out of the net. How can they be cast out of a reign in their hearts when they have never been within it, nor it within them? But if the kingdom be a commonwealth, attracting for various motives both good and bad, when the day comes the bad will be excluded.

The kingdom is likened to the sowing of wheat and tares in a field. The disciples are warned not to root up the tares. That will be done at the end of the age, when the age dawns. Then he will gather out of his kingdom them that do iniquity. But why and how can he gather them out of himself reigning in their hearts?

There is, again, the parable of the kingdom which represents it as a social feast to which there came a man without a wedding garment. We can understand one who had joined this gathering from the wrong motive or in the wrong spirit being cast out, but what on earth can be made of the story if the kingdom be the reign of God in the heart of such a churl?

We have dealt fully in the text with the command: 'Seek ye first the Kingdom of God and his justice,' and have shown that it cannot mean the reign of God in the heart of each disciple, for in this case the promise that no one should come to want would be cruelly misleading: The whole question of the alternative translations 'within you' or 'in your midst' has also been fully discussed, and the rendering 'within you' dismissed as impossible.

But it is urged that the much-quoted passage in Luke, 'the Kingdom of God is ἐντὸς ὑμῶν' (xvii. 21), contradicts this community interpretation. Now even if 'within you' be the right rendering, there need be no contradiction, for the ideal of a commonwealth, in which God's own justice and mercy should be made paramount, must first be an idea within the heart—not only in God's heart, but in many hearts inspired by him—before it becomes actualized and takes shape and dwells among us. Socialism is a collective idea, but it is first the dream of many hearts for which they will give their lives. This does not prove that socialism is the relation between an individual heart and a ruler. Home Rule was the dream held sacred within the hearts of many Irish folk. If it had not been within them, it would never have been realized 'without' in the outside world of affairs. So that even if 'within you' be the correct interpretation, there is here no contradiction.

People may say, what, after all, is the difference? Is this not only another controversy between theorists? What practical effect can it have on life? Reign or commonwealth—what does it matter? Do not many of the advocates of reign hold that if individual after individual accepted God as the ruler of his life, events of a world-shaking nature would be bound to happen? Would not the very face of the world be changed?

Is it not, after all, by the conversion of the individual to God that the world will at last be redeemed?

But to what God?

Throughout the gospels the approach to God is through the representative man, and through the love of the brethren. Jesus reveals the essential nature of God and of man, his child and care, as comradeship, as love, as commonwealth. The Christian conversion is not to some majestic God, ruling in heaven and imposing his regulations upon a race alien to himself. On this assumption, mankind is made up of so many million separate souls who must obey God. God tells them to be just to one another and to love one another; but who shall command the heart?

It is true that the Lord Jesus says: 'A new commandment I give unto you, that ye love one another'; but it is
not a new police regulation, but a commandment grounded
in the very law of man's being as revealed in him. If it is
an order imposed by the Majesty who reigns on high, and
who is not the very essence of men's life and of their relation
to one another in an organic body, it will never be obeyed,
because it can never be obeyed.

But if it be the revelation of one who was in the world
from the beginning, in whom all things consist, in whom
we live and move and have our being, it may be hard to
obey; sin and stupidity may keep us from that obedience,
and it may be with infinite difficulty that we find the way
home, but it will be home to which at last we come. In
commonwealth we shall have found him who is our life,
and who has written his laws in our hearts, and we shall
be travelling back by his grace into our proper nature as
revealed in him. For mankind was made by him to be
the body of God.

APPENDIX III

THE whole creation is God's attempt to express himself through his Word. You can look at God from three different angles, or in three different aspects. There is God the Father whom we could not know except He manifested Himself by speech and action. It is through His Son, His Word, and Energy, that we begin to know Him. There is also God the Spirit who binds the Father to the Son. We look on God then also as Spirit, the Spirit of Companionship. Now these are not merely three ways in which we look at God, but are actually three distinct though not contradictory expressions of God from everlasting to everlasting.

Theologians, such as Dr. Temple, Archbishop of York, and that great thinker, the late Dean Rashdall, following the early fathers and many medieval schoolmen, tell us that there are from everlasting three qualities in the one Being; sometimes they express this as three Essential Properties in the one God. This is what St. Athanasius meant by *tres personae*, for persons in those days did not mean distinct individualities as it does to-day, but three qualities in One Supreme Being.

Now we are not here concerned so much with the doctrine of the Holy Spirit as with that of the Son in his relation to the Father and to ourselves. The Son, being the second quality or property of God, is God from all time creating the universe, shaping, guiding, and sustaining it. It is God speaking and explaining himself, God expressing himself as Artist.

The universe is so vast as to be to us incomprehensible, we can only catch glimpses of its meaning. We are puzzled by the cruelties and waste that show themselves in the lowest forms of life, and yet are filled with awe and admiration for the structure of the minutest forms. But if we cannot understand or justify the cruelties, it must strike us also that we have in ourselves an instinct which revolts against them, and which responds to order, beauty, justice, and love.   There is, however, something in us which likes the disordered, the cruel, the evil, and ugly, but we are ashamed of this instinct and recognize it as no abiding part of us, as inhuman and unnatural.   It would seem, therefore, as if we were made in the image of a Being who is eternal and good and righteous, and that we are unfinished products who, when finally shaped and fashioned as that Being means us to be, will express Him and be like Him. There must be in us and in 'nature' something that has gone wrong and failed to fulfil as yet its original purpose. Is it that the Being who is shaping us has given us the possibility of choosing our own path?   Are we endowed with choice and will?   If so, what is that Being aiming at producing?   We do not like the title Superman, but would rather call it the Son of Man or simply Man.

What then is man?   He is an animal like other animals in many respects, but unlike them in that he has reason and will.   He can therefore be the subject of blame and of praise in a sense in which a cabbage or an amoeba cannot. It is true that you can blame or praise a dog or a cat or a horse, but not in the same measure as you can a human being.   The lower animals have, therefore, an embryo quality of reason and will, and a much more developed quality of affection; they are to some extent responsible beings, but only to a very slight extent, and also it must be remembered that we often have made for domestic animals arbitrary standards which are not natural to them, but only to ourselves.   Into this I cannot now enter. But it is evident that, when a man tortures a mouse, you can tell him that he is not quite himself, but you can hardly use the same argument with your cat, for the man is not fulfilling his nature by torture, while the cat apparently is.

God, then, gave to mankind the possibility of choice, for choice is of the essence of human nature, and if God were to create man at all, he must allow him the power of choosing right or wrong, otherwise he would have made not men but robots.

If man had chosen the right path from the beginning,

God might still have become incarnate in Jesus, as crown and goal of a long process. But mankind chose the wrong path and marred God's purpose. The Father could not force him into righteousness without destroying his will, so adopts the only method open to Him and sends His prophets and wise men into the world that they might draw men back into the path of life. But, for the most part, men turned a deaf ear to their pleading so that last of all God sent his Son; and the Word, who had only been partially revealed in the heroic personalities of all nations, was now made flesh and dwelt among us in the person of Jesus.

There is in the Incarnation a twofold action, that of man towards God and that of God towards man. Looked at from one aspect, man is striving up towards heaven, and through the long preparation and the aspirations of the Redemptionist Group and its daughter Mary, the child is at last born who fulfils the hopes of that Holy Remnant, and Mary's child is the Son of God and, more than that, Very God of Very God. That is one side of the truth. On the other hand, as we have shown, God has been continually striving to express Himself perfectly in the human race, striving to break through to man, and at last comes down and is incarnate and takes flesh of Mary.

Just as in the doctrine of the Kingdom of Heaven there is God's action from heaven and man's fulfilment of it on earth, so here is this dual action. It is a divine bursting through to man and a completion of the natural process, the flowering of the race into its true nature which is at the same time human and divine. So that we may invariably hold that Jesus is Very Man of Very Man and Very God of Very God.

As to whether or no Jesus previously existed, we venture to think, although some orthodox theologians doubt it, that he did. His 'before Abraham was, I am' suggests this, but in any case, whether he pre-existed or not, the Word who became incarnate in his person was from all time and before time. Now if Jesus existed from all time, what about the rest of mankind? It is possible that we also have pre-existed. The doctrine of reincarnation seems narrow, in that it limits the arena of man's existences before and after death to this earth. If there are limitless worlds, why

should all experience be confined to so small an arena?
All this is private speculation, but what we are bidden by
the Church to believe, and with sound reason, is that God
the Son or Word humbled himself and took our flesh
upon him and became incarnate in Jesus the Christ, our
Lord and Saviour.

Now it may be asked what is the method of God's
incarnation? Critics, both Roman and Anglican, whose
orthodoxy is unquestioned, insist on the fact of the virgin
birth, and yet distinguish between the virgin birth and the
incarnation. Orthodox theologians generally follow this
line, teaching that the doctrine of the incarnation is not
dependent on any particular method and that, if Jesus were
born of natural parentage, he might still be not only Very
Man of Very Man, but Very God of Very God. This
does not seem to be quite the position taken up by those
early Christians who denied the virginity of Mary, for the
Ebionites, who were primitive Palestinian Christians, denied
alike the virginity and the divinity, holding that Jesus was
the actual son of Joseph and Mary. It is impossible to
say whether their numbers were large or small, although
Justin Martyr in his Dialogue with Tryphon the Jew
(A.D. 150) speaks of them as a considerable body of men
'belonging to our race,' though not the majority.

Now it is interesting to note that these Ebionites accepted
only the Gospel of Matthew, and that this gospel as we
now have it is our best evidence for the virgin birth. It
looks, therefore, as if they knew the gospel in the more
original form of the writings of Matthew the publican,
before its rearrangement by a later Greek editor, and that
this earlier form did not contain the infancy narrative.
This does not, of course, prove that the Greek editor may
not have incorporated in the final form information, either
oral or written, based on a true tradition.

The genealogy in Matthew, which speaks of Jesus as
the son of Joseph, need not be taken too seriously, as this
kind of genealogy is what is called putative, that is, one
made out to satisfy Jewish opinion, as even Dr. Burkitt,
a most unconventional scholar, untrammelled by any bias
for or against the virgin birth, admits.

Now the evidence of St. Luke is of great importance in

that the infancy narratives are coming more and more to be considered as primitive and authentic. Taken at their face value they bear clear witness to the virgin birth. The gospel of St. Luke has sometimes been called the gospel of womanhood; he had great understanding of women, and Mary might well have confided to him secrets which she would not have disclosed to others, both because of his sympathy and of his profession as a doctor. But unfortunately it is not quite evident that his gospel does actually include the story of the virgin birth. Of late years much more value has been given to what are described as the Western Texts. Although these versions are late, they are now supposed to be based on manuscripts earlier than those used in the composition of our Authorized and Revised Versions. The most important of these texts, which we do possess, is Codex Bezae which can be consulted at Cambridge. Now the Lucan gospel of the infancy as based on these readings omits, as regards the Annunciation, 'How shall this be, seeing I know not a man?' and transposes verse 38 in its stead. The angel therefore announces that Mary has found favour with god and that she shall bear the Messiah of whose kingdom there shall be no end. 'And Mary said, Behold the handmaid of the Lord; be it unto me according to thy word. And the angel answered and said unto her, The Holy Ghost shall come upon thee, and the power of the highest shall overshadow thee; therefore also that holy thing which shall be born of thee shall be called the Son of God.' Now the mind of the ordinary Christian is so preoccupied with the virgin birth that he takes such an announcement as proving it, but in fact an angel might announce the birth of any holy prophet in such terms. On the other hand, even this form of the narrative does perhaps suggest something 'miraculous' in that it gives the analogy of Mary's cousin Elizabeth who had conceived in her old age, when conception was normally impossible. The only other clear reference to a virgin birth in Luke occurs in the next chapter. In verse 5, Joseph journeys to Bethlehem with 'Mary his betrothed, being great with child.' But several Syriac manuscripts substitute for 'betrothed' or 'espoused' the term 'wife,' i.e. we read γυνή instead of μεμνηστευμένη.

For the importance of these variants and of the Western Texts see Streeter's *The Four Gospels*, page 267, and Wilson's 'Acts of the Holy Apostles' appendix on the Western Texts.

It is noteworthy that even if these versions of St. Luke do not contain evidence of the virgin birth, these same versions of St. John do.

It is remarkable that the tradition of a virgin birth grew up on Palestinian soil which was peculiarly untainted by Manichean heresies against the flesh and against marriage. Evidence may be brought from the Fathers that it was a fairly primitive belief; although it does not occur in the original version of the Nicene Creed, the most binding and universal of all the creeds. It was inserted soon after by the second Œcumenical Council.

We may dismiss the argument for the virgin birth brought forward by those who quote St. Paul's 'Born of a woman, born under the law,' as it is evident that the author here does not mean born solely of the woman, but is stressing the fact that Jesus was an actual human being.

The apriorist assertion that such a miracle is impossible may be discounted for the reasons given in Chapter XIX, Part III, and even Thomas Huxley regarded it as absurd. Most Catholics would consider the question closed in the affirmative, but it is greatly to be desired that it should be once more reviewed by the Church in the light of modern criticism and of such evidence as is available. In any case, it must be remembered that the faith of the first Christians was built up, not on the virgin birth, which may well be a fact, but on the resurrection of our Lord Jesus Christ.

APPENDIX IV

THE HERESY OF THE SUBJECTIVE CHRIST

IT will, of course, be said, and with a considerable amount of truth, that every one who writes a life of Jesus will write it from his own particular view point. But although such a Life would be a colourless performance, unless the personality of the author to some slight extent came through, yet an author must try faithfully to reproduce the character of Jesus with as little of himself in the picture as may be. It is, I believe, permissible here and there to omit some story or incident which can fairly be shown to be an addition, especially is this the case where an addition seems to be the work of a single evangelist or, as in the case of St. Matthew, the later Greek editor. We have recorded one such apparent addition to our Lord's story of Jonah's preaching to the Ninevites, where Matthew alone adds the comment about the resurrection, a comment which seems to break the rhythm of the original.

But this would seem to be an entirely different matter from the practice of any writers who first form in their own minds a picture of what they think Jesus ought to be, and then deliberately take the censor's brush and blot out whole passages of his sayings and doings which contradict the character of their own personal and subjective Christ.

I shall take three or four examples of this method of the manufactured Jesus, the Jesus according to the gospel of subjective taste, but before so doing, I should like to write something on the general rule I have followed as to the criticism of passages in the New Testament.

All sound exegesis must be based on the following method: the whole of the evidence must be considered, and the many apparently contradictory sayings and actions must be appreciated. No solution will be satisfactory which blots out any part of the evidence. We have already pointed out that Jesus of Galilee was a genius and a poet rather than a philosopher who laboured at a kind of dull consistency; that his sayings are ultimately consistent we need not doubt, but on the surface they are often found to be in sharp contradiction.   It is these very contradictions which give us the true portrait of the Christ.

Now to our examples of the contrary method which seem to me to make havoc of the text.

The most glaring is, perhaps, in the attitude of the Lord's Day Observance Society and the Sabbatarians. They labour under difficulties which do not trouble most modern critics, in that they are frankly fundamentalist and must, therefore, accept the whole of the gospel narrative and every passage of the same as infallible.   Inconceivable as it may seem they yet maintain that Jesus was a Sabbatarian.   This they do in face of John's assertion that 'He not only broke the Sabbath . . .' (v. 18).   Over and over again we find Jesus breaking the Saturday Sabbath, and it is one of the principal theological counts against him brought by the Pharisees.   We have quoted his own liberating pronouncement that 'the Sabbath was made for man and not man for the Sabbath,' and to add to the difficulties of the Sabbatarians it must be remembered that the Jewish Sabbath was abolished by the inspired Christian community, and the Sunday, or Lord's Day or Day of the Sun, as it was called by the primitive Church, installed in its stead.   Christians had perforce at first to work on it, as they were mostly slaves and manual workers and had no choice in the matter, but when the Church was freed in certain respects on the passing of the Edict of Toleration, Christians were so far as was possible bidden not to work at their ordinary callings on the Day of the Sun, were told they should attend mass or the eucharist, and after that could devote the day to study, to doing good works, to prayer, but also to games and amusements of all sorts, so long as these were of an innocent character. [1]

It is unlikely that many students of this work will be inclined to take seriously the Sabbatarian heresy, but there may be among them not only total abstainers, but

[1] Readers who wish to pursue the study of this subject further should try to secure a copy of my *Day of the Sun*, now unfortunately out of print, or better still Hessey's Bampton lectures entitled *Sunday*.

abstainers who wrest the scriptures in the most shameless fashion to support their position. The teetotaller may quote St. Paul who says it is better not to indulge in any habit, however innocent in itself, if it is likely to cause a brother to stumble, if he also is honest enough to quote the apostle's advice to a bishop: 'Be no longer a drinker of water but use a little wine for thy stomach's sake.'[1] Our Lord himself had pronounced that if your right hand offend, cut it off and cast it from you; it is better to enter into life maimed than having two hands and two feet to be cast into hell. This advice would certainly cover the case of any one who was tempted to drink to excess, but it must also be noticed that the person who cuts himself away from fermented wine or any other form of alcohol is, though wise in so doing, entering life maimed. Better, then, to enter life unmaimed and whole if you are a normal being who can master your appetites and keep within the bond and balance of temperance. It is an impudent misnomer for societies existing to forward the interests of total abolition to call themselves 'Temperance Societies.' There does, however, exist a body calling itself 'The True Temperance Society,' which has every right to the title, as would all societies whose object is the moderate and temperate enjoyment of wine as of any other pleasure.

I was astonished at the recent performance of the Passion Play at Oberammagau to see that the Christ at the Cana Marriage Feast wave away the loving cup filled with the wine he had himself just created. One was the more puzzled in that the play is generally realistic and historically accurate.

Much more realistic was the picture, bravely published during the prohibition years, which caused such a scandal in the United States. The artist represented the wedding feast at Cana of Galilee being interrupted by prominent American prohibitionists, who are emptying the jugs of wine. For exhibiting this picture the secretary of the Society of Independent Artists at New York was fined twenty pounds, the charge being that the painting outraged public decency.

There are some teetotallers who assert that Jesus never

[1] I Timothy v. 23.

turned the water into wine, but into some nasty beverage
of the 'mineral water' type; the master of the feast must
have been scandalously drunk to have exclaimed: 'Thou
hast kept the good wine until now.' If prohibitionists
still insist that the beverage was not fermented wine they
must meet the fact that St. Paul uses the same Greek word
when he writes: 'Be not drunk with wine, wherein is excess.'
Abstainers must also remember the many occasions when
the Master was charged with eating and drinking with
publicans and sinners, and with being himself a wine-bibber.

Something should, however, be said in conclusion about
the nature of the wine of the Sacrament. We have already
shown that the Lord's Supper was a Passover meal and that
therefore the fruit of the vine which he consecrated was
that same fruit of the vine prescribed by Passover usage.
Although some modern Jews are in the habit of drinking
unfermented wine at the Passover, this was a custom unknown in the days of Jesus. Ample evidence to this effect
is brought forward in a report sponsored by the late Archbishop of Canterbury and prepared by such specialists on
Jewish history as Oesterley, Swete, Turner, and Woolley
under the chairmanship of Bishop Ryle. The report shows
conclusively that the fruit of the vine used at the Passover
was fermented and intoxicating wine mixed with a little
water, and they quote many primitive Christian authorities
to the effect that precisely the same fermented wine was
consecrated by our Lord and universally used by orthodox
Christians. Where this rule was broken by Catholics or
heretics the innovators were always condemned.

And now we come to the much more disagreeable task
of considering the position of those vegetarians and animal
lovers who seek to prove that Jesus never ate flesh nor even
fish, and on every occasion protested against the cruelty
and indifference of a section of the public who existed
then, and alas exist to this day, whom Henry Salt has aptly
called 'the Brutalitarians.'

The earliest Genesis legend gives an account of primitive
man as vegetarian. It is also certain that Isaiah looked
forward to an ultimate establishment of the kingdom in
which even the beasts would cease to prey upon each other,
a golden period when 'the wolf shall dwell with the lamb,

and the leopard shall lie down with the kid; and the calf
and the young lion and the fatling together; and a little
child shall lead them. And the cow and the bear shall
feed; their young ones shall lie down together: and the
lion shall eat straw like the ox. And the sucking child
shall play on the hole of the asp, and the weaned child
shall put his hand on the cockatrice' den. They shall not
hurt nor destroy in all my holy mountain: for the earth
shall be full of the knowledge of the Lord, as the waters
cover the sea.'[1]

Certainly in that blessed world man would no longer kill
his brothers and sisters, the lower animals, for sport or even
for food, and all honour to those who from humanitarian
motives are vegetarians or fruitarians in anticipation of that
good world of mercy and of grace. St. Paul himself seems
to look forward to this golden age in which the whole
creation liberated at last from the bondage of corruption
shall share in the blessings of Christ's kingdom. It is to
be remarked, as our humanitarian friends point out, that in
St. Paul it is Christ's ideal world which is to be actualized
among men. But when they seek to go further, and to
prove that the gospel itself yields the same evidence, one
must unfortunately enter a demurrer. There is, indeed, the
saying of Jesus to the effect that not a single sparrow falls
to the ground without the heavenly Father's concern, but
there is little else in the nature of evidence from the gospels
on which to build.

There is a certain amount of tradition to the effect that
two of the apostles were vegetarians, but it must be remembered that the twelve were mostly fisher-folk, and that
Jesus, instead of rebuking their calling, actually helped them
in securing a good catch. In the miracle of the five thousand he multiplies the fishes as well as the bread for the
feeding of a great crowd; and himself, after the resurrection, shares with his disciples a meal of fish.[2] Luke's
version of the story is even clearer: 'Have ye here anything
to eat? And they gave him a piece of the broiled fish.
And he took it and did eat before them.'[3] Some may
doubt the historicity of the resurrection and especially of
this act, but it cannot be doubted that the evangelists

[1] Isaiah xi. 6–9.   [2] John xxi. 9–13.   [3] Luke xxiv. 42 ff.

could not have inserted it if they had known their Master
to have been a vegetarian.

There is no suggestion in any of the gospels that Jesus
did not partake of roast lamb at the Paschal Feast, nor is
there any hint that in the expulsion of the traders from the
Temple courts he made a protest against the slaughter of
the beasts for sacrifice.   It is amazing that such protest
should not have been made, and that his anger should have
been reserved for the exploitation of men and not have
included this horrible exploitation of sheep and oxen.   It
may, of course, have done so, but there is certainly no
explicit evidence on this point.

It is, perhaps, legitimate to believe that when Jesus told
his disciples that he had many things to say to them but
that they could not bear them now, these things may have
included the more merciful treatment of the beasts and the
whole question of the rights of animals.   One cannot
doubt that Jesus looked forward to the golden age when
man should no longer prey on the lower animals, but should
treat them as brethren.   This coming age had been
anticipated by many of the saints who have been accepted
by wild animals as their closest friends.

And finally there is the much debated question of
pacifism.   We have dealt with this subject in the various
passages of the gospels which give us, on the one hand, the
non-resistance of Christ and his counsel to the same effect,
and on the other hand, his anger directed against his un-
merciful Sabbatarian opponents in Galilee, and the violence
of his language directed against the Pharisees of Perea
and of Jerusalem.   We have noted his gentleness and his
fury, his turning to the Father who makes his sun to shine
on the evil and on the good, and to that same Father who
destroyed the wicked murderers and burns up their cities;
the God who rains down fire and brimstone upon Sodom
and Gomorrah.

Many other passages have been dealt with on the one side
and the other, and it is with extreme difficulty and diffidence
that one has ventured to draw a composite picture of the
one Christ.   The records of the early Church yield the
same conflicting evidence.   One may read long passages
in a Patristic authority which would seem conclusively to

prove him a pacifist, until in those selfsame writings one notes his approval of Old Testament wars and of those apocalyptic wars which are to usher in the reign of Christ.

How again can one reconcile with a pacifist portrait of God or of his Messiah the violent deaths of Ananias and Sapphira,[1] and the inspired approval of St. Peter and his companions, for it was in the first flush of Christian enthusiasm that these things happened and as St. Luke assures us, under the guidance and inspiration of the Holy Ghost. The same may be said of the blinding for a season of Elymas by St. Paul and of this apostle's command that Christians should normally obey the magistrate, for he is God's minister and beareth not the sword in vain.

There may be, and I think one may say there must be, a kingdom beyond the kingdom where God will be all and in us all, and where every man will have been brought back into the universal fold. But Christ's immediate kingdom was, as has been pointed out, a new world from which many will be excluded or will have excluded themselves, many who will share the fate of the cities of the plain and in that dreadful destruction there will be the weeping and gnashing of teeth.

Now one cannot honestly exclude all this catastrophe and terror from the gospel picture. How are these apparently contradictory elements of gentleness and of fury to be applied to our own times? Certainly one may be assured that all imperial wars, all wars of national aggrandisement, under whatever specious terms they may be waged, must be ruled out by the Christian community. More certain is it that private quarrellings and murders and often even what is called 'standing up for one's own rights' will come under a similar condemnation.

But what of wars of national defence and wars in defence of the oppressed in one's own nation and of oppressed nationalities? Again, have not the workers and their sympathizers among the well-to-do classes the right to acquire liberty or to defend those liberties once gained against Fascist reactionaries and rebels? My reading of the gospels and of their interpretation by the early Church

[1] Although, in this case, it may have been their own conscience that struck them dead.

would suggest that they have.   The only kind of pacifism which one can respect is that active and practical pacifism expressed in a general strike engineered for some righteous end, or in some mass resistance to the manufacturing of arms, or their transport for some unrighteous cause.

The invention of poison gases and of other abominations, and the mechanized warfare of our times, has further complicated the question, but I would venture to suggest that in the Irish Rebellion of 1916 and in the Spanish resistance to armed rebellion there may be seen the action and the presence of Jesus Christ.

APPENDIX V

MR. T. A. JACKSON writes of 'the complete failure to disentangle any tangible personality from the tissue of myth, legend, tendencious distortion, and downright lying that constitutes the gospel record,' and quotes Dean Burgon as saying: 'The older the manuscripts the more corrupt the text,' and himself speaks of 'documents admittedly of composite origin and full of "interpellations" as well as blunders in transcription—documents which contradict each other on every vital issue—it is these documents which constitute the "evidence" of the historic Jesus.'

That there are serious discrepancies between the Synoptists no one denies. In copying ancient manuscripts various additions have crept in, and more serious sometimes are the omissions. A copyist will also occasionally alter a sentence to bring it into line with his own idea of what the author really meant. Sometimes such an alteration is suggested in the margin and the next copyist will believe it part of the text and so insert it; but when you have discounted all these alterations, additions, and compressions, there is a substratum left amply sufficient to give us the picture of a commanding and essentially consistent personality who dominates the stories and their respective authors. Canon Lilley of Hereford speaks in his *Religion and Revelation* of that 'secularization of the study of scripture which has, after two centuries, assumed the dimensions of a vast and highly specialized intellectual discipline known to us as Biblical criticism.'

The original manuscripts of the gospels as of the other literature of the New Testament have long since been lost. They were constantly being copied and recopied, copies old and worn out being replaced by new. The pogroms against the Christians always included a search for their scriptures and their wholesale destruction.

Among the oldest manuscripts that still exist are the Alexandrian (Codex A) and the Sinaitic (Codex Aleph) in the British Museum, also the Vatican (Codex B) in the Vatican Library, but none of these are before the fourth century. There is also the Codex Bezae in the library of the University of Cambridge.

Towards the end of the fourth century so many errors had crept into the Latin versions that St. Jerome determined at the request of the Bishop of Rome to make a revision and his work on the New Testament was completed in A.D. 385, and is almost as old as the earliest Greek manuscripts we have mentioned. It met with great opposition from the fundamentalists of his day and was called revolutionary and heretical, but Jerome, who was a profound and accurate scholar, replied to his critics with justifiable sarcasm, saying that 'a lyre is played in vain to an ass.' If these 'two-legged donkeys' prefer to drink of the muddy waters instead of the waters from the pure fountain head, let them. He gathered together all the best manuscripts available and subjected them to the minutest scrutiny, and thus produced the revised version of his time which we know as the Latin Vulgate.[1]

The earliest material used for writing manuscripts of the New Testament was probably sheets made from the fibre of the papyrus plant, a rather quickly perishing substance. It was not until the persecutions of the Church ceased and Constantine had given the Christians security that he ordered a number of more durable copies of the authentic scriptures to be made on parchment. The Vatican and Sinaitic manuscripts may have come into existence in this manner. The late J. M. Wilson, Canon of Worcester, writes 'that many thousands of later manuscripts are in existence, and that a manuscript's later date does not always prove its inferiority in accuracy to an earlier, as it may itself be the copy of a sounder text that preceded it.'[2]

The task of the textual criticism of the New Testament

---

[1] Much of the above information can be got in Paterson Smyth's *How we got our Bible*, S.P.C.K. 1906 edition. Streeter, in his *Four Gospels*, 1924, has an appendix on 'Jerome and the Codex Sinaiticus,' with a full discussion of the manuscripts probably used by St. Jerome.

[2] *The Origin and Aim of the Acts of the Apostles*, appendix i.

is, by examination of all these thousands of manuscripts, and of the hundreds of thousands of various readings, to discover what readings are to be selected so as most nearly to reproduce the original text. All these early Greek manuscripts have to be compared with early versions in other languages, Syriac, Latin, Coptic, etc. Many of these early translations may have relied on manuscripts much earlier than our four great manuscripts in Greek, and therefore may give readings closer to the original. There are also the numerous quotations of the New Testament scriptures in the Fathers, Apologists, and Opponents of the Christian Faith. These often yield matter by which manuscripts can be confirmed or corrected. All this research has been the work of many centuries of scholarship, and especially of the last hundred years, and is by no means yet complete.

These thousands of manuscripts, versions, and quotations fall into three groups, and are named from the places where they apparently originated and circulated. They are known as the Syrian, Alexandrian, and Western. The Syrian texts were largely relied on by our translators of the Authorized Version; the Alexandrian group was largely used by the scholars who gave us the Revised Version. The mis-named Western group had not been given much weight until after the Revised Version, but is now taking a high place in New Testament criticism. Canon Wilson, from whose book I have drawn most of these notes, says it is most completely represented in the Codex Bezae at Cambridge; it is a Greek text with a Latin translation, but the Latin may in some cases be more accurate than the Greek, and actually in some passages be the original. Often what used to be called 'Western interpolations are coming to be regarded as original readings.' F. C. Burkitt (*Two Lectures on the Gospels*) reminds us that the so-called Western texts have by far the best external claim to Apostolic antiquity. He gives a simple and valuable account of the Western group, and shows that it includes material from districts as far apart as African Carthage and Edessa of the Euphrates valley, places unexposed to 'the universal solvent of Greek culture,' and having apparently no intercourse one with the other. Where, then, texts from both these districts agree together, they may well give us a valuable and perhaps the original reading.

'The agreement of these two sources brings us back almost to the time when the four gospels first obtained their canonical position; and where Edessa and Carthage differ, we may call in the witness of the text of Alexandria to determine which of the two has preserved the ancient reading, and which presents us with the merely local variation.'

If readers want to pursue in detail the question of the Western text, they may be referred to Streeter's *The Four Gospels*. In Chapters III and IV he submits an outline 'of the evidence which compels us to recognize in what they called the "Western Text" two distinct types, an Eastern and (in a strictly geographical sense) Western Text.' He gives many reasons for the former unpopularity of this group, and for the reliability of many of its readings as evidenced by examples brought forward by himself and other modern textual scholars.

It is extraordinary that with so many thousands of manuscripts and versions with their multitudinous variety of readings, often contradictory, we should have so good a text of the gospels as undoubtedly exists and that it should present us with a vivid and life-like picture of the Messiah Jesus. To those who scorn textual criticism and the authors who defend this picture—to those who point to the contradictions among the critics themselves, it may be replied that the contradictions are certainly no greater than exist between physical scientists and also between experts of the medical profession. I do not think Bernard Shaw, although he points out the dangers arising from the pontifical utterances of a medical priesthood, would seriously question the great advances made in medicine, and especially in surgical discovery; no one, in fact, *in toto* rejects modern science because of its differences and contradictions, and we are certainly no more at liberty to reject the results of textual science which have in the main brought us back to a reasoned and critical reliance on the gospels and their picture of the human and divine Christ.

Vincent Taylor, in his *The Formation of the Gospel Tradition*, sums up as follows: 'I have no hesitation in claiming

that the tradition of the words of Jesus is far better preserved than we have any right to expect, and with much
greater accuracy than is to be found in the record of any
great teacher of the past.'

We should also make some note of the modern 'Form
Criticism,' a very recent development; which asks, what was
the nature of the tradition that lay behind the documents,
and how accurately does this tradition reproduce the events?
We must endeavour to push back the written sources to
the oral teaching that lay behind them.

Oral tradition received much emphasis in the nineteenth
century. (Westcott's *Introduction to the Study of the Gospels*.)
But this tradition, spread by word of mouth, was supposed
to contain a great volume of events and sayings in the life
of our Lord, from which each evangelist chose what he
considered most useful, for the purposes of his particular
gospel. No attempt was made to face the problem of
how such a narrative was formed, how preserved, and—
above all—what relation it had to the Church.   With the
rise of literary criticism this theory of oral tradition was
dropped, and for a while the talk of it was not considered
good form.   But the theory is with us again.

The real consideration of a supposed verbal source
from which the gospels were taken was made in a remarkable series of four volumes, all written quite independently,
and published just after the close of the War.   Their authors
are, respectively, Albertz, Bultmann, Dibelius, and Karl
Ludwig Schmidt.   While their results are very diverse, all
have in common the essential quality of endeavouring to
define sharply the nature of the first gospel tradition, and
to determine something of the laws that governed its formation and transmission.   The result has been to enrich New
Testament science with a new discipline that bears the name
of Form Criticism.

Form Criticism treats the fourth gospel as essentially
different from the Synoptics.   It makes a great point of the
study of 'the vital backgrounds' of the apocalyptic literature
and the Talmudic sources.   The title, 'Form Criticism,' is
used because it seeks to establish 'the authentic form of
Jesus' words, and the earliest information about his acts
can only be recovered from those sources which existed

before the gospels were written and upon which they were based.' These original sources can only be appreciated when placed against the background of the life and thought of their own day. The claim that such original sources can be recovered is made by Burton Scott Easton in his Hale Lectures entitled 'Christ and the Gospels.' This work deals fully with the recently discovered Russian version of Josephus, which we have already mentioned in the Appendix 'Jesus the Christ: Myth or History?' Professor Easton examines the Mandean literature, which belongs to a Mesopotamian sect who claim to be the descendants of the first followers of John the Baptist. According to their sacred scriptures, dating from perhaps the seventh to the tenth century or later, John had entrusted to them many divinely revealed truths, ceremonies, and sacraments. Jesus is supposed to have been a disciple of the Baptist, but to have distorted his teaching. John at once detected him to be an impostor, but baptized him on receiving his pledge of obedience, but Jesus broke the pledge and all manner of false doctrine was set loose in the world. The Mandeans were driven out of Palestine by the Jews towards the end of the first century (cf. the Christian emigration to Pella). The Mandeans have little or no knowledge of Christianity prior to the union of the State and the Church and their accounts of the Christians seem to be both late and faulty. Were they really followers of the Baptist, and not rather a gnostic sect with no primitive connection with Palestine? This sect seems to have been greatly influenced by Mohammedanism, and, therefore, it is probable that their accounts of John and of Jesus are grossly inaccurate. Professor Easton sees a connection between the Mandean writings and the fourth gospel, although the writer of this gospel sets himself out to contradict many of their assumptions.

Easton's attempt to go behind our existing gospel of Mark and to find a source which this evangelist used for his own purposes should be carefully studied. If such a source can be disentangled we should then have Quelle; L., or independent Lucan tradition; and the early written or oral sources of Mark. The 'Form Critics' consider that 'The Sayings' were fuller than what is generally called Q., and that both 'The Sayings' and L. are more primitive than Mark; in fact, they suggest that Mark not only knew this source, but embodied some of it in his narrative. I cannot find evidence of this, and their further suggestion that Mark is Pauline rather than Petrine and the arguments with which they support it, seems to me absurd.

Personally, I think that Form Criticism, which is the fashion of the moment, will soon be *démodé*, as directly it is related to the real historical background of the times, it exposes itself as based on a purely subjective and imaginary Jesus of the twentieth century.   That each Synoptic author, as also the author of the fourth gospel, colours his narrative to some extent by his own subjective predilections may readily be granted, but, for our own part, we still prefer the 'subjective' Christ of the early evangelists to the subjective 'Christ' of the twentieth-century American and German professors.   We have shown reason to believe that in spite of the personal colouring of the early writers they do present us with an authentic historical Jesus.

Readers will have seen as my story has been unfolded before them, the absurdity of Professor Easton's arguments on the secrecy of the parable, the detour through Syro-Phoenicia, the Sermon on the Mount, and the 'myth' of the Perean ministry.

There are many other extravagancies in his work with which we have no time to deal.

x

INDEX

INDEX

SOME MODERN AUTHORS CITED

MADE AT THE TEMPLE PRESS LETCHWORTH IN GREAT BRITAIN